T5-AFL-679

# OUR HYMNODY

## A MANUAL OF THE METHODIST HYMNAL

ROBERT GUY McCUTCHAN

WITH AN

INDEX OF SCRIPTURAL TEXTS

FITZGERALD SALE PARKER

Second Edition

ABINGDON PRESS
NEW YORK • NASHVILLE

OUR HYMNODY





M

SET UP, PRINTED, AND BOUND BY THE PARTHENON PRESS, AT NASHVILLE, TENNESSEE, UNITED STATES OF AMERICA

# CONTENTS

# Contents

# Contents



## BOOK III

# PREFACE

Our Hymnody: A Manual of the Methodist Hymnal, is the result of an interest the author has had in hymns and tunes since his childhood and of more than thirty years of critical study. It is intended to be just what its name implies. A manual is a book of information about something, not a commentary on it. This book gives information concerning each hymn and tune in *The Methodist Hymnal,* as well as of the chants, responses, and other aids to worship included therein. No directions for the singing of hymns have been made, for that would have caused the book to be entirely too large and unwieldy, and because, properly, such information should be given elsewhere. An attempt has been made to give accurate information concerning the source and first publication of both hymns and tunes, the changes in the texts of the hymns and in the melodies and harmonization of the music. A surprising amount of new information has been discovered, and a conscientious effort made to verify or disprove the many stories, most of them apocryphal, which have been given widespread credence. Some authentic incidents of both hymns and tunes have been included, and such have a real value.

A Calendar of the Hymnal has been provided, the thought being that there may be a coincidence in date between the delivery of a sermon or address and some incident connected with a hymn or tune.

Naturally in a work of this kind there is but little included that may be looked upon as original with the writer. The most reliable authorities have been consulted, without attempt to rewrite or paraphrase their work, and credit is given where credit is due.

The author wishes to express his gratitude and appreciation to those who have aided him in the preparation of the Manual. In addition to those whose published works he has consulted, to those members of the Joint Commission on the Revision of *The Methodist Hymnal* who have been most interested and helpful, and to the authors of hymns and the composers of tunes and their relatives and friends who have contributed much pertinent information, he desires to pay his respects to Professor Jerome C. Hixson, whose interest and advice have been a matter of many years and whose help in the preparation of the manuscript has been invaluable; to the Rev. John Telford, recently deceased, James T. Lightwood, the Rev. Thomas Tiplady, and others in the British Isles who have been of inestimable assistance in securing detailed information from British sources; to Dr. George C. Stebbins for authoritative information concerning the "gospel songs"; to Henry L. Mason, grandson of Lowell Mason, for factual data having to do with his grandfather's tunes; to Frank J. Metcalf, acknowledged authority on American composers of tunes and compilers of tune books; to Dr. Charles M. Boyd, of Western Theological Seminary; to Dr. Calvin W. Laufer, eminent hymnodist; to Professors Edwin B. Nichols and Gerhard Baerg for their criticisms; to Miss Olive Lewis and Miss Ruth Rooney for many hours spent in various libraries; and to Miss

Geraldene Reid Sherrill for her expert assistance in copying the manuscript and checking and verifying the various items.

The Scriptural Index was prepared by Doctor Fitzgerald Sale Parker, brilliant scholar of the Methodist Episcopal Church, South, whose death in July, 1936, saddened all who knew him.

To the author's wife, Caroline S. McCutchan, especial tribute is due. Not only have her interest and encouragement been constant through the years, but without her sympathetic assistance the preparation of the book would have been well-nigh impossible.

The MANUAL will be found useful by those who conduct classes in worship and music in our colleges and theological seminaries, by ministers of the gospel in a variety of ways, by choirmasters and organists in the preparation of music for public worship, and by the individual in private devotions.

The hymnal of the nonliturgical Protestant church may be considered analogous to the Book of Common Prayer of a liturgical body; the MANUAL may be looked upon as a textbook dealing with the *Hymnal.* A preacher is a teacher; the teacher should be familiar with his textbook.

It is dedicated to whatever uses it may be put in the worship of Almighty God and to the hastening of the coming of His Kingdom on earth.

ROBERT G. MCCUTCHAN

*Greencastle, Indiana*
*May 1, 1937*

## PREFACE TO THE SECOND EDITION

In the five years since the first edition of OUR HYMNODY appeared, a number of persons have sent the author items of further information about hymns and tunes treated. There seems to be a desire on the part of users of the book to make it as nearly perfect as a manual of this kind can be made. It is therefore especially gratifying to have the opportunity of incorporating in a second edition a score or more of corrections and additions, with corresponding new entries in the Calendar. That the changes involving known or suspected misstatements in the original edition are of minor significance has been most reassuring. The author is grateful to all those who by their interest have made possible this second edition.

ROBERT G. MCCUTCHAN

*Claremont, California*
*November 28, 1942*

# THE ANTECEDENTS OF THE METHODIST HYMNAL

Methodist hymnody may be said to have had its beginnings in America. When John Wesley, in 1737, published his first book of hymns at Charles-Town (now Charleston), South Carolina, he planted the seed which grew through many other lesser publications by himself and his brother, Charles, into his "Large Hymn Book" of 1780, entitled *A Collection of Hymns for the Use of the People called Methodists. The Charles-Town Collection* was not only the first hymnal published in America: it was the first book of hymns published for the use of the Church of England. The "Large Hymn Book," as John Wesley called it, was the main hymnic stay of British Methodism for nearly a century. With some additions, particularly those of 1831, it was in use until its revision and publication, with a Supplement, as *The Wesleyan Hymn and Tune Book,* in 1875. A further revision in 1904 constituted, thus, the lineal descendant of Wesley's "Large Hymn Book" of 1780. Other branches of the Methodist Church in Great Britain issued collections of hymns suited to their particular needs through the years, until all which were parties to the Methodist Union joined in the publication of *The Methodist Hymn-Book* of 1933.

In 1781 Robert Spence, a printer and bookseller of York, England, issued *A Collection of Hymns from various authors,* later enlarged and called *A Pocket Hymn Book—designed as a constant companion for the pious: collected from various authors,* the greater proportion of whose contents had been taken from compilations of the Wesleys, but without authority from, or acknowledgment to them. This book was received with favor by British Methodists, but in order to prevent its too extensive use by his followers, John Wesley, in 1785, published *A Pocket Hymn Book, for the use of Christians of all denominations,* which contained some popular hymns omitted from the "Large Hymn Book." John Wesley did not reprint this book, but, following the advice of the Conference, in 1787, had the Spence book reprinted under the title of that of 1785, omitting some of the hymns condemned as "grievious doggerel."

John Wesley had attached a number of *Psalms and Hymns* to his *Sunday Service of the Methodists of North America. With other occasional Services. London: printed in the year MDCCLXXXIV,* which he sent to America, in printed sheets, by Doctor Coke, together with a letter in which he advised

> All the travelling preachers to use (the liturgy) on the Lord's Day, in all their congregations, reading the litany only on Wednesdays and Fridays, and praying extempore on other days.

These books and the letter were properly presented to the Conference at Baltimore in December, 1784; the *Liturgy* and the *Psalms and Hymns* were adopted according to Wesley's wishes; and thus was the Methodist Episcopal

Church provided with its first official hymnal, called *A Collection of Psalms and Hymns.* Not giving satisfaction, it was used only a few years.

After the *Pocket Hymn Book,* however, had found its way across the Atlantic, it was soon as popular in this country as in England. A reprint of it, in 1790, became the second official American hymnal, and it, rather than the "Large Hymn Book" of 1780 or the *Psalms and Hymns* of 1784, became the nucleus of the hymnody of the Methodist Episcopal Church. The *Pocket Hymn Book* had not been copyrighted and was reprinted by various publishers. In 1802 Ezekiel Cooper, then book steward, revised it somewhat and issued, under copyright, *The Methodist Pocket Hymn Book, revised and improved: Designed as a constant Companion for the Pious of all Denominations. Collected from various authors.* It was the third hymnal to receive official approval.

The fourth came in 1808, when Bishop Asbury and Daniel Hitt presented to the Conference a *Supplement to the Pocket Hymn Book,* which was approved and issued as *A Selection of Hymns from various authors, designed as a Supplement to the Methodist Pocket Hymn Book, compiled under the direction of Bishop Asbury and published by order of the General Conference.* Printed separately for those who had the 1802 book, it was also bound up with it, and the two became known as "The Double Hymn Book."

The "Large Hymn Book" of 1780 seems to have been little known on this side of the Atlantic until 1814, when an edition of it was printed at Baltimore from the eighteenth London edition. A comparison of "The Double Hymn Book" with this showed a variation in text and called attention to many excellent hymns of which American Methodists had no knowledge.

The General Conference of 1820 ordered the publication of *A Collection of Hymns for the use of the Methodist Episcopal Church, principally from the Collection of the Rev. John Wesley . . . New York.* This fifth hymnal, compiled by the Book Agents and The Book Committee, was issued in 1821, and slightly revised in 1832.

After the disastrous fire of February 18, 1836, which destroyed the building of The Book Concern in New York City, and in which the plates of many of its publications, including those of the *Hymnal* were lost, a new issue was made necessary. This new edition, the sixth, was prepared by Dr. Nathan Bangs, book steward, who added a Supplement containing ninety hymns.

The next official *Hymnal* of the Church, the seventh, was that ordered by the General Conference of 1848, and issued the following year. This book served the Church until 1878, when the eighth, *The Methodist Episcopal Hymn and Tune Book,* appeared, having been compiled by order of the General Conference of 1876. This was the last official book of the Methodist Episcopal Church alone.

Many other books of hymns were used in Methodist churches both before and since the General Conference of 1784, but none of them had the official sanction of the Church.

The Methodist Episcopal Church, South, at its first General Conference in 1846, authorized the preparation of its first official hymn book, namely, *A Collection of Hymns for public, social and domestic worship,* issued by its publishing house, Nashville, in 1847. In 1851 it was amplified by *Songs of Zion: A Supplement to the Hymn Book of the Methodist Episcopal Church,*

*South.* This *Supplement* was somewhat enlarged in 1873, after extensive use by the Church for twenty-two years.

The propriety of publishing a "Tune-Hymn Book" was discussed at the General Conference of 1858, and an opinion generally favorable to the measure was expressed. The Book Agent and Editor were authorized to provide a book which would contain the hymns of the *Collection* of 1847 with musical settings. Such a book had already been prepared by Lemuel C. Everett, from whom the Book Agent secured exclusive rights for its publication under the title, *The Wesleyan Hymn and Tune Book: comprising the Entire Collection of Hymns in the Hymn Book of the Methodist Episcopal Church, South, with Appropriate Music Adapted to each Hymn.* It was issued in 1859.

*The New Hymn Book,* authorized by the General Conference of 1878, was issued in 1881. This book was compiled in response to a general appeal from certain churches of the denomination for a smaller and less expensive hymnal. It proved to be an abridgement of *Songs of Zion,* which is referred to in the Preface of the *New Hymn and Tune Book* as "the standard Hymn Book."

In 1889 there appeared the *Hymn Book of the Methodist Episcopal Church, South,* authorized by the General Conference of 1886. The limitation of the new book to eight hundred hymns was not followed, for it contained nine hundred and eighteen hymns, eleven doxologies, and fourteen chants. It was also printed with music under the title *Hymn and Tune Book of the Methodist Episcopal Church, South.* This was the last official hymnal of the Methodist Episcopal Church, South, alone.

After the organization of the Methodist Protestant Church in 1830, immediate use was made of a *Hymn Book* which had been compiled by John J. Harrod, of Baltimore, in 1828. This was superseded by the *Hymn Book of the Methodist Protestant Church,* authorized by the General Conference and published in 1838. The next hymnal, using the same title, was issued in 1859.

The delegates of the Northern and Western Conferences authorized the publication of the *Hymn Book,* which was published in 1860. In this year these Conferences withdrew from the Methodist Protestant Church, joining in 1867 to form the Methodist Church. Owing to the hastiness of the compilation of the book of 1860, a more suitable collection was deemed so desirable that in 1872 there was published *The Voice of Praise.* When the Methodist Church reunited with the Methodist Protestant Church in 1877, the official books of each body were approved, but there developed a strong sentiment for a single book with tunes. Accordingly, the plates and the publishing rights of Eben Tourjée's *The Tribute of Praise,* of 1874, were purchased; and, with revisions, it was republished, in 1882, as *The Tribute of Praise and Methodist Protestant Hymn Book.* This was the first hymnal of the Methodist Protestant Church containing both hymns and tunes.

After the latter book had been widely used for nineteen years, *The Methodist Protestant Church Hymnal,* 1901, was authorized by the General Conference of 1900. This was the last official hymnal of the Methodist Protestant Church alone.

In 1905 the Methodist Episcopal Church and the Methodist Episcopal Church, South, joined to issue *The Methodist Hymnal,* which served as the official hymnal of both churches for thirty years.

*The Methodist Hymnal* of 1935 is the joint product of the Methodist Episcopal Church, The Methodist Episcopal Church, South, and The Methodist Protestant Church. Is it too much to expect that the next generation of Methodists may publish a hymnal in which all other branches of the Church may join?

Clear in all these is the policy of the Church to include worthy hymns by many others than the Wesleys. John Wesley himself established a precedent for the inclusion of translations from the German in his first *Collection* of 1737; and hymns from Isaac Watts and others have ever appeared in Methodist hymnals. While the hymns of Charles Wesley, as is natural, have always outnumbered those of any other single writer, compilers of hymnals for the use of "the people called Methodists" have ever been alert to insert new contributions and to avail themselves of every possible source of suitable material. Thus we find in the latest *Hymnal,* selections from *The Scottish Psalter;* translations, or renderings, of Latin, Greek, German, Scandinavian, Welsh, and French sources; representative offerings from the books of other denominations, as well as from those of Jewish and Roman Catholic origin; from the field of sacred poetry; and from early twentieth-century and contemporary writers.

Methodism opened the way for a new church music. Whereas Doctor Watts conformed to familiar metrical schemes—namely, long, short, and common—for tunes already known, Charles Wesley wrote regardless of any known tunes, there having been no prejudice in the minds of Wesley's converts in favor of familiar melodies. Not only was an impetus given to the rewriting of texts, but frequently there was an actual suggestion of meters and rhythms from secular melodies. Those composers of the time who were writing for the Church were all members of the Established Church, and inasmuch as Nonconformists were not regarded with favor by educated musicians, there sprang up a new group of writers who saw in this new type of hymnody of Charles Wesley an especial opportunity for them. It was natural that the Methodists, being democratic and of the people, should have relied upon tunes of the folk style.

As Methodism became more of an organized institution, it began to conform to the general style of tunes in use in other denominations. And yet current all along there has been a common variety of everyday music that perhaps has kept Methodism nearer the soul of the people than are other denominations. In keeping with this instinct of Methodism, therefore, there have been included in this book some of the folklike camp-meeting tunes of a century ago. Keeping constantly in mind the cosmopolitan character of our Church, however, the makers of the present book have not forgotten to use things of the type of the German chorale, which John Wesley himself regarded so highly as to give precedent for using. As in the case of the hymns, all legitimate sources of tunes have been drawn upon. Here will be found music representative of great composers in the secular field; many examples of the late nineteenth-century school of English composers; examples of the work of Lowell Mason, his imitators and followers—their value all determined by years of use; the contribution of more recent and contemporary composers;

many "common" and "proper" tunes from the old psalters; and a few modified plainsong melodies. As stated in the Preface to *The Methodist Hymnal:*

> In the selection of music, those tunes emphasizing the melodic content were given preference. Care was taken to emphasize the associations of words and music that have grown familiar by long usage.

More than one hundred hymnals of recent and comparatively recent issue, and scores of older ones were scanned for suitable texts and music. Literally thousands of hymns and tunes were critically examined by the thirty-six members of the Joint Commission for material for possible Methodist use.

Not every student of *The Methodist Hymnal* will look with equal favor on every hymn, but there is sufficient variety to suit all qualities of taste among Methodism's varied millions. It is better to be happy over what has been included than to mourn over what has been excluded.

# BOOK I

## Notes on the Words and the Music of the Hymns, and Comments on the Authors, Translators, Composers, and Other Sources

# WORSHIP

## Adoration and Praise

**1—Holy, holy, holy—Reginald Heber**

**Nicaea—John Bacchus Dykes**

This great hymn to the Trinity is a paraphrase of Revelation 4. 8-11:

> And the four beasts had each of them six wings about him; and they were full of eyes within: and they rest not day and night, saying, Holy, holy, holy, Lord God Almighty, which was, and is, and is to come.
>
> And when those beasts give glory and honor and thanks to him that sat on the throne, who liveth for ever and ever,
>
> The four and twenty elders fall down before him that sat on the throne, and worship him that liveth for ever and ever, and cast their crowns before the throne, saying,
>
> Thou art worthy, O Lord, to receive glory and honor and power: for thou hast created all things, and for thy pleasure they are and were created.

Lord Tennyson is said to have told Bishop Welldon that he thought it the finest hymn ever written, taking into consideration its purity of language, its devotion, its spirituality, and the difficulty of treating such an abstract theme poetically.

Reginald Heber, born at Malpas, Cheshire, England, April 21, 1783, came of a cultured family and was, as Thackeray tells us in his *George the Fourth,* an English gentleman of the best sort—handsome, witty, competent, and of high character. He showed his poetic gift early in life, winning prizes for verse while he was a student at Brasenose College, Oxford. Once when Sir Walter Scott was having breakfast with Richard Heber, his half brother, Reginald, showed the company his poem "Palestine." Sir Walter called the youth's attention to the fact that no tools were used in the erection of the Temple. Such was Heber's genius that he immediately wrote the lines:

> No hammers fell, no ponderous axes rung;
> Like some tall palm the mystic fabric sprung.
> Majestic silence!

Heber served as Bampton lecturer from 1815, and preacher at Lincoln's Inn from 1822 until his appointment, in 1823, as Bishop of Calcutta. Although he had always felt drawn toward India, he had twice refused the bishopric there. Feeling that he had failed in his duty by not going, he let it be known that he would accept the post, saying he thought a clergyman should be like a "soldier, or sailor, bound to go on any service, however remote or undesirable, where the course of his duty leads him." For three years he labored unceasingly in India while the severe climate told mightily on his health. His servant found him dead in the bathroom of his home at Trichinopoly, India, on the morning of April 3, 1826. The poet Southey wrote for his monument this inscription:

> He performed his humblest as well as his highest duties carefully, with all his heart, with all his soul, with all his strength.

"Nicaea" was composed for this hymn for *Hymns Ancient and Modern,* 1861, one of seven tunes contributed by Doctor Dykes to its first edition. The tune received its name because of the fact that the doctrine of the Trinity was definitely established at the famous Council held at Nicaea, in Asia Minor, in 325. It was at this same Council that the Nicene Creed was adopted.

John Bacchus Dykes was born at Hull, March 10, 1823. His father, a staid banker, was prominent in musical circles as an amateur musician. That a dignified banker should name his child Bacchus after a scandalous heathen god is explained by the fact that it was an old family name. A one-time mayor of Hull named Bacchus married a Miss Huntington, to whose family Dykes's mother belonged; her father's name was Bacchus Huntington.

Young Dykes was very talented musically. He was taught violin and piano. While only a child he could play "by ear" almost anything he heard. Because of the especial appeal which the organ had for him, he used to have his sisters pump for him while he practiced, paying them a cent an hour for their labor. This practicing was done in his grandfather's church, St. John's, Hull, where John Bacchus was assistant organist at ten years of age. When the Dykes family later moved from Hull, the boy was presented with a gold watch and chain as an honorarium for his services. Dykes entered Cambridge in 1843, studying music throughout his course, and graduating four years later. He took Holy Orders and was appointed curate at Malton, Yorkshire. Two years later he was appointed precentor at Durham Cathedral. He was very happy in his work there, as it allowed him much time for composition, in which he was always interested. It was at Durham that he wrote most of his hymn tunes. An indefatigable worker, he worked out his hymn tunes wherever he happened to be—on the street, in a train, in the company of friends, even in the pulpit. In 1861 the University of Durham conferred on him the degree of Doctor of Music.

Of his appointment, a year later, as vicar of St. Oswald's, Durham, Philo A. Otis, in his *Hymns You Ought to Know,*[1] says:

> Soon after Dr. Dykes' appointment at St. Oswald's, a disagreement arose between him and the Bishop of the diocese, which proved to be a bitter contest and continued until Dr. Dykes' death. He was a High-Churchman, holding advanced ideas regarding the service of the sanctuary, with which his Bishop was not at all in accord. The Bishop was a Low-Churchman who disapproved of Dr. Dykes' services at St. Oswald's, regarding them as ritualistic and as an inroad of Popery. Dr. Dykes was successful in his work, and in consequence of the growing needs of St. Oswald, he required assistance, and applied (1873) to the Bishop for a Curate. The Bishop was willing to license the Curate on these conditions: that the Incumbent and Curate would give a written pledge that:

---

[1] Clayton F. Summy Co., Chicago.

1st. "The latter shall never wear a colored stole."
2nd. "Never have anything to do with incense."
3rd. "Shall never stand with his back to the congregation except when ordering the Bread."

Dr. Dykes considered this action of the Bishop illegal, and in this he was sustained by the judgment of many friends. He carried the case to the Court of the Queen's Bench in London, but was defeated; the court holding (January 19, 1874) that the Bishop had sole jurisdiction in such matters.

"Dr. Dykes," says his biographer, "never recovered from the shock. It is not too much to say that it killed him."

His death occurred at St. Leonards, January 22, 1876.

Doctor Dykes was one of the leading English hymn-tune writers of the last half of the nineteenth century who have so greatly influenced American hymn music. His tunes are less popular with American hymn singers than they were a generation ago. This is true also of the other English composers, such as Joseph Barnby (31), Arthur Sullivan (15), and others. The explanation is simple: American music is traditionally vocal and melodic. These English tunes were written by organists who were primarily instrumentalists. Add to that the fact that their tunes are overharmonized and the additional fact that they are not native to us, and the answer is found.

**2—Come, Thou almighty King**—Anonymous

**Italian Hymn** (Trinity)—Felice de Giardini

Although this hymn has been quite generally attributed to Charles Wesley, its author is unknown. As early as 1737 John Wesley began publishing hymns in booklets, and by 1780, when he had compiled the large *Collection of Hymns for the use of the People called Methodists,* he had issued many such booklets of hymns. One of these, published about 1757, is a very small one containing only two hymns. The date is uncertain because the title page to the little book has not been found. It may never have had one, and, indeed, it may not have been sponsored by either of the Wesleys. The second hymn in the booklet was a part of Charles Wesley's hymn on "The Backslider," beginning "Jesus, let Thy pitying eye." It is pure conjecture that "Come, Thou almighty King," the first one, was also by Charles Wesley, for it cannot be found in any known work of his. Some twelve or more years before the appearance of this hymn a version of the British National Anthem, "God save the King," had been launched and had attained immense popularity. The somewhat unusual meter of the Anthem intrigued writers of verse to copy its style extensively. As this hymn, that is, "Come, Thou almighty King," was first sung to the melody of the British Anthem, it had to follow its metrical pattern. The hymn has been translated, or rendered, into many languages, and its use in English-speaking countries is quite extensive.

"Italian Hymn," or "Trinity," was one of several tunes contributed by F. de Giardini to *The Collection of Psalm and Hymn Tunes sung at the Chapel of the Lock Hospital,* published in London in 1769, by the Rev. Martin Madan. There was an American edition in 1809. It is said that Lady Huntingdon was influential in having these tunes written for the book, generally referred to as the "Lock Collection," a source work of considerable value. In this book the tune, written in three-part harmony, was set to the words "Come, Thou almighty King" and was headed "Hymn to the Trinity, set by F. G." In different publications it has been called "Moscow," "Fairford," "Florence," "Hermon," and "Giardini's," as well as "Trinity" and "Italian Hymn." Why it has been called "Trinity" and "Giardini's" is obvious. The reason for the names "Italian Hymn" and "Moscow" are not difficult to find: it was composed by "the Italian" (as Giardini was known in England); and Moscow is the place where he died. For the use of the other names there seems to be no good reason. This multiplicity of names for hymn tunes is confusing. Compilers of hymnals seem to have no conscience in the matter. If the authentic name of the tune is not conveniently at hand, the compiler apparently goes to no trouble to search for it but chooses one which suits his fancy and lets it go at that. The original form of the tune was:

Felice de Giardini, violinist, born in Turin, Italy, April 12, 1716, began his musical career at Milan Cathedral, where he studied singing, clavier, and harmony under Paladini. His violin teacher, Somis, is best known because he taught Giardini. When very young Giardini played in the opera band (orchestra) in Rome and at San Carlo, Naples. He was fond of displaying his brilliant execution by means of ornamenting the accompaniment of songs with all sorts of runs, cadenzas, etc., until cured of his "inartistic propensities" by Jomelli, 1714-1774, an eminent opera composer, called the "Italian Gluck." During the performance of one of Jomelli's operas the composer sat near Giardini. The introduction of a brilliant cadenza of great length into the "ritornel" of a pathetic air, by the violinist, so enraged Jomelli that he gave the young man a box on the ear! In 1750 Giardini had a brilliant concert tour in Germany. Two years later he arrived in England and almost immediately took first rank among the violinists in the country, maintaining his position for thirty years. Because of his musical gifts he was not only in demand as an artist but as a teacher. His handsome pay from teaching probably had something to do with influencing royalty to recognize him socially. He was leader of the Italian Opera Band in London, becoming manager of the opera in 1856. His management was not successful and he suffered many losses. In 1784 he left England, apparently to retire and live in Italy, but he became restless and returned to London where, in 1790, he started a comic opera at the Haymarket Theatre. Upon its failure he took his troupe to Russia, where he was no more successful than in his last venture in London. Giardini was a prolific composer of operas, violin music, quartets, concertos, sonatas, etc. It is said that he was "capricious and splenetic"; that he spoke well of few and quarreled with many. Poverty-stricken and distressed, he died in Moscow, December 17, 1796.

**3—Before Jehovah's awe-full throne—Isaac Watts, altered**

**Old 100th—Genevan Psalter, 1551**

A paraphrase of Psalm 100, appearing first in Doctor Watts's *The Psalms of David imitated in the language of the New Testament,* 1719. It was in six stanzas of four lines each, beginning,

Sing to the Lord with cheerful voice;
Let every land His name adore;
The British isle shall send the noise
Across the ocean to the shore.

In the early American editions of Watts the third line was changed to read,

*America* shall send the noise.

John Wesley admired this hymn and selected four of its stanzas for use in his first book of hymns, the Charlestown (Charleston, South Carolina) *Collection* of 1737. He omitted the first stanza and changed the first two lines of the second from,

Nations attend before His throne
With solemn fear, with sacred joy,

to read,

Before Jehovah's awful throne
Ye nations bow with sacred joy.

In the 1935 edition of *The Methodist Hymnal* the word "awful" is spelled "awe-full" in order to convey more properly its original meaning. Watts's fourth stanza is omitted. The only other change from the original form is the use of the pronoun "His" in place of "Thy" in the last two stanzas, and the substitution of "shall" for "must" in the third line of the last stanza. In this form it is widely known, and has been translated into many languages. This hymn was sung in the hearing of thousands of Japanese who were stand ing on the shore watching the chaplain on Commodore Perry's flagship conduct divine service when the fleet was anchored in 1853-54 off the coast of Japan.

Isaac Watts, the eldest of nine children, was born at Southampton, England, July 17, 1674, into the Nonconformist family of Enoch Watts. His mother had descended from a Huguenot family which had fled to England to escape the persecutions which led to the St. Bartholomew Massacre. Enoch Watts was twice imprisoned for his Puritan beliefs. While her husband was incarcerated, Isaac's mother, with her baby in her arms, often came near the prison gate in order to sing psalms for him. The Watts family belonged to the Congregational church in Southampton, Enoch Watts being one of the deacons. This explains the apparent discrepancy in the story of Isaac's complaint about the dullness of the singing in the family church. Some writers say he spoke of it to his father; others, to one of the deacons. All are correct. The person to whom he spoke was both father and deacon. The young man was told to write something better if he did not like the psalms and hymns that were sung. This he proceeded to do, and the next Sunday he submitted his first hymn, "Behold the glories of the Lamb," in which the suggestion is made to

> Prepare *new* honours for His name
> And songs before unknown.

His first effort was so greatly appreciated that for two years a new hymn by him was sung each Sunday. Early in his life he showed promise of the poetic gift and an aptitude for study, for in his fourth year he began learning Latin. The Wattses kept a boarding school and after school hours Mrs. Watts used to employ the boys in writing verses, for which she offered a little copper medal as a prize for the most proficient. When he was eight, Isaac won a prize with,

> I write not for a farthing, but to try
> How I your farthing writers can outvie.

His father's imprisonment did not interfere with steady progress in Isaac's education. He was taught Greek, Latin, and Hebrew by the headmaster of the Grammar School at Southampton, and in 1690 entered a Nonconformist academy. A friend offered to bear the expenses of his education if he would prepare for the ministry in the Church of England. This Watts refused to do because it would necessitate his renouncing his dissenting belief, for none could be admitted to the schools receiving aid from the state without subscribing to the Articles of Faith of the Established Church. In good time he became a Congregational minister, and preached his first sermon, in 1698, at the age of twenty-four. Some two years before he had become the tutor of Sir John Hartopp's children at Newington. Here it was that he developed that love for children which gave us his *Divine and Moral Songs for Children,* 1715. In this book we find his moralizing verses about the "little busy bee" that "improves each shining hour"; the dogs that "delight to bark and bite"; the perfume of the rose; the industry of the ant. Here too we find that exquisite cradle song, "Hush, my babe, lie still and slumber." Soon after his ordination he went to London as assistant pastor of Mark Lane, but shortly found his health in such condition as to compel his withdrawal from active public life. He lived at the home of Sir Thomas and Lady Adney at Hertfordshire and London, and for more than thirty years he was a welcome guest of these friends he had originally gone to visit for a week.

Doctor Watts wrote many theological, philosophical, and poetic works but his fame rests upon his psalms and hymns. His versification of the psalms differed from that of others, for they were "imitated in the language of the New Testament, and applied to the Christian state of worship." He said, "My design is to accommodate the book of Psalms to *Christian worship.*" He wanted "to make David speak like a Christian of the eighteenth century." His hymns were epoch-making. His brother, Enoch, deserves credit for insisting that the hymns be published. Enoch wrote, "There is great need of a pen, vigorous and lively as yours, to quicken and revive the dying devotion of the age." He was not, as James Montgomery said, "the inventor of the English hymn." Others had written hymns before him, but he did establish the right of the metrical hymn to a place in modern Christian worship. Watts believed that songs for use by congregations should represent our word to God rather than God's word to us, to rephrase Dr. L. F. Benson's statement. Not all of his work was of high order, yet Doctor Johnson admitted him to his *Lives of the Poets*. Doctor Johnson, however, did not think too highly of some of Watts's work, for he says:

> His devotional poetry is, like that of others, unsatisfactory. The paucity of his topics enforces perpetual repetition, and the sanctity of the matter rejects the ornaments of figurative diction. It is sufficient for Watts to have done better than others what no man has done well.

Doctor Watts received recognition as a scholar. His *Logic* was long used as a textbook at Oxford, and the University of Edinburgh conferred upon him the degree of Doctor of Divinity. He died peacefully, November 25, 1748, in his seventy-fifth year. Of his work, Sir Roundell Palmer, Earl of Selborne, gives this estimate:

> No doubt his taste is often faulty, and his style very unequal. . . . It is true that in some cases dross is found in the original poems mixed with gold, but the process of separation without change is not difficult. As long as pure nervous English, unaffected fervour, strong simplicity, and liquid yet manly sweetness are admitted to be the characteristics of a good hymn, works such as these must command admiration.

As time goes on it is noticeable that Isaac Watts does not dominate the hymnals as he once did. In the 1905 *Methodist Hymnal* he was represented by fifty-one hymns and two doxologies; in the 1935 revision, by seventeen hymns and one doxology. This dropping of many of his hymns is true also in the case of the Presbyterian *Hymnal*. In the revision of *The Hymnal* of that denomination in 1911 there were forty-nine hymns by Watts; in the 1933 issue, twenty hymns and three responses. The reduction in the use of Watts's hymns in these newer hymnals is owing, not so much to the reduction of the total number of hymns in them, as to the general unsuitability of his work today.

There is much controversy over the origin, or derivation, of the tune known as "Old Hundred," or "Old Hundredth." It is agreed that it first appeared in the *Genevan Psalter,* 1551, where it was set to a metrical version of the 134th Psalm. The tune was brought to England by the Puritan refugees on their return from the continent. In 1561 there was printed in Geneva an edition of the *Anglo-Genevan Psalter,* containing William Kethe's version of Psalm 100 with this musical setting. Another edition of the same book, containing three fewer Psalms, appeared in London the same year. Which was issued first is a disputed point. The London edition contains this psalm and tune also. The name comes from the tune's association with Kethe's version of Psalm 100, with which this tune has been united for nearly four hundred years. It is not known how many of the tunes in the *Genevan Psalter* were original and how many adaptations. It was customary to take parts of various known melodies and combine them for use as new tunes. That is probably what happened in this case. During twelve of the sixteen years that Loys (Louis) Bourgeois was musical editor of the *Genevan Psalter,* 1541 to 1557, he lived with John Calvin, a fact which makes some authorities quite positive that Bourgeois wrote "Old 100th." It is more likely that he arranged it from parts of other melodies. Bourgeois was born at Paris about 1510 and died during the Massacre of St. Bartholomew's, August 25, 1572.

In the library of St. Paul's Cathedral, London, is a copy of this Geneva edition of the Psalter in which this tune appears as follows:

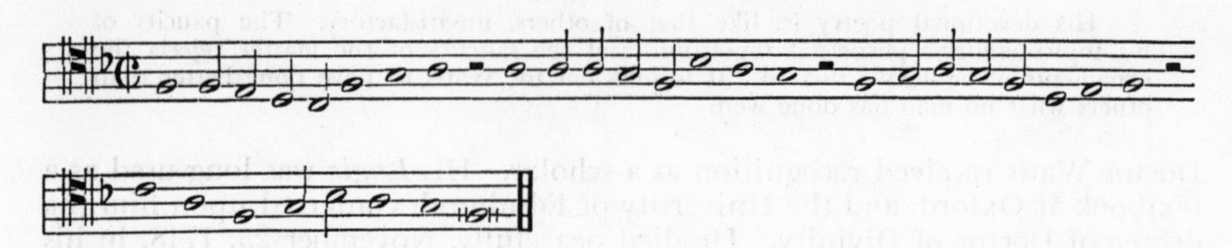

It is not included in Day's Psalter (No. 423) of 1562, but is found in the harmonized edition of the next year in the following form:

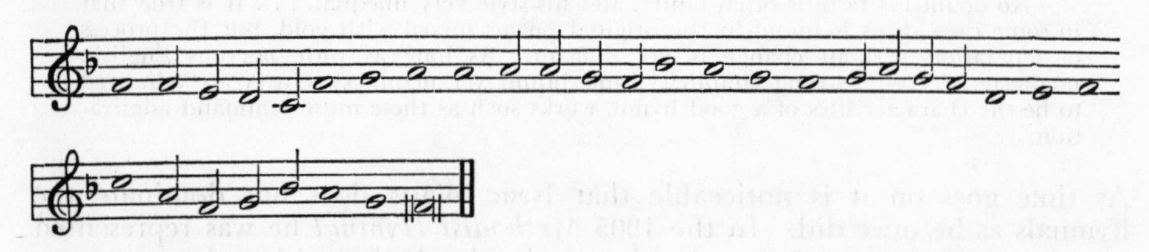

This is the version adopted by Ravenscroft in his *Psalter* of 1621 and is the one frequently (and erroneously) called the original. W. H. Havergal suggests the melody may have well been made up from four of the Gregorian hymn tunes from *The Evening Service.*

"Old 100th" has been attributed to Luther (by Handel, who probably did not know anything about it); to Guillaume Franc, author of musical notes in the 1564 *Genevan Psalter* (authorship attested by a local magistrate); to Claude Goudimel, a composer of the time (very doubtful); and to Bourgeois (as stated above). The original form (or rhythm—see No. 13) is being more and more printed in recent books, but because of the familiarity of congregations with the one in which the air consists of notes of equal value, it is not likely they will revert to it.

*The Genevan Psalter* had a gradual development. Starting in 1542 from a collection with thirty tunes, it went through various editions until, in 1562, it contained all of the Psalms. Clément Marot, d. 1544, the French poet, was the first Calvin psalmist. He was imprisoned as a boy for his Huguenot leanings, but later, when Court Poet (Francis I), he prepared some metrical versions of the Psalms, which became very popular, being sung to secular melodies of the day. Thirty of these renderings were probably the basis for John Calvin's first book of 1539. After Marot's death Calvin induced Théodore de Beza, d. 1605, to continue the work begun by Marot, and in 1551 an edition of *The Genevan Psalter* containing thirty-four Psalms in addition to those of the 1542 book was issued. It was from this old edition that "Old 100th" comes, as well as those other psalm tunes having the prefix "Old" (39 and 513).

**4—O worship the King—Robert Grant**

**Lyons—John Michael Haydn**

In the *Anglo-German Psalter* of 1561, William Kethe's version of Psalm 104 is found. The first stanza reads:

My foule praise the Lord
speake good of his Name
O Lord our great God
how doeft thou appeare,
So passing in glorie,
that great is thy fame
Honour and maieftie,
in thee fhine moft cleare.

It was this rendition of the psalm that suggested to Sir Robert Grant his much more elaborate hymn, which first appeared in Bickersteth's *Church Psalmody,* 1833. The first hymn, as it appears in this book, omits the well-known second stanza beginning,

O tell of His might, O sing of His grace,

and has included that beginning,

The earth, with its store of wonders untold.

Robert Grant, born (according to Julian) in 1785, more probably in 1779, was prominent in British letters and politics. He was called to the bar in 1807; was a member of Parliament, a director in the East India Company; made a privy councilor, and finally governor of Bombay. He died in Western India, July 9, 1838. His writings show a high poetic imagination. After his death his brother, Lord Glenelg, gathered together twelve of his hymns and poems and published them under the title *Sacred Poems.*

"Lyons" is credited to "Haydn" in an early edition of *The Boston Handel and Haydn Collection of Church Music.* This was first published in 1822 by the Society, edited by Lowell Mason (19). The tune came into such favor with Methodists that it was included in editions of *The Harmonist,* American Methodism's first official tune book, in the 1830's. It is one of some twenty-five tunes in that book which have survived in Methodist hymnody.

Johann Michael Haydn, born in the village of Rohrau, Lower Austria, September 14, 1737, a younger brother of the great Franz Joseph, was a remarkable singer as a boy. When his older brother's voice changed, Michael succeeded him as soloist at St. Stephens, Vienna, taking all the principal parts. Like his brother, he was also self-taught in music. He was interested in history, geography, and the classics. At the age of twenty-five he obtained a post at Salzburg, where he lived until his death. He seemed to be entirely happy there even though his salary was never more than two hundred and forty dollars per year with board and lodging. When Salzburg was taken by the French (1800), he lost all of his property. Although his brother and friends aided him, the Empress Maria Theresa, in order to aid him further, commissioned him to write a Mass for her. This he did, presenting it to her himself. At its first performance the Empress honored him greatly by singing the soprano solos. Michael Haydn, though untaught himself, was the teacher of many famous musicians, among them Carl Maria von Weber (200). Franz Joseph held Michael's compositions of sacred character in high esteem, insisting they were superior to his own. Michael wrote some three hundred and sixty works for the church, from which a number of our hymn tunes have been taken. Many of these have been attributed mistakenly to his better known brother. He was reticent about publishing his works. While somewhat rough in manner, he was honest, upright, warmhearted, and modest. Schubert said of him, after visiting his grave:

> The good Haydn! It almost seemed as if his calm, clear spirit were hovering over me. I may be neither calm nor clear, but no man living reverences him more than I do. My eyes filled with tears as we came away.

He was a very devout man, initialing all of his works with "O. a. M. D. Gl." (*Omnia ad Majorem Dei Gloriam.*)

He died at Salzburg, August 10, 1806.

**5—The God of Abraham praise**—Daniel ben Judah

**Leoni** (Yigdal)—Arranged from a Hebrew melody

This hymn is a rendering of the Yigdal, a Hebrew doxology which shares with Adon' Olam the place of honor at the opening of the morning and the close of the evening service in the synagogue. It is based on the thirteen Articles of Faith (usually called the Thirteen Creeds) formulated by Daniel ben Judah Dayyam, who spent eight years in improving it, completing it in 1404. This is not the only statement of the Jewish creeds, but it has outlived all others whether in Hebrew or in the vernacular. As used in *The Methodist Hymnal,* the version is substantially that made by Newton Mann (?) which is found in *The Union Hymnal for Jewish Worship,* published by the Central Conference of American Rabbis in 1914. The hymn begins "Praise to the living God," and is in five stanzas, the first, third, and last making this hymn.

"Leoni" (Yigdal) is an arrangement of an old folk motive common to

Jewish, Spanish-Basque, and Russian song. Bedřich Smetana, 1824-1884, Czech composer, uses this motive in his symphony, *Moravia,* thus:

In Josiah Miller's *Singers and Songs of the Church,* 1869, the following appears:

> The son of a Wesleyan minister said a few days ago, "I remember my father telling me that he was once standing in the aisle of the City Road Chapel during a conference in Wesley's time. Thomas Olivers, one of the preachers, came to him, and said, 'Look at this; I have rendered it from the Hebrew, giving it, as far as I could, a Christian character, and I have called on Leoni, the Jew, who has given me a synagogue melody to suit it; here is the tune, and it is to be called "Leoni."' "

The hymn to which reference was made is that with its first line, "The God of Abraham praise," numbered 4 in *The Methodist Hymnal,* 1905, and used in all Methodist hymnals since *The Pocket Hymn Book,* 1785. It was probably about 1770 when Olivers heard a chorister, Meyer Lyon, better known as Leoni, sing the Yigdal at the Great Synagogue, Duke's Place, London. He wrote the hymn immediately and shortly afterward published both hymn and tune as a leaflet entitled

A Hymn to the God of Abraham,

which passed through eight editions and was printed in *The Gospel Magazine* of April, 1775, before its inclusion in *The Pocket Hymn Book.* Olivers had been accompanied to the Great Synagogue by Joseph Rhodes, the precentor at the Foundery, who probably arranged the music.

Thomas Olivers, 1725-1799, orphaned before his fifth birthday, an apprentice to a shoemaker, was converted under the preaching of Whitefield and became a follower of John Wesley, who gave him charge of the editing of *The Arminian Magazine* and other literature for about twelve years. Owing to his negligence of many frightful errors in topography and his insertion of much matter without consultation with Wesley, another had to be secured for the work. Whatever his faults as an editor, his hymn is one of the "noblest in existence."

Meyer Lyon, Meier Leon, that is, Leon Chazzan (singer or precentor), in 1776 was appointed "singer" in the newly rebuilt Duke's Place Synagogue in London at an annual salary of £40, where "his attractive voice and wonderful singing attracted a great attendance of even Gentiles." He must have had some connection with the synagogue earlier, for Olivers heard him there in 1770. Later he was given opportunity of singing in opera at Covent Garden, assuming the Latinized name of "Leoni"; but owing to his lack of histrionic ability, and his refusal to sing on Fridays or on Jewish Festival days, he was unsuccessful. When he left the opera to return to the synagogue, he did so at a salary reduced to £32. In 1787 the Ashkenazic congregation at Kingston,

Jamaica, built a new synagogue and asked the London congregation for a reader. Leon went and remained there until his death in 1800.

The form in which the Yigdal is now chanted in the synagogues is:

It is probable, however, that the tune was not written in score in Leoni's time, but was sung in the manner in which it had been handed down from preceding generations of singers, and it may have been more like the version of Olivers than the one now in use. Whatever may be the truth of the matter, the melody is now known, in one form or another, all over the world.

**6—Ye watchers and ye holy ones**—John Athelstan Laurie Riley
**Lasst uns erfreuen**—From Geistliche Kirchengesäng

This hymn is one of universal praise couched in extravagant expression. It was doubtless suggested by the exhilarating melody to which it is set. In fact, Mr. Riley has stated that its career in England may be said to have begun in 1910 at The Church Pageant. Until *The English Hymnal* appeared with this hymn there had been no words which could be used with the peculiar meter of this fine chorale now so deservedly popular. Peculiarly fitted for men's voices, it is very effective when sung antiphonally.

"Lasst uns erfreuen" (Easter Alleluia) comes from a Cologne book of 1623 (*Geistliche Kirchengesäng*). It is an interesting example of the forcefulness of repetition, being built on a single unit of four notes, varied by repetition and inversion. It bears a strong resemblance to "Old 113th" (Lucerne—See No. 513), which, in turn, is quite similar to the 68th Psalm tune from *The Genevan Psalter,* composed or adapted by M. Greiter, c. 1500-1552. The arrangement in *The Methodist Hymnal* is by Ernest MacMillan (107), and appeared in *The Hymnary* (Canada), 1930. The name "Lasst uns erfreuen" comes from the Easter hymn, "Lasst uns erfreuen herzlich sehr," according to the German custom of naming the tune from the first line of the hymn to which it is set. It is also called "St. Francis."

J. Athelstan Riley, born at London, August 10, 1858, a member of the House of Laymen of the Province of Canterbury, educated at Eton and Pembroke Colleges, Oxford, M. A., 1883, was one of the compilers of *The English Hymnal,* 1906, to which he contributed three original hymns and seven translations from the Latin. One of the originals was a Saints' Day hymn, the first lines of which form the acrostic, "St. Bartholomew."

**7—Now thank we all our God**—Martin Rinkart
Translated by Catherine Winkworth

**Nun Danket**—Johann Crüger
Harmonized by Felix Mendelssohn-Bartholdy (33)

This hymn is a translation of the German, "Nun danket alle Gott," the first two stanzas of which are based on Ecclesiasticus 50. 22-24, and the third on the Gloria Patri. It is known as the German "Te Deum." Miss Winkworth, its translator, says it is to Germany what "Old 100th" is to England. When J. S. Bach (52) was about forty-five years old, during the period when he was writing the Leipzig cantatas, he became "sickened with the trivial rhyming of the 'madrigal' cantatas, on which, for nearly ten years he had been almost incessantly engaged," and yearned for a "stronger poetic diet. The old Protestant hymns supplied him with what he required." One of these old hymns, "Nun danket alle Gott," served him well. He also used the words from the Apocrypha for a five-part motett written many years later. The hymn must have been in his mind, however, for he used the words, "Who wondrous things hath done, wherein His world rejoices"—words which are in the hymn but not in Ecclesiasticus. There seems to be no connection between its composition and the Peace of Westphalia, as has so often been stated. The hymn is simply a general expression of thanksgiving. It has been quite generally sung on notable occasions of rejoicing as the laying of the cornerstones of the Reichstag building in Berlin, in 1884, and on the occasion of the declaration of peace at the close of the Boer War, when it was sung at Saint Paul's Cathedral in London.

Martin Rinkart, born at Eilenburg, April 23, 1586, theologian and musician, became archbishop at Eilenburg, Saxony, his birthplace, at the age of thirty-one. He received his education at the Thomasschule, Leipzig, where he was a foundation scholar and chorister, and at the University, where he studied theology. The greater part of his life was spent at Eilenburg amidst the horrors of the Thirty Years' War. Because this small city was inclosed by a wall, it attracted so many refugees during the Thirty Years' War that the people suffered from famine and pestilence. Being the only clergyman in the place for some time during the pestilence of 1637, Rinkart often read as many as forty or fifty burial services a day—in all about 4,480 of the eight thousand persons who died during the whole pestilence. Julian thinks that Rinkart wrote this hymn as early as 1636. He died at Eilenburg, December 8, 1649.

Catherine Winkworth, the translator, who was born at London, September 13, 1829, spent most of her early life near Manchester, later living with her family in Clifton, near Bristol. She died suddenly of heart disease in Savoy in July, 1878. Although greatly interested in higher education for women, a cause which she did much to further, her fame rests chiefly on her translations of German hymns into English. She issued *Lyra Germanica* in two series, the first in 1855 and the second in 1858; *The Chorale Book for England,* 1863, which contained translations of hymns as well as music; and an interesting biographical work, *Christian Singers of Germany,* 1869. So widely used are Miss Winkworth's translations that they undoubtedly have had more to do with the present interest in German hymns in English-speaking countries than have those of any other translator.

"Nun danket" gets its name from the first line of Martin Rinkart's hymn, following the German custom of naming chorales. The tune first appeared in the *Praxis Pietatis Melica,* 1648 (third edition), edited by Johann Crüger. The first edition was issued in 1636, according to Julian, and during the next one hundred years ran through fifty or sixty editions. Its original form was:

Mendelssohn (33) took the melody, altered it, harmonized it, and used it in his *Festgesang—Hymn of Praise* (or Thanksgiving). This work was first sung in Leipzig, Germany, on June 25, 1840, at a celebration held in that noted city of publishing houses, in honor of the invention of printing, some four hundred years before. Another famous tune from this work is that sung to "Hark, the herald angels sing" (86).

Johann Crüger was born near Guben, Prussia, April 9, 1598, and after attending various schools and making a tour of Austria, settled in Berlin in 1615, where he acted as private tutor for some years. In 1622 he was appointed cantor at the church of St. Nicholaus. He was one of the foremost musicians of his time, composing in all forms common in his day. His chief claim to greatness, however, is because of the excellent chorales he wrote, many of them, in one form or another, being in good repute today. He edited and contributed to the *Praxis Pietatis Melica,* the most important work in the field of hymnody produced during the seventeenth century. His death occurred at Berlin, February 23, 1662.

**8—Let all the world—George Herbert**

**All The World—John Porter**

This hymn, "Let all the world in every corner sing," is from *The Temple,* Antiphon 21; 1633. Some slight effort was made to introduce parts of *The Temple* into hymnals, but no very serious one until John Wesley included seven of them in his first collection (Charleston, South Carolina, 1737), and in *Hymns and Sacred Poems,* John and Charles Wesley, 1739, where more than forty are found, though much altered. Nothing was too commonplace for Herbert to use as a starting point for an expression of piety. The church key reminds him that "it is my sin that locks my hands." The floor-stones of his church typify patience and humility; the cement that binds them signifies love and charity.

Susannah Wesley introduced his poetry to her children, and Charles and John admired him greatly. It has been the Methodists who have kept his memory alive, for only recently has Herbert received wide recognition from hymnists of other denominations.

George Herbert was a member of the most important of the three Herbert families of England. His lineage was direct from Sir William Herbert, the first Earl of Pembroke, called Gwilim, or Black William, by the Welsh. Herbert was the chief glory of the Jacobean and Carolean poets, a remarkable group of kindred spirits, headed by Izaak Walton, 1593-1683. Born the same year, Walton outlived Herbert by fifty years, the former dying at forty. Among the group were Richard Crashaw, 1613(?)-1649, and Thomas Ken (later Bishop), 1637-1711, influenced by Herbert through Walton. Though not now represented in hymnals, Crashaw is well known for his translation of the "Dies Irae" and for his exquisite epigram:

Two went to pray? O rather say
One went to brag, the other to pray.

One stands up close, and treads on high,
Where the other dares not lend his eye.

One nearer to God's altar trod;
The other to the altar's God.

Gilman says this might have come from Herbert's pen, so dainty and worshipful it is. Thomas Ken lived in the home of Izaak Walton, where Herbert's life was revered "as a pattern of piety."

George Herbert, born at Montgomery Castle, April 3, 1593, married Jane Danvers after a courtship of three days, which had been arranged by interested friends. As a "King's Scholar" at Trinity, Cambridge, he became university "orator," a position which kept him at court much of his time making complimentary speeches "at the advent of royalty and distinguished personages." Such a great lover of music was Herbert that he devoted all of his spare time to its practice and was proficient on both lute and viol, with which he accompanied his hymns. It is from *The Temple* that most of his hymns were taken. *The Temple* was given to a friend, Nicholas Ferrar, his executor, three weeks before Herbert died. It was a record of his soul's spiritual conflicts with God. He told Ferrar to use it as he saw fit: that if Ferrar did not think it might turn to the advantage of "any dejected poor soul," he might burn it, for "I and it are less than the least of God's mercies." Walton gives numerous and touching anecdotes of his patience, gentleness, and generosity. "He seemed to be marked out for piety and to become the care of heaven." He arose from his bed on the Sunday before he died, asked for one of his instruments, and, upon its being handed to him, said:

My God, my God,
My music shall find Thee,
And every string
Shall have His attribute to sing.

Tuning it, he sang to its accompaniment:

The Sundays of man's life,
Threaded together on Time's string,
Make bracelets to adorn the wife
Of the eternal, glorious King:
On Sundays, heaven's door stands ope;
Blessings are plentiful and rife,
More plentiful than hope.

He died at Bremerton, near Salisbury, in February, 1632, and on March 3, following, was buried beneath the altar of his own church. On his deathbed he said, "I shall now suddenly (with Job) make my bed also in the dark; and I praise God, I am prepared for it." Izaak Walton wrote, "He pleased God and was beloved of Him; so that, whereas he lived among sinners, He translated him."

"Let all the world" was written especially for this hymn. Its meter is peculiar, and other settings did not seem to make the right appeal. Herbert called this poem "Antiphon," and wished the congregation to sing the first two lines as a chorus with the other four lines used as a solo. This setting, being in unison, lends itself admirably to that treatment.

"John Porter" is the nom de plume of a hymn-tune writer who prefers to remain anonymous.

**9—My God, I thank Thee, who hast made**—Adelaide Anne Procter

First tune: **Wentworth**—Frederick Charles Maker

Second tune: **Fowler**—Robert Guy McCutchan

The first line of this hymn was written to read "I thank Thee, O my God, who made." It is taken from Miss Procter's *Legends and Lyrics,* 1858. In its first form there were six stanzas. The three used in this book are 1, 2, and 5 of the original.

Adelaide Anne Procter, born at London, October 30, 1825, was the daughter of Bryan Waller Procter, English poet and author who wrote under the pseudonym of "Barry Cornwall." Her parents were personal friends of Charles Dickens, who often visited in the Procter home. Miss Procter showed unusual intellectual gifts as a young girl and later in her life became quite proficient in language and music. Her poetical works received wide recognition. After her death Dickens told of the publishing in *Household Words* of frequent contributions of one Mary Berwick, who he and the members of his staff thought was a domestic servant. On an occasion when he was dining with the Procters, Dickens showed them a proof of a poem by "a certain Miss Berwick." On the following day he learned that he had shown the poem to its author, Miss Procter. Dickens also wrote that during the fifteen months of her last illness, the poet never complained, and that her cheerfulness never left her. Miss Procter became a Roman Catholic in her twenty-sixth year. She died at London, February 2, 1864.

"Wentworth" appeared in *The Bristol Tune Book,* 1876 edition. It was written for this hymn. The music has been edited by the use of ties to avoid some bad accents which have militated somewhat against the general use of the tune heretofore.

Frederick Charles Maker was born in Bristol, England, 1844, and lived there until his death at the age of eighty-three. He began his musical career as a choir boy in the cathedral in that city. A very capable organist, he held several appointments, remaining for thirty years at the Rulland Park Congregational Church until his retirement in 1910. He became acquainted with Alfred Stone, conductor of festival choirs, and when Stone wanted some special tunes for *The Bristol Tune Book* which he was editing, Maker submitted several, one of which was "Wentworth." Mr. Maker became well and favorably known for his tunes, many of which are in use in the later hymnals. He died in 1927.

"Fowler" was written for *The Standard Hymnal,* issued in 1930. A tune which would avoid the unpleasant accents in "Wentworth" was wanted, and "Fowler" was the result.

Robert Guy McCutchan is the dean of the School of Music, DePauw University. Born at Mount Ayr, Iowa, September 13, 1877, he was educated at Park College, Missouri, at Simpson College, Iowa, at Berlin and Paris. For six years, from 1904, he taught at Baker University, Kansas, where he organized its Conservatory of Music, going to DePauw University as dean of the School of Music in 1911, where he is still located. Among his various activities he has been the Musical Editor of *Standard Hymns, The Junior American Church School Hymnal,* the editor of *The Methodist Hymnal,* 1935, and the author of this MANUAL.

**10—To Thee, Eternal Soul, be praise**—Richard Watson Gilder

**Worship**—Karl Pomeroy Harrington

In a letter written in 1907 to Dean W. F. Tillett, the author says this hymn "had a Methodist origin, as Wesley was in my mind, and it was first printed in the new (1905) *Methodist Hymnal.*" Doctor Gilder had been invited to take part in the celebration of the two hundredth anniversary of the birth of John Wesley at Wesleyan University, Connecticut, on June 3, 1903. For the occasion he wrote the poem "John Wesley," beginning,

> In those clear, piercing, piteous eyes behold
> The very soul that over England flamed!
> Deep, pure, intense; consuming shame and ill;
> Convicting man of sin; making faith live;
> And—this the mightiest miracle of all—
> Creating God again in human hearts.

Another stanza from this fine poem may well be quoted here:

> Let not that image fade
> Ever, O God! from out the minds of men,
> Of him Thy messenger and stainless priest,
> In a brute, sodden, and unfaithful time,
> Early and late, o'er land and sea, on-driven;
> In youth, in eager manhood, age extreme—
> Driven on forever, back and forth the world,
> By that divine, omnipotent desire,
> The hunger and the passion for men's souls!

He wrote the hymn, heading it

> Hymn. Thanksgiving for Saints and Prophets.

Doctor Gilder showed the hymn to Professor Caleb T. Winchester (561), whose guest at Middletown he was. Professor Winchester, widely known for his work, *Literary Criticism,* was, at the time, a member of the Joint Commission having in hand the preparation of a common hymnal for the use of the two largest branches of Methodism. The hymn made such a favorable impression on him that he asked and was granted the privilege of submitting it to the Joint Commission for inclusion in the new book. It was shortly afterward printed in Doctor Gilder's *The Fire Divine,* and has also found its way into other hymnals.

Richard Watson Gilder, the son of a Methodist minister, was born at Bordentown, New Jersey, February 8, 1844. His father, a teacher as well as a preacher, wisely encouraged the literary tastes which the youth manifested. Later in life when Doctor Gilder was the recipient of honorary degrees from universities, he was wont to speak of his "total freedom from collegiate training" and of his "general ignorance." As a schoolboy he edited his own paper, had some poems printed, and contributed a "youthful, formless novel" to a newspaper. He worked on a newspaper, for a time was part owner of another in Newark, New Jersey, and served for a while as a soldier in the Civil War. At the age of twenty-six he became assistant editor of *Scribners' Monthly* (later *The Century Magazine*), and eleven years later its editor. Doctor Gilder was an extremely busy man, making many public addresses, attending committee meetings, and engaging in all sorts of altruistic work. He was much interested in an international copyright law and in the work of the New York Tenement Commission, of which he was at one time chairman. He once served as a railway paymaster. "But," he said, "I am a poet. I would rather be that than all the rest put together." After suffering several breakdowns from overwork, he died the week before Thanksgiving, 1909.

"Worship" is one of twelve hymn tunes and an "Invocation Sentence," contributed by Professor Harrington to *The Methodist Hymnal* of 1905.

Karl Pomeroy Harrington, Professor Emeritus of Latin Language and Literature, Wesleyan University, Middletown, Connecticut, widely known as an educator and musician, was born in Somersworth, New Hampshire, June 13, 1861. Professor Harrington was one of the musical editors of *The Methodist Hymnal,* 1905. From the time of his graduation from Wesleyan University in 1882 to his retirement in 1929, Professor Harrington was actively engaged in teaching. He has held college positions in North Carolina and Maine as well as in Connecticut. He is a member of a number of learned societies, and is known to thousands of college men throughout the country because of his song "Mrs. Winslow's Soothing Syrup," which has been sung by college glee clubs for many years. It was written while he was teaching at the University of North Carolina. (See also No. 98.)

**11—Praise the Lord! ye heavens adore Him**—From the Foundling Hospital Collection, 1796

**Hyfrydol**—Melody by Rowland Hugh Prichard

This hymn is of unknown authorship. It first appeared as part of a four-page tract which was pasted in a 1796 music edition of *Psalms, Hymns, and Anthems of the Foundling Hospital,* and in a word edition of 1801. It probably was written after 1801, for it must have been pasted in both editions at the same time. The hymn is headed

Hymn from Psalm 148, Haydn.

*The Foundling Hospital Collection* was a collection of hymns and anthems compiled for the charity founded by Captain Thomas Coram in 1738. Captain Coram was a seaman, who afterward became a merchant captain. For a time he was engaged in shipbuilding at Taunton, Massachusetts, but returned to England in 1703. He was one of the promoters of the settlements in Georgia and in Nova Scotia. After the founding of the hospital he devoted the remainder of his life and all of his means to charitable enterprises. The Foundling Hospital maintained a chapel much frequented by fashionable folk and from its establishment made a special feature of training children in music. Handel (88) became greatly interested in the enterprise and upon completion of the chapel donated its organ. The Hospital owed much to Handel's support. Wishing to express his gratitude to the London public for favors shown him, he made a practice for several years of conducting a performance of the *Messiah* for the benefit of the charity. Not only did he do this, but John Hawkins, the musical historian, writes:

> By presenting the charity with a copy of the score and parts of this composition, he gave them such a title to it as seemed to import an exclusive right to the performance of it. This act of bounty was so ill understood by some of the governors of this foundation that they formed a resolution for an application to Parliament to establish their supposed right; in short, to prohibit, under penalties, the performance of the *Messiah* by any others than Mr. Handel and themselves. To facilitate the passing of a law for the purpose, Mr. Handel's concurrence was asked, but he was so little sensible of the propriety of it, that upon the bare mention of it he broke out into a furious passion, which he vented in the following terms: "For vat sal de Foundlings put mein oratorio in de Parlement?"

"Hyfrydol" is a very happy tune and an appropriate setting for such an exhilarating hymn. It first appeared in 1855 in the Welsh *Haleliwiah Drachefn,* literally "Hallelujah Again" (or afterward). Its marked characteristic is the simplicity of its melody, which, except for one note, is confined to the limits of a fifth—from *do* to *sol.* One of the strong tunes new to American Methodism, in its first form it began:

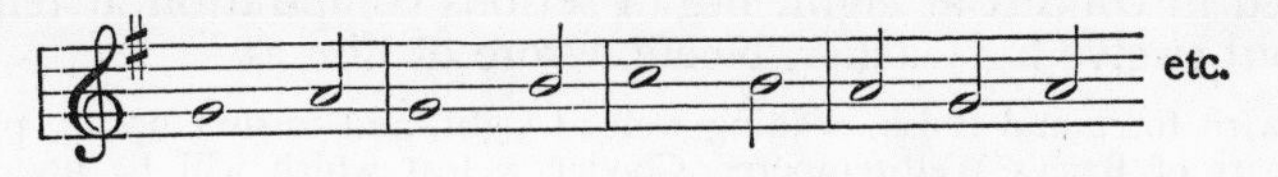


Rowland Hugh Prichard wrote "Hyfrydol" while in his teens. He was born near Bala, Wales, the seat of the Calvinistic Methodist College, in 1811. Here Prichard lived the greater part of his life, being engaged actively in church music, for he had a good voice and the ability to act as precentor. He contributed several tunes to Welsh periodicals, published a book, *The Singer's Friend,* made up mostly of his own compositions, and also compiled a little singing book for children. When he was sixty-nine years old he was given a position as assistant to a loom-tender in a woolen mill near Holywell (King's Head), where he died, January 25, 1887.

**12—Joyful, joyful we adore Thee—Henry van Dyke**

**Hymn to Joy—Ludwig van Beethoven**

The hymn comes from *Poems of Henry van Dyke,* published in 1911. A beautiful paean of joy, its every line is poetic, breathing man's gratitude to God, his Creator. It is also a nature hymn of the first order.

Henry van Dyke, born at Germantown, Pennsylvania, November 10, 1852, was one of America's most eminent men of letters, and he also gained fame as a preacher, a teacher, and as a diplomat. He graduated from Polytechnic Institute, Brooklyn, in 1869; from Princeton in 1873; from Princeton Theological Seminary in 1877, and was ordained a Presbyterian minister in 1879. He then served the United Congregational Church at Newport, Rhode Island, and the Brick Presbyterian Church, New York City, as pastor until 1900. After that, for twenty-three years, he was Professor of English Literature at Princeton. President Woodrow Wilson appointed him United States minister to the Netherlands and Luxemburg in 1913, which position he resigned in 1917. After his retirement in 1923 he devoted himself almost wholly to writing. He gained eminence as a lecturer, author, and editor, and was the recipient of many high honors, serving as Moderator of the General Assembly of the Presbyterian Church, Commander of the Legion of Honor, and President of the National Institute of Arts and Letters. He died at Princeton, April 10, 1933.

"Hymn to Joy" is taken from the last movement of the Ninth Symphony, Beethoven's masterpiece. Beethoven felt that he had exhausted all of his orchestral resources before writing this finale, and in order to express himself fully, he felt called upon to use the greatest of all instruments, the human voice. It is a fine example of the simplicity of the works of great men. It is also an example of the adaptation of one of the world's masterpieces in music to a hymn, and its effectiveness is greater because it has not been mutilated in any way. It seems particularly fitting that this tune should be used for this hymn.

Ludwig van Beethoven was born, probably, December 16, 1770, at Bonn, Germany, and died at Vienna, Austria, March 26, 1827. According to his own statement, he began working in music in his fourth year. His biographers tell us he played in concert at eight, began serious composition at ten, and when he was about twelve his teacher, Neefe, wrote of him as

> playing with force and finish, reading well at sight, and to sum up all, playing the greater part of Bach's Well-tempered Clavier, a feat which will be understood by the initiated.

At twelve years and four months he conducted an opera orchestra. It is strange that he did so little serious composing in his early life. Nevertheless, in his early attraction (in 1793) to Schiller's "Hymn to Joy," the principal motive of his colossal Ninth Symphony composed during the years 1817-1823, we have evidence of that deep thinking in his early life which characterized his later work. A study of his many notebooks tells of his remarkable tenacity of purpose and of his painstaking development of ideas, sometimes years elapsing before he is willing to submit them in finished form.

Beethoven was notoriously impatient of restraint and very independent. Most of his intimate friends were members of the aristocracy, yet never for a moment did he evidence any feeling of inferiority. He was very irascible, yet with all his remarkable genius he was possessed of a charming simplicity that was at times almost childlike. One writer, after meeting him, had the impression that he seemed like a very able man brought up on a desert island, who had been suddenly thrust into the world of everyday life.

Very fond of rough horse-play and practical joking, he was never willing to be placed on the receiving end. Some of his finest friendships were broken because of this unfortunate trait. His manners too were deplorably bad, but he had a strange attractiveness. Not only was this true so far as men were concerned, but it affected women also. Yet, except for a few unsubstantiated reports of youthful indiscretions, not the slightest suggestion of scandal was ever attached to his name. He lived a singularly clean life.

Apparently, he had no formal religion. But that he was deeply and sincerely religious there can be no doubt. On his writing table he had framed the following passages which he had copied and kept constantly before him:

> "I am that which is.
> "I am all that is, that was, and shall be.
> "No mortal man hath lifted my veil.
> "He is alone by Himself and to Him alone do all things owe their being."

A great lover of nature, he says: "No man on earth loves the country more than I do." And, "Woods, trees, and rocks give the response which man requires." And, again, "Every tree seems to say Holy, Holy."

Beethoven wrote no hymn tunes, as such, that we know of, but because of the deeply contemplative character of all of his works, "adaptations" have been numerous. Although many more of them were in common use a century ago than now, some are so genuinely devotional in character that they will doubtless be used as long as Christian hymnals are published.

**13—All people that on earth do dwell**—William Kethe

**Old 100th**—Melody from *Genevan Psalter,* 1551 (3)

There has been much controversy over the authorship of this classical version of Psalm 100, but most commentators now agree, passively, that it was the work of William Kethe. Belief is expressed that Kethe wrote this in long meter so that it might be sung to "Old 100th." It first appeared in Day's Psalter (423) or the *Anglo-Genevan Psalter* (3). Both books appeared the same year, 1561, but which was issued first has not been established. However that may be, we do know that it has been appearing in psalm and hymn books almost continuously for three hundred and seventy-five years. Although it first appeared in American Methodism in the Methodist Episcopal *Hymnal* of 1878, it was not in the 1880 *Hymnal* of the Methodist Episcopal Church, South, nor in the *Methodist Protestant Church Hymnal* of 1901. Lord Ernle (Rowland E. Prothers), in his *The Psalms in Human Life,* says this version of Psalm 100 "survives all changes of thought and fashion that the progress of four centuries has witnessed." Except for the use of the word "folk" instead of "flock" in the second stanza, and the omission of the interrogation point after "For why" in the first line of stanza four, it appears in *The Methodist Hymnal* exactly as in *The Scottish Psalter*.

William Kethe is supposed to have been a native of Scotland, but neither the date nor the place of his birth is known. He was one of the English reformers who fled to Frankfurt and Geneva to escape the wrath of Queen Mary. While on the Continent he is reported to have acted as messenger from Geneva to other English-speaking congregations there. Upon his return to England he acted as chaplain for the forces of the Earl of Warwick and is said to have been rector at Childe Okeford, Dorsetshire, from 1561 until his death, about 1593. The author of some religious ballads, he is reported to have been "no unready rhymer."

The musical version of "Old 100th" is that adopted by Ravenscroft in his *Psalter* of 1621 (3).

**14—Through all the changing scenes of life**—From Psalm 34. New Version
Tate and Brady, 1698

**Irish**—Melody from a Collection of Hymns and Sacred Poems, 1749

In its full rendering this psalm, in two parts, has eighteen stanzas of four lines each. Julian says its use in various forms is universal, although it never appears in modern books in its entirety. In this instance stanzas 1, 2, 7, and 8 of Part I, and stanza 18 of Part II are used. It appears exactly as in the original except for differences in spelling, and the changed rendering of the last line of stanza four, which read,

He'll make your wants His care.

The appearance of this hymn marks its restoration for Southern Methodism, for it was included in the *Hymn and Tune Book* of 1880. It is new to the two other branches of the Church.

*A New Version of the Psalms fitted to the Tunes used in the Churches,* by Nahum Tate, English poet-laureate under William III, and Dr. Nicholas Brady, "Chaplain in Ordinary," was issued in 1696. It was successor to the "Old Version," by Sternhold and Hopkins, 1562, the completed form of the *English Psalter*. While the "New Version" never completely supplanted the "Old Version," it did much to effect the transition from psalm to hymn singing. The hymn under consideration is an excellent example of the hymn-like tendencies of the "New Version."

"Irish" appeared in *Hymns and Sacred Poems,* published in Dublin in 1749, which may have been a product of John Wesley, for he and John F. Lampe (associated with Wesley in musical work) are known to have been in Dublin that year. This, however, is merely an assumption. The only known copy of *Hymns and Sacred Poems* is in the Warrington Library at Western Theological Seminary, Pittsburgh. "Irish" was one of a few tunes without names included at the end of the volume. "Irish Tune" was the name given to it in Caleb Ashworth's *Collection of Tunes,* about 1760. It has also been called "Dublin." It first appeared in the following form:

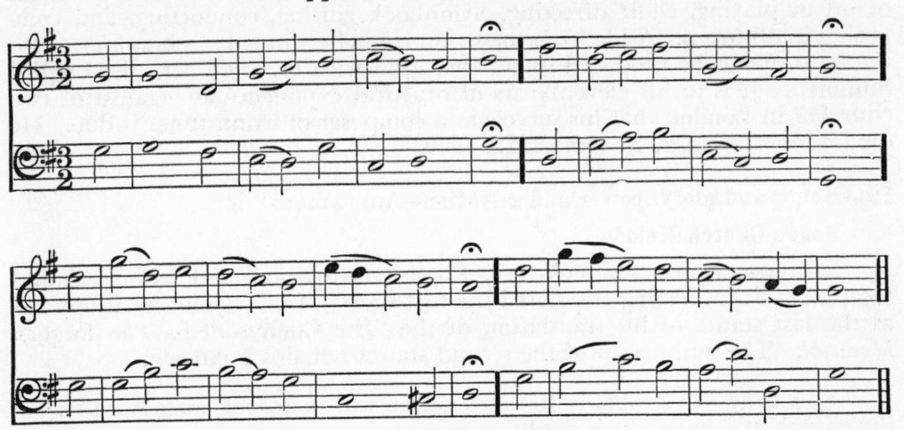

**15—Angel voices ever singing**—Francis Pott

**Angel Voices**—Arthur Seymour Sullivan

"For the dedication of an organ, or for a meeting of choirs" was the heading of this hymn which was first sung at the dedication of an organ in the Church of St. John the Evangelist at Wingate, England. Its first appearance in a hymnal was in *Hymns fitted to the Order of Common Prayer,* second edition, 1866, compiled by the author. An excellent processional for occasional use, no more effective hymn can be found for the dedication of an organ. It has been said that it "makes up in sweetness what it lacks in dignity."

Francis Pott, born at Southwark, a borough of London, December 29, 1832; educated at Brasenose College, Oxford; and for twenty-five years rector at Norhill, Ely, England, was noted for his translations from the Latin and Syriac as well as for his original hymns. His work has been favorably received and widely used. He died October 26, 1909.

"Angel Voices" has been criticized as being "feeble and dubious in its harmonic progressions" and "too frivolous," yet, like the hymn to which it is set, it has a "sweetness" that makes it a favorite with thousands of worshipers. Its first appearance was in 1872.

Arthur Seymour Sullivan, born May 13, 1842, at London, was the son of an Irish bandmaster. He became a choir boy at the Chapel Royal, London, when twelve years of age; at thirteen wrote an anthem, "O Israel," that attracted attention, and at fourteen, in open competition, became the first holder of the Mendelssohn Scholarship at the Royal Academy of Music, where he studied under such eminent teachers as Sterndale Bennett and Sir John Goss (264). With this scholarship, which made provision for study on the Continent, Sullivan made the most of his time in Germany, winning the "golden opinions" of his teachers. Upon his return to England, in 1861, he entered upon a career which was to make him famous for his varied activities of organ playing, choir directing, hymnbook editing, conducting, and composing in all forms. Aside from the hymn tunes he wrote, he is best known for the light operas he produced in collaboration with W. S. Gilbert, the English humorist. It is to his eleven years of practical experience as organist of two churches in London that his success as a composer of hymn tunes is due. He died at Westminster, November 22, 1900.

**16—Honor and glory, power and salvation**—Anonymous

**Rouen Church Melody**

Laurence Housman, 1865- , English artist, poet and author, should receive credit for having translated the first stanza of this hymn, for it appears as the last stanza of his translation of the "Iste Confessor" in *The English Hymnal.* The authorship of the second stanza remains unknown.

This tune was probably founded on an old plainsong melody in use in the church at Rouen. It is doubtless one of the sixteenth- or seventeenth-century "church melodies" which came out of the transition from the unmeasured type of song (plainsong) to that which was measured, that is, where the music was written in notes which of themselves indicated time values.

**17—From all that dwell below the skies**—Stanzas 1, 4, Isaac Watts (3)
Stanzas 2, 3, Anonymous

**Duke Street**—John Hatton

A paraphrase of the shortest psalm (117) by Isaac Watts, appeared in *Psalms of David,* 1719, in two stanzas, the first and fourth of this hymn. The attribution of the second and third to John Wesley has not been substantiated. In the Preface to the *Pocket Hymn-Book for the Use of Christians of All Denominations,* edition of 1786, Wesley says:

> A few years ago I was desired of many of our preachers to prepare and publish a small Pocket Hymn-book, to be used in common in our Societies. This I promised to do, as soon as I had finished some other business, which was then on my hands. But before I could do this, a Bookseller stepped in, and without my consent or knowledge, extracted such a Hymn-book, chiefly from our works, and spread several editions of it throughout the kingdom. Two years ago I published a Pocket Hymn-book according to my promise. But most of our people were supplied already with the other Hymns. And these are largely circulated still. To cut off all pretense from the Methodists for buying them, our Brethren in the late Conference at *Bristol* advised me to print the same Hymn-book which had been printed at *York.* This I have done in the present volume. . . .

Most present-day hymnals use only the original two stanzas of Watts. In the present Methodist book the order of stanzas has been changed from that in the edition of 1905, the second stanza of Watts being made the fourth of the hymn.

"Duke Street" appeared first in 1793 in *A Select Collection of Psalm and Hymn Tunes,* Glasgow, compiled by Henry Boyd, a teacher of psalmody. It had no name, but about 1805 it is found in *Euphonia,* a collection of tunes printed in Liverpool, called "Duke Street." It has also been called "Windle," "St. Helens," and "Newry." It appeared in *The Methodist Harmonist,* 1821, the first official tune book of the American church, called "Newry," and was set to "Jesus, from whom all blessings flow." Its connection with this hymn dates from about the middle of the last century, yet until the 1905 *Methodist Hymnal* was published Methodist Episcopal congregations were still singing it to "Old 100th."

John Hatton was born at Warrington, England, date not known. He was known as John of Warrington and lived in Duke Street, St. Helens, Windle, a fact which probably accounts for most of the names associated from time to time with his only known tune. It is said he was killed in 1793 in a stage-coach accident and buried in the Presbyterian Chapel in St. Helens.

**18—For the beauty of the earth**—Folliott Sanford Pierpoint

**Dix**—Abridged from a chorale by Conrad Kocher

"One of the most delightful hymns of thanksgiving in the language." It was written for the communion service, in eight stanzas, but seldom appears in that extended form. A universal hymn of praise, it has had very general use and is a favorite processional. "Lord of all" has been substituted for "Christ our God" in line 5 in each of the stanzas. The second line of stanza three originally read "For the heart and brain's delight," Mr. Pierpoint approving the change to "mind's delight."

Folliott Sanford Pierpoint, born October 7, 1835, at Bath, England, distinguished himself as a student of the classics at Queen's College, Cambridge. After leaving college he taught for some years, and, although he wrote much poetry, publishing a book of poems, he is known chiefly by this one hymn. He died in 1917.

"Dix" was named from its association with "As with gladness men of old" (90), by W. C. Dix, first used in *Hymns Ancient and Modern,* 1861. Its first appearance was in *Stimmen aus dem Reiche Gottes,* Stuttgart, 1838, a collection of new and old German hymns. The seven lines of the original melody were shortened to six for adaptation to the William C. Dix hymn. The original form was:

and it was set to "Treuer Heiland! wir sind hier."

Conrad Kocher, Ph.D., born at Dietzingen, Württemberg, December 16, 1786, was a tutor and teacher; a student of the works of Palestrina (156); a reformer of German church music; and editor of hymn collections. He went to St. Petersburg, Russia, as a tutor when seventeen years of age, and found time aside from his regular work to study pianoforte. His interest in music caused him to relinquish teaching for the musical profession, being encouraged by Clementi, the great pianist, whose friendship he had cultivated. While a student in Rome he became so thoroughly familiar with the works of Palestrina as to lead him to plan a general reform of church music in Germany. Returning to Stuttgart, he founded a School of Sacred Song which attracted such attention throughout Württemberg as to popularize four-part singing generally in the churches. In 1827 Kocher became organist at the Stiftskirche, Stuttgart, and occupied himself in the revision of hymnbooks and in writing new tunes for them. He died at Stuttgart, March 12, 1872.

**19—Let all on earth their voices raise—**Isaac Watts (3)

**Ariel**—Arranged by Lowell Mason

This hymn is Isaac Watts's metrical version of Psalm 96, published in his *Psalms of David,* 1719, with the title "The God of the Gentiles," the first two lines being,

Let all the earth their voices raise
To sing the choicest psalm of praise.

It has been considerably altered, and the meter changed from 8.8.8.D. to 8.8.6.D. The second stanza of the original, no longer included in the hymn, was:

The heathens know Thy glory, Lord;
The wond'ring nations read Thy word;
In *Britain* is *Jehovah* known;
Our worship shall no more be paid
To gods which mortal hands have made,
Our Maker is our GOD alone.

"Ariel" appeared in an early edition of the *Boston Academy Collection,* thus credited to Lowell Mason:

> This tune is taken from *Occasional Psalms and Hymn Tunes,* by permission of the proprietor of that work.

It is one of the many "arrangements" or "adaptations" by Lowell Mason, who purchased much musical manuscript from German publishers and used such material as suited his purpose for hymn tunes (No. 69).

Because no adequate biography of Lowell Mason has been written it seems advisable to give a somewhat extended account of his life and work.

Lowell Mason, Mus. Doc., was born January 8, 1792, at Medfield, Massachusetts, where, at sixteen years of age, he was a choir leader and a teacher of singing classes. Except for his statement that he spent twenty years of his life at nothing save playing on all available musical instruments very little is known of his boyhood. At twenty-three he went to Savannah, Georgia, where he held a position in a bank. His interest in music, however, kept him practicing, leading choirs, and teaching. While in Savannah he studied harmony with one F. L. Abel, who assisted him in 1818, in compiling a book of choral music. This collection of psalm tunes was based largely on William

Gardiner's *Sacred Melodies* (No. 28). Probably all that Abel had to do with the Mason book was to correct its harmonies. On a trip north some months after the completion of the manuscript, Mason tried to interest a Philadelphia publisher in the work. Being unsuccessful, he went on to Boston, where he tried to interest other publishers. Discouraged and about to return to Savannah, he met the severe but just critic, George K. Jackson, organist of the Handel and Haydn Society, whose endorsement led to the publication of the Society's *Collection of Church Music* in 1822. This organization did not do full justice to Mason in acknowledging him as its compiler, but Mason explained this by saying, "I was then a bank officer in Savannah, and did not wish to be known as a musical man, as I had not the least thought of ever making music a profession." In later editions of the book a statement is made that "the Society are happy to acknowledge their obligation to Lowell Mason . . . in the selection of the music and the arrangement of the harmony." This book made Lowell Mason known, for during the following thirty years or more it ran through some seventeen editions and had a sale of more than fifty thousand copies. Returning to Savannah, where he remained for five years, he became so famous as a choir leader that he was invited to return to Boston as leader of three of that city's choirs at a guaranteed salary of two thousand dollars a year. In Boston he served the choirs of the Hanover, Green, and Park Street Churches, later making a permanent connection with the Bowdoin Street Church, whose pastor was Lyman Beecher.

Mason had been urged to come to Boston by Amasa Winchester, the president of the Handel and Haydn Society. Elected to honorary membership, he declined for the reason that he preferred to begin his connection with the organization as an active member, yet within the year he was elected its president. It was customary at that time and for many years after for the president of the Society to act as its conductor. After five years he resigned in order to devote all of his time to the task of converting the people of Boston to the inclusion of music as one of the regular subjects in the public schools. He was able to accomplish this in 1838 after some years of arduous labor. Prior to this, in 1829, he made the acquaintance of W. C. Woodbridge, the geographer, who had studied the teaching of methods of Pestalozzi in Europe. Greatly impressed with the results obtained, and eager to adapt them to his musical work, Mason went to Europe to study Pestalozzi's methods more intensively. It was while in Germany that he made contact with Georg J. Nägeli (69) and studied with him. In order to demonstrate the worth of music as a study for children, he organized the Boston Academy of Music (with George J. Webb), and in 1832 began the instruction of children in classes held in the Bowdoin Street Church. While no fees were charged, a condition was attached that each child attend classes regularly for one year. It was through his perseverance in this work that he was finally permitted to experiment with one class in the public schools, although he received no pay for it. So well done and so greatly appreciated was the innovation that for many years he was closely associated with the Board of Education of the state of Massachusetts.

In 1834 he organized the first of his famous musical conventions as a means of teaching music to the general public. These conventions were first held in and near Boston, and were attended by any who wished to learn to read music by note. Many of these students in turn became teachers, and carried on the work of establishing and conducting singing classes. So phenomenally did the convention idea spread that, until late in the century, musical conventions were common in the East, South, and Middle West. The good accomplished by the followers of Lowell Mason through the carrying on of this work cannot be estimated.

The first degree of Doctor of Music conferred on any individual by an American college was granted him in 1835 by New York University. Universally esteemed, of sterling character, he was kind and generous. Through his musical conventions, through his publication of much material for their use, as well as for public and Sunday schools, Lowell Mason probably did more for music in America than any other single individual this country has produced.

In the writing of hymn tunes he excelled. He is one of the few Americans whose tunes have gained a strong foothold in English and European books. Henry L. Mason says in a letter:

> My grandfather left no data relative to his various hymn tunes. I have examined hundreds in order to obtain such meagre information as to details as I have been able to. He was an excessively active man and I presume as soon as he finished the composition of one hymn he rushed to some other activity. At all events, such journals that he did leave contain no information relative to the various hymn tunes.

It is a matter of regret that no adequate biography of Lowell Mason has been written. He died August 11, 1872, at Orange, New Jersey.

## Opening of Worship

**20—We gather together to ask the Lord's blessing**—Anonymous

**Kremser**—Netherland Folk Song, 1625
Arranged by Edward Kremser

Both hymn and tune are of folk origin, presumably. At least the source of neither words nor music is known. Only in recent years has this lovely hymn, almost carol-like in character, found its way into American hymnals.

Edward Kremser was a noted chorus master in Vienna during the late nineteenth and early twentieth centuries. He wrote many operettas, cantatas, part-songs, and much excellent music for the piano. Born at Vienna, April 10, 1838, he died there, November 27, 1914.

**21—Come, let us tune our loftiest song**—Robert Athow West

**Duke Street**—John Hatton (17)

The hymn first appeared in *Hymns for the use of the Methodist Episcopal Church,* 1849, with the heading, "Jesus reigns." While it is well known to Methodists it has not yet been included in the hymnals of other denominations.

Robert Athow West, an editor and author, was born at Thetford, England, in 1809. He came to America in 1843 and acted as official reporter of the historic General Conference of 1844. The next General Conference, 1848, appointed a committee of seven, one of which was Mr. West, to "prepare a Standard Edition of the Methodist Hymn Book." It was issued the following year. Mr. West, sometime editor of the *Columbia Magazine* and of the New York *Commercial Advertiser,* published *Sketches of Methodist Preachers,* 1848, and *A Father's Letters to His Daughter*. He died at Georgetown, D. C., February 1, 1865.

**22—Come, sound His praise abroad—Isaac Watts (3)**

**Silver Street—Isaac Smith**

The hymn is a rendering of the 95th Psalm which Isaac Watts included in his *Psalms of David,* 1719, giving it the title "A Psalm before Sermon." Originally in six stanzas, the last two are not now used for obvious reasons. They were:

But if your ears refuse
The language of his grace,
And hearts grow hard like stubborn Jews,
That unbelieving race;

The Lord in vengeance drest
Will lift his hand and swear:
*"You that despise my promis'd Rest*
*Shall have no portion there."*

The four stanzas used form a complete hymn and remain just as Watts wrote them.

"Silver Street" comes from *A Collection of Psalm Tunes in Three Parts,* c. 1770, where it is called "Falcon Street," the name which it is still given in England. It had attached to it the following refrain, which James T. Lightwood (453) says is still popular among English Methodists:

Both 1725 and 1735 are given as the date of Isaac Smith's birth. He was a clerk (precentor) to the Alie Street Meeting House, Goodman's Fields, London, a congregation of Dissenters, and it is said he was the first clerk among them to receive a salary. It was about one hundred dollars per year. However, he gave that up, going into a "reputable business," probably that of a linen draper. He did not relinquish his interest in music, for he furnished some tunes for the *Universal Psalmodist,* 1764, published by A. Williams, and himself issued the *Collection* referred to in the preceding paragraph. In the Preface to Smith's book he gives an insight into the psalm singing of the period, and some good advice. He says the clerk must always have a pitch pipe and, after having announced the hymn and given out the first line, should then sound the keynote, for if he does not give the exact key, there will be "shrieking on the high notes and growling on the low ones." The suggestion is also made that every congregation should appoint an hour or two each week for the practice of such tunes as may be thought proper. Similar advice has been given by many hymnologists since, but seldom has it been acted upon. He died about the year 1800.

**23—Come, Thou Fount of every blessing**—Robert Robinson

**Nettleton**—John Wyeth (?)

James Moffatt says:

> This hymn is as truly autobiographical as any of John Newton's, for Robert Robinson's youth had been wild and reckless. Six years before the hymn was written, a sermon on St. Matthew iii, 7 (But when He saw many of the Pharisees and Sadducees come to His baptism, He said unto them, O generation of vipers, who hath warned you to flee from the wrath to come?) by George Whitefield made an ineffacable impression on him, and after a lengthened period of deep spiritual concern, light and peace came to him.

It was written in 1758, three years after his conversion, during his ministry at Norfolk, and published a year later in *A Collection of Hymns used by the Church of Christ in Angel Alley, Bishopsgate* (of which there is a copy in the library of Drew Theological Seminary). It is a hymn for Whitsuntide, the fiftieth day after Easter, observed as a festival in commemoration of the descent of the Holy Spirit on the Day of Pentecost. For some time after the hymn appeared it was attributed to the Countess of Huntingdon but research has proven its writer to be Robinson.

Robert Robinson, born at Swaffham, Norfolk, England, September 27, 1735, of lowly parentage, was, after the death of his father, apprenticed to a barber in London, who often reprimanded him for paying more attention to his books than to his work. After his conversion by Whitefield he often heard John Wesley preach, and was assigned the oversight of a Calvinist Methodist chapel in Norfolk in 1758, the year he wrote this hymn. Leaving there shortly, he preached to an Independent congregation in Norwich, going, in 1759, to a Baptist church in Cambridge. His love of liberty led him from one denomination to another. From 1770 until his death he was constantly engaged in writing on various theological subjects. Robert Robinson was a man of fine intellect, but was said to be "as unstable as water." He died near Birmingham, June 9, 1790.

"Nettleton" has also been known as "Good Shepherd" and "Hallelujah." It received the last name because in the early days of its popularity it was always sung with a chorus,

Hallelujah! Hallelujah! We are on our journey home.

Originally in four-part time, this tune first appeared in the *Supplement* to John Wyeth's *Repository of Sacred Music,* 1813. In some books it is credited to the Rev. Asahel Nettleton, 1783-1844, the noted evangelist of the early nineteenth century, and in others it is anonymous. Doctor Nettleton compiled *Village Hymns,* 1825, a book with words only. Bennet Tyler, in his biography of Asahel Nettleton, does not indicate that Doctor Nettleton was in any way musically inclined. It seems safe to assume Wyeth's composition of this tune along with others known to have been written by him for the *Supplement* of 1813. When it first appeared in its present form, called "Nettleton," is a point for hymnologists to discover.

John Wyeth, born at Cambridge, Massachusetts, March 31, 1770, was from an old family which had purchased land and settled there prior to 1645. He learned the printers' trade and followed the printing and publishing business all of his life. Wyeth was in Santo Domingo at the time of the Haitian insurrection, escaping to the states disguised as a common sailor. He was postmaster at Harrisburg, Pennsylvania, under President Washington, but was removed by President Adams because of the "incompatibility of the office of postmaster and editor of a newspaper." In 1810 he issued his *Repository of Sacred Music,* and in 1813 a *Supplement* to it. He died at Philadelphia, January 23, 1858.

**24—Jesus, where'er Thy people meet**—William Cowper

**Malvern**—Lowell Mason (19)

This hymn was written to be sung at the first prayer meeting held in a large room in the Great House at Olney after the attendance had become too large to continue using the place where such meetings had been inaugurated (No. 313). It was afterward published in the *Olney Hymns,* 1779. It is founded upon Christ's promise to be present "where two or three are gathered together in My name." It is interesting to remember that the *Olney Hymns,* some of which are now sung all over the globe, were written for a small congregation in an English village.

William Cowper, the son of a clergyman "of good family," was born in Berkhampstead, Hertfordshire, England, November 26, 1731. It was unfortunate that such a timid child as he lost his mother when he was only six years old. When at a tender age he was removed from a country school to Westminster School, his life was made a constant terror by the ill treatment of older boys. After leaving school, he was articled to an attorney, in whose office he spent three years before preparing at Middle Temple for an appointment as clerk of the Journals in the House of Lords. Unnerved by this to the point of insanity, he was enabled by good care to regain a measure of health; but fits of melancholy recurred at intervals throughout his life. He held, until his death at East Dereham, April 25, 1800, a morbid belief that he was one of those who could not be saved. Living with close friends at Olney, he formed a lasting friendship with John Newton (27). Julian says,

> Though the most considerable poet who has written hymns, he has contributed little to the development of their structure, adopting the traditional modes of his time and Newton's severe canons.

Dean Tillett says, a "plaintive and refined tenderness runs through all of his hymns."

"Malvern" was at one time one of the most popular of Lowell Mason's hymn tunes, but it is now rapidly disappearing from compilations of hymns and tunes. *The Methodist Hymnal* is the only recent denominational book to include it. It first appeared in *The Psaltery,* Mason and Webb, 1847.

**25—Jesus, we look to Thee**—Charles Wesley

**Mornington**—Arranged from a chant by Garret Wellesley

While a number of the hymns of Charles Wesley which appeared in *The Methodist Hymnal* of 1905, and in *The Methodist Protestant Church Hymnal,* were not included in the book of 1935, this hymn has been restored to Methodism. Not since 1882 has it been found in any of the official hymnals of the three denominations joining in the most recent revision. It appeared first in the second volume of *Hymns and Sacred Poems,* 1749, with the title "At Meeting of Friends." As it appears here, it is composed of stanzas 1, 2, 4, 5, hymn 473, from the 1780 *Collection of Hymns,* by John Wesley, with the word "waiting" substituted for "bounding" in the third line of stanza four.

In the second series of the Drew Lectureship in Biography (1931), F. Luke Wiseman says of Charles Wesley:[1]

> He was richly endowed with the personal charm which makes and keeps friends, with dauntless courage, firm will, keen insight into character, strong intelligence, remarkable powers of expression, noble magnanimity. . . . To him it was granted by means of his extraordinary lyrical genius to express the adoration, lead the devotion, inform the mind, enlarge the understanding, quicken the imagination, purify the affection, guide the aspiration, build up the faith, enrich the experience, voice the call, inspire the testimony, provoke the zeal, unify the spirit of the Methodists, not only of his own time but of future generations. Even to-day if one wants to discover or to receive the essential spirit of Methodism or to do its characteristic work, one turns for inspiration not to John Wesley's *Sermons* nor to his *Notes on the New Testament,* nor to the Rules of Society, nor even to usages of the church called by his name, but to Charles Wesley's hymns.

And in the Preface to the published lectures, he says:

> It would be easy to select twenty hymns whose literary charm entitled them to a permanent place in the anthology of eighteenth-century lyrics. But their chief value lies in their delineation of spiritual experience. To Charles Wesley hymns were as natural a form of self-expression as was a *Journal* to his brother John.

Charles Wesley was born at Epworth, December 18, 1707, and died at Marylebone, March 29, 1788. Garret Wellesley offered to adopt him, but he

[1] *Charles Wesley: Evangelist and Poet.* The Abingdon Press.

had what his brother John said was "a fair escape" from worldly influence. Educated at Westminster School and Christ Church, Oxford, he accompanied General Oglethorpe to Georgia as his secretary, arriving at Savannah in February, 1736, after a journey of almost four months. Returning to England in December of the same year, he spent most of the following seventeen months at Oxford, preaching and discoursing informally as much as his health would permit. On Whitsunday, May 20, 1738, "the Methodist Apollos found peace with God and rejoiced in the hope of loving Christ." From that day he proclaimed a gospel whose "suitability and efficacy" for all had been demonstrated to him. He must have written hymns almost constantly, for his output was enormous—over sixty-five hundred. Like Schubert with his melodic instinct every thought that came to the mind of Charles Wesley seemed to shape itself in poetic form. Not only was he merely the "sweet singer" of Methodism, but more than any other he was successful in presenting religion and religious experiences in lyrical form. None other than John Julian, undoubtedly the greatest authority in English hymnody, said:

> It was Charles Wesley who was . . . perhaps, taking quantity and quality into consideration, the great hymn writer of all ages.

Charles S. Nutter:

> The poets of the eighteenth century did not rewrite and refine their works as those of the nineteenth have done. Wesley partook of the characteristic of the age, and instead of correcting and polishing what he had written, wrote more. Nothing but a consummate genius saved him from the perdition of voluminous writers.

Mortimer Collins:

> The magnetism of personal influence passes away; but the burning life of that wondrous psalmody, sung Sunday after Sunday by congregations full of faith, is imperishable.

Robert Southey:

> Perhaps no poems have ever been so devoutly committed to memory as these, nor quoted so often upon a deathbed. The manner in which they were sung tended to impress them strongly on the mind; the tune was made wholly subservient to the words, not the words to the tune.

S. W. Christophers:

> His name is balmy and immortal, not only because of his multitude of songs, but for the beautiful completeness and rich variety of his rhyme, the pleasant variations of his meter, his happy union of strong argument and melodious diction, and his genuine and tasteful setting of evangelical truth.

Louis F. Benson:

> Charles Wesley was the poet-laureate of Methodism with an ode for every occasion. Yet though "every occasion" provided him material for a song, John Wesley, in the obituary of his brother Charles, read at the Conference of 1788, said, "His least praise was his talent for poetry."

"Mornington" was arranged from a chant written by the Earl of Mornington (hence its name) about 1760. It appeared as a psalm tune in a collection issued about 1810. This was probably its first appearance in print, yet it had been in use in the Dublin Cathedral for some years prior to that date. The original form, still used in Dublin, is:

Garret Wellesley (or Wesley), first Earl of Mornington, father of the Duke of Wellington, was born July 19, 1735. He was the son of Richard Colley Wesley, the boy who was adopted by the grandfather of the Duke of Wellington (another Garret Wesley) when Charles Wesley declined the offer to become his heir. Richard Colley succeeded to the estates of the elder Wesley, a distant relative of the famous Wesley family of preachers, and took the name of the man who adopted him. The family name was changed from Wesley to Wellesley about 1790. The first Earl of Mornington is now known only as a musician. He was a well-known writer of madrigals, glees, and other part songs, some of which, being for the church, may be found in the choir books in St. Patrick's Cathedral, Dublin. In 1757 he founded an amateur singing society known as the Academy of Music, in which women sang in the chorus—an innovation at that time. He lived most of his life at Dublin, Ireland, where he was the first Professor of Music at Dublin University. He resigned this position in 1774 and removed to Kensington, where he died, May 22, 1781.

# Closing of Worship

**26—Lord, dismiss us with Thy blessing**—John Fawcett, altered

**Sicilian Mariners' Hymn**—Arranged from a Sicilian melody

The fact that there are four hymns having in common this first line probably accounts for controversies over its authorship. Julian discusses each of the hymns in detail, and concludes that this one was the product of John Fawcett. From 1773 to 1780 it appeared in different collections without credit; in 1786 it was signed "F" in a book published in York, and in both 1791 and 1800 in others signed "Fawcett." For a hundred and fifty years it has appeared substantially in this form in nearly every evangelical hymnal published. Originally in three stanzas, the third now rarely appears. The last line of the first stanza was,

In this dry and barren place.

John Fawcett, D.D., born at Lidget Green, Yorkshire, England, January 6, 1739 or 1740, came under the influence of George Whitefield when sixteen years old and was converted. For some time he attended the services of the Church of England, but in 1758 united with the Baptist communion. After preaching for two years he was ordained a Baptist minister in 1765, at Wainsgate, near Hebden Bridge (416). A chapel was built for him at Hebden Bridge and he lived in its vicinity during the remainder of his life. He declined the presidency of the Baptist Academy at Bristol. In 1811 Brown University, Rhode Island, conferred upon him the degree of Doctor of Divinity. In addition to his hymnal of 1782, Doctor Fawcett was the author of many books, one of them an *Essay on Anger,* being a particular favorite of George III, who offered its author any benefit he could confer. The offer was declined for the reason "that he lived among his own people, that he enjoyed their love, that God blessed his labors among them, and that he needed nothing which even a king could supply." He died July 25, 1817.

"Sicilian Mariners' Hymn" is of unknown origin, and no success has attended efforts to trace it. First appearing in the Rev. W. Tattersall's musical edition of Merrick's *Psalms,* called "Sicilian Hymn," it was included under this same name in *The Methodist Harmonist,* first official tune book among American Methodists. It is a restoration, for it was not included in the 1905 edition of *The Methodist Hymnal.*

**27—May the grace of Christ our Saviour**—John Newton

**Sardis**—Ludwig van Beethoven (12)

The hymn is taken from the *Olney Hymns,* John Newton's compilation of 1779, the same year John Wesley dated the Preface of his famous *Collection of Hymns for the use of the People called Methodists.* It is No. 101, one of the "Short Hymns after Sermon," based on 2 Corinthians 13. 14. The *Olney Hymns* were the joint product of John Newton and William Cowper, being composed for the prayer meetings or the church services at the Great House in Olney where John Newton preached. They were given out in the manner of Watts and Doddridge, after the sermon. Most of them were not of high poetic order, but neither Newton nor Cowper was attempting to write poetry—they were writing hymns. Newton, in his Preface to the *Olney Hymns,* says:

> There is a style and a manner suited to the composition of hymns, which may be more successfully, or at least more easily, attained by a versifier than by a poet. They should be *Hymns,* not *Odes,* if designed for public worship, and for the use of plain people. Perspicuity, simplicity, and ease, should be chiefly attended to; and the imagery and colouring of poetry, if admitted at all, should be indulged very sparingly, and with great judgment.

John Newton, vagabond, sailor, deserter from the British Navy, soldier of fortune, a slave trader, and at one time a slave himself, became a successful preacher and hymn writer. The redeeming features of his early life were his remembrance of a good Christian mother who died in his infancy, and his love for Mary Catlett. His sincere attachment for this girl never left him. Her influence over him was so strong that once he refrained from committing suicide for fear she might think ill of him.

After many degrading experiences in Sierra Leone he was induced, by a ruse, to return to England. En route he read the *Imitation of Christ,* which made such a profound impression on him that in time it completely changed his life. An apt student, he studied Greek and Latin as well as other subjects.

After several years of seeking ordination in the Church of England he was appointed in 1764 curate at Olney, where he met and became intimate with William Cowper (24).

After serving Olney for sixteen years, Newton was transferred to the rectory of St. Mary Woolworth, where he continued until his death at the age of eighty-two. He continued preaching until after he was eighty. When in his late years his eyes failed him so that he could not see to read his notes while preaching, he had an old servant accompany him to the pulpit, and, standing behind him, point out the lines of his manuscript. One morning he read the words "Jesus Christ is precious," paused, and then repeated them. Thinking Newton had become confused, the servant whispered, "Go on: go on, you said that before." Newton turned and said, "John, I said that twice, and I'm going to say it again." And his voice took on a different quality as he repeated more firmly than before, "Jesus Christ *is* precious!"

His epitaph, written by himself, tells, succinctly, his life story:

John Newton, Clerk,
Once an infidel and libertine,
A servant of slaves in Africa:
Was by the rich mercy of our Lord and Saviour
Jesus Christ,
Preserved, restored, pardoned,
And appointed to preach the Faith
He had laboured long to destroy.
Near sixteen years at Olney in Bucks;
And twenty-seven years in this church.

He was born in London, July 24, 1725, and died there, December 21, 1807.

"Sardis" is taken from the writings of Ludwig van Beethoven. It appears in his Romance in G, for violin, and is one of the best of the adaptations from his works. By whom it was arranged, or when, is not known. For more than one hundred years this tune was sung to the hymn, "May the grace of Christ our Saviour," at the close of the weekly meeting of the Presbyterian ministers in New York City. It may have been named "Sardis" for one of the churches mentioned in the New Testament.

**28—The Lord be with us as each day—John Ellerton, altered**

**Belmont—Adapted from Sacred Melodies, William Gardiner**

This is a hymn peculiarly suited for the close of an evening service. It was written by John Ellerton in 1870 at the request of a friend for use at the close of service on Sunday afternoons, when, as in summer, a strictly evening hymn would be unsuitable. First published in *Church Hymns,* 1871, it has since appeared in many hymnals. The first stanza has been changed from,

The Lord be with us as we bend,
His blessings to receive;
His gift of peace upon us send,
Before His courts we leave,

to read,

The Lord be with us as each day
His blessings we receive;
His gift of peace on all we pray,
Before His courts we leave.

John Ellerton was a successful preacher, teacher, and author, and his work in hymnology was of first importance. "No less than eighty-six hymns, original and translated, proceeded from his own pen," and he was widely consulted in matters hymnological during the last thirty years of his life. Not only did he publish a book of his own hymns, but he edited, or assisted in editing, six others, one of them being the famous *Hymns Ancient and Modern* (editions of 1875 and 1889). He refused to take out copyrights on any of his hymns, saying that if they were "counted worthy to contribute to Christ's praise in the congregation, one ought to feel very thankful and humble." He is called "Canon" Ellerton even though he was unable, because of his last illness, to be installed in that post in St. Alban's Cathedral Church. He was born in London, December 16, 1826; educated at King William's College (Isle of Man) and Trinity College, Cambridge; was ordained in 1850; and died at Torquay, June 15, 1893.

"Belmont" has been attributed to Samuel Webbe (35), his son, Samuel Webbe, Jr., to Wolfgang A. Mozart, and to William Gardiner, but there is no valid reason for believing that it came from any of these. Long a puzzle to hymn-tune specialists, it seems to have been arranged from an eight-line tune which appeared in William Gardiner's *Sacred Melodies,* 1812, with no name attached. The first half of this tune was:

It seems probable that it came from the Gardiner book and has been so credited in *The Methodist Hymnal.*

William Gardiner was born March 15, 1770, and lived, and died, November 16, 1853, in Leicester, England. There, while yet a boy, he wrote songs, signing them "W. G. Leicester." In his wide travels he tried to make the acquaintance of as many musicians as possible. He arranged an oratorio by selecting music from Haydn, Mozart, and Beethoven, affixing English words and writing the music for some of the necessary connecting passages. He wrote Beethoven asking him to write the overture, offering him one hundred guineas for it, and when he received no reply, decided his letter had never reached the great musician. He knew Beethoven and claimed, on good grounds, to have been the first to introduce that master musician's works in England. Gardiner was also acquainted with Mozart. To Haydn he had the pleasure of presenting a pair of stockings, in the "clocks" of which he had had woven the opening measures of the "Austrian Hymn" (382).

In 1812 he published the first of a six-volume work called *Sacred Melodies:* serviceable because it called attention to many excellent compositions. Sometime later, in *Music and Nature*—a curious work about nearly everything having to do with music and of no value whatever—he says:

> The piety of the Non-conformists has been married to unholy strains, and we have been deluged with a psalmody composed of light and impious trash. . . . To correct such levity and want of reverence, the author of these essays had the sanction of the late King, George IV, to make a selection of the best poetry, conjoined to the finest music, as a standard book of psalmody, which has been published.

**29—Saviour, again to Thy dear Name we raise**—John Ellerton (28)

Ellers—Edward John Hopkins

This hymn was written for a choral festival at Nantwich, Cheshire, England, in 1866, later being revised and abridged for use in *Hymns Ancient and Modern,* 1868. "Canon" Ellerton had organized the first choral society in the Midlands, which met for many years at Nantwich. Of its original version in six stanzas, the author's biographer says:

> By its condensation into four stanzas its spirit and power are wonderfully increased, and now it ranks with Bishop Ken's "Glory to Thee, my God, this night" (51), Keble's "Son of my soul, Thou Saviour dear" (56), and Lyte's "Abide with me, fast falls the eventide" (520), as one of the great evening hymns of the English Church.

Of this most popular hymn by Ellerton, W. Garrett Horder says, "It is as tenderly spiritual as it is ethically strong." The last line of the first stanza has been altered, in *The Hymnal* of 1935, to read,

> And still our hearts to wait Thy word of peace,

in place of,

> Then, lowly kneeling, wait Thy word of peace.

Otherwise it appears as its author revised it for *Hymns Ancient and Modern.* Its first stanza may be impressively used as a choral benediction. Doctor Benson (38) says that it seems the perfection of the blending of the corporate idea of worship with human individuality.

"Ellers" was composed for this hymn in 1869 by Dr. Edward J. Hopkins, who arranged it for voices in unison with an organ accompaniment varying with each stanza. Three years later its composer put it in four parts at the request of Samuel Smith, then arranging the *Appendix to The Bradford Tune Book.*

Edward John Hopkins, Mus. Doc., born at Westminster, London, June 30, 1818, "one of the last and certainly the greatest representative of the old school of English church musicians," was a child of the chapel, played services at Westminster Abbey before he was sixteen, and at that age secured the appointment of organist at Mitcham Parish Church. After serving there and at other churches in London, he went to Temple Church, where he remained for fifty-five years, until his retirement in 1898. Chaste melody, unobtrusive harmony, grateful inner parts, and a devotional fervor characterize his music. Highly respected as an editor of hymnals, he was selected to complete the *Wesleyan Tune Book,* 1876, after the deaths of H. J. Gauntlett (442) and George Cooper, who had started the work. He died at London, February 4, 1901.

## Morning Hymns

**30—Come, my soul, thou must be waking**—Friedrich Rudolph Ludwig von Canitz
Translated by Henry James Buckoll

**Haydn**—Arranged from Francis Joseph Haydn

This lovely morning hymn is a selection of four stanzas from a translation of the German "Seele du musst munter werden," by Baron von Canitz. It was some time after its first appearance anonymously in the *British Magazine* for July, 1838, until it was definitely established that Henry J. Buckoll was the translator.

Baron F. R. L. von Canitz, born in Berlin, November 27, 1654, and educated at Leyden and Leipzig, was chosen a member of the personal staff of the Elector Friedrich Wilhelm. As Ambassador, Chief Magistrate, and Privy Councilor, he executed for Friedrich III many important missions in which he toured over the greater part of Europe, including England. Baron von Canitz was regarded as "an ornament of the aristocracy." On the morning of his death, August 11, 1699, he asked to be carried to an open window so that he might see the sun rise again. He exclaimed:

> Oh, if the sight of this created sun is so charming and beautiful, what will be the sight of the unspeakable glory of the Creator himself!

After his death in Berlin his hymns were published anonymously.

Henry James Buckoll, born in Siddington, England, September 9, 1803, son of a clergyman, was educated at Rugby and at Queen's College, Oxford, after graduation returning as an assistant Master to Rugby, where he remained until his death, June 6, 1871. He made many translations from Bunsen's *Gesang und Gebetbuch,* some being included in various collections of English school hymnals, but few of which are known in America.

"Haydn" is from Symphony No. 93, in D major (Salomon Set No. 2), first movement, by F. J. Haydn. It has long been associated with this hymn.

Francis Joseph Haydn, Mus. Doc., son of a wheelwright, the second of a family of twelve children, was born in the small Lower Austrian village of Rohrau, March 31, 1732, and died at Vienna, May 31, 1809. The house in which he was born is still standing in its original form. When he was six years old, his father placed him in the school of a neighboring village, where he might be under the care of a relative. Here he learned to sing well and to play a little on most of the musical instruments available. Late in life he said,

> Almighty God, to whom I render thanks for all His unnumbered mercies, gave me such facility in music, that by the time I was six I stood up like a man and sang masses in the church choir, and could play a little on the clavier and the violin.

At eight he went to St. Stephens in Vienna to be one of the choristers. When his voice changed, he lost his place there and was thrown upon his own resources. For the next thirteen years he lived in Vienna, steadily progressing in his chosen field. In 1761 he was called by Prince Paul Anton Esterhazy to Esterhaz, where his duties were always pleasant, though numerous and heavy. In this beautiful spot he was destined to live the greater part of the remainder of his long, useful life. Except for two trips to England, where he was enthusiastically received, he traveled but little.

Known as "the father of modern instrumental music," and greatly influencing all other branches of the art, Haydn became one of the really great figures in the musical world. Composer in all the forms of his time, he is perhaps best known by his oratorio, *The Creation* (66). He was painstaking in his work, and all of his many scores were written in a neat and uniform style with surprisingly few erasures, "because I never put down anything until I have quite made up my mind about it." When he wanted to do a particularly good piece of work, he would wear the ring given him by the king of Prussia.

"Papa" Haydn, as he was affectionately called, was a devoutly religious man. He began every composition, no matter how small, with the inscription "In nomine Domini," and closed it with "Laus Deo." When an old man he said:

> I know that God has bestowed a talent upon me, and I thank Him for it; I think I have done my duty and been of use in my generation by my works; let others do the same.

One writer has said that after listening to a composition of Haydn's he always felt impelled to do some good work.

There is a cheerfulness and enthusiasm characterizing all of his music which makes it appeal alike to professional and amateur. Carpini, one of his biographers, says that "at the thought of God his heart leaped for joy, and he could not help his music doing the same."

In the catalogue of all graduates, Oxford, is the entry,

> Haydn, Joseph, Composer to His Serene Highness the Prince of Esterhazy, cr. Doctor of Music, July 8, 1791.

For his "exercise" he submitted the following:

*Canon cancrizans, a tre*

**31—When morning gilds the skies**—From the German, c. 1800
Translated by Edward Caswall

**Laudes Domini**—Joseph Barnby

This is said to be a translation of a German hymn whose source is unknown, but is so freely translated that it is practically a new hymn. It first appeared in the *Katholisches Gesangbuch* (56) with the title "A Christian Greeting." It was such a favorite with worshipers at Saint Paul's, London, that it was often printed on leaflets for distribution so that all might sing.

Edward Caswall, born at Yately, Hampshire, England, July 15, 1814, was the son of a distinguished clergyman of the Church of England, and the brother of another. He was a student at Brasenose College, Oxford, from which he graduated with distinction; took holy orders in the Church of England; became identified with the Tractarian movement; left the established church to enter the Roman, and joined John Henry Newman (514), then Father Superior of the Oratory of St. Philip Neri, near Birmingham. Here the remainder of his life was spent, marked by honest devotion to his clerical duties and a loving interest in the poor, the sick and afflicted, and little children. No higher praise could be given him than to quote "He loved God and little children." His translations of hymns from Latin have wider use than those of any other excepting those of Dr. John M. Neale (52). His original hymns, however, because of their doctrinal teaching, have been restricted to the use of the Roman Catholic Church. His death occurred at Birmingham, January 2, 1878.

"Laudes Domini" is a worthy name for a tune sung to this fine outburst of praise, even though Chancellor George Gardner said this one might be compared with the "clank, clank of machinery." Be that as it may, this has been the tune generally accepted as the proper setting for Doctor Caswall's translation since its first appearance in the Appendix to the original edition of *Hymns Ancient and Modern*. It is a good example of the type of English hymn tune which had such wide popularity at the beginning of this century. Sir Joseph Barnby, its composer, was quite impatient with the general feeling current during his hymn-tune writing days, that only tunes in the style of the seventeenth century were in good taste, and that all such writing to be acceptable should be modeled after them. He complained that critics were quite willing to admit the right of the seventeenth-century composers to write in the style of their time while denying Barnby and his contemporaries a similar right. "For my part," he says, "I have elected to imitate the old writers in their independent method of working rather than their works."

Joseph Barnby was one of the most prolific, if not one of the greatest of the late nineteenth-century group of hymn-tune writers. A precocious youth, he entered York Minster choir at seven, taught other boys at ten, was appointed organist at twelve, music master at a school at fifteen, finally attaining unusual distinction as a choral conductor in England, being knighted in 1892. In 1897 his two hundred and forty-six hymn tunes were published in a collection. Born in York, August 12, 1838, he died January 28, 1896, and was buried in London, where his funeral service was held in St. Paul's Cathedral.

**32—Christ, whose glory fills the skies**—Charles Wesley (25)

**Ratisbon**—Old German melody

Arranged in J. G. Werner's Choralbuch, 1815

"One of Charles Wesley's loveliest progeny," is the comment James Montgomery (39) made on this hymn which appeared in Wesley's *Psalms and Hymns,* 1740, and Dr. Alexander MacMillan says it is "one of the greatest morning hymns in our language, but it is more. It is a glorious hymn to Christ, the Sun of Righteousness, the Light of the World." This is the hymn (stanzas 2 and 3) which George Eliot describes Seth Bede, the young Methodist, repeating mentally as he "walked leisurely homeward" after leaving his brother on a February Sunday morning (*Adam Bede,* Chap. 38).

"Ratisbon" is from *Choralbuch zu den neuen sächsischen Gesangbüchern . . . von Johann Gottlob Werner,* Leipzig, 1815, set to "Jesu, meines Lebens Leben":

This, in turn, is from an older melody found in Neander's *Choralbuch* of 1680.

Johann G. Werner, who was born in 1777 near Leipzig, and who died at Chemnitz, July 19, 1822, was a well-known organist and teacher, composer of textbooks in organ, piano, harmony, and accompaniment, and sacred books of organ pieces.

**33—Come, O Lord, like morning sunlight**—Milton Smith Littlefield

**Trust**—Felix Mendelssohn-Bartholdy

The words, written by Doctor Littlefield in 1927, are from *The Hymnal for Young People,* 1928, edited by the author and Margaret Slattery.

The Rev. Milton Smith Littlefield, Presbyterian clergyman, born in New York City, August 21, 1864, was educated at Johns Hopkins and Union Theological Seminary, received the degree of Doctor of Divinity from Washburn College, and preached in and near his birthplace until his death, June 12, 1934. He was recognized as an authority in the field of hymnology, being president of the Hymn Society in 1927-28 and editor of two hymnals.

"Trust" is measures 1-6 and 15-16 from a hymn tune called "Contemplation," adapted from Mendelssohn's setting of Psalm 13 to English words by "C. B. Broadley, Esquire," for whom the work was composed in 1840.

Felix Mendelssohn-Bartholdy (who should also have Jakob Ludwig prefixed to his name) was born in Hamburg, February 3, 1809, and died at Leipzig,

November 4, 1847. He was a grandson of the eminent Jewish philosopher, Moses Mendelssohn. His father, Abraham, a banker in Berlin, wishing his children brought up as Protestant Christians, added the name, "Bartholdy," as a mark of distinction from the orthodox members of the family. Bartholdy was "former proprietor of the garden belonging to the family." Mendelssohn, one of the long line of famous German musicians, excelled as a composer of sacred music, particularly in the larger forms, his *Elijah, St. Paul,* and *Fest-gesang* (7) being works of the highest order. Several hymn tunes have been adapted from his *Songs Without Words* (40), a new and distinct contribution in writing for the pianoforte. He organized the famous Domchor in Berlin and established the great Leipzig Conservatory. His commanding position in the world's musical life during the second quarter of the last century was due to his gifts for social leadership and organization, his unusual intellectual equipment, his irrepressible vitality, and his undoubted genius. Before the age of ten he played in public and at twelve he was composing for the voice, the piano, and other instruments. He was responsible for the revival of interest in Bach (52), whose works had been forgotten for almost a century. Leading a life of incessant activity, he traveled extensively, making no fewer than eleven trips to England. There he was idolized by musicians and public alike, and was received with distinct honor by Queen Victoria. His most impressive works are those which reflect his natural buoyancy and his earnest religion.

**34—Awake, my soul, and with the sun**—Thomas Ken

**The Morning Watch**—Carl Fowler Price

Julian says this hymn is one of four that stand at the head of all in the English language. It is a part of Bishop Ken's wonderful "Morning Hymn" with one stanza, the second, added from his "Midnight Hymn." Thomas Ken wrote three hymns, "Morning," "Midnight," and "Evening" (51), while he was prebendary at Winchester College. Each closes with the famous long-meter doxology, "Praise God from whom all blessings flow," probably sung by more Christians than any other four lines ever written. In a *Manual of Prayers* for the boys of Winchester, published in 1674, Ken admonishes the scholars to "be sure to sing the Morning and Evening Hymn in your chamber devoutly." He followed the practice of singing the "Morning Hymn" each day before dressing, to the accompaniment of his lute or spinet. The boys were accustomed to sing the Latin hymn "Jam lucis orto sidere" (58), upon which the "Morning Hymn" was quite possibly modeled, yet only in the manner in which "a text of Holy Scripture suggests a sermon." In this cento stanzas 1, 3, 4, and 5, are from Ken's revised text of 1709, exactly. Stanza two (from the "Midnight Hymn") has been altered slightly. "Thy" is changed to "Thine," line 3; and the fourth line changed from,

> Dispels the sloth and clouds of night,

to,

> Dispels the clouds and dark of night.

Few hymns, if any, have lived for two and one quarter centuries with so little change.

Of the last stanza James Montgomery says:

> It is a masterpiece at once of amplification and compression; amplification, on the burthen, "Praise God," repeated in each line; compression, by exhibiting God as the object of praise in every view in which we can imagine praise due to Him;—praise, for *all* His blessings, yea, for "*all* blessings," none coming from any other source; praise by every creature, specifically invoked, "here below," and in heaven "above"; praise to Him in each of the characters wherein He has revealed Himself in His Word—"Father, Son, and Holy Ghost."

Thomas Ken was born at Berkhampstead, England, in July, 1637. After the death of his parents, when he was a child, he was reared in the home and under the care of Izaak Walton (of *Compleat Angler* fame), who had married Thomas's stepsister, Anne. Educated at Winchester and New Oxford, he took Orders and after holding several livings, returned as prebendary to Winchester, where he wrote his *Manual of Prayers,* from which his three most famous hymns are taken. Because of his absolute fidelity to his strong conscience and his great strength of conviction, he suffered much. Leaving Winchester to act as chaplain to Mary at The Hague, he incurred the displeasure of William for his remonstrance against William's treatment of the princess. His refusal of Nelle Gwynne the use of his house resulted in his being appointed Bishop of Wells and Bath, owing to the King's admiration for his independence. He was one of seven Bishops sent to the Tower for refusing to read the Declaration of Indulgence, and was deprived of his see, in 1691, for refusing to take an oath of allegiance to William III. After his retirement he gave the residue from his benefactions (about £700) to Lord Weymouth, with whom he lived until his death, March 19, 1711, retaining only his lute, "a sorry horse," and his Greek Testament, which is said to have opened of its own accord at 1 Corinthians 15. 10, "But by the grace of God I am what I am." Lord Weymouth gave the Bishop an allowance of £80 per year.

After his death his poetical works were published in four volumes, including *Hymns and Poems for the Holy Days and Festivals of the Church* which were highly prized by John Keble (35) and which suggested the *Christian Year.* Thomas Ken's character was saintly, he was bold, gentle, modest, and had a great love for mankind. Thomas Macaulay gives a just and true estimate of him:

> His moral character seems to approach, as near as human infirmity permits, to the ideal perfection of human virtue.

Many think the poet Dryden had him in mind when he wrote the lines concerning the "Good Parson":

> For, letting down the golden chain from on high,
> He drew his audience upward to the sky;
> And oft with holy hymns he charmed their ears;
> (A music more melodious than the spheres);
> For David left, when he went to rest,
> His lyre; and after him he sung the best.

The good man was buried "under the east window of the chancel just at sunrising" as he had requested, his friends singing his "Morning Hymn."

"The Morning Watch" was written in 1913 as a setting for William B. Oliver's hymn beginning, "Lord, in the morning let me hear Thy voice," and was first published in *The Daily Bible,* a magazine published by The World's

Morning Watch, a religious organization. Its composer changed it slightly in order that it might conform to the accents of this text.

Carl F. Price, son of a Methodist preacher, author, composer, and active Methodist layman for more than a quarter of a century, was born at New Brunswick, New Jersey, May 16, 1881. His activities have been numerous and varied, among them his services rendered as recording secretary of the New York City Society of the Methodist Episcopal Church for many years; as secretary of the National Board of the Epworth League; historian of the Methodist Historical Society; president of the Methodist Social Union; president of the Hymn Society; author of many books; editor of a number of hymnals, and composer of more than two hundred hymn tunes and cantatas. Although he is in the insurance brokerage business in New York, his greatest interest is in the field of hymnody, in which his many valuable contributions merit his rank as an author.

**35—New every morning is the love—John Keble**

**Melcombe—Samuel Webbe**

This hymn has been taken from John Keble's *Christian Year,* not a hymnal but a book of beautiful meditation poetry which had direct influence on sacred verse in throwing the "glamour of poetry" on the festal days of the church year. It is a part of a long poem of sixteen stanzas based on Lamentations 3. 22-23: "His compassions fail not. They are new every morning." The poem begins with the line, "Hues of the rich unfolding morn." Dean Tillett (117) thinks the *Christian Year* "is one of the greatest religious classics in the English language," and Julian says "what the Prayer Book is in prose the *Christian Year* is in poetry." It was published anonymously in 1827, five years after having been written, reaching its ninety-sixth edition in its author's lifetime.

John Keble, English divine and poet, was born at Fairford, Gloucester, England, April 25, 1792, and died at Bournemouth, March 29, 1866. After receiving his early educational training from his father, vicar of Coln, the boy at fourteen won a scholarship at Corpus Christi, Oxford. There he made a brilliant record in mathematics and the classics, being the second to earn "double first class honors." After his election to the Oriel fellowship when eighteen, an unprecedented honor for one so young, he was examining master and private tutor at Oxford, until the death of his mother, in 1823, called him to his birthplace to be with his father and sisters. His family attachments must have been strong, for, because he felt his loved ones needed his presence and care, he declined important preferment from his church. Public acclaim and money meant nothing to him, duty everything. At the death of his father, he married, when he was forty-three, and became vicar of Hursley (56), where he remained for the rest of his life. Though his professorship of poetry in Oxford required little more than one lecture in Latin each term, and though his famous Assize Sermon made him one of the leaders in the Oxford Movement, he preferred the quiet, uneventful life of the countryside. All of his life he lived in an atmosphere of culture and refinement: at his father's home at Oxford and at Hursley. His works reflect the fact that neither at home nor at college did he come into contact with anything coarse or common; a cultured and refined mind is necessary fully to enter into their spirit. His character and gifts of genius shone in his daily life. In his *Christian Year,* Cardinal Newman (514) says he "struck an original note and woke up in the hearts of thousands a new music, the music of a school long unknown in England." Its extraordinary popularity is illustrated by the incident related concerning the holiday planned by Lord Wilberforce and his four sons. Each was to take along a book to be read aloud, and when the time came for reading it was discovered that each had brought a copy of the *Christian Year.*

John Keble died peacefully in his seventy-third year. As a monument to him his friends and admirers established Keble College at Oxford, but "his real monument is in the altered lives of thousands whom he helped to serve."

"Melcombe" first appeared in the second part of a work called *An Essay on the Church Plain Chant,* 1782, set to "O Salutoris hostia." Here it is not assigned to anyone, but in *A Collection of Motets,* etc., issued ten years later, Webbe's name is attached, and in 1791 it was included as a hymn tune under his name in the Rev. Ralph Harrison's *Sacred Harmony,* Vol. II, with the name "Melcombe." Much interest attaches to *An Essay on the Church Plain Chant,* second part, for here also is found "Adeste Fideles" (96) in its first printed form.

Samuel Webbe is said to have been born in Minorca, an island east of Spain in the Mediterranean, in 1740, the exact date being unknown. An obituary notice in the *Gentleman's Magazine* (London, 1816) reports that his father died after accepting a government appointment, before his wife and son could join him there. Hence, the place of his birth is not known. Owing to the fact that, for some reason, young Samuel's mother did not receive any of the property which should have come to her, the boy's only early education was that which he received from her. In later years he referred with bitterness to his waste of seven years as cabinet maker's apprentice. When about twenty years of age he obtained employment as a music copyist, and, although able to earn scarcely enough to keep body and soul together (for he often worked from 5 A. M. until midnight), he found time to study French and Latin. His work created in him an interest in music, as such, and he determined to make himself a master of the subject. How well he succeeded is attested by the fact that he wrote some of the finest unaccompanied vocal music of all time. Webbe was also a noted organist, serving the Sardinian and Portuguese Chapels in London for some years. His interest in the study of languages increased so that before his death at London, May 25, 1816, he had attained some knowledge not only of Latin and French, but of Italian, German, Greek, and Hebrew, as well. He was much beloved and highly respected by those who knew him.

**36—We lift our hearts to Thee—John Wesley**

**Mornington** (25)—Arranged from a chant by Garret Wellesley (25)

"This is one of the few original hymns ascribed to John Wesley," says Dr. Charles E. Nutter in his *Hymn Studies,* 1884.

**One reason why it is thought to be his rather than Charles Wesley's is that it is only half-rhymed. Not a single known stanza of Charles Wesley's has that peculi-**

arity. The sublime thought expressed in the third line of the first stanza is borrowed from Plato: Lumen est umbra Dei.

The fourth stanza of the original has been omitted and "Thy" changed to "Thine" in line one, stanza two.

John Wesley, founder of Methodism, and without question the greatest religious force of the eighteenth century, is so well known to Christians of all denominations that only the barest outline of his life and work need be given here. The son of the Rev. Samuel Wesley, rector of Epworth in Lincolnshire, England, and his wife, Susannah, a woman of deep piety and great force of character, he was born at the Epworth rectory, June 28, 1703. After early education, guided by his mother, he proceeded to Charterhouse and Christ Church, Oxford, becoming Fellow of Lincoln and Greek Lecturer there in 1726. For a time he acted as curate for his father at Epworth. Under a commission from the society for the Propagation of the Gospel he undertook, in 1735, a mission to the new colony of Georgia, founded under the governorship of General Oglethorpe, and in 1737 published at Charleston (then Charlestown), South Carolina, the first American hymnbook. Returning to England early in 1738, he chanced to attend, on the night of May 24, a meeting in Aldersgate Street, London, where he heard some one reading Luther's preface to the Epistle to the Romans. It was then, Wesley said:

> About a quarter before nine, while he was describing the change which God works in the heart through faith in Christ, I felt my heart strangely warmed. I felt I did trust in Christ, Christ alone, for salvation; and an assurance was given me, that He had taken away *my* sins, even *mine,* and saved *me* from the law of sin and death.

His course from that moment was clear. For more than fifty years, "through evil report and good report," he did what he could to spread what he believed to be the truth about the everlasting gospel, and it is said that he traveled more miles, preached more sermons, made more converts, and wrote more books having practical value "than any man of his day, or perhaps of any day." Utterly worn out by his labors, he passed from this earthly life, March 2, 1791.

It is customary to say that John Wesley was the preacher and his brother, Charles, the hymn writer of the Methodist movement; but this is not strictly accurate, for John Wesley wrote hymns and Charles Wesley was an effective preacher. While it is not easy to ascertain the actual part he took in the writing of the original hymns of the Revival, he is known to have made more than thirty excellent translations from German, French, and Spanish hymnody. Attention should also be called to the many emendations he made of the hymns of his brother, Charles, and of Isaac Watts, most of them improvements. His thoughts were directed toward German hymnody through his association with the Moravians. In his sermon on "Knowing Christ after the Flesh," preached in 1789, he said:

> I translated many of their hymns for the use of our congregations. Indeed, as I durst not implicitly follow any man, I did not take all that lay before me, but selected those which I judged to be most Spiritual, and most suited to sound experience.

W. Garrett Horder, eminent English hymnodist, thought his translations "had never been surpassed" and considered him

> as great a translator as Charles is an original hymnist. For congregational use they are probably the finest translations in the English language, whilst they have the high honor of having opened to us the rich treasures of sacred song which Germany possesses.

John Wesley believed that hymns should not only be utilized for "raising the devotion," but for purposes of instruction and of establishing the faith of his followers—they were a sort of creed in verse. In the notable Preface to his large *Collection,* dated October 20, 1779, he wrote:

> In what other publication have you so distinct and full account of Scriptural Christianity; such a declaration of the heights and depths of religion, speculative and practical; so strong cautions against the most plausible errors, particularly those now most prevalent; and so clear directions for making your calling and election sure; for perfecting holiness in the fear of God?

He insisted hymns should be "a body of experimental and practical divinity." John Wesley had a "burning conviction" of the tremendous possibilities that lay in the people's part in the worship of Almighty God.

**37—At Thy feet, our God and Father—James Drummond Burns**

**St. Asaph—William Samuel Bambridge**

The text under which this hymn first appeared in *Psalms and Hymns for Divine Worship,* an English Presbyterian hymnal of 1867, was Psalm 65. 2:

> O Thou that hearest prayer, unto Thee shall all flesh come.

It was written as a hymn for the New Year, the fourth line of stanza 1 reading,

> To begin the year with praise.

"Year" was changed to "day" by the American hymnologists who first used it in this country, where it is becoming favorably known as a fine praise hymn for the morning service.

James Drummond Burns, born, February 18, 1823, at Edinburgh, Scotland, graduated from the University of Edinburgh and became the minister of the Free Church at Dumblane; but was compelled, because of ill health, to relinquish his work there; in 1848 he sought the warmer climate of the Madeira Islands, where he took charge of the work of the Presbyterian Church at Funchal. Returning to London in 1855, he became the minister of Hampstead Presbyterian Church. He died at Mentone, Southern France, November 27, 1864, where he had gone to escape the disagreeable London winter weather, and was buried in Highgate Cemetery, London. He was so recognized for his interest in hymnody that he furnished an article on the subject for the eighth edition of the *Encyclopedia Britannica.* His winsome personality, high character, and well-modulated voice made his preaching peculiarly effective.

"St. Asaph" was one of a number of compositions written in celebration of the recovery of Edward, Prince of Wales, from a severe attack of typhoid fever.

For his restoration to health services of joy and thanksgiving, held quite generally throughout the United Kingdom, were the inspiration for the writing of many hymns and anthems.

William Samuel Bambridge, born at Wainate, New Zealand, July 18, 1842, was brought to England at an early age and for a time was a chorister at Saint George's, Windsor. After graduating from Oxford he went to Marlborough College, where he taught music for forty-seven years (1864-1911). After his retirement he continued living at Marlborough until his death, in his eighty-first year, January 20, 1923.

**38—O splendor of God's glory bright**—Ambrose of Milan
Translated by John Chandler and Louis Fitzgerald Benson

**Wareham**—William Knapp

This is a translation of "Splendor paternae gloriae," a Latin hymn of the fourth century attributed to St. Ambrose, and although there is some uncertainty as to its authorship, the Benedictine editors of his works accept it. The hymn has had twenty-five or more translations, about half of them in common use being various centos. This is such a free rendering that it may be thought of as an adaptation rather than a translation. Originally it was a Morning Hymn to the Trinity, or, more properly, one exalting Christ as the Light of the World, but this is more in the nature of a prayer for guidance during each day.

Ambrose of Milan was not only one of the Fathers of the Western Church but one of the Fathers of modern Western Christian hymnody, for there is no question that he introduced two new forms into public worship in the Western Church—namely, the hymn and the antiphon. While it is true that in the early days any act of praise to God, provided it was sung, or declaimed, was called a "hymn," it is equally true that St. Ambrose was the first to introduce the metrical hymn into formal public worship and to give it a place beside the psalm and canticle. St. Augustine, in his *Confessions*, says,

> At this time[1] it was instituted that, after the manner of the Eastern Church, hymns and psalms should be sung, . . . which custom, retained from then till now, is imitated by many—yea, by almost all . . . congregations throughout the rest of the world.

He also had much to do with the organization of the early Christian musical system, but to what extent is not known. Certainly he did not invent the "Authentic Modes," but tradition has it that he did select and admit them to use for religious music. Whatever his actual musical contribution, the church at Milan, ever since he reformed its service in 384, has held to a tradition in the Ambrosian Chant that in some ways is distinct from general Roman Catholic Church usage.

Ambrose was born at Treves in 340 (?) and died at Milan, April 4, 397.

[1] The time of the conflict of St. Ambrose with the Arians. This occurred in 386.

Educated for the law, which he practiced until his thirty-fourth year, he was baptized and made Bishop of Milan. Scholarly, devout, sincere, an able orator and writer, he "shines upon us as a character most pure, serene, and brave."

> He accepted no invitations to banquets; took dinner only on Sunday, Saturday, and the festivals of celebrated martyrs; devoted the greater part of the night to prayer, to the hitherto necessarily neglected study of the Scriptures and the Greek fathers, and to theological writing; preached every Sunday and often in the week; was accessible to all, most accessible to the poor and needy; and administered his spiritual oversight, particularly his instruction of catechumens, with the greatest fidelity.

A model Bishop, indeed.

John Chandler, one of the earliest of the translators of Latin hymns, was born at Whitley, Surrey, England, June 16, 1806, and died at Putney, July 1, 1876. Graduating at Corpus Christi College, Oxford, he took Holy Orders and became Vicar of Whitley. His translations are the result of his desire for hymns of corresponding date to accompany the ancient Anglican prayers. Two collections of these were published, from which thirty or more hymns have been selected. His translations are quite free, yet, probably because of that fact, are more popular than many which conform more to the original.

Louis Fitzgerald Benson, eminent Presbyterian divine, was one of America's authoritative hymnologists for nearly a generation. Doctor Benson was born in Philadelphia, July 22, 1855, graduated from the University of Pennsylvania, School of Law, and after practicing law for some years attended Princeton Theological Seminary and was ordained a Presbyterian minister. His interest in hymnody was so great that he was considered one of the outstanding authorities in the field. Among his many published works, *The English Hymn, Its Development and Use,* stands a monument to his scholarship. For a generation he was sole editor of the Presbyterian *Hymnal.* His extensive and valuable hymnological library was given to Princeton Theological Seminary after his death, which occurred at Philadelphia, October 10, 1930.

"Wareham" ("All Saints" in the 1905 *Methodist Hymnal*) appeared as early as 1738 in a book by William Knapp, set to verses 5-10, Psalm 36, New Version, and headed "For ye holy sacrament," as follows:

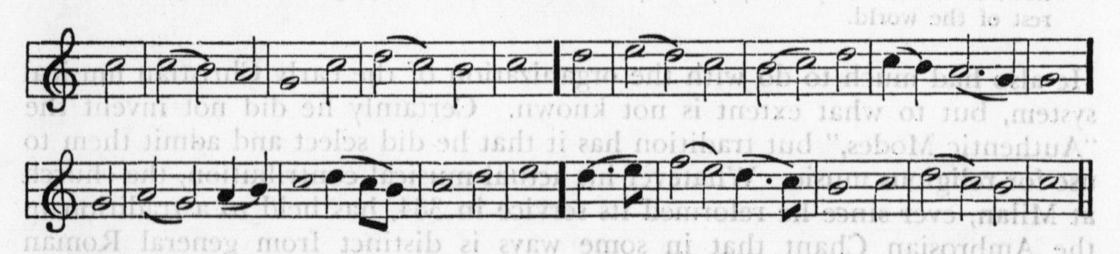

In this book it was called "Wareham," after the birthplace of the composer. In another book, *New Church Melody,* also by Knapp, published in 1754, this tune, in common time, called "Blanford Tune," appeared:

Here it was set to Psalm 139. It is common to all books of all denominations.

William Knapp, an Englishman, was of German descent. He was organist at Wareham, where he was born in 1698, and at Poole, where he died in 1768. Very little is known of him except that he was "a country psalm singer," that he wrote at least one excellent hymn tune, and that he was buried September 26, 1768, at Poole. He published *A Sett of New Psalm Tunes and Anthems in Four Parts,* in 1738, and another book, *The New Church Melody,* in 1754. "An Ejaculation," written by H. Price, of Poole, which appeared in *The London Magazine* in 1742, is of interest:

From pounce and paper, ink and pen,
Save me, O Lord, I pray;
From Pope and Swift and such-like men,
And Cribber's annual lay;
From doctors' bills and lawyers' fees,
From ague, gout and trap;
And what is ten times worse than these,
George Savage and Will Knapp.

At the time this was written Knapp was the parish clerk and George Savage sexton at St. James Church, Poole.

**39—Stand up and bless the Lord**—James Montgomery

**Old 134th (St. Michael)**—Adapted from Genevan Psalter, 1551 (3)

Written for a Wesleyan Sunday School anniversary held at Sheffield, England, on March 15, 1824, this hymn began

Stand up and bless the Lord,
Ye children of His choice.

James Montgomery changed the word "children" to "people" when, a year later, it was published in his *Christian Psalmist.* Its use is extensive wherever English hymns are sung. Truly a hymn for the sanctuary, the third stanza is particularly arresting:

O for the living flame
From His own altar brought,
To touch our lips, our minds inspire,
And wing to heaven our thought!

The son of a Moravian minister, who for a time was associated with John Cennick (199), later going to the West Indies as a missionary, where both he and his wife died, James Montgomery, born at Irvine, Scotland, November 4, 1771, was educated in a Moravian school. He intended to enter the ministry, but the Brethren, becoming dissatisfied with his progress, apprenticed him to a baker. Not caring for work of this sort, he ran away and secured a place in a ship chandler's shop. This also proving uncongenial, he went to London, where for a year he tried in vain to find a publisher for some poems he had written. When twenty-three he went to Sheffield to work for a bookseller, the publisher of *The Sheffield Register*. When the editor of the paper, because of political difficulties, had to leave Sheffield, Montgomery, who succeeded to the editorship, continued his work there for thirty-one years, publishing the paper under the name *The Sheffield Iris*. Twice imprisoned for publishing matter said to be inimical to the public interest (one of these articles being a song in celebration of the fall of the Bastille), he was a leader in wholesome enterprises—editing his paper, lecturing on poetry, interesting himself in the cause of foreign missions and in the Bible Society, quite generally over the country. He died at The Mount, Sheffield, April 30, 1854, and was honored by a public funeral. Doctor Julian, usually reserved, says of him:

> His ear for rhythm was exceedingly accurate and refined. His knowledge of Holy Scripture was most extensive. His religious views were broad and charitable. His devotional spirit was of the holiest type. With the faith of a strong man he united the beauty and simplicity of a child. Richly poetic without exuberance, dogmatic without uncharitableness, tender without sentimentality, elaborate without diffusiveness, richly musical without apparent effort, he has bequeathed to the Church of Christ wealth which could only have come from a true genius and a sanctified heart.

"Old 134th" ("St. Michael") is an adaptation of a tune appearing in the 1551 edition of the *Genevan Psalter*, where it was set to Marot's version of Psalm 101. In the *Anglo-Genevan Psalter* of 1561, it was set to Psalm 134; hence the name (3). Evidently, the tune did not prove to be popular, for it seems to have dropped out of use before 1600, not to be revived until 1836, when Dr. William Crotch (English musician, 1775-1847) included it in his *Psalm Tunes*, as "St. Michael." In its earliest form the melody was:

**40—Still, still with Thee—Harriet Beecher Stowe**

**Consolation—Arranged from Felix Mendelssohn-Bartholdy (33)**

This beautiful, intimately personal morning hymn was written at the request of Henry Ward Beecher, the brother of the author, for inclusion in *The Plymouth Collection* of 1855. While Mrs. Stowe gained fame and fortune through *Uncle Tom's Cabin*, many thousands, doubtless, who never heard of that book nor ever will hear of it, have sung or will sing this hymn. It probably was suggested by Psalm 139. 18:

> . . . when I awake, I am still with thee.

Harriet Beecher Stowe, who was born at Litchfield, June 14, 1811, and who died at Hartford, Connecticut, July 1, 1896, had published, during her life, more than forty volumes of her writings. She was a member of one of America's most illustrious families, her father being Lyman Beecher and her brother Henry Ward Beecher, as indicated above. When a young woman, she studied and taught in her sister's school in Hartford. Going to Cincinnati with her father when he was made president of Lane Seminary in 1832, she married a member of the Lane faculty, Professor Calvin E. Stowe, four years later. Her husband being in poor health, she found it necessary to do literary work. When Professor Stowe received an appointment at Bowdoin College, Maine, she seized her opportunity to do what she could to aid in the liberation of the slaves. *Uncle Tom's Cabin, Dred: A Tale of the Dismal Swamp,* and many magazine articles aided the abolition movement. Among her many works she issued one small volume of religious verse. In her later life she lived at Andover, Massachusetts, where her husband was a member of the Andover Theological Seminary faculty, and upon his retirement, at Hartford, where she died.

"Consolation" is the name given to No. 3, Book 2, *Songs Without Words,* by Mendelssohn, from which this tune is taken. It has also been called "Reynolds."

## Evening Hymns

**41—The radiant morn hath passed away—Godfrey Thring**

**Oldbridge—Robert Newton Quaile**

Under the heading "The Lord shall be thine Everlasting Light" (Isaiah 20), the hymn, written in 1864, first published in the author's *Hymns, Congregational and Others,* 1866, was chosen as the opening one for the Appendix to *Hymns Ancient and Modern,* 1868. The hymn, its writer has said,

> was composed as an "afternoon" hymn, as in most of the parishes in that part of Somersetshire in which I lived, the sacred service was nearly always held in the afternoon and not in the evening, whilst all the hymns in the hymnbooks in common use were for the late evening or night. I wrote "The radiant morn hath passed away" to supply this want.

Originally in five stanzas, the fourth has been omitted, and the second changed from,

> Our life is but a fading dawn:
> Its glorious noon how quickly past!
> Lead us, O Christ, when all is gone,
> Safe home at last,

to,

> Our life is but an autumn sun;
> Its glorious noon how quickly past!
> Lead us, O Christ, our lifework done,
> Safe home at last.

The author made the change when a correspondent called his attention to the fact that the dawn does not fade—it grows brighter. This hymn had been admitted to collections in the United States only recently, yet it has been sung as an anthem by choirs quite generally for a generation or more.

Godfrey Thring, brother of the famed educator, Edward Thring, was born at Alford, Somersetshire, England, March 25, 1823, educated at Balliol College, Oxford, and died at Plouck's Hill, Guilford, September 13, 1903. Twelve years after his graduation, meanwhile serving various churches, he succeeded his father, John Gale Thring, as rector of Alford. After acting as rural dean for nine years, in 1876 he became prebendary of East Harptree in Wells Cathedral, retiring from active work in 1893. While rector of Alford he had begun publishing the collections of hymns that were to make him so influential that his brother Edward could write, sixteen years later:

> Be sure that no painting, no art work you could have done, by any possibility could have been so powerful for good, or given you the niche you now occupy. As long as the English language lasts, sundry of your hymns will be read and sung, yea, even to the last day, and many a soul of God's best creatures thrill with your words. What more can a man want? Very likely if you had had all that old heathendom rammed into you, as I had, and all the literary artists slicing and pruning, and been scissored like me, you would just have lost the freshness and simple touch which make you what you are. No, my boy, I make a tidy schoolmaster and pass into the lives of many a pupil, and you live on the lips of the Church. So be satisfied. And what does it matter, if we do the Master's work?

Compiler of several hymn books, it is said his *Church of England Hymn Book,* 1880, set a higher literary standard than any other like book of the period. This book was almost austere because of Thring's objection to anything savoring of sentimentality. As a boy he had led a severely restricted life. His father had wanted a career in the army, but submitted to a strong-willed mother and took holy orders. "The duties thus assumed were not, perhaps, entirely congenial to him, but they were discharged with conscientious care and fidelity." So, life in the Thring home has been described as "just, but hard." William Budd Bodine thinks that because the childhood was "rugged" there was "no lack of strength in the manhood. It had been better, however, if there had been more gentleness in the training." Possibly more of Godfrey Thring's hymns would now be in common use had there been more gentleness shown the boy.

"Oldbridge" was written in 1903 and first published in *The English Hymnal,* 1906. As a fitting tune for this hymn in unusual meter, it finds its way into denominational hymnody for the first time in America through *The Methodist Hymnal.*

Robert Newton Quaile, the son of an Irish Methodist minister, was born in County Limerick, Ireland, in 1867. He is an amateur musician, being engaged in business at Mallow, County Cork. In 1920, as one result of the difficulties through which Ireland was passing, all of his possessions were burned, and, after middle life, he had to make a new start. He has contributed three other tunes to the *Methodist Sunday School Hymnal* (English).

**42—Again as evening's shadow falls**—Samuel Longfellow

**Abends**—Herbert Stanley Oakeley

While Samuel Longfellow was pastor of the Second Unitarian Church, Brooklyn, from 1863 to 1869, he inaugurated a series of Vesper Services and wrote this hymn for use in them. In 1859 he prepared a little book of *Vespers,* since the appearance of which its excellence has brought it into general favor for evening services.

Samuel Longfellow, brother of the famous poet, was himself a poet of good repute and a Unitarian minister of high standing. He was born at Portland, Maine, June 18, 1819, and died there, October 3, 1892. In addition to serving several New England churches as well as one in Brooklyn, he found time to compile two hymnals, a book of poetry, part of which was original, to write the life of his brother, Henry W. Longfellow, and to do other literary work. The vesper service owes its popularity to him.

"Abends" was written by Doctor Oakeley as a setting for "Sun of my soul, Thou Saviour dear" because he felt that "Hursley" (56), which bears a resemblance to a drinking song by Mozart, was not a suitable tune for such a fine hymn. It was written for the *Irish Church Hymnal,* 1873.

Herbert S. Oakeley, born at Ealing, Middlesex, England, July 22, 1830, was educated at Rugby, Christ Church, Oxford (A.B. and M.A.), at Dresden, and at Leipzig. An organist of unusual gifts, he had a remarkable facility in improvisation. From 1865, for twenty-six years, he was professor of music in the University of Edinburgh, was knighted in 1876, and made Composer in Scotland to Queen Victoria in 1881. He was influential in promoting public performances of the best music at the famous annual Reid Concert in Edinburgh. His scholarship was noteworthy, nine institutions honoring him by giving him doctorate degrees. While he wrote numerous vocal numbers with piano or orchestral accompaniment, he is known for a few of his hymn tunes. "Abends" seems to be the most favored of them. It appears three times in *The Methodist Hymnal.* He died at Eastbourne, October 26, 1903.

**43—God that madest earth and heaven**—Reginald Heber (1)
Frederick Lucian Hosmer

**Ar Hyd Y Nos**—Welsh traditional melody
Harmonized by Luther Orlando Emerson (224)

The original hymn was of but one stanza, the first here, which appeared in Bishop Heber's posthumous *Hymns,* 1827. It was written for "Ar Hyd Y Nos," the old Welsh melody to which it is set in this book. The second stanza was written by Doctor Hosmer for the *Hymn and Tune Book* of 1914.

Frederick Lucian Hosmer, D.D., born at Framingham, Massachusetts, October 16, 1840, was a descendant of James Hosmer, one of the first settlers at Concord in 1635. Graduating from Harvard in 1872, and ordained a Unitarian minister, he served churches in Massachusetts, Ohio, Illinois, Missouri, and California, where he continued to live after his retirement until his death in Berkeley, June 7, 1929. In 1908 he delivered a series of lectures on hymnody at Harvard University. Julian says Hosmer was the strongest and most original of Unitarian hymn writers of the last quarter of the nineteenth century. His hymns are used extensively not only in the United States but many of them are familiar to Congregationalist and Unitarian groups in England.

"Ar Hyd Y Nos," a very old Welsh air, may be found in many collections of ballads under the title "All through the night." It first gained prominence as a popular tune long ago in England, where it was sung to

Here beneath a willow weepeth
Poor Mary Ann.

It is first found in printed form in Edward Jones's *Welsh Bards,* 1784. Bishop Heber heard a Welsh harper playing this tune in the hall of a house where he was visiting. Retiring to a quiet corner, he wrote the stanza to fit it. The Bishop's sister, Mary, included the stanza and tune in the Choir book in use at the church at Hodnet (1). Like most fine melodies, it has been put to a variety of uses both sacred and secular.

**44—Day is dying in the west**—Mary Artemisia Lathbury

**Chautauqua** (Evening Praise)—William Fiske Sherwin

Of this hymn W. Garrett Horder, the eminent English hymnologist, wrote:

> It is one of the finest and most distinctive hymns of modern times. It deserves to rank with "Lead, kindly Light," of Cardinal Newman, for its picturesqueness and allusionness, and above all else for this, that devout souls, no matter what their distinctive beliefs, can through it voice their deepest feelings and aspirations.

Horder was one who welcomed the "emotional side of hymnody." "Pious moderation," he said, "has been the curse of hymnody." The hymn has been criticized, however, for having overdone, somewhat, the beautiful simplicity and grandeur of Isaiah 6. 3. However that may be, of all the evening hymns it has come to have first place in the hearts of Americans, and is held in affectionate regard by Christians throughout the world. It was written in 1877 at the request of Dr. John H. Vincent, the founder of the original Chautauqua Assembly on western New York's beautiful lake of that name (originally the site of a Methodist camp-meeting ground). The hymn requested was to be sung at the vesper service held on the lake shore. There is some question as to the date of the writing of the hymn, but S. W. Duffield has written that Miss Lathbury informed him it had been composed in the summer of 1880. Doctor Bestor, however, has written the author, "It is safe to assume it was written in 1877."

Mary Artemisia Lathbury, who was born at Manchester, New York, August 10, 1841, and died at East Orange, New Jersey, October 20, 1913, was the daughter of a Methodist local preacher, and had two brothers who were ministers of that church. More important than her work as a professional artist, her gifted work in writing verse has made her name a household word. Miss Lathbury contributed to periodicals for children and young people and served in an editorial capacity for the Methodist Sunday School Union, of which Doctor Vincent was the secretary. Through him she became associated with the Chautauqua movement, and became known as the "Laureate of Chautauqua." She is also remembered as the founder of the "Look Up Legion" which was based on Edward Everett Hale's four rules of good conduct:

Look up, not down;
Look forward, not back;
Look out, and not in,
And lend a hand.

"Chautauqua" ("Evening Praise") was written by W. F. Sherwin for Miss Lathbury's hymn in 1877. It is generally used in the United States as the setting for this hymn, but has not been popular in England. So completely has this tune become fixed in the musical memory of Americans that it and the words "Day is dying in the west" have become synonymous.

William Fiske Sherwin was born at Buckland, Massachusetts, March 14, 1826, and died at Boston, April 14, 1888. His successful leadership of choirs during his boyhood was responsible for his selection by Doctor Vincent to organize the choruses at Chautauqua. He was for a time a student of Lowell Mason (19), later teaching vocal music at the New England Conservatory of Music, Boston. An unusually successful organizer and director of amateur choruses, a writer in *The Independent,* some years ago, said he "was a genial tyrant of the baton, who would scold his chorus until they cried, and then heal all hearts with his 'Day is dying in the west.' "

**45—Now on land and sea descending**—Samuel Longfellow (42)

**Vesper Hymn**—Dimitri Stepanovitch Bortniansky

The hymn comes from *Vespers,* published in 1859, and is one of the most beautiful from that collection of verses (42).

No definite information concerning the source of the tune "Vespers" has been found.

Dimitri Stepanovitch Bortniansky was a protégé of the Empress Catherine of Russia and became choirmaster of what was known from 1796 as the "Imperial Kapelle." For his systematization of modern Russian church music he has been known as its father, and as "the Russian Palestrina." Tschaikowsky edited his works in ten volumes. Bortniansky was born at Gloukoff, in the Ukraine, October 28, 1752, and died at St. Petersburg, September 28 (October 7, 9 ?), 1825.

**46—The shadows of the evening hours**—Adelaide Anne Procter (9)

**St. Leonard**—Henry Hiles

*Legends and Lyrics,* Miss Procter's principal work, from which this evening prayer was taken, first published in 1858, ran through many editions, which probably accounts for the various publication dates given, namely, 1858, 1861, and 1862. Julian gives the date as 1862, the year in which the enlarged edition of *Legends* was issued.

"St. Leonard," written for this hymn for a festival held at Manchester, England, in 1867, was published the same year by Dr. Henry Hiles in *Twelve Tunes to Original or Favorite Hymns.*

Henry Hiles, Mus. Doc., who was born at Shrewsbury, England, December

31, 1826, and died at Worthing, October 20, 1904, was a late nineteenth-century English composer of repute, who wrote textbooks dealing with the theory of music. He held positions as organist in various churches, and was lecturer on harmony and composition at Owen's College, Manchester, at Victoria University, and finally at the Manchester College of Music. When the Cheetham Hill Methodists found their tune books too old-fashioned for modern use, a committee was appointed to prepare a more modern one and chose Doctor Hiles as its editor. The product was *The Wesley Tune Book* of 1872, a book which marked a considerable advance in English hymn music. He was also founder, proprietor, and editor of the *Quarterly Musical Review,* 1885-1888.

**47—Softly now the light of day**—George Washington Doane
**Mercy**—Louis Moreau Gottschalk
Arranged by Edwin Pond Parker (295)

The hymn is from *Songs by the Way,* published by George W. Doane the year he became Professor of Belles Lettres in Trinity College, Hartford, Connecticut, 1824. As a heading for this hymn, "Evening," Psalm 141. 2 was quoted:

> Let my prayer be set forth before thee as incense; and the lifting up of my hands as the evening sacrifice.

Somewhere George Washington Doane, D.D., wrote these lines, which well apply to his own life:

> "What is that, Mother?"
> "The eagle, boy!
> Proudly careering his course of joy,
> Firm on his mountain vigor, relying,
> Breasting the dark storm, the red bolt defying,
> His wing on the wind, and his eye on the sun,
> He swerves not a hair, but bears onward, right on."

Certainly, he himself "swerved not." He was born at Trenton, New Jersey, May 27, 1799; graduated from Union College at nineteen; attended General Theological Seminary and was ordained a deacon in the Protestant Episcopal Church at twenty-two, being made priest two years later. At twenty-five he was Professor at Trinity College, and coeditor of *The Episcopal Watchman;* at twenty-nine he was assistant at Trinity Church, Boston, and rector at thirty-one. When only thirty-three he was made Bishop of New Jersey, establishing his cathedral at Burlington, where he was to found St. Mary's Hall and Burlington College. A successor to Bishop Doane has written:

> He was a pioneer in the work of education, ahead of his time in a good many things, and his name is remembered, not by the troubles he was compelled to face, but by his greatness as a man and a bishop.

Bishop Doane's son, William Croswell Doane (59), also a bishop, writes:

> My father's poetical writings were simple necessities. He could not help them. His heart was so full of song. It oozed out in his conversation, in his sermons, in everything that he did. Sometimes in a steamboat, often when the back of a letter was his only paper, the sweetest things came. And with his heart so full of it, nothing ever touched it, but it pressed some out.

There is a tradition at St. Mary's Hall that "Softly now the light of day" shall be sung at each weekly chapel service during the school year. He died April 27, 1859.

"Mercy" is an adaptation of one of Louis M. Gottschalk's compositions for piano, entitled "The Last Hope." This arrangement is by Dr. Edwin P. Parker, late distinguished Congregational minister at Hartford, Connecticut (295).

Louis Moreau Gottschalk was born at New Orleans, Louisiana, May 8, 1829, his father an Englishman, his mother a French woman. A musical prodigy, he began the serious study of violin at six, but soon turned to piano as, for him, a more fitting medium of expression. When only twelve years of age he was taken to Paris, where he presented himself to take the examinations for entrance to the Conservatoire, but the judges refused to give him a hearing. Ten years later, however, he himself was one of the judges. Chopin said to him: "I predict you will become a king of pianists." His popularity as a concert artist was so extraordinary that he was able to give eighty concerts in New York during the winter of 1855-56. He refused P. T. Barnum's offer of twenty thousand dollars and all expenses for a year's contract. A great favorite in Spanish American countries, probably no other artist traveled more extensively in concert giving. Most of his public programs featured his own compositions. Late in his life he suffered severely from fevers, and on one occasion shortly before his death he stopped while playing a piece, "La morte," seeming to have a premonition of his death. He died suddenly at Rio de Janeiro, December 18, 1869.

**48—At even ere the sun was set**—Henry Twells

**Abends** (42)—Herbert Stanley Oakeley (42)

This evening hymn was written at the request of Sir Henry W. Baker (353), secretary of the committee which compiled *Hymns Ancient and Modern,* who felt another evening hymn was needed for the Appendix to the first edition of the book. The author has given the following account of its writing:

> Being at that time headmaster of a large grammar-school—the Godolphin School, Hammersmith—I wrote it one afternoon while the boys were under examination (paper work), and I was supposed to be seeing "all fair." I am afraid I could not have been very energetic or lynx-eyed in my duties that day, but I little anticipated the popularity the hymn would attain. . . . Copies have been kindly sent to me in Greek, Latin, German, French, Welsh, and Irish. I like to think it may have brought souls nearer Christ, and if so, I heartily thank God for it.

Of the eight stanzas written originally by Canon Twells, the following (4 and 5) have been omitted—wisely, it is felt:

And some are pressed with worldly care,
And some are tried with sinful doubt;
And some such grievous passions tear,
That only Thou canst cast them out.

And some have found the world is vain,
Yet from the world they break not free;
And some have friends who give them pain,
Yet have not sought a friend in Thee.

The first line as here printed is as Canon Twells wrote it. Prebendary Thring (41) and others took exception to its first form as not being in keeping with the old Jewish law which forbade the people bringing their sick before sunset. The hymn was based on Mark 1. 32: "And at even, when the sun did set, they brought unto Him all that were diseased." While the author was willing to allow "ere" to be changed to "when," he insisted that his original form was not inconsistent with Luke's account of the incident (Luke 4. 40): "Now when the sun was setting, all they that had any sick with divers diseases brought them unto Him." As included in most of the better hymnals issued since 1868, the first line reads in nearly all cases,

At even, when the sun was set.

Henry Twells, M.A., born March 23, 1823, at Ashted, Birmingham, England, was active in the preparation of *Hymns Ancient and Modern,* 1861, and served on the committee which prepared the Appendix of 1868. For the Appendix he wrote the first of six hymns now included in that epoch-making hymnal. A native of Birmingham, a graduate of Cambridge University, a preacher of note, a builder of churches, one interested in missionary work in the parishes he served, a friend of the lowly, Henry Twells lived a quiet life of many interests. At Bournemouth, England, the health resort to which place he had retired because of failing health, he recovered sufficiently to act as priest-in-charge of the new church of St. Augustine, which he built and partly endowed with his own funds. He died there, January 19, 1900.

**49—Now God be with us**—Petrus Herbert
Translated by Catherine Winkworth (7)

**Nightfall**—Joseph Barnby (31)

Petrus Herbert helped edit the *Gesangbuch* of the Bohemian Brethren, 1566, to which he contributed the hymn beginning,

Die Nacht ist kommen, drin wir ruhen sollen.

Miss Winkworth included it in her *Chorale Book for England,* 1863, and again in her *Christian Singers of Germany,* 1869. Originally in five stanzas of seven lines each, one of which was a metrical rendering of the Lord's Prayer, a sixth (stanza 4, this book) was added by Johann H. Schein (1586-1630) in his *Cantonial* of 1627.

First of Protestant churches the Bohemian Brethren (Unitas Fratrum) published a hymnbook, which appeared in the Bohemian language in 1501. It contained versions of the old Latin hymns with many originals, most of which were by John Huss and Bishop Luke of Prague, the latter its editor. The better known book of 1505 followed, also in Bohemian, and shortly after the middle of the century enlarged and revised editions appeared in German and Polish. It is from the German edition of 1566 that this hymn is taken.

The hymns of the Brethren were a power in the Church and the land. They gave life to public worship; they were familiarly sung in the homes of the nobles and of peasants; they set forth the pure Gospel in strains that captivated thousands of hearts in the Roman Catholic Church and brought them to a knowledge of free grace in Christ Jesus.

—From the Preface to *The Liturgy*, etc., of the Unitas Fratrum.

We have been told that the hymn was probably written under "persecution and oppression." Dr. Charles Seymour Robinson suggests:

> The Christians of the present day, who live so tranquilly in the light of modern advancement and peace, are fortunate in being permitted to tone up and strengthen their piety with some of these old songs of faith which bore the warrior souls of Reformation times on through the perils of the martyr days.

Petrus Herbert, the date of whose birth is not known, seems to have been of Moravian extraction, a native of, or a resident at Fulnek. A man of considerable influence among the Bohemian Brethren, he was ordained to their priesthood and acted as their ambassador on many important missions, one of which was to confer with Calvin. His contribution of ninety hymns to the 1566 enlarged and revised German edition of the Brethren's hymnbook, and the inclusion of one hundred and four in the 1639 edition, sixty-eight years after his death, set him out as one of the great religious poets of the sixteenth century. He died at Eibenschütz in 1571.

"Nightfall," called "Horeb" by its composer, Sir Joseph Barnby, in his *Hymn Tunes,* 1897, is appropriately named for Herbert's hymn and is a satisfactory setting, yet the optional tune suggested, "Flemming" (327), is superb when sung by a competent chorus of male voices.

**50—Saviour, breathe an evening blessing**—James Edmeston

**Evening Prayer**—George Coles Stebbins

This hymn is from James Edmeston's *Sacred Lyrics,* 1820, with this introduction:

> At night their short evening hymn, "Jesu Mahaxaroo" ("Jesus, forgive us"), stole through the camp.
>
> —Salte's *Travels in Abyssinia.*

So impressed was the author with the above quotation that he composed the two eight-line stanzas, "Saviour, breathe an evening blessing." Julian says it has taken rank with the first evening hymns in the English language, and has been translated into several others, yet it has not been included in most of the better-known hymnals published in England in recent years. In this country, until it became wedded to its present music, it was quite generally sung to Bortniansky's "Vesper Hymn" (45).

James Edmeston, born at Wapping, London, September 10, 1791, and educated at Hackney, was an eminent English architect and surveyor whose great aim and desire was to write sacred poetry. He is said to have written more than two thousand hymns, for years composing each week a new one, which he read at family worship on Sundays. He was a good friend of and a constant visitor to the London Orphan Asylum. Indicative of his great love for children, he named one of his books of verse *Infant Breathings.* He won a prize of £20 for a collection of fifty hymns suitable for cottage prayer meetings. He died at Homerton, a suburb of London, January 7, 1867.

"Evening Prayer" was written as a response to be sung after prayer at the morning service at Tremont Temple, Boston, in 1876, while its composer was in charge of the music there. He writes in his *Reminiscences:*

> Two years afterward, while these meetings in Providence were in progress, I was reminded of that music, and the thought came to me that if I could find a hymn suited to it, it might be worth publishing. With this in mind I began looking through such church hymn books as came to my hand, and "Saviour, breathe an evening blessing" caught my eye, and was finally chosen.

"Evening Prayer" was first published in *Gospel Hymns No. 3.*

George Coles Stebbins was a descendant of Rowland Stebbins, who settled at Springfield, Massachusetts, in 1634. He was born, February 26, 1846, in northwestern New York, where he attended country school and worked on his father's farm. His attendance at singing school at the age of thirteen so awakened in him his natural love for music as to encourage his making it his profession. Aside from some little study of singing under private teachers, his musical education was confined to the country singing school. A year after his marriage, in 1868, he found employment in Chicago as a clerk in the music store of Lyon and Healy and as director of music in the First Baptist Church. Active in the musical affairs of Chicago, he was a charter member of the famous Apollo Club, a tenor soloist whose services were in demand; so it was that he had the opportunity of making the acquaintance of leaders in the evangelistic song field. In 1874 he moved to Boston, where he first led the singing in the church of Dr. A. J. Gordon, two years later, in 1876, being given charge of the music in Tremont Temple. In this eventful year for him, he wrote "Evening Prayer," met Dwight L. Moody, and returned to Chicago, where his association with Moody and Sankey began. From that time, he was for many years one of the leading musical figures in the great evangelistic campaigns at home and abroad. He was one of the editors of the series of *Gospel Hymns* and editor of the *Northfield Hymnal.* His songs are among the best of their kind.

**51—All praise to Thee, my God, this night**—Thomas Ken (34)

**Tallis' Canon (Evening Hymn)**—Thomas Tallis

This, with the exception of one line and two words, is the first four and last stanzas from Bishop Ken's *Evening Hymn,* 1709. The third line of stanza three is from the 1695 rendering, and "Judgment Day" has been substituted for "awful day" in the last line, same stanza. In the last line of the first stanza "Thine" has replaced "Thy" (See No. 34).

"Tallis' Canon," also known as "Evening Hymn," "Tallis Hymn," "Canon," "Brentwood," "Suffolk," "Magdalen," and, in the Foundery collection (295), as "Cannon Tune," is one of the most famous tunes in general use.

The form in which it is written is known as "canon"—that is, "one voice begins a melody, which is imitated precisely, note for note, and (generally), interval for interval, by some other voice, either at the same or a different pitch, beginning a few beats later and thus, as it were, running after the leader. . . . It is the strictest and most regular species of imitation." "Canon" is from the Greek word meaning "rule" or "standard." A composition in this form, then, is one written strictly according to rule.

In this case the melody begins in the soprano, the tenor entering in exact imitation at the fifth note. In order that the imitation be complete throughout, the first four notes of the tenor part as written must be added at the close. The imitation is between the soprano and the tenor only, the alto and bass parts being free. Originally the tenor had the melody and the imitation was in the soprano, as was usual at the time it was written.

The tune was first printed, probably, in 1567, but its first printing in connection with these words was in 1732 in *The Harmonious Companion,* by Smith and Prelieur. It "had probably been associated with them earlier, perhaps from the beginning." Various dates are given for its writing: 1560, 1565, 1567. Available evidence seems to point to 1567 as correct. In several late hymnals the tune has been altered so that it is no longer in canonic form. The alteration has not improved the composition.

Thomas Tallis (Talys or Tallys) was probably born before 1520 although that is the date usually given. (Groves gives c. 1505.) A noted English composer and organist, during the reigns of Henry VIII, Edward VI, Mary, and Elizabeth, he was a Gentleman of the Chapel Royal and joint organist with William Byrd. These gentlemen, in 1575, secured the exclusive privilege of printing music and ruled paper for a term of twenty-one years. One of Tallis's most interesting compositions is a song of forty parts for eight five-voiced choirs. He died November 23, 1585, and was buried in the church at Greenwich, and an epitaph was engraved on a brass plate and placed in a stone before the altar rails. When the church was torn down to make way for a new one, this plate was lost. However, the wording of the epitaph had been preserved by Stowe in his *Survey of London,* and after the passage of one hundred and fifty years, a copy was made and placed in the present church. The epitaph, written in verse, follows:

Enterred here doth ly a worthy wyght,
Who for long tyme in mufick bore the bell:
His name to fhew, was Thomas Tallys hyght,
In honeft uertuous lyff he dyd excell.

He feru'd long tyme in chappel with grete prayfe.
Fower fouereygnes reygnes (a thing not often feene)
I mean kyng Henry and prynce Edward's dayes,
Quene Mary, and Elizabeth our quene.

He maryd was, though children he had none,
And lyu'd in loue ful thre and thirty yeres
Wyth loyal fpowfe, whos name yclept was Jone,
Who here entomb'd, him company now bears.

As he dyd lyue, fo alfo did he dy,
In myld and quyet fort, O happy man!
To God ful oft for mercy did he cry,
Wherefore he lyues, let deth do what he can.

**52—The day is past and over**—Anonymous. 6th century
Translated John Mason Neale

**Du Friedensfürst, Herr Jesu Christ**—Bartholomäus Gesius
Harmonized by Johann Sebastian Bach

This is one of the loveliest of all evening hymns. It has been attributed to St. Anatolius (d. 458) by John M. Neale, translator, but this claim has been disproved. The author is unknown. The hymn is from *The Great After-Supper Service of the Greek Church.* Its first translation appeared in 1853, and was included in Doctor Neale's *Hymns of the Eastern Church,* in 1862. In the second edition of this work, which appeared the same year, it was revised, and with the exception of a change from the first to the third person throughout, and the additional change of two words ("sin" to "dark" in the fourth line of the second stanza, and "fear" to "dark" in the corresponding line of the third stanza) it stands as revised by its author. Doctor Neale comments:

> This little hymn, which, I believe, is not used in the public service of the Church, is a great favorite in the Greek Isles. Its peculiar style and evident antiquity may well lead to the belief that it is the work of our present author (Saint Anatolius). It is, to the scattered hamlets of Chios and Mitylene, what Bishop Ken's Evening Hymn is to the villages of our own land; and its melody is singularly plaintive and soothing.

John Mason Neale was born at London, January 24, 1818, of good stock noted for intellectual strength. After the death of his father (in Neale's fifth year) he was trained by his mother, to whom he paid tribute. After graduating from a grammar school (receiving some special tutoring) he went to Cambridge, where he gained a scholarship in Trinity College. He missed taking honors in the classical course because of his dislike for the required mathematics. He earned lesser honors, however, and, as a graduate, prizes for work of literary merit no less than eleven times. Although he identified himself at Cambridge with the church movement, similar to that under way at Oxford, and lived to see it triumph, yet he did not follow Newman and others into the Roman Church. So poor was his health, owing to lung trouble, that he never held other than a minor position. To better his health, he spent the year 1843-44 in Madeira. Later, when he was offered a place at Perth paying £100 a year, he could not take it on account of the climate.

Instead, he was obliged to go to St. Grinstead where, while acting as warden of Sackville College (an almshouse), he founded the sisterhood of St. Margaret. This developed greatly, and he established an orphanage, a school for girls, and a home for fallen women. He was accused of enticing a sister into St. Margaret's Home, getting her to leave all of her money to the sisterhood, and then sending her to a post where she might be exposed to scarlet fever and die from that disease. Upon the occasion of her funeral Doctor Neale was mobbed and received serious bodily injuries. None who knew him, however, believed the slander.

He was a curious combination of gentleness and firmness. He spent nearly half of his life at St. Grinstead at an annual salary of £27, most of which he gave away. He was one of the most eminent of Latin and Greek scholars, and, although he lived in comparative obscurity, he became world famous as a result of his writings. In view of his precarious health it is almost incomprehensible how he could carry on the work of development at St. Margaret's and do the immense amount of literary work that he did. He died at East Grinstead, August 6, 1866.

His first original contribution was *Hymns for Children,* published in 1842. It reached its tenth edition the year after his death. Following *Hymns for Children* came *Hymns for the Young.* In the same year (1844) he published *Songs and Ballads for Manufacturers,* in which he says his aim was "to set forth good and sound principles in metaphors which might, from their familiarity, come home to the hearts of those to whom they were addressed." Eleven years later, in 1855, he issued a similar work, *Songs and Ballads for the People.* Illustrative of their aggressive and controversial character are such vigorous themes as "The Teetotallers" and "Why don't you go to meeting?" He also published small works with such titles as *Hymns for the Sick, Readings for the Aged,* etc. His *Sequences, Hymns, and Other Ecclesiastical Verses* is probably his most outstanding original work. But it is in the field of translation that he is pre-eminent. His work as a translator of Latin is outstanding. His translation of the *Hora Novissima* (from which work we get the great hymns, "Jerusalem, the Golden" and "For thee, O dear, dear country") is the only one in common use, although several others have been made by other eminent scholars. Many had translated Latin hymns, but Doctor Neale was the first to attempt this work from the Greek. This was a much more difficult task for, he says, "in attempting a Greek canon, from the fact of its being in prose (metrical hymns are unknown) one is all at sea."

One of the outstanding qualities of Doctor Neale's work is its splendid masculinity. Even in his sermons this feature is notable. When we consider that he spent the greater part of his life ministering and preaching to women, we may wonder sometimes that there are not traces of femininity in his writings, but Doctor Littlefield, who wrote an interesting account of his life, tells us that because he had only women to deal with, "he aimed at showing them the masculine side of Christianity, its strength, as well as its beauty."

The tune by Bartholomäus Gesius (Gese), or more familiarly Barthel Göss, is found in *Geistliche deutsche Lieder,* Frankfort, 1601. Gesius was the editor of this book which contained hymns by Martin Luther and other writers of the Reformation. He became one of the older Lutheran cantors, and, following custom, first studied theology. Cantor at Frankfort for the last eighteen years of his life, he was the composer of many works, important in showing the thoroughly liturgical character of the early Lutheran Church. He was born about 1555, at Müncheberg, near Frankfort-on-Oder, Germany, and died at the latter place in 1613.

The harmonization of the tune is by Johann Sebastian Bach.

He, whose ancestors "sounded A for all Germany" for two hundred years, was born at Eisenach, March 21, 1685. No adequate sketch of his life and works can be given here, nor is it necessary, for information concerning him should be available in any library, no matter how meager its resources. It is enough to say that through self-education and self-discipline throughout his life he became one of the great masters of all time. Conscious of his own powers, he chose to follow the inclination of his creative genius regardless of immediate success. While his greatness was to an extent recognized and reverenced during his lifetime, it was a century before there was adequate understanding of what he had done for the art of music. An orthodox Lutheran, he was a devoutly religious man. Sir Hubert Parry, in his *Johann Sebastian Bach, the Study of a Great Personality,* 1909, says that, to Bach, music was the apparatus of worship; religion was the foundation of his sterling character. The little pieces he wrote for his children's clavier exercises were prefaced,

In nomine Jesu,

and he seldom omitted the petition "Jesu juva" when he sat down to write, nor did he often fail to add "Soli Deo Gloria" to his finished scores. He died of apoplexy at Leipzig, July 28, 1750.

**53—Now the day is over**—Sabine Baring-Gould
**Merrial**—Joseph Barnby (31)

This was written for and sung by the children of Horbury Bridge, England, while its author was curate in charge of that mission district. Of the original eight stanzas, the second, which was "written down" for the children, and the last, in doxology form, have been wisely omitted. The hymn was first printed in *The Church Times,* February 16, 1867, and the next year included in the Appendix to *Hymns Ancient and Modern,* where it was set to the tune "Eudoxia" (308) by the author of the lines. The hymn was based on Proverbs 3. 24, "When thou liest down, thou shalt not be afraid: yea, thou shalt lie down, and thy sleep shall be sweet."

Sabine Baring-Gould, born at Exeter, England, January 28, 1834, from 1854 to 1906 published eighty-five books on a variety of subjects—religion, travel, folklore, mythology, history, fiction, sermons, popular theology—besides editing a quarterly review of ecclesiastical art and literature. It is said that he has more book titles listed in the literary catalogue of the British Museum than any other writer of his time. Born at Exeter, he lived much of his early life in Germany and France, was educated at Clare College, Cambridge, took Holy Orders, and served various parishes until 1881. Then, exercising his rights as squire of the estate in Lew Trenchard, Devon, inherited from his father, he appointed himself rector and spent the remainder of his life there. He is given recognition by H. C. Coles, editor of Grove's *Dictionary,* for his pioneer work in the collecting of English folk songs. It is said that Baring-Gould influenced Cecil J. Sharp to devote his life to folk-song research. James Moffatt says he was "a man of extraordinary range of interests, and of inexhaustible versatility and industry." He died at the age of ninety at Lew Trenchard, January 2, 1924.

"Merrial" is as well-known and deservedly popular as any tune written by Sir Joseph Barnby. Although a universal favorite for choir use in evening services, it is difficult for congregations to sing well because of its lack of definite melody in any one voice. Barnby did not give it any name in his

*Hymn Tunes,* referring to it as "1st Setting." It was written in 1868. Apparently, it is not a popular setting for this hymn in England, for an examination of twenty English hymnbooks issued in late years disclosed the fact that all use the Baring-Gould tune, "Eudoxia."

**54—The day Thou gavest, Lord, is ended**—John Ellerton (28)

**St. Clement**—Clement Cotterill Scholefield

This was written as an Empire hymn, though meant for use at missionary meetings. Queen Victoria chose it as one of the hymns to be used at her Diamond Jubilee Service held on the same day by thousands of churches throughout the British Empire. Written in 1870, it appeared the next year in *Church Hymns* (S. P. C. K.) in varied form. Two changes in text and the omission of a stanza make this differ slightly from the author's 1871 revision. "Sanctify" was changed to "hallow now" in line four, stanza one; and the last line of the third stanza from,

Nor dies the strain of praise away,

to,

Nor die the strains of praise away.

"St. Clement," the name of this tune, may have been adapted from the first name of Rev. C. C. Scholefield, its composer, or it may have been given in honor of Clement Marot, the sixteenth-century poet. Marot gave us a metrical version of the Ten Commandments which appeared in the French Psalter, 1549, with a musical setting written or adapted by Loys Bourgeois (3), who lived with John Calvin from 1545 to 1557. This tune has come down to us and is in some of the modern hymnals associated with the words of the hymn beginning "The day Thou gavest, Lord, is ended." While "St. Clement" in no way resembles the old tune, the name may have some bearing on this old association of words and music. "St. Clement" was written expressly for these words, and appeared in *Church Hymns with Tunes,* 1874.

Clement Cotterill Scholefield, M.A., born at Edgbaston, England, June 22, 1839, the son of William Scholefield, long a Member of Parliament from Birmingham, was a self-taught musician and writer of hymn tunes. He was a clergyman, graduating from St. John's College, Cambridge, and for a time was chaplain of Eton College, Windsor. While he had no formal musical training, he excelled as a pianist. He died at London, September 10, 1904.

**55—I love to steal awhile away**—Phoebe Hinsdale Brown

**Woodstock**—Deodatus Dutton, Jr.

Writing in the late 1880's, the Rev. F. M. Bird, sometime Professor of Rhetoric and Christian Evidences, Lehigh University, has said that the talents and work of Mrs. Brown, the writer of this hymn, "are superior to those of any other female hymnist of America." Yet this is her only hymn to be found in collections now in use, and a somewhat extended search has failed to find it in any other book than *The Methodist Hymnal.* Perhaps its infrequence is due to the fact that it is too personal for general congregational use. One who loves to "steal awhile away" does not care to sing about it with others. Without any intention of writing a hymn, Mrs. Brown wrote this poem to relieve an overflowing heart. The author, greatly burdened by domestic cares, used to walk in the late evenings along a lane and through a neighbor's garden so that she might escape "from little ones and care, and spend the hours of closing day" in prayer. The neighbor, in whose garden she walked, rebuked her, and these verses, headed,

My Apology for My Twilight Rambles
Addressed to a Lady

were written under the sting of the rebuke. She wrote "from little ones and care" for, she has written:

> I had four little children, a small, unfinished house, a sick sister in the only finished room, and there was not a place, above or below, where I could retire for devotion without a liability to be interrupted.

The poem consisted of nine stanzas, from which five were selected by Dr. Asahel Nettleton (23) for inclusion in *Village Hymns,* 1824, together with three other hymns by the same writer. Four of the stanzas have been included here, and while some slight changes have been made they stand practically as orginally written. A full and interesting account of the poem and its writing is given by Dean Tillett (117) in *Hymns and Hymn Writers of the Church.*

Phoebe Hinsdale Brown, born at Canaan, New York, May 1, 1783, was left an orphan before her second birthday and lived with her grandparents until nine, when she was sent to live with a sister. This sister's husband was a rough fellow, keeper of the county jail, and her life until she was eighteen was one of "privation, cruel treatment, and toil." She did not learn to write until after she was eighteen years of age, when some interested friends made it possible for her to have three months' schooling—all she ever received. After her marriage to a house painter, a poor but worthy man, she lived successively at East Windsor and Ellington, Connecticut; Monson, Massachusetts; and at Marshall, Illinois, where she died, October 10, 1861. She was buried at Monson. Most of her writing was done while she lived at Ellington, Connecticut. Her son, Dr. S. R. Brown, first American missionary to Japan, said she was a "most devoted mother, wife, and Christian; . . . the tale of her early life . . . is a narrative of such privations, cruel treatment and toil, as it breaks my heart to read." While modern congregations probably would show little interest in most of Mrs. Brown's hymns, there is one, a part of which, at least, might well be included in modern books. It begins,

> O Lord, Thy work revive,
> In Zion's gloomy hour,
> And make her dying graces live
> By Thy restoring power.

N. D. Gould in his *History of Church Music in America,* 1853, says of Deodatus Dutton, Jr., born at Monson, Massachusetts, December 22, 1808, and of this tune "Woodstock":

> His skill and taste were of the most promising order, and the tune of "Wood-

stock," with the words, "I love to steal awhile away," will be associated with his name, and handed down to future ages, and be sung by many on earth, while he is singing the song of Moses and the Lamb in heaven.

It is interesting to note that the composer of this tune was born in Monson, Massachusetts, where Mrs. Brown, the writer of the hymn, lived for a while and lies buried. The composer died at New York City, December 16, 1832, when only twenty-four years of age.

**56—Sun of my soul, Thou Saviour dear—John Keble (35)**

**Hursley—Adapted from Katholisches Gesangbuch**

William Stead, in *Hymns That Have Helped,* gives this eighth place, while it is ninth in the list of hymns of "first rank" in *Anglican Hymnology.* It was first published as No. 2 in Keble's *The Christian Year* (35), headed

EVENING

Abide with us; for it is toward evening, and the day is far spent. St. Luke xxiv: 29.

This cento of six stanzas is from a poem of fourteen, written on November 25, 1820. Doctor Bodine writes:

> John Keble believed in the *Ocean of God's love.* That belief, in a special sense, makes him my brother.
>
> Out upon that ocean you and I are sailing. The winds are rough at times; the waves beat high. But our Father is at the helm, and the port is not far off. There, with Keble and with all of God's saints, may you and I find rest and joy forevermore.

"Hursley," "Pascal," "Paris," "Stillorgan," or "Framingham," evolved from a melody which appeared in the *Katholisches Gesangbuch,* Vienna, n.d., but which is thought to have been 1774. It was with the words of the hymn beginning:

Grosser Gott, wir loben dich

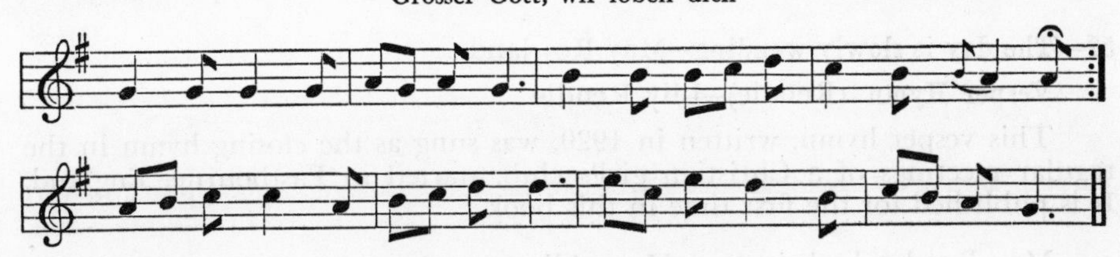

As it became popular, its use was extended to Protestant tune books, in the first of which, Schicht's *Choral-buch* (Leipzig, 1819), it appears, set to the same words:

It appeared in France five years later in *Choix de Cantiques,* then in England in the second volume of *A Sequel to Melodia Sacra,* Dublin, c. 1844, set to "Jesus and shall it ever be," in its present form, with the last line repeated, as was then the custom, thus:

"Hursley," the choice of Doctor Keble and his wife as the most fitting setting for "Sun of my soul," and named from the parish where they lived for so many years, was first associated with this hymn in 1855, when from "MS. music in the possession of Rev. W. J. Irons, D.D." it appeared in the *Metrical Psalter* of Doctor Irons (150) and Henry Lahee (537). The first American appearance was in *The Boston Handel and Haydn Society Collection of Church Music,* c. 1830, but the melody had been changed somewhat. It was there called "Framingham" and the hymn began,

Come hither, all ye weary souls.

The last edition of *The Methodist Hymnal* and other books have given Peter Ritter, 1760-1846, credit for having composed the tune, or for having adapted it from a melody by Mozart. But this is not at all probable, for Ritter was still only in his teens when it appeared in its first form. Sir Herbert S. Oakeley (42) was of this opinion and gave it as his reason for writing "Abends," the alternative tune suggested. He was mistaken, for Mozart produced *Le Nozze di Figaro* in 1786. Sir Herbert said "to hear 'Sun of my soul, Thou Saviour dear,' sung to a lively tune unsuited to sacred words often had the effect of driving me out of the church." Lightwood (453) suggests that "Hursley" certainly has not lived up to Oakeley's characterization, "a lively tune." It is one of the best-known and sincerely loved of all hymn tunes.

**57—The day is slowly wending**—May Rowland

**Vesper Hymn** (Rendle)—Lily Rendle

This vesper hymn, written in 1920, was sung as the closing hymn in the regular meetings of a Christian girl's club, started in Eastbourne, England. It is published for the first time in this book.

May Rowland, christened Mary Alice, was born September 21, 1870, in Oxfordshire, England. Her upbringing amid country scenes, far away from towns, and the beauties of nature helped to foster a poetic tendency. She was educated in Somerset, beside the Severn Sea, and brought up a member of the Church of England, being confirmed by the Bishop of Bath and Wells (then Lord Arthur Hervey) in Wells Cathedral. Having written many poems chiefly of historic or patriotic interest, some of which were published in magazines or newspapers, she left Oxfordshire and went to Eastbourne in 1902. As a helper in church work her chief pleasure was to teach boys, and for some years she was a leader of a Bible class both in Oxfordshire and in the parish of All Souls', Eastbourne. The vicar of the latter parish, the Rev. Evan J. Hopkins (son of the celebrated Keswick preacher), asked Miss Rowland to write a hymn suitable for the open-air services that he held in the streets of the parish during the World War. Accordingly, she wrote a "Hymn for a Night Procession," the success of which encouraged her to write sacred verse. When the Hymn Society of New York issued their appeal for a "Hymn for Airmen," Miss Rowland succeeded in winning the contest, in which there were twelve hundred and seventy-six competitors from all parts of the world. Since then, she has written several other hymns and also a poem "To the Girls of England," dedicated by permission to the Prime Minister (then the Rt. Hon. Stanley Baldwin) in view of the greater political responsibilities resting on the younger generation.

"Vesper Hymn" was written in 1930 by Miss Rendle for this hymn.

Lily Rendle was born at London, May 14, 1875, and received her education there and in Paris. By hard work, unassisted by others, she won a gold medal with an associateship in the Guildhall School of Music. She did much studying of piano playing and singing and developed into a concert artist and composer, receiving favorable recognition for her work. For some years she has lived in Eastbourne so that she might more adequately care for her parents. Miss Rendle and Miss Rowland have done much work together. When Miss Rowland won the prize offered by the Hymn Society of New York for a hymn for airmen in 1928, the text was submitted to composers in competition for musical setting. Miss Rendle was successful in this contest, which was open to composers from any part of the world, and both women were greatly surprised to learn that they had lived within a mile of each other for some time, yet had never met. Since that time their artistic association has been close. Miss Rendle also has a gift for versification. At her last concert in London the program contained eighteen of her songs, for several of which she had written both words and music.

**58—Now cheer our hearts this eventide—From *The Yattendon Hymnal***

**Jam Lucis—Plainsong melody**

The Rev. James Mearns, assistant editor of Julian's *Dictionary of Hymnology,* says this translation of "Ach bleib bei uns" was made to provide a hymn for weekday evenings. This translation by Robert Bridges, late Poet Laureate of England, to go with Bach's setting, was included in his *Yattendon Hymnal,* 1899, a beautifully printed book of one hundred hymns set to "masterpieces" which "are, without question, of an excellence which sets them above either the enhancement of ruin or time." Most of the tunes were from the *Genevan Psalter* (3) and were arranged in four parts for unaccompanied singing. Forty-four of the hymns in this book were translated, adapted, or written by Mr. Bridges with an eye to fitting the tunes, as he explains:

> Where the hymn has to be translated from a foreign language, some reconstruction is generally inevitable, and it can follow no better aim than that of mutual enforcement of words and music. And the words owe a courtesy to the music; for if a balance be struck between the words and music of hymns, it will be found to be heavily in favor of the musicians, whose fine work has been unscrupulously altered and reduced to dullness by English compilers, with the object of conforming it in rhythm to words that are unworthy of any music whatever.

After Doctor Bridges, a physician and highly cultivated musician, as well as poet, settled in Yattendon to devote himself to literary work, he took charge of the congregational singing in the local parish church. The result of that interest was *The Yattendon Hymnal,* which Doctor Dearmer (79) says is "easily the most distinguished of individual pioneer contributions to modern hymnody."

Nicolaus Selnecker (Selneccer or Seleneccer), born at Hersbruck near Nürnberg, December 5, 1532, was a church organist at the age of twelve. An eminent theologian, preacher and musician, he wrote the music for many of his hymns. Because of the many theological controversies in which he engaged he moved frequently from place to place. He wrote some one hundred and seventy-five controversial and theological works as well as one hundred and thirty hymns. He was one of those who developed the Motett Choir of St. Thomas's Church, Leipzig, later made famous by J. S. Bach (52). He died, May 24, 1592, at Leipzig. "Ach bleib bei uns" has been the inspiration for many of the "Abide with us" hymns.

"Jam Lucis," a fine example of plainsong melody, was sung to the hymn "Jam lucis orto sidere" thus:

The present form is taken from Giovanni Guidetti's *Directorium Chori,* 1582, a work in which he was joined by Palestrina (156). It seems to have been adapted from the older melody. In the Preface to the *Directorium,* the result of a commission given to Palestrina by Gregory XIII to revise the services of the Roman Church, Guidetti, Palestrina's pupil, makes it clear that the pupil had all of the drudgery of the work, while the master did the final revising.

# GOD

## Majesty and Power

**59—Ancient of Days, who sittest throned in glory**—William Croswell Doane

**Ancient of Days**—John Albert Jeffery

This fine hymn of praise and prayer was written in 1886 for the bicentenary celebration of the charter which made Albany, New York, the first chartered city in America. It was revised somewhat by its author for inclusion in *The Hymnal* of the Protestant Episcopal Church, 1892. A hymn to the Trinity, or for occasions of national thanksgiving, it may also be used as a processional, especially for the larger and more formal festivals.

William Croswell Doane, first Bishop of the Diocese of Albany, Protestant Episcopal Church, was born at Boston, March 2, 1832, and died at Albany, May 17, 1913. He received his college education at Burlington College, New Jersey, founded by his father, Bishop George W. Doane (47), who later ordained him. After serving churches in Burlington, New Jersey; Hartford, Connecticut, and Albany, New York, he was consecrated Bishop. Bishop Doane was long an honored figure in American life. Fearless in expressing his opinion on public questions, he was actively interested in the bettering of social and moral conditions. He held honorary degrees from Trinity, Columbia, Hobart, and Union Colleges, and from Oxford, Cambridge, and Dublin Universities. His principal literary work was a biography of his father in four volumes, including a memoir. He also published several books on religious subjects and a book of verse entitled *Rhymes from Time to Time.* From 1902 he was Chancellor of the Regents of the University of the State of New York.

"Ancient of Days" was written by Dr. J. Albert Jeffery for this tune at the time he was organist at All Saints' Cathedral, Albany, New York, under Bishop William C. Doane. It was written for four voices with an organ accompaniment which has been omitted from this hymnal.

John Albert Jeffery, Mus. Doc., an Englishman, born at Plymouth, October 26, 1854, succeeded his father as organist at St. Andrew's Cathedral in his birthplace, when he was fourteen years of age. The honorary degree of Doctor of Music was conferred upon him after his graduation from Leipzig Conservatory of Music, where he had been a pupil of the great organist, Reineke. He also studied with Liszt at Weimar. Doctor Jeffery came to America in 1876 to have charge of the department of music of St. Agnes School in Albany, founded by Bishop Doane, and to act as organist and choirmaster at All Saints'

Cathedral. Later he went to Boston, where he became a well-known teacher at the New England Conservatory of Music. Doctor Jeffery died June 14, 1929, at Brookline, Massachusetts.

**60—Praise to the Lord**—Joachim Neander
Translated by Catherine Winkworth (7)

**Lobe den Herren**—From Praxis Pietatis Melica, 1668

Canon Percy Dearmer says this magnificent song of praise is perhaps the finest there is, considering the tune to which it is sung. Founded on Psalm 103. 1-6, and Psalm 101, the translation is by Catherine Winkworth. It is undoubtedly the noblest contribution of Neander.

Joachim Neander, whose real name was Neumann (Newman), was born in 1650, educated and died, May 31, 1680, at Bremen, Germany. The grandfather of the poet (another Joachim, d. 1651), assumed the Greek form—Neander. He is known as "the first poet of the Reformed Church in Germany." Neander was a careless youth, but was converted at a service at St. Martin's Church, Bremen, where he had gone to criticize and make mischief. He became the tutor of five young men from well-to-do families in Franfurt-am-Main, and together with them spent some time at Heidelberg. He seems to have been deeply affected by the beautiful scenery. Receiving an appointment in a school at Düsseldorf, he had many unpleasant experiences, owing mainly to his unwillingness to comply with regulations of the school. He was suspended from his duties for a period of two weeks, but upon signing a declaration, "without mental reservations," that he would cause no further trouble, was reinstated, though in a somewhat minor capacity. Deeply humiliated by his disciplining, he went into a decline, dying of consumption some three years later, at the age of thirty. The legend that he lived in a cave for some months during his "banishment" is probably without basis of fact. Neander wrote sixty hymns and set them to music, publishing them under the curious title *A und Ω, Joachim Neander Glaub- und Liebesübung.*

"Lobe den Herren" first appeared in *Ander Theil des Erneuerten Gesangbuch,* second edition, 1665, Stralsund, set to the hymn *"Hast du denn, Liebster."* In 1680 it was transferred to this hymn of Neander's and has been so associated ever since. In the present form it comes from Crüger's *Praxis Pietatis Melica,* 1668. The melody greatly loved by the Germans was sung to this hymn on the occasion of their great Thanksgiving celebration on January 9, 1871, in celebration of their victory over France. In its original form it was:

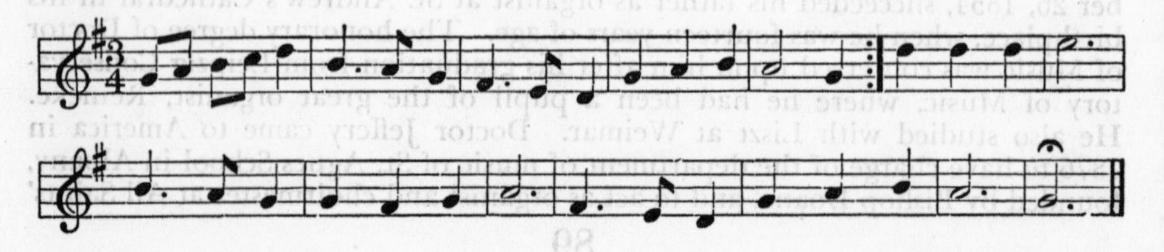

**61—The Lord our God is clothed with might—Henry Kirke White**

**Tappan—George Kingsley**

One of ten hymns ascribed to H. Kirke White, this one, entitled "The Eternal Monarch," was first published in *Hymns Partly Collected and Partly Original,* 1812, compiled by Dr. William B. Collyer (195). This hymn on the Divine Sovereignty is said by Dr. C. S. Robinson to have a poetic fervor and loftiness of imagination unusual in religious lyrics.

Henry Kirke White, born March 21, 1785, son of a butcher of Nottingham, England, showed unusual precocity at an early age. His eldest sister has told how their mother was "obliged to change the tone of her voice" in order to get the boy to stop reading and "come to dinner." His father wanted Henry to follow him and be a butcher, but was prevailed upon, first to permit him to work in the local hosiery mill, and, later, through the efforts of the boy's mother, to take a clerkship in the offices of a firm of attorneys in order that he might study law. He became skilled in drawing, and learned to play the piano quite well "by ear." He also had some mechanical skill, for he made with his own hands, all the fittings for the little room which had been placed at his disposal and which he called his study. When only fifteen years of age he was not only doing the work of a law clerk and reading the subject, but was also busily engaged in studying Greek, Latin, Italian, Spanish, and Portuguese. He found time also to gain a "very respectable knowledge of chemistry" and to be interested in astronomy and electricity. Although a skeptic in his boyhood, he became converted. To satisfy his deep love of learning and to prepare himself for a career in the church, he spared no efforts to secure a college education. Although he realized little or nothing in financial gain, from the publication of a small volume of verse he thus attracted the attention of interested friends who made possible his entrance at St. John's College, Cambridge. Two years to the month from the time he left the law office to prepare for college entrance, October 19, 1806, he was dead. Henry Kirke White had literally worked himself to death. The English poet, Southey, published his *Remains* with an excellent short biography; Lord Byron composed some beautiful lines addressed to him, and in his honor a Boston admirer erected in All Saints' Church, Cambridge, a monumental tablet. Dean Tillett's (117) eulogy is worthy of quotation:

> His rare poetic genius, his victory over skepticism and subsequent faith and piety, his hard struggle with poverty, and early death invest the story of his life with more than ordinary pathos.

"Tappan" was written for a five-line hymn, "There is an hour of peaceful rest," by William B. Tappan (133), and appeared first in *The Sacred Choir,* 1839, edited by George Kingsley, its composer.

George Kingsley was born in 1811 and died March 13, 1884, at Northampton, Massachusetts. A self-taught musician, he became sufficiently proficient to hold the position of organist at Old South and Hollis Street Churches, Boston; to be a teacher of music at Girard College, Philadelphia; to be supervisor of music in the Philadelphia public schools, and to become prominent in musical affairs in New York, where he moved from Philadelphia. He wrote many hymn tunes, furnishing more than forty for Charles Everest's *The Sabbath,* 1873. During his last years he lived in his old home at Northampton. All of the music furnished at his funeral service had been written by him.

**62—Lord of all being, throned afar**—Oliver Wendell Holmes

**Keble**—John Bacchus Dykes (1)

One critic has stated that, outside the Bible, this hymn is probably the finest statement of God's omnipresence in the English language. Although written in 1848, it was not published before its appearance at the end of the closing chapter of *The Professor at the Breakfast Table,* in the *Atlantic Monthly,* in 1859. The author's title for it, "A Sun-Day Hymn," had this introduction:

> Peace to all such as may have been vexed in spirit by any utterance these pages may have repeated! They will doubtless forget for the moment the difference in the hues of truth we look at through our human prisms, and join in singing (inwardly) this hymn to the source of the light we all need to lead us, and the warmth which alone can make us all brothers.

Oliver Wendell Holmes, born August 29, 1809, son of a Congregational minister of Cambridge, Massachusetts, became one of the most distinguished graduates of Harvard University. So sympathetic was he that he gave up his Boston practice to become Professor of Anatomy and Physiology at the Medical School of his Alma Mater. Although teaching was his major occupation, he gained fame as a man of letters, being one of the famous group of New-England literati to which Longfellow, Bryant, Lowell, and Whittier belonged. He was chiefly instrumental in the founding of the *Atlantic Monthly,* was a charming speaker, wit, novelist, poet, and humanist. He was a freethinker, yet "believed more than some and less than others," and liked "those who believed more better than those who believed less." He attended church regularly because "there is a little plant called 'reverence' in the corner of my soul's garden, which I love to have watered once a week." The honorary degree of Doctor of Laws was conferred on him by Harvard and Edinburgh Universities; Cambridge made him Doctor of Letters; and Oxford, Doctor of Civil Law. He died in Boston, October 7, 1894, and was buried in Mount Auburn Cemetery.

"Keble," one of Doctor Dykes's strongest tunes, was written for the hymn beginning "Sun of my soul" (56), by John Keble, and first appeared in the Revised Edition of *Hymns Ancient and Modern,* 1875.

**63—The Lord Jehovah reigns**—Isaac Watts (3)

**Millennium**—Composer unknown. Early American (?)

This is from Doctor Watts's *Hymns and Spiritual Songs,* Book II, 1709. Owing to its appearance in Wesley's *Psalms and Hymns,* 1738, it has long been associated with Methodism. It was the last stanza of this hymn that Martha Thompson, a servant girl in London, sang so continuously, after hearing it at a John Wesley meeting, that her employers had her judged insane and confined in an asylum. John Wesley, being informed of her plight, secured her release and helped her on her way to Preston, where she engaged in the dressmaking and millinery business. At the time of her death she gathered her children and grandchildren about her bed and begged them to sing,

And will this Sovereign King
Of glory condescend,
And will He write His name,
My Father and my Friend?
I love His name,
I love His word:
Join all my powers
And praise the Lord.

The source or origin of "Millennium" is not known. Some books indicate it is English; certainly it seems to have come into this country by way of the South, although its progress has not been traced. Its case may be similar to that of the tune "Saltash" or "Pleading Saviour," brought to this country by the ancestors of the east Kentucky and Tennessee mountaineers. Long popular as a camp-meeting tune, this was used by Henry Ward Beecher in his *Plymouth Collection,* 1855. Now it is found in *The Methodist Hymn Book* (British), 1933, credited to *"Plymouth Collection* (U. S. A.), 1855."

**64—Immortal, invisible, God only wise—Walter Chalmers Smith**

**Joanna—Welsh melody—Arranged by Van Denman Thompson (153)**

This brilliant hymn of praise to "God only wise" was first printed in Dr. W. Chalmers Smith's *Hymns of Christ and Christian Life,* 1867. W. Garrett Horder introduced it into English hymnody in his *Congregational Hymns,* 1884, and after its inclusion in *The English Hymnal,* 1906, its use became widespread. It was based on 1 Timothy 1. 17: "Now unto the King eternal, immortal, invisible, the only wise God, be honour and glory for ever and ever. Amen."

Walter Chalmers Smith was born at Aberdeen, Scotland, December 5, 1824, and educated at its Grammar School and University and at New College, Edinburgh. Ordained a minister of the Scottish Church, he afterward became identified with the Free Church of Scotland, held various pastorates, and served as its moderator in 1893, the Jubilee Year. His death occurred September 20, 1908. The hymns of this author of merit have a richness of thought and a vigor of expression that should bring more of them to the attention of hymnologists.

"Joanna," a fine Welsh melody, known in England as "St. Denis," is probably from a ballad of about 1810, "Can Mlynedd i 'Nawr" ("A hundred years from now"), although the *Journal* of the Welsh Folk Music Society (Vol. I) suggests other possible sources. It first appeared as a hymn tune in John Roberts' *Caniadan y Cyssegr* (*Sacred Songs*), 1839, called "Palestrina." This arrangement was made for this book by Dr. Van Denman Thompson in 1933.

**65—All creatures of our God and King**—Francis of Assisi
Translated by William Henry Draper

**Lasst uns Erfreuen** (6)—Geistliche Kirkengesäng, Cologne, 1623 (6)

This is a paraphrase of the famous *Sun Song,* or *Song About Creatures,* which St. Francis of Assisi wrote in Italian. It was made by the Rev. William H. Draper, who translated other fine hymns from the Latin as well as from the Greek. It first appeared in a small collection of the translator's own hymns in 1926, then was included in *School Worship.* Under great difficulties St. Francis wrote this remarkable *Song About Creatures,* in the unusually hot summer of 1225, when he was ill and so suffering from loss of sight, that he was unable to have his eyes exposed to any light. During this illness the good man lay helpless and, according to J. Jörgensen, in his *San Francesco de Asis,* he was

> plagued by a swarm of field-mice who probably had their home in the straw walls of the hut, and who eventually ran over his face so that he had no peace day or night. And yet it was precisely in this wretched sickness that he composed his wonderful masterpiece.

There is much dispute as to the real authorship of many of the hymns that are usually ascribed to St. Francis, but none concerning this *Song of the Sun.* "Matthew Arnold has singled it out as the utterance of what is most exquisite in the spirit of his century." It is a charming expression of St. Francis' childlike delight in God's good works.

St. Francis of Assisi was one of the most beautiful, as well as one of the strangest personalities among the early Italian Christian leaders. He it was who took poverty as his bride and tried literally to go forth and preach repentance and forgiveness of sins with no thought of reward. He gave up all his earthly possessions when a young man, and thereafter until his death suffered the severest poverty. He was particularly interested in preaching to the poor and forsaken, treating with especial tenderness lepers and other outcasts. These expressed their great joy by saying, "He hears those whom even God will not hear." His great humility and lovableness drew many followers to him. To these he said:

> Fear not, in that ye seem few and simple-minded. Preach repentance to the world, trusting in Him, who hath overcome the world that His spirit speaks through you. You will find some to receive you and your word with joy, if still more to resist you and mock you. Bear all that with patience and meekness. Take no heed of your simplicity or mine. In a short time the wise and noble will come to preach with you before princes and people, and many will be turned to the Lord. He has shown it to me, and in mine ears there is a sound of the multitude of disciples who are to come to us out of every people.

He founded the famous Order of Franciscans. Though he started out with no thought of founding any order, yet by so doing he loosed forces that resulted in one of the greatest revivals of religion the world has ever seen. Francis was born in 1182 and died October 4, 1226, at Assisi in Italy, the son of Pietro Bernardone, one of the substantial merchants of the place. Probably none other has so seriously attempted to imitate Christ's own way of living.

William Henry Draper, D.D., born at Kenilworth, England, December 19,

1855, was educated at Keble College, Oxford, ordained in 1880, held various appointments as curate, vicar, and rector until 1919, when he became Master of the Temple, London. He translated hymns from the Greek, published two hymnals, and edited others. His death occurred August 9, 1933, at Clifton, Bristol.

**66—The spacious firmament on high—Joseph Addison**
**Creation—Francis Joseph Haydn (30)**

Addison's hymn, based on Psalm 19. 1-6, appeared in *The Spectator,* London, in its issue of Saturday, August 23, 1712, at the close of an article on "Faith and Devotion," which discussed the best means of "strengthening and confirming faith in the mind of man." He said:

> Faith and devotion naturally grow in the mind of every reasonable man, who sees the impressions of divine power and wisdom in every object on which he casts his eye. The Supreme Being has made the best arguments for His own existence, in the formation of the heavens and the earth, and these are the arguments which a man of sense cannot forbear attending to, who is out of the noise and hurry of human affairs. . . . The Psalmist has very beautiful strokes of poetry to this purpose in that exalted strain (Psalm xix). As such a bold and sublime manner of thinking furnishes very noble matter for an ode, the reader may see it wrought into the following one.

Lord Selbourne says it is "a very perfect and finished composition, taking rank among the best hymns in the English language."

Joseph Addison, son of the Rev. Lancelot Addison, the author of *Devotional Poems,* 1699, and one time Dean of Lichfield, born May 1, 1672, at Milston, Wiltshire, England, was the greatest English writer of his time and one of the greatest of all time. Originally intended for the Church, he was educated at the Charterhouse and at Magdalen College, Oxford. His study of law and politics, however, fitted him for various important secular posts, one of which was that of chief secretary for Ireland. In 1699 some political friends secured for him a pension permitting extensive travel on the Continent. He happened to be in Dublin in 1703 when his Charterhouse school friend, Richard Steele, published the first number of the *Tatler,* Addison's contributions to which demonstrated his ability as an essayist. After the passing of the *Tatler* in 1711, Addison played the leading part in establishing the famous *Spectator,* a nonpolitical paper, issued daily from March 1, 1711, to December 6, 1712, whose purpose it was to "bring philosophy out of the closets and libraries, schools and colleges, to dwell in the clubs and assemblies; at tea tables, and in coffee houses." How well it succeeded is attested by John Wesley, who, a short time before his death, in talking with Adam Clarke about the beginnings of Methodism, told how

> God raised up Mr. Addison and his associates to lash the prevailing vices and ridiculous and profane customs of the country, and to show the excellence of Christianity and Christian institutions. The *Spectators,* written with all the simplicity, elegance, and force of the English language, were everywhere read, and were the first instrument in the hands of God to check the mighty and growing profanity, and call men back to religion and decency and common sense. Methodism, in the order of God, succeeded, and revived and spread scriptural and experimental Christianity over the nation. And now what hath God wrought!

Dr. Samuel Johnson, who differed politically with Addison, paid him this tribute:

> Whoever wishes to attain an English style, familiar, but not coarse, and elegant but not ostentatious, must give his days and nights to the volumes of Addison.

Lord Macaulay said of Addison:

> [he was] the unsullied statesman, the accomplished scholar, the consummate painter of life and manners, the great satirist, who alone knew how to use ridicule without abusing it; who, without inflicting a wound, effected a great social reform; and who reconciled wit and virtue after a long and painful separation, during which wit had been led astray by profligacy and virtue by fanaticism.

He died at Holland House, Kensington, June 17, 1719, and his body lay in state in the Jerusalem Chamber of Westminster Abbey.

"Creation" is an adaptation of a part of the magnificent chorus, "The heavens are telling," from Haydn's oratorio, *The Creation.* This chorus is considered a model of writing for four voices and as such has not been excelled by any other composer. Haydn said: "Never was I so pious as when composing *The Creation.* I knelt down every day and prayed God to strengthen me for my work."

The setting of this tune to this hymn appears to be confined to American compilers of hymnals, and only of comparative recency. Another shorter adaptation from the same chorus, called by the same name, or "Haydn," was in use with another hymn as early as 1837 (*Songs of Zion,* Thomas Whittemore), but the use of the present form, by Methodists at least, began with the *Hymnal of the Methodist Episcopal Church,* 1878. I. B. Woodbury (137) used it with this hymn in *The Dulcimer,* 1850.

**67—A mighty fortress is our God**—Martin Luther
Translated by Frederick Henry Hedge (139)

**Ein' Feste Burg**—Martin Luther

Luther wrote both words and music of this famous hymn, thus described by the German poet, Heinrich Heine:

> A battle hymn was this defiant song, with which he and his comrades entered Worms (April 16, 1521). The old cathedral trembled at these new notes, and the ravens were startled in their hidden nests in the towers. This hymn, the Marseillaise Hymn of the Reformation, has preserved its potent spell even to our own days, and we may yet soon use again in similar conflicts the old mailed words.

In assigning the date 1529 to the first singing of the hymn, Julian offers no explanation for Heine's apparent error in the date, 1521. Certainly, it was not only Luther's greatest contribution to hymnody but the greatest hymn of the Reformation. There have been sixty-three translations into English worthy of notice by Julian, the most forceful being that of Thomas Carlyle beginning

> A safe stronghold our God is still.

This is the rendering used by the British Methodists.

The German princes gained the name "Protestant" at the Diet at Speyer because of their protest against the revocation of their liberties and it was probably for this occasion that the hymn was written. There it was that "Luther, with his hymns, entered a protest before all the German people against endeavoring to obstruct the gospel" (Lauxman).

Founded upon Psalm 46, it has been the inspiration of great gatherings of people, being sung at countless celebrations in Germany, England, and America, and once by the whole army of Gustavus Adolphus before the battle of Leipzig, September 17, 1631. James Moffatt says it is "the greatest hymn of the greatest man in the greatest period of German history."

"Ein' Feste Burg," the tune, is excellent from every standpoint. It is thrilling, and has a dignity, a solidarity, and an authority seldom equaled. It has held a powerful attraction for composers of ability, great and small, Bach using it in a cantata by the same name. Dudley Buck, an American composer, made it the climax of a male quartet. The most conspicuous example of its use is that of Meyerbeer in his historical opera, *Les Huguenots,* 1836. Mendelssohn (33) takes it as the theme for a movement in his *Reformation Symphony.* Wagner makes effective use of it in his *Kaisermarsch,* written to celebrate the triumphant return of Emperor William in 1871 at the close of the Franco-Prussian war. O. Nicolai employed it in his *Fest-Ouvertüre.*

Martin Luther was born at Eisleben, November 10, 1483, and was educated at Magdeburg, Eisenach, and Erfurt. A highly educated Augustinian monk, he became a priest, and in 1508 was made professor of theology, at Wittenberg, where, nine years later, his famed ninety-five theses protesting against indulgences were presented. His views, which were placed before the Diet at Worms, were rejected. By holding him prisoner at the Wartburg for a year, the friendly Elector of Saxony saved his life. While in this confinement, he completed the first part of his translation of the Bible. Two years after his release he issued his first book of hymns, four of which were written by him. Twenty-one years later, 1545, he had increased the number of his own hymns to thirty-five, for some of which he is credited with having written tunes. Though playing well on the flute and lute, and having a good knowledge of polyphony, he was not a composer. In his writings he made frequent discriminating references to music:

> I am not of the opinion that through the gospel, all arts should be banished and driven away, as some zealots want us to believe; but I wish to see all arts, principally music, in the service of Him who gave and created them. Music is a fair and glorious gift of God. I would not for the world forego my humble share of music. Singers are never sorrowful, but are merry, and smile through their troubles in song. Music makes people kinder, gentler, more staid and reasonable.

Luther's doctrines of the right of private judgment, salvation by faith, and the universal priesthood of believers called for radical changes in the established forms of worship. With the aid of Johann Walther, his chief musical adviser and editor of his hymnals from 1524 to 1551, he emphasized congregational singing with such orders as he considered essential to the success of the Reformation. His further insistance that all participation by the people be in the vernacular instead of Latin did much to strengthen the movement. He said, "It is my intention to make German Psalms for the people—spiritual songs, that is, whereby the word of God may be kept alive in them by singing."

He provided hymns in metrical form and supplied melodies which were adapted or borrowed from folk or part songs, or were especially written for them. Known as "Chorales" these melodies were important in fostering a new style in church music by combining it with one already popular. The development of the chorale had a tremendous effect on the trend of music and hymn writing which followed the Reformation. Luther's leadership for this movement so long in need of organization emphasized the right of the people to write their own hymns and sing them in their own language. Doctor Nutter says that modern hymnody dates from the Reformation and that we owe our hymnbook "to the same grand man who gave us the Bible." Martin Luther died at Eisleben, February 18, 1546.

## Providence

**68—God moves in a mysterious way**—William Cowper (24)

**Dundee (French)**—From the Scottish Psalter, 1615

That William Cowper had many personal experiences of "perplexities and sorrows" there can be no doubt, but there is doubt as to the authenticity of the stories so frequently told in connection with this hymn. One is to the effect that, during one of his fits of despondency, he drove to the Thames intent upon suicide, one of his obsessions being that God had decreed he take his own life. His disordered mind interpreted as providential obstacles the presence of a porter and the low level of the water in the river. This so impressed him that he immediately wrote this hymn. Another version is that Cowper thought it the Divine Will that he go to a certain point on the river Ouse and drown himself, but the driver of the carriage lost his way and had to return to the poet's home. Still another tells of his having a premonition of the loss of his reason, and while walking alone in the fields he composed these lines. It is difficult to verify such stories; James Moffatt thinks there is no basis for them. Certainly, the hymn was written at a time when Cowper's mind was clear. The "joyous note of Christian confidence" does not suggest the workings of a mind in disorder, although "it was drawn from Cowper by much sorrow."

This was his last contribution to *Olney Hymns* (27), and James Montgomery (39) tells us it was written "in the twilight of departing reason." It has been referred to as the most powerful hymn ever written on the subject of Divine Providence. First appearing anonymously in John Newton's (27) *Twenty-six Letters on Religious Subjects, to which are added Hymns* (1774), it was then included in the *Olney Hymns.* Its original title was "Light shining out of darkness."

In a letter from Dr. Archibald Alexander, written to comfort Dr. Nicholas Murray at the time of the death of his only son, from scarlet fever, there is this paragraph:

> Read Cowper's hymn, "God moves in a mysterious way." Christ seems to say, "What I do you know not now, but you shall know hereafter. All things work together for good to them that love God."

There is some confusion concerning the two tunes commonly known as "Dundee." The tune here used first appeared as one of the twelve "common" tunes (to distinguish them from "proper" tunes which were attached to particular hymns) appearing in 1615 in a book called *Psalms of David,* A. Hart, Edinburgh, where it was called "French Tune." It came to England in 1621 in Ravenscroft's *Whole Booke of Psalms,* being indexed among the "Scottish Tunes" and called "Dundy." The melody was in the tenor part. It has been frequently credited to Christopher Tye, 1553, but the one supposed to have been taken from Tye is in minor and is known as "Windsor" and "Eaton," as well as "Dundee." In *The Methodist Hymnal* these tunes are listed as "Dundee" (French) and "Dundee" (Windsor), respectively.[1]

It is probable that "Windsor" is the tune referred to by Robert Burns in his "Cotter's Saturday Night" (136).

Of the 1615 edition of the *Scottish Psalter,* James Love says it is "one of the most handsome, and, in regard to the musical department, one of the most correctly printed of all editions up to this date."

**69—How gentle God's commands**—Philip Doddridge

**Dennis**—Arranged from Hans Georg Nägeli, by Lowell Mason (19)

This hymn first appeared in the author's posthumously published *Hymns Founded on Various Texts in the Holy Scriptures,* London, 1755, under the heading "God's care a remedy for ours." It was based on 1 Peter 5. 7: "Casting all your care upon Him; for He careth for you." In the original the first two lines of the second stanza were,

While Providence supports
Let saints securely dwell,

and the second line of the fourth stanza,

Down to the present day.

Not even John Wesley could have found fault with the "hymn tinkerers" (338) who improved these lines. In this form it has been called "an artistic expression of true religion." The climax of the last stanza—the exchanging of a burden for a song—is beautiful poetic imagery.

Philip Doddridge, D.D., a friend and contemporary of Isaac Watts (3), said his was one of several lamps "kindled at Watts's torch." Born in London, June 26, 1702, the son of an oil merchant, he received his early religious training from his mother, who taught him Bible stories from some Dutch tiles which covered a portion of the walls of the family living room. Left an orphan when quite young, he declined an offer from the Duchess of Bedford, to educate him for the ministry of the Established Church, choosing to enter a Non-conformist school at Kibworth instead, becoming pastor there when only twenty-one. Eight years later, in 1729, he began his work as precentor and divine at the seminary which he was called to establish at Northampton. There he remained for the rest of his active life. During the twenty-two years

[1] For a full discussion of these two tunes the reader is referred to *The Music of the Church Hymnary,* Cowan and Love: Henry Frowde, Edinburgh, 1901.

of his stay at Northampton two hundred young men from England, Scotland, and Holland prepared for their life's work under his tutelage, most of them entering the dissenting ministry. Born with a weak constitution, he easily fell a victim to tuberculosis and was compelled to give up his work in 1750. Friends provided money for him to seek relief in Portugal, but it was too late. He died in Lisbon the next year (October 26) and was buried in the English cemetery there. Aberdeen University conferred on him the degree of Doctor of Divinity.

Like all of the direct followers of Watts, Doddridge's hymns were homiletical, that is, they were written under the emotional stress of composing the sermon which they followed and which they were intended to emphasize. That was the reason his hymns were not published during his lifetime. The one manuscript copy of the author was enough, for the hymn was read ("lined out") by the precentor and sung line by line by the congregation. Doctor Doddridge wrote more than four hundred hymns but only a few of them are in common use today. Where *The Methodist Hymnal* of 1905 contained twenty-three, that of 1935 has but eight.

"Dennis" was arranged for this hymn by Lowell Mason (19) from a melody by Hans G. Nägeli, and first appeared in *The Psaltery,* 1845, edited by Mason and George J. Webb (487). While the tune is often associated with other hymns, if this one is included in a book, "Dennis" is certain to be selected for it.

Hans Georg Nägeli (whose first name was Johann but which is generally used in its abbreviated form) was a noted Swiss composer and publisher of music. The excellence of his printing has received widespread approval, for it was exceedingly well done for his time, and accounts for his acting as publisher for Beethoven, Clementi, Cramer, and other leading composers. He evidently held a high opinion of himself, for he had the effrontery to add four measures (between 27 and 28, first movement) to Beethoven's Sonata Op. 31, No. 1, which he published. This gratuitous contribution, says Sir George Grove, "will prevent Nägeli from being forgotten as long as Beethoven sonatas are being studied." He revived interest in male-chorus singing, wrote music which was popular in churches and schools, and did much to aid teaching music in elementary schools along Pestalozzian lines (19). Lowell Mason thought well of him, for in the Preface to the *Boston Academy's Collection of Church Music,* 1836, he says:

> No man in modern times has done more, perhaps, to promote the cause of music education and church music than H. G. Nägeli, to which great object he has been almost entirely devoted for many years. His psalm and hymn tunes are in a style both simple and novel, easy of performance, and yet often pleasing and effective.

In another book, published in 1839, Mason says (Preface to *The Modern Psalmist*):

> During a recent tour in Europe it was a leading object . . . to obtain materials for a work like this. In the prosecution of this design he (the editor) visited many of the most important cities and obtained from distinguished composers of different nations much manuscript music; and also a great variety of recent musical publications, English, German, and French, which had not before reached this country.

It was from this "manuscript music" and publications that Doctor Mason made so many "arrangements" and "adaptations."

Nägeli was born[1] May 26, 1773, carried on his music publishing business, and died December 26, 1836, in Zürich.

**70—The Lord's my Shepherd, I'll not want**—Scottish Psalter, 1650

**Martyrdom (Avon)**—Hugh Wilson

This is the metrical rendering of the 23rd Psalm as it appeared in the *Scottish Psalter* of 1650. In the development of congregational singing during the Reformation, followers of Luther made serious efforts to introduce a choralelike style into England and Scotland. Choosing, however, to become followers of Calvin, the conservative Scots adopted the former's type of church song, that is, the metrical psalm.

Briefly, the Church of Scotland has had three stages of psalm singing. The first was one of preparation, when the versions known as the *Dundie Psalmes* were in use. The second, which shows the influence of Marot and Beza, as well as that of Sternhold and Hopkins, brought forth the *Psalter*, of 1564-65. This continued to be used, though not without opposition, for nearly a century (1650), when the *Psalter* of that date was issued. Julian says, "It has survived all proposals to modernize it, save in orthography, and remains to this day the only version of the psalms used by Presbyterian Scotland" (74).

"Martyrdom," or "Avon," as it was named in the last edition of *The Methodist Hymnal,* and as it is frequently named in other books, seems to be the only psalm tune by Hugh Wilson which has survived, although he wrote several. It was first printed on slips for use in classes, and was written in common (4/4) time instead of triple (3/4) time, as it has long appeared in church singing books. Said to have been well known twenty-five years before its appearance in any book of psalm or hymn tunes, it was published in *Sacred Music Sung in St. George's Church, Edinburgh,* in 1825. Two years later it again appeared in *The Seraph, a Selection of Psalms and Hymns,* published in Glasgow. In this book a footnote states: "The above tune, 'Fenwick,' or 'Martyrdom,' and by some called 'Drumclog,' was composed by Mr. Hugh Wilson, a native of Fenwick." In the legal controversy over its authorship plenty of evidence was secured to establish Wilson's claim.

Doctor Moffatt calls attention to the fact that a writer many years ago said, "I well remember the day it ['Martyrdom'] was sung in St. George's, Edinburgh, for Doctor Thompson then said to me, 'O man! I could not sing for weeping.'" While it is quite generally known as "Martyrdom," it has suffered much from naming, having been called, at times, "Avon," "Fenwick," "Drumclog," "Inverness," and "All Saints."

Hugh Wilson was born at Fenwick, Ayrshire, Scotland in 1764 (was baptized December 2). He learned the shoemaking trade from his father, John Wilson, and received his education in the village school and by self-

[1] While 1768 is given in *The Methodist Hymnal* (and in all other hymnals the author has examined) as the year of Nägeli's birth, Grove, Baker, Riemann, Pratt, and other reliable historians agree on the date given here.

study. By teaching the villagers some of the ordinary school subjects and music, he was able to add somewhat to his income. To the study of mathematics and kindred subjects he applied himself assiduously. His hobbies seem to have been the making of sundials and the writing of hymn tunes, one of each being in use to this day: the sundial in the town of his birth, Fenwick, and the hymn tune in many, if not all, of the better hymnbooks of the last century. Shortly before 1800 he removed from Fenwick to Pollokshaws, where he became acquainted with William Dunn, a millowner, in whose mills in Duntocher he was later employed in a position of responsibility. Wilson was interested in religious work, having acted as manager of what is now the United Presbyterian church at Duntocher, and was one of the two founders of the first Sunday school there, where he died, August 14, 1824. A plain stone marks his grave in the churchyard of Old Kirkpatrick.

**71—How are Thy servants blest, O Lord**—Joseph Addison (66)

**Praetorius**—Harmoniae Hymnorum Scholae Gorlicensis

This hymn, originally with ten stanzas, was written aboard ship on the Mediterranean during a storm, and printed in *The Spectator* (66) on Saturday, September 20, 1712, with this introduction:

> Great painters do not only give us Landskips of Gardens, Groves, and Meadows but very often employ their Pencils upon Sea-Pieces. I could wish you would follow their example. If this small Sketch may deserve a Place among your Works, I shall accompany it with a Divine Ode, made by a Gentleman upon the conclusion of his Travels.

Of the author's continental travels from 1699 to 1702, we read in Lord Macaulay's essay on Addison in the *Edinburgh Review,* July, 1843:

> In December, 1700, he embarked at Marseilles. As he glided along the Ligurian coast, he was delighted by the sight of myrtles and olive trees, which retained their verdure under the winter solstice. Soon, however, he encountered one of the black storms of the Mediterranean. The captain of the ship gave up all for lost, and confessed himself to a capuchin who happened to be on board. The English heretic, in the meantime, fortified himself against the terrors of death with devotions of a very different kind. How strong an impression this perilous voyage made on him appears from an Ode, "How are Thy servants blest, O Lord!"

It is frequently referred to as the "Traveler's Hymn."

"Praetorius" appeared in *Harmoniae Hymnorum Scholae Gorlicensis,* a book of Latin and German hymns, published at Görlitz in 1599, set to a hymn beginning,

Für dein empfangen Speis und Trank,

in a form so nearly like that in use here as to be worth quoting:

When it appeared ten years later in a book by Michael Praetorius, *Musae Sioniae* (Part VI, 1609), it was given his name because it was thought to be his composition.

Michael Praetorius, 1571-1621, was a voluminous writer on musical subjects (*Musae Sioniae* being a fifteen volume work), a composer of much music for the church, and was organist and Kapellmeister, as well as secretary, to the Duke of Brunswick.

**72—This is my Father's world—Maltbie Davenport Babcock**

**Terra Beata—Franklin Lawrence Sheppard**

The three stanzas comprising this are made up of six four-line ones from a poem of sixteen, published in *Thoughts for Everyday Living*, in 1901, the year of its author's death. It is said that when Doctor Babcock, a great lover of nature, would frequently go in the early morning to the top of a hill north of Lockport, New York, his first pastorate, in order to get the full benefit of the fine view of Lake Ontario and the country lying between, he would say, "I am going out to see my Father's world." George Herbert (8) might have said,

In the rustling grass I hear Him pass,
He speaks to me everywhere.

There can be no doubt that "God is Ruler yet" when He can be seen in "rocks and trees," in "skies and seas," in "the lily white," and in "the morning light."

Maltbie Davenport Babcock came from a family socially prominent in Syracuse, New York, where he was born, August 3, 1858, and where he graduated from the University. After attending Auburn Theological Seminary, he was ordained a minister of the Presbyterian Church and began preaching at Lockport. From there he went to Brown Memorial Presbyterian Church, Baltimore, where he was so popular with the students of Johns Hopkins University that a room was set aside for him in one of the University buildings, where he might hold conferences with them. He was chosen to succeed Dr. Henry van Dyke (12) at the Brick Presbyterian Church, New York City. In his college days he was prominent in athletics and led the college glee club and orchestra. He died in Naples, Italy, May 18, 1901, while on a trip to the Holy Land.

"Terra Beata," happy or blessed earth, was said, by Franklin L. Sheppard, to be an arrangement made in 1915 of an old English melody, but it has also been stated that he was the composer of the tune. He did not wish to claim it, for it seemed to him to be reminiscent of a tune he had learned from his mother as a boy. There is no doubt, however, that it was original with him.

Franklin Lawrence Sheppard was a business man, born in Philadelphia, August 7, 1852, but who carried on his business in Baltimore. Confirmed an Episcopalian, he later united with the Presbyterian Church and was quite active in its councils. Music being his avocation, he played the organ, was the successful director of Sunday-school music, and editor of *Alleluia,* 1915, a Sunday-school songbook, which had a remarkable sale of approximately a half million copies. He died in Germantown, a suburb of Philadelphia, February 15, 1930.

**73—Be still, my soul: the Lord is on thy side**—Katharina von Schlegel
Translated by Jane Laurie Borthwick

**Finlandia**—Jean Sibelius
Arranged for The Hymnal, 1933

The fine hymn on waiting for God is taken from Miss Borthwick's *Hymns from the Land of Luther,* second series, 1855, where it appears as a translation of Fräulein von Schlegel's hymn "Stille, mein Wille, dein Jesus hilft siegen," which appeared in the *Neue Sammlung Geistlicher Lieder,* Wernigerode, 1752. It might well have been founded on portions of Psalm 46. 10-11: "Be still, and know that I am God: The Lord of hosts is with us."

Our only definite knowledge of Katharina von Schlegel is that she was born October 22, 1697, and a lady attached to the small ducal court at Cöthen, Germany. Her name does not appear on the roll of the Protestant nunnery at Cöthen, where it has been stated she lived, nor is there a record of the date or place of her death. Only one of her hymns has passed into English usage.

Jane Laurie Borthwick, born April 9, 1813, was the elder daughter of James Borthwick, manager of the North British Insurance Office, Edinburgh, and sister of Sarah Borthwick Findlater (427). She spent some time in Switzerland, where a friend suggested that she translate some German hymns which interested her, but it was not until her father made a similar suggestion that she joined with her sister in the work of translation entitled *Hymns From the Land of Luther,* in four series, 1854-62. There were one hundred and twenty-two hymns included, sixty-nine of which were by Miss Borthwick. Her signature of her later translations, "H. H. L.", was suggested by the title of the series of books, and she was "sorely vexed" when her identity was betrayed in *Lyra Britannica.* A devout Christian, she was deeply interested in both home and foreign missions. She died at her birthplace, Edinburgh, in 1897.

"Finlandia" is an arrangement of a part of Jean Sibelius' Tone Poem *Finlandia,* made for *The Hymnal* of the Presbyterian Church, 1933.

Jean Sibelius was born at Tavastelius, Finland, December 8, 1865, and was given a classical and legal education at the University of Helsingfors. He gave this up, however, because of a strong musical urge, manifested in his youth, and entered the Helsingfors Conservatory, where he made an impression later as teacher of violin and theory. Never allowing himself to be dominated by any foreign teacher, his definite Finnish personality was so strongly evidenced in his compositions that he was looked upon as the representative national composer of Finland, and was granted a pension which enabled him to retire in 1897. Since that time he has lived quietly, written much, has made occasional visits abroad (to the United States in 1914), and is looked upon as a musical patriot.

**74—The man who once has found abode**—Psalm 91
United Presbyterian Book of Psalms

**Tallis' Canon (Evening Hymn)** (51)—Thomas Tallis (51)

This rendition of Psalm 91 in which God's care of His people is so abundantly proclaimed and to which is presented the thought of One who will keep once we are saved, is the first four of eleven stanzas taken without change from *The Psalter,* "the Scottish version of the Psalms revised, and new versions adopted by the United Presbyterian Church of North America," 1871 (copyright 1872). In *The Psalms in Worship,* a compilation of papers read at two conventions held in 1905 (at Pittsburgh and Chicago) "to promote the claims of the Psalms in worship," Dr. J. C. K. Milligan says:

> After the organization of the United Presbyterian Church of North America in 1858, almost the first work was arrangements for the revision of the *Scottish Psalter;* and in 1871 the completed Book was adopted with substantial unanimity. In a conservative spirit the Common Meter Version was preserved, but it was thoroughly amended. . . .

Speaking of the *Scottish Psalter* of 1650 (70), the Rev. W. E. McCullock has said:

> It is impossible to estimate the influence which the Scottish Version has wielded upon the spiritual destinies of mankind. Through generation after generation it was woven into the very life of the Scottish people. It furnished them their home-songs and their battle songs, and was their mainstay through their long and terrible struggle for civil and religious liberty. It was not confined to Scotland, but was adopted by the Presbyterians of England and America, and became their song-book for a century. Thus far-reaching in its grasp upon the minds and hearts of men, it stimulated the intellect, put stamina into the moral fiber, and created a virile type of Christian character which the passing of many generations has not worn out. He who believes in the eternity of influence will not look with light regard upon the Scottish Psalter.

The difficulties in the way of psalm versification are great; if a translation from the Hebrew is attempted, they are very great, for Hebrew poetry has neither rhyme nor meter. The use of much poetic license is necessary, since each line must accord with the poetic measure and additions to or subtractions from the original must be made. To keep close to the original text, to conform as nearly as possible to the Authorized and Revised translations, to provide a variety of meters in order to avoid monotony in singing, and yet express the thought with clearness and elegance of style is a task of extreme difficulty. How remarkably all of this was accomplished by those who provided the *Scottish Psalter* has been attested by its wide and extended use (70).

This four-part form of "Tallis' Canon" is substantially that made by Thomas Ravenscroft, c. 1621, and while this has some differences in the alto and bass voice leadings, the canon between the soprano and tenor has not been disturbed. (See No. 51 for the original two-voiced form.)

## Love and Mercy

**75—God is love; His mercy brightens**—John Bowring

**Stuttgart**—Adapted from a melody in Psalmodia Sacra, Gotha

This bright, happy hymn, emphasizing in the last line of each stanza God's wisdom and His love, has found its place in nearly all hymnals. It is taken from John Bowring's *Hymns,* published when the author was thirty-three years of age, the same year he became editor of *The Westminster Review.* In *Hymns* the first stanza was repeated as the last, and in this book the third line of the third stanza has been changed from,

> From the mist His brightness streameth,

to read,

> Thro' the gloom His brightness streameth.

*Hymns,* 1825, by John Bowring, was written as a sequel to his *Matins and Vespers,* London, 1823. In the Preface to the latter the author wrote:

> I have often witnessed, with complacency and delight, the consoling influence produced by the recollection of some passage of devotional poetry, under circumstances the most disheartening, and suffering the most oppressive. Should any fragment of this little book, remembered and dwelt upon in moments of gloom and anxiety, tend to restore peace, to awaken fortitude, to create, to renew, or to strengthen confidence in heaven, I shall have obtained the boon for which I pray—the end to which I aspire. . . . To be useful is my first ambition; that obtained, I am indifferent to the rest.

This desire, similar to the one expressed in the Preface to Hymns (149), has been abundantly fulfilled.

John Bowring, philanthropist, publicist, biographer, statesman, historian, financier, naturalist, poet, great linguist, and one of the most brilliant men of his time, was born at Exeter, England, October 17, 1792, the son of a manufacturer of woollen goods. He left school at the age of fourteen to assist his father, and later became a clerk for a merchant in Exeter. Through contact made with foreigners he acquired, in his father's wool business, and through his native genius a knowledge of Spanish, Portuguese, Italian, German, and Dutch before he was sixteen. In his late life he boasted of the fact that he knew two hundred languages and could speak one hundred. Much of the time between his twentieth and thirtieth years was spent in foreign travel, looking after commercial interests. His interests were political rather than commercial, however, and he attracted attention through his writings, for a time editing the radical *Westminster Review,* securing election to Parliament, and holding important government positions, among them consul at Canton, governor of Hong Kong, and general superintendent of trade with China. In 1828 the University of Groningen conferred on him the degree of LL.D., and he was knighted by the Queen in 1854. Of his works edited in thirty-six volumes, only a few of his hymns are remembered. He was a Unitarian, "though in faith and spirit he was nearer to orthodoxy than the radical wing of his own denomination." It has been said that he was on the side of everything good and true. He died at Exeter, November 23, 1872.

"Stuttgart" is from *Psalmodia Sacra,* published at Gotha, Germany, in 1715. It was probably arranged by Christian Friedrich Witt (1660-1716), who with one A. C. Ludwig edited the collection. Witt was court Kapellmeister at Friedenstein in Gotha. The original form of the tune, set to "Sollt es gleich bisweilen scheinen," was:

**76—There's a wideness in God's mercy—Frederick William Faber**

**Wellesley—Lizzie S. Tourjée**

This cento is stanzas 4, 6, 8, and 13 from thirteen stanzas written by F. W. Faber, entitled "Come to Jesus," which appeared in his *Hymns,* 1862. In many books the hymn consists of six stanzas, the first two being used in addition to those found in *The Methodist Hymnal.* They are:

Souls of men! why will ye scatter
Like a crowd of frightened sheep?
Foolish hearts! why will ye wander
From a love so true and deep?

Was there ever kindest Shepherd
Half so gentle, half so sweet
As the Saviour who would have us
Come and gather round His feet?

The third stanza, while not so singable as the others, might well be quoted:

It is God: His love looks mighty,
But is mightier than it seems!
'Tis our Father; and His fondness
Goes far out beyond our dreams.

How much more the fourth stanza means following after these! The ninth stanza suggests how man belittles God:

But we make His love too narrow
By false limits of our own;
And we magnify His strictness
With a zeal He will not own.

Not always is the best judgment used in the selection of stanzas for a hymn. "The greatest poet is he who faithfully interprets the inner world of the emotion of his fellows"—(R. Pearsall Smith).

Frederick William Faber, D.D., born at Calverley Vicarage, Yorkshire, England, June 28, 1814, was educated at Balliol and University Colleges, Oxford, being elected a fellow at the latter. He was descended from Huguenot stock and brought up a strict Calvinist. Taking orders, he was appointed rector of Elton, Huntingdonshire, where he remained for three years, introducing certain advanced ritualistic practices which probably influenced his transference to the Roman communion. Although in his early days in Oxford he had been anti-Roman in his writings, he was influenced by John Henry Newman (514) to the other extreme.

It was not until after he became a Catholic that he published his hymns. These he wrote because of a deficiency of hymns suitable for English Catholics, as he says in his Preface to *Jesus and Mary; or Catholic Hymns for Singing and Reading*. Although ignorant of music, he began by writing some eleven hymns to fit certain tunes with which he was familiar. Favorable comment on them by a musical friend encouraged his further effort. The *Olney Hymns* and those of John and Charles Wesley were his models, for he felt the Catholics did not have "the means of influence which one school of Protestants has in Wesley's, Newton's, and Cowper's hymns, and another in the more engaging works of the Oxford writers."

Of Faber's total of a hundred and fifty hymns, corresponding in number to that of the Psalms, most are too doctrinal, too personal, or too emotional to have wide use outside the Roman Church. His devotional works, like most of his hymns, are "curiously wanting in the sense of proportion, their emotionalism is at times all but hysterical." He was a man of charming personality with a remarkable voice and a persuasive eloquence that made his preaching unusually effective. Doctor Faber died September 26, 1863.

"Wellesley" was written by Miss Tourjée, either in the winter of 1877 or the spring of 1878, while she was a student at Wellesley College.

Lizzie S. Tourjée, 1858-1913, was the daughter of Dr. Eben Tourjée, founder of the New England Conservatory of Music, one of the musical editors of the *Hymnal of the Methodist Episcopal Church with Tunes,* 1878, and editor of *The Tribute of Praise,* 1882. Dr. Hamilton C. Macdougall, professor emeritus of music, Wellesley College, gives the following information:

> Mrs. Franklin Estabrook, who died in 1913, was in Wellesley College from September, 1877, to June, 1878, and was then Lizzie S. Tourjée. That seems to be all the information we have about her. . . . When I came to Wellesley in 1900, I found her tune in use, and when the Wellesley *Song Book* came under my editorship in 1914 I printed "Wellesley" in the *Song Book;* it had previously been in our *In Excelsis* Wellesley supplement. The tune was not quite correct in its voice leading, and I wrote Mrs. Estabrook asking for permission to print as slightly revised by me: the permission was promptly given.

**77—Praise, my soul, the King of Heaven**—From Psalm 103
Henry Francis Lyte

**Regent Square**—Henry Smart

Taken from the first (1834) edition of Henry F. Lyte's *Spirit of the Psalms,* written primarily for use in his own church in Lower Brixham, in southern England. While the *Spirit of the Psalms* was enlarged in 1836, it is from the smaller book that most of his hymns are taken. This is the happiest of Lyte's versions of the Psalms, most of them being characterized by "sadness, tenderness, and beauty." This rendering is so free that it can scarcely be considered a "version"; rather it might well be said to have been based upon

Psalm 103. Of this hymn, written originally in five stanzas, with the omitted fourth bracketed for omission if desired, the fifth line has been changed from "Praise Him, praise Him," to "Alleluia! Alleluia!"—a change quite generally found in contemporary books.

Henry Francis Lyte was born in Ednam, southeast Scotland, the birthplace of James Thomson (the author of *The Seasons*), on June 1, 1793. He was educated at the Royal School of Enniskillen and at Trinity College, Dublin, Ireland, and served his Church in England. For a time he considered studying medicine, but changed his mind and took up theology. Three times during his university years he won the English poetry prize. In 1818, three years after taking Orders, he underwent a remarkable spiritual change, the result of an unusual religious experience. He wrote:

> A neighboring clergyman, with whom I was intimate, and who bore the highest character for benevolence, piety, and good sense, was taken ill, and sent for me. I went to attend him, and witnessed all the workings of his mind and body for some weeks until he expired. . . . He died, I rejoice to say, happy under the belief that though he had deeply erred, there was One whose death and sufferings would atone for his delinquencies, and be accepted for all that he had incurred. I was greatly affected by the whole matter, and brought to look at life and its issues with a different eye than before; and I began to study my Bible and preach in another manner than I had previously done.

For twenty-five years he labored at Lower Brixham, Devon. When he went there, he found conditions quite unfavorable to the growth of morality or religion, but the changes he wrought with his incessant labor were remarkable. The people were rough, but warmhearted, and responded readily, for, says one of his choir members, "He had the gentlest expression, and most winning manner possible." He is best known for having written "Abide with me" (520). He died November 20, 1847, at Nice.

"Regent Square" was written for *Psalms and Hymns for Divine Worship,* 1867, a book designed for use among English Presbyterians. It is an excellent example of the best in English hymn-tune writing. Only eleven years elapsed between its publication in England and its inclusion in the *Hymnal of the Methodist Episcopal Church,* 1878. Two years later it was used in *The Hymn and Tune Book* of the Methodist Episcopal Church, South, but it did not come into Methodist Protestant hymnody until 1901. It is an excellent processional tune if allowance be made for an additional measure before beginning the second and ensuing stanzas.

Henry Thomas Smart, known only as Henry Smart, was born in London, October 26, 1813, the son of another Henry, who was a violinist and piano manufacturer. Declining a commission in the Indian army, the younger Smart studied law; but when he found he did not like it, he began to develop his natural musical aptitude. He was largely self-taught, though he did have some lessons from W. H. Kearns, a violinist prominent in London musical circles the middle of the last century. Smart's first appointment was as organist at Blackburn, Lancashire, where he first attracted attention with an anthem written for the tercentenary of the Reformation in 1835. It was here also that he wrote "Lancashire" (278), at the request of the Methodists. Returning to

London in 1838, he was organist at three prominent churches, being in active service until his death. Having suffered many years from an affliction of the eyes, he became totally blind by 1865. This did not interfere with his composing, however, although thereafter it was necessary for him to dictate all of his work to his daughter, who acted as his amanuensis. The organ afforded him his best means of musical expression. He was an able player, a very sympathetic accompanist for the church services, an excellent improviser, a voluminous and creditable composer. He had a considerable knowledge of organ building. While his writings for the Church are not extensive, he produced more than two hundred and fifty secular works. He edited two noteworthy tune books—namely, *The Presbyterian Hymnal,* for the use of the United Presbyterian Church of Scotland, and the *Chorale Book,* a model for later harmonizers of hymn tunes. Lightwood says that Smart in this book has done for the English hymn tune what Bach did for the German chorale, and adds: "He has done it equally well, but with greater fidelity to the original."

He died July 6, 1879, less than a month after the British government had granted him a pension of about £100 per year in acknowledgment of his services in the cause of music. His family did not benefit from it in any way.

**78—O Will of God beneath our life**—George Angier Gordon

**St. Magnus**—Jeremiah Clark

This hymn was brought to the attention of the Joint Commission on the Revision of the *Hymnal* at a meeting held at Lake Chautauqua, New York, in July, 1933, by Dr. John W. Langdale, who has said that it will "test the quality of those who would assay it. It has to be mastered by the intelligence before it can satisfy the emotions." Dr. George A. Gordon, "the stateliest preacher of the present century," ministered for more than forty years at Old South Church, Boston. Frequently Doctor Gordon wrote poems which, with his sermons, were published continuously in pamphlet form by his church. This hymn, which he wrote for Easter of 1915, appears for the first time in the present *Methodist Hymnal.*

George Angier Gordon, born January 2, 1853, was the son of an overseer of the estate of Pitodrie, parish of Oyne, Aberdeenshire, Scotland. He emigrated to America in 1871 and worked at various manual trades until it was possible for him to enter the Congregational Theological Seminary at Bangor, Maine. Through the friendship of the Rev. Luther H. Angier, from whom he adopted his middle name, the way was opened for him to attend Harvard University, where, after only two years, he advanced to the Senior class. One of America's leaders in the pulpit, his ministry of forty-three years at Old South Church, Boston, was a notable one. Intensely loyal to Harvard, he was her University preacher, member of her Board of Overseers, and president of her alumni association. Doctor Gordon was "a philosopher who knew how to preach, and a theologian with real insight and power." He died at Boston, October 29, 1929.

"St. Magnus" first appeared in Henry Playford's *Divine Companion or David's Harp new tun'd,* 1709, without a name, and without credit. In

*Harmonia Perfecta,* issued in 1730 by Nathaniel Gawthorne, the second Nonconformist "professor of music" to go about the various meetinghouses instructing the congregations in singing, it was called "Nottingham." Rechristened "St. Magnus," it was credited to Jeremiah Clark in William Riley's *Parochial Psalmody,* 1762, which Lightwood (453) says was the only church tune book of any importance issued during the second half of the eighteenth century.

Jeremiah Clark, who was born in London in 1670, and who died there December 1, 1707, was a chorister in the Chapel Royal under Dr. John Blow; organist at Winchester College; organist and vicar choral at St. Paul's; and joint organist of St. James's Chapel Royal with Dr. William Croft (169). Clark had entertained "a hopeless passion for a very beautiful lady in a station of life far above him; his despair of success threw him into a deep melancholy," says John Hawkins in his *History of Music,* 1776. Of a melancholy temperament, he died by his own hand. Unable to decide whether he should commit suicide by hanging or drowning, he tossed a coin, which struck on its edge in the soft ground when it fell. He went home and shot himself with a "screw pistol."

He wrote operatic and instrumental music and songs, as well as anthems and hymn tunes. The only work he published himself was some "Choice Lessons" for the harpsichord for the use of Queen Anne, whose music master he was.

**79—To the Name that is salvation**—Percy Dearmer

**Oriel**—C. Ett, Cantica Sacra

The author of this hymn says it was written to provide "another hymn about God," for use with this tune, "Oriel," for the enlarged edition of *Songs of Praise,* 1931.

Percy Dearmer, D.D., Canon of Westminster from 1931, born in London, February 27, 1867, was educated at Westminster School, abroad, and Christ Church, Oxford. From 1901 to 1915 he served as vicar of the Church of St. Mary the Virgin, Primrose Hill. From 1915 to 1919 he served in the Great War. Returning to England, he became Professor of Ecclesiastical Art in King's College, London, and Lecturer in Art. His publications are many and valuable. A noted authority in the field of hymnody, he edited the *English Hymnal,* both editions of *Songs of Praise* (1925 and 1931), and *Songs of Praise, Discussed.* He was also a poet of distinction. Doctor Dearmer died at London, May 29, 1936.

"Oriel" comes from *Cantica Sacra in usum studiosae Juventutis* . . . Casparus Ett, 1840. It was set in four parts to "Pange lingua gloriosi" by Venantius Fortunatus (161), and while it is not definitely known whether it was written or arranged by Ett, it has not been traced to any earlier source. In *Easy Music for Church Choirs,* Part III, 1853 (124), Ett is named as its composer.

C. Ett is the manner in which the name of Kasper, Casper, or Gaspard Ett is always printed in modern tune books. He was born at Erringen,

Bavaria, January 5, 1788, and died at Munich, May 16, 1847. At nine years of age he became a choir boy in a Benedictine Abbey, studied at the Electoral College, Munich, and from 1816 was court organist at St. Michael's Church there. He rendered valuable service in reviving and producing old sacred musical works of the sixteenth to eighteenth centuries, which he took as models for his own compositions. Of these only a few appeared in print. All of his manuscripts have been preserved in the Munich library.

**80—O, my soul, bless God the Father**—From Psalm 103

United Presbyterian Book of Psalms, 1871 (77)

**Stuttgart** (75)—Adapted from a melody in Psalmodia Sacra, 1715 (75)

This is an excellent paraphrase of Psalm 103, which a comparison with the text will show:

The Psalm—Bless the Lord, O my soul: and all that is within me,
bless his holy name.
Bless the Lord, O my soul, and forget not
all his benefits.

The Paraphrase—O, my soul, bless God the Father;
All within me bless His name;
Bless the Father, and forget not
All His mercies to proclaim.

The Psalm—Who forgiveth all thine iniquities; who
healeth all thy diseases;
Who redeemeth thy life from destruction; who
crowneth thee with loving-kindness and tender mercies. . . .

The Paraphrase—Who forgiveth thy transgressions,
Thy diseases all who heals;
Who redeems thee from destruction,
Who with thee so kindly deals.

It is a splendid rendering of verses 1 and 2, 3 and 4, 12 and 13, 17, 18, and 21 and 22. Further comparison with Henry F. Lyte's hymn (77) will show the difference between a hymn suggested by a psalm and a metrical rendering of one.

In the *Book of Psalms* the first stanza reads,

O my soul, bless thou Jehovah,
All within me bless His name;
Bless Jehovah and forget not
All His mercies to proclaim.

With one other very slight change in the second stanza and the use of "the Father" in place of "Jehovah" in the last stanza the paraphrase has not been altered.

**81—Let us with a gladsome mind**—John Milton

**Innocents**—From The Parish Choir

John Milton wrote this paraphrase of Psalm 136 when he was only fifteen years old, still a pupil at St. Paul's. Originally, the paraphrase contained twenty-four two-line stanzas with the refrain. Milton lived in a day when metrical versions of the Psalms were about the only things available for congregational singing. Their stilted style must have so grated on Milton's poetic ear as to interest him in writing something better. It does not need to be said that Milton is not known primarily for his hymn writing. In fact his influence in that field is slight.

John Milton, the famous blind poet, was born in London, December 9, 1608, and died there November 8, 1674. His works are so familiar and biographical details so numerous and easily available that only very slight mention of him need be made here. Milton's literary life is divided into three clearly marked periods: his earlier and shorter poems, such as his "Ode on the Morn of Christ's Nativity"; his political and controversial writings, such as his "Areopagitica," on the freedom of the press; and his more extended works, such as "Paradise Lost." Much of his best work was done while he was a comparatively young man. He became totally blind in 1652.

The tune "Innocents" has long puzzled students of hymn tunes. It appeared in a magazine, *The Parish Choir,* Vol. III, the organ of the "Society for Promoting Church Music," where it is appointed as a tune to be sung to an Innocents' Day hymn. There was little interest shown in this magazine of the middle of the last century and it lived only three years. The origin of "Innocents" is not known. There is some possibility of its being an arrangement of a tune by Handel (in the opera *Siroe*), because of its slight resemblance to "Christmas" (88). It may have been the setting for a song called "The Sun," probably dated about 1850, and found in a book of manuscript songs by one Joseph Smith, who lived in a small place near Birmingham, England, in the early part of the last century. In this book appears the following little song which is certainly not "Innocents" as we know it, but which may have suggested it:

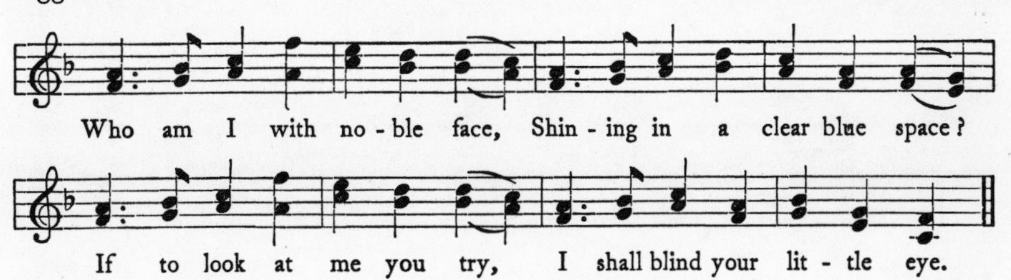
Who am I with no - ble face, Shin - ing in a clear blue space?
If to look at me you try, I shall blind your lit - tle eye.

It became popular as a hymn tune after its appearance in *Hymns Ancient and Modern,* 1861, the original edition.

**82—High in the heavens, Eternal God**—Isaac Watts (3)

**DePauw**—Robert Guy McCutchan (9²)

This "imitation" of a part of Psalm 36 (verses 5-9 inclusive) is one of three which Isaac Watts made for *The Psalms of David Imitated in the Lan-*

*guage of the New Testament.* It is composed of stanzas 1, 2, 4, and 6, with only minor changes. The original form of stanza 3 was:

My God! how excellent Thy grace,
Whence all our hope and comfort springs!
The sons of *Adam* in distress
Fly to the *shadow* of Thy wings.

The first word of the last line, stanza 1, was "which"; and "the Lord" has been changed to "my Lord" in stanza 4, line 2. The hymn was headed "The perfections and providence of God; or, general providence and special grace."

"DePauw" was written in the summer of 1928 at Lake Winona, Indiana, as a setting for Theodore Williams's hymn, "Thou rulest, Lord, the lights on high." It first appeared in *The Standard Hymnal,* 1930.

# JESUS CHRIST

## Advent and Nativity

**83—O come, O come, Immanuel**—From the Latin, 12th century
Stanza 1 Translated by John Mason Neale (52)
Stanzas 2, 3 Translated by Henry Sloane Coffin

**Veni Immanuel**—Ancient plain song, 13th century

The first stanza of the hymn is the revision of Dr. J. M. Neale's translation of 1851, which appeared in the "trial copy" of *Hymns Ancient and Modern,* 1859. It is the first of the Seven Greater Antiphons which are sung at Vespers (Anglican) in Advent, beginning December 17, one being sung each evening until Christmas Eve. These Antiphons, or "Great O's," as they are frequently called, are:

O Sapientia, quae ex ore altissimi.
O Adonay et dux domus Israel.
O Radix Jesse qui stas in signum populorum.
O Clavis David et spectrum domus Israel.
O Oriens, splendor lucis aeternae.
O Rex gentium et desideratus.
O Emanuel, rex et legifer.

Sometime during the thirteenth century five of the "Great O's" were made into a metrical hymn, "changing the order and adding a refrain," which has had wide use through translations by Doctor Neale and others. Doctor Neale's translation appears in *The Abingdon Hymnal* as follows:

O come, O come, Emmanuel,
And ransom captive Israel;
That mourns in lonely exile here,
Until the Son of God appear.

Rejoice! Rejoice!
Emmanuel
Shall come to thee,
O Israel!

O come, thou Rod of Jesse, free
Thine own from Satan's tyranny;
From depths of hell thy people save,
And give them vict'ry o'er the grave.

O come, thou Dayspring, come and cheer
Our spirits by thine advent here;
Disperse the gloomy clouds of night,
And death's dark shadows put to flight.

O come, thou Key of David, come,
And open wide our heavenly home;
Make safe the way that leads on high,
And close the path to misery.

O come, O come, thou Lord of might!
Who to thy tribes on Sinai's height,
In ancient times didst give the law,
In cloud, and majesty, and awe.

Stanzas two and three, as the hymn appears in *The Methodist Hymnal,* were written by Dr. Henry Sloane Coffin, in 1916, while minister of the Madison Avenue Presbyterian Church, New York City.

"Veni Immanuel" has not been traced to any earlier source than *The Hymnal Noted,* Part II, 1856, where it is said to be "From a French Missal in the National Library, Lisbon." The Rev. W. Hilton, of the English College, Lisbon, has made an examination of all of the missals in that library but has failed to find this tune. It is more than likely that this tune has been made from several plainsong phrases as most of these have been found among the many settings of the Kyrie eleison. Probably the adaptation to suit Doctor Neale's translation of the five "Great O's" was made by Thomas Helmore, editor of *The Hymnal Noted,* and one of the pioneers in the revival of the use of the Gregorian Tones in the Anglican service. In any case it is a fine tune even if it is a "modern imitation," as "A Minister" says in *A Guide for Methodist Choirs.* Because of the popularity of this tune and hymn it has seemed wise to discuss them at some length.

Henry Sloane Coffin, D.D., LL.D., was born in New York City, January 5, 1877. He graduated from Yale College, A.B., 1897, M.A., 1900, studied at New College, Edinburgh, and the University of Marburg, and holds honorary degrees from Union Theological Seminary, New York University, Yale, Harvard, and Amherst. Ordained to the Presbyterian ministry in 1900, he has served Bedford Park and Madison Avenue Churches, New York, was associate Professor of Practical Theology, Union Theological Seminary, and since 1926 has been its president. Noted preacher and lecturer, writer of many books, member of many learned societies, Doctor Coffin is one of the recognized leaders in contemporary religious thinking. He was chairman of the committee that compiled *Hymns of the Kingdom of God,* 1910.

**84—Come, Thou long expected Jesus**—Charles Wesley (25)

**Hyfrydol** (11)—Rowland Hugh Prichard (11)

This hymn, one of Charles Wesley's first, was No. 10 in *Hymns for the Nativity of our Lord,* a small book of twenty-four pages containing eighteen hymns, published in 1744. It is strange that it was not included in the *Wesleyan Hymn Book* until the edition of 1875, nor in any of the Methodist books in America until 1878. It is only fair to say that this hymn has never had deserved general use, for the reason that it has not had a proper musical setting.

"Wilson," the tune associated with it in *The Methodist Hymnal* of 1905, was a poor adaptation of the tenor solo, "If with all your hearts," from Mendelssohn's oratorio *Elijah.* One of the most beautiful of solos, it was not intended to be sung by a congregation and would not lend itself to such treatment. "Hyfrydol" (11) is a tune worthy of this hymn, and has proven to be one of the most effective and popular of the modern hymn tunes.

**85—Hail, to the Lord's Anointed**—James Montgomery (39)
**Ellacombe**—Gesangbuch der Herzogl. Wirtemburgischen Katholischen Hofkapelle

S. W. Christopher asks:

> Can anything be more sublime than Psalm 72? Could there be a more perfect harmony of the Divine and the human in prayer and praise? And who does not thank God for the man who threw that song into English meter, so happily as to give it all the charms of new music, so effectually as to naturalize it to the purest taste and to the warmest hearts of Christian England? James Montgomery did this when he taught us to sing—
>
> "Hail to the Lord's Anointed,
> Great David's greater Son!"

There is general agreement among hymnologists that this is James Montgomery's finest rendering of any of the psalms. Written for a Christmas ode, it was sung at one of the British Moravian settlements (Fulneck) on Christmas Day, 1821. The next month after its composition and first use it was started on its foreign career, being sent in manuscript to one George Bennett, then on a missionary tour in the South Seas. On the following April 14, Montgomery read it at the close of his address before a Wesleyan missionary conference at Liverpool. The president of the conference, Dr. Adam Clarke, was so greatly impressed with it that he asked permission to include it in his *Commentary,* then about to be published. The following month it appeared in the *Evangelical Magazine* with the heading "Imitation of the 72nd Psalm, Tune Culmstock." It has since gone around the globe, and is an ever popular hymn for the Advent season.

Doctor Julian says:

> Of all Montgomery's renderings and imitations of the psalms, this is the finest. It forms a rich and splendid Messianic hymn. Its success has been great, partly due at the first to the publicity given to it by Dr. Adam Clarke in his *Commentary on the Bible,* in which it appeared in 1822 with a special note at the end of his exposition of Psalm 72:
>
> I need not tell the intelligent reader that he has seized the spirit, and exhibited some of the principal beauties, of the Hebrew bard; though (to use his own words in a letter to me) his "hand trembled to touch the harp of Zion." I take the liberty here to register a wish, which I have strongly expressed to himself, that he would favor the Church of God with a metrical version of the whole book.

Doctor Benson (38) points out that while Montgomery did much to elevate the taste of the dissenting churches as to their hymns, he also kept close to the Scriptures and was "true to the ends of edification."

"Ellacombe" is found as "Melody No. 1b" in a collection made for use in the private chapel of the duchy of Wirtemburg. The collection is known as *Gesang Buch—der Herzogl. Wirtemburgischen Katholischen Hofkapelle,* 1784. It found its way into English hymnody, however, after its publication in 1833 by X. L. Hartig in *Vollständige Sammlung der gewöhnlichen Melodien zum Mainzer Gesangbuche,* in the following form:

86—Hark! the herald angels sing—Charles Wesley (25)
Altered by George Whitefield

Mendelssohn—Felix Mendelssohn-Bartholdy (33)
Adapted by William Haymen Cummings

All will agree with Doctor Bodine's statement:

> When we wish to give utterance to our feeling of Christmas joy, it is Charles Wesley who shouts for us:
>
> Hark! the herald angels sing,
> "Glory to the new-born King;
> Peace on earth and mercy mild;
> God and sinners reconciled."

This hymn with its familiar tune makes a great song—perhaps the most popular English hymn in the world. It is the only one of Charles Wesley's hymns included in the *Book of Common Prayer* of the Church of England. How it came to be included there is something of a mystery, though it is thought some printer in the eighteenth century, needing some material to fill a blank space, inserted it after the psalms as a hymn for festival use. In spite of some attempts for its displacement, it has remained because of the love the people have for it.

Like all of our greatest hymns, with the exception of "Jesus, Lover of my soul" (338), this is not now sung in its original form. Written in 1739, shortly after Charles Wesley "consciously believed," it began,

> Hark! how all the welkin rings
> "Glory to the King of Kings."

It was published in *Hymns and Sacred Poems* that same year, being in ten four-line stanzas, six of which are now generally used. It was revised and included in the 1743 edition of the same book headed "Hymn for Christmas Day." George Whitefield included it in his *Collection* of 1753, with the first two lines changed to,

> Hark! the herald angels sing,
> "Glory to the new-born King."

In 1760 the Rev. Martin Madan made further changes in the last two lines of the present first stanza (2 of the original), making

Universal nature say
"Christ the Lord is risen today,"

read,

With th' angelic hosts proclaim,
"Christ is born in Bethlehem."

There were further slight alterations made in R. Conger's *Collection* in 1774, and in that of De Courcy in 1775. It was added to *The Supplement* of the *New Version* of Tate and Brady (1782), in three stanzas of eight lines each, with the first two lines of the hymn repeated as a refrain to each stanza. This, with some recent changes in the first and second stanzas, is the form in which it comes to us. Because of its excellence the whole of the hymn as Wesley wrote it is given here:

Hark, how all the welkin rings
"Glory to the King of Kings,
Peace on earth and mercy mild
God and sinners reconciled."

Joyful all ye nations rise,
Join the triumph of the skies,
Universal nature say
"Christ the Lord is born today."

Christ, by highest heaven adored,
Christ, the everlasting Lord,
Late in time behold Him come
Offspring of a Virgin's womb.

Veil'd in flesh, the Godhead see,
Hail the Incarnate Deity!
Pleased as man with men to appear
Jesus! our *Immanuel* here!

Hail the heavenly Prince of Peace!
Hail the Sun of Righteousness,
Light and life to all He brings,
Risen with healing in His wings.

Mild He lays His glory by,
Born—that man no more may die,
Born—to raise the sons of earth,
Born—to give them second birth.

Come, Desire of Nations, come,
Fix in us Thy humble home;
Rise, the woman's conquering seed.
Bruise in us the serpent's head.

Now display Thy saving power,
Ruin'd nature now restore;
Now in mystic union join
Thine to ours and ours to Thine.

*Adam's* likeness, Lord, efface;
Stamp Thy image in its place;
Second *Adam* from above,
Reinstate us in Thy love.

Let us Thee, though lost, regain,
Then the Life, the Inner Man;
O! to all Thyself impart,
Form'd in each believing heart.

George Whitefield, born at Gloucester, England, December 16, 1714, died at Newburyport, Massachusetts, September 30, 1770, educated at St. Mary le Crypt School and Pembroke College, Oxford, and ordained a deacon in 1736, began preaching for the Methodists in 1737, two years after joining the Society. From 1737 until his death he spent his time in the British Isles and the American colonies, being "the connecting link between the revival movement in England and America." He was closely associated with Lady Huntingdon (143) in her work of founding chapels. His famous chapel in Totten ham Court Road was opened in 1756; rebuilt in 1899. Here, as elsewhere, his preaching attracted great numbers of people and resulted in many conversions. On his second visit to America enthusiasm greeted him everywhere he went, especially in New England, then in the midst of the Great Awakening. On his later visits to this section a coolness toward him gradually developed. Dr. W. W. Sweet says, "Whatever limitations Whitefield may have had, he was one of the chief 'human factors in the greatest religious overturning New England has ever experienced.'" Whitefield lies buried under the pulpit of Old South Presbyterian Church, Newburyport, Massachusetts.

"Mendelssohn," named after its composer, Ludwig Felix Mendelssohn-Bartholdy, is also known as "Jesu Redemptor," "Bethlehem," "St. Vincent," "Berlin," and "Nativity." It is taken from the *Festgesang* (No. 7), written in 1840, which was composed to celebrate the anniversary of the discovery of printing. It is adapted from the "Lied," second number of the work. In 1855 Dr. W. H. Cummings set it to the words "Hark, the herald angels sing." Mendelssohn, not liking the translation W. Bartholomew had made of the "Lied," said:

> I think there ought to be other words to No. 2, the "Lied." If the right ones are hit at, I am sure that piece will be liked very much by the singers and the hearers, but it will *never* do to sacred words. There must be a national and merry subject found out, something to which the soldierlike and buxom motion of the piece has some relation, and the words must express something gay and popular, as the music tries to do it.

William Haymen Cummings, Mus. Doc., was noted as a tenor singer. Born in Sidbury, Devon, England, August 22, 1831, he attained prominence at an early age. He sang in the United States in 1871, and subsequently. He was an authoritative singer of Bach's Passion Music. Doctor Cummings succeeded Sir Joseph Barnby (31) as principal of the Guildhall School of Music, London. He died June 6, 1915.

**87—Angels, from the realms of glory**—James Montgomery (39)

**Regent Square** (77)—Henry Smart (77)

This first appeared in the Sheffield, England, *Iris,* a newspaper of which James Montgomery was the editor, on December 24, 1816. Its first appearance in a hymnal was in Thomas Cotterill's (207) *Selection,* 1819. It was included as one of "three new carols" in *The Christmas Box,* 1825, the first complete book issued by the religious Tract Society of England, the first of the popular "Christmas Books."

In 1928 it appeared in the excellent *Oxford Book of Carols,* where it is set to the old French tune used in this book at 108. Doctor Dearmer says the hymn resembles an early nineteenth-century translation of the French carol "Les anges dans nos campagnes," which is sung to "Gloria" (108). When it first appeared in the *Iris,* it had the title "Nativity," but when its author used it in his *Christian Psalmist,* 1825, it was titled "Good tidings of great joy to all people."

> . . . for comprehensiveness, appropriateness of expression, force and elevation of sentiment, it may challenge comparison with any hymn that was ever written, in any language or country.

**88—While Shepherds watched their flocks by night**—Nahum Tate

**Christmas**—Arranged from George Frederick Handel

Some time soon after Tate and Brady (See No. 14) issued their *New Version* of the Psalms, there was added a *Supplement,* containing a few hymns by Nahum Tate, which was bound in with the book. The first *Supplement* of which there is a known copy was dated 1700. In this edition there were sixteen hymns, one of which was "While Shepherds watched their flocks by night," a paraphrase of Luke's story of the shepherds. The other fifteen are all forgotten. It is quaint and picturesque, and being greatly loved, has been translated into almost, if not all, of the living languages, and into classical Latin. In 1745 it appeared in the Draft of the *Scottish Translations and Paraphrases,* the first stanza being,

> While humble Shepherds watched their Flocks
> in Bethlehem's Plains by Night,
> An Angel sent from Heav'n appeared
> and fill'd the Plains with Light.

The hymn appears in modern books as Tate wrote it with the exception of the last two lines of stanza five. The original,

> Of angels, praising God, and thus
> addresst their joyful song,

has been changed to read,

> Of angels praising God on high,
> Who thus addressed their song.

This change seems to be peculiar to American Methodist books. Whether or not it improves the hymn is open to question.

Nahum Tate, born in Dublin, in 1652, son of Faithful Tate, an Irish clergyman, produced, in 1696, with Nicholas Brady, the *New Version* of the Psalms, which gradually superseded the *Old Version* of Sternhold and Hopkins. He wrote largely for the stage. Though Tate was but a mediocre poet, court influence made him poet laureate of England in 1690 and historiographer-royal in 1702. He died at London, August 12, 1715.

He did some work under the superintendence of Dryden, but the classicists of the period scorned him. A man of "intemperate and improvident" habits, he died within the bounds of the British mint, then a refuge for debtors.

"Christmas" is an adaptation of a melody from one of George F. Handel's operas, *Siroe,* 1728. Although there have been many "arrangements" or "adaptations" from Handel's numerous works, he wrote only three hymn tunes. These were written upon the request of Charles Wesley, who met Handel at the home of a mutual friend.

George Frederick Handel, born at Halle, Prussia, February 23, 1685, but for fifty years a resident of England, was the founder of the traditional English oratorio. He was a contemporary of Johann S. Bach (52), being born in the same year, but outliving Bach by nine years. Historians of music now call the first half of the eighteenth century from these dominant figures, the age of Bach and Handel.

Handel was the son of a German surgeon, who intended him for a career in law. The boy's musical urge was so strong, however, as to attract the attention of one of his father's aristocratic patrons, who had the boy given careful instruction by a good teacher. Being adept at composing and quickly mastering the clavier, organ, violin, and oboe, he was taken to Berlin as a prodigy when only eleven years old. When seventeen he entered the new University at Halle and received the appointment as organist at the Cathedral. After a year he went to Hamburg, where, during three years, he played in the opera orchestra, wrote four operas, and won recognition as an organist. For three years (1707-1710), he traveled in Italy, studying Italian operatic styles and composing extensively. Upon his return he secured the position as choirmaster to the Elector of Hanover, who immediately gave Handel leave of absence for further travel. Going to England, he gained immediate success with his operas. After only a brief return to Germany, he journeyed again to England, where he overstayed his leave sufficiently to gain the ill will of the Elector. This would not have mattered greatly had not this same Elector of Hanover become King George I of England in 1714. Nevertheless, he regained the favor of the king by composing the famous "Water Music" with which he serenaded his Royal Highness. He was fifty-three years of age before he began the type of composition that has immortalized his name. Until that time he had devoted himself largely to the composition and presentation of the then conventional type of Italian opera in London. But once started in the field of oratorio writing, he kept it up until his death, April 14, 1759. Burney, the historian, who knew him well, gives this picture of him:

> The figure of Handel was large, and he was somewhat unwieldy in his actions;

> but his countenance was full of fire and dignity. His general look was somewhat heavy and dour, but when he did smile, it was the sun bursting out of a black cloud. There was a sudden flash of intelligence, wit and good humor beaming in his countenance which I hardly ever saw in any other. . . . His smile was like heaven.

After his death Handel's body was placed in the Poet's Corner of Westminster Abbey.

> He died as he lived, a good Christian, with a true sense of his duty to God and man, and in perfect charity to all the world.

**89—Joy to the world! the Lord is come**—From Psalm 98

**Antioch**—Arranged from George Frederick Handel (88)

With the exception of one word this free rendering of the last part of Psalm 98 by Isaac Watts is as it appeared in the 1719 edition of his *Psalms of David Imitated, etc.* For the first line of the second stanza Watts wrote,

> Joy to the earth! the Saviour reigns.

"Antioch" is said to be an arrangement from the *Messiah,* the oratorio by which Handel is best known. Some authorities state it is a sort of medley, the opening phrase being taken from the chorus, "Lift up your heads," and that part set to the words "and heaven and nature sing" (four measures), from the introduction to the tenor recitative, "Comfort ye, my people." It is also said to have been arranged by Lowell Mason. It appeared in his *Modern Psalmist,* 1839, where it is said to be "from Handel." In the index of this book it has placed before it an asterisk, indicating, as stated in the Preface, that it is a tune that has "either been arranged, adapted, or composed for this work, or taken from other recent works of the Editor." L. F. Benson says it was composed (or first appeared) in 1836.

J. T. Lightwood refers to the tune in the following paragraph:

> Students of Handel are aware how fond he is of the phrase:

> This has been used by some unknown artist to commence a tune very popular in some places, known as "Comfort," or "Antioch." It seems to be of American origin, and its source is usually stated to be "from Handel"; but Professor Prout, to whom I wrote on the subject, gives it as his opinion "that it is very far from Handel."

In the *Union Tune Book, a selection of Psalm and Hymn Tunes, suitable for use in Congregations and Sunday Schools,* arranged by Thomas Clark of Canterbury, published in London in 1842 (first edition, 1837), the following tune, called "Jerusalem," is found:

In *The Dulcimer,* I. B. Woodbury, 1850, this tune is called "Media" and is said to be "arranged from the *Surrey Chapel Music.*" The arrangement is somewhat different from that by Mason.

Charles Dingley says it is "also ascribed to C. Thompson." In Mason's early books the middle portion of the tune was for soprano and alto only. Someone later supplied tenor and bass parts, making it all in four-part harmony.

It has also been called "Comfort," "Holy Triumph," and "Messiah."

**90—As with gladness men of old**—William Chatterton Dix

**Dix** (18)—Abridged from a chorale by Conrad Kocher (18)

This Epiphany hymn, first published in the author's *Hymns of Love and Joy,* 1861, was written during an illness of Mr. Dix the previous year. A better text of the first two lines of the second stanza is that approved by the author for use in *Hymns Ancient and Modern*—namely:

As with joyful steps they sped,
Saviour to Thy lowly bed.

It was pointed out that Joseph and Mary had found shelter in a house before the arrival of the Wise Men. The original version, however, is still in quite general use in the United States, and is doubtless the most popular of its author's hymns. The Earl of Selborne includes this in his list of the better hymns written in the latter part of the last century. While this hymn was included in *The Methodist Episcopal Hymn Book* of 1878, it was omitted from *The Methodist Hymnal* of 1905. It is found in the *Methodist Protestant Church Hymnal* of 1901.

William Chatterton Dix, son of John Dix, a surgeon of Bristol, England, author of the *Life of Chatterton,* was born June 14, 1837. Educated at the Bristol Grammar School, he became manager of a marine insurance company at Glasgow. He was the author of several volumes of poetry and devotional works and his renderings of hymns from the Greek and Abyssinian are noteworthy. In 1866, in a paper on "English Church Hymnody," prepared by Lord Selborne for the York Church Conference, the writer said,

> I may be permitted to say that the most favorable hopes may be entertained of the future prospects of British hymnody, when among its most recent fruits is a work so admirable in every respect as the Epiphany Hymn of Mr. Chatterton Dix . . . "As with gladness men of old."

Mr. Dix died at Clifton, September 9, 1898.

**91—All my heart this night rejoices**—Paul Gerhardt
Translated by Catherine Winkworth (7)

**Stella** (Parker)—Horatio William Parker

Fröhlich soll mein Herze springen
Dieser Zeit,
Da vor Freud
Alle Engel singen.
Hört, hört, wie mit vollen Chören
Alle Luft
Laute ruft:
Christus ist geboren!

This is the original first stanza of Paul Gerhardt's carol-like hymn, which Miss Winkworth translated for her *Lyra Germanica,* 1858, second series. Of the fifteen stanzas written by Gerhardt Miss Winkworth translated only ten, for she says,

> In many instances even fine hymns are weakened by repetition or disfigured

> by verses of decidedly inferior merits; this is especially the case with Paul Gerhardt, notwithstanding the remarkable beauty of his works.

Three of the ten translated stanzas, 1, 4, and 5, comprise this cento. Lauxman says the hymn is "a glorious series of Christmas thoughts, laid as a garland on the manger at Bethlehem."

Paul Gerhardt, born March 12, 1607, was the son of the burgomaster of the little town of Gräfenhainichen, Saxony. Miss Winkworth tells us:

> The whole of his youth and early manhood fell in the time of war. That it must have been a period full of disappointment and hope deferred for him is clear enough when we find a man of his powers at the age of forty-five still only a private tutor and candidate for holy orders. In 1651 he was living in this capacity in the family of an advocate named Berthold, in Berlin. He had already written many hymns, but was as yet unable to publish them; and he was in love with Berthold's daughter, but had no living to marry upon. About the close of that year, however, the living of a country place called Mittlewalde was offered him; he was ordained, and in 1655 he at last married Anna Maria Berthold. At Mittlewalde he passed six quiet years, during which he began to publish his hymns, which immediately attracted great attention, and were quickly adopted into the hymnbooks of Brandenburg and Saxony. His name thus became known, and in 1657 he was invited to the great church of St. Nicholas, in Berlin, where his life was soon both a busy and honorable one. He worked most assiduously and successfully in his pastoral duties; he brought out many hymns, which were caught up by the people much as Luther's had been of old; and he was the favorite preacher of the city, whom crowds flocked to hear. He is described to us as a man of middle height, of quiet but firm and cheerful bearing; while his preaching is said to have been very earnest and persuasive, and full of Christian love and charity, which he practiced as well as preached by never turning a beggar from his doors, and receiving widows and orphans who needed help and shelter into his own house. His religion and his temperament alike made him cheerful, and not all the many disappointments of his life seem ever to have embittered his mood.

The terrible times of the Thirty Years' War were rich in sacred poetry. One of many who suffered from all its horrors truly said, "The dear cross hath pressed many songs out of me." Gerhardt, who undoubtedly holds first rank among hymn writers of Germany, wrote many of them "under circumstances which would have made most men cry rather than sing." He died at Lübben, June 7, 1676.

"Stella," written by Horatio W. Parker especially for this hymn, first appeared in the Protestant Episcopal *Hymnal* of 1894. In the Preface to *The Hymnal* of 1903, of which Doctor Parker was the editor, he says, "Clearly, we need not more tunes, but better ones, attaining a higher standard of musical worth and dignity." In this instance he has not only given us one more tune but a better one than that provided theretofore for this hymn.

Horatio William Parker was born in Auburndale, Massachusetts, September 15, 1863, his father an architect and his mother the daughter of a Baptist preacher. Until his fourteenth year he showed no inclination toward music—quite the reverse. But at fifteen he began composing of his own accord, and in two days wrote tunes for all of the fifty poems in Kate Greenaway's "Under the Window." Living near Boston, he had opportunities for studying with some of the best teachers in America. He was one of George W. Chadwick's

(316) first pupils. At the age of eighteen he went to Munich, where for three years he studied with Rheinberger. Upon his return to America he found a place in New York City, teaching at the National Conservatory of Music, of which, at that time, Antonin Dvorak was the head, but devoted most of his time to church music. In this latter interest he went to Boston as organist and choirmaster of Trinity Church during the encumbency of Phillips Brooks. In 1894 he was appointed professor of music of Yale, a position which he held until his death. He was very active and for years he was rushing from one appointment to another in Philadelphia, New York, Boston, and New Haven. Notwithstanding that he composed nearly one hundred works, he is best known for his *Hora Novissima,* the text for which was translated from the famous Latin hymn of Bernard by his mother. This work has been and still is included in the repertoires of the best choral organizations in America. It was the first work by an American composer to be given at the famous Three Choirs Festival at Worcester, England. Doctor Parker was as greatly admired in England as in his own country. Cambridge University conferred on him the degree of Doctor of Music in 1902. He was the winner of two ten thousand dollar prizes offered for operas composed by an American. Without doubt Horatio Parker was one of the most outstanding musicians America has produced. He died at Cedarhurst, New York, December 18, 1919.

**92—It came upon the midnight clear—Edmund Hamilton Sears**

**Carol—Richard Storrs Willis**

This hymn, entitled "Peace on earth," was sent to the editor of *The Christian Register,* Boston, a year before its publication, in December, 1850. It is one of the first of the carol-like hymns that seem to have sprung from American poets. Hymns stressing the social message of Christmas—"Peace on earth, good will toward men"—are distinctly American. This was the first one of its kind to be welcomed into British hymnody, being included in Bishop Bickersteth's *Hymnal Companion* in 1870, twenty years after its first appearance. The Rev. Dr. Morrison, who first published it, wrote, "I always feel that, however poor my Christmas sermon may be, the reading and singing of this hymn are enough to make up for all deficiencies."

Edmund H. Sears, born in Berkshire County, Massachusetts, April 6, 1810, and educated at Union College and Harvard Divinity School, was a Unitarian preacher, author, editor, and hymn writer. The author wrote to Bishop Bickersteth, "Though I was educated in the Unitarian denomination, I believe and preach the divinity of Christ." The greater part of his ministry was spent at Wayland, Massachusetts. Most of his hymns and poems were printed in the *Monthly Religious Magazine,* of which he was associate editor for twelve years. He died at Weston, January 14, 1876.

"Carol" is an arrangement by Uzziah C. Burnap of Richard S. Willis's "Study No. 23," made in 1850, the year this hymn was first printed.

Richard Storrs Willis, born in Boston, February 10, 1819, was the son of the founder of *The Youth's Companion.* Educated at Yale, he spent some time in Germany, and upon his return, while teaching colloquial German to Yale students, was advised by Charles A. Dana to go into journalism. He edited the *Musical Times,* later the *Musical World,* and the American edition of the life of his friend, Mendelssohn (33), whom he had met in Germany. He also wrote some books on the subject of church music. In his later life he lived in Detroit, Michigan, where he died, May 7, 1900.

**93—Christians, awake! salute the happy morn—John Byrom**

**Yorkshire**—John Wainwright

John Byrom one day asked his daughter what she would like for a Christmas present, and she replied, "Please write me a poem." On the next Christmas morning (1749), when she came to the breakfast table, she found on her plate a sheet of paper on which had been written a poem headed "Christmas Day. For Dolly." In one of his notebooks is found this entry:

> Christmas, 1750: The singing men and boys with Mr. Wainwright came here and sang "Christians, awake!"

It is from this poem of forty-eight lines that this hymn was taken. Owing to the fact that the poem was not divided into stanzas, the task of selecting the lines most suitable for use as a hymn has been no small one for editors. The length of the present selection is just one half that of the original. Thomas Cotterill (207) with James Montgomery (39) issued the ninth edition of *A Selection of Psalms and Hymns for Public and Private Use,* 1819, which was the first hymnbook to include a selection of John Byrom's lines for use as a hymn. The selection, doubtless made at the instigation of Montgomery, was one of six stanzas of six lines each, in which form it may be found in *Hymns Ancient and Modern.* As this was entirely too long, three stanzas were marked for optional use. It is interesting to note that two of the stanzas marked for possible omission have been included (as stanzas 2 and 3) in later books. Its marked out-of-door flavor makes it unusually attractive.

John Byrom, son of a linen-draper, was born at Manchester, England, February 29, 1692. He entered Trinity College, Cambridge, in 1708, became a fellow of the college in 1714, and took his M. A. degree two years later, but declined to take Holy Orders. Soon after he married his cousin. He studied medicine but gave up its practice to go to London to teach a system of shorthand writing which he had invented. A friend of John and Charles Wesley, he taught them the shorthand in which Charles Wesley wrote many of his hymns and in which his brother John wrote his *Journals.* Indicative of the fact that he did not seek publicity as an author, he signed his verses that appeared in *The Spectator* with the pseudonym "John Shadow." Interesting references to the evangelical revival in England are found in his *Journal and Letters.* John Wainwright said of him: "He has all the wit and humor of Doctor Swift, together with much more learning, a deep and strong understanding, and, above all, a serious vein of poetry." It was Byrom who originated "Tweedle-dum and Tweedle-dee" in his well-known epigram upon Handel and Buononcini, whose friends were quarreling over their relative merits as composers:

Some say, compared to Buononcini,
That mynheer Handel's but a ninny;
Others aver that he to Handel
Is scarcely fit to hold a candle.
Strange all this difference should be
'Twixt Tweedledum and Tweedledee.

Palgrave in his *Treasury of Sacred Song* said he "was one of the many men of strong feeling in whom faith burned 'like a hidden flame' throughout the eighteenth century." Upon succeeding to the family property through the death of an elder brother, Byrom removed to the family home near Manchester, where he spent the last part of his life quietly following his literary pursuits. He died September 28, 1763.

"Yorkshire"—some insist more properly "Stockport," as it was originally named—was sung first on Christmas Day, 1750, in the parish church of Stockport, England, probably having been written only a short while before. While it was included in only a few of the tune books until the middle of the nineteenth century, all the while it was sung by the English people as one of their most popular carol tunes to the words "Christians, awake!" It is sung now almost exactly as it was written by John Wainwright, who is thought to have been the organist at Stockport Church at the time (122).

John Wainwright, who was born in Stockport, England, was baptized April 14, 1723, and was buried there January 28, 1768, settled in Manchester as "singing man" in the Collegiate Church there, now the Cathedral. While he composed some anthems and other hymn tunes, and published a *Collection of Psalm Tunes, Anthems, Hymns, and Chants, etc.*, 1766, he is known by this one tune, "Stockport," or "Yorkshire."

**94—Love came down at Christmas—Christina Georgina Rossetti**

**Garton**—Traditional Irish melody

This little poetic gem, "where so much is said in so little space," first appeared in Christina G. Rossetti's *Time Flies; A Reading Diary,* 1885, with this last line,

Love the universal sign.

In a later edition the poem was greatly improved by the author's revision to,

Love for plea and gift and sign.

This hymn is not included in Doctor Julian's *Dictionary of Hymnology* because at the time of the publication of his *Supplement* in 1907 it had not been included in any hymnal.

Christina Georgina Rossetti was born in London, December 5, 1830, a member of an exceptionally brilliant family. She was the daughter of Gabrielle Rossetti, scholarly Italian refugee, and sister of Dante Gabrielle Rossetti, painter and poet, and William Michael Rossetti, author and critic. An elder sister, Maria Francesca Rossetti, who entered the Anglican sisterhood, is known to scholars by the *Shadow of Dante.* While Christina shared the studies of her gifted brothers and sisters, she was subjected to the more or less questionable influence of the eccentric Englishmen and the Italian exiles who were followers of her father. In her girlhood she had a peculiarly religious beauty of face that attracted the attention of the Pre-Raphaelite group of painters and she sat as a model not only to her brother, Dante, but to Millais and others. Such was her devotion to the Church of England that she felt compelled to decline an offer of marriage from a Roman Catholic, for whom she had a deep affection; consequent sorrow and disappointment affected her poetic writings. She loved children and had a remarkable gift of expressing lofty and subtle sentiments in language so simple and clear that any child might understand. Sir Edmund Gosse says at her best she may challenge comparison with the most admirable of the English poets. She had a fixed religious faith, held herself aloof from the world, was timid, and almost nunlike. During the last months of her life she suffered terribly from an incurable disease and died December 29, 1894.

Only comparatively recently have her poems been looked upon as hymnic material. Her verses appear for the first time in American Methodist hymnals in the 1935 book. "All that we need to know about her, save that she was a great saint, was that she was a great poet."

"Garton," a fine traditional Irish melody, one of the loveliest of the carol-like tunes, is said to be a favorite in County Donegal, Ireland.

**95—Thou didst leave Thy throne and Thy kingly crown**—Emily Elizabeth Steele Elliott

**Margaret (Elliott)**—Timothy Richard Matthews

The hymn was first printed in 1864 as a leaflet for use at St. Marks' Church, Brighton, England; in 1870 it was published in the *Church Missionary Juvenile Instructor,* which the author was editing at the time; was included in her *Chimes of Consecration,* 1880. With the exception of only a few changes it appears in this book as in the last named book. In many hymnals the words of the refrain are the same throughout the hymn, the change in the last stanza being somewhat confusing.

Emily Elizabeth Steele Elliott, daughter of the scholarly author of *Horae Apocalypticae,* was born at Brighton, England, July 22, 1836, and died at London, August 3, 1897. Forty-eight of the hymns constituting Part II of her *Chimes for Daily Life* were printed separately as *Under the Pillow,* a book, with tunes, especially for hospitals, infirmaries, and the sick generally. Her better-known aunt, Charlotte Elliott (198), also published an *Invalid's Hymn Book.*

"Margaret," or "Elliott," was written for this hymn by Timothy R. Matthews, and it was first published in *Children's Hymns,* 1876, a book issued by the Society for the Promotion of Christian Knowledge. Mr. Matthews called it "Margaret" but others have given it the name "Elliott" after Miss Elliott, the writer of the words.

Timothy Richard Matthews, an English clergyman and musician, who was born at Colmworth Rectory, near Bedford, England, November 4, 1826, and died at Tetney, Lincolnshire, January 5, 1910, was educated at Bradford Grammar School, and at Gonville and Caius College, Cambridge. He composed more than a hundred hymn tunes, some morning and evening services, a Christmas carol, and was the editor of the well-known *Village Organist* in its original form. He was a long-time friend of Sir George Elvey (170).

**96—O come, all ye faithful, joyful and triumphant**—Anonymous. Latin, 18th century. Translated by Frederick Oakeley, and others

**Adeste Fideles (Portuguese Hymn)**—Source unknown, 18th century melody

This popular translation of the Latin hymn "Adeste Fideles" is of unknown authorship and date. It may have had its origin in either France or Germany, probably the former, for it was sung there a great deal. No manuscript copies have been found dating earlier than the middle of the eighteenth century. Julian lists thirty-eight translations into English, that of Canon Oakeley originally beginning "Ye faithful approach ye," in 1841, and used at Margaret Street Chapel, London, until its publication as "O come, all ye faithful," in Murray's *Hymnal*, 1852. Although it was never published by the translator, the singing of it at the Chapel attracted attention. While there are eight stanzas in the original Latin, only three (1, 7, and 8) are now in common use:

1. Adeste, fideles,
Laeti triumphantes;
Venite, venite in Bethlehem;
Natum videte
Regem Angelorum:
Venite adoremus Dominum.

7. Cantet nunc hymnos,
Chorus Angelorum:
Cantet nunc aula celestium,
Gloria
In excelsis Deo!
Venite adoremus Dominum.

8. Ergo Qui natus
Die hodierna.
Jesu Tibi sit gloria:
Patris Aeterni
Verbum Caro factum!
Venite adoremus Dominum.

Its popularity is due to its measure, its lilt, and its fine tune. Doctor Oakeley's original text has been included in Roman Catholic hymnals, but slight changes and the omission of the greater part of the hymn are common to Protestant books.

The translation used in the 1905 *Methodist Hymnal* was by Edward Caswall (31).

Frederick Oakeley, D.D., was born at Shrewsbury, England, September 5, 1802, the son of a former governor of Madras. Educated privately and at Oxford, he became a fellow at Balliol College, and took orders in the Church of England, being prebendary at Lichfield Cathedral, preacher at Whitehall, and incumbent of Margaret Chapel, London. Interested in the Oxford Movement, he published pamphlets of such controversial nature that he was forced to resign all of his appointments in the English Church. He followed John H. Newman (514) into the Roman Church and for many years was canon of the diocese of Westminster. His publications were numerous, some having considerable value. He died January 29, 1880.

Nothing is known of the writer of the tune "Adeste Fideles," or "Portuguese Hymn," as it is also called. For a long time this tune was supposed to have been written by one of two men, father and son, both named John Reading. The elder was an English organist who died in 1692. His son, 1677-1764, was also a well-known organist and choirmaster. One reason for attributing the tune to one of these men is the appearance of the title "Air of Reading, 1680," over the tune in a book *Home Music, the Congregational and Chorister's Psalm Book, &c.,* issued by Vincent Novello in London, in 1843. It was set to Psalm 106. The following note appears in connection with the tune:

> This piece obtained its name of "The Portuguese Hymn" from the accidental circumstance of the Duke of Leeds, who was a director of the Concert of Ancient Music, many years since (about the year 1785), having heard the hymn first performed at the Portuguese Chapel, and who, supposing it to be peculiar to the service in Portugal, introduced the melody at the Ancient Concerts, giving it the title of "The Portuguese Hymn," by which appellation this very favorite and popular tune has ever since been distinguished; but it is by no means confined to the choir of the Portuguese Chapel, being the regular Christmas hymn, "Adeste Fideles," that is sung in every Catholic chapel throughout England.

That accounts for the name "Portuguese Hymn," but other evidence goes to show that neither of the Readings wrote the tune.

The claim that this tune was written by Marcos Antonio da Fonesca (1762-1830), a Portuguese musician known as "Il Portogallo," is invalidated by the fact that it appeared eleven years before he was born.

It appears in a small book, *An Essay on the Plain Chant,* London, 1782 (35). This book was issued in three parts, and it is in Part Second that this tune is found. The heading is "Part Second, containing several Anthems, Litanies, Proses, and Hymns, as they are sung in the Public Chapels in London." This is the earliest printed book in which it has been found. There is preserved in the library at Stonyhurst College, Lancashire, a volume in manuscript under date of 1751, which contains the hymn "Adeste Fideles," set to this tune. It is the work of John Francis Wade, apparently an itinerant whose business was to copy music for Roman Catholic institutions and families. The hymn, in four stanzas, is entitled "In Nativitate Domini Hymnus."

**97—The first Noel, the angel did say**—Old English carol

**The First Noel**—Traditional melody from W. Sandys' Christmas Carols

This cento is taken from William Sandys' *Christmas Carols Ancient and Modern,* 1833, with only slight changes. Another "rougher" version had appeared in Davis Gilbert's *Ancient Christmas Carols* in 1823. The entire carol consists of nine stanzas, of which 1, 2, 3, 4, and 6 are used here.

Stanza 2 is not quite correct historically—the shepherds did not see the star. It is more for Epiphany than Christmas, for since the fifth century, in the Western Church, Epiphany commemorates the coming of the Magi as the occasion of the manifestation of Christ to the Gentiles. This carol makes an excellent seasonal processional.

William Sandys was born in London in 1792 and died there February 18, 1874. He was a lawyer, yet an enthusiastic musical amateur, playing the 'cello well. His other interests may be noted from some of his book titles: *A History of Freemasonry; Specimens of Cornish Dialect; History of the Violin;* and a monograph, *Christmastide: Its History*. He did great service in calling attention to the beauty and interest of carols and did much not only to preserve them but to stimulate interest in them. With Charles Dickens, he did much to restore interest in the celebration of Christmas as a Christian festival in England. Parliament had forbidden its observance in 1644, and, although Charles II revived the feast, it did not fully take on its Christian significance until the beginning of the nineteenth century. Hitherto the occasion, observed as a time of feasting and merrymaking when the waits sang carols, could not be looked upon as a form of religious observance. The prosaic and formal world of the seventeenth century ignored the carol. Sandys was one of the most influential in restoring it to favor.

"The First Noel" is the traditional tune for this carol. The French word "Noël" (English—"Nowell") may have some association with the Latin *novella* (news), but it more likely came from the Provençal *nadal,* a corruption of the Latin *natalis* ("birthday").

**98—There's a song in the air!**—Josiah Gilbert Holland
**Christmas Song**—Karl Pomeroy Harrington (10)

This modern Christmas carol by J. G. Holland, first published by the author in his *Complete Poetical Writings,* 1879, has attained great popularity during the last twenty-five years. Its first appearance in any hymnal was in *The Methodist Hymnal* of 1905, and, largely because of the lovely tune "Christmas Song," written for it by Professor Harrington, it became popular almost at once. This is one of the best of Holland's poems.

Josiah Gilbert Holland, born at Belchertown, Massachusetts, July 24, 1819, and who died at New York City, October 12, 1881, for a time attended the Northampton, Massachusetts, high school, but because of poor health was not able to complete its courses required for graduation. For a time he taught school, carried on a business in photography, and conducted a writing school. At the age of twenty-one he began the study of medicine, graduating from Berkshire Medical College, and tried practicing his profession in Springfield. Successively abandoning the practice of medicine and the teaching profession, he established a weekly paper which lived six months, later joining the editorial forces of the Springfield, Massachusetts, *Republican,* making himself widely known as the writer of the "Timothy Titcomb Letters." Their humor and common sense gained for them general favor. Mr. Holland planned *Scribner's Magazine,* of which he was editor from its beginning until his death.

Some of his novels appeared in its columns. He published four or five books of poems, that which met with the most favor being "Bitter Sweet."

"Christmas Song," one of the loveliest of carol tunes, was written by Professor Karl Harrington (10) in July, 1904, while he was vacationing at his summer cottage at North Woodstock, New Hampshire. Of the three settings of these verses in the last *Hymnal,* this was the only one sung. It is this tune that has made "There's a song in the air" probably the most loved Christmas song among the school children of America.

**99—Long years ago o'er Bethlehem's hills—Leigh Richmond Brewer**

**Weihnacht—Karl Pomeroy Harrington (10)**

The author of this carol, Bishop Brewer, wrote it in 1892 just before Christmas. It was written as a Christmas greeting and remembrance to a friend who had just given him five thousand dollars to assist in carrying on certain missionary work in the Protestant Episcopal diocese in Montana. It was written in five four-line stanzas. The last stanza, not included in the hymn, was:

God bless all those who help to give
From burdens a release!
God send his blessings on their homes
And fill their lives with peace!

These stanzas were first set to music by C. Whitney Coombs, once as a solo and again as a quartet. Bishop Brewer, however, was not satisfied with these as he wanted the song sung by children at Christmas festivals. Mr. Coombs tried to make such a setting but was not successful, and the hymn never became favorably known until its inclusion in *The Methodist Hymnal* of 1905 with an entirely new musical setting by Professor Karl P. Harrington. It has not been used in other denominational hymnbooks. In Julian's *Dictionary of Hymnology* the hymn is erroneously credited to C. Whitney Coombs, who first composed music for it. Julian secured his information from the first edition of the 1905 book where the wrong credit was given.

Leigh Richmond Brewer was born at Berkshire, Vermont, in 1839, and died at Helena, Montana. Educated at Hobart College and General Theological Seminary, he served churches in New York state from his ordination until his consecration as Missionary Bishop of Montana, where he served until his death in 1916.

"Weihnacht," that is, Holy Night (Christmas Eve), is a fitting name for this excellent Christmas music, written by Professor Karl P. Harrington in 1903 or 1904, and first published in 1905, in *The Methodist Hymnal.*

**100—O little town of Bethlehem—Phillips Brooks**

**St. Louis—Lewis Henry Redner**

In 1865 Phillips Brooks, then a young preacher in Philadelphia, spent some time in the Holy Land. On the day before Christmas he rode from Jerusalem to Bethlehem and went into the fields where, we are told, the shepherds were abiding. On that Christmas Eve he attended a service at the ancient Church of the Nativity, not far from the place where Christ was born. Three years later he wrote this hymn for the children of his Philadelphia Sunday school to sing at their Christmas service. It was given its present musical setting by the organist of Holy Trinity Church, of which Doctor Brooks was the rector, Lewis H. Redner, also superintendent of the Sunday school there. The hymn and tune were printed on leaflets and became known locally, but it was not until about twenty-five years later that it was included in *The Hymnal* of the Protestant Episcopal Church. Its first appearance in a book was in 1874, when the Rev. William R. Huntington, of Worcester, Massachusetts, edited a hymnal for Sunday schools. Doctor Ninde says,

> Unnumbered multitudes who will never hear the matchless voice of the great preacher, or even read one of his sermons, are singing with grateful joy, "O little town of Bethlehem."

Originally in five stanzas, the fourth has not been included in hymnals, the author himself omitting it from some of his later copies of the poem. It is:

> Where children, pure and happy,
> Pray to the Blessed Child;
> Where misery cries out to thee,
> Son of Mother mild;
> Where charity stands watching,
> And faith holds wide the door,
> The dark night wakes, the glory breaks,
> And Christmas comes once more.

Phillips Brooks, born December 13, 1835, a native of Boston, tried teaching in Boston Latin School after his graduation from Harvard, but proved a "conspicuous failure." He then attended the Episcopal Theological Seminary, Alexandria, Virginia, and was ordained in 1859, serving the Church of the Advent and Holy Trinity, Philadelphia, before going to the famous Trinity Church, Boston. There he became the "dominant pulpit force of all New England" because "he dared preach Jesus Christ" in that Unitarian stronghold. In 1891, after refusing many offers of preferment, he was made Protestant Episcopal Bishop of Massachusetts. Doctor Brooks learned hymns at his home when a boy. It is said that he knew two hundred by heart when he entered Harvard and was heard singing them each morning in his room after arising from his bed. He wrote other carols, but he was not a poet: he was a preacher, one of the most eloquent America has produced. Lovable, warmhearted, his delight in the society of children was one of his most interesting characteristics. A bachelor, he kept several dolls at his rectory so that his nieces might have them to play with when they visited him. His verses about the Christ Child are the most beautiful he ever wrote. He died January 23, 1893. When told of Bishop Brooks's death, a little girl of five exclaimed "Oh, mama, how happy the angels will be!"

> Posterity will never see his princely form towering six feet and a half in height; and his majestic face, combining the thoughtfulness and fire of Webster with the sweetness of Fénelon or Fletcher; and his massive frame, impressing one at first as a giant, yet so filled with light and life that he seemed as radiant as an angel.

"St. Louis" was written by Lewis H. Redner at the request of Doctor

Brooks. On the Saturday night preceding the day he wished to use it, Doctor Brooks asked Mr. Redner to set it to music. Sometime during the night the melody was evolved and it was harmonized early in the morning ready in time for Sunday school. Several other tunes have been written for these verses and have been published, but there is such an affinity here between hymn and tune that they are now inseparable in this country. While the words have extensive use in England, the tunes there generally used are "Forest Green," a traditional air, and "Bethlehem" (not 391), a tune written for it by Sir Joseph Barnby (31).

Lewis Henry Redner was organist at Holy Trinity Church, Philadelphia, and superintendent of the Sunday school there during the incumbency of Phillips Brooks. He was born at Philadelphia in 1831 and died at Atlantic City in 1908. At the age of sixteen, after attending public school in Philadelphia, he was employed by a real-estate firm and showed such aptitude for the business that he was made a member of the firm at the age of twenty-one. Later going into business for himself, he became a wealthy real-estate operator. His interests, other than those of his business, were in church work, particularly that of the Sunday school, and music. With Doctor Brooks he organized the Sunday school at Trinity Chapel, where "St. Louis" was first sung, with six teachers and thirty-six children. During his superintendency of nineteen years the school and Bible classes increased to more than one thousand in number. Mr. Redner served as organist in four different churches in his native city during his lifetime. He never married, making his home with his sister, Mrs. Sarah H. Sagers. From a tribute paid him by Dr. Floyd W. Tomkins, of Holy Trinity, the following is taken:

> He held to the old paths, not in any blind conservatism which forbade growth, but with the firm conviction that the religion of our fathers is still needed to bring men to God. . . . That such a man has lived and done his work is but another proof of the undying presence of Christ with His Church.

**101—The Kings of the East are riding—Katharine Lee Bates**

**Wallace—Clarence Grant Hamilton**

Mrs. George Sargent Burgess, niece of Miss Bates, has stated that this hymn was written prior to 1915 and that it was first published in a magazine "with illustrations," but she was unable to furnish the name of the magazine, as "my records of my aunt's go back only to 1915."

Katharine Lee Bates, LL.D., was born at Falmouth, Massachusetts, August 12, 1859. Her college education was obtained at Wellesley, and after her graduation she engaged in teaching at the Natick High School and at Dana Hall before returning to her Alma Mater as an instructor in English literature. She was advanced to a full professorship in 1891, continuing as such until her retirement from active teaching in 1925. The editor of many editions of classic texts in American and English literature, the author of seventeen books, she published her first poems in 1887. Wellesley honored her with its LL.D., as did Middlebury and Oberlin Colleges with the degree of Litt.D. She died at Wellesley, March 29, 1929.

"Wallace" was written for this hymn of Miss Bates for the *Wellesley Song Book,* 1914.

Clarence Grant Hamilton, Mus. Doc., was born at Providence, Rhode Island, June 6, 1865, and received his education in the city schools of Providence and at Brown University. After his graduation from college in 1888, he taught in his home city until 1904, going from there to Wellesley College. There he was made associate professor, and later professor of music. In addition to his teaching, he has acted as organist at the Congregational Church, has composed piano pieces, songs, and anthems, and has written several books about music. His *Outlines of Music History,* first issued in 1908, is an authoritative work. He died in 1935.

**102—We three kings of Orient are—John Henry Hopkins, Jr.**

**Kings of Orient—John Henry Hopkins, Jr.**

This carol from Doctor Hopkins's *Carols, Hymns, and Songs,* 1862, is the story, in verse, of the kings of the Orient bearing gifts to the Infant Jesus.

John Henry Hopkins, Jr., D.D., son of a Bishop of Vermont, was born at Pittsburgh, Pennsylvania, October 28, 1820; educated at the University of Vermont; for some time was preacher at Williamsport, Pennsylvania; and died at Troy, New York, August 13, 1891. He published at least two books of poems, from one of which, *Poems by the Wayside,* 1883, several hymns have been taken, though none of them appear in *The Methodist Hymnal.*

"Kings of Orient" was written for this hymn by its author, John H. Hopkins, Jr.

**103—In Bethlehem 'neath star-lit skies—Grace May Stutsman**

**Waits' Carol—Grace May Stutsman**

This hymn and tune by Miss Stutsman were printed on a card and sent to her friends as a Christmas greeting in 1927. Contrary to the usual procedure in song writing, both words and music were composed simultaneously. This fine contribution to the store of modern carols is particularly effective when sung antiphonally.

Grace May Stutsman, a native of Melrose, Massachusetts, received her early education from private tutors, and, for a brief period, in the public schools of Indianapolis, Indiana. She attended Boston University and graduated from the New England Conservatory of Music, winning the Endicott prize in song composition together with a scholarship for graduate work. During Miss Stutsman's preparation for a career as a concert pianist, she became so interested in music education that she made an extended survey of methods and materials used in teaching public-school methods in the principal cities of the East and Middle West. For a time she was head of the department of music in the Wykenham Rise School for Girls, leaving this appointment to lecture on adult education in Musical Appreciation for the Extension Division of the Massachusetts State Board of Education. In recent years Miss Stutsman has been acting as music critic and analyst for *The Christian Science Monitor,* Boston, and *Musical America,* New York. She has written much for various newspapers and magazines. Most of her composition in various musical forms has been done for her own enjoyment, or that of her friends.

"Waits' Carol" was especially arranged by its composer for *The Methodist Hymnal* of 1935.

**104—In the bleak midwinter—Christina Georgina Rossetti (94)**

**Cranham—Gustav Holst**

This literary gem was published in Christina G. Rossetti's *Poetical Works,* 1904, as "Before 1872." A welcome addition to our hymnals, it was first used as a hymn in the *English Hymnal,* 1906, at once became popular, and has been included in many of the best late collections.

"Cranham" was written by Gustav Holst for this hymn. It was first published in *The English Hymnal* in 1906. The composition, as simple and unpretentious as the words, has had much to do with the popularity of the song.

Gustav Theodore Holst, eminent English composer and teacher, was born at Cheltenham, England, September 21, 1874, and died at London, after an operation, May 25, 1934. His great-grandfather came to England from Sweden in 1808. Early discouraged by symptoms of neuritis from preparation for piano concertizing, he took up the study of organ and trombone and, when only seventeen years old, held a responsible position as organist. For five years he was trombonist in the Scottish Orchestra and later played with the Carol Rosa Opera Company. Upon the completion of his musical education at the Royal College of Music he taught composition there. During the Great War he was sent to Salonika by the Y. M. C. A. to take charge of musical activities. He visited in America in 1923 and was Cramb Lecturer at the University of Glasgow in 1925. The fine quality of religious sentiment with which all his fifty works are imbued is especially characteristic of his outstanding *Hymn of Jesus.* Written in 1919, it was hailed as the greatest work by an English composer of the twentieth century, and will probably outlast his other compositions. Although handicapped by painful illness, a marked timidity, and a hypersensitiveness to criticism, his energy and enthusiasm seemed endless, and he attained high rank as a teacher and composer.

**105—Infant holy, Infant lowly—From the Polish**
English words by Edith Margaret Gellibrand Reed

**W̧ Zlobie Lezy (Polish Carol)—Arranged by Edith Margaret Gellibrand Reed**

This beautiful Nativity song is an adaptation from the Polish carol "W̧ zlobie lezy" (In manger lying) made by Miss Reed c. 1925.

Edith Margaret Gellibrand Reed was born at London, March 31, 1885, and died there, June 4, 1933. She was educated at Clifton High School, St. Leonard's School, St. Andrews, and at the Guildhall School of Music, London. She was an Associate of the Royal College of Organists and assisted Percy Scholes in editorial work. During Doctor Scholes's absence in France during the World War she carried on the editing of *The Music Student, Music and Youth,* and *Panpipes,* continuing as editor of the two last-named publications after the close of the war. She visited America twice in the interests of *Music and Youth.* In addition to her editorial work she wrote two Christmas mystery plays and was the author of one volume of *Story Lives of the Great Composers.* She lived a particularly active life, being devoted to hiking, sailing, swimming, and camping. Miss Reed walked around most of the coast of England and Wales.

**106—Silent night, holy night**—Joseph Mohr
Translation compiled from various sources

**Stille Nacht**—Franz Grüber

These words were given to Franz Grüber, the composer of the music, by his friend, Joseph Mohr, the author of the words, as a Christmas present in 1818. The presentation was made on Christmas Eve when preparations were being made for a celebration to be held in the schoolhouse of the village of Arnsdorf, where Grüber was the teacher. The same evening the recipient of the gift wrote the music with which all are familiar and he with other friends sang it to a guitar accompaniment played by the author. The song was taken up by itinerant minstrels and sung by them over much of South Germany and Austria. It seems to have been introduced into American hymnody by Charles L. Hutchins, who used it in his *Sunday School Hymnal* in 1871. The translation used in *The Methodist Hymnal* has been compiled from various sources.

Joseph Mohr was born at Salzburg, Austria, December 11, 1792, and died at Wagrein, December 4, 1848. He was ordained a Roman Catholic priest in 1815 and spent all of his life serving churches in the vicinity of his birthplace. Whether or not he wrote other hymns is not known. This is the only one that has been translated into English.

Franz Grüber, an Austrian, was born at Hochburg, November 25, 1787, and like his friend, Joseph Mohr, lived all of his life not far from Salzburg. He was schoolmaster in the little village of Arnsdorf and served as parish organist. It is not known that he ever wrote any other music than this tune, certainly none other which has been published. He died June 7, 1863, at Hallein.

**107—Gentle Mary laid her Child**—Joseph Simpson Cook

**Tempus Adest Floridum**—A Spring Carol, c. 14th century
Arranged by Ernest MacMillan

This hymn, which appeared first in *The Hymnary of the United Church of Canada,* 1930, was Doctor Cook's only contribution to hymnody.

Joseph Simpson Cook, D.D., born in Durham County, England, December

4, 1859, came to Canada in his early manhood and studied at Wesleyan College of McGill University, in Montreal. He went into the United Church of Canada and died at Toronto, May 27, 1933.

"Tempus Adest Floridum" is the first line of "A Spring Carol" which Dr. J. M. Neale (52) turned into a Christmas carol by writing the "Good King Wencelas" legend in verse. It is to be regretted that the tune has become so definitely associated with "Good King Wencelas" as to give the general impression that it originated as a Christmas song. Such is not the case; it originally was a spring carol. No matter what its first association, it is a jolly tune quite fitting for this lovely Nativity hymn. It is found in *Piae Cantiones,* compiled by Theodoricus Petrus of Nyland, Finland, 1582, while he was a student at Rostock, near Lübeck. It was from the British Minister at Stockholm that this very rare book came into the possession of Doctor Neale. This copy of *Piae Cantiones,* probably unique, containing many exquisite sixteenth-century tunes, some used by the Reformed Lutherans of Finland and Sweden, is now in the British Museum. With the Rev. Thomas Helmore, Doctor Neale selected from it carols which were published as *Carols for Christmastide,* 1835, and *Carols for Eastertide,* 1854.

Sir Ernest Campbell MacMillan, Mus. Doc., son of Dr. Alexander MacMillan, secretary of the Committee on Church Worship and Ritual which prepared *The Hymnary of the United Church of Canada,* was born at Mimico, Ontario, August 18, 1893. When only ten years of age he appeared as organist in Massey Music Hall, Toronto; at thirteen he became an Associate of the Royal College of Organists; and four years later, a Fellow. In the same year he graduated as Bachelor of Music from Oxford University. His education was received at various institutions in Canada, England, Scotland, and France. Happening to be on a visit to the German musical center, Bayreuth, at the outbreak of the World War in 1914, he was interned in the Ruhleben prison camp. A leader in the musical activities carried on in this camp, he composed *England,* a major work for soli, orchestra, and chorus, which won for him Oxford's coveted degree of Doctor of Music. At the termination of the war he returned to Canada and located in Toronto, where he made an immediate impression by his outstanding musical personality. In 1926 he succeeded Dr. A. S. Vogt as principal of the Toronto Conservatory of Music, and a year later as dean of the Faculty of Music of the University of Toronto. He was knighted in the list of birthday honors of the late King George in 1935. Doctor MacMillan has earned an enviable reputation as a composer, a conductor, and as a concert organist. He has a prodigious memory, easily carrying in his mind not only the notes of the most intricate compositions, but, in the case of vocal works, the words as well. To Doctor MacMillan should go the credit for the remarkable progress the Toronto Symphony Orchestra has made in recent years.

**108—Harken, all! What holy singing**—Anonymous

Gloria—Old French carol

These words were taken from a mystery play entitled *The Nativity,* published in 1922. The author is not known.

"Gloria" is the name given to a tune sung to an old French carol beginning "Les anges dans nos campagnes" (87).

**109—What Child is this, who, laid to rest**—William Chatterton Dix (90)

**Greensleeves**—Old English melody

This is one of the many Christmas carols written by William C. Dix. His *Christmas Customs and Christmas Carols* contain several others.

"Greensleeves," an old English melody, in *New Christmas Carols,* 1642, was used to the words of a New Year carol. A fine, rollicking tune, quite typical of the happiness of the old carol, it may be used very effectively as a solo, or with the soprano singing the words of the stanzas while the other voices hum an accompaniment, all parts singing the words of the refrain.

**110—Good Christian men, rejoice**—From the Latin
Translated by John Mason Neale (52)

**In Dulci Jubilo**—14th century German melody—Harmonized by Winfred Douglas

This carol appearing in Doctor Neale's *Carols for Christmastide,* 1853, can hardly be called a translation from the Latin. In fact, the poem upon which it is founded is more German than Latin. Doctor Neale's free rendering was made to accord with the old carol tune, named from the first line of the old macaronic (that is, mixed language) poem, "In dulce jubilo." This "patois carol" came from the time—the late 14th century—when the creeping of the vernacular into sacred song was first noted. This practice aided the early reformers in introducing congregational singing in the vernacular into their services of worship. Luther, it will be remembered, violated at will all German rules of word order in fitting German words to tunes with which the people were familiar. Because of the importance of this carol and the very great interest in it, it is quoted in full with a free translation in a parallel column:

| | |
|---|---|
| In dulce jubilo | In sweet shouting (or jubilation) |
| Nu singet und seyt fro! | Now sing and be joyful! |
| Unsers herzen wonne | The joy of our hearts |
| Leyt in praesepio | Lies in a manger |
| Und leuchtet als die sonne | And shines like the sun |
| Matris in gremio | In the lap of his mother. |
| Alpha es et O! | Alpha and Omega! |
| | |
| O Jesus, parvule, | O tiny Jesus, |
| Nach dir ist mir so we; | For you I long so much; |
| Tröst mir myn gemüte, | Comforting soul, |
| O puer optime, | O best of boys, |
| Durch aller juncfrawen güte, | Through all thy mother's grace, |
| O princeps gloriae. | O Prince of Glory. |
| Trahe me post te! | Draw me after thee! |
| | |
| O patris caritas! | O love of the Father! |
| O Nati lenitas' | O gentleness of the Son! |
| Wir weren all verloren | We should all be lost |
| Per nostra crimina; | Through our crimes |
| So hat er uns erworben | But he has gained for us |
| Coelorum gaudia. | Joys of heaven. |
| Eya, wär wir da! | O that we were there! |

| | |
|---|---|
| Ubi sunt guadia | Where are there joys |
| Nirgend mer denn da? | Ever more than these? |
| Da die engel singen | Where angels are singing |
| Nova cantica, | New songs, |
| Und die schellen klingen | And the bells are ringing |
| In Regis curia. | In the court of the King. |
| Eya, wär wir da! | O that we were there! |

Canon Charles Winfred Douglas, America's leading authority in the field of Protestant liturgical music, was born at Oswego, New York, February 15, 1867; received his Mus. Bac. degree from Syracuse University in 1891; was a student at St. Andrew's Divinity School, Syracuse; studied church music in England, France, and Germany (plain chant under Mocquerean at Solesmes); and received his Doctorate degree in music from Nashotah House, Wisconsin, in 1916. He served churches as organist in Syracuse, New York City, Denver, and Fond Du Lac, Wisconsin, and while in Denver was minor-canon, then canon, at St. John's Cathedral. Canon Douglas has written and lectured on musical subjects, conducted summer schools of church music, adapted English texts to Russian church music, edited hymnals, and is a well-known author of books. At present he is the director of music at St. Mary's Convent (Protestant Episcopal), Peekskill, New York.

# Life

**111—Fairest Lord Jesus, Ruler of all nature—From the German, 17th century**
**Crusader's Hymn—From Schlesische Volkslieder, 1842**
**Arranged by Richard Storrs Willis (92)**

Because of the great popularity of this hymn and tune in the United States it may be well to discuss them at some length. Although the tune, in a form similar in many respects to "Crusader's Hymn," is popular in England, the words to which it is sung are either those of Doctor Watts's rendering of Psalm 122 (second part), beginning,

How pleased and blest am I,

or, particularly among the Methodists, that by Benjamin Rhodes, the first line of which is,

My heart and voice I raise.

The hymn beginning "Fairest Lord Jesus" seems not to be known in England. In a search through some thirty odd present-day books it has not been found.

Its popularity (both hymn and tune) in America dates from 1850, when Richard Storrs Willis included it in his *Church Chorals and Choir Studies.* For a time Mr. Willis's name was attached to the hymn, the impression given being that he had either written or translated it. He, however, disclaimed any literary connection with it and stated that he did not know where he had found it.

The same year that Willis published his book there appeared in *Evangelical Christendom,* an English journal, this article:

> An unexpected treasure was discovered in 1850 in the guise of a Crusader's Hymn. It was found in Westphalia amid a number of other curious relics, and according to the traditional text by which it was accompanied this hymn used to be sung by the German Pilgrims on their way to Jerusalem. It may, therefore, be regarded as a national air of that time.
>
> A musical note calls this one of the most remarkable discoveries of modern research. It achieved great popularity at the time of its discovery. It has already become a chief favorite with the people, and is sung by all classes and ages from the shepherd on the hillside to the lisping urchin in the nursery. At a missionary meeting lately held in the Principality of Lippedetmold (Lippe-Detmold) it was commenced by three voices only, yet, ere the third verse was reached, hundreds joined in the heart-stirring song of praise. From that period it has been progressing from meeting to meeting through the Rhinish provinces and thus bids fair to rival the popularity of P. Gerhardt's celebrated hymn "Befiehl du deine Wege" ("Commit thou all thy ways.")
>
> We are told how the Halls of Köthen echoed to its melody, and there, where a few years since, the Friends of Light held their sittings and triumphed in the thought of having deposed King Jesus from His throne, this hymn was eagerly copied and traveled thence to many distant and far-scattered villages.

The tune referred to (accompanying the article) is that given by Willis. It was printed on a leaflet set to an English translation of the German "Schönster Herr Jesu," a hymn dating from 1677. Neither the author of the hymn nor its translator is known.

A variant of this tune, called "Ascalon" (referred to above), came into English hymnody in 1861, when Doctor Gauntlett (442) used it in his *Congregational Psalmodist,* the source being given as "Crusaders' Melody."

The "unexpected treasure" of *Evangelical Christendom* had been published in a book of Silesian folk songs (Schlesische Volkslieder), Leipzig, 1842. This book was the joint product of the labors of Dr. Heinrich August Hoffmann (1798-1874), distinguished poet and philologist, and Ernst Friedrich Richter (1808-1879), the successor to Moritz Hauptmann at the Thomasschule in Leipzig. In the Preface to this book Doctor Hoffmann says:

> In the summer of 1836 I visited a friend in the country. Toward evening I heard the haywardens sing. I made inquiries. They sang folk songs which to me seemed worthy of collection. For this purpose I associated myself with my friend Richter. We divided the work between us; to him fell the musical portion, to me the rest.

The tune which the English call "Ascalon" was one of the songs the "haywardens" sang. It is

set to "Schönster Herr Jesu."

The hymn beginning, "My heart and voice I raise," by the Rev. Benjamin Rhodes (1743-1815), became very popular with English Methodists before the middle of the last century. It had associated with it a tune called "Dalston," a tune in the proper meter found in Rippon's *Selection of Psalm and Hymn Tunes,* 1806, where it was taken presumably from Aaron Williams (227). This was used extensively for about fifty years. There is a resemblance to "Crusaders' Hymn" in the first part of the tune, which appears in Williams's *Psalmody in Miniature,* 1778:

While all this was going on, this melody ("Crusaders' Hymn") appeared in *The Legend of St. Elizabeth,* by Franz Liszt, finished in 1862. In the Preface to *St. Elizabeth,* Liszt expressed his thanks to Herrn Cantor Gottschlag for calling his attention to the "Pilgrims' Song" which he had used in the work. C. A. Barry (1830-1915), an English writer on musical subjects, in his Preface to the English version of the Liszt oratorio, wrote:

> The "Trio," as it may be regarded, which occurs twice in the Crusaders' March, and again in the sixth scene, is derived from an old Pilgrims' Song, supposed to date from the time of the Crusaders.

Barry later gave the acknowledgment to Liszt as his authority for saying that the song dated from the time of the Crusaders.

Not longer ago than 1916 (October) an article appeared in the *Musical Times,* London, stating that the "original source [of the tune] has now been traced to a melody in a choralbuch by J. G. Schicht in 1819. This tune—

is no more the "Crusaders' Hymn" than "Dalston," yet there is some similarity in the first measures of the two. Probably there is no connection whatever.

All that is known definitely is that the hymn, "Schönster Herr Jesu," appeared in the *Münster Gesangbuch,* in 1677, and the tune called "Ascalon" in Hoffmann and Richter's *Silesian Folksongs* of 1842. But how may one reconcile the "arrangement" by Richard Storrs Willis in 1850, the "discovery" referred to in *Evangelical Christendom* the same year, and the "Pilgrims' Song" used by Liszt? The inference is that the tune that Liszt used was probably the folk tune, and that "Ascalon" was the result of Richter's editing of it. If that is the case, then Willis has given us the original melody. It is hoped that additional research may bring to light new facts concerning this interesting tune.

**112—I know not how that Bethlehem's Babe—Harry Webb Farrington**

**Shirleyn—Earl Enyeart Harper**

In 1910 Harvard University sponsored a competition for a Christmas Hymn. Harry Webb Farrington, then a graduate student there, won the prize with this hymn which he hesitated to submit because its style was so simple and unpretentious. Though it received the unanimous vote of the committee of judges, probably they did not know when they voted that the hymn had been composed in less than half an hour. George Herbert Palmer, late Alford Professor of Natural Religion, Harvard University, has said this is "a perfect poem." It has become, deservedly, one of our most loved Christmas hymns because it says so much in so few lines.

Harry Webb Farrington was born at Nassau, Bahama Islands, July 14, 1880. He was educated at Syracuse University, Boston University School of Theology, and Harvard University. Greatly interested in children, he organized the Week Day Church School at Gary, Indiana, in 1914, at the time that young industrial city was finding its conglomerate racial problem a difficult one. Going to France at the beginning of the World War to serve the *Foyers du Soldat,* he received an honorary commission in the Seventh and Tenth Cuirassiers. Upon his return from the war Farrington devoted a large part of his time to lecturing to children in the public schools. In 1920 and 1921 he published, each year, a volume of his poems. He has written other excellent hymns (555) and some books dealing with the lives of such distinguished Americans as George Washington, Benjamin Franklin, Abraham Lincoln, and Theodore Roosevelt. An ordained Methodist Episcopal minister, he was a member of the New York East Conference. He died October 25, 1931.

"Shirleyn" was written especially for this hymn by Dr. Earl Enyeart Harper while compiling *The Abingdon Hymnal,* 1928. The prize tune "Veritas" selected for the hymn not having proved entirely satisfactory, Doctor Harper submitted "Shirleyn" to the author's widow, and only after its approval by her did he include it in the book he was then editing. Acting upon the suggestion of Mrs. Farrington, "St. Agnes" is offered as an alternative tune.

Earl Enyeart Harper, LL.D., son of a Methodist preacher, was born at Craig, Missouri, March 28, 1895, and received his education at Nebraska Wesleyan University, Boston University School of Theology, Harvard University, and the University of Chicago. Ordained a minister of the Methodist Episcopal Church in 1914, with subsequent pastoral charges in the Nebraska and the New England Conferences, he was instrumental in having the General Conference of his Church at Springfield, Massachusetts, in 1924, appoint its first Commission on Music, of which he was the first chairman. As a member of the Joint Commission which revised *The Methodist Hymnal,* 1935, he was a member of the special Editorial Committee which was appointed to complete the work. From 1927 to 1936 he was president of Evansville College, and since April, 1936, has been president of Simpson College. He is active in the educational affairs of his Church, being a member of its Board of Education.

Doctor Harper is a musician of training and attainment. He holds the degree of Bachelor of Music as well as that of Bachelor of Arts from Nebraska Wesleyan University, his major subject being piano. For a time he planned to make music his profession, but the urge toward the ministry was too strong to be overcome. While insisting that music is only an avocation with him, Doctor Harper is known as a leader in the field of church-music education. He organized the first interchurch choir in Boston; was instructor in church music, Boston University; taught choral as well as instrumental music at La Salle Junior College, Auburndale, Massachusetts; has lectured extensively throughout the United States on church music; has written books on the subject; was editor of *The Abingdon Hymnal,* 1928; compiled the *Junior-Intermediate Anthem Book,* 1924, and has acted as precentor at the last two General Conferences. Doctor Harper's contribution to the present *Methodist Hymnal* was very great.

**113—We would see Jesus; lo! His star is shining**—John Edgar Park

**Cushman**—Herbert Barclay Turner

President J. Edgar Park, of Wheaton College, Massachusetts, has written the author concerning this hymn:

> It was written for a hymnal published by the Pilgrim Press of Boston (*Worship and Song*) and the lady in charge returned it, I remember, thinking some of the lines could be improved. The line "Light of the village life from day to day" came as the result of the revision. . . . The tune ("Cushman") to which it is set in the hymnal in which it was first published was in my mind as I wrote it. The hymn is a "Song of Youth."

John Edgar Park is the son, grandson, great-grandson, and father of ministers of the gospel. He was born at Belfast, Ireland, March 7, 1879, and was educated at New College, Edinburgh, Royal University, Dublin, and Princeton Theological Seminary. He has been the recipient of honorary degrees from Tufts College (D.D.) and Wesleyan University (LL.D.). Doctor Park has been the pastor of churches in New York and Massachusetts, was a member of the faculty of Boston University School of Theology, 1925, and since 1926 has been president of Wheaton College at Norton, Massachusetts. He has written many books and is a distinguished educator. Doctor Park delivered the Beecher lectures at Yale in 1935.

"Cushman" was written by the Rev. Herbert B. Turner for the hymn beginning,

> We would see Jesus, for the shadows lengthen,

by Anna B. Warner, while he was editing *Hymns and Tunes for Schools* at Hampton Normal and Agricultural Institute, Hampton, Virginia. In this book, issued in 1907, "Cushman" first appeared.

Herbert Barclay Turner, D.D., born at Brooklyn, New York, July 17, 1852, was graduated in 1874 from Amherst College, which later granted him the D. D. degree. After studying for the ministry at Union Theological Seminary, the Rev. Mr. Turner preached in a small parish in Massachusetts and at the Congregational Church in Washington, Connecticut, before going to the Hampton Institute in Virginia. For more than thirty-three years chaplain there, he was made chaplain emeritus upon his retirement in 1925. He edited, or assisted in editing, three books of hymns and tunes. He died at Washington, Connecticut, May 1, 1927.

**114—Light of the world, we hail Thee—John Samuel Bewley Monsell**

**Salve Domine—Lawrence White Watson**

Doctor Monsell wrote this as a missionary hymn and published it in his *Hymns of Love and Praise,* 1863. In the present *Methodist Hymnal* it was included with the hymns dealing with the Life of Christ, believing it would have much wider use than if placed in the Missions section. Its brightness and buoyancy add to its beauty.

John Samuel Bewley Monsell, LL.D., was the son of Archdeacon Monsell, of Londonderry, Ireland, where he was born, March 2, 1811. After graduation from Trinity College, Dublin, he devoted himself to the work of the ministry. While rector of St. Nicholas Church, Guildford, he died April 9, 1875, as the result of an accident which befell him while watching workmen making some alterations in his church. Doctor Monsell said:

> We are too distant and reserved in our praises. We sing not as we should sing to Him and of Him who is chief among ten thousand, the altogether lovely.

Certainly he carried out this principle in his own life, for his rectory at Guildford was "an ideal household, full of the beauty of holiness, with genial brightness and gaiety playing like sunshine over all the troubles of life." One of his best-known hymns has as its first line,

> O worship the Lord in the beauty of holiness.

W. Garrett Horder, English hymnologist, thought highly of his hymns:

> His deep religiousness, his tenderness of spirit, his lyric nature, all combined to give the Church verses which have done much, and will probably do more, to express and deepen her worshiping emotion.

He published eleven volumes of poems, including nearly three hundred hymns, of which "only a few are of enduring excellence."

"Salve Domine" was written for James Montgomery's hymn, "Hail to the Lord's Anointed," by Lawrence White Watson, and was first published in *The Book of Common Praise,* the hymnbook of the Church of England in Canada, 1909. A letter from Mr. Watson's son says the tune

> was written by him in 1909 and published locally (i. e., Charlottetown, P. E. I.). He wrote it as an alternative tune to the words of the hymn "Hail to the Lord's Anointed" in the Church of England—Episcopal—hymnbook, and it was sung in St. Peter's Cathedral for a year or two until the Canadian Hymnal of the Church of England was published and the tune was then published in this book and used throughout Canada.

There is a discrepancy in dates in these two statements. James Edmund Jones, a member of the Compilation Committee of the *Book of Common Praise* and the author of its annotated edition, is the authority for the statement that it was published in 1909.

Lawrence White Watson was born at Charlottetown, Prince Edward Island, Canada, May 2, 1860, and died there July 17, 1925. Following musical study at a local Roman Catholic convent, he became, at eighteen years of age, organist at St. Peter's Cathedral, Episcopalian, in Charlottetown, where, with a short interruption for medical study at the University of Edinburgh, Scotland, he continued as organist until five years before he died. The composer's son, Mr. G. R. D. Watson, writes that, in addition to his father's musical activities, he had

> many hobbies which he enjoyed, and his life was a full one. He did a bit of painting, principally in oils, but his sepia etching and illuminated addresses gave him his greatest pleasure. He was also a keen botanist and did considerable research work for the Dominion government in connection with the Island's flora. A new species of violet, which he discovered, was named after him by the government—*Viola Watsoni*. He was also interested in geology and natural history and was president of the local Society for a number of years.

Mr. Watson was also the composer of "The Island Hymn." His son says:

> Perhaps I had better explain why it is called "The Island Hymn." The Province of Prince Edward Island is a small one but has a very beautiful rolling landscape; the population is about 80,000, but as there is no manufacturing there, numbers of the young people, like myself, moved to other parts of Canada and the United States. They are very fond of their small island and always speak of it as *The Island*.
>
> Miss L. M. Montgomery, who was born on Prince Edward Island, and who was the author of the popular book, *Anne of Green Gables,* wrote the words of "The Island Hymn" and father wrote the music. It was intended to be sung with the Canadian National Anthem, "O Canada," throughout the Province in the schools, on National occasions, and at times in the churches, but it is not in any sense a National Hymn.

**115—What Grace, O Lord, and beauty shone**—Edward Denny

**This Endris Nyght**—Old English carol, 15th century

This hymn was published in 1839 in *A Selection of Hymns,* issued by its author, Edward Denny. It was given the title, "The Forgiving One," and was based upon Psalm 45. 2: "Thou art fairer than the children of men: grace is poured into thy lips: therefore God hath blessed thee for ever."

Though Sir Edward Denny, Bart., of Tralee Castle, County Kerry, Ireland, had a rental income of about $65,000 a year, he lived simply in a cottage in Islington, London, and devoted his time to the study of prophetic books and to his philanthropies. He gave liberally to the poor and to religious causes. His religion was real to him and manifested itself in his dealings with his fellow men. It is said his rents were so fair that he was almost alone in England in not having them reduced by government authorities. He belonged to the Plymouth Brethren, a sect holding peculiar millenarian views, and was one of their prominent leaders in London. He wrote a number of hymns, but most of them so emphasized the peculiar doctrines of this sect as to make them undesirable for general use. He was born October 2, 1796, and died at London, June 13, 1889.

"This Endris Nyght" is a carol tune of the fifteenth or sixteenth century. It was sung to the carol beginning,

> This endris nyght (The other night)
> I saw a sight,
> A star as bright as day;
> And ever among (and now and then)
> A maiden sung
> "Lullay, by by, lullay."

It may be found in manuscript in the library of the British Museum, set for three voices, the melody being in the tenor.

**116—How beauteous were the marks divine**—Arthur Cleveland Coxe

**Canonbury**—Robert Schumann

While yet a student, at the age of twenty-two, A. Cleveland Coxe (Cox at that time), in 1840, published a book of his own poetry, called *Christian Ballads,* from which this hymn was taken. Originally in five stanzas, the fourth has been omitted. Changes in its wording have been slight. In stanza 2 "mild" replaces "calm" in the first line, and in the third line of the third stanza it has been changed from

> So meek, forgiving, Godlike, high,

to read,

> So meek, so lowly, yet so high.

Arthur Cleveland Coxe, D.D., LL.D., was born at Mendham, New Jersey, May 10, 1818, where his father, the Rev. Samuel Hanson Cox, later one of the leaders of the Presbyterian Church, was then preaching. From his boyhood he had serious differences of opinion with his father, which led to his leaving the Presbyterian for the Protestant Episcopal Church upon graduation from New York University, and also to the changing of the spelling of his name. He studied at the General Theological Seminary (Episcopalian); was ordained; served several churches; and in 1865 was consecrated Bishop of Western New York, residing thereafter in Buffalo, until his death, July 20, 1896, at Clifton Springs, New York. Not until 1892 did any of his hymns appear in the official hymnal of his own Church, although other denominations used them freely. A member of the Hymnal Commission of the Protestant Episcopal Church, he asked his associates not to include any hymns of his writing, and his wishes were respected. Bishop Coxe was a man of unusual gifts: great personal charm, wonderful eloquence, a scholar of distinction, and a poet whose master-motive was his love of Christ, his love of souls.

"Canonbury," taken from one of the fou. pieces comprising Robert Schumann's "Nachtstücke," op. 23, began to creep into our hymnals the latter part of the last century, and it is such a favorite now that it is found in nearly all books of sacred song, whatever their character. It seems to have won a permanent place in the hearts of all lovers of beautiful hymn tunes.

Robert Alexander Schumann, who was born at Zwickau, Saxony, June 8, 1810, and died at Endenick, near Bonn, July 29, 1856, was one of the great figures of the musical fraternity. Although he early manifested exceptional musical talent, precociously attempting composition in his seventh year, and writing for chorus and orchestra at eleven, his mother unsympathetically insisted that he study law; and not until his father's death was he able to gain her consent to devote himself wholly to the study and practice of music. In his contacts with the world he was quiet and reserved, but in the family circle he could be quite cheerful and gay. Clara Wieck Schumann, his wife (one of the greatest piano players the world has ever produced), and his children were devoted to him. From 1833 tendencies toward insanity became increasingly evident, and, after an attempt at self-destruction by throwing himself into the Rhine, he had to be cared for in a hospital for the insane until his death two years later. Schumann was a pioneer in musical journalism and, being a leader in the new Romantic school, took pains in his critical writings to explain carefully what it was all about. He was a master in the field of writing short pieces for the piano, as a song writer was unrivaled, and is the acknowledged founder of the modern school of piano technic.

**117—O Son of God incarnate**—Wilbur Fisk Tillett

**Incarnation**—Alfred Wooler

This hymn on the Incarnation first appeared on the front page of the *Christian Advocate,* Nashville, October 28, 1921. Dean Tillett has provided this explanatory note:

> My thought in writing this hymn may be expressed as follows: I felt that a new hymn on the Incarnation was needed and it seemed fitting that it should be of doctrinal as well as devotional significance and value. Christ is designated by St. John as the "Logos," the *Word* of God. A word is a thought-bearer, a love-bearer, and a will-bearer from one person to another. The best messenger a King can send to his subjects in a distant realm is his own son, who as a personal word bears most effectively the mind and heart and will of the Sovereign to his people. Christ is the personal "Word of God," and as such is the most effective bearer of the thought and love and will of God to the human race. Whatever else, or more, was accomplished by the Incarnation, this is a large part of the divine purpose in the Word becoming flesh and dwelling among us. It is because the Son of God became the Son of Man that He was, and is, God's best revealer to men of the mind and heart and will of God.

The hymn has not been published in any other hymnal.

Dean Wilbur Fisk Tillett, D.D., LL.D., distinguished theologian, was three times honored by the Methodist Episcopal Church, South, with appointments on its hymnal commissions—in 1886, 1904, and 1930. He was made chairman of the Committee on the Selection of New Hymns of the Joint Commission which prepared *The Methodist Hymnal* of 1935. Dean Tillett was born at Henderson, North Carolina, August 25, 1854, received his education at Randolph-Macon College, Princeton, and Princeton Theological Seminary, and received honorary doctorate degrees from Randolph-Macon College, and Wesleyan, Southwestern, and Northwestern Universities. After preaching at Danville, Virginia, for two years, in 1882 he went to Vanderbilt University, where he served successively as Chaplain and Tutor in Theology, Adjunct Professor and Professor of Systematic Theology, Professor of Christian Doctrine, Dean of the Theological Faculty and Vice-Chancellor of the University. He was made Dean Emeritus in 1919. Author of note, authority in the field of hymnology, contributor to magazines, four times a delegate to the General Conference of his Church, one of the great preachers of his Church, a scholar of note, and a Christian gentleman, Dean Tillett was for a generation one of the great educational leaders of the South. He died, full of honors and of years, at his home on the campus of Vanderbilt University, Nashville, Tennessee, June 4, 1936.

"Incarnation" was written for this hymn by Alfred Wooler at the request of the author, Dean W. F. Tillett. The tune, with the hymn, has been printed in leaflet form, but this is its first appearance in any hymnbook.

Alfred Wooler, Mus. Doc., was born at Shipley, Yorkshire, England, May 11, 1867. Starting his musical career as a boy soprano, he has been a singer and chorus director for more than sixty years. He is well known as a tenor soloist in western New York, where he has also served as an adjudicator in many musical contests. The composer of more than one thousand songs, anthems, cantatas, and a few piano pieces, he won a prize in 1911 for the best anthem in an international contest. Though, for the most part, self-taught, Doctor Wooler has studied harmony and counterpoint with Hugh A. Clarke, professor of music, University of Pennsylvania, and took examinations for his degrees of Mus. Bac., 1903, and Mus. Doc., 1908, from the University of New York.

**118—O Master Workman of the race—Jay Thomas Stocking**

**St. Michel's—From W. Gawler's Hymns and Psalms, 1789**

This hymn was written by Doctor Stocking while on a short vacation to his summer camp in the Adirondacks in the spring of 1912. It happened that soon after he had been asked by The Pilgrim Press of Boston to write a hymn for a book about to be issued, he went on a short fishing trip to his camp, on which he found carpenters at work putting it in livable condition. While not engaged in fishing he watched the men at work, and, he says,

> The figure of the carpenter, as applied to Jesus, flashed on me as never before, and I sat down and wrote the hymn, almost, if not quite, in the exact form in which it now appears.

It is a challenging hymn for young people, dealing, as it does, with the boyhood and young manhood of Jesus.

Jay Thomas Stocking, D.D., born at Lisbon, New York, April 7, 1870, was educated at Amherst, Yale Divinity School, and the University of Berlin. Ordained a Congregational minister in 1901, he served his Church in New England, New Jersey, Missouri, and Washington, D. C.; wrote several books; was active in educational and interdenominational affairs; was a member of learned societies, and was active in the work of the Federal Council of Churches. He was called as minister to the Congregational Church at Newton Center, Massachusetts, in 1935, but died there January 27, 1936, serving only a few months. Doctor Stocking was a member of the Commission on International Justice and Good Will of the Federal Council of Churches.

"St. Michel's" in many English and American books is said to be a "German melody" and in some German books it is called an "Old English melody." It appeared sometime after 1784 (possibly not so late as 1789) in a collection of *Psalms and Hymns,* London, by William Gawler set to "Creator Spirit, by whose aid," a long-meter hymn, and was called "St. Michel." Its expansion into a common-meter double tune was not difficult, as will be seen:

The fact that this was written for girls' voices accounts for its being written in the key of B-flat. *Psalms and Hymns* was issued for the use of the children of an orphan asylum at Lambeth, where its compiler was organist. "St. Michel's" may be found in different books under the several names: "St. Maria," "Beulah," "Woolrich Common," and "St. Michel."

William Gawler, organist, composer, and publisher of music, is said to have been born at Lambeth, London, in 1750. He died there March 15, 1809. In 1785 while organist at the "Asylum of Refuge for French Orphans, Lambeth," he published the book of hymns and psalms referred to, following it some time later with a supplement, or another edition, containing additional hymns and tunes. Gawler compiled other tune and instrumental instruction books and did some composing. The Lambeth "Asylum" was the first of its kind in England to provide a home for fatherless girls. Almost from the beginning the children received training in music and some well-known English musicians have held appointments there as organists and teachers.

**119—Brightest and best of the sons of the morning**—Reginald Heber (1)

**Morning Star**—James P. Harding

This Epiphany hymn by Reginald Heber appeared in the November, 1811, number of *The Christian Observer,* while its author was vicar of Hodnet. Bishop Heber had great pleasure in hearing this and another of his hymns, "The Son of God goes forth to war" (285), sung "better than I ever heard them in a church before," on the occasion of the dedication of a church at Meerut, India, where, in a "remote situation, in sight of the Himalaya Mountains," he found an excellent organ in one of the "earliest, the largest, and handsomest churches in India." The manuscripts of this and other hymns of Bishop Heber are preserved in the British Museum. These hymns were written in two small school exercise books, probably belonging to his children. On one side are problems in Euclid and on the other the hymns in the neat, clear handwriting of the Bishop.

"Morning Star," by James P. Harding, appeared in American tune books as early as 1901. The author of this MANUAL has been unable to trace it to any book published in America earlier than *The New Psalms and Hymns,* 1901, Richmond, Virginia, the Presbyterian Committee of Publication. It was written in 1892 for use at Gifford Hall Mission, located in one of the worst slum districts in London, and was a part of the music of an anthem. Its brightness and carol-like quality should make it one of the most popular of the songs for the Christmas season. While it was the setting for this hymn in *The Methodist Hymnal* of 1905, it does not seem to have become widely known.

Our Christmas hymn and carol singing should not be confined to the Sunday nearest Christmas Day. Advent songs might properly be sung some weeks before Christmas, and Epiphany hymns, such as this, would be entirely in order for some time after, for they may quite fittingly close the celebration of the Christmas festivals.

James P. Harding was born in 1859 and died in 1911; was for thirty-five years organist at St. Andrew's Church, Islington, London; and he composed other church music than hymn tunes. He is said to have been interested in providing music for children's festivals held at Islington. He was for many years engaged in work in the Civil Service, and aside from his sacred musical compositions was the composer of many other works, some of which were composed particularly for the Musical Association in connection with the Civil Service.

Mr. W. Edmund Harding, for nearly sixty years a friend and benefactor of Gifford Hall Mission, London, was his brother, and of the two a friend has written:

> These two men were magnificent specimens of the true gentleman, gifted, both of them, each in his particular way above the ordinary, possessing a charm of character unique, with wit and wisdom wonderfully united. They lived glorious lives, seeking ever the material and spiritual well-being of the poor.

**120—We may not climb the heavenly steeps—John Greenleaf Whittier**

**Serenity—William Vincent Wallace**

This hymn is taken from a poem of thirty-eight stanzas by John G. Whittier, entitled "Our Master," first published in *The Panorama and Other Poems,* 1856. Nearly every one of the stanzas in the long poem has been used in some cento or other. W. Garrett Horder, who says "Our Master" is Whittier's finest hymn, has made a selection of nine stanzas which does not include any used in *The Methodist Hymnal.* Many American books begin the hymn with the first stanza, some using the second also. Many agree with Dean Tillett in thinking the first two stanzas make a finer beginning for a hymn than the one used in this book:

1. Immortal Love, forever full,
Forever flowing free,
Forever shared, forever whole,
A never-ebbing sea!

2. Our outward lips confess the Name
All other names above;
Love only knoweth whence it came
And comprehendeth love.

John Greenleaf Whittier, the "Quaker Poet," was born on a farm in the valley of the Merrimac River, near Haverhill, Massachusetts, December 17, 1807. He stayed on the farm of his father until he was twenty years old, doing the work necessary on a New England farm. Coming into possession of a volume of Burns's poems when but a boy, his imagination was fired and he began writing verses. When he was nineteen years old, an older sister sent some of his verses to William Lloyd Garrison, the abolitionist leader, who became interested in young Whittier and sought him out. A friendship was formed which lasted through nearly forty years. Whittier was influenced by Garrison's extreme antislavery views and became an ardent champion of the abolition movement. For a time he attended Haverhill Academy, supporting himself by doing some teaching and by working at the shoemaker's trade. A lifelong member of the Society of Friends, he always used their mode of speech and wore their style of dress.

Although F. J. Gillman, author of *The Evolution of the English Hymn,* calls Whittier America's foremost hymn writer, Whittier was not a hymn writer, as such; the few hymns of his authorship did not have any extended use. But in the fact that many hymns have been culled from his works, he was akin to Beethoven: we know of no tunes which Beethoven wrote for hymns, but some of the noblest ones we have were taken from his more extended works. (See Nos. 12, 27, 150, 581, 606, 629.)

Said Whittier:

> I am not really a hymn writer for the good reason that I know nothing of music. Only a very few of my pieces were written for singing. A good hymn is the best use to which poetry can be devoted, but I do not claim that I have succeeded in composing one.

He is also said to have remarked that "two hundred years of silence had taken the 'sing' out of the Quakers." However that may be, John Greenleaf Whittier "is one of the sweetest singers in our choir" of hymn writers. Lowell said of him:

> There never was a man born who had more of the swing
> Of the true lyric bard and all that kind of thing.

Dean Tillett made this comment on his religious poems:

> He always magnified the goodness and love of God for man and man's love for and service of his fellow-man as that which proves far better than creeds and ceremonies could that one possesses the Christian character. Whittier's poems are pervaded by the ethical and religious element more largely, perhaps, than is true of any other great English poet of modern times.

In one of her last poems, "John G. Whittier," Phoebe Cary wrote:

> But not thy strains with courage rife,
> Nor holiest hymns, shall rank above
> The rhythmic beauty of thy life,
> Itself a canticle of love.

He died at Hampton Falls, New Hampshire, September 7, 1892.

"Serenity" is taken from William V. Wallace's "Waft ye winds."

Although the composer wrote much music for the piano as well as many operatic works, he will doubtless be known longer for having written this lovely melody than for any other thing he did. It is fittingly named.

William Vincent Wallace, born at Waterford, Ireland, March 11, 1812, was one of the most picturesque and unusual of composers. Because of dissatisfaction with things generally, he left his later home in Dublin, where, since boyhood, he had been prominent musically, and went with his family into the wilds of Australia. Here, and in the South Sea Islands, in South America, Mexico, and elsewhere, he led an unusual life. A brilliant violinist, he gave highly successful concerts in all of the countries where he lived or visited. He was paid for his concerts in whatever medium of exchange happened to be at hand. One time he received a hundred sheep, another, some game cocks. The daughter of a chieftain in Australia interceded for his life after he had been sentenced to die; he narrowly escaped death in an explosion on a steamboat; lost his fortune in the failure of a New York piano factory in which he was interested. He wrote several operas, the most successful, *Maritana,* still being sung. Because of failing eyesight he was unable to finish an opera requested by the Grand Opera in Paris. Forced to abandon writing, he visited the United States on a highly lucrative concert tour, and after a residence in London, went, on his physician's orders, to the Pyrenees, where he died at Chateau de Bages, October 12, 1865.

**121—O Son of Man, Thou madest known**—Milton Smith Littlefield (33)

**Brookfield**—Thomas Bishop Southgate

This hymn was first published in *The School Hymnal,* 1920. Only recently have hymns suggested by the early life of Jesus been written. This, suggesting "the soundness of common things," is one of the best.

"Brookfield" first appeared in the *Congregational Church Hymnal,* London, 1887, a book which contained the best tunes then available for congregational singing. Its music was ably edited by Dr. E. J. Hopkins, for many years organist at the Inner and Middle Temple, London.

Thomas Bishop Southgate was born June 8, 1814, at Hornsey, Middlesex, England, and died November 3, 1868, at Highgate Rise, London, where he had been organist at St. Anne's Church since 1853. He was educated at the Chapel Royal, where he was a chorister, later studying harmony with Sir John Goss (264) and organ with Samuel S. Wesley (324).

**122—Stay, Master, stay upon this heavenly hill**—Samuel Greg
**Yorkshire** (93)—John Wainwright (93)

This hymn comes from *Scenes from the Life of Christ,* by Samuel Greg. It closes the chapter on Transfiguration.

Samuel Greg was a millowner at Bollington, near Maclesfield, a town between London and Manchester. Born at Manchester, England, September 6, 1804, he was a student at Edinburgh University. Ill for many years, he was without pain during little of the thirty years before his death at Bollington, May 14, 1876. The sermons which he had preached to his work people were published in *A Layman's Legacy,* a year after his death. In a prefatory note to this book Dean Stanley wrote he had "rarely met with a man so profoundly penetrated with the true sentiment of religious veneration." A school friend (Doctor Martineau) said of him:

> A purer aspiration for truth, a readier devotion to all clear light, a simpler trust in a divine light hid within every cloud, I do not believe was ever found in a human mind.

Knowledge of these facts about the author cannot help giving one a deeper appreciation of the significance of this lovely hymn on the Transfiguration. In the last stanza one can almost hear the man admonishing his working people.

"Yorkshire" was written as a carol tune to Byrom's "Christians, Awake." J. A. Lightwood (453) says the name is a complete misfit as it has no relation to Yorkshire County. John Wainwright, its composer, was born, and later was an organist, at Stockport, which is the name sometimes given the tune. However, when it first appeared in print it was called "Mortram," probably a misprint for "Mottram." The first publication of this tune did not fall to its composer, Wainwright, but, rather, to one Caleb Ashworth, a Non-conformist preacher who liked, and claimed for his own, this tune which he had heard, publishing it in one of the "collections" of psalms and hymns he occupied his spare time in compiling. Ashworth excused his plagiarism by saying that he gave good advertising to the literary and musical property of others. "Yorkshire" has always been associated with "Christians, Awake," but it seemed such an excellent setting for the Greg hymn it was deemed wise to use it. The meter of this hymn (10s 6l) is one for which good musical settings are hard to find. It seemed also that "Yorkshire" was too good a tune to be used only with a Christmas hymn (93).

**123—There's a light upon the mountains**—Henry Burton

**Mt. Holyoke**—Maurice L. Wostenholm

The hymn, written by Doctor Burton in 1910, was first published in *The Hymnal of Praise* in 1913.

Henry Burton was born November 26, 1840, on a farm at Swannington, Leicestershire, England, in a house where his ancestors had lived for two centuries. All the members of his family were ardent Methodists, his grandfather being a class leader, and his grandmother being the founder of the first Wesleyan Methodist juvenile missionary society. At the age of fifteen he was converted at a service held in his father's barn, which, during the enlargement of the chapel he regularly attended, was being used as a meetinghouse. The large family—father, mother, and ten children—emigrated from England to northern Illinois in 1856. Young Burton went to Beloit, Wisconsin, to attend the Academy, remaining until he had graduated from Beloit College in 1862. Three days after his graduation he went to supply the pulpit which the brother of Frances E. Willard had been compelled to relinquish as a result of poor health. After six months of preaching at Monroe, Wisconsin, he returned to England, in 1865, to enter the Wesleyan Methodist ministry, in which he continued for forty years after his ordination in 1869. His "St. Luke" in the *Expositor's Bible* and his *Gleanings from the Gospels* made him known in the literary world. Many selections from his book of poems, *Wayside Songs,* lent themselves to musical settings. Beloit College honored him with the D. D. degree in 1900. Doctor Burton died at West Kirby, Cheshire, England, April 27, 1930.

"Mt. Holyoke," called "There's a Light upon the mountain" by its composer, Doctor Wostenholm, was written for this hymn in 1908 at the request of Doctor Burton.

Maurice L. Wostenholm, Mus. Doc., was born at Hastings, England, in 1887, the son of a Wesleyan Methodist minister, the Rev. Henry Wostenholm. Educated under private teachers, at Durham, and at Trinity College, London, he became one of England's most prominent organists, serving many years at Central Hall, Birmingham. From 1918 until his retirement in 1931 from all professional duties because of ill health, he was also music master at King Edward School, Birmingham. Doctor Wostenholm was selected as musical adviser by the committee which compiled *The Methodist Hymn Book* for the United Methodism of Great Britain, but because of the condition of his health was forced, in 1932, to give up this important work.

**124—Ye fair green hills of Galilee**—Eustace Rogers Conder

**Stella** (English)—Founded on an old English melody

This good hymn on the example of Christ's life was contributed by Dr. E. R. Conder to the *Congregational Church Hymnal* (English), 1887.

Eustace Rogers Conder was subordinate to his father, Josiah Conder, as a hymn writer. He was born near St. Albans, England, April 5, 1820, and died at Poole, July 6, 1892. After studying for the Congregational ministry at Spring Hill College, and at London University, where he received a gold medal for superior work in philosophy, he preached for seventeen years, during which, in addition to his regular duties, he trained men for the mission fields. After leaving Poole, he was stationed at Leeds until the year of his death, 1892. He has several published works, among them being *Sleepy Forest,* a book of fairy tales for children.

"Stella" is based on an old English melody that has been known in North England "from time immemorial." There the children sang the old song as a part of a game, thus:

Sweet Mary, sweet Mary, my age is sixteen;
My father's a farmer on yonder green;
He has plenty of money to dress me in silk.
But there's no bonny laddie will take me a walk.

One morning I rose, and I looked in the glass,
I said to myself, "What a handsome young lass!"
My hands by my hinches[1] I gave ha! ha! ha!
But there's no bonny laddie to take me a walk.

The tune came into use about 1850, when Henri F. Hemy (256) arranged it to go with a hymn beginning "Hail, Queen of Heaven, the ocean star," in *Easy Music for Church Choirs,* a book for use in Catholic churches. He used it again in the *Crown of Jesus Music,* another Catholic book, which he edited in 1864. This book has been one of the principal sources for modern "arrangements" of tunes from various sources. In the meantime, however, the following tune, called "Coventry," appeared in the first Sunday-school tune book issued by the Wesleyan Methodists, said to have been adapted by one A. J. Hubbard:

[1] North-country dialect—"sides."

There is a world of life and light,
Where death and care no longer blight,
Where music fills the balmy air,
And angels with bright wings are there,
With harps of gold in mansions fair.

This was the setting for an eight-syllable five-line stanza which called for the omission of the fourth phrase of the music, making it somewhat awkward.

Added impetus to the respectability of this tune came from its inclusion in the *Music of the Appendix to the Hymnal Noted,* known as the *St. Alban's Tune Book,* originally issued in 1875. *The Hymnal Noted,* first issued in 1852, was the result of that queer reactionary effort of Doctor Neale (52) and the Rev. Thomas Helmore to limit hymn singing to English versions of the old pre-Reformation hymns set to plainsong melodies. The notation was utterly foreign to the church musicians and the book was doomed to failure. However, the *St. Alban's Appendix* was just as extreme in the opposite way and was filled with really singable tunes taken from both sacred and secular sources. It, like the *Crown of Jesus Music,* is a treasure house of "arrangements" or "adaptations." "Stella" as used in *The Methodist Hymnal* appears almost note for note as in *St. Alban's Tune Book.*

## Passion

**125—Ride on! ride on in majesty**—Henry Hart Milman

**St. Drostane**—John Bacchus Dykes (1)

No other English hymn has proven so popular for Palm Sunday as this. When Bishop Heber was making a collection which should include representative works of the best living poets of his time, he received the manuscript of this hymn, and, in acknowledging it, wrote Doctor Milman:

> You have indeed sent me a most powerful reinforcement to my projected hymn book. A few more such and I shall neither need nor wait for the aid of Scott and Southey.

This book, *Hymns Written and Adapted to the Weekly Church Services of the Year,* was issued by Bishop Heber's widow in 1827, the year after his death. The hymn has not been improved by changing the third line of the first stanza from

Thine humble beast pursues his road,

to

O Saviour, meek, pursue Thy road,

and by the omission of the original fourth stanza—

Ride on! ride on in majesty!
The last and fiercest strife is nigh;
The Father on His sapphire throne
Expects His own anointed Son.

There is no finer poetry in our hymnals, and it is a pity that we have not had written for it a tune strong enough to carry the climax in the last stanza. Doctor Milman wrote this hymn at the age of thirty, the year he was elected professor of poetry at Oxford University, 1821.

Henry Hart Milman, D.D., English historian and ecclesiastic, was born at London, February 10, 1791, and died at Sunninghill, Ascot, September 24, 1868. He was educated at Greenwich, Eton, and at Brasenose College, Oxford, where he became a Fellow. His career at Oxford was exceedingly brilliant. Among his accomplishments there was the winning of the coveted Newdigate Prize with his *Belvidere Apollo,* considered "the best of the Oxford prize poems." After his ordination in 1816 he received the living at St. Mary's, Reading; was appointed professor of poetry at Oxford; was Bampton Lecturer; was made canon of Westminster and rector of St. Margaret's; and finally was appointed dean of St. Paul's Cathedral. Though a dramatist and a translator of Greek plays, he is best known as a historian. His *History of the Jews,* 1830, aroused so much opposition that it had to be withdrawn and revised. Doctor Milman edited Gibbon's *Decline and Fall of the Roman Empire,* and wrote a *Life of Gibbon.* He was the author of thirteen hymns.

"St. Drostane" was written by Doctor Dykes for the words "Ride on, ride on in majesty!" for the *Congregational Hymn and Tune Book,* London, compiled by the Rev. R. R. Chope in 1862. It appeared in the revised and enlarged edition of *Hymns Ancient and Modern* in 1875. Since that time it has come into large use in its association with this fine hymn for Palm Sunday.

**126—Lift up your heads, ye mighty gates**—George Weissel
Translated by Catherine Winkworth (7)

Truro—From Thomas Williams's Psalmodia Evangelica

This is taken from Miss Winkworth's translation of George Weissel's Advent hymn, published in her *Lyra Germanica,* first series, 1855, consisting of five eight-line stanzas. This cento is composed of the first four lines from stanzas 1, 4, and 5, with changes from the first to the third person in the last. The third line of this stanza has also been changed from

Let me Thy inner presence feel

to

Thine inner presence let us feel.

This hymn of triumph for the entry of the King of Glory, recalls Psalm 24. 7:

> Lift up your heads, O ye gates; and be ye lift up, ye everlasting doors; and the King of glory shall come in.

Miss Winkworth, however, has the following at the head of the hymn in her book:

> Rejoice in the Lord alway: and again I say unto you, Rejoice. . . . The Lord is at hand. From the Epistle to the Philippians 4. 4.

The last lines of the first stanza give the clue to Miss Winkworth's citation:

> Life and salutation doth He bring,
> Wherefore rejoice and gladly sing
> Praise, O my God to Thee!
> Creator, wise in Thy decree!

George Weissel, one of the most important of the earlier Prussian hymn writers, was born near Königsberg in 1590. His education was thorough, for after attending the University of Königsberg, he studied for short periods at Wittenberg, Leipzig, Jena, Strassburg, Basel, and Marburg. For three years he was rector of the school at Friedland, but returned to Königsberg for further study at the University. In 1623 he became pastor of the Altrossgart Church there, where he remained until his death, on August 1, 1635.

> His hymns, about twenty in all, are good in style, moderate in length, and varied in meter. . . . The majority are for the quarter festivals of the Christian year.

"Truro" appeared first in *Psalmodia Evangelica,* 1789, a collection of three-part psalm and hymn tunes, in two volumes, compiled by Thomas Williams (?). No composer's name is given. It has been quite generally assigned to Charles Burney (1726-1814), the musical historian, but without apparent reason. Burney had other tunes in the book properly credited to him, and Lightwood (453) suggests that had Burney written it, he would have made due claim to it, "for the doctor was not the kind of man to let any offspring of his go unacknowledged." A fine tune of its kind, it is a matter of regret that its composer is unknown.

**127—Hosanna, loud hosanna**—Jeannette Threlfall

**Ellacombe**—Gesangbuch der Herzogl. Wirtemburgischen Katholischen Hofkapelle, 1784 (85)

This Palm Sunday hymn for children was published in Miss Threlfall's volume of verse, *Sunshine and Shadow,* 1873. It is the most widely used of any of her compositions.

Jeannette Threlfall, the daughter of a wine merchant, was born at Blackburn, Lancashire, England, on March 24, 1821. Early left an orphan, she was a "beloved inmate" of the homes of relatives. She met with two serious accidents, the first laming and mutilating her for life, and the second leaving her helpless. A woman of beautiful character, she was cheerful and always more interested in others than in herself. Her sacred poems and hymns, written with ease in "idle moments," were sent anonymously to various periodicals, later collected and issued in a volume called *Woodsorrel:*[1] *or, Leaves from a Retired Home,* in 1856. In later years she selected some fifteen poems from this work, added fifty-five others, and issued them in the book called *Sunshine and Shadow,* from which this hymn is taken. Bishop Christopher Wordsworth speaks of her poems as those "in which considerable mental powers and graces of composition are blended with pure religious

[1] Taken from the Italian word "alleluja," so-called because it blooms between Easter and Whitsuntide, when songs ending with "alleluia" or "hallelujah" are sung in the churches.

feeling, and hallowed by sound doctrine and fervent devotion." She died at the home of her daughter, Sarah A. Aston, and her husband, Dean's Yard, Westminster, November 30, 1880.

**128—All glory, laud, and honor**—Theodulph of Orleans
Translated by John Mason Neale (52)

**St. Theodulph**—Melchior Teschner, 16th or 17th century

This hymn, which is used as a processional in all Christian churches, both Protestant and Catholic, was probably written when Theodulph was imprisoned in the cloisters of the Cathedral at Angers in 821. Theodulph, who had been sent to France by Charlemagne and made Bishop of Orleans, was suspected by King Louis I, called Pious, of complicity in the rebellion of the king's nephew. While walking in the procession on Palm Sunday, 821, King Louis heard sung from the cloisters this song by Theodulph, which so pleased him that he ordered the Bishop restored to his see and the hymn to be sung as the processional for Palm Sunday thereafter. This story comes to us from the year 1516, but Julian questions its authenticity, for, he says, it is almost certain that Theodulph was never really restored, that Louis I was not in Angers after 818, and that Theodulph died in Angers in 821. The original hymn consisted of seventy-eight lines of which the twenty-four found in *The Methodist Hymnal* are most commonly used.

Theodulph of Orleans is said to have been born in Italy where, before being sent to France by Charlemagne, he was the abbot of a monastery in Florence. He is known for having written this hymn, which because of the tune attached to it as well as its worth for its own sake, is known throughout Christendom.

"St. Theodulph" was named for Theodulph, author of the Latin hymn beginning "Gloria, laus et honor." The tune comes from a little tract of six leaves published in Leipzig in 1615, containing a hymn by Herberger, "Valet will ich dir geben," having two melodies set to it by Melchior Teschner, both for five voices. This is the second one and has come down through all the years with only slight change of melody. It is supposed to have been written in 1613. The original was:

With some elaboration Bach uses this in his *St. John's Passion*. Its ritualistic use—always as a processional on Palm Sunday—is interesting.

According to the Sarum use the first four stanzas were to be sung before leaving the church by seven boys "in loco eminentiori," near the south door. In the use of

York, the boys of the choir seem to have gone up to a temporary gallery over the door of the church, and there sang the first four stanzas. After each of the first three stanzas, the rest of the choir, kneeling below, sang stanza one as a refrain. At the end of stanza four the boys began the refrain and the rest of the choir, standing up, sang it along with them. In the Hereford use the procession went to the gates of the town. These being shut, seven boys of the choir went to the summit and there sang the hymn. In the uses of Tours and Rouen it was also sung at the gates of the city. According to the modern Roman use it is sung when the procession returns to the church; two or four singers entering the church, and when the door has been closed, facing it and singing the hymn while the rest outside repeat the chorus.

Melchior Teschner was a Lutheran cantor at Fraustadt, Silesia, early in the seventeenth century. The date of his birth and death are not known, but it is thought he died about 1615. He is known chiefly because of his tune, "St. Theodulph."

**129—When, His salvation bringing**—John King

**Tours**—Berthold Tours

"And the children crying in the temple, and saying, Hosanna to the Son of David" (St. Matthew 21. 15).

The hymn deals with the Triumphal Entry of Christ into Jerusalem, and is quite familiar, being one of the hymns one learns in childhood. The use of such hymns as this should not be confined to any particular season of the year. There seems to be no question now but that it was written by John King. It was included in *The Psalmist,* London, 1830, by Henry and John Gwyther, but Magistrate James Edmund Jones, of Toronto, thinks it probably appeared earlier in *Psalms and Hymns,* published at Wellington, Salop, in 1817. The hymn, found in many books, was credited to "J. King" in *The Psalmist,* and many books gave his first name as Joshua.

John King, an Englishman, born, it is stated, in 1789, was graduated from Queen's College, Cambridge, in 1814; was at one time curate at Eyton Church, Wellington; became an incumbent at Christ Church, Hull, where he held a benefice, discharging certain ecclesiastical functions; and died there, September 12, 1858.

"Tours" (Toor) was written in 1872 and published the same year in *The Hymnary,* edited by Sir Joseph Barnby (31). It was originally in the key of F.

Berthold Tours was born at Rotterdam, Holland, December 17, 1838. After studying with his father and at the conservatories in Brussels and Leipzig, he went to Russia, where he remained two years. Coming to London in 1861, he engaged in teaching, composing, and playing the violin in the better orchestras, among them that of the Royal Italian Opera. While organist at the Swiss Church, Holborn, he became musical adviser and editor to Novello and Co., the great English publishing house. Of his numerous compositions, the best are all religious, being services for the Anglican Church, anthems, and hymn tunes. He died at London, March 11, 1897.

**130—O Thou Eternal Christ of God—Calvin Weiss Laufer**

**Percival-Smith—Calvin Weiss Laufer**

The author of the hymn and the composer of the music, Dr. Calvin W. Laufer, has contributed the following information:

> This hymn was written on Palm Sunday afternoon, 1933. It was the writer's privilege to attend a very stimulating Palm-Sunday service, which had a great deal to do with the inspiration that produced the hymn.
>
> At first there were only three stanzas. The third stanza of the hymn, as it now appears, was suggested by a friend who felt the importance of Christ being identified with the world of affairs. A euphonious and lyric expression of that relation was rather difficult, but there are friends who feel that this is one of the strongest stanzas in the hymn.
>
> The first musical setting identified with the hymn was Psalm "Old 22nd," and wedded to which it had been struck off for private circulation. A few months later, however, my own tune, "Percival-Smith," was composed and in the minor key in the hope of expressing the dramatic progress of the Lord's march into Jerusalem and since then through the world. The tune was dedicated to Alfred Percival Smith, a devoted friend and a distinguished elder in the Presbyterian Church of Overbrook, Philadelphia.

Calvin Weiss Laufer, D.D., Presbyterian clergyman, was born at Brodheadsville, Pennsylvania, April 6, 1874, and received his education at Franklin and Marshall College, Pennsylvania, and at Union Theological Seminary, New York. After his ordination, in 1900, he served pastorates at Long Island City, New York, and at West Hoboken, New Jersey. From 1919 to 1924 he was field representative of the Presbyterian Board of Publication and Sunday-school work, in the latter year becoming the representative of his Church's Board of Christian Education, and since 1925 has also been the assistant editor of its musical publications. He is the author of many books and, with Dr. Clarence Dickinson, edited the 1933 edition of the Presbyterian *Hymnal*. A writer of hymns, a devotional poet, and a musician of attainment, Doctor Laufer has made a notable contribution to the Church at large. His home is at Philadelphia.

**131—Lift high the triumph song today—Ernest Frank McGregor**

**Suomi—Finnish Cavalry march. Thirty Years' War**

The hymn was first printed on the back of an Order of Service for Easter Day, 1931, for use in the First Congregational Church, of Norwalk, Connecticut. On the previous Sunday the choir of this church had sung Maunder's cantata, "From Olivet to Calvary." Doctor McGregor had prepared a sermon to accompany the cantata, and failing to find a quotable poem with which to close, he wrote the words of this hymn and used them in the sermon for that day. The text of the sermon was Luke 19. 37-38: "And when he was come nigh, even now at the descent of the mount of Olives, the whole multitude of the disciples began to rejoice and praise God with a loud voice for all the mighty works that they had seen; saying, Blessed be the King that cometh in the name of the Lord: peace in heaven, and glory in the highest." On Easter Sunday, following, the choir of Doctor McGregor's church sang this hymn, set to an arrangement of music from Maunder, as an anthem. In 1932 it was printed on sheets that were pasted in the backs of the hymnals used in the

Norwalk church. Its first appearance in any hymnal is in *The Methodist Hymnal,* 1935.

The only change made in the text of the hymn was to make the word "grandly" read "nobly" in the last line of the hymn. This change received the approval of the author.

Ernest Frank McGregor, Ph.D., born October 7, 1879, at Alexandria, New Hampshire, graduated from the University of Minnesota in 1901, and for his theological training went to Yale, where he received the B. D. degree in 1904, the M. A. in 1906, and the Ph.D. in 1910. While doing his graduate work he held pastorates at Avon and Clinton, Connecticut. During the World War he served as a Y. M. C. A. secretary with the United States Navy. He went to the Congregational Church in Norwalk, Connecticut, as its pastor in 1912.

"Suomi" is a part of a Finnish cavalry march dating from the Thirty Years' War. It makes a stirring processional hymn.

**132—Into the woods my Master went—Sidney Lanier**

Lanier—Peter Christian Lutkin

Although, like certain other hymns, this is regarded by many as beautiful poetry unsuitable for use as a hymn, this poem has taken such hold on the hearts of believing Christians as to find its place in many modern hymnals. The best known work of Sidney Lanier, it was written at Baltimore, dated November, 1880, entitled,

A Ballad of Trees and the Master,

and was published soon after.

Sidney Lanier was born at Macon, Georgia, February 3, 1842. He came naturally by his religious and artistic bent, for both are dominant traits in his ancestry. After showing in childhood an absorbing interest in music, he early developed exceptional skill as a violinist and a flutist. He was a voracious reader of the best type of imaginative literature. After self-preparation he entered Oglethorpe College, Milledgeville, Georgia, a small Presbyterian college. Volunteering for service in the Confederate Army, he served as private, scout, signal officer, and blockade runner. Made prisoner in the war, he suffered failure in health from prison life, and was dismissed from Point Lookout in 1865.

From that time on, his life was a mere struggle for existence. He taught school and was clerk in a hotel—all the while studying and writing. He joined his father in a law office in Macon in 1870, but ill health compelled him to live elsewhere. For that reason he went to San Antonio, Texas, where he met many musical and literary people, and was encouraged to give himself wholly to music and poetry. Thus he found his way to Baltimore, where he secured an engagement as first flutist in the Peabody Orchestra. In 1879 he was appointed lecturer on English literature at the recently established Johns

Hopkins University. A year later he was so ill that he had to remain seated while he lectured. In the summer of 1881 he went to the North Carolina mountains, hoping the climate might help him, but his condition was such that nothing could be done for him and he died, September 7, 1881, near Tryon.

Sidney Lanier's accomplishments, both intellectually and in the number of works he produced, are quite remarkable in the light of his many unavoidable difficulties, such as the conditions under which he began life; the effect of the Civil War, not only in its interruption of his studies, but in its complete undermining of an already weak constitution; and his constant struggle against poverty and disease. Nevertheless, he left twenty-four volumes, ten of them poetical works. His poetic thinking was modern in its attempt to express his faith in a beneficent God in a confused and contradictory world. Dr. Henry N. Snyder, in his article on Lanier in *The Library of Southern Literature,* says the number of those who care for his poetry is growing surely and steadily and that "A Ballad of Trees and the Master" is one of at least three of his poems which offer an appeal to the discriminating taste of the critic and have received the approbation of the "great common heart of the world."

"Lanier," named for the poet, was written for this hymn for *The Methodist Hymnal* of 1905 by Dean Peter C. Lutkin, one of the musical editors of that book. While many consider this suitable only for choir use, it is now so familiar that the average congregation will sing it well if but given the opportunity.

Peter Christian Lutkin, Mus. Doc., was born at Thompsonville, Wisconsin, March 27, 1858, the youngest of six children. Two years after the Lutkin family moved to Chicago (1869), both parents died suddenly and young Peter was thrown on his own resources. His early education was obtained in the Chicago public schools and in the Choir School of the Protestant Episcopal Cathedral, where for some years he served as its contralto soloist, the first boy soloist in the Middle West. At the age of fourteen he began playing the organ at the Cathedral even though he had, up to that time, received very little formal training in music. Good fortune in attracting the attention of some of the leading musicians of the city opened to him attractive opportunities for study. Advancing rapidly, he acted as instructor in piano at Northwestern University from 1879 to 1881, although at that time there was no music department there. After four years' study in Berlin, Paris, and Vienna, he returned to Chicago to become organist and choirmaster at St. Clement's Episcopal Church, later going to St. James's Episcopal Church. In 1896 he organized the Northwestern University School of Music, and shortly afterward was given the title of Dean.

A pioneer in the field of music education in America, Dean Lutkin greatly influenced the development of music curricula in other institutions. He was a choral conductor of note, one of the founders of the American Guild of Organists, a guiding spirit in the Music Teachers' National Association, a composer of much excellent sacred music, an authority in the whole field of church music and hymnology, the musical editor of several hymnals, and a fine Christian gentleman.

The Rev. George Craig Stewart, Protestant Episcopal Bishop of the Diocese of Chicago, said of him:

> Dean Lutkin's attitude to music was that of a high priest in the temple of a divine revealing art. He considered himself a steward of the mysteries of God, and communicated to his pupils that high sense of a spiritual vocation which alone gives dignity and nobility to life.

Dean Lutkin died at Evanston, Illinois, December 27, 1931.

**133—'Tis midnight; and on Olive's brow—William Bingham Tappan**
**Olive's Brow—William Batchelder Bradbury**

This hymn, entitled "Gethsemane," is taken from a book of *Poems* by William B. Tappan, published in 1822. The third line of the second stanza, which has been altered, originally was written:

> E'en the disciple that He loved.

While its sadness is almost depressing, it continues to hold its place as one of the worthy Passiontide hymns.

William Bingham Tappan was born October 24, 1794, at Beverly, Massachusetts, and after the death of his father, when the boy was twelve years old, he was apprenticed to a clockmaker. Just as soon as he became of age he went to Philadelphia, where he sought work, doing the only thing he knew how to do—make and repair clocks. In 1822 he became associated with the American Sunday School Union and retained that connection for the remainder of his life. Being licensed a Congregational minister in 1840, he engaged in evangelistic work in the West, as well as in the East, and was unusually successful. He was at all times greatly interested in the work of the Sunday schools. The Rev. Mr. Tappan published no less than ten books of his own poetry, most of which was merely commonplace, yet from them have been taken those hymns of his which are still used. He died suddenly of cholera at West Needham, Massachusetts, June 18, 1849.

"Olive's Brow" was written for this hymn by W. B. Bradbury and first published in *The Shawm,* 1853, by Bradbury and Root. This book, which was a "Library of Church Music, embracing about one thousand pieces, consisting of psalm and hymn tunes adapted to every meter in use . . . ," included a special index for "all the Peculiar Metres of the Methodist hymnbooks as used in the North, these hymns being differently marked from those of the other religious denominations." There were thirty-three of these "Peculiar Metres," being marked "1st P. M.," "2d P. M.," etc.

William Batchelder Bradbury was born at York, Maine, October 6, 1816, and until his family moved to Boston when he was fourteen years of age, he had never seen a piano or organ. He became a member of Lowell Mason's singing classes and progressed so rapidly in his study of music that after some months he was asked to become organist at a small church. The salary offered young Bradbury was twenty-five dollars per year. Upon his discovery that the organ was one of the old type requiring the player to pull up the keys after depressing them, he asked for a salary of fifty dollars a year on the ground that the required amount of work would be double that of the ordinary organist! Being sent to Machias, Maine, by Doctor Mason to take charge of some classes in music, he remained there somewhat more than a year. After short, unsatisfactory residences in St. Johns, New Brunswick, in Boston, and in Brooklyn, he went to the Baptist Tabernacle, New York City, where he did remarkable work in the teaching of music to children. He organized the Juvenile Music Festivals which were for years a feature of New York's musical life, and were largely responsible for the introduction of music into the public schools of that city. He was especially competent in the teaching of children and in the writing of music for the Sunday schools. In 1847 Bradbury went for further study to Europe, where he was under the tutelage of some of the greatest teachers then living. Upon his return to America he devoted himself almost wholly to the editing and compiling of songbooks, of which he produced about sixty. With his brother he went into the business of manufacturing pianos, the long famous Bradbury piano. He was associated with Lowell Mason (19), Thomas Hastings (204), and George F. Root (439) in musical Normal Institute work in the East during the 1850's. Mr. Bradbury died at his home in Montclair, New Jersey, January 7, 1868.

**134—O come and mourn with me awhile**—Frederick William Faber (76)

**St. Cross**—John Bacchus Dykes (1)

Originally in twelve stanzas with the refrain, "Jesus, our Love, is crucified," after each, the poem was first published in Father Faber's *Jesus and Mary,* 1849. The refrain was evidently suggested by the line, "My Lord, my Love, was crucified," in an earlier hymn by John Mason, 1683. This line was used by Charles Wesley in his hymn beginning "O Love divine, what hast Thou done!" (137). The line as used by Faber was changed to read "Jesus, our Lord, is crucified." The first stanza originally read,

O come and mourn with me awhile:
See, Mary calls us to her side;
O come, and let us with her mourn:
Jesus, our Love, is crucified!

Faber, naturally a sentimentalist, followed the general custom of his time in overaccentuating those scenes which, as is suggested by Doctor Dearmer (79), are treated with such "noble reticence" in the New Testament.

"St. Cross," written for this hymn by John Bacchus Dykes, was one of seven of his tunes included in the original edition of *Hymns Ancient and Modern,* 1861.

**135—There is a green hill far away**—Cecil Frances Alexander

**Meditation**—John Henry Gower

This hymn, one of the finest for children and one of the really great hymns on the atonement, came from *Hymns for Little Children,* 1848. It is based on that section of the Apostles' Creed: "Suffered under Pontius Pilate, was crucified, dead and buried." Mrs. Alexander found difficulty in teaching the children of her Sunday-school class the meaning of the Apostles' Creed and wrote several little poems couched in language easily understood by children, in order that it might be made clear. This hymn is one of them. It was written at the bedside of a child who was very ill. Upon her recovery the child claimed the hymn as her own. Others will be found at Nos. 442 and 447. The French composer, Charles Gounod (1818-1893), who has given to this hymn a musical setting, which has made it a favorite solo in thousands of churches the world over, has said that many of Mrs. Alexander's hymns set themselves to music; he regarded this as the most perfect hymn in the English language.

Cecil Frances Alexander, the author, was born Cecil Frances Humphreys, at Dublin, Ireland. Hymnologists give the date as 1823, but in the *Dictionary of National Biography* it is given as 1818. She married the Rev. W. Alexander, who became Archbishop of Armagh and Primate of all Ireland. Mrs. Alexander is known in every country as a writer of hymns for children. A. S. Gregory said she combined the winsome simplicity which charms and instructs a little one with "the power to speak to the child in the heart of a man." Many of her hymns were written for her Sunday-school class and were read to its members before being published. She died October 12, 1895.

"Meditation" was written for the hymn "There is a land of pure delight," and first appeared in Mr. Gower's *Original Tunes,* in 1890. It is a perfect setting for Mrs. Alexander's lovely hymn and is widely used with it.

John Henry Gower was born at Rugby, England, May 25, 1855, and attained prominence there as a concert organist, and later as a professor at Trent College. Coming to America, he engaged in mining interests in Denver, but continued his organ playing at St. John's Cathedral, and the Central Presbyterian Church. During the Columbian Exposition in 1893 he acted as organist at the Church of the Epiphany, Chicago. He died at Denver, July 30, 1922.

**136—Behold the Saviour of mankind**—Samuel Wesley

**Dundee (Windsor)**—Melody from Este's Psalter, 1592

This hymn, sincerely loved by Methodists and used only in Methodist collections of hymns, was written by the Rev. Samuel Wesley, father of John and Charles Wesley. It was one of the few things saved when the rectory at Epworth burned for the second time in 1709. The paper on which the hymn was written was found in the garden, singed by the flames, after the fire. Charles Wesley, Jr., has written on the leaf:

> The words by my grandfather, the Rev. Samuel Wesley. Probably the music was adapted by Henry Purcell or Dr. Blow. A Hymn on the Passion: the words by the Rev. Samuel Wesley, Rector of Epworth, in the diocese of Lincoln.

The hymn had six stanzas; and because of the interest the "people called Methodists" have in it, the two stanzas, two and six, not included in *The Methodist Hymnal,* are given here:

Though far unequal our low praise
To Thy vast sufferings prove,
O Lamb of God, thus all our days,
Thus will we grieve and love!

Thy loss our ruin did repair;
Death by Thy death is slain;
Thou wilt at length exalt us where
Thou dost in glory reign.

The hymn has been included in this book largely for its historic interest. John Wesley included it in his first collection, that made at Charleston, South Carolina, in 1737, headed,

On the Crucifixion.

It was sung by Charles Wesley when he was imprisoned with Mr. Bray in a cell at Newgate Prison with a party of condemned criminals. Writing of the occasion, he says, "It was one of the most triumphant hours that I have known." The next morning he sang it again at Tyburn when ten of the criminals were hanged.

Samuel Wesley, father of John and Charles Wesley, was born at Whitechurch, Dorsetshire, England, in 1662, the son of John Wesley, who was vicar of that parish until he was compelled by the Act of Uniformity to resign his living. He seemed destined for the Non-conformist ministry but his interest in the Established Church was so aroused by a course in controversial reading that he changed his views and became a confirmed Churchman. His early education had been obtained at a Non-conformist academy in London, but he determined to enter Oxford, although it was necessary for him to walk the whole distance from London to do so. In spite of his straitened circumstances he was able to remain there until he had earned his degree from Exeter College, Oxford. After taking Holy Orders, he was appointed to a curacy that paid him £28 per year. He held various curacies and chaplainships until 1697, when he was appointed rector at Epworth where he remained until his death, April 25, 1735. Several books of his were published, one of which, a *Heroic Poem on the Life of our Blessed Lord and Saviour Jesus Christ,* written in 1693, and dedicated to Queen Mary, led to the Epworth appointment. Another of his works was *The History of the Old and New Testament, attempted in verse; and adorned with three hundred and thirty sculptures.* Samuel Wesley had little of the poetic gift, but what he had he devoted to religious writing. His greatest contribution to poetry lay in his being the father of his three famous children: Samuel, Jr., John, and Charles.

In 1553 a book dedicated to Edward VI was printed with the inscription,

HYNDER NOT MUSYKE

and the following title page:

The
Actes of the Apostles
translated into Englyshe Metre and
dedicated to the Kynges most excellent
Majestye by Christopher Tye
Doctor in Musyke and one of the
Gentylmen of hys graces most honourable
Chappell, wyth notes to
eche Chapter, to synge and also to
play upon the Lute
Very necessarye
for studentes after theyr studye,
to fyle theyr wyttes and also
for all Christians that
cannot synge to
read the good and
Godlye Storyes
of the lyves of Christ and Hys
Apostles.

In this book is found the melody which has been made into "Windsor," as it is known in England and America, or "Dundee," as it is known in Scotland, set to chapter 3, as follows:

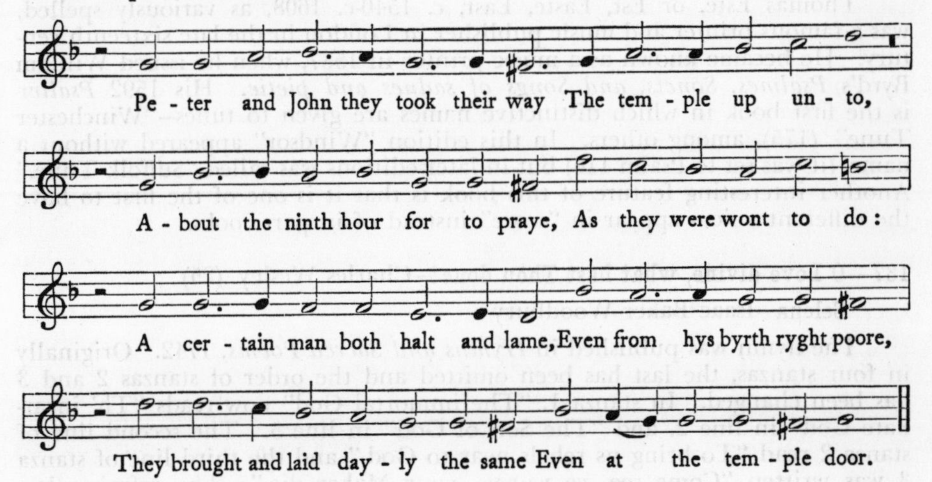
Pe - ter and John they took their way The tem - ple up un - to,
A - bout the ninth hour for to praye, As they were wont to do:
A cer - tain man both halt and lame, Even from hys byrth ryght poore,
They brought and laid day - ly the same Even at the tem - ple door.

William Damon (or Daman), "late one of Her Maiesties Musitions," issued a *Booke of Musicke* in 1591, which contains the tune in this modified form:

Certain changes were made in the melody in books by Thomas Este, 1592; A. Hart, 1615; Ravenscroft, 1621; and Raban, 1633 and 1635. It came to its present form about the beginning of the nineteenth century. This is undoubtedly the tune referred to by Robert Burns in his *Cotter's Saturday Night,* when he says:

> The sire turns o'er, wi' patriarchal grace,
> The big ha'-Bible, ance his father's pride:
> . . . . . . . . . . .
> And "Let us worship God!" he says, with solemn air.
>
> They chant their artless notes in simple guise;
> They tune their hearts, by far the noblest aim;
> Perhaps "Dundee's" wild warbling measures rise,
> Or plaintive "Martyrs," worthy of the name;
> . . . . . . . . . . .
> Compar'd with these, Italian trills are tame;
> The tickl'd ears no heartfelt raptures raise
> Nae unison hae they with our Creator's praise.

Frances R. Havergal (161) says: "The Scotch claim it as a national tune. Burns believed it to be such." Robert Burns thought it to be "The sweetest far of Scotia's holy lays."

Thomas Este, or Est, Easte, East, c. 1540-c. 1608, as variously spelled, was a famous printer and music publisher in London in the late sixteenth century. He became known as a music printer in 1587, when he issued William Byrd's *Psalmes, Sonets, and Songs of sadnes and pietie.* His 1592 *Psalter* is the first book in which distinctive names are given to tunes—"Winchester Tune" (175), among others. In this edition "Windsor" appeared without a name (it was set to Psalm 116) but in later editions was called "Suffolk Tune." Another interesting feature of this book is that it is one of the first to have the different voices appear in "score" instead of in part-books.

**137—O Love divine, what hast Thou done!**—Charles Wesley (25)

**Selena**—Isaac Baker Woodbury

The hymn was published in *Hymns and Sacred Poems,* 1742. Originally in four stanzas, the last has been omitted and the order of stanzas 2 and 3 has been changed. In stanza 1, "The immortal God" now reads "Th' incarnate God" in line 2, and "The Son of God" in line 5. The second line of stanza 2 read "To bring us rebels near to God," and the third line of stanza 3 was written "Come see, ye worms, your Maker die." The refrain (last line) of each stanza was taken from St. Ignatius' Epistle to the Romans, written on his way to martyrdom. The cross was ever in Charles Wesley's heart. In this hymn it makes one of its strongest appeals:

> The Son of God for me hath died.

"Selena" appeared in I. B. Woodbury's first book, *The Anthem Dulcimer,* 1850, set to the hymn, "Asleep in Jesus." The tune had a place in hymnals for many years but has now been dropped from most of them.

Isaac Baker Woodbury has had it said of him that at the time of his death his tunes were sung by more people in America than those of any other writer. He was born at Beverly, Massachusetts, October 23, 1819, and learned the trade of blacksmithing. Self-educated in music, both in this country and in Europe, he attained great prominence as a writer of hymn tunes and sacred songs. *The Lute of Zion,* a very popular book of the second half of the last century, and several others were the result of his labors, usually with the aid of some coworker. He wrote extensively and could accomplish a great deal in a short space of time. Exhausted by his work, he remarked, only a few weeks before his death, "No more music for me until I am in heaven." Only thirty-nine years old, he died at Columbia, South Carolina, October 26, 1858, where he had gone to spend the winter in the hope of regaining his health. In the Preface to the *New Lute of Zion,* 1856, he says,

> The music is not designed for the fastidious and scientific musician whose highest delight, and perhaps sole worship, is music as an art, but for those who love to worship God in the simple song of praise.

**138—Near the cross her vigil keeping**—From the Latin, 13th century
Translation compiled by Louis Fitzgerald Benson (38)

**Stabat Mater**—French Church melody

This translation of a part of the "Stabat Mater dolorosa" was compiled from many by Dr. L. F. Benson, and is probably better suited to the use of Protestants than any single one that has been made. The "Stabat Mater" was one of the five medieval hymns, or sequences, retained by the Roman Catholic Church after the reform of its service books in the sixteenth century. Liturgically and historically there is a difference between the hymn and the sequence, but in modern Protestant hymnals no distinction is made. The sequence evolved from the "jubilus," or "sequentia," the prolongation of the last syllable of the Alleluia, sung between the Epistle and the Gospel, in the Roman Mass. St. Augustine said, "He who sings a jubilus speaks no words; it is a song of joy without words; it is the song of a heart dissolved with joy, . . . its joy is too great to put into words." The custom of lengthening the Alleluia by means of the "jubilus" was at first a practical one: to occupy the time taken by the officiant in passing from the lectern to the pulpit side of the chancel. Soon it was extended for its own sake, reaching its height in the eighth or ninth centuries, when some of them became quite elaborate melodies. There was difficulty in remembering passages of such intricacy and length, and, it seems, some monks at Jumieges thought of the plan of writing words for these tunes, giving to each note a syllable. Somehow the practice became known at the monastery of St. Gall, where Notker Balbulus (840-912) developed it by writing for it some rhythmical, but nonmetrical, verse. So the "jubilus," a tune without words, gave birth to the "sequence," or "prose," words to which any fitting tune might be set. So many sequences were written that it became necessary to exclude all but a limited number from the regular service.

The "Stabat Mater dolorosa," which so vividly depicts the sorrow of Mary the mother of Jesus as she stood at the cross, is one of the most widely known and best loved of all of the sequences. It has seemed to have a particular attraction for composers, for Palestrina, Haydn, Rossini, Dvorak, and others have written some of their most beautiful music for its words. It has been translated many times by different scholars, but the question of its authorship is still an open one, although it has been quite generally ascribed to Jacopone da Todi, d. 1306. The use of this hymn is, of course, restricted to Good Friday services, and should be sung very slowly and solemnly.

"Stabat Mater" seems to have come into English usage through France, being based on a melody which appeared in the *Mainz Gesangbuch,* 1661:

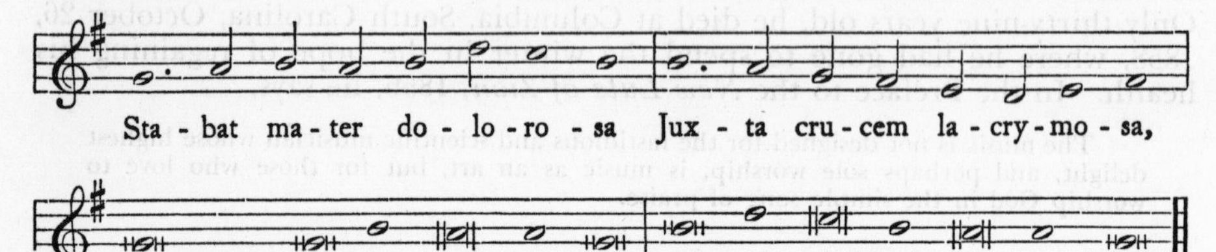
Sta - bat ma - ter do - lo - ro - sa Jux - ta cru - cem la - cry - mo - sa,
Dum pen - de - bat fi - li - us, Dum pen - de - bat fi - li - us.

**139—"It is finished!" Man of Sorrows!**—Frederick Henry Hedge

**Christi Mutter**—Corner's Gesangbuch, 1625

This hymn by Dr. F. H. Hedge is a part of that beginning,

'Twas the day when God's Anointed,

written originally for a confirmation service held at Bangor, Maine, Good Friday, 1843.

Frederick Henry Hedge, D.D., was born at Cambridge, Massachusetts, December 12, 1805, and educated in Germany and at Harvard University. After serving Unitarian congregations as pastor in Massachusetts, Maine, and Rhode Island, he was made Professor of Ecclesiastical History at Harvard, later becoming Professor of German Literature. He was sometime editor of *The Christian Examiner,* and with Dr. F. D. Huntington, compiled *Hymns for the Church of Christ,* for Unitarian churches. His death occurred at Cambridge, August 21, 1890.

"Christi Mutter" comes from *Gross Catolisch Gesangbuch,* 1625, compiled by David Gregor Corner (1587-1648), at the time a priest at Roz, Austria. While this was a very large collection of Catholic hymns, he is said to have made an even larger one in 1631. Corner is not known to have written any hymn tunes, probably selecting them from any available source.

**140—There is a fountain filled with blood**—William Cowper (24)

**Cleansing Fountain**—Early American melody

Dr. J. B. Reeves, Professor of English Literature at Westminster College and author of *The Hymn as Literature,* says this is one of Cowper's finest hymns. Few have caused more controversy than this owing to the imagery used in the first stanza. Dr. James Moffatt says:

Attempts have been made to improve it, but they have proved disastrous failures. . . . It must be taken as Cowper wrote it or not at all.

Saintsbury, in his *History of English Prosody,* insists:

No finical or Philistine dislike of the phraseology ought to blind any lover of poetry to the wonderful tranced adoration of the movement of "There is a fountain filled with blood."

James Montgomery tried to improve it by writing:

From Calvary's Cross a fountain flows
Of water and of blood,
More healing than Bethesda's pool,
Or famed Siloam's flood.

He felt the original stanza was

objectionable, as representing the fountain as being filled, instead of springing up; I think my version is unexceptionable.

However that may be, Cowper's stanza still holds its place.

The hymn, probably written in 1771, was first published in a *Collection of Psalms and Hymns* made by Doctor Conyer, rector of St. Paul's Church, Deptford, England, in 1772, and then in *Olney Hymns,* 1779, where it was headed,

Praise for the fountain opened.

It was based on Zechariah 13. 1: "In that day there shall be a fountain opened to the house of David and to the inhabitants of Jerusalem for sin and for uncleanness."

John Mason Good, a London physician and man of letters, was so fond of it that he frequently repeated it while walking in the street. At his request his daughter repeated it to him as he lay dying. The line, "E'er since by faith I saw the stream," seemed to strike him forcibly, and he said, "All the promises are yea and amen in Christ Jesus."

"Cleansing Fountain" is doubtless an old American melody. Asa Hull, in his *Pilgrims' Harp,* as did others in their books, called it "Western Melody." As was suggested in the 1905 *Methodist Hymnal,* it may have been "arranged from" Lowell Mason's tune "Cowper," which is frequently used with this hymn. It is entirely possible that Lowell Mason may have heard it before writing "Cowper." It is a stirring tune, however, and sounds very much as though it might have been an early camp-meeting favorite.

**141—O sacred Head, now wounded**—Authorship uncertain
Translated by Paul Gerhardt (91)
Translated by James Waddell Alexander

**Passion Chorale**—Hans Leo Hassler
Harmonized by Johann Sebastian Bach (52)

This hymn is a translation of a translation. The poem, known as the

Salve mundi salvatore,

from which it is taken, is ascribed to St. Bernard of Clairvaux (188), although it has not been discovered in manuscript form earlier than the fourteenth century. In spite of the belief by Archbishop Richard C. Trench, author of *Sacred Latin Poetry,* that internal evidence pointed to its authorship by St. Bernard, this, like that of so many of the old Latin hymns, is open to question. As Bernard lived from 1091 to 1153, it must have come from the early part of the twelfth century. The poem was one of seven parts, each addressed to a different part of Christ's body—namely, the feet, the knees, the hands, the side, the breast, the heart, and the face, and was entitled,

> A rhythmic prayer to any one of the members of Christ suffering and hanging on the Cross.

In a manuscript in the Town Library at Nürnberg containing the poem, there is a notation after the last stanza of the third part, which says:

> As now St. Bernard had spoken these words with quiet earnestness of desire, the image on the cross bowed itself and embraced him with its wounded arms, as a sure token that to it this prayer was most pleasing.

Paul Gerhardt, German hymnist, translated this Latin poem into German, and it is from part seven,

> Salve caput cruentatum,

of his translation, beginning,

> O Haupt voll Blut und Wunden,

that Dr. J. W. Alexander made his hymn. R. Lauxman, in his *Koch,* says,

> Bernard's original is powerful and searching, but Gerhardt's hymn is still more powerful and more profound, as redrawn from the deeper spring of evangelical Lutheran, Scriptural, knowledge, and fervency of faith.

Gerhardt's hymn was headed,

> To the suffering face of Christ.

Of Doctor Alexander's translation, Dr. Philip Schaff, one time Professor of Sacred Literature in Union Seminary, New York, a specialist in German hymnody, has written:

> The classical hymn has shown an imperishable vitality in passing from the Latin into the German, and from the German into the English, and proclaiming in three tongues, and in the name of three Confessions—the Catholic, the Lutheran, and the Reformed—with equal effect, the dying love of our Saviour, and our boundless indebtedness to Him.

James Waddell Alexander, D.D., an eminent Presbyterian clergyman of the early middle of last century, was born March 13, 1804, at Hopewell, and died July 31, 1859, at Sweetsprings, Virginia. For a time Professor of Ecclesiastical History at Princeton Seminary, from which he had graduated, Doctor Alexander later served churches of his denomination as pastor in Virginia, New Jersey, and New York City. Though he was the author of many books, it is for his translations of German and Latin hymns that he is best known.

"Passion Chorale" first appeared in a work, *Lustgarten Neuer Teutscher Gesäng—Componirt durch Hanns Leo Hassler von Nürmberg,* 1601. It was set to a love song entitled "Mein G'müt ist mir verwirret," in this form:

Apparently, it was first set to a hymn in 1613 in *Harmoniae Sacrae,* Gorlitz, the words being "Herzlich thut mich verlangen." Later it became associated with "O Haupt voll Blut und Wunden." This tune was greatly loved by Bach, who used it five times in his *St. Matthew Passion.* Philipp Spitta, in his voluminous and authoritative *Life of Bach,* has this to say about the use of the chorale in that work:

> Bach has distinguished one of the chorales introduced from the rest by repetition, thus making it the center of the church sentiment of the whole work. Among the fourteen simply set chorales included in the work in its original form, the melody, "O Thou whose Head was wounded," occurs five times; it was a favorite melody with Bach, and there is no other that, throughout his long life, he used so frequently or more thoroughly exhausted as to its harmonic possibilities for every variety of purpose. It comes in three times in the second part: first when Jesus silently bows to His fate at Pilate's decision. . . . It was a beautiful idea to associate the pious submissiveness of Jesus with a congregational meditation on it; . . . Apparently, Bach felt chiefly the need for bringing in the melody; . . . The second time the chorale is sung is in the second section, immediately before the progress to the cross, when the soldiers have crowned the Saviour with thorns and mocked Him and smitten Him; and we here have the first two verses of the hymn addressed to the head of Christ.
>
> Nothing more suitable could be found for this place, and the effect is consequently deeply touching. The third time it is the last chorale of the work, and it comes in after the words, "But Jesus cried with a loud voice and departed." . . . This climax has always been justly regarded as one of the most thrilling of the whole work.

As used in the *Hymnal,* it is, in the main, a combination of harmonizations by Bach. The melody has been slightly altered.

Hans Leo Hassler, born at Nuremberg, Bavaria, October 25 or 26, 1564, was one of three distinguished sons of Isaac Hassler, eminent organist at Nuremberg. In the obituary of Isaac, a part of the sermon preached at his funeral, it was stated that he had

> carefully brought up and trained his son, Hans Leo, in the fear of God, in the free arts, and especially in the praiseworthy art of music.

When he was about twenty years of age, Hans went to Venice for study, and he may have been the first of a long line of German music students who went to Italy to further their knowledge of music. Although he did not remain in Venice for any great length of time, he was greatly influenced by what he learned there. Upon his return he remained at his post as a private organist at Augsburg until after the death of his patron in 1600, when he returned to Nuremberg. There, a year later, he published his *Lustgarten,* containing thirty-two German songs and eleven instrumental Intradas (introductions). After eight years at Nuremberg he received the appointment as organist to the Electoral Chapel at Dresden, but he was in ill health and unable to do much other than take care of his regular services. His death occurred June 8, 1612, while he was on a visit to Frankfurt with the then Elector of Saxony.

**142—Alas! and did my Saviour bleed—Isaac Watts (3)**

**Martyrdom (Avon) (70)—Hugh Wilson (70)**

In July, 1707, Isaac Watts issued his epoch-making *Hymns and Spiritual Songs. In three books:* I. *Collected from the Scriptures.* II. *Composed on Divine Subjects.* III. *Prepared for the Lord's Supper.* This hymn was one of those "composed on divine subjects," and, as Dr. Charles S. Robinson said,

> It is likely that more conversions have been credited, in the wide round of Christian biography, to this hymn . . . than to any other in the English language.

The hymn was in six stanzas, the second seldom, if ever, used. In its original form the omitted one read,

> Thy body slain, sweet Jesus, Thine—
> And bath'd in its own blood—
> While the firm mark of Wrath Divine
> His Soul in Anguish stood.

The fifth stanza is the only one which has escaped change. Line 4, stanza 1, now reads,

> For sinners such as I?

There was quite general objection to the original,

> For such a worm as I?

and for many years the books of other denominations than Methodist, and at least one branch of this Church in England, have made the change noted or have used the line,

> For such an one as I?

Line 2, stanza 2, originally read,

> He groaned upon the tree.

Line 3, stanza 3, as Doctor Watts wrote it, was,

> When God, the mighty Maker, dy'd,

and "my" was changed to "mine" in the last line of stanza 4.

The incident related of former Governor A. H. Colquitt, of Georgia, an influential Methodist layman, by Bishop Warren A. Candler in his *High Living and High Lives,* is worthy of repetition here:

> Just before he arose to address the meeting the choir sang one of the sweetest hymns of Watts. It seemed to fill him with holy rapture. When he rose to speak,

his handsome face shone with supernatural brightness, his lustrous eyes were filled with tears, and his utterance was choked with emotion as he said impulsively: "Oh, how I love that song! It was my mother's song. And today, if I could hear her sing it again, I should have greater joy than if I had heard all the choirs of heaven."

"Alas! and did my Saviour bleed!"—that was the song they sang. Because his Saviour bled and died that men might live, this noble man has found at last the eternal home and the "vanished hand" for which he sighed.

Fanny Crosby (231) tells, in her autobiography, how "my very soul flooded with celestial light" at the time of her conversion, when this hymn was sung.

**143—Sweet the moments, rich in blessing**—Stanzas 1-3, Walter Shirley
Based on James Allen
Stanza 4 from Cooke and Denton's
Church Hymnal, 1853

**Dorrnance**—Isaac Baker Woodbury (137)

This Good Friday hymn is based on one of James Allen's which appeared in the *Kendall Hymn Book,* 1757, beginning,

While my Jesus I'm possessing.

The Rev. Walter Shirley, who assisted Lady Huntingdon in revising the collection of hymns used in her chapels, rewrote Allen's hymn, beginning with the second stanza, for the Countess of Huntingdon's book, 1770 edition. From this collection it has gone into many others, but has suffered such extreme revision as to be quite different from the original, although retaining its sentiment. The fourth stanza was taken from Cooke and Denton's *Church Hymnal,* 1853. The hymn has been known to Methodists in America since 1859, for it was included in the *Methodist Protestant Hymnal* of that year. It is found in the *Wesleyan Hymn and Tune Book,* Methodist Episcopal Church, South, 1869, and in *The Hymnal of the Methodist Episcopal Church,* 1878. It was not included in *The Methodist Hymnal* of 1905, although another version of it may be found in the *Methodist Protestant Hymnal* of 1901.

James Allen, born at Gayle, Wensleydale, Yorkshire, England, June 24, 1734, was educated with the view of taking Holy Orders, but left Cambridge University to join the Inghamites, an English denomination which combined Methodist and Moravian doctrines, later affiliating with the Sandemanians (Glassites), a Scottish sect believing in the community of property, and emphasizing love feasts and weekly communion services. Still unsatisfied, he built a chapel on his estate at Gayle, his birthplace, and ministered there until his death, October 31, 1804. He was the editor of and principal contributor to the *Kendall Hymn Book,* 1757.

The Honorable and Rev. Walter Shirley, M.A., who was born in 1725, in Ireland, was a friend of George Whitefield and the Wesleys, and often preached in their chapels. He became greatly interested in Lady Huntingdon's religious work and was especially helpful in preparing hymns for her chapel services, contributing several from his own pen. Although sympathizing with Lady Huntingdon's efforts to establish a "connection" of her own, he still retained his standing in the Anglican Church, serving a parish in Ireland until his death, April 7, 1786.

Selena, Countess of Huntingdon, born August 24, 1707, at London, was deeply religious from her early girlhood, and Christian tenets ruled her life. She was a member of the first Methodist Society in Fetter Lane, London, and the first Methodist Conference was held at her home in June, 1744. Being more in sympathy with the doctrines held by George Whitefield than with those of the Wesleys, she followed Whitefield when the break between them came. She spent her money lavishly in building chapels and supplying preachers for them. Although it was her desire to remain in the Church of England and have her chapels used for the deepening of the spiritual life of her time, she finally withdrew and attempted to establish a "Connection." At the time of her death at London, June 17, 1791, some sixty chapels had been built by her.

Lady Huntingdon gave hymn singing a prominent place in her chapel services and had compiled for their use *A Select Collection of Hymns.* It has not been definitely established that she wrote any hymns herself, although some, among them, "Come, Thou Fount of every blessing," have been attributed to her.

Canon William Cooke was one of the editors of *The Church Hymnary,* 1870-72, a complete manual of English Church song, whose music, edited by Sir Joseph Barnby, was so important that it became known as "Barnby's Hymnary." In 1853 Canon Cooke, with the Rev. William Denton, an English churchman, issued *The Church Hymnal.* It was from this book that the last stanza of our hymn, "Sweet the moments, rich in blessing," was taken. There had been added twelve lines to the Allen hymn, four of which were selected for use as this closing stanza.

"Dorrance" came from *The Choral,* 1845, by Isaac B. Woodbury and Benjamin F. Baker, his associate.

**144—Beneath the cross of Jesus—Elizabeth Cecilia Clephane**

**St. Christopher—Frederick Charles Maker** (9[1])

This hymn is from *The Family Treasury,* a magazine popular in Scottish homes at the time it was written. Three years after Miss Clephane's death, two poems appeared anonymously under the heading,

Breathings from the Border.

The editor of the magazine, the Rev. W. Arnot, in a note, said:

> These lines express the experiences, the hopes, and the longings of a young Christian lately released. Written on the very edge of this life, with the better land fully in view of faith, they seem to us footsteps printed on the sands of Time, where those sands touch the ocean of Eternity. These footprints of one whom the Good Shepherd led through the wilderness into rest, may, with God's blessing, contribute to comfort and direct succeeding pilgrims.

One of these poems was "Beneath the cross of Jesus." No more effective hymn can be found for use in Good Friday services than this, its spirit of devotion and the excellence of its poetry making it peculiarly acceptable. It should be used more widely in evangelistic services, for, as Dr. Charles C. Washburn has written:

> Miss Clephane knew that it is "by grace we are saved," and not of our own selves or our words of deserving—"lest any man should boast."

Ira D. Sankey (237) used it, to another tune, with telling effect in the famous Moody and Sankey meetings.

Elizabeth Cecilia Clephane was born in Edinburgh, Scotland, June 18, 1830, but her family shortly removed to Melrose on the River Tweed near Abbotsford, Sir Walter Scott's home. She died February 19, 1869, at Bridgend House, near the bridge referred to by Scott in *The Abbot* and *The Monastery*. She was devoted to philanthropic work, expending all of her allowance for that purpose, and she and her sister even sold their horses and carriage that they might give more to the poor.

"St. Christopher" was written for this hymn by F. C. Maker, and it first appeared in the Supplement to *The Bristol Tune Book* of 1881, noted in another place, No. 190.

**145—Above the hills of time the cross is gleaming**—Thomas Tiplady

**Londonderry**—Irish traditional melody

This hymn by the Rev. Thomas Tiplady was submitted in manuscript to the Joint Commission having in hand the preparation of *The Methodist Hymnal*. The following year, 1932, it was published in *Songs of a Cinema Church*, London, a small book of sacred poetry by its author, of which a critic in *The Methodist Recorder* has said:

> Hymns are rarely poetry, say the critics, but there is poetry of high order in this little collection, and frequent evidence that the poet has been inspired not by the muse alone, but also by the Holy Spirit.

The Rev. Tiplady had in mind the "Londonderry Air" when it was written. Written in four stanzas of four lines each, it was given the heading,

Above the Hills of Time.

With the approval of the author, the third line of the second stanza was made to read,

And so for Thee, O Christ,

instead of,

And for the love of Christ.

Thomas Tiplady was born of Methodist parents on January 1, 1882, in the village of Gayle, Wensleydale, Yorkshire, England, being one of a family of ten children. He received an elementary education and worked as a "half-timer" in a cotton mill at the age of ten, leaving school at thirteen. In the evenings he took private lessons and attended the technical school. Accepted for the Wesleyan Methodist ministry in 1905, he spent three years in the Richmond Theological College, London. At his first appointment he founded the Portsmouth City Guildhall Mission, under the direction of the Home Mission Committee. For five years he served in the East End of London, having charge of the Old Ford Mission in the Poplar and Bow Circuit, and then enlisting as a chaplain was attached to the Queen's Westminster Rifles and served with this regiment throughout the Somme and Arras campaigns in France. After being invalided home with trench fever, he returned to the army in France and was stationed at Abbeville until after the Armistice.

At the invitation of the Methodist Episcopal Church he spent five months in America in 1919, speaking in all parts of the United States in the interests of the Missions Centenary Celebrations and emphasizing the need for American Mission work in Europe. On his return to England he was appointed to the Buxton Road Church, Huddersfield, and accepted his present post as Superintendent of the Lambeth Mission, London, in 1922.

The Lambeth Mission, built by the Rev. Adam Clarke, the famous Bible commentator, was reconstructed in 1928 by the Rev. Mr. Tiplady at a cost of fifty thousand dollars. In developing a new kind of Mission work, he has made use of moving-picture films in Christian work, and every Sunday evening during the last several years he has had a film service consisting of a liturgical service with a sermon, a film, and an epilogue in which slides, illustrating the Scriptures, are used. During the six days of the week, from 2 P. M. until 11 P. M., he gives cinema exhibitions in the Mission Hall, while using an adjoining hall for the religious work of the Mission. In 1933 he helped to found the Religious Film Society in London.

In 1931 the Rev. Mr. Tiplady paid a return visit to America as a delegate to the Ecumenical Conference of Methodism held at Atlanta, Georgia, where he read a paper on "The Press and Motion Pictures as International and Ethical Factors." He is the author of a number of books and has written many hymns.

"Londonderry" has become so popular as a hymn tune in England, it is said, that it would be disastrous to the sale of any hymn book to omit it. The tune is an arrangement of the famous Irish melody, "The Londonderry Air." If any criticism may be directed against it, it is that it may become commonplace through too much use, for it has been subject to numerous "arrangements," and set to a wide variety of texts, both sacred and secular. The fact remains, however, that it is a very beautiful tune with a telling climax at just the right place to make it most effective. Ernest Newman, noted English music critic, after discussing the analyses of this tune that have been made in attempting to explain its extraordinary hold on people, says:

> All of which is perfectly true; but does it, after all, throw more than the most meager light on the question of *why* the Londonderry Air is one of the loveliest melodies ever written? Of course it does not. The particular handling of a climax could be paralleled in a thousand other songs that have nothing like the aesthetic value of the Londonderry Air. The triumph of this latter, then, is not the result of its "form"; or at least not of its form alone, but of the rare suffusion of the form by something rich and rare that is not in the other songs. The only name we can give to this something is imagination.

F. E. Weatherby, who arranged it for "Danny Boy," said that Thomas Moore's words, "The Minstrel Boy," were such a perfect fit that he hesitated to compete with them, but that his song was sung by both Sinn Feiners and Ulstermen alike all over the world, and that it was as great a favorite in England and America as in Ireland.

**146—Never further than Thy cross**—Elizabeth Rundle Charles

**Aletta**—William Batchelder Bradbury (133)

The hymn was first published in *The Family Treasury,* in February, 1860, later being included in Mrs. Charles's *Poems,* 1867. W. Garrett Horder thought so highly of her work that he included three of her hymns in his *Worship Song,* this being one of them. The first line of the second stanza has been changed from

> Gazing thus our sin we see,

to

> Here, O Christ, our sins we see,

and the original fourth stanza has been omitted. It was:

> Symbols of our liberty
> And our service here unite;
> Captives, by Thy cross set free,
> Soldiers of Thy cross, we fight.

Elizabeth Rundle Charles, or, as she signed her name for some years before her death, "Rundle-Charles," was born in Tavistock, Devonshire, England, January 2, 1828, and, at the age of twenty-three, married Andrew P. Charles, a lawyer. A gifted woman, she was an accomplished linguist, poet, painter, musician, and author. She was a popular historian and wrote much of early life in England, of Martin Luther, of John Wesley and his work, and of the English civil wars. Widely read in America, her best-known work was the *Chronicles of the Schönberg-Cotta Family,* 1863. Mrs. Charles not only wrote original hymns but made valuable translations from the Latin and German. Dorothy Greenwell, the English poet, wrote, after a visit from Mrs. Charles: "That woman always brings and leaves a sense of comfort. . . . Tender and unassuming, . . . she has an unusually unfettered and even daring mind." She died at Hampstead, March 28, 1896.

"Aletta" first appeared in *The Jubilee,* 1857, compiled by W. B. Bradbury, set to a six-line hymn beginning,

> Weary sinners, keep thine eyes,

with a note saying it might be used with a four-line hymn "by omitting the repeat." Once widely used, it is now seldom found in contemporary hymnbooks. It typifies the quite uninteresting kind of tune which seemed to be the favorite output of the less able followers of Lowell Mason (19). There were many such tunes in the numerous books of the period.

**147—Ask ye what great thing I know**—Johann Christoph Schwedler
Translated by Benjamin Hall Kennedy

**Hendon**—Abraham César Malan

Benjamin Hall Kennedy edited a book of fifteen hundred hymns entitled *Hymnologia Christiana,* 1863, in which appears this translation by him of Johann C. Schwedler's "Wollt ihr wissen was mein Preis?" headed,

Jesus the Crucified, or Love to Christ.

Johann Christoph Schwedler, born at Krobsdorf, Silesia, December 21, 1672, and educated at the University of Leipzig, was a powerful preacher, especially effective in prayer. It is told that his services lasted from six in the morning until two or three in the afternoon, while he preached to relays of people who came to hear him. Most of his active life was spent at Niederweisse, where he acted as assistant minister, diaconus, and pastor, and where he died suddenly during the night of January 12, 1730.

Benjamin Hall Kennedy, English hymnodist, author, and scholar, known for his Latin textbooks and editions of some of the classics, was born at Summer Hill, near Birmingham, November 6, 1804, and died at Cambridge, where he had been elected Honorary Fellow of St. John's College, April 6, 1889.

"Hendon" probably appeared first in America in *Carmina Sacra,* Lowell Mason, 1841, but is said to have been first published in France in 1827. A more fitting tune for this stirring hymn would be difficult if not impossible to find. The series of direct questions with the thrilling answer,

Jesus Christ, the crucified,

with its splendid tune, makes this hymn one of the most challenging of the new hymns included in *The Methodist Hymnal.* A very unusual effect may be obtained by singing it antiphonally.

Henri Abraham César Malan was a man of varied interests: he not only wrote hymns, but tunes for them; he was interested in blacksmithing and carpentering; he had a printing press, and was an artist as well as a mechanic. Well educated, a master in the College at Geneva, after he lost his appointment because of an unorthodox sermon he had preached, he built a chapel in his own garden and preached there for forty-three years. As an evangelist in Belgium, France, England, and Scotland, he became well known. The Rev. H. Leigh Bennett, one time prebendary of Lincoln Cathedral, said:

> The greatest name in the history of French hymns is that of César Malan of Geneva. The general store of hymns has grown up almost entirely from a number of small contributions; Malan alone emulates the wealth of production exhibited by Watts and Wesley. Like Watts, he gave the first great impulse toward the general recognition of hymns in public worship; like Charles Wesley, he was the poet and interpreter of a great religious movement craving devotional expression. The first idea of composing hymns seems to have been suggested to him by a friend in 1821.

Malan wrote more than one thousand hymns and set tunes to them—a remarkable achievement. He was born at Geneva in 1787, and died at Vandoeuvres, near there, in 1864.

**148—When I survey the wondrous cross—Isaac Watts (3)**

**Eucharist—Isaac Baker Woodbury (137)**

Crucifixion to the world, by the cross of Christ

is the heading to this hymn of Doctor Watts which first appeared in his *Hymns and Spiritual Songs, Book III,* 1707. There the first two lines were:

When I survey the wondrous cross
Where the young Prince of Glory dy'd.

In the enlarged edition of 1709, the second line was revised to read,

On which the Prince of Glory dy'd.

It was in five stanzas, with the fourth in brackets for optional use:

His dying crimson like a robe,
Spreads o'er His body on the tree;
Then I am dead to all the globe,
And all the globe is dead to me.

With the exception of the use of the word "offering" for "present" in the second line of the last stanza, the four stanzas are as Doctor Watts finally published them. This change was first made by Canon Hugh Stowell (317) when he was preparing *A Selection of Psalms and Hymns Suited to the Services of the Church of England,* in 1831. It has met with the general approval of hymnodists, but this is the first Methodist book to make the change. This hymn did not appear in American Methodist books until 1849 and English Methodism did not include it until 1875. It is without doubt one of the very greatest hymns in the English language. Dr. David R. Breed says, in his judgment, it holds first place, and Matthew Arnold was of the same opinion. On the day of Arnold's death, April 15, 1888, he had attended the church of Dr. John Watson (Ian Maclaren), where this hymn had been sung after the sermon. Shortly before he died he was heard to repeat the third stanza. Dr. William B. Bodine says, "There may be a few others equally great, but there is not one that is greater." Its greatness is evident; it needs no explanation, no analysis; it needs only to be sung to be realized.

As the basis for the hymn, Doctor Watts indicated the scriptural reference, Galatians 6. 14: "But God forbid that I should glory, save in the cross of our Lord Jesus Christ, by whom the world is crucified unto me, and I unto the world."

"Eucharist" was called "Olivet" when it first appeared in I. B. Woodbury's *New Lute of Zion,* 1856. The change in name was made to avoid confusing it with the better known "Olivet" (176) of Lowell Mason (19). Methodists are alone in the use of this tune for this hymn, nearly all other denominations using the tune "Hamburg" (334).

**149—In the Cross of Christ I glory**—John Bowring (75)

**Rathbun**—Ithamar Conkey

On Sir John Bowring's gravestone may be found the first line of his immortal hymn,

In the cross of Christ I glory.

It was published in the author's *Hymns* of 1825, and like "When I survey the wondrous cross" (148), was based on Galatians 6. 14. Many writers have called attention to the interesting fact that this hymn should have been written by one who held Unitarian beliefs. It was given the title,

Glorying in the Cross.

When the siege of Pekin was lifted, at the time of the Boxer Rebellion, the missionaries gathered around the altar in the Temple of Heaven, that mysterious shrine which was visited by the Emperor of China, and by no one else, once each year, and sang this hymn, which so well expressed the spirit which had sustained them during the trying, dangerous weeks.

"Rathbun" was written in 1849 by Ithamar Conkey while organist at Central Baptist Church, Norwich, Connecticut. The *Norwich Bulletin* of June 24, 1907, had this article on "Rathbun":

> Doctor Hiscox was . . . pastor of the church. He had prepared a series of seven sermons from "The Words on the Cross."
>
> One Sunday during the series it was a very rainy day. Mr. Conkey was sorely disappointed that the members of the choir did not appear, as only one soprano came. Mr. Conkey was so discouraged and disheartened that after the prelude he closed the organ and locked it and went to his home on Washington Street. The pastor and choir gallery were at opposite ends of the church, and he could leave without attracting the attention of the congregation.
>
> That afternoon he sat down at the piano for practice; the thoughts suggested in the series of sermons Doctor Hiscox had prepared and the words of the hymn suggested to be sung, "In the Cross of Christ I glory," passing and repassing through his mind. He then and there composed the music which is now so universally familiar in churches of every denomination, known as "Rathbun." He admitted afterward the inspiration was a vivid contradiction of his feelings at the morning service.
>
> He prepared the scores for his choir, and the following Saturday evening it was rehearsed, and Sunday at the morning service in the Central Baptist Church, Norwich, Connecticut, it was sung for the first time. . . . Mr. and Mrs. Beriah S. Rathbun were both members of the choir. Mrs. Rathbun was the leading soprano. Mr. Conkey named it "Rathbun" as a compliment to her. She was then twenty-four years old. She died when she was twenty-nine years old.

Ithamar Conkey was born at Shutesbury, Massachusetts, May 15, 1815, and died at Elizabeth, New Jersey, April 30, 1867. He was best known as a bass singer in New York City, but before going there in 1850, was organist and choir director at Norwich, Connecticut. While in New York he became a recognized authority as an oratorio singer.

## Resurrection

**150—Sing with all the sons of glory**—William Josiah Irons

**Hymn to Joy** (12)—Ludwig van Beethoven (12)

This hymn comes from Dr. W. J. Irons's *Psalms and Hymns,* 1873, where it is headed,

Easter

William Josiah Irons, D.D., who was born at Hoddesdon, England, September 12, 1812, and who died at London, June 18, 1883, was educated at Queen's College, Cambridge. After taking Holy Orders, he served several churches, was one time Bampton Lecturer, and became prebendary of St. Paul's Cathedral, London. He is noted for having made the finest translation of the famous Latin hymn, "Dies Irae," which Canon Ellerton (28) says was "a truly wonderful achievement, for he has solved a difficulty which has baffled almost everyone who has attempted it." In addition to his able translations of hymns, Doctor Irons has also contributed a number of excellent originals, only a few of which, however, have had extensive use outside his own church. Doctor Julian thought highly of his hymns, for he says, "Their high excellence, variety of subjects and meters, intense earnestness, powerful grasp of the subject, and almost faultless rhythm, must commend them to the notice of hymnbook compilers."

**151—Come, ye faithful, raise the strain**—John of Damascus, 8th century

Translated by John Mason Neale (52)

**St. Kevin**—Arthur Seymour Sullivan (15)

The first two stanzas of this hymn are taken from Dr. J. M. Neale's translation of Ode I from a Greek Canon for St. Thomas's Sunday (Greek Church), the first Sunday after Easter, also known as Little Easter or Low Sunday, written by St. John of Damascus. The third stanza is a form of doxology provided for an early edition of *Hymns Ancient and Modern.* In the Historical Edition of that work, 1909, it was rewritten and "brought into correspondence with the Greek."

The first stanza consists of the first four lines of the first stanza and the second four lines of the third stanza (each with some alterations) of Doctor Neale's translation. The second stanza is the corresponding one of the original translation with lines three and four changed completely, and "Thanks" substituted for "Laud" as the first word of the last line. The first three stanzas from Doctor Neale as well as the first two of *The Methodist Hymnal,* all which concern us here, are printed in parallel columns so that the extent of the alterations may be seen:

"Come, ye faithful, raise the strain
"Of triumphant gladness!
"God hath brought His Israel
"Into joy from sadness:
"Loosed from Pharaoh's bitter yoke
"Jacob's sons and daughters;
"Led them with unmoistened foot
"Through the Red Sea waters."[1]

'Tis the Spring of souls today;
Christ hath burst His prison;
And from three days' sleep in death,
—As a sun, hath risen.
All the winter of our sins,
Long and dark, is flying
From His Light, to whom we give
Laud and praise undying.

Now the Queen of seasons, bright
With the Day of Splendor,
With the royal Feast of feasts,
Comes its joy to render:
Comes to glad Jerusalem,
Who with true affection
Welcomes, in unwearied strains,
Jesus' resurrection.

Come, ye faithful, raise the strain
Of triumphant gladness:
God hath brought His people forth
Into joy from sadness.
Now rejoice, Jerusalem,
And with true affection
Welcome in unwearied strains
Jesus' resurrection.

'Tis the spring of souls today:
Christ hath burst His prison,
From the frost and gloom of death
Light and life have risen.
All the winter of our sins,
Long and dark, is flying
From His light, to whom we give
Thanks and praise undying.

The Greek Church canon consists of a number of odes, usually eight, for although there are theoretically nine (there are nine scriptural canticles employed at Lauds, the early morning service in the monastic houses), the canon never has a second ode, because it may be recited only during Lent. This is the only rendering from the Greek by Doctor Neale that, in any sense, can be called a translation; others are such free renderings as to be only looked upon, rightfully, as being suggested by the Greek lines. Doctor Neale has explained this in his Preface to the first edition to *Hymns of the Eastern Church,* 1862:

> There are difficulties . . . to which it is well to revert . . . in attempting a Greek Canon, from the fact of its being in prose—(metrical Hymns . . . are unknown) —one is all at sea. What measure shall we employ? why this more than that? Might we attempt the rhythmical prose of the original, and design it to be chanted? Again, the great length of the Canons renders them unsuitable for our churches, as *wholes.* Is it better simply to form centos of the more beautiful passages? or can separate Odes, each necessarily imperfect, be employed as separate Hymns? And above all, we have no pattern to direct our labour.

The hymn, in four stanzas, was first printed as a part of an article on Greek mythology by Doctor Neale, in *The Christian Remembrancer* of April, 1859, then in *Hymns of the Eastern Church,* 1862.

John of Damascus, saint in both Greek and Latin churches, last of the Christian Fathers of the Greek Church, was a scholar, theologian, and hymn writer. Born at Damascus (date unknown), he was educated by the learned Italian, Cosmas, said to have been purchased in a slave market by St. John's father. He held an important office in Damascus, but became involved in the Iconoclastic controversy in the eighth century and, disposing of all of his

[1] In the office books of the Greek Church the inverted commas are used at the beginning of each line to indicate a "hirmos," that is, the first stanza or strophe of a standard (original) ode in a Greek canon. This serves as a model for the succeeding odes.

worldly possessions, retired to the monastery of St. Sabas, built on a rock overhanging the brook of Kedron, between Jerusalem and the Dead Sea, where he spent his time in writing hymns and theological works. Late in his life he was ordained a priest in Jerusalem. He is held in high esteem in the Greek Church, and Doctor Neale considers him the greatest of the Greek poets. His death occurred on December 4 (the day on which he is commemorated in the Greek calendar), about 780.

"St. Kevin," by Sir Arthur Sullivan, appeared first, to this hymn, in *The Hymnary,* 1872, edited by Sir Joseph Barnby (31). As was the case with all other tunes in this book, it was given no name. In the *Hymn Tunes,* 1902, of Sullivan, it is called "St. Kevin."

**152—Sing, men and angels, sing**—John Masefield

**Masefield**—John Porter (8)

This splendid new Easter hymn, here published for the first time in any hymnal in the United States, was taken from John Masefield's *Easter,* a play published in 1929. No more beautiful lines can be sung at Eastertide than those expressing the love of a Master who

> Has given us light and spring
> And morning breaking.

John Masefield, LL.D., poet laureate of England, was born at Ledbury, Herefordshire, June 1, 1875. In his youth he was a sort of vagabond, spending his years in England, America, and at sea. These early experiences are reflected in his writings and give them a human character they otherwise might not have. He has written many books of poetry and prose, and is the author of many plays.

"Masefield," the tune, was written for this hymn because the tune, "Lemon's Farm," to which it is sung in England, did not seem suitable for American Methodist congregations, and the members of the Joint Commission which prepared *The Methodist Hymnal* for publication, thinking highly of the new hymn, were desirous of securing a musical setting that would make it attractive and useful.

**153—Alleluia! Alleluia! Hearts to heaven and voices raise**—Christopher Wordsworth and others

**Longden**—Van Denman Thompson

This hymn comes from Bishop Wordsworth's *Holy Year,* second edition, 1863, and is founded upon 1 Corinthians 15. 20: "But now is Christ risen from the dead, and become the first-fruits of them that slept." "Saviour" has been substituted for "victim," line 5, stanza 1, and "won" for "gained" in line 4, stanza 3. Stanza 2, omitted from most hymnals, was included in *Church Hymns,* London, 1871, a book issued by the Society for the Promotion of Christian Knowledge. It will serve admirably as a processional or hymn-anthem for Easter Sunday.

Christopher Wordsworth, who was born at Lambeth, England, October 30, 1807, and who died at Harewood, March 20, 1885, was a nephew of the poet Wordsworth, and the son of Christopher Wordsworth, Master of Trinity College, Cambridge. Educated at Winchester and Trinity College, he was a brilliant student and showed considerable prowess as an athlete. After serving as Fellow and Classical Lecturer of his college, Public Orator for the University, Head Master of the school at Harrow, a canon at Westminster, and rector of a quiet parish in Berkshire, he was made Bishop of Lincoln. Although he was a diligent writer, among other things preparing a *Commentary* on the whole Bible, he is doubtless best known for his *Holy Year,* first published in 1862. He insisted that "the first duty of a hymn is to teach sound doctrine, and thus save souls," and while his didactic treatment of most of his own hymns made them unfit for general use, some of them are of excellent quality. Canon Ellerton (28) said he was

> a most holy, humble, loving, self-denying man. And the man is reflected in his verse. To read one of his best hymns is like looking into a plain face, without one striking feature, but with an irresistible charm of honesty, intelligence, and affection.

"Longden" was written for this hymn by Dr. Van Denman Thompson, in 1933. After having it accepted for *The Methodist Hymnal* he used it as the setting for the chorus, "Once more confusion rules a world," in *The Evangel of the New World,* an oratorio written by him for the Sesqui-Centennial Celebration of the founding of the Methodist Episcopal Church. It is familiar to thousands of choir singers throughout the United States.

Van Denman Thompson, Mus. Doc., was born at the village of Potter Place, town of Andover, New Hampshire, December 10, 1890. His father was a storekeeper and bookkeeper, and one time postmaster at the village of Wilmot Flats. Doctor Thompson was largely self-educated in music, beginning to compose when he was only ten years of age. His formal education was obtained at Colby Academy, Harvard University, and at the New England Conservatory of Music, which he entered at the age of seventeen and from which he graduated after being in attendance but one year, an almost unprecedented happening. Given a scholarship in composition by G. W. Chadwick (316), he continued an additional year at the Conservatory doing graduate work. He taught one year at Woodland College, Jonesboro, Arkansas, and, in 1911, went to DePauw University, where he has since remained. In 1919 he won the prize offered by the National Federation of Music Clubs for a composition for the organ and he has won a prize in song competition. His *The Evangel of the New World,* an oratorio, composed for the Sesqui-Centennial Celebration of the founding of the Methodist Episcopal Church, is a work of extraordinary merit. It was first performed at Baltimore, Maryland, during the Sesqui-Centennial Celebration in 1934. The composer of many anthems, songs, pieces for organ and piano, he is also a concert organist of note.

**154—Christ the Lord is risen today—Charles Wesley (25)**
**Easter Hymn—From Lyra Davidica**

William T. Stead, in *Hymns That Have Helped,* said:

> This hymn has long been accepted as the best Easter hymn. Yet it is curious to note that John Wesley dropped it out of the Wesleyan Hymn Book in 1780, and it did not regain its place until 1830.

It is not only one of Charles Wesley's finest hymns, but there are few, if any, others that are sung more frequently at Easter services. The use of the "Alleluia" after each line is in keeping with an early Christian custom. "Hallelujah!"[1] was the usual salutation on Easter morning.

The hymn is one of Charles Wesley's "Hymns for Easter Day" in *Hymns and Sacred Poems,* 1739. Seven of the original eleven stanzas have been omitted.

"Easter Hymn," called "The Resurrection," appeared in *Lyra Davidica, or a Collection of Divine Songs and Hymns, partly Newly Composed, partly translated from the High German, and Latin Hymns: and set to easy and pleasant tunes, for more General Use,* London, 1708. The only known copy of this book is now in the British Museum. It contained only twenty-five tunes and thirty-one hymns. In the Preface the unknown compiler says it has been his desire to introduce "a little freer air than the grave movement of the psalm tunes, as being both seasonable and acceptable." He also says:

> In Germany, where they have abundance of divine songs and hymns, set to short and pleasant tunes, the peasant at his plow, the servants at their labour, the children in the street . . . make use of these for the expression of their mirth; and have no such custom as we unhappily labour under, of ballads and profane songs.

"The Resurrection" tune appeared in this book set to the anonymous hymn, "Jesus Christ is risen today" (155). In 1789 Charles Burney made the statement that "Hanover" (169) and the "Easter Hymn" were the only new tunes that had been adopted in the church services in England for a hundred years. Its inclusion in *Lyra Davidica* set a precedent for hymn tunes which was to have a far-reaching effect. John Wesley included it in his *Foundery Tune Book,* 1742, but substituted his brother's hymn for the anonymous one. It has been attributed to Dr. J. W. Worgan, to Henry Carey (489), and to Handel (88), but, in each case, on insufficient evidence. While it is doubtful if the name of its composer ever will be known, Lightwood (453) says "there is probably no tune in Christendom so universally sung on any festal day as is the Easter hymn, with its rolling 'Hallelujah,' on Easter morning."

**155—Jesus Christ is risen today**—From the Latin, 14th century

**Llanfair**—Robert Williams

The first English version of the anonymous fourteenth-century hymn beginning,

> Surrexit Christus bodie
> Humano pro solamine.
> Alleluia,

is found in *Lyra Davidica,* 1708 (154), as follows:

> Jesus Christ is risen today, Halle-Hallelujah.
> Our triumphant Holyday
> Who so lately on the cross
> Suffer'd to redeem our loss.

[1] Hallelujah: Praise the Lord. "Alleluia" is the Greek form of the Hebrew word. Its use in liturgies and offices is common from the earliest times.

Haste ye females from your fright
Take to Galilee your flight
To his sad disciples say
Jesus Christ is risen today.

In our Paschal joy and feast
Let the Lord of life be blest,
Let the Holy Trine be prais'd
And thankful hearts to heaven be rais'd.

THE RESURRECTION (Original form)

Je - sus Christ is risen to - day, Hal - le- Hal - le - lu - jah!
Our tri - um-phant Ho - ly - day, Hal - le - Hal - le - lu - jah!
Who so late - ly on the Cross, Hal - le - Hal - le - lu - jah!
Suf - fered to re - deem our loss, Hal - le - Hal - le - lu - jah!

The Halle-Hallelujah followed each line. It went through various alterations, appearing in the Supplement to the *New Version,* Tate and Brady (14), issued about 1816. There it was composed of three stanzas, 1 and 2, as used in *The Methodist Hymnal,* but without a doxology. The doxology now generally used (stanza 3) appeared in *Hymns and Sacred Poems,* 1740.

"Llanfair" (thlahn-viar), called "Bethel" in Robert Williams's manuscript book, where it is dated July 14, 1817, is taken from Dr. Joseph Parry's (338[3]) *Peroriaeth Hyfryd,* 1837, where it was said to have been harmonized by John

Roberts, Henllan. That is the information given in *The Handbook to the Church Hymnary,* 1927, edited by Dr. James Moffatt. James T. Lightwood (453), however, in *The Music of the Methodist Hymn-Book,* London, 1935, calls attention to the fact that others have claimed this tune as their own, and cites the Rev. E. Ebrard Rees, an authority on Welsh tunes, who has made a wide search in his effort to trace it, as saying:

> Many of the early Welsh tunes appeared under various titles and various authors. To avoid trouble some of them were designated 'Welsh Air' (Alaw Gymreig); but many of them were traditional Welsh airs that were put down on paper by people who claimed them as their own. *Llanfair* seems to belong to this class.

Robert Williams, born at Mynydd Ithel, Llanfechell, Anglesey County, Wales, about 1781, was blind from birth. He became a skilled basket maker and so was enabled to become self-supporting. A good amateur musician with a superior voice, "he had a quick ear to take in all the notes; and if he heard a tune once, he could then write it out without a single mistake." He died at Mynydd Ithel in 1821.

**156—The strife is o'er, the battle done**—Authorship uncertain
Translated by Francis Pott (15)

Victory—Giovanni Pierluigi da Palestrina

This is from the Latin Easter hymn, "Finita jam sunt praelia," generally given with double Alleluia prefixed. It is known to English readers through this translation by Francis Pott and by that of J. M. Neale (52), "Finished is the battle now," of equal merit with this. Mr. Pott translated this in 1859 from *Symphonia Sirenum,* Cologne, 1695, and included it in his *Hymns Fitted for the Order of Common Prayer,* 1861. The period to which this Latin hymn belongs has been a puzzle to hymnodists. J. M. Neale and S. W. Duffield attribute it to the twelfth century; John Julian and Percy Dearmer say it has not been traced earlier than the *Hymnodia Sacra,* Münster, 1753, while J. A. Jones and John H. Telford, English authorities, and James Moffatt agree that it was probably written by some German Jesuit in the seventeenth century, as it is in the Jesuit book referred to, printed in Cologne in 1695. While the Latin hymn is a puzzle, the translation is also a problem because of the many changes made in the text. The original translation was revised by Mr. Pott himself in 1861, and in 1875. After its first printing, 1861, it immediately began to appear in other English publications, usually in a much altered condition. That which is used here is practically the rendition of 1859, and is the one quite generally used in the United States. Mr. Pott wrote J. A. Jones that he could tell him nothing about his hymns, as there was nothing interesting to tell. This hymn was first rendered into English by Dr. J. M. Neale, who published it in his *Mediaeval Hymns,* 1851.

"Victory" was made by Dr. William Henry Monk (520) for the Original Edition of *Hymns Ancient and Modern.* An earlier adaptation had been published in *The Parish Choir* (No. 81), in 1851. The music for the Alleluias is not taken from Palestrina. The twelve measures of music set to the three-line stanzas are taken almost exactly from Palestrina's "Gloria" from "Magnificat Tertii Toni," a part of a work entitled "Magnificat Octo Tonorum," published by the composer in 1591. Since Doctor Monk adapted this tune to this hymn it has become one of the best known of the Easter songs.

Giovanni Pierluigi (da Palestrina) took his name from the town of his birth, the old Praeneste, home of Pliny the younger, a resort much frequented in summer by prominent Romans of the time, among them Hadrian and Marcus Aurelius. There has been great uncertainty as to the year of his birth, varying dates from 1514 to 1529 being given, but late investigators have produced evidence pointing to 1525 as the correct one. Nothing is known definitely of his early life other than that his parents occupied a fairly good social position which made it possible for him to have the then common educational advantages. He probably studied music in Rome for four years from the age of fourteen. At nineteen he was given the position of organist in his home church. His marriage three years later was of considerable advantage to him financially. In 1551 he was taken to Rome to act as choirmaster at St. Peter's, his extraordinary ability leading to his appointment, in 1555, by express command of the Pope, to the college of singers of the Papal Chapel. This was a gross violation of a rule of the Chapel, which stipulated that none but priests were eligible for membership. Palestrina was not only not a priest —he was married and the father of four sons. After some six months, therefore, he, with other ineligibles, was dismissed. He then became choirmaster successively at St. John Lateran, Santa Maria Maggiore, was employed in various capacities by the Pope, and in 1571 was again called to St. Peter's. Here he remained in ease and honor for the last twenty years of his life. He died at Rome, February 2, 1594.

His renown rests chiefly on his connection with the debate over church music at the Council of Trent, and because he was one of two musicians ever to have conferred upon them the title of Composer to the Papal Choir. The Council of Trent in 1562 took up the sharp debate which had been raging for some years over the proper style of music for public worship. The prominent school of Netherlandic composers practiced using popular airs as themes for their masses and motets, even tolerating the use of the original secular words, while the counterpoint proceeded with the regular Latin text. When this type of church song reached Rome, such trouble ensued at once, that the whole matter was discussed at Trent. It was decided, after much debate, that all music for public worship be set to the prescribed Latin texts alone, and that the writing in parts be so restricted as to leave the words and the sense of the text obvious to the worshiper. As a model for music for the Church there was presented to the Council a Mass, which Palestrina had written some years before, in conformity to these principles. Pope Marcellus II, to whom it was dedicated, had made special effort in 1555 to purify church music. Even though other composers had written in an equally plain and unadorned style, Palestrina became known later on as the "Saviour of church music," and there were many exaggerations and perversions of this story. Nevertheless, he was without question the greatest composer of the Catholic Church, as well as of the Roman school. His work marks the culmination of *a cappella* church music within the limits of strict simple contrapuntal composition in the Gregorian modes. The number of works produced by Palestrina was enormous, among them being no less than ninety-three masses. The well-known publishing house of Breitkopf and Härtel, Leipzig, has published his complete works in a monumental edition of thirty-three volumes.

**157—Joy dawned again on Easter-Day**—Authorship uncertain
Translated by John Mason Neale, alt.
(52)

**Splendour (Puer nobis nascitur)**—Michael Praetorius

This hymn is from Part III of the ancient Latin hymn "Aurora lucis rutilat," from the fourth or fifth century, found in the Junius manuscript of the eighth century and in most of the Breviaries. It has been ascribed to Ambrose (38), although Doctor Duffield states it belongs to a group of hymns which are

> known to be mere paraphrases of Ambrose's own homilies, or imitations of his hymns, (yet) they are as frequently found to possess his spirit and almost the very forms of his verse.

Julian says, "It *may* be his; but is not specially referred to as such by any early writer." It is long and is usually divided into parts. Of the five stanzas in Part III (Claro Paschali gaudio), the four here used are those found in *The Hymnary,* London, 1872, known as "Barnby's." This version is altered somewhat from that which first appeared in *The Hymnal Noted,* J. M. Neale, 1852.

"Splendour" (Puer nobis nascitur) is taken from *Musae Sioniae,* an extraordinary collection of religious part songs, some of which are original, written or arranged for from four to thirty voices. It is in nine parts and contains one thousand two hundred and forty-four songs. This tune, from Part VI, 1609, was set to "Geborn ist Gottes Söhnelein," evidently a variant of a fifteenth-century tune used with the carol, "Puer nobis nascitur," beginning,

> Unto us a boy is born!
> King of all creation
> Came He to a world forlorn,
> The Lord of every nation.

The earliest printed form of the tune seems to be that found in *Christlichs Gesangbüchlein,* Cyriak Spangenberg, printed at Eisleben in 1568, as follows:

The present form is probably by Praetorius, for it is not found earlier than in the *Musae Sioniae.*

Michael Praetorius (Prätorius), whose father's name was Michael Schultze, was born February 15, 1571, and died on the fiftieth anniversary of his birth,

February 15, 1621. He was born at Kreuzberg, Thuringia, and died at Wolfenbüttel. Several of the well-known German musicians whose family name was Schultz, or Schultze, assumed the Latinized form, Prätorius. The word "Schultze" may mean "headman" of a town or village; hence may be translated, "Praetor."

Little is known of his early life except that he attended the University of Frankfurt-on-the-Oder, where he studied philosophy. Upon the death of an elder brother, upon whose support he relied, he was given the post of organist in the town. Where he received his preparation for this work is not known, but that it was adequate may be judged from the fact that he became kapellmeister at Lüneburg; then, entering the service of the Duke of Brunswick, he became in turn organist, kapellmeister, and secretary. He was appointed prior of a monastery near Goslar, though he was not required to reside there.

Though the service of Praetorius in fostering the then new style of vocal music with instrumental accompaniment was great, it is his literary work which is most highly regarded. *Syntagma Musicum,* in three volumes, 1615-19, with Appendix, 1620, his greatest work, was written in Latin and German. Volume II is the most elaborate and valuable of all treatises on instruments and instrumental music through the sixteenth century. It is one of the most remarkable examples of musical scholarship in existence. He was the most important writer on musical subjects during the early part of the seventeenth century.

**158—Away with gloom, away with doubt!**—Edward Shillito

**Blairgowrie** (Thompson)—Robert George Thompson

This hymn comes from *Jesus of the Scars,* a book of poems by Edward Shillito. Its first publication as a hymn was in *The Methodist Hymn-Book,* London, 1933.

Edward Shillito, M.A., Victoria University, B.A., Oxon, is Literary Superintendent of the London Missionary Society. He was educated at Owens College, Victoria University, and at Mansfield College, Oxford. Poet and author, he has published several volumes.

"Blairgowrie" (Thompson) was written for this hymn by Robert George Thompson at the request of the editors of *The Methodist Hymn-Book,* London, 1933. There is another tune by Doctor Dykes (1) with this name (266), but the two may be distinguished by noting that in such cases the name of the composer is placed in parentheses after the tune name.

Robert George Thompson was born in Middlesbrough, England, in 1862, and spent all of his life there and in the neighboring town of Stockton-on-Tees. His education was received at the Wesleyan Day School and the Westminster Training School. In music he was largely self-taught. A member of the college band, he played the clarinet, but because of that instrument's tendency to "squawk" he became disgusted with it and gave it up. For some years he was an assistant master at the Wesleyan Day School, which he had attended as a boy, and he acted as organist in churches of different denominations during the greater part of his adult life. He organized the Wesleyan

Choir Union, consisting of more than thirty choirs from the district in which he lived, and conducted an annual Festival in Middlesbrough Town Hall, in which a chorus of a thousand voices participated. He was especially gifted in training choirs of children, and it was his custom to use these choirs in augmenting the soprano section of his choruses. In addition to a cantata, *Arise, Shine,* many of his anthems attained considerable popularity. At the time of his death, early in 1934, he was organist at Park Methodist Church, Middlesbrough.

**159—The day of resurrection**—John of Damascus (151)
Translated by John Mason Neale (52)

**Rotterdam**—Berthold Tours (129)

This is Doctor Neale's translation of St. John Damascene's Canon for Easter Day, called "the Golden Canon," or "The Queen of Canons." Doctor Neale has given us the following paragraphs preceding this rendering of the "glorious old Hymn of Victory" in his *Hymns of the Eastern Church,* 1862:

> The circumstances under which the Canon is sung are thus eloquently described by a modern writer. The scene is at Athens.
>
> "As midnight approached, the Archbishop, with his priests, accompanied by the King and Queen, left the Church, and stationed themselves on the platform, which was raised considerably from the ground, so that they were distinctly seen by the people. Everyone now remained in breathless expectation, holding their unlighted tapers in readiness when the glad moment should arrive, while the priests still continued murmuring their melancholy chant in a low half-whisper. Suddenly a single report of a cannon announced that twelve o'clock had struck, and that Easter day had begun; then the old Archbishop elevating the cross, exclaimed in a loud, exulting tone, 'Christos anesti,' 'Christ is risen!' and instantly every single individual of all that host took up the cry, and the vast multitude broke through and dispelled forever the intense and mournful silence which they had maintained so long, with one spontaneous shout of indescribable joy and triumph, 'Christ is risen!' 'Christ is risen!' At the same moment the oppressive darkness was succeeded by a blaze of light from thousands of tapers, which communicating one from another, seemed to send streams of fire in all directions, rendering the minutest objects distinctly visible, and casting the most vivid glow on the expressive faces full of exultation, of the rejoicing crowd; bands of music struck up their gayest strains; the roll of the drum through the town, and further on the pealing of the cannon announced far and near these 'glad tidings of great joy'; while from hill and plain, from the sea-shore and the far olive-grove, rocket after rocket ascending to the clear sky, answered back with their mute eloquence, that Christ is risen indeed, and told of other tongues that were repeating those blessed words, and other hearts that leap for joy; everywhere men clasped each other's hands, congratulated one another, and embraced with countenances beaming with delight, as though to each one separately some wonderful happiness had been proclaimed;—and so in truth it was;—and all the while, rising above the mingling of many sounds, each one of which was a sound of gladness, the aged priests were distinctly heard chanting forth a glorious old hymn of victory in tones so loud and clear, that they seemed to have regained their youth and strength to tell the world how 'Christ is risen from the dead, having trampled death beneath His feet, and henceforth they that are in the tombs have everlasting life!' "

With the exception of the first word " 'Tis" which has been omitted, and three lines, this rendering is that of Doctor Neale as printed in his *Hymns of the Eastern Church.* Line 6 of stanza 1 read,

From this world to the sky,

and lines 5 and 6, stanza 3,

> Invisible and visible
> Their notes let all things blend.

"Rotterdam" is named after the birthplace of its composer, Berthold Tours, who wrote this tune in 1875. It is an excellent processional tune and, with this hymn, might well be used on Sundays other than Easter.

**160—Life is good, for God contrives it**—Percy Dearmer (79)

**Trefaenan**—From a Welsh traditional melody

Doctor Dearmer says this hymn was written by him to carry the tune "Trefaenan" in an effort to "improve the musical character of the long Easter season," and because the Easter season has suffered from a lack of "stirring and beautiful tunes." He also objected to the surfeit of references to the "Paschal Lamb and the Red Sea" which were taken from the old Latin hymnals. He has succeeded in giving one of the best of modern Easter hymns to recent books. It was first published in the Enlarged Edition of *Songs of Praise,* London, 1931.

"Trefaenan" is an arrangement of a Welsh traditional melody made by the Editor of *The Methodist Hymnal,* 1935, in order to avoid the use of a musical phrase in the original which might have given rise to merriment if used in a hymnal in the United States. It is doubtless familiar to many:

**161—"Welcome, happy morning"**—Venantius Fortunatus
Translated by John Ellerton (28)

**Hermas**—Frances Ridley Havergal

This hymn is John Ellerton's paraphrase of "Salve festa dies," written near the close of the sixth century by Fortunatus, Bishop of Poitiers. It is a part of a long poem beginning, "Tempora florigero rutilant distincta sereno." First appearing in Brown-Borthwick's *Supplementary Hymn and Tune Book,* 1869, in six stanzas, it has been included, usually in abbreviated form, in countless books of sacred song. The poem was addressed to Fortunatus' friend, Felix, Bishop of Nantes, and was written sometime before 582.

Canon Ellerton, in a letter to Dr. Godfrey Thring, notes that Cranmer, writing to Henry VIII, on October 7, 1544, mentions that he had tried to make a translation of the "Salve festa dies." This was probably the first attempt to translate a Latin hymn directly into English.

"Welcome, happy morning," was sung by Jerome of Prague on his way to the stake to be burned.

Referring to this hymn, A. S. Walpole, in *Early Latin Hymns,* says:

> In it he dwells with much poetical force and with deep religious feeling upon the beauty of spring, which has come in her gayest attire to greet her risen Lord. He endows nature with a soul, much as a modern poet might. No writer has with

truer insight or keener observation portrayed her outburst of rejoicing after the winter of her discontent than Fortunatus has done in this poem. Each verse brings a fresh trait, a new point of beauty and of exultation, and all this rejoicing is brought into connexion with the resurrection of Christ.

Venantius Honorius Clementianus Fortunatus, not content with the three names he had been given, assumed a fourth, Theodosius. He was born at Treviso, upper northeast Italy, about 530. Nothing is known of his parentage or early training. During his education at Ravenna, where he excelled at versifying and oratory, he was threatened with blindness. His friend, Gregory of Tours, learning of his affliction, sent for bathing his eyes some oil taken from a lamp which burned before the altar of St. Martin in a church in that city. Greatly relieved, Fortunatus made a pilgrimage to Tours, and remained in Gaul for the rest of his life.

Fortunatus is said to have been the first Troubadour, for, prior to his becoming officially associated with the Church, he roamed about from place to place, writing verses and singing songs for festive occasions of all kinds. Arriving at Poitiers, he became enamoured of the beautiful Queen Radegund —who had left her husband, Clothaire II, the Frankish king, and established the convent of St. Croix—and made that city his home. He became the close friend of Queen Radegund and her devoted maid, Agnes, and frequently visited them at the convent. Under the influence of these pious women, he took Holy Orders, and after the death of the Queen, was elected Bishop of Poitiers, serving from 597 to 609, the year of his death.

His writings, chiefly poetical, are extensive and varied in kind, ranging from lively casual verse to hymns of grandeur. His finest work, the Easter processional hymn, "Vexilla Regis prodeunt," translated by Doctor Neale (52) and forming the hymn beginning "The royal banners forward go," is in many hymnals. This is

one of the grandest hymns of the Latin Church, in which in glowing accents, its author invites us to contemplate the mystery of love accomplished on the Cross.

He has been called the last of the classic poets.

"Hermas," one of the most popular of Miss Havergal's tunes, was written in 1871 as a setting for her Ascension hymn for children, "Golden harps are sounding," which hymn she wrote in the short space of about ten minutes. A day or two after writing the hymn she composed the tune, which is a bright and happy one, well suited for use as a children's processional.

Frances Ridley Havergal, youngest daughter of the noted English psalmodist, the Rev. W. H. Havergal, was born at Astley, Worcestershire, December 14, 1836. She was a brilliant woman, but suffered from ill health the greater part of her life. It was not possible for her to follow any systematic course of study during her childhood, but later she did some work at Düsseldorf, in Prussia. Her ability to acquire a knowledge of languages was remarkable. Not only was she well versed in French and German, but was also familiar with Latin, Greek, and Hebrew, being able to read both the Old and New Testaments in the original. Gifted with an unusual memory, she was able to play much from Handel, Beethoven, and other masters of music, and she is said to have committed to memory the whole of the New Testament, the Psalms, Isaiah, and the Minor Prophets.

Miss Havergal was not a great poet, but because of an unusual personality, a sweetness of nature, and a kindly feeling for her fellows, she endeared herself to a multitude through her verses. She attracted confidences and, because of the burden of her correspondence, as a result of it she said she hoped "the angels would have orders to let her alone a bit when she first got to heaven."

Once asked by a correspondent how she composed her poetry, she replied:

> I can never set myself to write verse. I believe my King suggests a thought and whispers me a musical line or two, and then I look up and thank Him delightedly and go on with it. That is how the hymns and poems come. The Master has not put a chest of poetic gold into my possession and said, "Now use it as you like!" But He keeps the gold and gives it me piece by piece just when He will, and as much as He will and no more. . . . I often smile to myself when people talk about "gifted pen" and "clever verses," etc., because they don't know that it is neither, but something really much nicer than being "talented" or "clever."

Her life was one of complete and happy consecration. Dr. E. W. Welch, in *Romance of Psalter and Hymnal,* has said:

> She does not profess to meet intellectual needs or answer the deepest questions of life. She gives highly spiritual teaching in devout language. Some minds find her too mystical, too unhuman, too purely spiritual; others are led by her to a more perfect tr st and a more constant joy in Christ.

She died at Caswall Bay, near Swansea, Wales, June 3, 1879.

## The Everliving Christ

**162—O for a thousand tongues to sing**—Charles Wesley (25)

**Azmon**—Carl Gotthelf Gläser
Arranged by Lowell Mason (19)

"If I had a thousand tongues, I'd praise Christ with all of them," were some words spoken to Charles Wesley sometime in May, 1738, by Peter Böhler, the Moravian missionary, whose doctrine of faith led Charles Wesley to seek after it, "first as a faint longing, soon after as a vehement desire." This quest bore fruit on May 21, 1738, the day of his conversion. These words had stirred Wesley so much that near the first anniversary (1739) of his conversion, he wrote a hymn beginning,

> Glory to God, and praise, and love,

entitled "For the Anniversary Day of One's Conversion," which contained eighteen stanzas, six of which (7-12) comprise this hymn. The entire hymn was first published in *Hymns and Sacred Poems,* 1740, headed "Invitation of Sinners to Christ"; in the seventeenth edition, 1773, it was reduced to eleven stanzas, and in the "Large Hymn Book" of John Wesley, 1780, to nine. The number of stanzas used since in different Methodist hymnals has varied. After reading the entire hymn, surely no one will question the wisdom of the selection made for the 1878 *Hymnal of the Methodist Episcopal Church,* which is used in the 1935 book. These six stanzas are exactly as Charles Wesley wrote them with the exception of one word: In line 2, stanza 1, his brother, John, changed

My dear Redeemer,

to

My great Redeemer.

Because of the great love Methodists have for it, the entire hymn is printed here:

Glory to God, and praise, and love,
Be ever, ever given,
By saints below and saints above,
The church in earth and heaven.

On this glad day the glorious Sun
Of Righteousness arose;
On my benighted soul He shone,
And filled it with repose.

Sudden expired the legal strife;
'Twas then I ceased to grieve;
My second, real, living life
I then began to live.

Then with my *heart* I first believed,
Believed with faith Divine;
Power with the Holy Ghost received
To call the Saviour *mine.*

I felt my Lord's atoning blood
Close to *my* soul applied,
*Me, me* He loved—the Son of God
For *me,* for *me* He died!

I found, and owned His promise true,
Ascertained of my part;
My pardon passed in heaven I *knew,*
When written on my heart.

O for a thousand tongues to sing
My dear Redeemer's praise!
The glories of my God and King,
The triumphs of His grace.

My gracious Master, and my God,
Assist me to proclaim,
To spread through all the earth abroad
The honours of Thy name.

Jesus, the name that charms our fears,
That bids our sorrows cease;
'Tis music in the sinner's ears,
'Tis life, and health, and peace!

He breaks the power of cancelled sin,
He sets the prisoner free;
His blood can make the foulest clean,
His blood availed for me.

He speaks; and, listening to His voice,
New life the dead receive,
The mournful, broken hearts rejoice,
The humble poor *believe.*

Hear Him, ye deaf; His praise, ye dumb,
Your loosened tongues employ;
Ye blind, behold your Saviour come;
And leap, ye lame, for joy.

Look unto Him, ye nations; own
Your God, ye fallen race!
Look, and be saved through faith alone;
Be justified by grace!

See all your sins on Jesus laid;
The Lamb of God was slain,
His soul was once an offering made
For *every soul* of man.

Harlots, and publicans, and thieves
In holy triumph join;
Saved is the sinner that believes
From crimes as great as mine.

Murderers, and all ye hellish crew,
Ye sons of lust and pride,
Believe the Saviour died for you;
For me the Saviour died.

Awake from guilty nature's sleep,
And Christ shall give you light,
Cast all your sins into the deep,
And wash the *Ethiop* white.

With me, your chief, you then shall *know*,
Shall feel your sins forgiven;
Anticipate your heaven below,
And own that love is heaven.

William T. Stead said:

> The first man whom this hymn helped was Charles Wesley himself. . . . It may be said to strike the key-note of the whole of Methodism, that multitudeness chorus whose voices, like the sound of many waters, encompassed the world.

Alexander MacMillan writes:

> This splendid hymn is an outstanding expression in song of the *jubilant confidence* and *evangelical certainty* which characterized the message of the Wesleys.

Would that more preachers today had more of that "jubilant confidence" and "evangelical certainty"!

It is said few men ever quoted passages from the *Hymn-Book* with greater effect than the eccentric "Billy" Dawson, an old-time lay preacher in England. On one occasion when he was preaching his celebrated sermon on "Death on the White Horse," he announced this hymn and on coming to the stanza beginning,

See all your sins on Jesus laid,

paused and said:

> Come and see! What? I do not ask you to come and see the preacher, to hear the voice of thunder, but to come and see yourselves, your sins, and your Saviour, "See all your sins on Jesus laid."

There is a widespread belief that this hymn has been used as No. 1 in all

Methodist hymnals since John Wesley gave it that place in his book of 1780. That is true of the Methodist Church in England and of the Methodist Episcopal Church in the United States. Neither the *Primitive Methodist Hymnal* nor the *United Methodist Church Hymnal* (both English) had it as No. 1 before the union of the English Methodist churches, nor did it have that place in the *Hymn and Tune Book* of the Methodist Episcopal Church, South, 1889, which was the official book of that denomination until it joined with the Methodist Episcopal Church in issuing the joint *Methodist Hymnal* of 1905. In the *Methodist Protestant Church Hymnal,* 1901, and later editions, "Holy, holy, holy! Lord God Almighty!" is the first hymn in the book. In the light of the heading given this hymn by John Wesley in his *Hymns* of 1753, "Invitation of sinners to Christ," and after a careful rereading of its text, the Joint Commission decided it would be much more fitting to use it to open that section of the *Hymnal* entitled "The Everliving Christ" than to continue to place it as the first hymn in the general Worship section.

"Azmon" is Carl G. Gläser's only tune in common use in modern hymnals. It has been called "Denfield" and "Gaston" as well as "Azmon." It was first arranged as a 4/4 tune, then as 6/8; again as 3/4, and still later, as now, as 3/2. It is a favorite hymn tune in this country and popular as a school song in Germany. It does not seem to be used much in England. In the Preface to *The Modern Psalmist,* which Mason published in Boston in 1839,[1] he gives a "list of European authors, specimens of whose works are contained in this volume, together with dates showing at about what period they flourished." In this list is

Glaser, J. M., German, 1780

No mention is made of Carl G. Gläser in this book, yet in *The Sabbath Hymn and Tune Book,* 1859, by Mason and others, this tune called "Denfield," is credited to C. G. Gläser. It seems not to have been popular when first published, for it did not appear in any of Mason's compilations for twenty years—1839 to 1859. Today it has a place in all denominational hymnals.

Carl Gotthelf Gläser was born May 4, 1784, at Wessensfels, Germany, and died at Barmen, April 16, 1829. He was a student at the Thomasschule, Leipzig, a student of law at Leipzig University, but became a music teacher, director, and finally a music dealer at Barmen, where he published chorales, school songs, and piano music. He was a pianist and violinist as well as an author and composer.

**163—The head that once was crowned with thorns**—Thomas Kelly

**St. Magnus** (78)—Jeremiah Clark (78)

This first appeared in Thomas Kelly's *Hymns . . . not before Published,* 1820 edition, based on Hebrews 2. 9, 10: "But we see Jesus, who was made a little lower than the angels for the suffering of death, crowned with glory and honour; that he by the grace of God should taste death for every man. For it became him, for whom are all things, and by whom are all

[1] See comment on Mason's statement in The Preface to this book at No. 69.

things, in bringing many sons unto glory, to make the captain of their salvation perfect through sufferings." In six stanzas, of which the first three and the last are used here, with the title, "Perfect through suffering," it was evidently intended by the author to be used as an Ascension Day hymn.

Thomas Kelly, son of an Irish judge, was born July 13, 1769, at Kellyville, near Athy, County Queens, Ireland. Educated at Trinity College, Dublin, he intended making the law his profession but his great interest in evangelical religion led him to take Orders in 1792. He began preaching in Dublin, but his energetic espousal of the doctrine of justification by faith caused the archbishop to close to him all pulpits in the Dublin diocese. Thus leaving the Established Church, he was able, being a man of independent means, to found a new sect, now extinct, and to build churches at Athy, his birthplace, and elsewhere. A man of superior learning, great humility of mind, a magnetic preacher, he made himself greatly beloved by the poor of the community in which he lived through his great generosity, especially during the year of the great famine, 1847. One poor man in Dublin is said to have cheered his wife by saying: "Hold up, Bridget! Bedad, there's always Mr. Kelly to pull us out of the bog after we've sunk for the last time."

One of his great interests was the writing of hymns and the compiling of hymnals. In 1804 he issued *Hymns on Various Passages of Scripture,* which went through various editions, each including new hymns, until 1853, the year before he died, the final one containing 765. In the Preface to his last book he wrote:

> It will be perceived by those who read these hymns, that though there is an interval between the first and last of nearly sixty years, both speak the same great truths, and in the same way. . . . Nothing that he has seen or heard has made the least change in his mind that he is conscious of, as to the grand truths of the gospel. What pacified the conscience then, does so now. What gave hope then, does so now. Other foundation can no man lay than that is laid, which is Jesus Christ.

At one time he issued a companion volume containing tunes of his own composition fitted to every variety of meter in his hymnal.

A man of good spirit, his hymns abound in expressions of joy, praise, faith, and hope. When, on his deathbed, a friend quoted

> The Lord is my Shepherd,

Mr. Kelly replied,

> The Lord is my *everything.*

He died at Dublin, May 14, 1854.

**164—All hail the power of Jesus' Name!**—Edward Perronet, stanzas 1-4
John Rippon (315), stanza 5

First Tune: **Coronation**—Oliver Holden
Second Tune: **Miles' Lane**—William Shrubsole
Third Tune: **Diadem**—James Ellor

The nature of the story of this hymn and its first tune is such that the two cannot well be discussed separately. While living in Canterbury, Edward Perronet met and became friendly with William Shrubsole, then a chorister at Canterbury Cathedral. At the age of twenty Shrubsole wrote the tune now called "Miles' Lane" for the hymn "All hail the power of Jesus' Name." This tune, under the title "Shrubsole," was published with the first stanza of the hymn in *The Gospel Magazine,* Augustus M. Toplady's journal, in November, 1779. In answer to appeals the remainder of the hymn appeared in the same journal in April, 1780. There were eight four-line stanzas in the original. No name was signed to the hymn and its authorship was a matter of speculation for a number of years. Doctor Julian gives full particulars as to how Perronet's claim to it has been established. The original has been much edited, altogether to its betterment. The last stanza, beginning,

O that, with yonder sacred throng,

is the product of John Rippon. The hymn has rarely, if ever, been used in its original form.

This is an instance in which a tune launched a hymn. After its appearance in *The Gospel Magazine* it became immediately immensely popular, especially among the Dissenters, and has remained so, particularly in England, where hymn and tune ("Miles' Lane") are referred to as the "English Te Deum." Its original form may be seen on page 206.

"Miles' Lane" certainly began appearing in American songbooks by the early 1850's. Sung to this unusually powerful and vigorous tune, the hymn is capable of producing a profound effect. When E. P. Scott, a missionary in India, ventured into the mountain stronghold of some murderous natives who had never heard of the gospel of Christ, he was suddenly confronted by members of the tribe who pointed their spears at his breast. Thinking death was near, Scott, who had taken a violin with him, took it from its case and, closing his eyes, began playing and singing this hymn. When he began the stanza, "Let every kindred, every tribe," he opened his eyes and was relieved to note a decided change in the demeanor of his captors. They invited him to join them, and he immediately began two and one-half years of successful work among them. His health failing, he was compelled to return to America for rest. Upon his departure some of the tribesmen followed him for thirty or forty miles entreating him to return to them, for they said, "There are tribes beyond us who have never heard the glad tidings of salvation!" Upon the recovery of his health he did return to them, laboring there until his death.

The Perronet family was of French extraction, the grandfather of Edward Perronet coming to England from Switzerland in 1680. The family were French Huguenot refugees. The Rev. Vincent Perronet, Edward's father, Vicar of Shoreham, was a close friend and confidant of John and Charles Wesley. There are many references to him in the records left by the Wesley brothers. He was sometimes called "The Archbishop of Methodism."

Edward Perronet, born in 1726 (exact date uncertain), was educated at home under a tutor. There is a question as to whether or not he ever attended Oxford University. Because of his growing dislike for the Church of England, in which he had considered taking Holy Orders, he, instead, threw himself with enthusiasm into the work of evangelism being carried on by the Wesleys,

Miles' Lane
(Early form of William Shrubsole's tune)
tr
tr
All hail the Pow'r of Je - su's Name, Let An - gels pros - trate fall;
crown him,
Bring forth the Roy - al Di - a - dem, crown him,
To crown him,
Chorus
tr
Crown him Lord of all.
tr
Crown him Lord of all.

and was with John Wesley at Bolton when a mob filled the street before the house in which they were staying. Perronet ventured out of the house and the mob immediately closed in, threw him down and rolled him in the mire; so that when he scrambled from them and got into the house again, one could scarce tell what or who he was.

It was at Edward Perronet's house that Charles Wesley met Mrs. Vazielle, who had aroused the interest of his brother, John. When Perronet told Charles that his brother was thinking of marrying the lady, Charles "refused his company to the chapel and retired to mourn with my faithful Sally."

John Wesley had great admiration for Perronet and wanted to hear him preach, but Perronet seemed determined that he should not. Seeing Perronet in his congregation one day, Wesley calmly announced the former would preach the next morning. Perronet, feeling he could not go against Wesley's wishes, appeared in the pulpit at the proper time, announced the hymn, led in prayer, and then explained that he had not been asked to preach and had not consented to do so, but would deliver at that service the finest sermon that had ever been preached. He then read the Sermon on the Mount with no word of comment, after which he brought the service to a close.

Edward Perronet and his brother, Charles, both Methodist preachers, favored separation of their group from the Church of England when that question was under discussion. This movement was opposed by the Wesleys. Perronet had written *The Mitre, a Sacred Poem,* 1757, sharply criticizing the Church. He discontinued selling it at Wesley's protest, but continued giving copies of it away. This caused a break between Perronet and the Wesleys, and also led to an estrangement between Perronet and the Countess of Huntingdon (142), whose chaplain he had been at Canterbury. He then served an independent church in that city until his death, January 2, 1792.

William Shrubsole, who wrote the tune "Miles' Lane," was born at Canterbury in January, 1760, and sang in the Cathedral choir there for seven years, during which he also studied organ playing. At twenty-two years of age he succeeded to the post of organist at Bangor Cathedral, but remained there only about a year, being dismissed because of dissatisfaction caused by his associating too much with the Dissenters. He had been warned of the consequences of "attending conventicles." Leaving Bangor he went to London and engaged in music teaching. Almost immediately he became attached to one of Lady Huntingdon's chapels (Spa Fields), where he remained as organist for the rest of his life. While living in Canterbury he had become the intimate friend of Edward Perronet, the author of the hymn, "All hail the power of Jesus' Name." Perronet became so attached to Shrubsole that he made him one of the executors of his will and left him some property. A clause in the will states the property was left Shrubsole because of

that fine, disinterested affection he has ever shown me from our first acquaintance, even when a proverb of reproach, cast off by all my relatives, disinherited unjustly, and left to sink or swim as afflictions and God's providence should appoint.

William Shrubsole, baptized January 13, 1760, is now known solely for having written this tune. He died at London, January 18, 1806. The composer of "Miles' Lane" must not be confused with the hymn writer of the same name who was so actively interested in the London Missionary Society.

"Coronation," set to Perronet's hymn, appeared in Oliver Holden's second book, *The Union Harmony,* issued in 1793, and, in America at least, its popularity has been permanent. In the older books the third line of the tune appears, as Holden wrote it, to be sung as a duet between the tenor and bass. In *The Sabbath,* compiled by C. Everest, Philadelphia, 1873, occurs this footnote:

> The third line of Coronation has been arranged to furnish choirs with their appropriate parts. This will not prevent the congregations from singing the tune in their accustomed manner.

The reason for calling the tune "Coronation" is quite obvious—"And crown Him Lord of all." The small organ upon which Holden played when he composed this tune may still be seen in the Old State House, Boston, in the rooms of the Bostonian Society.

Oliver Holden was born at Shirley, Massachusetts, September 18, 1765, lived there until he was twenty-one years old, and then moved to Charlestown. After the burning of Charlestown by the British, Holden, a carpenter by trade, made much money in helping to rebuild it. He became a large operator in real estate, was a prominent Mason, was elected to his state legislature, and was in all respects a leading citizen. Much interested in music, he owned a music store, led singing schools and the church choir, wrote music, and compiled songbooks. He donated the land upon which a Baptist church was built in Charlestown, and later, almost unaided, built another, for many years popularly called the Puritan Church. Of this, he was the leading figure, and acted as its preacher throughout its life. He died on September 4, 1844.

"Diadem" was composed by James Ellor for a Sunday School Anniversary of the composer's home church. A generation or two ago most of the inhabitants of Droylsden, Ellor's birthplace, worked at hatmaking during the day and then spent their evenings practicing singing and playing the hymns for the following Sunday's services at the Wesleyan Chapel. Under the leadership of Ellor these services attracted more than local notice, and people from a considerable distance attended any of these services that might have special significance. One day in 1838, when he was nineteen years of age, Ellor brought to the factory a new tune he had composed for "All hail the power of Jesus' Name!" Work was immediately suspended until it was "solfa-ed" a few times. Its reception was so enthusiastic that copies were made for distribution in order that it might be sung as the feature of the forthcoming anniversary. It was so popular that it soon became the custom to use it on all anniversary occasions "for miles around." It is one of the many fine hymn tunes produced by English Methodists who had received no formal musical training. Possibly that is a reason for their homely, human appeal.

James Ellor was born at Droylsden, a typical Lancashire, England, village about three miles from Manchester, in 1819. He was a hatter, working at his trade during the week and leading the singing at the local Wesleyan Chapel on Sundays. Sometime before 1843 he gave up working at his trade and took a position with a railway that was being constructed near Manchester. In 1843 he came to America, where for some time he worked at his trade of hatmaking. Little is known of his late years except that for some years before his death, 1899, he was nearly blind.

**165—Look, ye saints, the sight is glorious**—Thomas Kelly (163)

**Cwm Rhondda**—John Hughes

The hymn was entitled "The Second Advent" in the third edition of Thomas Kelly's *Hymns on Various Passages of Scripture,* 1809. It is based on Revelation 11. 15:

> And the seventh angel sounded; and there were great voices in heaven, saying, The kingdoms of this world are become the kingdoms of our Lord, and of his Christ; and he shall reign for ever and ever.

Doctor Julian says it ranks with many of the best hymns by Watts and Charles Wesley. Its original four stanzas have not been changed in any way. It was introduced to American Methodism through *The Hymnal of the Methodist Church,* 1878.

"Cwm Rhondda" is the name of the principal coal town in Glamorganshire, Wales. *Cwm* means "valley"; *Rhondda* is the name of a particular valley in the coal district in South Wales. Mrs. Hannah H. Hughes, widow of the composer, gives this information:

> My late husband, Mr. John Hughes, composed the hymn tune "Rhondda," in 1907. Owing to the fact that there was another tune composed by Mr. M. O. Treherbert by this name, it was changed to "Cwm Rhondda" a few years later. It was undoubtedly his "masterpiece," and is sung in almost every country. He was inspired to compose this hymn tune on a Sunday morning when he attended Divine Service at Salem Chapel, situated in quiet country surroundings.

The tune was written for the Anniversary Services at Capel Rhondda, Pontypridd, in 1907. In less than twenty-five years it has been used on more than five thousand festival programs in Great Britain.

John Hughes, composer of "Cwm Rhondda," who rose from a doorboy at Glyn Colliery (at twelve years of age) to the position of an official in the traffic department of the Great Western Colliery Company, was born at Dowlais, Wales, in 1873. He was a lifelong member of Salem Baptist Church and succeeded his father there as deacon and precentor. Mr. Hughes was the composer of many Sunday-school marches, anthems, and hymn tunes. He died on May 14, 1932.

**166—Hail, Thou once despised Jesus!**—John Bakewell

**Autumn**—Arranged from François Hippolyte Barthélémon

Two stanzas of this hymn were first published in *A Collection of Hymns Addressed to the Holy, Holy, Holy, triune God, in the Person of Christ Jesus, our Mediator and Advocate,* 1757. In 1760 it appeared in M. Madan's *Collection of Psalms and Hymns,* substantially as used in this book. Augustus M. Toplady (204) included it in his *Psalms and Hymns,* 1776, omitting the second stanza and making the remainder "subservient to his stern Calvinistic views." The various editings are not important enough to warrant taking the space to enumerate them in a MANUAL such as this, yet the hymn as now generally used seems to have been the product of Bakewell and Toplady, and possibly Madan. The only portion that can be said, without question, to be Bakewell's is the first stanza and the first four lines each from stanzas 3 and 4. Dean Tillett has said:

> The hymn is worshipful and at the same time is strongly doctrinal. The atonement and intercession of Christ are plainly taught. It has been widely used, and has strengthened the faith and inspired the worship of unnumbered disciples.

John Bakewell was born at Brailsford, Derbyshire, England, in 1721, and died at Lewisham, near Greenwich, March 18, 1819. His early years are clouded in obscurity. When eighteen years of age he read Thomas Boston's *Fourfold State,* which turned his thoughts to religion, and he began to preach in 1744, the year of the first Methodist Conference. Upon his removal to London he met and became a friend of John and Charles Wesley, M. Madan, Augustus M. Toplady, and other evangelical preachers. In 1749 he became one of John Wesley's local preachers. For a time he conducted the Greenwich Royal Park Academy, where he introduced Methodism, holding the first class meeting at his house. Among several of John Bakewell's interesting connections with early Methodism: he was present when John Fletcher was ordained at Whitehall; he was the host of Thomas Olivers when the latter wrote "The God of Abraham praise." When John Wesley dined with him on his wedding day and was shown over the house, he is said to have exclaimed, "Fine enough, in all conscience, for a Methodist!"

In the *Methodist Magazine* for July, 1816, there appeared a letter on brotherly love written by Bakewell, submitted for publication by a friend, which concludes with this prayer:

> May God in his infinite goodness grant that we, and all serious Christians, of every denomination, may labour for a perfect union of love, and to have our hearts knit together with the bond of peace; that following after those essential truths, in which we all agree, we may all have the same scriptural experience, and thereafter attain one and the same kingdom of glory.

John Bakewell is buried in City Road Chapel near his friend John Wesley. This epitaph appears on his tombstone:

Sacred to the Memory
of
John Bakewell,
late of Greenwich
who departed this life March 18, 1819,
age ninety-eight.
He adorned the doctrine of God, our Saviour,
eighty years,
and preached His Glorious Gospel
about seventy years.
"The memory of the just is blessed."

"Autumn" is an instance of the carelessness with which compilers of tune books accept, seemingly without question, statements concerning composers of tunes even though they may be meticulous in their care in the case of authors of texts. Sometimes a bewildering array of composers or sources has been associated with some one tune. "Autumn" is said to have been written by Louis von Esch (?); François H. Barthélémon; Ludovich Nicholson (?); arranged by George F. Root (439); a Spanish melody; Spanish from Marechio (?); a Scotch melody; "probably from the eighteenth century," and arranged from Psalm 42 in *The Genevan Psalter,* 1551 (3).

Dr. Louis F. Benson (38), in discussing the Genevan melodies, says that they have left no trace among us other than "a reminiscence embodied in the familiar 'Autumn.' . . ." Upon that suggestion, apparently, this tune has been said to have been taken from *The Genevan Psalter* of 1551. The author has not seen a copy of the 1551 book, but has found the setting of the forty-second psalm in the editions of 1564, 1595, and 1701, finds them alike, and assumes no change has been made in the melody of this particular psalm tune from its beginnings. It is:

PSEAV. XLII. TH. DE BE.

*Le Prophete empeſché par ſes ennemis d'eſtre en l'aſſemblee du peuple ſainct, en fait une gran complainte, & proteſte qu'il y eſt de cœur, encores qu'il ſoit abſent de corps: declare ſes calamités, s'aſſeure & conſole ſoy-meſme en la bonté de Dieu. Pſeaume pour ceux que les infideles empeſchent de ſe trouuer en l'Egliſe.*

Ainſi qu'on oit le cerf bruire,
Pourchaſſant le frais des eaux, Ainſi mõ cœur
qui ſouſpire, Seigneur, apres tes ruiſ-
ſeaux, Va touſiours criant, ſuiuant Le
grand, le grand Dieu viuant. Helas, donques
quand ſera ce Que verray de
Dieu la face?

...urs & nuicts pour ma viande
...pleurs me vay ſouſtenant,
...oy qu'on me demande,
...eſt ton Dieu maintenant?
...e ſon en me ſouuenant,
...n troupe i'alloy' menant,
...ant, chantans, groſſe bande
...aye au temple ſon offrande.

D'ou vient que t'esbahis ores
Mon ame, & fremis d'eſmoy?
Eſpere en Dieu: car encores
Sera-il chanté de moy,
Quand d'vn regard ſeulement
Il guerira mon torment.
Las! mon Dieu, ie ſen mon ame,
Qui de grand deſir ſe paſme.

Car i'ay de toy ſouuenance
Depuis outre le Iordain,
Et la froide demeurance
De Hermon pays hautain,
Et de Miſar autre mont.
Vn gouffre l'autre ſemond,
Lors que tonnent ſur ma teſte
Les torrens de ta tempeſte.

Tous les grans flots de ton onde
Par deſſus moy ont paſſé:
Mais ſur vn poinct ie me fonde,
Que n'eſtant plus courroucé,
De iour tes biens m'enuoyras,
De nuict chanter me feras,
Priant d'vne ame rauie,
Toy ſeul autheur de ma vie.

Ie diray, Dieu ma puiſſance,
D'où vient qu'en oubli ſuis mis?
Pourquoy vi-ie en deſplaiſance,
Preſſé de mes ennemis?
Ie ſen leurs meſchans propos
Me naurer iuſques aux os,
Quand ils diſent à toute heure,
Où fait ton Dieu ſa demeure?

D'où vient que t'esbahis ores,
Mon ame, & fremis d'eſmoy?
Eſpere en Dieu, car encores
Sera-il loué de moy:
D'autant qu'il eſt le Sauueur,
Me preſentant ſa faueur.
Bref, pour conclurre, mon ame,
C'eſt le Dieu que ie reclame.

The above is a facsimile of part of a page taken from a 1564 edition of *The Genevan Psalter.*

Translated into modern notation, without time signature or measure bars, to indicate psalm-tune rhythm, it reads:

In the modern *Chants Chrétiens* (the author has an edition of 1841 and has seen others), no changes have been made except rhythmically, and the one note in the second measure from the last, as will be noticed from this form found there:

That tune certainly is not "Autumn," and beyond the first few notes contains not even, as Doctor Benson says, a "reminiscence" of it.

Some time after 1796 a song with harp accompaniment, ascribed to F. H. Barthélémon, the eminent violinist, was published with words taken from *The Monk,* by Matthew Gregory Lewis (1775-1818). Often called "Monk" Lewis, the English romance writer and dramatist, and one time member of Parliament, was mentioned by Byron in *English Bards and Scotch Reviewers,* in this fashion:

> Wonder-working Lewis, Monk or Bard,
> Who fain would'st make Parnassus a churchyard;
> Even Satan's self with thee might dread to dwell,
> And in thy skull discern a deeper hell.

In an advertisement to *The Monk,* Lewis says,

> The poem "Belerma and Durandarte" is translated from some stanzas to be found in a collection of old Spanish poetry, which contains also the popular song of Gayferos and Melisandra, mentioned in *Don Quixote,*

which probably accounts for the tune being ascribed to Spanish origin, and undoubtedly accounts for the name "Balerma" given to Robert Simpson's tune mentioned below. William Chappell (1809-1888), English music historian and author of *Popular Music of the Olden Time,* in two volumes, 1855-1859, says:

> The melody is quite unlike Spanish music or any kind of sixteenth-century music. I should say it is not older than the last century, and far more likely to have been composed within the present by a singer or violinist who had a feeling for melody.

With regard to its being "a Scotch melody," George F. Graham (1789-1867), erudite Scottish musician and critic, author of the critical, biographical, and historical notes to *The Songs of Scotland, adapted to their Appropriate Melodies,* 1848-49, speaks of it as being Barthélémon's composition.

1. Sad and fear - ful is the sto - ry Of the Ron - ces - val - es
2. Oh, Be - ler - ma! oh, my dear one! For my pain and pleas- ure
fight; On those fa - tal plains of glo - ry, Per - ish'd
born, Seven long years I served thee, fair one, Seven long
man - y a gal - lant knight. There fell Du - ran - dar - te,
years my sea was scorn. And when now, thy heart re
nev - er Verse a no - bler chief - tain named; He be -
ply - ing, To my wish - es burns like mine, Cru - el
fore his lips for ev - er Closed in si - lence thus ex-claimed:
fate, my bliss de - ny - ing, Bids me ev - 'ry hope re - sign.

For the ten stanzas of this poem, about the slaying of Durandarte, a brave knight, by the Moors at the siege of Roncesvalles (Roncevaux) in 788, the tune is unmistakably "Autumn." There seems to be no basis whatever for ascribing it to any other than Barthélémon.

There is a familiar tune called "Balerma" which was used twice in *The Methodist Hymnal* of 1905 (242 and 260), said to have been arranged by

Robert Simpson (1790-1832), a Scottish weaver. This arrangement was found among some papers left by Simpson shortly after his death, and was published the year following. It seems to have been suggested by this song of Barthélémon's.

François Hippolyte Barthélémon, son of a French officer and an Irish lady, one of the most eminent violinists of his time and a composer of note, was born at Bordeaux, July 27, 1741, and died at London, July 20 (23?), 1808. He married Mary Young, a niece of Mrs. Lampe, whose husband, late in 1746, wrote the first book of original tunes to Charles Wesley's hymns, entitled *Hymns of the Great Festivals, and Other Occasions.* Barthélémon entered the army but was persuaded by his friend the Earl of Kellie to resign and make music his profession. Settling in London about 1765, he became a brilliant violinist and composed much music for the theater and the public gardens but very little for the Church. His only known hymn tune is "Morning Hymn," which was written for and should always be used with Thomas Ken's "Awake, my soul, and with the sun" (34). His last years were filled with misfortune, and he died a broken-hearted paralytic.

**167—Hark! ten thousand harps and voices**—Thomas Kelly (163)

**Harwell**—Lowell Mason (19)

This hymn, based on Hebrews 1. 6, "And again, when He bringeth in the firstbegotten into the world, He saith, And let all the angels of God worship Him," is taken from the second edition of the author's *Hymns on Various Passages of Scripture,* 1806. Of the original seven stanzas, 1, 6, and 7 are used, unaltered. The "Hallelujahs" and "Amens" were added by Lowell Mason when he wrote "Harwell" for it. The Joint Commission charged with compiling the *Methodist Hymnal,* 1935, not always wisely softened all the "Hallelujahs" into "Alleluias." Sometimes a Methodist feels the need of shouting "Hallelujah!"

"Harwell" is one of the best known of Lowell Mason's original tunes. Written in 1840, it first appeared in his *Carmina Sacra,* 1841. The tune appears here in its original form. It had been edited—not to advantage—in the 1905 edition.

**168—O could I speak the matchless worth**—Samuel Medley

**Ariel** (19)—Lowell Mason (19)

This hymn appeared first in the third edition of the author's *Hymns,* 1789, with the title, "Praise of Christ." Of the original six stanzas beginning,

Not of terrestrial mortal themes,

2, 6, and 8 are used.

Samuel Medley was born June 23, 1738, at Cheshunt, Hertsfordshire, England, where his father kept a school. He was well educated and was apprenticed to an oil dealer, but not liking the business, joined the Royal Navy. At the time in England, one objecting to an apprenticeship could fill out his time by joining the navy. He was obliged to retire from active service after being severely wounded in a battle with the French fleet off Port Lagos, in 1759. Taken to the home of his grandfather, he was converted by the prayers of that good man. He joined the Baptist Church, successfully conducted a school, and then began a preaching experience which was climaxed by twenty-seven years' work, from 1772, at Byrom Street Church, Liverpool, where his popularity was extraordinary. Doctor Julian lists twenty of his hymns which have had common use, especially in his own denomination. W. R. Stephenson said:

> Their charm consists less in their poetry than in the warmth and occasional pathos with which they give expression to human experience.

Most of his hymns were printed first on leaflets, commencing in 1786. He died after a long and painful illness, July 17, 1799, at Liverpool.

**169—Ye servants of God, your Master proclaim**—Charles Wesley (25)

Hanover—William Croft

This was No. 1 in *Hymns to be Sung in a Tumult,* included in *Hymns for Times of Trouble and Persecution,* 1744. It was one of four hymns literally intended "to be sung in a tumult," which were published in a booklet. Stanzas 1, 4, 5, and 6 of the original six stanzas of the hymn are used here. The other two are worthy of being quoted.

2 The waves of the sea Have lift up their voice,
Sore troubled that we In Jesus rejoice;
The floods they are roaring, But Jesus is here,
While we are adoring He always is near.

3 When devils engage, The billows arise,
And horribly rage, And threaten the skies;
Their fury shall never Our steadfastness shock,
The weakest believer Is built on a rock.

Two changes in the text have been made. In line 3, stanza 3, the original,

> Our Jesus's praises The angels proclaim,

was changed to read,

> The praises of Jesus the angels proclaim,

and line 4, stanza 4,

> And thanks never ceasing, And infinite love,

was made to read,

> And thanks never ceasing for infinite love.

The ten years from 1739, when Charles Wesley went to Bristol, to 1749, when he was married, were strenuous ones for the Methodists, preachers and laymen alike. The *Journal* gives many instances of serious assaults being made upon them. In the midst of such persecution, who but a Charles Wesley could write hymns "to be sung in a tumult"? These men and women knew they would be persecuted—be set upon and beaten—yet the great poet of Methodism wrote hymns for them to sing! No wonder the Wesleyan Revival was such a triumph.

This hymn is finding its way into an increasing number of books. Doctor MacMillan thinks

> the reason is not to be found in its value as literature, for Charles Wesley has produced hymns far greater in this respect, but there is in it the very spirit of adoring praise, and a fervid enthusiasm which must find utterance.

"Hanover" first appeared in the sixth edition of the *Supplement to the New Version* by Tate and Brady, 1708 (see No. 14), without a name. It was said to be "A New Tune to the 149th Psalm of the New Version and the 104th of the Old." "St. Anne" (384) also saw its first appearance in this book. While the name of no composer appeared with either tune, both are quite generally credited to Doctor Croft, who is supposed to have edited the work.

John Wesley seems to have supplied its first name, calling it "Bromswick" (probably by way of complimenting the then reigning house of Brunswick) in his *Foundery Collection,* 1742. Evidently, it met with favor by the early Methodists, for it was again used by John Wesley in his *Sacred Melody,* 1765, this time called "Tally's," doubtless because he thought it had been written by Thomas Tallis (51). For a time it was said to have been composed by Handel (88), but as he did not arrive in England until 1710, two years after it appeared in the *Supplement,* it is hardly probable that he had anything to do with it. Credit was given to Handel in American Methodism's first tune book, *The Methodist Harmonist,* 1821, yet it was omitted in later editions. It came into its name "Hanover" during the reign of George III, although it was also called "St. George" in some books. It is a famous tune and has long been associated with these words. It is played daily on the bells of old St. Clement's Church, London.

William Croft, who was born in 1678 (baptized December 30, 1678) at Nether Ettington, Warwickshire, England, and who died August 14, 1727, at Bath, was one of the Children of the Chapel Royal, and became famous as an organist and composer. He was made a Doctor of Music by Oxford University in 1713, his exercise being two odes, one in English, one in Latin, on the Peace of Utrecht. In his youth he wrote some sonatas, odes, and songs, and for the theater. But his real contribution was his music written for the Church. It is said he influenced Handel to a considerable extent. His best known tunes are important historically as being the earliest examples of the English psalm tune, in distinction to the Genevan style.

> They required quicker singing, and the glorious rhythmical impulse of "Hanover" and its triple measure worked at once a distinct originality.

Sir John Hawkins, in his *History of Music,* 1776, says that William Croft

> was a grave and decent man, and being a sincere lover of his art, devoted himself to

> the study and practice of it. The bent of his genius led him to church music; nevertheless, he composed and published six sets of tunes for two violins and a bass, which in his youth he made for several plays. He also composed and published six sonatas for two flutes, and two solos for a flute and a bass. The flute . . . being formerly a favorite instrument in this country.

He is also noted for his anthems, continues Hawkins, quite naïvely, most of which are

> in that grand and solemn style of composition which should ever distinguish music appropriate to the service of the Church. Many of the anthems were made on the most joyful occasions, that is to say, thanksgiving for victories obtained over our enemies during a war in which the interests of all Europe were concerned.

Doctor Croft died of an illness "occasioned by his attendance on his duty" at the coronation of George II. On a monument erected to his memory is an epitaph, a part of which reads:

> In his celebrated works, which for the most part he consecrated to God, he made a diligent progress; nor was it by the solemnity of the numbers alone, but by the force of his ingenuity, and the sweetness of his manners, and even his countenance, he excellently recommended them. Having resided among mortals for fifty years, behaving with the utmost candor (not more conspicuous for any other office of humanity than a friendship and a love truly paternal towards all whom he instructed), he departed to the heavenly choir, . . . that, being near, he might add his own Hallelujah to the concert of angels.

**170—Crown Him with many crowns—Matthew Bridges and Godfrey Thring (41)**

**Diademata**—George Job Elvey

This selection of stanzas comprising this hymn consists of 1 and 3 from Matthew Bridges' original which first appeared in the author's *Hymns of the Heart,* 1851, with the title,

In Capite Ejus Diademata Multa, Apoc. xix. 12;

then in his *Passion of Jesus,* 1852, with the title changed to,

Third Sorrowful Mystery, Songs of the Seraphs, Apoc. xix. 12.

Stanza 2 is by Godfrey Thring, and stanza 4 is a composite: lines 1-4 Bridges; 5-8, Thring.

At the Centenary Thanksgiving of the London Bible Society held in November, 1905, at Albert Hall, the presiding officer, the Marquis of Northampton, after reading congratulatory messages from all of the Protestant rulers of Christendom, said: "Now that we have read these messages from earthly rulers, let us turn our minds to the King of kings. We will sing, "Crown Him with many crowns."

Matthew Bridges, born July 14, 1800, at Malden, Essex, England, was brought up in the Church of England, but in 1848 he entered the Roman Catholic Church, following John Henry Newman (514) and others interested in the Oxford Movement. He began writing poetry and prose in 1825, continuing until he had published several volumes. Aside from poetry his chief intellectual interest was in the field of history. The last years of his life were spent in the Province of Quebec, Canada, where he died, October 6, 1894.

"Diademata" was written for this hymn by Dr. G. J. Elvey for the Appendix (1868) to the Original Edition of *Hymns Ancient and Modern.* Its name is taken from the Latin title given the hymn.

George Job Elvey, born March 27, 1816, at Canterbury, England, was an organist and composer who began his career as a choir boy at Canterbury Cathedral. He studied with his brother and at the Royal Academy of Music, London. When only nineteen he received the appointment as organist of St. George's Chapel, Windsor, a post which he held for forty-seven years, until his retirement. In 1838 he graduated from Oxford as a Bachelor of Music, and two years later was granted the Doctorate degree in music from the same institution. He was knighted in 1871, after his composition of a Festival March for the wedding of the Princess Louise. His connection with the Chapel at Windsor caused him to have charge of the music for many important events of state. Most of his works are for the Church, many of the larger ones having been sung by choir and festival organizations. While Doctor Elvey did not contribute many hymn tunes, those he did write are models of what a good one should be. "No one could be long in his presence without being struck by his devout, religious spirit, and it was this spirit that went into all of his work." He died December 9, 1893, at Windlesham, Surrey, and was buried outside of the west front of the Chapel he had served for so many years.

**171—Rejoice, the Lord is King**—Charles Wesley (25)
**Darwall**—John Darwall

The hymn, from Charles Wesley's *Hymns for Our Lord's Resurrection,* 1746, was doubtless based on Philippians 4. 4: "Rejoice in the Lord alway: and again I say, Rejoice." Stanzas 1-3 of the original six-stanza hymn are used unaltered. While the resurrection note is sounded in the second stanza, it is an excellent processional hymn for general occasions.

Handel (88) composed music for three of Charles Wesley's hymns, this being one of them. Wesley had met the great composer at the home of a Mr. Rich, lessee of Covent Garden, London, who had arranged for Handel to produce some of his operas at that theater. Mrs. Rich, who had been converted under the preaching of the Wesleys, is said to have asked Handel to set music to "Rejoice, the Lord is King," "Sinners, obey the gospel word," and "O Love Divine, how sweet Thou art!" This he did, writing "Gospal," "Cannons," and "Fitzwilliam" to go with these hymns, respectively. None of these settings are familiar to American Methodists, but in the recent *Methodist Hymn-Book,* published in England in 1933, "Gospal" is used as the setting for this hymn, continuing a practice of nearly two hundred years.

"Darwall," composed by the Rev. John Darwall, was originally called "Darwall's 148th" because it had been set to the new version of that Psalm in

Aaron Williams's (227) *New Universal Psalmodist,* 1770. It is widely used with this hymn. Following is the form in which it first appeared:

It will be noticed the melody began on A instead of D, as in this book. A

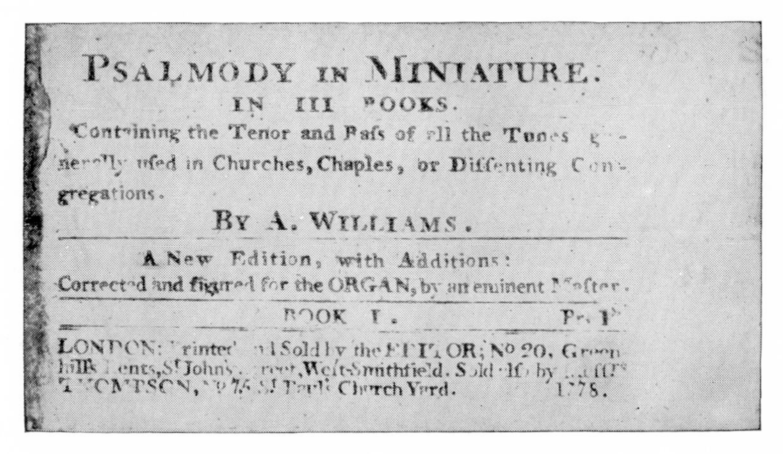
PSALMODY IN MINIATURE.
IN III BOOKS.
Containing the Tenor and Bass of all the Tunes generally used in Churches, Chaples, or Dissenting Congregations.
BY A. WILLIAMS.

A New Edition, with Additions:
Corrected and figured for the ORGAN, by an eminent Master.

BOOK I. Pr. 1

LONDON: Printed and Sold by the EDITOR; No 20, Greenhill's Rents, St John's Street, West-Smithfield. Sold also by ... THOMPSON, No 75 St Paul's Church Yard. 1778.

small book (see illustration above), *Psalmody in Miniature. In III Books. Containing the Tenor and Bass of all the Tunes generally used in Churches, Chapels, or Dissenting congregations,* 1778, is of interest not only because it is "a curious little tune-book . . . a very much minified form of Aaron Williams's *Universal Psalmodist,"* but because it contains "Darwall's 148th" with the melody beginning on D. This little book is

> A New Edition, with Additions: Corrected
> and figured for the Organ, by an eminent Master.

In the "Advertisement" (Preface) this statement is made:

> Though this Edition is posthumous, the Tunes were figured and corrected during the Author's life, and by his desire. The other Improvements are what himself intended had his life been spared.

This is quoted because it shows the change in the first note of the melody was made as early as eight years after its first appearance. When this change was made has been a matter of concern to hymn-tune specialists.

The words (first stanza) for which this famous tune was written should be of interest as they are not now easily accessible:

> Ye boundless realms of joy,
> Exalt your Maker's fame,
> His praise your tongues employ
> Above the starry frame!
> Your voices raise,
> Ye Cherubim
> And Seraphim,
> To sing His praise.

It is interesting to note how the melodic line of the tune follows the suggestion of the words.

John Darwall, English clergyman, poet, and good amateur musician, known now only for having written this tune, composed a tune for each of the one hundred and fifty psalms (in two parts only), some of which gained currency. He also wrote some hymns, among them "A Christmas Hymn and Tune," "A Charity Hymn and Tune," and "A Hymn to Which Is Prefixed a Biographical Notice," and published two volumes of sonatas for the pianoforte. He was born at Haughton, Staffordshire, England, in 1731 (baptized January 13), and was educated at Manchester Grammar School and at Brasenose College, Oxford, which he entered when only fourteen years of age. After graduation he became curate and later vicar of St. Matthew's, Walsall, where he served for twenty years. He died at Walsall, December 18, 1789.

# THE HOLY SPIRIT

## The Holy Spirit

**172—Come, Holy Spirit, heavenly Dove—Isaac Watts (3)**
**St. Martin's—William Tans'ur**

The hymn is taken from Doctor Watts's *Hymns and Spiritual Songs,* edition of 1709, in five stanzas, entitled "Breathing after the Holy Spirit: or, Fervency of Devotion Desired." Doctor Julian says:

> About twenty texts are now in common use, each differing from the other in some detail, and all joining in rejecting certain expressions in the original. . . . In its various forms the use of this hymn is extensive.

Stanzas 1, 3, and 5 are as in the original. Doctor Watts wrote:

> 2 Look how we grovel here below,
> Fond of these trifling toys!
> Our souls can neither fly, nor go,
> To reach eternal joys.
>
> 4 Dear Lord! and shall we ever live
> At this poor dying rate;
> Our love so faint, so cold to Thee
> And Thine to us so great?

The changes in the second stanza have been traced to George Whitefield's *Collection,* and line 1, stanza 4, was changed by John Wesley, who objected to addressing the Deity too familiarly.

"St. Martin's" was first published in the second edition of *The Royal Melody Compleat, or the New Harmony of Zion,* London, 1740, and was marked "Composed in four parts: W. T." The initials stood for William Tans'ur, the compiler of the book. It has been widely used in the United States ever since its introduction through the early New England singing-school books. The tune is reminiscent of the florid style of hymn-tune writing of the early eighteenth century.

William Tans'ur, English composer and writer on musical theory, was probably born in 1706, although he informs us in the Preface to *The Elements of Musick display'd,* 1772, that the year was 1700. The records of the parish of Dunchurch, Warwickshire, state that William "Tanzer" was baptized November 6, 1706. Tans'ur says he was born at Dunchurch, and as it is not probable that his parents neglected to have him baptized until his sixth year, 1706 is probably the correct date. Why and when the name was changed from "Tanzer" to "Tans'ur," and why the apostrophe was used, is not stated, although most of the details of his biography are obtained from the prefaces and imprints of Tans'ur's several books. He compiled a number of tune books, wrote some verses, and was the author of two very creditable works on the theory of music: *A New Musical Grammar,* 1746-1756, and *The Elements of Musick display'd,* 1772. He died at St. Noet's, October 7, 1783.

**173—Holy Spirit, Truth divine**—Samuel Longfellow (42)
**Mercy** (47)—Louis Moreau Gottschalk (47)

Stanzas 1-4 from a six-stanza hymn first published in *Hymns of the Spirit,* 1864, one of three books compiled by its author, Samuel Longfellow, and Samuel Johnson (405). It was entitled "Prayer for Inspiration." Doctor Longfellow was convinced that the Divine Spirit only should be the object of man's devotion, yet he held Jesus "in high and loving regard" as a teacher.

**174—I worship Thee, O Holy Ghost**—William Fairfield Warren
**Cooling**—Alonzo Judson Abbey

William Fairfield Warren wrote this hymn in 1877 for publication in the *Hymnal of the Methodist Episcopal Church,* 1878. Written at the request of the editors, it has proved such a useful hymn that it has been included in other collections.

William Fairfield Warren, LL.D., was born of old New-England stock in Williamsburg, Massachusetts, March 13, 1833, and died at his Brookline home, in his ninety-seventh year, December 6, 1929.

He pursued his formal education in the district school and East Greenwich Academy; Wesleyan University, Connecticut, where he graduated in 1853; Andover Theological Seminary; the Universities of Berlin and Halle. His broader education he continued to the very end of his long life through unremitting study and research, publishing his results in books and learned journals. His intellectual interests were as wide as the whole field of human knowledge, and as deep as its subsoil in philosophy and religion.

Doctor Warren was ordained as a minister of the Methodist Episcopal Church in 1855, and in 1859-60 was pastor of the Bromfield Street Church in Boston. For the next five years he was professor of systematic theology in the Missionsanstalt, Bremen, Germany. Invited to fill the same chair in the theological seminary just transferred from Concord, New Hampshire, to Boston, he returned to share, as acting president, in the plans that led to the establishment of Boston University in 1869. Although reluctant to leave his studies or to reduce his teaching, he accepted as president the task of organizing the new University. For half a century he was the leader in determining the policies—many of them innovations—the aims, and the standards of this nonsectarian institution.

Doctor Warren's work within the Methodist Church was varied and untiring. In scores of ways he made himself felt for the right handling of problems connected with freedom for incisive scholarship in theology, history, and biblical learning; with the place of women in the organization of the Church; with the organic law of the Church itself; with the members of foreign birth and speech; with the Negro; with the reuniting of the Northern and Southern Methodists; with the church schools, colleges, and seminaries;

with missions, other benevolent activities, and interdenominational relations. He was a wise and quiet leader, never seeking recognition, but ever giving the full measure of his insight, sympathies, and skilled power to the needs and opportunities of the Church.

Though endowed with a gift of poetical expression, both in meter and in the free rhythm of address and oral prayer, Doctor Warren never published any collection of his verses. He wrote the hymn, "I Worship Thee, O Holy Ghost," because, as he told a friend, many Christians were unintentionally thinking too little about the Holy Spirit of the Infinite.

"Cooling" was first published in *The American Choir,* 1858. Alonzo Judson Abbey was born in 1825 at a little place called Olive, Ulster County, New York, which was located about the center of what is now the Ashokin Reservoir supplying water to New York City. The entire town was wiped out when the reservoir was built. As compiler, or coeditor, Mr. Abbey issued nine books; he was a voluminous writer of tunes, and occasionally furnished the words of his offerings. In *The Triad,* 1866, more than one hundred tunes have his initials attached to them. Several of the texts for which he supplied tunes were written by Kate M. Topping, his second wife, sister of his first wife. His death occurred March 24, 1887, at Chester, New Jersey.

(This information was supplied by Frank J. Metcalf.)

**175—Come, Holy Ghost, our hearts inspire—Charles Wesley (25)**

**Winchester Old—From Este's Psalter (136)**

One of Charles Wesley's finest hymns, this is from *Hymns and Sacred Poems,* 1740, with "prolific Dove" changed to "celestial Dove" in stanza 3, line 1. The hymn had the title,

**Before Reading the Scriptures.**

"Winchester Old" seems to have been based on the second half of the setting to chapter 8 in Christopher Tye's *Actes of the Apostles* (136), 1553, which was the following:

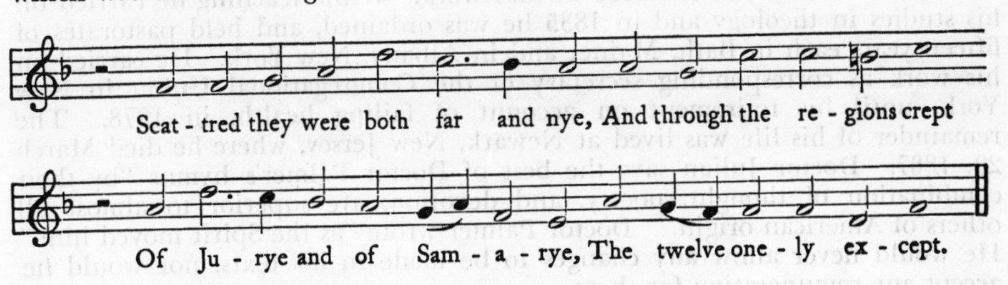
Scat - tred they were both far and nye, And through the re - gions crept
Of Ju - rye and of Sam - a - rye, The twelve one - ly ex - cept.

The harmonization shows the next note from the last to be a misprint for E.

The arrangement in *The Methodist Hymnal* was set to Psalm 84 in *The Whole Booke of Psalmes,* Thomas Este, 1592, where the name of G. Kirby was attached to it.

**176—Come, Holy Ghost, in love**—Founded on Veni Sancte Spiritus, 12th or 13th century—Ray Palmer

**Olivet** (213)—Lowell Mason (19)

This hymn, which was founded upon, rather than translated from, the Latin "Veni Sancte Spiritus," of the twelfth or thirteenth century, was first printed in *The Sabbath Hymn and Tune Book,* Andover, 1859. It was written by Dr. Ray Palmer, who had formed the habit of translating hymns during his leisure hours. In medieval times it was known as the "Golden Sequence." Doctor Julian says it is "almost impossible to present an adequate translation." Critics are not in agreement as to its authorship, variously accrediting it to Robert II of France; to Hermanus Contractus; to Archbishop Stephen Langton of Canterbury, in the early thirteenth century, and to Pope Innocent III. Some are frank enough to say its author is unknown. While they do not agree as to who wrote it, they are unanimous in praising it. Archbishop Trench has said:

> It is the loveliest of all the hymns in the whole cycle of Latin sacred poetry; . . . [it] could only have been composed by one who had been acquainted with many sorrows, and also with many consolations.

Clichtovaeus wrote:

> It is above all praise. . . . I well believe that the author (whoever he was), when he composed this piece, had his soul transfused by a certain heavenly sweetness, by which, the Holy Spirit being its author, he uttered so much sweetness in so few words.

Ray Palmer, D.D., son of Judge Thomas Palmer, Rhode Island, was born in Little Compton, November 12, 1808. His father supervised his education at home until he was thirteen, when he went to Boston and began clerking in a dry-goods store. He joined the Park Street Congregational Church under Dr. Sereno E. Dwight, who recognized his bright mind and helped him to secure admission to Phillips Andover Academy, from which he graduated in three years. After his graduation from Yale in 1830 he went immediately to New York, where he taught in a school for girls. Later he went to New Haven to continue in that work. While teaching he carried on his studies in theology and in 1835 he was ordained, and held pastorates of fifteen years each in Bath, Maine; and in Albany, New York. He carried on his work as corresponding secretary of the Congregational Union in New York, until his retirement on account of failing health, in 1878. The remainder of his life was lived at Newark, New Jersey, where he died March 29, 1887. Doctor Julian says the best of Doctor Palmer's hymns "by their combination of thought, poetry, and devotion, are superior to almost all others of American origin." Doctor Palmer wrote "as the Spirit moved him." He would never allow any changes to be made in his texts, nor would he accept any remuneration for them.

**177—Our blest Redeemer, ere He breathed**—Harriet Auber

**St. Cuthbert**—John Bacchus Dykes (1)

This was one of two hymns for Whit-Sunday by Miss Auber published by her in *The Spirit of the Psalms,* 1829, six of the seven stanzas being used here. In some hymnals the change of its meter by the addition of two syllables to the last line of each stanza, into Common Meter, is an unjustifiable mutilation. The hymn also appears frequently with a Doxology, which was not a part of the original. The omitted stanza is,

He came in semblance of a dove,
With sheltering wings outspread,
The holy balm of peace and love,
On earth to shed,

which, as Doctor Dearmer says, "follows the common error of making the reference to a bird too specific." The hymn did not come into immediate use, but once it became known attained great popularity. One of the finest of our hymns on the Holy Spirit, it has been translated into several languages. There has been current a story that this hymn was written with the diamond from a finger ring on a windowpane by the author. This story is based on the report of an anonymous writer, "Eusebius," that the Rev. Dawson Campbell had lived in the house formerly occupied by Miss Auber and that he had tried to secure permission from the owner of the place to remove the windowpane for preservation as a curiosity. The landlord declined, and later investigation showed the particular pane of glass had been removed and had become lost. This story is told in the Historical Edition of *Hymns Ancient and Modern,* a scholarly work, without questioning its foundation. Doctor Dearmer (79) says the story "has been denied," and Dr. James Moffatt states it is "no more than a pleasant myth."

Harriet Auber, whose name suggests French ancestry, was the great-granddaughter of Pierre Auber (Aubert), of Normandy, who came to England as a refugee after the Revocation of the Edict of Nantes. Most of the eighty-nine years of her life were lived in cultured seclusion in the quiet villages of Broxbourne and Hoddesdon, Hertfordshire, England. She was born at London, October 4, 1773, and died at Hoddesdon, January 20, 1862.

"St. Cuthbert" was composed by Doctor Dykes for these words for the Original Edition of *Hymns Ancient and Modern,* 1861. It is one of seven tunes by Doctor Dykes published in the first edition of this famous hymnbook.

**178—Spirit of Life, in this new dawn—Earl Marlatt**

**Maryton**—Henry Percy Smith

Doctor Marlatt has written the following account of the circumstances attending the writing of this hymn:

> The hymn, "Spirit of Life," originally called "God is a Spirit," was written in answer to a question put to me by a student in a Church-History class. We had been studying the various councils through which the Church tried to define "The Trinity." I had shown—very lucidly, I thought—how all problems were solved and all differences resolved in the near-miraculous formulation of the Nicene Creed.
>
> "In any case," I added, "it makes God a many-sided, social Being immediately immanent in present experience, rather than the isolated potentate of postexilic and early Christian worship."

I thought that summary just about settled the matter and was ready to move on to an equally final solution of the problem of immortality, when one of my students shattered my complacency with a devastating question: "Do you suppose you could say that in plain United States so that a dumb-head like me can understand it?"

"Did you want me to sing it?" I asked, a little resentful of the reflection on my explanation.

"Well," he said, "it would help a lot if you could."

Away from the classroom and my outraged academic dignity, I took his suggestion seriously and wrote this hymn for him. He approved it because it expressed in terms that he could understand and sing my conception of the Trinity, not three persons in One, but three cosmic, continuing manifestations of the one creative, redeeming, consoling Power, of whom Jesus said, "God is a Spirit, and they that worship Him must worship Him in spirit and in truth."

Earl Marlatt, Ph.D., christened Earl Bowman Marlatt, was one of twin boys born into a Methodist preacher's family in Columbus, Indiana, May 24, 1892. After graduation from DePauw University, he studied at Harvard, Boston University, Oxford, England, and the University of Berlin. For one year he did newspaper work in Kenosha, Wisconsin, leaving this work to enter the United States Army, where he served during the World War as second lieutenant of field artillery. In 1923 he became associate Professor of Philosophy in Boston University; Professor since 1925. The same year he won the Golden Flower at the May Day Poetry Tournament in Boston. In 1931 his Alma Mater conferred on him the honorary degree of Doctor of Letters. Member of many learned societies, a poet of distinction, he has written many hymns of excellence. He was the Associate Editor of *The American Student Hymnal,* 1928. A writer of prose as well as poetry, Doctor Marlatt has contributed widely to American journals and has been honored by election to the presidency of both the Boston Browning Society and the Boston Authors' Club.

"Maryton," or "Sun of my Soul," was written as a setting for "Sun of my soul, Thou Saviour dear," and was published in *Church Hymns with Tunes,* 1874. (See No. 259.)

Henry Percy Smith, 1825-1898, an English clergyman, was educated at Balliol College, Oxford. After holding various appointments in England, he was for a time chaplain at Cannes, and later canon of Gibraltar.

**179—Spirit of God, descend upon my heart**—George Croly

**Morecambe**—Frederick Cook Atkinson

This is from George Croly's *Psalms and Hymns for Public Worship,* 1854, only one edition of which was issued and the greater part of that was destroyed by fire. Copies of this book are very scarce. It contained twenty-five psalms, fifty hymns, and six longer poems, of which ten psalms, twelve hymns, and the poems are by the compiler. The scriptural text of the hymn is Galatians 5. 25:

> If we live in the Spirit, let us also walk in the Spirit.

George Croly was born in Dublin, Ireland, August 17, 1780. After his education at Trinity College there, he took Holy Orders, and, until about thirty years of age, labored in Ireland. For the remaining fifty years of his life he engaged in literary work in London, leaving numerous works dealing with biographical, historical, and scriptural subjects. In addition to his writing his career in London as a preacher was unique, particularly at St. Stephen's, a church in a poor section of the city, where he opened a pulpit which had been closed for a hundred years. A fundamentalist in religion and politics, he was opposed to liberalism of any kind. He dropped dead November 24, 1860, while walking on the street in Holborn.

"Morecambe," originally called "Hellespont," was written and published in 1870 as a leaflet, set to "Abide with me," for use in the church at Mannington, England, where its composer was then serving as organist.

Frederick Cook Atkinson was born August 21, 1841, at Norwich, England, and for eleven years (1849-1860) was chorister and assistant organist at the Cathedral there. After taking his Bachelor's degree in music at Cambridge and acting as choirmaster and organist at churches in Bradford for some years, he returned to Norwich as organist at the Cathedral in which he had been a chorister as a boy. He died at East Dereham in 1897.

**180—Breathe on me, breath of God—Edwin Hatch**

**Trentham**—Robert Jackson

This hymn by Doctor Hatch, based on John 20. 22, ". . . He breathed on them, and saith unto them, Receive ye the Holy Ghost," first appeared in print in a privately printed pamphlet called *Between Doubt and Prayer*, 1878, with line 2, stanza 3, written,

Blend all my soul with Thine.

Its first appearance in a hymnal was in *The Congregational Psalmist Hymnal*, by Dr. Henry Allon, in 1886.

Edwin Hatch, D.D., born at Derby, England, September 4, 1835, was educated at King Edward's School, Birmingham, and at Pembroke College, Oxford. While at the University he was closely associated with Burne Jones and Swinburne, and before graduation contributed to magazines on a number of different subjects. The son of Non-conformists, he took Orders in the Church of England and for a time labored in an east end parish in London. For some years he was in Canada, first as professor of classics in Trinity College, Toronto, then as rector of the Quebec High School. Returning to Oxford in 1867, he held various appointments, becoming university reader in ecclesiastical history in 1884. An acknowledged master in the field of historical research, his profound learning made him respected in intellectual circles all over the world. His famous Bampton Lectures "On the Organization of Early Christian Churches," delivered in 1881, which made a profound impression in Germany, showed him to be "one of the most original and erudite students of early Christian history that England had produced." Doctor Hatch wrote few hymns, this being the only one which has attained wide circulation. Doctor Moffatt pays him this tribute: "Profound as his learning was, his published sermons show that his piety was as simple and unaffected as a child's." He died at Oxford, November 10, 1889.

"Trentham" was originally written for "O perfect life of love" by Sir Henry Williams Baker (353). It first appeared, according to James T. Lightwood (453), in *Fifty Sacred Leaflets,* 1888.

Robert Jackson, who was born at Oldham, England, in 1842, and who died there in 1914, received his musical education at the Royal Academy of Music and was for a time organist at St. Mark's Church, Grosvenor Square W., London. In 1868 he returned to his birthplace to become his father's successor as organist and choirmaster at St. Peter's Church, remaining there in that capacity for forty-eight years and retiring in 1914. As his father had held the same position for the same number of years, St. Peter's Church has the distinction of having had its music provided by father and son for nearly a century.

**181—Send down Thy truth, O God**—Edward Rowland Sill

**Garden City**—Horatio William Parker (91)

The hymn, a prayer "For the outpouring of the Holy Spirit," was taken from *The Hermitage,* 1867, a book of poetry. Though written at the close of the war between the states, when there was still much strife and hatred between the North and South, its appeal to "cleanse" of "hate and strife," in the light of political developments since the World War, is just as challenging now as when it was written.

Edward Rowland Sill, born at Windsor, Connecticut, April 29, 1841, and educated at Yale, was for some years (1874-82) professor of English literature at the University of California. He died at Cleveland, Ohio, February 27, 1887.

"Garden City" was first published in 1890. Dr. L. F. Benson (38) in *The Hymnody of the Christian Church,* commenting upon Parker's contempt for popularity, is authority for the statement that Parker would recall this tune if he could. Doctor Parker's prize opera, *Mona,* may be performed again and be heard by a few hundreds of people, but it is safe to assume that "Garden City" will be heard and sung by millions during the lives of the hymnals now carrying it.

**182—O Spirit of the Living God**—Henry Hallam Tweedy

**St. Leonard** (46)—Henry Hiles (46)

Doctor Tweedy, the author of this fine new hymn on the Holy Spirit, tells of the motive back of its writing in a letter to the author:

> "O Spirit of the Living God" was written just before the churches proposed to celebrate the supposed anniversary of Pentecost. Some of the old Pentecostal hymns were to me unsatisfactory, and I was eager to interpret the symbolism of the story in Acts in a way that modern men could understand and sincerely mean. Unless I am mistaken, *The Methodist Hymnal* is the first to use this. My memory is that my colleague, Professor Halford E. Luccock, asked for it and sent it to the Committee.

Henry Hallam Tweedy, D.D., since 1909 professor of practical theology at Yale Divinity School, was born August 5, 1868, at Binghamton, New York, and was educated at Yale, Union Theological Seminary, and at Berlin, Germany. He has held pastorates at Utica, New York, and Bridgeport, Connecticut. One of the few effective hymn writers, his hymns are being received with great favor, for he unfailingly writes in "language all men understand."

**183—Spirit of faith, come down—Charles Wesley (25)**

**Bealoth**—From Mason's Sacred Harp

This hymn consists of stanzas 1, 2, and 4 of the five-stanza hymn published in the small booklet of thirty-two hymns entitled *Hymns of Petition and Thanksgiving for the Promise of the Father,* 1746. The second line of stanza 3 originally read,

> The great atoning Lamb,

which was changed by John Wesley when he included it in his *Collection of Hymns for the Use of the People called Methodists,* 1780, with the omission of the original third stanza. It came into American Methodist hymnals in the *Supplement to the Pocket Hymn Book,* authorized by the General Conference of 1808. Since 1849 it has appeared as here used.

"Bealoth," or "Phillput," was taken from *Mason's Sacred Harp, or Eclectic Harmony, A New Collection of Church Music,* Lowell Mason and Timothy B. Mason, Cincinnati, 1843. There has been much speculation concerning its origin, for it has been attributed to a number of composers, some of whom could not possibly be seriously considered. Claims have been put forth for Lowell Mason, Lemuel C. Everett, and for the latter's brother, Asa Brooks Everett. While the Everetts issued a great many singing-school books in the second quarter of the last century, this tune has not yet been said to have been published in any of them. It has not been found in any book published earlier than *Mason's Sacred Harp*. Henry L. Mason, grandson of Lowell Mason, has written the author:

> There is a characteristic quality to the tunes Mason wrote. . . . I do not believe my grandfather wrote this tune; I should be surprised if any conclusive evidence is brought to bear showing that he did.

Until such evidence is discovered it seems wise to assign it to the book referred to.

The tune is a very popular one among all denominations in the South. The Disciples of Christ have long used it as the setting for "I love Thy kingdom, Lord." This was the hymn to which it was set in *Mason's Sacred Harp*. As written there (and as it usually appears) the first phrase is:

Because of the bad accent, it was changed for the Charles Wesley hymn with which the Methodists always sing it.

# THE GOSPEL

## The Call

**184—Come, every soul by sin oppressed—John Hart Stockton**
**Stockton—John Hart Stockton**

Both hymn and tune appeared in either 1874 or 1875. It is one of the type of gospel songs which has proven valuable in evangelistic meetings and has come into wide use in both the British Isles and America. When it first appeared, the chorus used was the old familiar,

Come to Jesus,
Come to Jesus,
Come to Jesus now.

Ira D. Sankey (237) changed it to

Only trust Him,

because the other words had been used so much they had become trite. Sankey included it in *Sacred Songs and Solos,* which he published in England and which still has a large circulation there. In this book it has as a text, Matthew 11. 29:

Take my yoke upon you, and learn of me; . . .
and ye shall find rest unto your souls.

In Mr. Sankey's use of this song, he frequently changed the words of the Refrain to,

I will trust Him,

and,

I do trust Him.

He tells of a missionary in England who had the door of his heart opened "to let the Master into his soul in all His fullness," as a result of hearing the first stanza sung at a Soldiers' Home. This missionary wrote: "I have ever since been happy serving Him with my whole heart. I am now a missionary to my comrades."

While songs of this kind more often than not "embody more sentiment than thought" in both text and music, they have a certain value that justifies their inclusion in a book designed primarily for the use of churches of diverse classification and membership. It is frankly a hymn of invitation (the tune has been called "Invitation"), and it may well be said that when Methodist churches cease calling upon people to repent of their sins they will no longer be Methodist churches for that was the very soul of the Wesleyan Revival which made the Methodist Church possible.

John Hart Stockton was born of Presbyterian parents at New Hope, Pennsylvania, April 19, 1813. Converted at a Methodist camp meeting held at Paulsboro, New Jersey, in the summer of 1832, he joined the Methodist Episcopal Church in 1838; was licensed to exhort in 1844 and to preach in 1846; was received on trial in the New Jersey Conference in 1853, and into full relationship in 1857. He had difficulty in settling the question of becoming an "Itinerant," but finally said, "Here am I, send me." Twice he took the "supernumerary relation" because of ill health. After his last withdrawal from active pastoral work in 1874, he published *Salvation Melodies* that year, and *Precious Songs* in 1875. Always active in evangelistic work, he was a valuable assistant in the notable Moody and Sankey meetings held in Philadelphia. Ira D. Sankey (237) wrote him, saying:

> I thank my Heavenly Father for enabling you to write so much sweet music, as well as words; and I hope you may long be spared to bless the world with your "precious songs." I wish you to accept our regards for one whose songs have been blessed to tens of thousands in the lands beyond the seas.

While talking with friends on the afternoon of March 25, 1877, after having attended the morning service of worship at the Arch Street Church, Philadelphia, he was suddenly stricken, and after a few minutes passed away.

**185—God calling yet! Shall I not hear?**—Gerhard Tersteegen
Translated by Jane Borthwick (73)

**Federal Street**—Henry Kemble Oliver

A variant of Jane Borthwick's translation of Gerhard Tersteegen's hymn, "Gott rufet noch; sollt ich nicht endlich hören," which was included in the second edition (1735) of his *Geistliches Blumen-Gärtlein* (*Spiritual Flower Garden*), with the title, "To-day if ye will hear His Voice." It was translated in the original meter (11. 11. 11. 11.) as one of the *Hymns from the Land of Luther,* by the Borthwick sisters (73), but was considerably changed, to reduce it to Long Meter, in *The Sabbath Hymn Book,* Andover, 1859. It is most widely used in this country in its altered form. One of the best of the invitation hymns, it stresses God's gracious call to us to turn to Him, and what our answer should be.

Gerhard Tersteegen, "the greatest poet of the mystical school of the seventeenth and eighteenth centuries," and who wrote one hundred and eleven hymns varying in merit, was born at Mörs, in Westphalia, November 25, 1697, the son of a merchant. His parents intended him for the Reformed Church, but after the death of his father his mother's limited resources were so exhausted by sending him through Latin school that he was unable to complete his education at the University. After serving an apprenticeship of one year, at sixteen he engaged in the business of making silk ribbons, living in a modest cottage near Mühlheim, eating one meager meal a day, and giving all that he could save to the poor. Never in robust health, such privation further weakened him and, doubtless, was in large measure responsible for a spiritual depression which settled on him for five years. Upon his recovery, he wrote a solemn covenant with God, signing it with his own blood. It is said he worked at his loom ten hours each day, prayed for two more, and then devoted not less than two hours to writing on religious subjects and to discussing spiritual matters with friends. Reports of his good works spread so that multitudes came to him for spiritual guidance. His wants during his later years were provided for by his followers, and a house between Mühlheim and Eberfeld was set aside for him to use as a retreat for those who wished to be near him. This was known as "the Pilgrims' Cottage." Tersteegen did not spend all of his time at his retreat but traveled about over the district, and, for some years, made annual pilgrimages to Holland. After his twentieth year he ceased attending the services of the Reformed Church and refused to take communion with "open sinners," yet he formed no sect and lived the life of a celibate and ascetic. His correspondence grew to immense proportions and new editions of his hymns and other writings were in constant demand. Gerhard Tersteegen was "a gentle, heaven-inspired soul, whose hymns are the reflection of a heavenly, happy life." He died at Mühlheim, April 3, 1769.

"Federal Street" was published by Lowell Mason (19) in the *Boston Academy's Collection of Church Music*, 1836. It was inspired by its composer, Henry Kemble Oliver, musing over the last stanza of Anne Steele's (389) hymn on the death of a child, which began "So fades the lovely, blooming flower." It is to this last stanza, slightly altered, that the tune appears in Doctor Mason's book. The tune had been written in 1832 and had been laid aside. Two years later, Lowell Mason, then conducting a class in Salem, Massachusetts, asked if any of its members had written any tunes. Oliver, one of the class, submitted "Federal Street," which appealed to Mason, who asked for, and obtained permission to use it.

Federal Street is a street in Salem, where the composer lived, and where his wife was born, lived, and died.

Henry Kemble Oliver was born at Beverly, Massachusetts, November 24, 1800, and died at Salem, August 12, 1885. He was a great lover of music, yet he did not make it his profession, for his father so disapproved of his son's musical inclinations that he forbade the boy having anything to do with it. In spite of the parental disapproval, young Oliver found time to attain a certain proficiency on several instruments. He took a part of his college course at Harvard, but graduated from Dartmouth. After his graduation he taught school; was manager of some cotton mills; was Adjutant-General of his state; was State Treasurer of Massachusetts during the Civil War; and was Mayor of Salem, Massachusetts, for four years before his retirement. Yet withal he found time to compose and publish much sacred music.

**186—Come, sinners, to the gospel feast**—Charles Wesley (25)

**Uxbridge**—Lowell Mason (19)

A part of one of the *Hymns for those that seek and those that have Redemption in the Blood of Jesus Christ*, 1747, bearing the title,

The Great Supper, Luke xiv. 16-24.

Stanzas 1, 2, 12, 20, and 24 are taken from a long hymn of twenty-four with only slight changes. One of them was necessary because of Charles Wesley's predilection for the use of polysyllabic words in his hymns. Line 2, stanza 5, was,

> This is the acceptable day,

which would not "sing" well to a long-meter tune.

Some of the omitted stanzas are quaint and worth remembering:

> Your grounds forsake, your oxen quit,
> Your every earthly thought forget,
> Seek not the comforts of this life,
> Nor sell your Saviour for a wife.
>
> "Have me excused," why will ye say?
> Why will ye for damnation pray?
> Have you excused—from joy and peace?
> Have you excused—from happiness?
>
> Excused from coming to a feast!
> Excused from being Jesu's guest!
> From knowing *now* your sins forgiven,
> From tasting *here* the joys of heaven.
>
> Excused, alas! why should you be
> From health, and life, and liberty,
> From entering into glorious rest,
> From leaning on your Saviour's breast.

This is the hymn Jesse Lee sang on the Common just before preaching the first Methodist sermon ever delivered in Boston, a day in July, 1790. Unable to find a pulpit from which to preach, he was forced to find a place in the open. In his *Short History of the Methodists,* Jesse Lee says:

> I was appointed this year to the town of Boston, in order if possible to establish the Methodist doctrine and discipline, and to raise up a people for the Lord. . . . On one occasion, I went out on the common, and standing on a table, began to sing with only a few persons present. But having prayed and begun to preach, the number increased so that there were two or three thousand attentive hearers. The number was still greatly increased the next Sabbath day, at the same place, at six o'clock in the afternoon.
>
> This may be considered the beginning of Methodism in Boston. . . . Methodist preaching was a strange thing in that part of the world. . . . In Boston it was hard to procure a place to preach in, and the word took but little hold on the minds of the hearers.

"Uxbridge" appeared as early as 1830 in the ninth edition of *The Boston Handel and Haydn Society Collection of Church Music,* where it was set to the words,

> At anchor laid, remote from home,

the first line of a cento from A. M. Toplady's (204) hymn beginning,

> Empty'd of earth I fain would be,

a "Petitionary Hymn," of 1757. "Uxbridge" was used in the 1837 edition of *The Harmonist,* the first American Methodist tune book, set to another invitation hymn,

Draw near, O Sons of God, draw near,

by Charles Wesley. The quality of the melody seems to make it an appropriate setting for hymns of this character. There are at least three other tunes by this same name, but they are not commonly used in American churches.

**187—Come, ye sinners, poor and needy—Joseph Hart**

**Greenville—Jean Jacques Rousseau**

This is taken from *Hymns composed on Various Subjects, with the Author's Experience,* 1759, originally in seven stanzas, headed,

Come and welcome, to Jesus Christ.

Through various editings it has acquired its present form. The first line appears in many books as in the original:

Come, ye sinners, poor and wretched.

The spirit of Joseph Hart's ministry is expressed in his simple, warm, and persuasive hymn.

Joseph Hart was born in London about 1712. Little is known of his early life except that he had a Christian home and that he received a fair education. After his conversion he preached from 1760 to the year of his death, 1768, at an old wooden meetinghouse in Jewin Street, London, where he attracted a large congregation. His life, for seven years, was, he says,

> an uneasy, restless round of sinning and repenting, working and dreading. At length the Lord was pleased to comfort me a little by enabling me to appropriate, in some measure, the merits of the Saviour to my own soul. In this blessed state my continuance was but short, for, rushing impetuously into notions beyond my experience, I hasted to make myself a Christian by mere doctrine, adopting other men's opinions before I had tried them; and set up for a great light in religion, disregarding the internal work of grace began in my own soul by the Holy Ghost. This liberty, assumed by myself and not given by Christ, soon grew to libertinism, in which I took large progressive strides, and advanced to a dreadful height, both in principle and practice. In a word, I ran such dangerous lengths both of carnal and spiritual wickedness, that I even outwent professed infidels, and shocked the irreligious and profane with my horrid blasphemies and monstrous impieties. . . . In this abominable state I continued for more than ten years. . . . Then I began by degrees to reform a little, and to live in a more soberly and orderly manner. . . . For several years I went on in this easy, cool, smooth, and indolent manner, with a lukewarm, insipid kind of religion. . . . But the fountains of the great deeps of my sinful nature were not broken up. . . . Nor was the blood of Christ effectually applied to my soul. I looked upon His death, indeed, as the grand sacrifice for sin, . . . yet I was so far from seeing or owning that there was such a necessity for His death, and that it could be of such infinite value as represented, that I have often resolved . . . that I never would believe it. After a time, I fell into a deep despondency of mind, and, shunning all company, I went about alone, bewailing my

sad and dark condition. . . . This suffering was aggravated by physical infirmity and pain, and in this sad state I went moping about till Whit Sunday, 1757, when I happened to go in the afternoon to the Moravian Chapel in Fetter Lane. The minister preached from Rev. iii. 10. I was much impressed. I was hardly got home, when I felt myself melting away into a strange softness of affection which made me fling myself on my knees before God. The alteration I . . . felt in my soul was as sudden and palpable as that which is experienced by a person staggering and almost sinking under a burden when it is immediately taken from his shoulders.

Joseph Hart was simple, earnest, and much beloved by his people. He died on May 24, 1768, at London. Twenty thousand persons attended his funeral services, and an obelisk was erected in Bunhill Field in 1875, more than one hundred years after his death, to perpetuate his memory.

"Greenville," "Rousseau," or "Rousseau's Dream," as it is more appropriately named in some books, is taken from a little song in the opera *Le Devin du Village,* by Rousseau. It was sung first, in 1752, at Fontainebleau. In the opera it appeared thus:

There is a story to the effect that Rousseau fell asleep one day and had a vision of God in heaven, surrounded by angels singing this melody, when, immediately upon awakening, he wrote it out. It is a beautifully quaint old tune, and has been deservedly popular ever since it was written. It seems to have been used first in England as a hymn tune, about 1825. In this country it has been popular for more than a century, for it is found in the second edition of the *Handel and Haydn Collection of Church Music,* 1823. In the Appendix to *Musica Sacra,* tenth edition, 1836, Thomas Hastings (204) has appended this note to the tune:

Originally a piece of secular music, invented during a dream in the night, by the infidel Rosseau. We have never been partial to the tune; but as it is found in the best collections, we are constrained to give it place.

How many tunes have been given a place because they have appeared in the "best collections"!

Jean Jacques Rousseau, born at Geneva, June 28, 1712, who wrote this tune, has given us his *Confessions,* which throw a great deal of light on his unusual life. He ran away from home when he was sixteen, experimented in many occupations, failing in most of them, but after discovering that he was an original and forceful thinker, greatly influenced education in Europe, and became one of the great forces in modern literature. Because of his political views he was forced to leave France and for a time lived in England. Always interested in music, he composed an opera, *Le Devin du Village,* which was enthusiastically received at Fontainebleau. This success so turned his head that though he continued to work at music, he had but scant success. His life was very unhappy, and it is thought he committed suicide. He died at Ermenonville, near Paris, July 3, 1778.

**188—Of Him who did salvation bring**—Ascribed to Bernard of Clairvaux
Translated by Anthony Wilhelm Boehm
Altered by John Christian Jacobi

**Rockingham** (Mason)—Lowell Mason (19)

This is from the Latin hymn "Jesu dulcis memoria," known as the "Joyful Rhythm of St. Bernard on the Name of Jesus." Dr. Philip Schaff, in his *Christ in Song,* says it is "the sweetest and most evangelical . . . hymn of the Middle Ages." Its extensive use is unique in hymnody. Some few hymns have been translated into English more often, but no others have had made from them so many deservedly popular centos. This translation, one of three in use in *The Methodist Hymnal* (See Nos. 345 and 348), came into English through the German translation of Anthony Wilhelm Boehm, about 1712. This was altered by John C. Jacobi some eight years later, further changes being made by persons unknown, to produce the hymn beginning,

Of Him who did salvation bring,

included in M. Madan's *Psalms and Hymns,* 1760. It has been used by Methodists in America since the days of Bishop Asbury.

Bernard of Clairvaux, born in 1091 at Les Fontaines, near Dijon, Burgundy, France, whom Luther thought "the greatest monk that ever lived," was educated at Chatillon. Studious, and by nature a recluse, he spent some time at a small monastery at Citeaux, before he founded the one at Clairvaux which became world famous. He became the most influential man of the twelfth century, and his advice was sought by kings and high ecclesiastics. His eloquence is said to have been almost irresistible. Of his hymns, Dr. Richard S. Storrs has written:

> I do not overestimate these hymns; but they show his profound evangelical spirit, how the meek and sovereign majesty of the Lord continually attuned and governed his thoughts, and how the same hand which wrote letters, treatises, notes of sermons, exhortations to pontiffs, reproofs of kings, could turn itself at pleasure to the praises of Him in whose grace was his hope, in whose love was his life. If these hymns had not remained after he was gone, we should have missed, I think, a lovely luster of his work and his fame.

Bernard died August 20, 1153.

Anthony Wilhelm Boehm, a German writer of whom little is known, is said to have been born in 1673, and to have died in 1722.

John Christian Jacobi, born of German parentage in 1670, was from 1708, for forty-two years Keeper of the Royal German Chapel, St. James's

Palace, London. Among his publications was *A Collection of Divine Hymns, Translated from the High Dutch,* 1720, which was issued in enlarged form in 1722 under the title, *Psalmodia Germanica.* He died at London, December 14, 1750.

"Rockingham" (Mason) was one of Lowell Mason's original tunes appearing in 1830. It is frequently called "Rockingham New" to distinguish it from the excellent tune of the same name by Dr. Edward Miller, misnamed "Miller" in the 1905 *Methodist Hymnal.*

**189—Blow ye the trumpet, blow!**—Charles Wesley (25)

**Lenox**—Lewis Edson

This is Hymn III of seven in Charles Wesley's *Hymns for the New Year,* in six six-line stanzas, published in 1750. It has been attributed without reason to Augustus M. Toplady (204), who was only ten years old when this hymn was published. One of the finest of Charles Wesley's hymns, dealing with his favorite theme, full atonement, it has extensive use in all English-speaking countries. Stanzas 1, 2, and 6 are used, without change except for the last line, which Wesley wrote,

Return to your eternal home.

The meter 6. 6. 6. 6. 8. 8. has been called "Trumpet Meter" because it is the meter of this hymn.

"Lenox" is a revised "fuguing tune," of the type made popular by William Billings and others in the late eighteenth century in New England, not many of which have survived. As late as 1895, however, "Lenox" was printed as a "fuguing tune" in *The Presbyterian Hymnal.* The last half of the tune, as it was written by its composer, may be seen at page 238.

"Lenox" first appeared in 1782 or 1783 in a book called *The Chorister's Companion.* It was used with striking effect by Dr. Van Denman Thompson (153) in *The Evangel of the New World,* 1934, an oratorio written for the celebration of the one hundred-fiftieth anniversary of the founding of the Methodist Episcopal Church.

Lewis Edson, born January 22, 1748, at Bridgewater, Massachusetts, was a blacksmith by trade, living in western Massachusetts, eastern New York, and at Woodstock, Connecticut, where he died in the spring of 1820. He held singing schools in various places and had a reputation as "a great singer."

**190—Come to the Saviour now**—John Murch Wigner

**Invitation**—Frederick Charles Maker (9[1])

The hymn, dated 1871, was taken from *Psalms and Hymns for School and Home,* 1882, an English Baptist hymnal. It was in five stanzas, 1, 4, and 5 being used with a change of only one letter: in line 2, stanza 3, "burden" has

**Original form of the last half of the "fuguing tune" "Lenox," taken from *The Chorister's Companion*.**

**In some of the older books, after the harmonization had been modernized, the melody was written as follows:**

been pluralized. "Invitation" was the title of the hymn. The author's father was the editor of the hymnal in which it was first published.

John Murch Wigner, son of an English Baptist clergyman, born at Lynn, Essex, England, June 10, 1844 (Julian, June 19), educated at Lynn Grammar School and at London University, was for many years connected with the India Home Civil Service, with offices in London. He belonged to his father's church and was greatly interested in working with young people. The date and place of his death have not been ascertained.

"Invitation" took its name from the title to this hymn, for which it was composed by Frederick Charles Maker. It appeared in *The Bristol Tune Book* of 1881, among some new tunes added in that edition. This book was compiled by Alfred Stone and others as a collection of tunes which might be adapted to a number of Non-conformist hymnals issued about the middle of the last century, when it was customary to print most of the hymnals in word editions only. As stated in the Preface of the 1881 *Bristol Tune Book:*

> The first edition of the "Bristol Tune-Book," published in 1863, provided for about 100 varieties of metre. This number was increased to nearly 200 by the issue of the Second Series in 1876. Since then still further varieties have been introduced, to provide for which a small Supplement is now added, containing tunes, Nos. 713 to 751.

"Invitation" is No. 723.

**191—Sinners, turn: why will ye die?**—Charles Wesley (25)

**Hollingside**—John Bacchus Dykes (1)

This is Hymn xiii from *Hymns on God's Everlasting Love, Part II,* in sixteen eight-line stanzas, headed,

> Why will ye die, O house of Israel
> Ezek. xviii. 31,

of which these are the first three, unchanged except that it has "ye" for "you," and vice versa, in several of the lines.

"Hollingside" was written for the hymn, "Jesu, Lover of my soul," and was contributed by Doctor Dykes to the Original Edition of *Hymns Ancient and Modern,* 1861 (338).

**192—Come, said Jesus' sacred voice**—Anna Letitia Barbauld, née Aikin

**St. Bees**—John Bacchus Dykes (1)

The hymn is from the revised edition of Mrs. Barbauld's *Poems,* 1792. It appears as in the last two editions of *The Methodist Hymnal:* the first two stanzas, and the first half of the third with the first half of the fourth stanzas of the original. It is a paraphrase of Matthew 11. 28.

Anna Letitia Barbauld, daughter of John Aikin, D.D., an English Dissenting minister, was born at Kibworth-Harcourt, Leicestershire, England, June 20, 1743, and married a French Protestant preacher, Rochemont Bar bauld, who for a time conducted a school in addition to his pastoral work. She early showed the poetic trend of her mind. While her father objected to her obtaining the classical education she desired, he permitted her to read Latin and Greek. With a vigorous mind she possessed a fine imagination. Mrs. Barbauld is best known by her *Hymns in Prose for Children,* 1781, which passed through several editions and which was translated into several languages. She died at Newington Green, March 9, 1825.

"St. Bees" was written by Doctor Dykes for a book published by Richard R. Chope, an English clergyman, called *Congregational Hymn and Tune Book,* in 1862 (revised and enlarged edition of the first edition of 1857). It was one of several of Doctor Dykes's tunes appearing in the work, two of which were prize-winning tunes. The book referred to was not a denominational one, but was compiled with the purpose in view of encouraging congregational singing in the English Church.

**193—Art thou weary, art thou troubled**—From the Greek, 8th century
John Mason Neale (52)

**Stephanos**—Henry Williams Baker (353) and
William Henry Monk (520)

This hymn appears more frequently with its first line

Art thou weary, art thou languid.

Two other changes have been made:

Is there,

line 1, stanza 3, was made

Hath He,

and Bishop E. H. Bickersteth, in his *Hymnal Companion,* 1870, changed the third line of the last stanza from

Angels, Martyrs, Prophets, Virgins,

to its present reading. The hymn was given by Doctor Neale in the first edition of his *Hymns of the Eastern Church,* 1862, as a translation of a hymn by St. Stephen, the Sabaite, 725-794, but in the third edition he explained there was so little of the original Greek in it that in any future edition it would be placed in the appendix. It is one of the great hymns of all time, and since its inclusion in *Hymns Ancient and Modern* (Appendix, 1868) has found its way into hymnals of all denominations of English-speaking peoples.

Obviously an antiphonal hymn, the questions may be sung by the choir, the congregation responding with the answers, or it may be used very effectively by having the choir and congregation read the first two lines of each stanza, with the minister replying. There are many occasions when hymns may be read to advantage.

"Stephanos" appeared in 1868 in the Appendix to the Original Edition of

*Hymns Ancient and Modern.* The melody by Sir Henry W. Baker was harmonized by Dr. W. H. Monk.

**194—"Come unto me, ye weary"**—William Chatterton Dix (90)

**Meirionydd**—Welsh hymn melody—William Lloyd

The hymn was first published in *The People's Hymnal,* London, 1867. The text has been changed somewhat from time to time. Some time before his death, Mr. Dix sent a manuscript copy of his hymn to Mr. F. A. Jones, who wrote *Famous Hymns and Their Authors,* London, 1902. In the letter accompanying the manuscript, Mr. Dix gave this information concerning the circumstances under which it was written:

> I was ill and depressed at the time, and it was almost to idle away the hours that I wrote the hymn. I had been ill for many weeks, and felt weary and faint, and the hymn really expresses the languidness of body from which I was suffering at the time. Soon after its completion I recovered, and I always look back to that hymn as the turning point in my illness.

It first appeared in American Methodist hymnals in 1905, where it was set to the tune "Savoy Chapel," by John B. Calkin (502).

"Meirionydd" was found in manuscript form in a book formerly in the possession of William Lloyd. Its form has been changed, but any alterations that were made must have been some improvement for it would be difficult to change its present form without altering its whole character. The composer's name for it was "Berth." "Meirionydd" is the Welsh name for the county (Merioneth) lying immediately south of Carnarvon, the home of the composer. The word is pronounced as it is spelled in English (Mer-i-on-eth') with a rather pronounced accent on the last syllable. It is one of the best tunes new to American Methodism.

William Lloyd, the composer of "Meirionydd," was probably a farmer and cattle dealer in Rhos Goch, Llaniestan, Carnarvon, Wales, where he was born, in 1786, and where he died, in 1852. He was a self-educated musician, having a good singing voice and being an able singer, and his home was a gathering place for singers whom he taught. Traveling frequently in England, he heard much good congregational singing, and his love for music caused him to go about in different parts of the Lleyn Promontory, a district in Wales little known and quite unattractive, conducting singing societies.

**195—Return, O wanderer, return**—William Bengo Collyer

**Woodworth** (198)—William Batchelder Bradbury (133)

The hymn appeared in the *Evangelical Magazine,* in May, 1806, and in the author's *Hymns, partly collected and partly original, designed as a supplement to Dr. Watts' Psalms and Hymns,* 1812. Stanzas 1, 2, 4, and 5, unaltered, from a six-stanza hymn with the title "The Backslider," are used.

William Bengo Collyer, D.D., born April 14, 1782, at Blackheath, near London, enrolled at Homerton College when only sixteen. and began to preach at twenty years of age. Dr. Joseph Belcher, who knew him well, says he was, for fifty years, by far the most popular Non-conformist minister in England, and that he was almost the only Dissenting preacher to be heard by royalty, to whom, as to all others,

> he preached in the most faithful manner the doctrines of the cross, in a style combining simple elegance, fervent feeling, and an indomitable adherence to "the truth as in Jesus."

The following is a part of a biographical sketch quoted by Doctor Julian in his *Dictionary of Hymnology:*

> Dr. Collyer was eminent in his day as an eloquent Evangelical preacher, when formalism in worship, and Arianism in doctrine, prevailed. He was a man of amiable disposition, polished manners, and Christian courtesy; popular with rich and poor alike.

He died at Peckham, January 8, 1854.

**196—Behold! A Stranger at the door**—Joseph Grigg
**Bera**—John Edgar Gould

This hymn, originally in eleven four-line stanzas, was first published in a pamphlet, *Four Hymns on Divine Subjects,* London, 1765, another of which was "Jesus, and shall it ever be" (258).

Joseph Grigg, who is said to have begun writing hymns when he was only ten years old, was born about 1720, the exact date and place not being known. After an early life spent in poverty he worked as a mechanic until his twenty-fifth year, when he dropped all other pursuits to devote his time wholly to religious work. He became assistant pastor of the Silver Street Presbyterian Church, London, from which he retired upon the death of his associate, the Rev. Thomas Bures. Retiring to St. Albans after his marriage to a wealthy widow, he devoted himself to literary work. A friend, writing an elegy after his death, said he was "the friend of the poor, the charm of the social circle, and the attractive and useful preacher." He died at Walthamstow, Essex, October 29, 1768.

"Bera" first appeared in a *Collection of Church Music,* New York, 1849, compiled by George F. Root (439) and Joseph E. Sweetser (217).

John Edgar Gould, the composer of "Bera," was born at Bangor, Maine, in 1822, and died at Algiers, Africa, March 4, 1875. In New York he became a member of a firm dealing in pianos and other musical merchandise, and later moving to Philadelphia, he engaged in the same business, with William G. Fischer (245) as his partner. Interested in music, he was a choral conductor, a composer of psalm and hymn tunes, and a publisher of music books. He was associated with Edward S. White in issuing *The Modern Harp,* 1846, and *Harmonia Sacra,* 1851. Mr. Gould's death occurred while on a trip taken for the benefit of his health. His widow has written that he wrote the tune "Pilot" (269) and played it on his piano the night before he embarked on shipboard for his last earthly voyage.

**197—O Jesus, Thou art standing—William Walsham How**

**St. Hilda—Justin Heinrich Knecht, and
Edward Husband**

This popular and useful hymn was written in 1867 by Doctor How and published the same year in a Supplement to a collection of *Psalms and Hymns* compiled by the author and the Rev. Thomas B. Morrell, first in 1854. In few hymns has the gospel call been more earnestly urged. Doctor How said:

> I composed the hymn early in 1867, after I had been reading a very beautiful poem entitled "Brothers, and a Sermon." The pathos of the verses impressed me very forcibly at the time. I read them over and over again, and finally, closing the book, I scribbled on an old scrap of paper my first idea of the verses beginning "O Jesus, Thou art standing." I altered them a good deal subsequently, but I am fortunate in being able to say that after the hymn left my hands it was never revised or altered in any way.

Jean Ingelow wrote the poem, "Brothers, and a Sermon," in which she describes two brothers listening to an old parson preaching in a fishing village church:

> The parson knew that he had lost the eyes
> And ears of those before him for he made
> A pause, . . .
> . . . then with a sigh
> Fronted the folk, lifted his grand gray head,
> And said, as one that pondered now the words
> He had been preaching on with new surprise,
> And found fresh marvel in their sound, " 'Behold!
> Behold!' saith He, 'I stand at the door and knock.' "
>
> Then said the parson: "What! and shall He wait,
> And must He wait . . . ?
>
> "Open the door with shame if ye have sinned;
> If ye be sorry, open it with sighs.
> Albeit the place be bare for poverty,
> And comfortless for lack of plenishing,
> Be not ashamed for that, but open it,
> And take Him in that comes to sup with thee;
> 'Behold!' He saith, 'I stand at the door and knock.'
>
> ". . Speak then, O rich and strong:
> Open, O happy young, ere yet the hand
> Of Him that knocks, wearied at last, forbear;
> The patient foot its thankless quest refrain,
> The wounded heart for evermore withdraw."

The famous picture by Holman Hunt, "The Light of the World," which hangs in Keble College, Oxford, and which has produced a very marked religious effect, also influenced the writing of this hymn.

William Walsham How, born December 13, 1823, at Shrewsbury, England, filled a long line of quite diversified ecclesiastical duties until appointed Bishop of Wakefield in 1888, after having declined the Bishopric of Manchester, without even speaking of it to his wife, and that of Durham, one of the most distinguished posts in the Anglican Church. Seemingly he was entirely without worldly ambition. "It is impossible to say whether the virtues or the graces of the Christian character were more conspicuous in his life." He was an intimate friend of Canon Ellerton (28), and was associated with him in hymnological work. Through his hymns he greatly enriched worship in all English-speaking countries. His most effective ones are simple and unadorned, and will doubtless outlive his other literary works. He wrote hymns for children, who knew him, and loved him, and ran to greet him; in London he was known as "the poor man's Bishop," "the people's Bishop," "the omnibus Bishop," for he was a commoner who lived, worked, walked, and rode with his people. Francis Pigou, Dean of Bristol, wrote of him:

> Walsham How . . . was a man of great personal piety, which shone transparently in him. . . . His well-known hymns are fragrant with it. All brought into contact with him were conscious of it. He was not a man of great intellectual power, but he was, like St. Barnabas, "a good man, full of faith and of the Holy Ghost"; and his ministry was singularly owned and blessed of God. It is true that more men are won to God by holiness than by cleverness.

There is much that may be pondered with profit in the conclusion of a supplementary chapter of Bishop How's biography (by his son) written by Dr. Boyd Carpenter, at the time Bishop of Ripon:

> It is the fate of a hymn writer to be forgotten. Of the millions who Sunday after Sunday sing hymns in our churches, not more than a few hundred know or consider whose words they are singing. The hymn remains; the name of the writer passes away. Bishop Walsham How was prepared for this; his ambition was not to be remembered, but to be helpful. He gave free liberty to any to make use of his hymns. It was enough for him if he could enlarge the thanksgivings of the Church or minister by song to the souls of men. There will be few to doubt that his unselfish wish will be fulfilled. Some of his hymns . . . will continue to be sung for long years to come; they will cheer and console the hearts of millions; many who hear will take up their burden and their hope again. We are told that when Melanchthon and his comrades, shortly after Luther's death, fled to Weimar, they heard a child singing the stirring words of Luther's "Ein' Feste Burg" (67). "Sing, dear daughter, sing," said Melanchthon, "you know not what great people you are comforting." Even so the voice of the hymn writer carries comfort to unknown hearts and to after ages.
>
> The writer dies; the hymn remains; the song goes on; tired men listen and find rest. Struggling men are encouraged to struggle on again; statesmen, philanthropists, the broken-hearted and the despairing, are helped. Sing on: you know not what great people you are comforting. Such a reward is better than fame. It is as if, even after life is ended, the power to give a cup of cold water to a fainting soul in the name of Christ was not denied to the singer of the Church.

In addition to the collection of *Psalms and Hymns* from which this hymn is taken, Bishop How was joint editor of *Church Hymns,* 1871, sponsored by the Society for the Promotion of Christian Knowledge, Arthur S. Sullivan (15), musical editor, and in 1886 a collection of his *Poems and Hymns* was issued. Bishop How died at Wakefield, August 10, 1897.

"St. Hilda," also known as "St. Edith," was suggested by a tune written by Justin H. Knecht and published in *Vollständige Sammlung,* Stuttgart, 1799. In 1871 the Rev. Edward Husband took the first two lines of Knecht's tune and added the rest to make the present one. The melody of the tune by Knecht is:

This is the tune called "Knecht," and should not be confused with "St. Hilda."

Justin Heinrich Knecht was professor of Belles Lettres at Biberach, Württemberg, where he was born September 30, 1752, and where he died December 1, 1817. He allowed his love for music to win him away from his professorship to become the town musician. Called to Stuttgart to have charge of the Court and theater orchestra, he was unsuccessful, doubtless because of lack of training, so that he returned to Biberach to his former position. Although he was a voluminous writer, much of his work was commonplace.

Edward Husband, 1843-1908, was an English clergyman with a bent for music. He was vicar of St. Michael's and the Church of All Angels in Folkstone. He was interested in church music and was a well-known lecturer on that subject.

# Repentance

**198—Just as I am, without one plea**—Charlotte Elliott

**Woodworth**—William Batchelder Bradbury (133)

This undoubtedly ranks with the finest hymns in the English language, and it has been translated into almost all of the European languages, as well as into many others. Written in 1834, it was first published in the 1836 edition of *The Invalids' Hymn Book,* to which, in its various editions, Miss Elliott contributed more than one hundred hymns. It was headed with the text from St. John 6. 37: ". . . him that cometh to me I will in no wise cast out." Stories associated with the writing of the hymn are for the most part apocryphal. The one of the young girl on her way to a dance being questioned by her minister could not be true, for Miss Elliott was an invalid, forty-five years old when she wrote it. While she was a friend of Dr. César Malan, and undoubtedly was greatly influenced by him, there seems to be no conclusive evidence that he used the words "just as you are" in conversation with her. Miss Elliott's niece has given the facts concerning its writing, which, briefly, are: Miss Elliott was living at Westfield Lodge, Brighton, in 1834. Her brother, the Rev. H. V. Elliott, was arranging a bazaar in order to raise money to assist in the building of a college where the daughters of poor clergymen might be educated at low expense. Miss Elliott, being ill and unable to assist in the final preparations, lay on her bed, tossed about

With many a conflict, many a doubt

as to her usefulness. On the day following, while all of the other members of the family were at the opening of the bazaar, a feeling of peace and contentment came over her, and she wrote this hymn, one of the most helpful ever penned. This is her brother's testimony:

> In the course of a long ministry, I hope I have been permitted to see some fruit of my labor, but I feel that far more has been done by a single hymn of my sister's.

This simple, candid expression of trust and personal confession, which has appealed to the public mind in a way few others have done, does not need a story of any kind to aid in carrying its message. "Perhaps there is no hymn in the language which has been more blessed in the raising up of those that are bowed down."

Charlotte Elliott was born at Clapham, England, March 18, 1789, and died at Brighton, September 22, 1871. She spent the first thirty-two years of her life with her father at Clapham, removing to Brighton in 1823, though spending some time at Torquay, Devonshire. She was an invalid for the last fifty years of her life. During her girlhood she wrote humorous poems and was interested in music and drawing. In 1822 her father was visited by Dr. César Malan (147), who ventured to ask Miss Elliott if she were a Christian. Somewhat resenting the question at first, she gave serious thought to religious matters, and in a short while was a happy believer, her soul at peace in her Saviour. Her highly cultured and well-developed mind is reflected in her hymns, there being in all about one hundred and fifty, many in common use. Her ill health did not prevent her keeping actively at literary work. For a time she edited *The Christian Remembrancer Pocket Book,* originally edited by a Miss Kiernan, of Dublin. Although she edited four books of verse, her best-known book was *The Invalids' Hymn Book,* 1834-41, previously compiled by Miss Kiernan, but before publication rearranged by Miss Elliott, who added thirty-two of her own hymns to the first edition. She continued adding hymns of her own writing until the various editions contained 112. Miss Elliott wrote:

> My Heavenly Father knows, and He alone, what it is, day after day, and hour after hour, to fight against bodily feelings of almost overpowering weakness and languor and exhaustion, to resolve, as He enables me to do, not to yield to the slothfulness, the depression, the irritability, such a body causes me to long to indulge, but to rise every morning determined on taking this for my motto, "If any man will come after me, let him deny himself, take up his cross daily, and follow me."

"Woodworth" was first published in 1849 in the *Third Book of Psalmody,* or the *Mendelssohn Collection,* as it was perhaps better known. The book was by Thomas Hastings (204) and W. B. Bradbury, who jointly edited and published four books. It was first used with the hymn "The God of Love will sure indulge," but it took the words, "Just as I am, without one plea," to make it universally known. It is one of hundreds of simple tunes written during the middle of the last century which mark the transition between the

Lowell Mason sort of tune and the gospel song. Some of the monotony of the original harmonization has been relieved here, but it is printed in its original form at No. 195. "Woodworth" appears in some of our most critically edited hymnals.

**199—Jesus, my All, to heaven is gone—John Cennick**

**Duane Street—George Coles**

The hymn, considerably altered, was taken from *Social Hymns for the use of Religious Societies, Generally Composed in Dialogue, Part II,* Bristol, 1743. The author's title was,

Following Christ the sinner's Way to God.

John Cennick, born into a family of Quakers, December 12, 1718, at Reading, Berkshire, England, was brought up in the Church of England. He fell under evil influences on his visits to London during his fifteenth and sixteenth years, but on Easter, 1735, became "seriously impressed" as he was walking the streets of the city. His conversion was not brought about until in September of his twenty-first year. John Wesley had visited him in the spring of that year, 1739, and wrote:

> I came to Reading, where I found a young man who had in some measure known the powers of the world to come. I spent the evening with him and a few of his serious friends, and it pleased God much to strengthen and comfort them.

Wesley was so impressed with Cennick that he appointed him as a teacher of the children of the colliers at Kingswood, where he also began to act as a lay preacher and to write hymns. Charles Wesley sympathized with his efforts and corrected his verses before publication. Doctrinal differences with the Wesleys caused him to break with them in 1740, Cennick establishing a new sect and gaining a few followers. These he took with him when he began to assist Whitefield in his work. This connection he maintained until 1749, when he was ordained a deacon in the United Brethren Church. His labors with the Brethren led him to Germany and to Ireland. He died in London, July 4, 1755.

"Duane Street," a stirring melody by George Coles, was written in 1835 for James Montgomery's (39) hymn beginning "A poor way-faring man of grief," from his poem "The Stranger," but has been associated with this hymn by several generations of Methodists.

George Coles, born in Stewkley, England, January 2, 1792, who kept a diary for more than fifty years, tells us that in his youth music was his only recreation and that he became so fond of it that he lost interest in the sports of other boys. He emigrated to America when a young man, joined the New York Conference of the Methodist Episcopal Church, and spent the remainder of his life in its service. For twelve years he was assistant editor of *The Christian Advocate* and for three years editor of *The Sunday School Advocate* and other literature for Sunday schools. He became quite proficient as a flutist and enjoyed playing in an amateur trio composed of two flutes and a cello. Frank J. Metcalf says three of his tunes, none of which are now in use, were included in *The Methodist Harmonist.* He died at New York City in 1858.

**200—Depth of mercy! can there be**—Charles Wesley (25)

**Seymour**—Carl Maria von Weber

This hymn with the title,

After a Relapse into Sin,

is from *Hymns and Sacred Poems,* 1740, John and Charles Wesley. Written in thirteen four-line stanzas, 1, 2, 13, and 9 have been selected, with two changes: line 2, stanza 3, "sins" substituted for "fall"; line 2, stanza 4, originally read,

Shows His wounds and spreads His hands.

The Rev. J. Ward, in *Round and Through the Wesleyan Hymn Book,* tells this incident:

> An actress in one of the principal theaters, while passing through the streets, heard singing in a cottage. Intrigued, she looked in and saw a few poor people, one giving out the lines
>
> "Depth of mercy, can there be
> Mercy still reserved for me?"
>
> the others singing. Accepting an invitation to enter, she was much impressed. Securing a copy of a book containing this hymn, she was led to give her heart to God. Her theatrical manager called her to take part in a new benefit play the following week. She did not wish to do it, but upon his urging, consented. At her first appearance on the stage she sang not the song she was supposed to sing, but "Depth of mercy." The sensation created was remarkable.

"Seymour," or "Weber," is from the opening chorus of *Oberon,* Weber's last opera. It is a great favorite, frequently being used with "Softly now the light of day" (47). Dr. W. H. Monk (520), musical editor of *Hymns Ancient and Modern,* reported that in answer to an advertisement asking for tunes for the proposed work, he received more suggestions that this one be used than for any other. Yet he did not use it.

Carl Maria Friedrich Ernest von Weber was born at Eutin, northern Germany, December 18, 1786, and died at London, June 5, 1826. With the exception of J. S. Bach (52), Weber probably had the longest musical pedigree of any of the great musicians. He grew up in the theater, his father being the director of a troupe consisting largely of members of the family, with his mother the leading soprano. His early career was somewhat "checkered," early dissipation doubtless being a contributing cause to his premature death from consumption. He excelled in the field of operatic composition, creating the German romantic opera. It is said no German musician of the last century

> exercised a greater influence over his own generation and that succeeding it than Weber; indeed, there is scarcely a branch of artistic life in which his influence is not still felt.

**201—Jesus, the sinner's Friend, to Thee**—Charles Wesley (25)

**Federal Street** (185)—Henry Kemble Oliver (185)

This hymn is a selection of stanzas 1, 2, 10, and 12 from a thirteen-stanza hymn which first appeared in *Hymns and Sacred Poems,* 1739, based on Galatians 3. 22: "But the scripture hath concluded all under sin, that the promise by faith of Jesus Christ might be given to them that believe." Three words have been changed: "dark" replaced "fall'n," and "lost" replaced "cursed" in stanza 2, while "lost" has been substituted for "damned" in the last line.

# Faith

**202—Father, I stretch my hands to Thee**—Charles Wesley (25)

**Naomi**—Hans·Georg Nägeli (69)

This is from a six-stanza hymn, 1, 2, 5, and 4, unchanged, found in *A Collection of Psalms and Hymns,* 1741, with the title,

A Prayer for Faith.

"Naomi," by Hans G. Nägeli, was brought to America by Lowell Mason, who published it first in a periodical called *Occasional Psalm and Hymn Tunes,* in 1836. It came into his *Modern Psalmist,* 1839, set to "Father, whate'er of earthly bliss," and at once it gained popularity, being included in many other books.

**203—Father of Jesus Christ, my Lord**—Charles Wesley (25)

**Evanston**—Karl Pomeroy Harrington (10)

The hymn is from *Hymns and Sacred Poems,* 1742, based on Romans 4. 16, *et seq.* John Wesley included it in his large *Collection* of 1780, but reduced the number of stanzas from the original twenty to eleven. The selection here is unchanged.

"Evanston" was written in the key of A-flat by Professor Harrington for the hymn, "Jesus, immortal King, arise!" and was first published in *The Methodist Hymnal,* 1905. This is one of a number of tunes whose pitch was lowered in the interests of congregational singing.

**204—Rock of Ages, cleft for me**—Augustus Montague Toplady

**Toplady**—Thomas Hastings

In *The Gospel Magazine* of October, 1775, an article entitled "Life a Journey" appeared with the pseudonym "Minimus," used sometimes by A. M. Toplady as his signature. A part of the article, which gives the root from which this hymn grew, was:

> Yet, if you fall, be humbled; do not despair. Pray afresh to God, who is able to raise you up, and to set you on your feet again. Look to the blood of the Covenant, and say to the Lord, from the depth of your heart,

"Rock of Ages, cleft for me,
let me hide myself in thee!
Foul, I to the fountain fly:
wash me, Saviour, or I die."

Make those words of the apostle, your motto: "Perplexed, but not in despair; cast down, but not destroyed."

In the following March (1776) the same magazine carried a curious article enumerating human sins and holding out the hope (Galatians 3. 13) that "Christ hath redeemed us from the curse of the law; being made a curse for us." The whole closes with a four-stanza elaboration of the lines which had appeared the previous October, entitled,

*A living and dying* PRAYER *for the* HOLIEST BELIEVER *in the World.*

1

Rock of Ages, cleft for me,
Let me hide myself in Thee!
Let the Water and the Blood,
From Thy riven Side which flow'd,
Be of Sin the double Cure,
Cleanse me from its Guilt and Pow'r.

2

Not the labors of my hands
Can fulfill the Law's demands:
Could my zeal no respite know,
Could my tears forever flow,
All for Sin could not atone:
Thou must save, and Thou alone!

3

Nothing in my hand I bring;
Simply to Thy Cross I cling;
Naked, come to Thee for Dress;
Helpless, look to Thee for grace;
Foul, I to the fountain fly:
Wash me, Saviour, or I die!

4

Whilst I draw this fleeting breath—
When my eye-strings break in death—
When I soar through tracts unknown—
See Thee on thy Judgment-Throne—
Rock of Ages, cleft for me,
Let me hide myself in Thee!—A. T.

In addition to subsequent minor changes by Toplady himself, some significant ones were made by Thomas Cotterill (207) and others. Although it would be useless to discuss these changes here, it is enough to say that the "recognized Methodist version" is substantially that which Cotterill used in his *Selection of Psalms and Hymns,* 1815. When one of the learned members of the Editorial Committee charged with the completion of the work of compiling this book raised the question as to whether an additional "editing" might be advisable, Bishop Edwin Holt Hughes, in his inimitable way, quieted any discussion which might have arisen by suggesting that it "would be just as well not to do any tinkering with the Rock of Ages."

Doctor John Julian thinks no other English hymn has taken such a strong hold upon the mind of the English-speaking world, and calls attention to its influence on men of learning. No matter in what light it is regarded, whether as sacred lyric poetry or as an "epitome of certain well-known passages of Scripture," it is of very high order. It is one of the "choicest specimens of sacred poetry that have gradually grown up in the soil of religious sentiment." It has been a stay and comfort in days of peril and in the hour of death.

When Albert, Queen Victoria's consort, lay dying in December, 1861, he used frequently to repeat portions of this hymn. He said, "If in this hour I had only my worldly goods and dignities to depend upon, I should be poor indeed."

It has been criticized as a "medley of confused images," and "accumulated, if not misplaced metaphors," yet so eminent a critic as Saintsbury says, "Every word, every syllable, in this really great poem has its place and meaning."

In a letter to Harriet Beecher Stowe (40), Oliver Wendell Holmes (62) wrote of its wonderful power and solemnity, how it impressed him more than any other hymn, and called it the Protestant "Dies Irae," though it has "more of hope and less of terror." Like others, he stressed its richness in material imagery:

> The imagination wants help, and if it cannot get it in pictures, statues, crucifixes, etc., it will find it in words. That, I believe is the reason why "Rock of Ages" impresses me more than any other hymn—for I think it does.

One who was present at Gladstone's funeral at Westminster Abbey when this hymn was sung, said,

> To have written words which should come home to people in moments of high, deep, and passionate emotions, consecrating, consoling, uplifting: . . . there can hardly be anything worth better doing than that.

There is no foundation in fact to the story of its composition on a stormy day, when the author sought shelter in a cleft of limestone rock at Burrington Combe in the Mendip range of hills in southern England. The story seems to have been invented about 1850.

Augustus Montague Toplady was born in Farnham, Surrey, England, November 4, 1740, the son of a major in the British army who was killed at the siege of Carthegena in 1741. His mother, a woman of deep piety and strength of character, placed him in Westminster School, London, a school not least noted for having been attended by so many poets, among them such superior hymn writers as George Herbert (8), Charles Wesley (25), William Cowper (24), John Dryden, and others. Circumstances led the mother to remove to Ireland, and the boy continued his education at Trinity College, Dublin. In relating the circumstances of his conversion, which was brought about in his sixteenth year, he has said:

> Strange that I who had so long sat under the means of grace in England should be brought right unto God in an obscure part of Ireland, midst a handful of people met together in a barn, and by the ministry of one who could hardly spell his own name. Surely, it was the Lord's doing and is marvellous.

Dr. A. B. Gossart, author of *Three Centuries of Hymns,* takes exception to a part of this statement, saying:

> The present writer happens to know that the lay preacher, a Wesleyan Methodist, was James Morris, and his text was Ephesians vi. 13; and that he was not the illiterate man Toplady's words would have us believe. Likewise, he had far more brain power than his convert, and was a born orator, though reticent and lowly-minded.

Augustus M. Toplady took Orders in the Church of England in 1762, and sometime afterward was appointed vicar of Broadhembury, Devonshire. When the climate there told severely on his health, he became, in 1775, preacher for the French Calvinists at Leicester Fields, London. Earl Selborne's summary of Toplady's work and character is worthy of quotation:

> Few writers of hymns had higher gifts than Augustus Montague Toplady, author of "Rock of Ages," known to everybody, and by some esteemed the finest in the English language. He was a man of ardent temperament, enthusiastic zeal, strong convictions, and great energy of character. "He had," says one of his biographers, "the courage of a lion, but his frame was brittle as glass." Between him and John Wesley there was a violent opposition of opinion, and much acrimonious controversy; but the same fervor and zeal which made him an intemperate theologian gave warmth, richness, and spirituality to his poems; few of which, however, have the character of hymns suited for divine worship. In some of them . . . the setting is too artificial; but his art is never inconsistent with a genuine flow of real feeling.

He died of consumption at London, August 11, 1778.

"Toplady" first appeared in *Spiritual Songs for Social Worship,* 1831, compiled by its composer and Lowell Mason (19). It was written in three parts for "Air, 2nd Treble," and Bass, in the key of D.

Thomas Hastings, Mus. Doc., was born at Washington, Connecticut, October 15, 1784, and died at New York City, May 15, 1872. With Lowell Mason (19) and William B. Bradbury (133), he stands as one of the great leaders in the advance of church music in America during the greater part of the last century. Of the six hundred and more hymns of Hastings' authorship, Professor F. M. Bird, of Lehigh University, has said:

> His aim was the greater glory of God through better musical worship; and to this end he was always training choirs, compiling works, and composing music. His hymn work was a corollary to the proposition of his music work; he wrote hymns for certain tunes; the one activity seemed to imply and necessitate the other. Although not a great poet, he yet attained considerable success. If we take the aggregate of American hymnals published during the fifty years prior to 1892 or for any portion of that time, more hymns by him are found in common use than by any other native writer. Not one of his hymns is of the highest merit, but many of them have become popular and useful. . . The sum of what can be said in his behalf is that the hymns are in his style and that they have not been claimed by others.

He wrote a thousand or more hymn tunes. These are not all easy to identify, for his *noms de plume* were many. He said,

> I have found that a foreigner's name went a great way, and that very ordinary tunes would be sung if "Palestrina" or "Pucitto" were over them, while a better tune by Hastings would go unnoticed.

Most of them are unnoticed now, but it is remarkable how many have lived. He issued approximately fifty volumes of music books, Mason, Bradbury, and others collaborating with him in some of the hymn books and books of sacred songs, but, for the most part, they are his collections.

His boyhood was spent on the farm of his father, a physician as well as a farmer. When he was twelve years of age, the family moved to Clinton, New York, where at eighteen he was the leader of the village choir. His only preparation for his lifework was the education he received at country schools. For some years he was editor of a religious paper at Utica, New York, and he also published some books on music and kindred subjects. He was an indefatigable worker, "not laying aside his pen until three days before his death," according to his son, Thomas S. Hastings, one-time president of Union Theological Seminary.

A perfect albino, very nearsighted, yet having the ability to read from a book held upside down, he was said to have been an excellent choral conductor, often conducting while reading from a book held in the hands of some person standing facing him.

His first work, *The Utica Collection,* a pamphlet with tunes by himself written for use in his singing schools, was issued sometime before 1816. In that year it was combined with *The Springfield Collection,* a book in which all of the tunes were by Europeans, to make *Musica Sacra,* a very popular collection for a quarter of a century.

Most of his tunes and hymns are forgotten, but he was a great leader in his day, holding aloof from the cheapening tendencies of the music then in vogue, constantly keeping before him the ideal of devoutness in music for church worship. "His monument is his music; this man made the tune for 'Rock of Ages.'"

**205—Jesus, Thy blood and righteousness**—Nicolaus Ludwig Zinzendorf
Translated by John Wesley (36)

**Ombersley**—William Henry Gladstone

John Wesley's "spirited but rather free" translation of Zinzendorf's hymn, containing twenty-four stanzas, of which 1, 2, 7, and 8 constitute this hymn, first appeared in *Hymns and Sacred Poems,* 1740, with the title,

The Believer's Triumph.

The last stanza closed with the couplet,

For all Thou hast a ransom given,
Purchased for all peace, life, and heaven,

but was changed to its present reading before Wesley included it in his *Collection* of 1780.

John Wesley had made the acquaintance of Moravian hymnody while in Georgia, and upon his return to England resolved to go to Herrnhut "to see the place where the Christians lived." Here he was further impressed by attending their services and love feasts and listening to their singing. His contributions to hymnody rest on the fine translations he made of some of the Moravian hymns and not on the few originals which have been attributed to him.

Zinzendorf's original, "Christi Blut und Gerechtigkeit," from which John Wesley made his translation, was first published in an appendix to the Herrnhut *Gesangbuch.* In a later edition of Zinzendorf's *Geistliche Lieder,* 1845, it is headed,

On St. Eustachius,

which may mean that it was written on the island of St. Eustatius, Dutch West Indies, or on St. Eustachius's Day. The first four lines of the hymn were taken by Count Zinzendorf from Paul Eber's hymn beginning,

In Christi Wunden schlaf ich ein.

Count Nicolaus Ludwig von Zinzendorf, born at Dresden, May 26, 1700, was the son of the Prime Minister of the State of Saxony. The Zinzendorf family was noble, wealthy, and religious. While at school he founded the Order of the Mustard Seed, its members pledging themselves to lives of personal service and to missionary effort. When twenty-two years of age, he set apart a portion of his estate as a refuge for the persecuted descendants of the Moravian Brethren and founded Herrnhut, where five years later he went to live. Exiled on the charge of preaching false doctrines, he was not allowed to return from Stralsund, where he had gone incognito to pass the required examinations for ordination. He spent the ten years of this exile in a preaching pilgrimage which carried him from St. Petersburg to the West Indies, four of which were spent in this country with his followers. Following his consecration as a bishop at Berlin, in 1737, he became the leader at Herrnhut, devoting so much of his fortune to the work that he died poor. He was the author of more than two thousand hymns, most of them of little merit. His death occurred at Herrnhut, May 9, 1760.

"Ombersley" first appeared in *The Hymnary,* 1872, set to "Jesus shall reign where'er the sun." It was included ten years later in *A Selection of Hymns and Tunes, made and arranged by W. H. Gladstone. (1882.) Not for sale.* Of this book, Sir Walter Parratt (1841-1924), who succeeded Sir George J. Elvey (170) as organist at St. George's Chapel, Windsor, said, "It is the only book I know in which there are no bad tunes."

William Henry Gladstone, eldest son of England's great statesman, William E. Gladstone, born at Hawarden, England, June 3, 1840, was a good amateur musician. In his college days at Oxford music seemed to be his greatest interest. Not only was he a good singer, being a member of the Bach Choir and other singing organizations, but he played the organ well and often played the service at the church at Hawarden, the family home. He was a student of the history of music, especially the development of Anglican church music. Some of the several anthems, hymn tunes, and chants of his composing are used at St. Paul's Cathedral. For twenty years he held a seat in the House of Commons. He died at London, July 4, 1891.

**206—Strong Son of God, immortal Love**—Alfred Tennyson

**Keble** (62)—John Bacchus Dykes (1)

This great hymn of faith is composed of stanzas 1, 3, 4, and 5 from the

*Introduction* (dated 1849) to *In Memoriam,* by Lord Tennyson, a series of elegies on Arthur H. Hallam, his intimate friend, first published anonymously in 1850.

Alfred Tennyson, son of the rector of Somersby, England, was born August 6, 1809, and educated at Louth Grammar School and Trinity College, Cambridge. With his brother, Charles, he issued a volume of poems when only eighteen. His *Poems,* published in 1842, at once gained him a place with the foremost English poets. Twice declining knighthood, he was finally persuaded by Gladstone to accept a peerage, and became, in 1884, Baron of Aldworth and Farringford. In 1850 he had been made Poet Laureate of England, succeeding William Wordsworth. He died at Aldworth, October 6, 1892.

**207—By Thy birth and by Thy tears**—Robert Grant (4)
Altered by Thomas Cotterill (413) and others

**Gethsemane**—Richard Redhead

The poem, "Saviour, when in dust to Thee," from which these stanzas were taken, was first published in *The Christian Observer,* 1815, in five eight-line stanzas, entitled "Litany." It appeared again in H. V. Elliott's *Psalms and Hymns,* 1835, with a protest over its mutilation. Thomas Cotterill (413) had made a selection of lines aggregating four stanzas of four lines each for the eighth edition of his *Selection of Psalms and Hymns,* 1819, and probably he was the object of the protest. Later others, among whom one changed Cotterill's first line,

By Thy birth and early years,

to its present reading, made further alterations to give the hymn its present form. This *Selection* of Thomas Cotterill (eighth edition) had a marked influence on the hymnody of the Church of England during the thirty years from 1821 to 1850, and a large majority of the hymns which appeared there, most of them altered and (or) emendated by Cotterill and James Montgomery (39), are still in use in England and America.

"Gethsemane," "Petra," or "Ajalon," or more correctly "Redhead No. 76," is from Richard Redhead's *Church Hymn Tunes, Ancient and Modern,* 1853. He did not give names to his tunes but signed them with his own name, followed by a number. This tune is a favorite setting for "Rock of Ages" (204).

Richard Redhead, born at Harrow, England, March 1, 1820, received his musical education as a chorister at Magdalen College, Oxford, where he came under the influence of the Rev. Frederick Oakeley (96), who invited him, in 1839, to become organist at one of the churches (Margaret Street Chapel) prominent in the Oxford movement. Twenty-five years later he went to the church of St. Mary Magdalene, Paddington, where for thirty years he was in charge of its music. A skilled trainer of boys' voices, he excelled as "an accompanist of devotional spirit, whose extemporizing seemed inspired by his faith." He died at Hallingley, Sussex, April 27, 1901.

## Forgiveness

**208—How can a sinner know**—Charles Wesley (25)

**Old 134th (St. Michael)** (39)—Adapted from the Genevan Psalter, 1551 (3)

The hymn, originally in eight eight-line stanzas, entitled,

The Marks of Faith,

is from *Hymns and Sacred Poems,* 1749. This selection is made up of lines 1-12 and 29-32, unaltered from its appearance in John Wesley's large *Collection* of 1780.

**209—Amazing grace, how sweet the sound**—John Newton (27)

**Amazing Grace**—Early American melody

The hymn consists of the first four stanzas of six, entitled,

Faith's Review and Expectation,

taken, unaltered and unabridged, from the *Olney Hymns,* 1779. It was based on 1 Chronicles 17. 16, 17: "And David the king came and sat before the Lord, and said, Who am I, O Lord God, and what is mine house, that thou hast brought me hitherto? And yet this was a small thing in thine eyes, O God; for thou hast also spoken of thy servant's house for a great while to come, and hast regarded me according to the estate of a man of high degree, O Lord God." The hymn is not used in modern English collections but is popular in America. It is one of the many hymns written by John Newton out of his experience, for he had been wretched, he had been "lost" and "blind," and had passed

Through many dangers, toils, and snares.

John Newton knew, as many men have come to know,

How precious did that grace appear
The hour I first believed!

"Amazing Grace" is evidently an old tune from the Southeastern states. Joe S. James, publisher of the *Original Sacred Harp,* 1929, says it appears on page 8 of the *Southern Harmony,* William Walker, 1835, and believes it was composed early in the nineteenth century, but has found no composer given in books he has examined. It may be a variant of an old tune called "Loving Lamb."

**210—I heard the voice of Jesus say**—Horatius Bonar

First tune: **Vox Dilecti**—John Bacchus Dykes (1)

Second tune: **Truman**—Joseph Perry Holbrook

The hymn, based on St. John 1. 16, "And of his fullness have all we received, and grace for grace," is from Horatius Bonar's *Hymns, Original and Selected,* 1846. One of the most beautiful of Doctor Bonar's hymns, "so beautiful in its simplicity," it was written at Kelso while he was ministering there. His son has said it was written several years before its publication. No changes have been made from the final copy in Doctor Bonar's notebook.

He blended into perfect unity three sayings of Jesus:

Come unto me, all ye that labour and are heavy laden, and I will give you rest.—St. Matthew xi. 28.

Whosoever drinketh of the water that I shall give him shall never thirst.—St. John iv. 14.

I am the light of the world: he that followeth me shall not walk in darkness, but shall have the light of life.—St. John viii. 12.

The title to the hymn,

The Voice from Galilee,

is entirely fitting, while the whole hymn is an excellent illustration of the personal note sounded in so many of Doctor Bonar's offerings, his use of first personal pronouns having had much to do with their appeal to minds of all types.

Horatius Bonar, D.D., foremost of the Scottish hymn writers, was born at Edinburgh, December 19, 1808, the son of the solicitor of excise for that city. Educated at the High School and University of Edinburgh, he was ordained at Kelso when thirty years of age, and was given charge of the work in North Parish. In 1843 he, with his church, joined the movement which led to the founding of the Free Church of Scotland. Part-time editor of the Free Church periodical, *The Border Watch,* he later became editor of the *Journal of Prophecy.* Although at Kelso he had frequently said, "Here I am, and here I must remain until my Lord comes to me, or for me"; nevertheless, after much persuasion he went to the larger Chalmer's Memorial Church, Edinburgh, named after Thomas Chalmers, leader of the Free Church movement and its first moderator, whose pupil Doctor Bonar had been in the University of Edinburgh. In 1883 Doctor Bonar himself had the honor of being elected moderator of the General Assembly of his Church. He died at Edinburgh, July 31, 1889.

Doctor Bonar, like Beethoven, kept a notebook in which he jotted down ideas or fragments of verse as they occurred to him and which he thought might be of later value. He told a friend he had no record nor remembrance of how or when his many hymns had been written, but he believed he had done most of them when traveling on railway trains. He seemed to write them casually, when he was not busy with other matters.

One said of him that he was always visiting, another that he was always preaching, another that he was always writing, another that he was always praying.

James Bonar, joint editor of the Scottish *Free Church Hymn Book,* has written:

Doctor Bonar's hymns satisfy the fastidious by their instinctive good taste; they mirror the life of Christ in the soul, partially, perhaps, but with vivid accuracy; they win the heart by their tone of tender sympathy; they sing the truth of God in ringing notes; and, although, when taken as a whole, they are not perfect, . . . a singularly large number have been stamped with approval, both in literary circles and in the Church.

"Vox Dilecti," Voice of the Beloved One, shows Doctor Dykes at his best. He has given us a tune well worthy of study. The first half, Jesus' invitation, in G minor; the glad acceptance, in the relevant major, is an example of artistry not always found in hymn tunes. That Doctor Dykes felt strongly as to the fitness of the music to which hymns are set is indicated in a letter to Dr. W. H. Monk, dated August 24, 1874, concerning some tunes he was writing for *Hymns Ancient and Modern:*

> I never think of setting a hymn that *is* worthily set, where the tune can be got. That would be merely silly caprice, or vanity, or presumption. But if a hymn does *not* appear to me worthily set, then, I own, I am often induced, I may say, sometimes almost *compelled,* to try to do my best for it.
>
> I know so well the teaching power of hymns, if they are happily wedded, that I am very anxious to do my best (as far as God is pleased to help me) to add to the number of those useful and felicitous unions. . . . My one desire is this: that each hymn should be so set to music (by whomsoever God wills to select for that purpose) that its power of influencing and teaching may be best brought out. All other considerations must be subordinate to that.

"Vox Dilecti" appeared in the Appendix to *Hymns Ancient and Modern,* 1868.

"Truman" doubtless appeared in one of the many books compiled by its composer. The statement that it is of the gushing, gospel song type used in few hymnals, is no disparagement of gospel songs. But it is not an adequate setting for Doctor Bonar's exquisite hymn, which Dr. David R. Breed has said is "one of the most ingenious hymns in the language." Certainly, there is nothing ingenious in this tune.

Joseph Perry Holbrook was born near Boston in 1822. Composer of hymn tunes and compiler and editor of several books, the best known being *Songs of the Sanctuary,* he was one of the musical editors of *The Hymnal of the Methodist Episcopal Church,* 1878. He died in 1888.

**211—Arise, my soul, arise**—Charles Wesley (25)

**Lenox** (189)—Lewis Edson (189)

The hymn is given as it was published in *Hymns and Sacred Poems,* 1742, with the title,

**Behold the Man.**

It is one of Charles Wesley's most jubilant hymns; one which has furnished to many souls a medium for expressing their happiness. Dr. Charles C. Washburn in *Hymn Stories,* 1935, says:

> In this hymn Charles Wesley gives expression to the spiritual life of Methodism, and at one period in the life of this great body it expressed, vocally, the personal experience of its individual members. Throughout its lifetime "Arise, my soul, arise," has been the conclusive means of bringing thousands of earnest seekers to an ultimate stand and conviction, or realization of adoption in the family of God.

Dr. Van Denman Thompson (153) makes striking use of this hymn and the tune "Lenox" in *The Evangel of the New World.*

> The God we know is the Father of the prodigal: we hear His pardoning voice, and draw nigh with confidence.

**212—O happy day, that fixed my choice**—Philip Doddridge (69)

**Happy Day**—Adapted from Edward Francis Rimbault

This hymn, without the Refrain, appeared in the edition of Doctor Doddridge's *Hymns* published in 1819 by John Doddridge Hymphreys, the author's great-grandson, except the last two lines of stanza four, which read,

With ashes who would grudge to part,
When called on angel's bread to feed.

It is otherwise, doubtless, as Doddridge wrote it. The Refrain was added when the evangelistic adaptation of the Rimbault tune was made. It was published with the title,

Rejoicing in our Covenant engagements to God. II Chron. xv. 15.

"Happy Day" is said to have been adapted from a work of Dr. E. F. Rimbault. This is true of the Refrain at least, for that is taken from his

Pretty little song, "Happy Land,"

which, William H. Husk says, "had an extensive popularity." It begins:

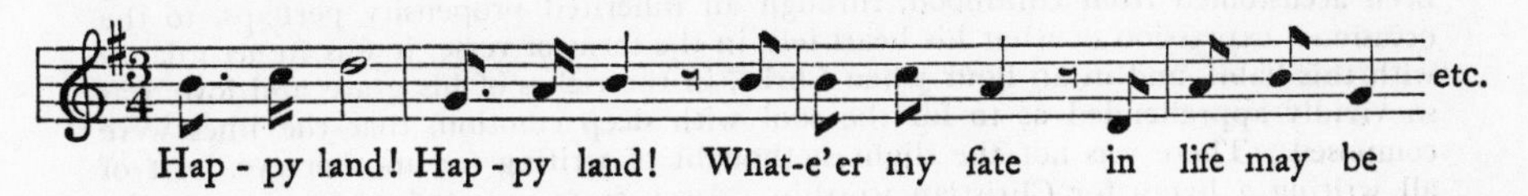
etc.
Hap - py land! Hap - py land! What-e'er my fate in life may be

Set to John Cennick's hymn, "Jesus, my All, to heaven is gone" (199), and with "Happy day, happy day," as its chorus, with this hymn given second place, this tune appeared in *The Wesleyan Sacred Harp, . . . by Rev. W. McDonald, of the Maine Conference, and S. Hubbard, Esq.*, Boston, 1854. Though it has not been traced to any previously printed book, it may have been current earlier, for the compilers in their Preface say, "Many of the tunes—not altogether *new*—have never appeared in a work of this kind before."

This is still another example of a transitory popular melody being given a greatly extended lease on life by being taken into a hymnal. The learned Doctor Rimbault doubtless never dreamed that his "pretty little tune" would become familiar to millions of Christians through their singing,

Happy day, happy day,
When Jesus washed my sins away.

Edward Francis Rimbault, LL.D., was born at Soho, London, June 13, 1816, and died there September 26, 1876. Living in London all of his life, he was a scholar of attainment, a musician, a voluminous writer, and a compiler of numerous and various collections of musical works and works about music. At the age of sixteen he became organist at Swiss Church, Soho, London. He was offered, but declined, the chair of professor of music at Harvard University. Most of his teaching in music was received from his father, but for a time he was a pupil of Samuel Wesley (633).

## Consecration

**213—My faith looks up to Thee—Ray Palmer (176)**
**Olivet—Lowell Mason (19)**

This, Doctor Palmer's first and best hymn, was first published in Thomas Hastings' (204) *Spiritual Songs for Social Worship,* 1831, entitled,

Self-Consecration.

Doctor Palmer's account of the writing of this hymn and the circumstances which led Lowell Mason to write the tune, "Olivet," cannot be improved upon:

> Immediately after graduating at Yale College, in September, 1830, the writer went to the City of New York to spend a year in teaching in a select school for young ladies. This private institution, which was patronized by the best class of families, was under the direction of an excellent Christian lady connected with Saint George's Church. . . . The writer resided in the family of the lady who kept the school, and it was there that the hymn was written. It had no external occasion whatever. Having been accustomed from childhood, through an inherited propensity perhaps, to the occasional expression of what his heart felt, in the form of verse, it was in accordance with this habit, and in an hour when Christ, in the riches of his grace and love, was so vividly apprehended as to fill the soul with deep emotion, that the lines were composed. There was not the slightest thought of writing for another eye, least of all writing a hymn for Christian worship. Away from outward excitement, in the quiet of his chamber, and with a deep consciousness of his own needs, the writer transferred as faithfully as he could to paper what at the time was passing within him. Six stanzas were composed and imperfectly written, first on a loose sheet, and then accurately copied into a small morocco-covered book, which for such purposes the author was accustomed to carry in his pocket. This first complete copy is still (1875) preserved. It is well remembered that when writing the last line, "A ransomed soul," the thought that the whole work of redemption and salvation was involved in those words, and suggested the theme of eternal praises, moved the writer to a degree of emotion that brought abundant tears.
>
> A year or two after the hymn was written, and when no one, so far as can be recollected, had ever seen it, Dr. Lowell Mason met the author in the street in Boston, and requested him to furnish some hymns for a *Hymn and Tune Book,* which, in connection with Doctor Hastings of New York, he was about to publish. The little book containing the hymn was shown him, and he asked for a copy. We stepped into a store together, and a copy was made and given to him, which, without much notice, he put into his pocket. On sitting down at home and looking it over, he became so much interested in it that he wrote for it the tune "Olivet," to which it has almost universally been sung. Two or three days afterward we met again in the street, when, scarcely waiting to salute the writer, he earnestly exclaimed: "Mr. Palmer, you may live many years and do many good things, but I think you will be best known to posterity as the author of "My faith looks up to Thee!"

Probably no other hymn by an American has become so well known the world around. Translated into many languages, included in numerous hymnals and other books of sacred song, it is universally praised. As Doctor Ninde suggests, "Had it been intended for the public eye, it could never have been written."

**214—My God, I love Thee, not because**—Anonymous. From the Latin
Translated by Edward Caswall (31)

**Molleson**—Douglas Fletcher

This hymn, of unknown origin, has been ascribed to St. Francis Xavier, but authoritative criticism has declined to associate his name with any part of it. Dating from the seventeenth century, it appeared in *Coeleste Palmetum,* a book published in Cologne in 1669, and is believed to be the Latin form of a Spanish sonnet. Edward Caswall would not have translated this hymn for his *Lyra Catholica,* 1849, it has been said, if he had known it was not by St. Francis. Yet by doing so he has given us a widely used hymn with perhaps his best verse, expressing beautifully the thought,

We love Him because He first loved us.

"Molleson," written by Douglas Fletcher in 1924, has its first printed appearance in this book.

Douglas Fletcher, the composer of "Molleson," the son of a Church of England organist, was born in the county of Wiltshire, England, January 3, 1884. From his earliest years he has been deeply interested in religious music and at the age of twelve served as assistant organist in a small Baptist church in Swindon. At this same age he won a county scholarship by competitive examination which enabled him, during the next four years, to acquire a scientific and technical education at the Swindon and North Wiltshire Technical Institute and thereby lay the foundation for his future career as an industrial chemist. After arriving in America, he continued his studies in chemistry at the Cooper Union Institute in New York until he obtained his diploma as a graduate chemist. During the years that have followed he has labored continuously as an industrial chemist in the paint and varnish industry.

While an inherent love of music has served to make it a great source of recreation for his hobby side of life, he has devoted much leisure time to the serious study of piano, organ, and harmony. He "firmly believes that hymn tunes should interpret the verse in an inspiring, reverent, and dignified style with a tuneful appeal that will enable the average congregation to join heartily in the singing," after hearing one verse for the first time. In furtherance of this ideal, he has during the past several years composed new melodies for approximately one hundred and fifty standard hymns found chiefly in the Episcopal and Methodist hymnals.

**215—O the bitter shame and sorrow**—Theodore Monod

**St. Jude**—Charles John Vincent

This text is the only one of several of this hymn which the author endorsed. He particularly objected to the repetition of the last line in order to make it conform to a six-line tune. It was written in July, 1874, while M. Monod was in England, a guest of Lord and Lady Mount-Temple at their home, Broadlands, in Hampshire (or Hants), at the close of a series of private meetings. He gave the stanzas the title,

The Altered Motto.

Some time shortly after, without his knowledge, the words were printed on the back of some invitations to the first public "consecration meetings" which were held at Oxford the latter part of August of the same year. While never intended for a hymn, these stanzas have found their way into many books of sacred song.

Theodore Monod was born at Paris, France, November 6. 1836, and after taking degrees of Bachelor of Science and Master of Arts at the University of Paris, became a student of the law. Coming to America and completing his theological course at the Western Theological Seminary, Pittsburgh, Pennsylvania, he was licensed to preach in the Presbytery of Allegheny in January, 1861, and in July of the same year was ordained pastor of the Second Presbyterian Church, Kankakee, Illinois, where he remained for two years. Returning to France in 1864, he became pastor of the Chapelle du Nord and of the Reformed Church in Paris; was agent of Home Missions in France; and was editor of *Le Libérateur.* M. Monod was the author of several books, his *Le don de Dieu* was translated into English ("Life More Abundant"). He was an evangelical preacher who made himself felt beyond the confines of his own denomination. His death occurred at Paris, February 26, 1921.

"St. Jude" must not be confused with the tune "Galilee," improperly named "Jude" in *The Methodist Hymnal,* 1905, set to "Jesus calls us, o'er the tumult" (233). This tune was written by Charles John Vincent for the Revised and Enlarged Edition of *The Hymnal Companion to the Book of Common Prayer,* 1877, edited by Bishop E. H. Bickersteth (354), the musical editor being J. T. Cooper. Bishop Bickersteth states that Mr. Cooper was not responsible for the selection of the tunes. This explanation is given because of the current statement that Doctor Vincent had been musical editor of the *Hymnal Companion.* "St. Jude," which first appeared in the edition of 1877, was written especially for that work, set to this hymn.

Charles John Vincent, Mus. Doc., born at Houghton-le-Spring, Durham, England, September 19, 1852, was the son of a dealer in musical merchandise and an organ builder at Sunderland. A chorister at Durham Cathedral, he studied music with the eminent organist, Dr. Philip Armes. Vincent's career was a varied one. He held several important posts as organist; studied at Leipzig; was sent to South Africa and Australia as an examiner for Trinity College; was one of the founders of *The Organist and Choirmaster;* became a publisher of music, and founded a firm dealing in pianos. After an active life in business he retired to Hendon. He died at Monte Carlo, February 23, 1934. He is buried in the cemetery at Monaco, "A place of beauty which he loved so much," according to his daughter, Dorothy Vincent.

**216—Prince of Peace, control my will**—Mary Ann Serrett Barber

**Aletta** (146)—William Batchelder Bradbury (133)

The hymn was taken from a poem which appeared in *The Church of England Magazine,* in March, 1838, headed,

**He is our Peace,**

the words taken from Ephesians 2. 14. The poem was in four stanzas of eight lines each. This hymn was compiled by taking the first stanza with the change of only one word ("way" was made "gate"), and by the selection of various lines from the remainder—some altered slightly, others completely changed from the original poem.

Mary Ann Serrett Barber, contributor of verse to *The Church of England Magazine* and author of several books, was an Englishwoman of Huguenot descent, born in 1801. From 1847 to 1864 she was the editor of the *Children's Nursery Magazine;* she was interested in all religious work; with her sister was the support of her invalid father: and from an annual income of £1,000, aided more than two hundred children in Africa, India, and North America. She died at Brighton, March 9, 1864.

**217—Lord, in the strength of grace**—Charles Wesley (25)

**Greenwood**—Joseph Emerson Sweetser

The hymn was taken from Charles Wesley's *Short Hymns on Select Passages of Scripture,* Vol. I, 1762. Written as in one stanza with the heading,

> Who is willing to consecrate his services this
> day unto the Lord? xxix. 5 (I Chronicles),

it has been made into two stanzas without change of any kind in its wording. It is a fine short consecration hymn which should have wide use.

"Greenwood" was written by Joseph E. Sweetser for the hymn "We lift our hearts to Thee," and was included in *A Collection of Church Music,* 1849, popularly known as the "Root and Sweetser Collection."

Joseph Emerson Sweetser was an English organist who came to America in his young manhood and became organist at the Church of the Puritans, New York City. He joined with George F. Root (439) in publishing what became known as the "Root and Sweetser Collection" of church music, 1849, a very popular book for many years. Mr. Sweetser, concerning whose life details are lacking, was born in 1825 and died in 1873.

**218—O Love divine, how sweet Thou art!**—Charles Wesley (25)

**Ariel** (19)—Lowell Mason (19)

This hymn comes from *Hymns and Sacred Poems,* 1749, one of six with the same title,

> Desiring to Love.

This cento consists of three stanzas from seven. Dean Tillett (117) refers to this as a "truly magnificent hymn," in which the author is "in his happiest vein; he never sang a sweeter song than this. As sung to the tune 'Ariel,' it truly aids devotion."

**219—Saviour, Thy dying love**—Sylvanus Dryden Phelps

**Something for Jesus**—Robert Lowry

This hymn, written in 1862, was first published in *The Watchman and*

*Reflector.* Soon after its appearance in the Baptist publication, Dr. Robert Lowry asked Dr. S. D. Phelps, its author, to supply some hymns for a work he then was preparing for publication. This, with others, was given Doctor Lowry, who used it in *Pure Gold,* 1871, using the heading,

> "Lord, what wilt Thou have me to do?"
> Acts 9. 6.

It has gained wide circulation since having been included in *Gospel Hymns* (No. 1), 1875, being found in many books not overly friendly to gospel songs. On Doctor Phelps's seventieth birthday, Doctor Lowry wrote him:

> It is worth living seventy years even if nothing comes of it but one such hymn as
> "Saviour! thy dying love
> Thou gavest me;
> Nor should I aught withhold,
> Dear Lord, from thee."
>
> Happy is the man who can produce one song which the world will keep on singing after its author shall have passed away. May the tuneful harp preserve its strings for many a long year yet, and the last note reach us only when it is time for the singer to take his place in the heavenly choir.

William F. Sherwin (44) tells of the third stanza changing the whole trend of the life of a young lawyer, who gave up his profession to enter religious work to which he gave his whole heart. Doctor Phelps said, "Doctor Lowry has given wings to my hymn."

Of his father, William Lyon Phelps has written:

> He was always deeply gratified by the success of one of his hymns, "Saviour, Thy dying love," and he wished that "author of the hymn" be put on his gravestone in the New Haven cemetery. It was.

Sylvanus Dryden Phelps, D.D., born at Suffield, Connecticut, May 15, 1816, was educated at the Connecticut Literary Institute, Brown University, and at Yale Theological Seminary. For twenty-eight years he was pastor of the First Baptist Church, New Haven. One time editor of *The Christian Secretary,* at Hartford, Doctor Phelps published several books of poetry and prose, his *Holy Land* passing through nine editions. He began writing hymns in his college days, his first efforts being temperance hymns for children. Of his many offerings of gospel songs, this is the best known.

Doctor Phelps died at New Haven, November 23, 1895.

"Something for Jesus" was written by Dr. Robert Lowry to these words for *Pure Gold,* a small Sunday-school collection, of which more than one million copies were sold. It is one of Doctor Lowry's most popular tunes.

Robert Lowry, D.D., born March 12, 1826, at Philadelphia, was a Baptist preacher, a college professor, an administrator of ability, and a popular orator. He did not take up the study of music seriously until after his fortieth birthday. Highly gifted with musical and versifying talent, he wrote both words and music for many of his songs. Asked whether he wrote the music to fit the words or vice versa, he said:

> I have no method. Sometimes the music comes and the words follow, fitted insensibly to the melody. I watch my moods, and when anything strikes me, whether

words or music, no matter where I am, at home, or on the street, I jot it down. Often the margin of a newspaper or the back of an envelope serves as a note book. My brain is a sort of spinning machine, I think, for there is music running through it all the time. I do not pick out my music on the keys of an instrument. The tunes of nearly all the hymns I have written have been completed on paper before I tried them on the organ. Frequently the words of the hymn and the music have been written at the same time.

Doctor Lowry said he would rather preach a gospel sermon to an appreciative, attentive congregation than write a hymn, yet his hymns and tunes have been remembered long since his sermons have been forgotten. His songs have helped millions, his sermons reached only a few thousands. He died at Plainfield, New Jersey, November 25, 1899.

**220—Majestic sweetness sits enthroned**—Samuel Stennett

**Ortonville**—Thomas Hastings (204)

This, one of thirty-eight hymns by Samuel Stennett published in *Rippon's Selection,* 1787 (315), was entitled,

Chief Among Ten Thousand; or, The
Excellencies of Christ. Cant. v. 10-16,

and was made up of nine stanzas, the first being,

To Christ, the Lord, let every tongue
Its noblest tribute bring:
When He's the subject of the song,
Who can refuse to sing?

This selection consists of stanzas 3, 4, 7, and 9. Line 2, stanza 1, was originally:

Upon His awful brow.

Samuel Stennett, D.D., was born, probably in 1727, at Exeter, England. He came from a line prominent for more than a century in the English Baptist Church and in Baptist hymnody. With his father's family he moved to London at the age of ten, and at twenty became his father's assistant at the Baptist Church in Little Wild Street, Lincoln's Inn Fields. Later, upon the death of his father, he was ordained its regular minister. For twenty years he preached each Saturday morning at the Sabbatarian Baptist Church, London. A writer of elegance of style, he issued a number of books on religious subjects, some short poems, and thirty-eight hymns contributed to *A Selection of Hymns from the best authors, intended as an Appendix to Dr. Watts's Psalms and Hymns,* the famed *Selection* of 1787 (315) compiled by his friend, Dr. John Rippon. He enjoyed the personal friendship of George III, and held the close friendship of John Howard, noted philanthropist, who was a member of his congregation. In 1763 the University of Aberdeen conferred on him the degree of Doctor of Divinity. He died at London, August 24, 1795.

"Ortonville" was composed by Thomas Hastings, the compiler of the book from which it was taken, *The Manhattan Collection,* 1837. Written in the key of C, and set to this hymn, the tune appeared with this note, "The Swell as indicative of great tenderness, is here required," referring to the knee-action "swells" of the old reed-organs. This ranks second in popularity, among Hastings' many tunes, to "Toplady" (204).

**221—Master, speak! Thy servant heareth**—Frances Ridley Havergal (161)
**Amen, Jesus Han Skal Raade**—Anton Peter Berggreen

This hymn, in nine stanzas, was written by Miss Havergal on Sunday evening, May 19, 1867, at Weston-super-Mare, a seaside resort of Somersetshire, England, on the English channel. Stanzas 1, 6, 8, and 9 are used. It was first published in *Ministry of Song* in 1869, its title being,

Master, Say On!

While no mention of a text is made, evidently it was suggested by the conversation between Samuel and Eli (1 Samuel 3. 1-10), one of the most dramatic passages of the Old Testament. The first line of the hymn epitomizes the life of its author.

"Amen, Jesus Han Skal Raade" (Amen, Jesus, He shall reign), a favorite setting among Lutherans to John Newton's hymn beginning,

One there is above all others,

was written in 1849, and was published in 1853 in the composer's *Psalm Tunes.*

Anton Peter Berggreen, born at Copenhagen, Denmark, March 2, 1801, was intended by his parents for the law, but began studying harmony and composing at the age of fourteen. Although a composer of works on a large scale, he is best known for his *National Songs,* in eleven volumes; for his thirteen-volume *Songs* for use in schools; and for his collection of *Psalm Tunes,* now quite generally used in Danish churches. During the time that he held the position of organist at Trinity Church, Copenhagen, from 1838 until shortly before he died, he was responsible for the organization of the musical associations among the laboring classes still popular in his country. For many years he was Professor of Singing at the Metropolitan School and inspector of the public schools of his native city. He died at Copenhagen, where he had lived all of his life, November 9, 1880.

**222—Jesus, Thy boundless love to me**—Paul Gerhardt (91)
Translated by John Wesley (36), altered
**Yoakley**—William Yoakley

The hymn first appeared in *Hymns and Sacred Poems,* 1739, headed,

Living by Christ—From the German.

John Wesley was in Georgia when he translated this hymn of Gerhardt's. It was in sixteen stanzas, reduced to nine in his *Collection* of 1780, of which stanzas 1, 3, and 9 are used with changes in the first: "fear" in the second line has been substituted for "pain"; the last two lines changed from,

Thine, wholly Thine alone—I am,
Be Thou alone my constant flame,

to,

Thine, wholly Thine alone I'd live,
Myself to Thee, entirely give.

In John Wesley's *Plain Account of Christian Perfection* he says:

> In the beginning of the year 1738, as I was returning from Savannah, the cry of my heart was—
>
> O grant that nothing in my soul
> May dwell but Thy pure love alone;
> O may Thy love possess me whole,
> My joy, my treasure, and my crown!
> Strange fires far from my heart remove;
> My every act, word, thought, be love.

This is the second stanza of the original, omitted from this edition of *The Methodist Hymnal.*

Paul Gerhardt's hymn appeared in Crüger's *Praxis Pietatis Melica,* 1653, a source book for tunes (60), but Wesley doubtless took it from the Herrnhut *Collection* of Count Zinzendorf (205). Its first line was,

> O Jesu Christ, mein schönstes Licht.

It is one of the finest of all hymns on the love of Christ and has had wide circulation through many denominational books.

"Yoakley." In the light of the recently revived interest in the tune "Yoakley," the author of this MANUAL has made great effort to learn something definite of its history and of its composer, but has been unable to trace it to any earlier source than *Carmina Sacra,* or *Boston Collection of Church Music,* 1841, compiled by Lowell Mason. It was used there as the tune for

> The Lord my pasture will prepare,

the first hymn Joseph Addison (66) published in *The Spectator,* and was credited:

> Arranged from a tune by William Yoakley.

This book, like others by Mason, contained "specimens from distinguished composers of the present day in Europe." Certain questions arise: Did Mason discover "a tune by William Yoakley" during his English visit of 1837? If so, the date usually given for the birth of William Yoakley, 1820, is probably an error, as it is not probable a seventeen-year-old youth would have produced a tune which would have attracted Mason's notice. Who arranged the tune for *Carmina Sacra?* Probably Lowell Mason. What was the tune from which it was arranged? Who was William Yoakley? These are questions which remain to be answered.

**223—Blessed Master, I have promised**—Charles Albert Dickinson

**Bullinger**—Ethelbert William Bullinger

When this hymn was written the author doubtless had in mind the Christian Endeavor pledges, each of which begins,

> Trusting in the Lord Jesus Christ for strength, I promise Him that I will strive to do whatever He would (like to) have me do.

Charles Albert Dickinson was born at Westminster, Vermont, July 4,

1849. A graduate of Harvard University and a Congregational minister, he was interested in young people, in the organization of their religious work, and particularly in the writing of hymns for them. Compelled, on account of ill health, to relinquish active work in the ministry, he removed to California in 1899. He died there in 1906.

"Bullinger" was written in 1874, and set to

Jesu, Refuge of the weary,

while Doctor Bullinger was curate at Walthamstow, Essex, England.

Ethelbert William Bullinger, D.D., born at Canterbury, December 15, 1837, was an English clergyman, a graduate of King's College, London, who held curacies in several parishes. So serious was his avocational interest in music that it led him to study with such men as John Pyke Hullah, noted for his teaching of singing in classes, and Dr. W. H. Monk (520). The degree of Doctor of Divinity was conferred upon him in 1881 by the Archbishop of Canterbury. Doctor Bullinger died at London, June 6, 1913. He is known now solely for having written this overly sentimental tune, in many cases made more so by the lengthening of the last phrase to

**224—Lord, I am Thine, entirely Thine**—Samuel Davies

**Sessions**—Luther Orlando Emerson

This hymn by Samuel Davies, with the title,

Self-Dedication at the Table of the Lord,

originally had seven stanzas, of which 1, 3, 4, and 6 are used here, unchanged. It was published in 1769 in *Hymns adapted to Divine Worship in two books,* published by the Rev. Thomas Gibbons, D.D., who wrote a life of Isaac Watts (3). This hymn and fifteen others, all he wrote, were published in Doctor Gibbons's *Hymns,* Doctor Davies having entrusted his sermons and other writings in manuscript to him.

Samuel Davies, D.D., born November 3, 1723, at Summit Bridge, Delaware, was a Presbyterian minister who succeeded Jonathan Edwards as president of New Jersey College, now Princeton University. He was intellectually vigorous, a man of piety, whose life was fully useful. After his ordination in 1747 he spent many years in evangelistic and missionary work in Virginia. He visited England in 1753 as an emissary of New Jersey College. He died at Princeton, February 4, 1761.

"Sessions" was written for a choir at Salem, Massachusetts, where Dr. L. O. Emerson first taught. Concerning this tune he has written:

In the year 1847 I was living in the city of Salem, Massachusetts. One pleasant summer Sabbath day after returning from church, being alone in my house, I took up my hymn book, and on opening it my eyes fell upon the hymn beginning "Sinner, O why so thoughtless grown?" My attention was at once fixed upon it. I read the whole hymn through several times, and the impression it made upon me grew stronger and stronger at each repetition. I had a longing to give expression in some way to my emotions. After a season of prayer, I went to the piano and at once played the tune just as it came to me. There was no hesitancy about it, no effort made. It was all done in a minute. I played it again and again, and felt at the time it had life-giving power, and would live.

Luther Orlando Emerson, Mus. Doc., born at Parsonsfield, Maine, August 3, 1820, member of a musical family, compiled more than seventy books of sacred songs and hymns. So great was his love for music that he chose to practice it rather than medicine, for which he had by study prepared himself. It was natural that his reputation was great during the late nineteenth century, for he had conducted more than three hundred musical conventions in this country and in Canada. W. S. B. Matthews, musical historian and critic, thought him the best melodist of all the gospel-song writers. He received the degree of Doctor of Music from Findlay College, Ohio. His home was in Boston, where for some time he was organist and musical director at the Bulfinch Street Church. Doctor Emerson died at his home at Hyde Park, near Boston, October 1, 1915.

**225—Take my life and let it be**—Frances Ridley Havergal (221)

**Messiah**—Louis Joseph Ferdinand Hérold
Arranged by George Kingsley (61)

This beautiful and useful consecration hymn, originally in eleven two-line stanzas, was written by Miss Havergal at Areley House, February 4, 1874, and first printed in her *Loyal Responses,* 1878. Miss Havergal's own account of the writing of this hymn was:

> Perhaps you will be interested to know the origin of the consecration hymn, "Take my life." I went for a little visit of five days. There were ten persons in the house; some unconverted and long prayed for, some converted but not rejoicing Christians. He gave me the prayer, "Lord, give me all in this house!" and He just *did.* Before I left the house every one had got a blessing. The last night of my visit I was too happy to sleep, and passed most of the night in renewal of my consecration, and these little couplets formed themselves and chimed in my heart one after another till they finished with *"Ever,* only, ALL for Thee."

Many years after writing this hymn, Miss Havergal wrote, "I had a great time early this morning renewing the never regretted consecration."

"Messiah" is an arrangement of one of Louis J. F. Hérold's tunes by George Kingsley, who was adept at "arranging" the music of better composers than himself. It appeared in his *The Sacred Choir,* 1839.

Louis Joseph Ferdinand Hérold, born at Paris, January 28, 1791, composer of the opera, *Zampa,* and many others, was also an excellent pianist and composer for that instrument. He was a prodigious worker and seemed at all times to be consumed with the desire to create music. Only a few days before he died of an affliction of the lungs, he said to a friend, "I am going too soon; I am just beginning to understand the stage." His death occurred at Les Ternes, January 13, 1833.

**226—O Jesus, I have promised**—John Ernest Bode

**Angel's Story**—Arthur Henry Mann

The hymn was written about 1866, in six eight-line stanzas, when John E. Bode was rector of Castle Camps, Cambridgeshire, England. It was first printed on a leaflet

For the newly confirmed,

by the Society for the Promotion of Christian Knowledge in 1868, and was published in the Appendix to that Society's *Psalms and Hymns,* 1869. It is particularly suited to those who are about to partake of their first communion, being written for the occasion of the confirmation of its author's children.

John Ernest Bode, born at London, February 23, 1816, son of William Bode of the General British Post Office, was educated at Eton, Charterhouse, and Christ Church, Oxford. After tutoring for six years at Christ Church, he took Holy Orders and ministered at three parishes, spending fourteen years at Castle Camps, Cambridgeshire. He was honored by being asked to deliver the Bampton Lectures at Oxford University in 1855. He died on October 6, 1874. The Rev. Mr. Bode may be classed among the "one-hymn writers," for although he wrote two volumes of verse containing many hymns on various church festivals, this is the only one of sufficient merit to gain a permanent place.

"Angel's Story" was written by Dr. A. H. Mann for the hymn by Mrs. E. H. Miller, beginning,

I love to hear the story
Which angel voices tell,

the same hymn for which George F. Root (439) wrote "Ellon," and which was first called "Angels' Story." The tune first appeared in *The Methodist Sunday School Hymnbook,* London, 1881.

Arthur Henry Mann, Mus. Doc., who was born May 16, 1850, was trained as a chorister in the cathedral of his native city of Norwich, England. He served many appointments as organist, among them that of the University of Cambridge. Musicians will be interested in knowing that Doctor Mann edited Thomas Tallis's (51) famous motet for forty voices. Honorary Master of Arts, Cambridge, a Fellow of King's College, he wrote much music for both voice and organ, and was editor of *The Church of England Hymnal.* He died at Cambridge, November 19, 1929.

## Songs of Salvation

**227—Come, we that love the Lord**—Isaac Watts (3)

**St. Thomas**—Aaron Williams

The hymn was in Isaac Watts's *Hymns and Spiritual Songs,* 1707, entitled,

Heavenly Joy on Earth.

John Wesley included it in his Charlestown (Charleston, South Carolina) *Collection* of 1737, with the heading,

Heaven begun on earth.

Originally in ten four-line stanzas, 1, 3, 8, and 10 are used in this book. Stanza 1 is as in the original except for two words: "that" has replaced "who" in the first line, and "His," "the" in the last line. John Wesley changed "we" to "ye" (second word) and it is so used in many hymnals. Stanza 2 has "children," line 3, where Doctor Watts had written "fav'rites." Stanza 3, line 3, was written "celestial fruits." Stanza 4 is unchanged. Since its use by John Wesley editors have felt free to change the order of stanzas and alter the text at will. Julian says such differences may be counted by the hundred. It is a fine hymn for revival use—so fine that it was placed as the first of the "Songs of Salvation" in *The Methodist Hymnal.* This was the hymn used by Dr. Samuel West in early New-England days to rebuke the members of his choir who were inclined to allow the congregation to struggle through the hymns without their aid, doubtless feeling it beneath them to sing anything other than the "special pieces." Doctor West announced this hymn, read it through, and then said, "Please commence at the second verse."

"St. Thomas," or "Williams's," is found in Aaron Williams's *Universal Psalmodist,* 1770, and is the first tune (in two parts) in Book III, *Psalmody in Miniature* (mentioned at No. 171), one of his most important books. There is confusion as to its exact source. It is said to have been taken from the second of a four-movement piece in a Williams's collection of 1762, and to have appeared in J. F. Wade's *Cantus Diversi,* 1751 (315[1]). While it is true there is a tune called "St. Thomas" which was taken from the *Cantus Diversi,* it is not this tune, but is in 8. 7. 8. 7. 4. 7. meter, and begins:

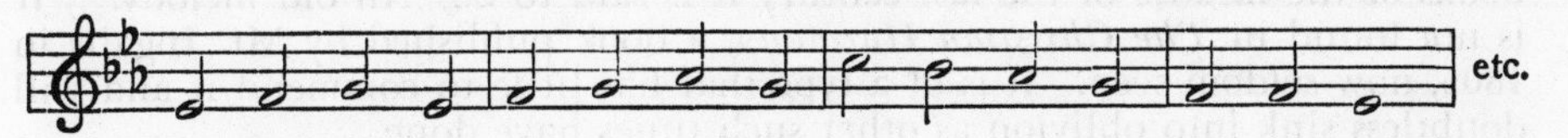


It has been attributed both to Williams and to Handel (88). There is no doubt but that it is Williams's tune, yet editors of Methodist tune books have not always been certain of it. The first American Methodist tune book, *The Methodist Harmonist,* 1822, and its revision of 1833, gave Handel as the composer; the edition of 1837, Williams; 1878, Handel; and 1905, Williams. It is one of those vigorous old English tunes which has stood the test of more than one hundred and fifty years on both sides of the Atlantic.

Aaron Williams is thought to have been born at London, the date usually given being 1731. Little is known of him except that he seems to have had various occupations—composer of music, its engraver, publisher, and teacher, as well as clerk of the Scotch Church, London Wall. He published a number of important collections of tunes. He died at London in 1776.

**228—O for a closer walk with God**—William Cowper (24)

**Naomi** (202)—Hans Georg Nägeli (69)

The hymn is complete as William Cowper wrote it, December 9, 1769. It was first published in the second edition of William Conyer's *Collection of Psalms and Hymns,* 1772, and was included in the *Olney Hymns,* 1779, headed

Walking with God. Genesis v. 24.

The scriptural reference reads, "And Enoch walked with God: and he was not; for God took him." It is one of the most tender and beautiful of Cowper's hymns and is in general use wherever English is spoken.

**229—And can it be that I should gain**—Charles Wesley (25)

**Fillmore**—Jeremiah Ingalls

This hymn was written by Charles Wesley in 1738, probably shortly after his conversion, and is a word picture of his personal experience. First appearing in *Hymns and Sacred Poems,* 1739, with the title,

Free Grace,

in six stanzas, 1, 4, and 6 comprise this cento. The author wrote "God" instead of "Lord" in the last line of the first stanza. Stanza 5, omitted here, is said by Dr. C. S. Nutter to be

> full of the spirit of Methodism, and reveals the secret of its early success:
>
> 5 Still the small inward voice I hear,
> That whispers all my sins forgiven;
> Still the atoning blood is near,
> That quenched the wrath of hostile Heaven:
> I feel the life His wounds impart;
> I feel my Saviour in my heart.

"Fillmore" was doubtless composed by Jeremiah Ingalls, although in tune books of the middle of the last century it is said to be "An old melody." It is not found in *The Christian Harmony,* a book published by Mr. Ingalls in 1805, now seldom seen. It is of a type that has little to commend it and will doubtless sink into oblivion as other such tunes have done.

Jeremiah Ingalls, born at Andover, Massachusetts, March 1, 1764, the great-grandson of one of the settlers of that town, was a farmer, a cooper, a tavern keeper, and a singing master. In N. D. Gould's *History of Church Music in America,* 1853, he tells of places where singing schools were held in the early days:

> The next important question was, "Where shall the school be kept?" Lecture rooms were then scarcely known. A common schoolhouse was too dull and lonely a place. A hall in a public house, then called a tavern, was the only place to meet the approbation of the majority. Besides, the terms for the use of the hall were generally made easy; for it was understood by all parties that the profits arising from the sales in the barroom, to scholars and spectators, would amply compensate for the use of the room.

Possibly Ingalls was thus able to profit doubly from the teaching of singing: both as tavern keeper and master. While living at Newbury, Vermont, he was leader of the choir in the Congregational church and wrote several of his tunes for that organization. He does not seem to have written any of them for any particular set of words. His family was large and musical, the sons playing violin, clarinet, flute, and bassoon, with the father playing the bass viol. Jeremiah Ingalls died at Hancock, Vermont, April 6, 1828.

**230—I lay my sins on Jesus—Horatius Bonar (210)**

**St. Hilda** (197)—Justin Heinrich Knecht (197)
Edward Husband (197)

This hymn, written while Doctor Bonar was an assistant at St. James's Church, Leith, Scotland, is probably his first. He began hymn writing because he found the children listless and indifferent during worship services, for, while they were fond of music and enjoyed singing, the texts of the psalms and hymns were, for the most part, beyond their years. Doctor Bonar wrote the hymns for them "in a desire to provide something which children could sing and appreciate in divine worship." Of this hymn its author has said that while it might be good gospel it was not good poetry. Entitled,

The Substitute,

it appeared in the first series of *Songs in the Wilderness,* published by Doctor Bonar in 1843. It was in four stanzas, the third omitted here, and the only alteration is the change of the first word of the last line, "And" replacing "To."

**231—Pass me not, O gentle Saviour—Fanny Jane Crosby**

**Pass Me Not**—William Howard Doane

The hymn, written in 1868, was contributed to Doctor Doane's *Songs of Devotion,* 1870, the original showing some slight differences from this text. The changes made have been an improvement. In stanza 1 "calling" is better than "smiling," and stanza 2 is immeasurably improved by being made to read,

Let me at Thy throne of mercy,

instead of,

Let me at a throne of mercy.

"Merits," stanza 3, line 1, has become "merit." Stanza 4 is unchanged.

Many earnest Christians recall this simple little song with feelings of gratitude, knowing it was instrumental in bringing about their conversion.

Fanny Jane Crosby, born at South East, Putnam County, New York, March 24, 1820, blind from infancy due to the ignorance of a country physician who applied hot poultices to her inflamed eyes, was one of the most prolific of all writers of sacred songs. Her songs and hymns are numbered by the thousand, most of them without value. Julian says she wrote 2,000, but for two firms of publishers alone, she is said to have furnished 5,959, and for publishers of gospel songbooks (Philip Phillips (525), Robert Lowry (219), Ira D. Sankey (237), and W. H. Doane) 1,500 more. Much of her writing was done to order, she having been commissioned by one publishing house to furnish three songs each week for an indefinite period, which she was able to do. The few of her songs which have survived have done so mainly because of the tuneful melodies which were made for them. Her texts will not support stronger tunes. Through Ira D. Sankey many of her songs became immensely popular in England.

Miss Crosby was educated at the New York School for the Blind. For eleven years, until her marriage to Alexander van Alstyne, a musician, also blind, she was a teacher in the institution which she attended as a pupil. Her first poems were published when she was only eight years old, and for about eighty years she continued to write. The books in which her verses were published sold into the millions, and for more than a generation she was better known than any other writer of sacred verse.

Mrs. van Alstyne was a close friend of Grover Cleveland, with whom she became acquainted when both were employed at the New York School for the Blind, she a teacher, and the future President a secretary. So long as churches continue to put forth evangelistic effort, Fanny Crosby's songs will continue to be sung. A lifelong member of the Methodist Episcopal Church, she died at Bridgeport, Connecticut, February 12, 1915.

"Pass Me Not" was written by William H. Doane especially for Fanny Crosby's text, and it was published in *Songs of Devotion,* 1870.

William Howard Doane, Mus. Doc., was born at Preston, Connecticut, February 3, 1832, and died at South Orange, New Jersey, December 24, 1915, while visiting at the home of his daughter. From childhood he was interested in music, singing in public at six years of age; joining a choir at ten; was considered an exceptionally good flutist at twelve; a year later he began playing a string bass; and at fifteen was quite proficient as a player on the reed organ. He began writing melodies in his childhood. The boy began his business career as a clerk in the offices of his father's cotton mill; later he became an expert accountant. After some experience in New England and Chicago in the business of the manufacture of wood-working machinery, he moved to Cincinnati where he was, from 1860, manager, later president, of a firm manufacturing that product. Following the appearance of his first book in 1862, he compiled forty or more, mostly of the gospel-song type. He also wrote some twenty-three hundred vocal and instrumental numbers, several of them being cantatas, of which "Santa Claus," a Christmas cantata by him, launched the flood of cantatas coming from various publishers in recent years. Denison University, Ohio, conferred the degree of Doctor of Music on him in 1875.

> There is scarcely a place on earth where civilization has pushed its way that the influence of Doctor Doane has not been felt. To almost every soul in civilized countries some of his songs are familiar, and as it is the Christian missionary chiefly who extends our civilization, we doubt if any of late years have gone forth to the foreign field without some of Dr. Doane's songs as a part of his equipment.

**232—I need Thee every hour—Annie Sherwood Hawks**

**I Need Thee Every Hour**—Robert Lowry (219)

The hymn was published in *Royal Diadem,* for the Sunday school, by Robert Lowry and W. H. Doane, a small, end-fold book issued in 1873, having the text, "Without Me ye can do nothing."—John 15. 5. The first four stanzas of the original five are used without change. It was first sung in November, 1872, at a meeting of the National Baptist Sunday School Association held in Cincinnati. The words of the refrain were added by Doctor Lowry. Mrs. Hawks has said this of it:

> Whenever my attention is called to it I am conscious of great satisfaction in the thought that I was permitted to write the hymn, "I need Thee every hour," and that it was wafted out to the world on the wings of love and joy, rather than under the stress of a great personal sorrow, with which it has so often been associated in the minds of those who sing it.
>
> I remember well the morning . . . when in the midst of the daily cares of my home . . . I was so filled with the sense of nearness to the Master that, wondering how one could live without Him either in joy or pain, these words, "I need Thee every hour," were ushered into my mind, the thought at once taking full possession of me. . .
>
> For myself the hymn was prophetic rather than expressive of my own experience at the time it was written, and I do not understand why it so touched the great throbbing heart of humanity. It was not until long years after, when the shadow fell over my way—the shadow of a great loss—that I understood something of the comforting in the words I had been permitted to write and give out to others in my hours of sweet security and peace.

Annie Sherwood Hawks was born at Hoosick, New York, May 28, 1835, and during her long residence in Brooklyn was a member of the Hanson Place Baptist Church, where, for eight years, Doctor Lowry, who encouraged her to write hymns, was her pastor. Her songs were contributed to popular Sunday-school books. "I need Thee every hour" is the only one which has survived. Mrs. Hawks died at Bennington, Vermont, January 3, 1918, where she had made her home with her daughter after the death of her husband.

"I Need Thee Every Hour" had been called "Need" in recent books, but in deference to the wishes of the widow of the composer, the title to the gospel song for which it was written has been used. As has been the case with most of the gospel songs, each has its own tune, especially written for it, and is seldom, if ever, used with any other text.

**233—Jesus calls us, o'er the tumult—Cecil Frances Alexander (135)**

**Galilee—William Herbert Jude**

The hymn, contributed to *Hymns for Public Worship,* issued by the Society for the Promotion of Christian Knowledge in 1852, was founded on St. Matthew 4. 18, the beginning of the Gospel for St. Andrew's Day, observed in those churches following the Calendar. The second stanza, omitted in this *Hymnal,* is:

> As of old, St. Andrew heard it
> By the Galilean lake,
> Turned from home, and toil, and kindred,
> Leaving all for His dear sake.

It has been adopted in the United States and Canada as the hymn of the Brotherhood of St. Andrew. Doctor Bodine, in *Some Hymns and Hymn Writers,* says:

> I have heard it sung by a dozen men at a chapter meeting, in some little room. I have heard it sung by a thousand men, and more, in the great congregation, and

always with power. For enthusiasm there is nothing in our Church (Episcopal) that compares with a great Brotherhood convention, assembled from every part of our land. How striking the fact that this multitude of mighty men should follow the lead of a woman in their chosen song!

"Galilee" was written in 1874 by William H. Jude for this hymn and it was published in *Congregational Church Hymns,* London, 1887. It was misnamed "Jude" in the 1905 edition of *The Methodist Hymnal.*

William Herbert Jude, an English organist, composer, and lecturer on musical subjects, was born at Westleton, Suffolk, in September, 1852. He served as organist at the Blue Coat Hospital, Liverpool; at Stretford Town Hall, near Manchester, and was editor of the *Monthly Hymnal.* He is said to have been the founder of the Purcell Society, but the revised (third) edition of *Grove's Dictionary of Music and Musicians,* 1935, does not include his name in the list of members of the original committee which founded the Society, February 21, 1876. At that time Jude would have been but twenty-five years old, hardly of an age to assume the leadership of so important a society. He died at London, August 7, 1922.

**234—Lord Jesus, I love Thee**—William Ralf Featherstone
From the London Hymn Book

**Gordon**—Adoniram Judson Gordon

This hymn, whose author was unknown when *The Methodist Hymnal* was issued, was found by Dr. A. J. Gordon in *The London Hymn Book,* 1864, and he wrote the tune "Gordon" for it, which made it known to congregations in the United States. After *The Methodist Hymnal* was released, October 1, 1935, Dr. George C. Stebbins (50) furnished the following information concerning its authorship:

> A few years ago a friend of mine by the name of Mr. Frederick Steele spent a good deal of time in tracing the authorship of hymns that had come into general use with no name definitely ascribed to them, and one of them is the one mentioned above. He ascertained that the author of that hymn was a man by the name of William R. Featherstone, a Canadian.

The hymn had appeared in books in this country as early as 1870, but it did not become popular until Doctor Gordon made this setting. The words, "Lord Jesus," occurring in each stanza, were originally "My Jesus."

William Ralf Featherstone, 1842-1878, a Canadian by birth, wrote the hymn, "My Jesus, I love Thee," when he was only sixteen years of age. The author sent the text to his aunt, Mrs. E. Featherstone Wilson, then living at Los Angeles, California, who approved of it and suggested to her nephew that it be published. A diligent search has failed to bring to light any facts concerning Mr. Featherstone.

Adoniram Judson Gordon, D.D., born April 19, 1836, at New Hampton, New Hampshire; one of the editors of *The Service of Song for Baptist Churches,* 1871; editor of *The Vestry Hymn and Tune Book,* 1872; was educated at Brown University, and Newton Theological Seminary; was ordained pastor of the Baptist Church at Jamaica Plains, Massachusetts, in 1863, later being called to succeed Dr. Baron Stowe at Clarendon Street Baptist Church, Boston, and was one time editor of *The Watchword,* a monthly publication. Brown University conferred the Doctor of Divinity degree upon him in 1878. He was a descendant of John Robinson, of Leyden, and was named after Adoniram Judson, the pioneer missionary to Burmah. He died at Boston, February 2, 1895.

**235—Thou, my everlasting portion**—Fanny Jane Crosby (231)

**Close to Thee**—Silas Jones Vail

This, one of Fanny Crosby's many prayer hymns, with its tune was first published in *Songs of Grace and Glory,* 1874, compiled by W. F. Sherwin (44) and Silas J. Vail, the composer of "Close to Thee," with which the hymn is always associated.

Silas Jones Vail, born at Brooklyn, New York, October 6, 1818, left his home when a young man to go to Danbury, Connecticut, to learn the trade of making hats. Upon his subsequent return to New York City, he clerked in a store. Later he was successful in a business of his own. In 1863 he compiled *The Athenaeum Collection,* which contained ten new songs by Stephen Foster. He had a connection with Horace Waters, an intensely religious man, one of the founders of the Prohibition Party, who made a fortune publishing cheap Sunday-school songbooks, and, with W. F. Sherwin, Vail compiled for Waters, in 1874, the little book containing this song. He died at Brooklyn, May 20, 1884.

**236—Saviour, more than life to me**—Fanny Jane Crosby (231)

**Every Day and Hour**—William Howard Doane (231)

Ira D. Sankey, in *My Life,* tells of the writing of this gospel song:

> Tune preceded words in this instance. It was in 1875 that Mr. Doane sent the tune to Fanny Crosby, and requested her to write a hymn entitled "Every day and hour." Her response in the form of this hymn gave the blind hymn writer great comfort and filled her heart with joy. She felt sure that God would bless the hymn to many hearts. Her hope has been most fully verified, for millions have been refreshed and strengthened as they have sung it.

It was first published in 1875 in *Brightest and Best,* with the name "Every Day and Hour," and the text,

Cleanse me from my sin.—Ps. 51: 2.

Later in the same year it was included in the first of the *Gospel Hymns,* the title given to a series of evangelistic songbooks issued from 1875 to 1891.

The remarkable enthusiasm with which these books were received by the public was responsible for the name "Gospel hymns" being given to all songs of like character, although neither the name nor the type was new. They had been appearing since early in the century, both in England and in the United States, and had had wide use at religious gatherings other than the regular services of public worship, such as prayer meetings, revivals, etc. Essentially folklike, in that they consisted of easily remembered words with a simple melody and harmonization, the hold they took on the public mind was extraordinary. They came in direct competition with the accepted pattern for hymn settings, and in many respects, especially in their singable melodies and flowing rhythm, they gave real relief from a certain dullness that was common to many of the established tunes. Each had its "chorus," probably borrowed from the camp meeting, and this feature in time came to be an abomination. Though many of them have a real charm and permanent worth, the commercial element became so dominant by 1870 that the whole movement began to lose caste among those concerned with keeping church music on a dignified plane. It has been estimated that more than fifteen hundred books of this type of song were issued before 1900, with their sales running into fabulous figures, Sankey's books alone selling above fifty million copies. This extraordinary development constituted a phenomenon which will receive the dispassionate attention of the musical historian. As a popular musical movement its like had not occurred before.

**237—I have a Saviour, He's pleading in glory**—Samuel O'Malley Clough (Cluff)
**I am praying for you**—Ira David Sankey

The words of this song were found by Ira D. Sankey, printed on a leaflet, while in Ireland with Dwight L. Moody in 1874. This was the second text for which he supplied music, and he reports the song was used with profit at the great Moody and Sankey meetings in London. It has proved a valuable gospel song, with an appeal for all classes of men. It was suggested for inclusion in this book by a well-known professor of philosophy in a mid-Western university. Bishop Edwin Holt Hughes is responsible for some changes being made from the original text.

Samuel O'Malley Clough (or Cluff) is said to have been an Irish clergyman who left the Established Church to affiliate with the Plymouth Brethren, in Ireland, from which he later seceded, leading what was perhaps the most important of the lesser schisms in that Church during the lifetime of its founder, J. N. Darley. Clough sponsored a doctrine of sanctification similar to that of R. Pearsall Smith in America. This division took place in 1881, but the sect is now nearly, if not quite, extinct. David J. Beattie, who in 1936 was engaged in writing a history of the Brethren movement, wrote that he had "not yet come across S. O'M. Clough."

There has been some confusion concerning the spelling of the name of the author of "I have a Saviour." Julian and authorities on the Brethren movement spell the name "Clough." Ira D. Sankey used the spelling "Cluff," which has been generally followed by compilers.

Ira David Sankey was born at Edinburgh, in western Pennsylvania, August 28, 1840. Of this boy who joined the Methodist Episcopal Church at seventeen years of age, his father said, "I'm afraid that boy will never amount to anything; all he does is to run about the country with a hymnbook under his arm." This interest in religious music, augmented by hearing Philip Phillips (525) sing, was manifest by his leading the singing at various Sunday-school conventions and later becoming one of the world's greatest evangelistic singers. Toward that career, he was secretary and president of the Y. M. C. A.

in Newcastle, Pennsylvania, where later he constructed a $40,000 building for the organization. It was in his association with Dwight L. Moody, the great evangelistic preacher, that his name became a household word on both sides of the Atlantic. Probably he as much as anyone else lived to demonstrate the power of music as a religious force. He was one of the original compilers of *Gospel Hymns,* discussed in the preceding number. His *Sacred Songs and Solos,* published first in 1873, is still current. His *My Life, and the Story of the Gospel Hymns,* issued in 1905, is a source work of information about gospel songs. After Mr. Sankey had prepared the manuscript of this work for publication, it was destroyed by fire, and, although he had lost his sight, he dictated its contents to an amanuensis, publishing it in 1906.

Mr. Sankey was modest about his gift of singing. He said:

> I am no musician; indeed, I am no singer; I was never taught to sing. . . . As to my singing there is no art or conscious design in it. I never touch a song that does not speak to me in every word and phrase. Before I sing I must feel, and the hymn must be of such a kind that I know I can send home what I feel into the hearts of those who listen. I find it much more difficult to get good words than good music. Our best words come from England; the music which best suits our purpose comes from America. Your composers, apparently, do not care to write simple songs such as we need. We can get plenty of the grand and solid style, but though that is useful now and again, our services could not thrive upon it.[1]

He died at Brooklyn, August 13, 1908.

**238—Blessed assurance, Jesus is mine**—Fanny Jane Crosby (231)

**Assurance**—Mrs. Joseph Fairchild Knapp

This song was copyrighted by Mrs. Knapp in 1873. The date of its first publication has not been ascertained, although certain books say it was taken from *Glad Tidings* (?). Mrs. Knapp wrote the tune, took it to Mrs. van Alstyne, and after playing it over for her, asked, "Fanny, what does that tune say to you?" After a few moments' thought the reply came, "Blessed assurance, Jesus is mine!" That phrase, suggested by Mrs. Knapp's music, was developed and the two, always together, are now known to thousands of Christians who are assured that Jesus is theirs.

Mrs. Joseph Fairchild Knapp, born at New York City in 1839, was Phoebe Palmer, daughter of Dr. Walter Palmer, before her marriage in 1885. She showed unusual musical talent as a child both as a singer and composer, writing many songs for children. In one of the books issued by her the Opening Note says that her work

> is not the result of a hasty combination of the efforts of the scissors and the paste bottle. Its hymns and tunes have been composed, not hurriedly, nor only to fill the pages which they occupy, but each one with a view to taking its place in leading the devotional thoughts of worshipping throngs of children in the praise of God.

This book, *Notes of Joy,* has in it a page headed "Words of Cheer" by Bishop Simpson, who compiled a book with her called *Bible School Songs,* 1873.

During her lifetime Mrs. Knapp was well known as a writer of verse and of music. On one of her visits to England she was invited to visit Sheffield

[1] *Studies in Worship Music.* Second Series. John S. Curwin. 1885.

and was "given such a reception as was never before accorded a musician in that city." Her husband was the founder of the Metropolitan Life Insurance Company, and at his death left his wife an annual income of $50,000. Both Mr. and Mrs. Knapp, members of the Methodist Episcopal Church, dispensed much of their wealth in charitable and philanthropic work. Mrs. Knapp died at Poland Springs, Maine, July 10, 1908.

**239—Softly and tenderly Jesus is calling**—Will Lamartine Thompson
**Softly and tenderly**—Will Lamartine Thompson

Both hymn and tune by Will L. Thompson.

Will Lamartine Thompson was born November 7, 1847, and died September 20, 1909, at East Liverpool, Ohio, where he made his home all of his life. He was educated at Mt. Union College, Ohio, and at the Boston Conservatory of Music. Near the close of his work at Boston, while on a visit to Nahant Beach, he wrote the song, "Gathering up the shells by the seashore," which immediately became very popular and brought him attention and a small fortune for that day. Some time later he wrote and published the popular "Come where the lilies bloom so fair." While he wrote other secular songs, some of them patriotic, his greatest interest was in sacred song, and it was in this field that he spent most of his effort. One who knew him well writes:

> Will L. Thompson, who always wrote both the words and music, lives in his songs that give wings to the gospel and still bring strength and comfort to many souls. . . . His musical gift was matched by a fine character and a beautiful spirit. . . . Simplicity, sincerity, humility, and righteousness marked his life.

At a time when Dwight L. Moody lay very ill, and visitors were forbidden, Mr. Thompson called to make inquiry as to his condition. Hearing of Thompson's presence, Moody insisted upon his visitor's admittance to the sick room, and greeted him: "Will, I would rather have written 'Softly and tenderly Jesus is calling,' than anything I have been able to do in my whole life."

**240—What a Friend we have in Jesus**—Joseph Scriven
**Converse**—Charles Crozat Converse

This hymn was written about 1855 and was probably first published in *Social Hymns, Original and Selected,* H. L. Hastings, Richmond, Virginia, in 1865, in spite of the statement by the editor of *Silver Wings,* the little Sunday-school book first containing the familiar tune, "Converse" (also called "Erie"): "Words from the Genevan Presbyterian Church (of Brooklyn) Collection. Music by Karl Reden." When Ira D. Sankey (237), with P. P. Bliss (254), was compiling *Gospel Hymns* (No. 1), he discovered this song and, just before the book was printed, substituted it for another by Doctor Converse. Thus, he says, "the last hymn that went into the book became one of the first in favor." The hymn was written by Joseph Scriven to comfort his mother in a time of sorrow, and he did not intend it for the eyes of others. At a time when he was ill a friend visiting him saw a manuscript copy of "What a Friend we have in Jesus," and as a result of questioning, the author admitted he had written it. Sometime later another friend inquired if it were true he had written the text and Mr. Scriven replied, "The Lord and I did it between us."

Joseph Scriven, born at Dublin, Ireland, in 1820, was educated at Trinity College, Dublin, emigrating to Canada at the age of twenty-five. As a result of the drowning of his fiancée on the eve of their intended marriage, he was afflicted with melancholia the remainder of his life. He was devoutly religious and devoted his life and all of his property to Christian uses, delighting to do for others manual labor for which he would accept no pay. On one occasion, as he was seen with a wood-saw and sawbuck trudging along a street in Port Hope, Canada, a stranger made inquiry as to who he was, wanting to employ him for other work. He was told, "You cannot get that man; he saws wood only for poor widows and sick people who are unable to pay." It is said he would give away his warm clothing to those who gave evidence of being cold. Although he was eccentric, living with several families in succession, and showing other peculiarities, he was a good man, eager to help all whom he could. On October 10, 1886, his body was found in a "water-run" near Lake Rice, Canada, where he had lived for a time. Whether his death came about as the result of accident or design has never been definitely determined. Those to whom he had given assistance, and other friends, erected a monument to his memory at Lake Rice.

"Converse" was first published in a small Sunday-school book called *Silver Wings,* copyright and published in 1870, but the name of the compiler is not given. In this little book are thirteen songs by "Karl Reden," and one by C. C. Converse, credited to "Karl Reden," the *nom de plume* of Doctor Converse, is one of the best and most popular of the gospel tunes, and is winning a place in most carefully edited hymnals.

Charles Crozat Converse, LL.D., born at Warren, Massachusetts, October 7, 1832, was an American musician, lawyer, philologist, and inventor. Receiving his musical training in Germany, at Berlin and Leipzig, he returned to America and took up the study and practice of law. Most of his active professional life was spent at Erie, Pennsylvania, but in his last years he lived at Highwood, New Jersey, where he died, October 18, 1918. Under the pen name of "Karl Reden" he wrote interestingly and authoritatively on many subjects. It was Doctor Converse who led in the movement to establish the use of the pronoun "thon."

**241—I've found a Friend, O such a Friend—James Grindlay Small**

**Friend—George Coles Stebbins (50)**

The hymn was first published in *The Revival Hymn Book,* second series, 1863, and then in the author's *Psalms and Sacred Songs,* 1866.

James Grindlay Small, born at Edinburgh, Scotland, in 1817, was educated at the Royal High School and at the University of Edinburgh, where he was a student under Dr. Thomas Chalmers. He joined the Free-Church movement of 1843 and four years later became minister of that Church in

Bervie, near Montrose. Certain peculiarities of speech and manner interfered with his preferment, but those who knew him loved him for his gentleness and beautiful character. His greatest enthusiasm aside from his church duties was for psalmody, leading him to compile two books of sacred song, in addition to writing two volumes of verse. He died February 11, 1888, at Renfrew on the Clyde.

"Friend" was written in 1878 while Mr. Stebbins was engaged in a revival meeting at Providence, Rhode Island, and was published the same year in *Gospel Hymns*, No. 3, the first one of the series with which its composer was connected.

**242—He leadeth me: O blessed thought!**—Joseph Henry Gilmore
**He Leadeth Me**—William Batchelder Bradbury (133)

The following is Doctor Gilmore's account of the writing of this hymn:

> The hymn was written in the spring of 1862, at the residence of Dea. Thomas Wattson, Philadelphia. I had been talking, at the Wednesday-evening lecture of the First Baptist Church, about the twenty-third Psalm, and had been especially impressed with the blessedness of being led by God, of the mere fact of His leadership altogether apart from the way in which He led us, and what He was leading us to. At the close of the service we adjourned to Dea. Wattson's pleasant home, at which I was stopping, and still held before our minds and hearts the thought which I had just emphasized. During the conversation . . . the blessedness of God's leadership so grew upon me that I took out my pencil, wrote the hymn just as it stands today, handed it to my wife, and thought no more of it. She sent it, without my knowledge, to the *Watchman and Reflector*, and there it first appeared in print. Three years later I went to Rochester, New York, to preach for the Second Baptist Church. President Anderson took me to their place of worship on the day after my arrival, and, on entering the chapel, I took up a hymnbook, thinking, "I wonder what they sing!" The book opened at "He leadeth me," and that was the first time I knew that my hymn had found a place among the songs of the church. I shall never forget the impression made upon me by coming in contact then and there with my own assertion of God's blessed leadership. This is the story of "He leadeth me" substantially as I told it when first asked to tell it, except that I then said (which shows how little the fact of authorship impressed me), "The refrain has since been added by another hand." Afterward I found among my deceased wife's papers the original copy of the hymn and was surprised to find that I wrote the refrain myself.

Joseph Henry Gilmore, D.D., born at Boston, April 29, 1834, was educated at Phillips Andover Academy, Brown University (from which he graduated with highest honors), and at Newton Theological Seminary. Variously, he taught Hebrew at Newton; preached at the Baptist Church at Fisherville, New Hampshire; was secretary to his father, a governor of New Hampshire, at the same time acting as editor of the Concord *Daily Monitor;* again took up preaching at Rochester, New York; again taught Hebrew, this time at Rochester Theological Seminary; and finally became professor of logic, rhetoric, and English literature at the University of Rochester. In addition to these duties he found time to contribute editorials to papers, to write reviews of books, to publish a textbook for schools, and to write hymns. He died at Rochester, July 23, 1918. An unusual memorial to Doctor Gilmore was provided by the United Gas Improvement Company of Philadelphia by way of a tablet placed on the annex to the company's building at Broad and Arch

Streets, that city, which now occupies the former site of the home of Deacon Wattson, where this hymn was written. A Baptist clergyman of the city pointed out the brown-stone dwelling to an official of the gas company, saying, "The old building has a remarkable history; a wonderful hymn, 'He leadeth me,' was written there." When the new building was erected, the officials decided the spot should be marked and placed the tablet on the Arch Street side where it may now be seen.

"He Leadeth Me" first appeared in *The Golden Censer,* 1864, a Sunday-school book compiled by its composer, W. B. Bradbury (133). The musical element of this combination of verse and tune promoted its popularity and fixed it in the minds of worshipers.

**243—Holy Spirit, faithful Guide—Marcus Morris Wells**

**Holy Spirit, Faithful Guide—Marcus Morris Wells**

Marcus Morris Wells lived in New York State all of his life, being born at Otsego, October 2, 1815, and dying near Hardwick, where he was following the occupation of farmer and maker of farm implements, July 17, 1895. Early in life he was converted in a mission at Buffalo. Of the origin of this hymn and tune he has written:

> On a Saturday afternoon in October, 1858, while at work in my cornfield, the sentiment of the hymn came to me. The next day, Sunday, being a very stormy day, I finished the hymn and wrote a tune for it and sent it to Professor I. B. Woodbury.

The hymn and tune were first published in the November number of the *New York Musical Pioneer,* edited by Isaac B. Woodbury (137). It gradually came into use in denominational hymnals and was popular for some time, but apparently is losing its interest for few books of recent years include it.

**244—My hope is built on nothing less—Edward Mote**

**The Solid Rock—William Batchelder Bradbury (133)**

This "grand hymn of faith" in six stanzas of four lines each, with a refrain, in its original form beginning,

> Nor earth, nor hell, my soul can move,

entitled,

> Jesus, my All in All,

was written by Edward Mote probably in 1834. His story of the writing and first publication of it appeared in an issue of *The Gospel Magazine,* London:

> One morning it came into my mind as I went to labour, to write an hymn on the "Gracious Experience of a Christian." As I went up Holborn I had the chorus,
>
> On Christ the solid Rock I stand,
> All other ground is sinking sand.
>
> In the day I had four first verses complete, and wrote them off. On the Sabbath following I met Brother King as I came out of Lisle Street Meeting, . . . who informed me that his wife was very ill, and asked me to call and see her. I had an early tea,

> and called afterwards. He said that it was his usual custom to sing a hymn, read a portion, and engage in prayer, before he went to meeting. He looked for his hymn-book but could find it nowhere. I said, "I have some verses in my pocket; if he liked, we would sing them." We did; and his wife enjoyed them so much, that after service he asked me, as a favour, to leave a copy of them for his wife. I went home, and by the fireside composed the last two verses, wrote them off, and took them to Sister King. . . . As these verses so met the dying woman's case, my attention to them was the more arrested, and I had a thousand of them printed for distribution. I sent one to the *Spiritual Magazine,* without my initials, which appeared some time after this. Brother Rees, of Crown Street, Soho, brought out an edition of hymns (1836), and this hymn was in it. David Denham introduced it (1837) with Rees's name, and others after. . . . Your inserting this brief outline may in future shield me from the charge of stealth, and be a vindication of truthfulness in my connection with the Church of God.

The form in which it is usually found, that in *The Methodist Hymnal,* appeared in 1836 in *Hymns of Praise, A New Selection of Gospel Hymns, combining all the Excellencies of our Spiritual Poets, with many Originals.* London, 1836.

One of the last things said by the Rev. Joseph Knapp, familiarly known as "Elder Knapp," the successful evangelist who published *The Evangelical Harp,* was:

> "I have come to the everlasting hills!
> On Christ the solid Rock I stand,
> All other ground is sinking sand."

Edward Mote was born at London, January 21, 1797, the son of the keeper of a public house. Of his youth Mote said: "My Sabbaths were spent in the streets at play. So ignorant was I that I did not know there was a God." While a cabinetmaker's apprentice he formed the habit of going to church and was influenced for good by the preaching of one of Lady Huntingdon's adherents, John Hyatt, at the time preacher at Tottenham Court Road Chapel. After changing his church membership several times, he moved to Southwark, the borough south of the river Thames in the city of London, where he established a business as a cabinetmaker and began writing for the press. In 1852 he entered the Baptist ministry as a preacher at Horsham, Sussex, where he met with unusual success. Largely instrumental in securing the building used for his services, the members of his congregation expressed their gratitude by offering to deed it to him. This he refused, saying, "I do not want the chapel, I only want the pulpit; and when I cease to preach Christ, then turn me out of that." Just before his death, which occurred at Southwark, November 13, 1874, he said, "The truths I have preached I am now living upon; and they will do to die upon."

"The Solid Rock" was written in 1863 and appeared the following year in W. B. Bradbury's *Devotional Hymn and Tune Book,* the only new Baptist hymnal which appeared during the Civil War.

**245—O sometimes the shadows are deep**—Erastus Johnson

**The Rock of Refuge**—William Gustavus Fischer

The source of this gospel song has long been obscure. Dean Tillett (117) in *Our Hymns and Their Authors,* commenting on the hymns in *The Hymn and Tune Book of the Methodist Episcopal Church, South,* 1889, and published the same year, has this note:

> This is one of the most popular of modern hymns. Words and tune seem well adapted to each other, and have helped to comfort many a sad heart. It is based on Ps. lxi. 2: "When my heart is overwhelmed, lead me to the Rock that is higher than I."

With Dr. C. S. Nutter, Dean Tillett prepared *The Hymns and Hymn Writers of the Church,* an annotated edition of *The Methodist Hymnal* of 1905, in which he again refers to the hymn:

> . . . Few modern hymns have won their way into the hearts of the people more truly than this songful sigh of the tempest-tossed soul. . . . We have no facts concerning the origin of this hymn.

On July 13, 1936, the Rev. George E. Heath, pastor of the Wesley Methodist Episcopal Church, Worcester, Massachusetts, wrote the author of this MANUAL, in part as follows:

> A short time ago a woman who was worshiping in our congregation spoke with me about the Hymn numbered 245 in our new Hymnal as having been composed by her father. She called my attention to the fact that a question mark appears in the Hymnal regarding his dates of birth and death. I told her that if she would write me the facts, I would be glad to forward them to the editor of the Hymnal so that in a subsequent edition the full information might be included.

Inclosed with this letter was another by Mrs. Julia Johnson Howe, daughter of Erastus Johnson, author of this hymn, in which she said:

> I copy the notes of the writing of the hymn "The Rock of Refuge," from the back of father's book:
>
> "At a convention of the Y. M. C. A. in 1873 at Carlisle, Pennsylvania, which I attended as a delegate from Pittsburgh, Pennsylvania, John Wanamaker was president. About the close of the first session a telegram came from Philadelphia announcing the failure of Jay Cook, in whose bank Wanamaker had $70,000, which to him at that time was a serious matter and the loss of which might result in his financial undoing.
>
> "Soon followed reports of other failures throughout the country, indicating a general panic and, of course, throwing a pall of gloom over the convention. As an expression of the common feeling I wrote this hymn.
>
> "Mr. William Fisher (Fischer) was at the convention, who with my brother, William (since Reverend), led the singing. Mr. Fisher set the hymn to music and it immediately became popular in the convention."

The hymn and refrain appeared in *The Hymnal of the Methodist Episcopal Church,* 1878. The words of a refrain in somewhat similar form,

> Lead me to the Rock that is higher than I,
> Higher than I, higher than I,
> Lead me to the Rock that is higher than I,

found as early as 1823 in *Mercer's Cluster,* were long popular in the Southland.

Erastus Johnson was born April 20, 1826, in a logging camp in the town of Lincoln, Maine, on the west bank of the Penobscot about sixty miles above Bangor, died at Waltham, Massachusetts, June 16, 1909, and was buried at

Jackson, Maine. His life was singularly active, varied, and interesting. A poor boy, having but little opportunity for schooling in his childhood, his active mind embraced every opportunity afforded for self-improvement. At fifteen years of age he entered the Academy at Calais, Maine, where he remained for two years, taught school for six years, and then entered Bangor Theological Seminary. His health having failed and the loss of his sight being threatened, he followed the advice of his physician and took a sea voyage, embarking on the ship *Gold Hunter* for California. Before rounding Cape Horn the crew of the ship mutinied and Johnson, being the only man on board who knew anything about navigation, was pressed into service to take the ship on to San Francisco, which he was able to do without mishap. He led the life of a rancher in California for eight years, lived on a farm in the state of Washington for eleven years, was connected with the petroleum industry in Pennsylvania for twenty years, farmed again near Jackson, Maine, for another eight years, and then retired to live at Waltham, Massachusetts. He published a book of poems most of which are of family interest only, played the organ well, was a lifelong student of the Bible, a fluent speaker, and was always interested in religious work. Writing of his brothers and sisters in the diary he always kept, he said, "Of the thirteen, not one ever took a glass of intoxicating drink, nor used tobacco, nor got rich, nor used a profane word."

William Gustavus Fischer was born October 14, 1835, at Baltimore, and when only eight years of age would start the singing in a German church in his home city. He became well educated in music, studying at night while learning the bookbinding trade in Philadelphia. Becoming a teacher of singing and piano playing, well and favorably known as a choral conductor not only in that city but as a leader of Welsh singing societies, for ten years he was Professor of Music at Girard College. While thus engaged he became interested, with J. E. Gould (196), in the retail piano business, which flourished. Contrary to the custom of song writers of his day, he did not compile any books, but under the firm name of Gould and Fischer, issued some "Sunday School Leaflets." He died at Philadelphia, August 13, 1912.

**246—I am coming to the cross—**William McDonald

**Coming to the Cross—**William Gustavus Fischer (245)

The author has told the story of the hymn:

> The hymn was written in 1870, in the city of Brooklyn, New York, while I was pastor in that city. I had felt the need of a hymn to aid seekers of heart purity while at the altar. I had desired something, simple in expression, true to experience, and ending in the fullness of love. The tune composed by Mr. Fischer, with the first two lines of the chorus, I had seen, and was much pleased with their simplicity. And as I was sitting in my study one day, the line of thought came rushing into my mind, and I began to write, and in a few minutes the hymn was on paper. It was first sung at a National Campmeeting, held at Hamilton, Mass., June 22, 1870. It has been translated into many languages, and sung all round the globe.

The date of its first publication was probably May, 1872, in the *Advocate of Christian Holiness Extra,* a pamphlet containing *Music for Camp Meetings,* which was "given as a premium to every new subscriber to *The Advocate of*

*Christian Holiness*." The first of sixteen songs, it is in five stanzas with the refrain for the last beginning,

Still I'm trusting, Lord, in Thee.

In addition to the omission of the fourth stanza, there are two minor changes in the text. Doctor Julian says the song first appeared in *The Baptist Praise Book* of 1871, but according to Dr. Henry S. Burrage, this book was not issued until 1872. (See *Baptist Hymn Writers,* p. 665.)

William McDonald, born at Belmont, Maine, in 1820, joined the Maine Conference of the Methodist Episcopal Church in 1843, transferred to other Conferences, and served several churches in the North and West. From 1870 he engaged in evangelistic work with the Rev. J. S. Inskip, who advocated "Christian Holiness" as a "second blessing." One time editor of *The Christian Witness,* successor to *The Advocate of Christian Holiness* (journal of the National Association for the Promotion of Holiness, of which he was the vice-president), he published some ten volumes on religious subjects and seven books of sacred music. He died at Monrovia, California, in 1901.

**247—There were ninety and nine**—Elizabeth Cecilia Clephane (144)

**The Ninety and Nine**—Ira David Sankey (237)

A sister of Miss Clephane, who was in the audience at the Moody and Sankey meeting where this song was first sung, told Mr. Sankey these words were written for a friend, who caused them to be printed in *The Children's Hour,* 1868, from which they found their way into other publications. Later the poem appeared in *The Family Treasury* as one of the "Breathings on the Border" (see No. 144). In 1874 Mr. Sankey discovered the verses in a newspaper he had purchased to read on the train while en route from Glasgow to Edinburgh. He had discarded the paper, but just before reaching his destination he recovered it and clipped from it the poem that is now familiar to all Christians. On the second day of the Edinburgh meetings, after short addresses by Doctor Andrew Bonar and others, on the subject of "The Good Shepherd," Mr. Moody suddenly asked Mr. Sankey to sing something appropriate. Remembering that he had with him the newspaper clipping, he placed it on the music rack of the organ and improvised the tune now so familiar. He has stated that no changes have ever been made in the tune since its first singing. Probably no other gospel song has ever been more popular. The composing of the tune gave Mr. Sankey the "most intense moment" of his life, and it became one of his most famous songs. While Miss Clephane's "sermon on the love of Christ" and Mr. Sankey's melody will never die so long as English songs are sung, "only in the last great day will it be known how many wandering sheep have been brought to Jesus by its means." It was first published in *Sacred Songs and Solos,* issued by Mr. Sankey in 1874.

**248—Jesus, keep me near the cross**—Fanny Jane Crosby (231)

**Near the Cross**—William Howard Doane (231)

This is from *Bright Jewels,* 1869, a book compiled by W. B. Bradbury

(133) for Bigelow and Main. Miss Crosby wrote the words to fit a tune which W. H. Doane, its composer, had submitted to her.

**249—I love to tell the story—Katherine Hankey**

**Hankey—William Gustavus Fischer (245)**

This hymn is a cento from Part II of a long poem on the life of Jesus written in 1866 by Katherine Hankey. The first section, written on January 29, was entitled "The Story Wanted," and it is from this that the well-known "Tell me the old, old story" is taken. This hymn was made from selections from the second part, written in November, with the title "The Story Told." In order to conform to the gospel-song type, then popular, Mr. Fischer, composer of the tune, added this refrain. It is quite probable that the hymn and tune as now sung were first issued by the mercantile firm of Gould and Fischer, as a part of the "Sunday School Leaflets," referred to at No. 245, although the hymn had appeared with a different tune, by W. H. Doane (231), in 1870. It was customary in the 1860's and 1870's for dealers in musical merchandise to issue small collections of gospel songs as a means of advertising their business. Such were the *Musical Leaves,* put out by Philip Phillips (525) at Cincinnati, beginning in 1864. As a matter of historical interest the wording of the title page and a part of the Preface to *Musical Leaves,* No. 1, is given:

MUSICAL LEAVES
Every Song a Gem.
Published
Every Four Months by
Philip Phillips & Co.
Dealers in
Pianos, Melodeons
and Organs.
Pike's Opera House, Cincinnati.

No one can for a moment doubt but Music forms one of the chiefest attractions of the Sabbath-school, and should be conducted in such a manner as to keep the young minds continually feasting on something *new, awakening,* and adapted to the times and their natures. True, there are many most excellent singing-books gotten up for this purpose, and every Sabbath-school should have one or more of them. But, in getting and using books, we have noticed that but a small portion of the pieces are sung, no matter how fine they may be. If the Sabbath-schools could afford to get all the good books published, and select from them, it would be a fine idea; but that would be too expensive. Consequently, we have gotten up a little book, in pamphlet form, containing twenty-four *new* songs, of the very *choicest* kinds, adapted to the Sabbath-school, Anniversary Occasions, Monthly Concerts, etc. . . .

We have given the book the name of "MUSICAL LEAVES." It will be published every four or six months, with an entire new set of songs, for Sabbath-schools. We also add to the back part of the book a complete Catalogue Price-list for Piano Fortes, Melodeons, Harmoniums, Excelsior and Cabinet Organs, and it is for this reason we sell them to Sabbath-schools at actual *net cost;* which we think would be preferred rather than pay double its present price without the catalogue. As earnest lovers of the Sabbath-school cause, we hope that Superintendents, Teachers, and all interested, will not fail to bring this matter before the Sabbath-schools at their earliest convenience.

Seven hundred thousand *Musical Leaves* were sold.

"I love to tell the story," with three other texts set to music by W. G.

Fischer, appeared as early as 1872 in *Music for Camp Meetings,* referred to at No. 246, where the words are credited "by permission," and in *The Emerald,* published the same year, where the tune (since named "Hankey") is credited to *Joyful Songs* (?). The following notations accompany the song in *Music for Camp Meetings:*

"I would rather," said Bishop Hamline, "be Brainard, wrapped in my bearskin, and be spitting blood upon the snow, than to be Gabriel."

COURAGE.—I told the judge, as to this matter (of preaching the gospel), I was at a point with him; for, if I was out of prison today, I would preach the gospel again tomorrow, by the help of God.—BUNYAN.

Katherine Hankey, known as Kate Hankey, and whose real given name was Arabella Catherine, was born at Clapham, England, in 1834. She was the daughter of a banker who was a member of the Clapham Sect of Evangelicals, a group under the guidance of William Wilberforce, founder of *The Christian Observer,* a religious periodical which would admit "a moderate degree of political and common intelligence." Under this influence, while still a schoolgirl, Miss Hankey became deeply interested in teaching in a Sunday school. She was a refined, consecrated woman, organizing among the working girls, and those of her own social circle, Bible classes of which several members became devoted religious workers. On a trip to South Africa, where she traveled often in oxcarts to look after an invalid brother, she became so deeply interested in missions as to devote thereto the receipts from the sale of her writings. This devout Christian died at London in 1911.

**250—Rescue the perishing**—Fanny Jane Crosby (231)
**Rescue**—William Howard Doane (231)

This hymn, a great favorite of Frances E. Willard and Francis Murphy, temperance crusaders, was written by Miss Crosby upon her return from a visit to one of the worst slum districts in New York City, where she had heard harrowing tales of the lost and perishing. Doctor Doane set it to music and published it in *Songs of Devotion,* 1870, since when it has become a rallying song for Christian workers in all parts of the world. It is the only one of Fanny Crosby's songs to be included in *Hymns Ancient and Modern.*

**251—Take time to be holy**—William Dunn Longstaff
**Holiness**—George Coles Stebbins (50)

For long the only information obtainable concerning this gospel song and its writer was that given by Ira D. Sankey (237) in *My Life.* He says W. D. Longstaff lived at Sunderland, England; that he wrote these stanzas after hearing a sermon preached at New Brighton on,

Be ye holy as I am holy,

probably the text from 1 Peter 1. 16: "Because it is written, Be ye holy; for I am holy"; and that it was first published in *Gospel Hymns* (No. 6) and *Sacred Songs and Solos,* both issued in 1891. Recently, certain facts were disclosed by Doctor Stebbins, composer of the tune "Holiness." The words

"Take time and be holy," spoken by Dr. Griffith John, a missionary to China at a conference in that country, were repeated at a meeting at Keswick, England. On the night of the same day the hymn was written. It was first published in an English publication about 1882, and later in *Hymns of Consecration,* used at Keswick.

William Dunn Longstaff, son of a land- and ship-owner in the days of the primacy of wooden vessels, was born January 28, 1822, at Sunderland, England, on the North Sea. Being a man of independent means, he devoted much of his wealth to philanthropic enterprises. He followed the Rev. Arthur A. Rees when the latter seceded from the Established Church and founded Bethesda Free Chapel. Longstaff supported the new enterprise by providing for needed alterations and additions to the building, and by acting as its treasurer. Among his close friends he numbered Dwight L. Moody, Ira D. Sankey, and William Booth of the Salvation Army, who, with other religious leaders, were frequent guests in his home. Sydney E. Watson, of Bethesda Chapel, Sunderland, has contributed this interesting incident:

> I remember being told by an old friend, a contemporary of his (Longstaff), that when Moody and Sankey began their work in England, Bethesda was the second church that received them. The founder and pastor of Bethesda, A. A. Rees, was an outstanding character and in his way, a great man. He doubted the propriety of allowing anyone to sing solos in his church and would not at first agree to Sankey coming to join Moody at Bethesda. He stipulated, however, that if Sankey would come and interview him he would consider. Eventually Sankey came and was taken by Mr. Rees to the house of W. D. Longstaff to give a trial solo, accompanying himself on Mr. Longstaff's harmonium. The result was that Sankey passed his examination with honors and joined Moody in the forthcoming campaign.

Mr. Longstaff died at Cambridge Terrace, Sunderland, April 2, 1894.

"Holiness" was written by Doctor Stebbins in 1890. The words had been handed him in the early spring of that year by a friend who had clipped them from some periodical. They were placed among Doctor Stebbins's papers

> and were quite forgotten till late in that year when, spending a winter in India assisting Dr. George F. Pentecost, also Bishop Thoburn, in evangelistic and conference work, happened to recall them and found I had brought them with me. I at once decided to set music to them and in a short time had made the setting and sent it on to Mr. Sankey in New York.

**252—I am Thine, O Lord, I have heard Thy voice—Fanny Jane Crosby (231)**

**I am Thine—William Howard Doane (231)**

This was first published in *Brightest and Best,* for Sunday Schools, in 1875, with the title,

Draw Me Nearer.
"Let us draw near with a true heart."—Heb. 10. 22.

**253—Take the Name of Jesus with you—Lydia Baxter**

**Precious Name—William Howard Doane (231)**

First published in *Pure Gold,* 1871, the song was written in 1870 by Mrs.

Baxter for Doctor Doane, who was then preparing this little book for publication. He includes the name of Mrs. Lydia Baxter "among the Excellent Hymn Writers who have Contributed directly to this Work." It is one of the most popular gospel songs on the Name of Jesus.

Lydia Baxter was born September 9, 1809, at Petersburgh, New York, and died at New York City, June 22, 1874. With her sister, also a convert under the preaching of the Rev. Eben Tucker, a Baptist missionary, she led a movement which resulted in the forming of a Baptist church at Petersburgh. After her marriage she moved to New York City, where, though an invalid for many years, her home became a center for gatherings of Christian workers coming to her for inspiration and advice. Many of her songs were widely used in the Moody and Sankey movement. She published a volume of verse in 1855 entitled *Gems by the Wayside.*

**254—Brightly beams our Father's mercy—Philip Paul Bliss**

**Lower Lights—Philip Paul Bliss**

This song was included in *The Methodist Hymnal* because of the urgent requests for it which came from many devout Christians whose homes are on the seacoast or on the shores of the Great Lakes, and members of whose families are engaged in work which keeps them much of the time upon the water. It was suggested to Mr. Bliss by a passage from one of Dwight L. Moody's sermons:

> On a dark, stormy night, when the waves rolled like mountains and not a star was to be seen, a boat, rocking and plunging, neared the Cleveland harbor. "Are you sure this is Cleveland?" asked the captain, seeing only one light from the lighthouse. "Quite sure, sir," replied the pilot. "Where are the lower lights?" "Gone out, sir." "Can you make the harbor?" "We must, or perish, sir!" With a strong hand and a brave heart the old pilot turned the wheel. But, alas, in the darkness he missed the channel, and with a crash upon the rocks the boat was shivered, and many a life lost in a watery grave. Brethren, the Master will take care of the great lighthouse; let us keep the lower lights burning.

The song first appeared in *The Charm,* by P. P. Bliss, in 1871.

Philip Paul Bliss, whose father was musical and deeply religious, was born in a log cabin in the woods of Clearfield County, northern Pennsylvania, July 9, 1838. He left home at the age of eleven and worked on farms, in lumber camps, and in sawmills for about five years, getting what schooling he could. When about twelve he joined the Baptist Church after attending a revival meeting near Elk Run, Pennsylvania. Under the influence of W. B. Bradbury (133) he established himself as a music teacher in 1860, going about with an old horse, Fanny, and a twenty-dollar melodeon. He sold his first song in 1864 to Root and Cady, music publishers, Chicago, about the time he went to Chicago to work for them. Conducting singing classes and conventions for this firm throughout the nearby states, he gained a reputation as a speaker and leader of singing, and a vocal soloist. He also contributed articles dealing with musical subjects to the firm paper, *The Musical Visitor.* On one occasion he wrote of speaking before a "general association of ministers," where he was conducting the singing, saying:

> There is a deal of mighty fine *talking*, a *few* earnest *prayers*, but very little hearty *singing*. Why is it that so few ministers sing? Wouldn't it improve their voices, and *hearts* too?

And another time he wrote:

> I don't believe ministers' and deacons' families are a whit worse than other folks, but I do believe that every Christian family should be a praise-giving band, and, if possible, "psalm singers."

Mr. Bliss had a remarkable voice, full, resonant, and with a range from low D-flat to high A-flat. It was from choice that he devoted his life to Christian work—singing, speaking, writing, composing verse and songs, setting music to the words of others, and editing and compiling song books. He published the first book of *Gospel Songs* in 1874, beginning the series of *Gospel Hymns,* with Ira D. Sankey (later with others), a year later. Although a poor man, Mr. Bliss gave to the evangelistic cause for which he had joined forces with Major W. D. Whittle in 1874 all his royalties—amounting to some thirty thousand dollars—from the enormous sale of these books.

His death was tragic. While he was returning to Chicago from a trip to the East in company with Mrs. Bliss, the train on which they were riding was wrecked near Ashtabula, Ohio. Though Mr. Bliss could have escaped when the wreckage caught fire, he remained to try to extricate his wife, who was pinned down under a car seat. But it was too late: Mr. and Mrs. Bliss, together with nearly one hundred others, perished on the night of December 29, 1876.

**255—True-hearted, whole-hearted—Frances Ridley Havergal (221)**

**True-hearted, Whole-hearted—George Coles Stebbins (50)**

This song, with its setting by Doctor Stebbins, became immensely popular through its use at Christian Endeavor conventions in the 1890's. Its marked rhythm and aggressive tone in both words and music have done much for the retention of its hold on young people. Miss Havergal included it in her *Loyal Responses,* 1878. The original third stanza has been omitted since its first publication in *Gospel Hymns* (No. 6), 1891.

"True-hearted, Whole-hearted," the tune, was written by Doctor Stebbins in the spring of 1878, while he was engaged in evangelistic services at New Haven, Connecticut. Originally written for male voices in four parts, it was rearranged for mixed voices before its publication in *Gospel Hymns.*

# THE CHRISTIAN LIFE

## Discipleship

**256—Faith of our fathers! living still—Frederick William Faber (76)**

**St. Catherine—Henri Frederick Hemy**
Adapted by James George Walton

The hymn, taken from Doctor Faber's *Jesus and Mary; or Catholic Hymns for Singing and Reading,* was written in four stanzas, with 1, 3, and 4 used in this book. Stanza 2, originally reading,

Faith of our fathers! Mary's prayers
Shall win our country back to Thee;
And through the truth that comes from God
England shall then indeed be free,

has been changed thus for Protestant use:

Faith of our fathers! we will strive
To win all nations unto Thee,
And through the truth that comes from God
Mankind shall then be truly free.

In the present *Hymnal* the controversial stanza has been omitted:

Our fathers, chained in prisons dark,
Were still in heart and conscience free:
How sweet would be their children's fate,
If they, like them, could die for Thee!

The hymn is an exceptionally fine expression of Christian aspiration.

"St. Catherine," known in England as "Tynemouth," appeared in Part II, *Crown of Jesus Music,* 1864, set to a hymn beginning,

Sweet Saint Catherine, maid most pure,
Teach us to meditate and pray,

headed,

St. Catherine, Virgin and Martyr,

the melody, with organ part, by H. F. Hemy. The hymn was in ten lines and only the first sixteen measures of the melody are used, the last eight being supplied by James G. Walton (1821-1905) when he adapted it for use in *Plain Song Music for the Holy Communion,* 1874.

Henri Frederick Hemy, an Englishman, was for many years an organist at St. Andrew's Catholic Church at Newcastle-on-Tyne, where he was born November 12, 1818. He taught music at Tynemouth, became professor of music at Ushaw Catholic College, near Durham, and subsequently removed to Hartlepool, northeast England, where he died in 1888. He wrote a *Royal Tutor for the Pianoforte,* 1858, which had extensive use, and he gained a fine reputation as a teacher of piano playing. He also compiled two books of sacred music, the better known being *Crown of Jesus Music,* 1864, a book in which there are very few original tunes. Most of them are arrangements of melodies of others, yet it is very popular in Catholic churches in England.

**257—My gracious Lord, I own Thy right**—Philip Doddridge (69)
**Holborn Hill**—St. Alban's Tune Book

This is from Doctor Doddridge's *Hymns,* 1775, and is entitled,

"Christ's Service, the Fruit of our Labours on Earth."
Philippians i: 22,

which is, "But if I live in the flesh, this is the fruit of my labor: yet what I shall choose I wot not." It has been considerably changed in form since it was first published, but it would be of no interest to discuss such changes here. A fine discipleship hymn, it may be used with profit for communion, especially for young people just coming into an active church relationship.

"Holborn Hill," sometimes called "Penitence," appeared as No. 116, *St. Alban's Tune Book,* to be sung to,

O Christ, Thou art the Light and Day,

W. J. Copeland's translation of the Ambrosian hymn,

Christe, qui lux es et dies,

in the Appendix of *The Hymnal Noted,* first issued in 1852, where it, as the other tunes in the book, has no composer's name given. The Preface says it has been newly arranged and harmonized, this probably having been done by Thomas Morley, organist at St. Alban's, who is thanked for his assistance in preparing the book for publication.

*St. Alban's Tune Book,* as it is commonly called, has as its proper title, *Music of the Appendix to the Hymnal Noted,* c. 1866. *The Hymnal Noted,* sponsored by John M. Neale (52), with the assistance of Thomas Helmore, marked a new departure in Church of England hymnody, and was one of the results of the Tractarian movement. Doctor Neale, having introduced the beauties of pre-Reformation hymns, contended they should be sung only to their plainsong melodies. Without much vogue, *The Hymnal Noted* received its greatest acclaim because of the excellent congregational singing at St. Alban's Church, Holborn. This singing, however, was not itself from *The Hymnal Noted,* but from its excellent Appendix, whose hymns had as settings not Gregorian tones or plain tunes, but a wide selection of very singable tunes gathered from sources secular as well as sacred. The demand for these Appendix tunes, because so eminently congregational, resulted in the publication of the *St. Alban's Tune Book,* about 1866,[1] from which many excellent tunes have been taken.

**258—Jesus, and shall it ever be**—Joseph Grigg (196)

**Federal Street** (185)—Henry Kemble Oliver (185)

This hymn, said to have been written by Joseph Grigg when only ten years of age, was first published in its original crudity in the author's *Four Hymns on Divine Subjects wherein the Patience and Love of our Divine Saviour is displayed,* 1765, with the title,

Ashamed of Me.

In order to make it useful, emendation was necessary, the result being five versions of the hymn, each of which has had some use. This is the one which appeared in Rippon's *Selection,* 1787, with the statement that it had been "Altered by B. Francis," and with the more fitting title,

Not Ashamed of Christ.

In this form it seems to have been more widely used than in any of its others.

**259—O Master, let me walk with Thee**—Washington Gladden

**Maryton** (178)—Henry Percy Smith (178)

This greatly loved modern service hymn, according to Doctor Gladden's statement, was not intended for a hymn, but was written in 1879 for the magazine, *Sunday Afternoon,* of which the author was then editor, and where he placed it in "The Still Hour," a section of the periodical filled with devotional reading. In three eight-line stanzas, it was entitled:

Walking with God.

Doctor Gladden has written:

> Dr. Charles H. Richards found the poem . . . and made a hymn of it by omitting the second stanza, which was not suitable for devotional purposes.
>
> It had no liturgical purpose and no theological significance, but it was an honest cry of human need, of the need of divine companionship.

In this form it was published in *Songs of Christian Praise,* 1880. The omitted stanza is:

O Master, let me walk with Thee
Before the taunting Pharisee;
Help me to bear the sting of spite,
The hate of men who hide Thy light,
The sore distrust of souls sincere
Who cannot read Thy judgments clear,
The dullness of the multitude,
Who dimly guess that Thou art good.

[1] There seems to be lack of agreement as to this date. In J. H. Lightwood's *Hymn Tunes and Their Story,* 1923, the date is given as 1875, but in his later book, *The Music of the Methodist Hymnal,* 1935, he gives it as 1865. James Edmund Jones, in the annotated edition of *The Book of Common Prayer,* 1909, gives 1866. There is a possibility of a typographical error in the Lightwood book of 1923. The failure of English publishers of hymn and tune books to date them has led to a great deal of confusion as to exact dates, and in many cases it is impossible to fix them.

Dr. Earl Marlatt (178) thinks this hymn suffers dangerous possibility of loss of deeper meaning through overuse. The fact that its author placed it in "The Still Hour" carried with it the implication that it could best be used in "moments of quiet consecration."

Washington Gladden, LL.D., great leader for civic righteousness, was born at Pottsgrove, Pennsylvania, February 11, 1836. Following his education at Williams College, he served, as a Congregational minister, parishes in New York, Massachusetts, and in Ohio. At Columbus, Ohio, for thirty-two years his ministry was so outstanding it attracted the attention of the nation—his militant preaching and writing tended to mold the thought of his generation. For four years he was editor of *The Independent,* a periodical wielding a wide influence because of its fearlessness. This hymn alone, had he done no other writing, would have given him a place among the leaders in awakening the new social consciousness. His social creed, as declared in his *Recollections,* 1909, was:

> Because the Christian life is the noblest life; because it is more blessed to give than to receive, and better to minister than to be ministered unto; because the good of life is not found in separating yourself from your fellows, but by identifying yourself with them—therefore, let us be Christians.
>
> If the Church would dare to preach and practice the things which Jesus Christ commanded, she would soon regain her lost power.

Doctor Gladden died at Columbus, July 2, 1918.

"Maryton" (178) was written by Canon Smith as a setting for "Sun of my soul, Thou Saviour dear" (56), and first appeared in *Church Hymns with Tunes,* 1874. Doctor Gladden expressed a decided preference for "Maryton" as the most fitting setting for his hymn. It was particularly distasteful to him to find his texts used with different tunes, frequently denying permission for their use unless his wishes were complied with. In this case, certainly, his preference was justified.

**260—"Take up thy cross," the Saviour said—Charles William Everest**

**Germany**—William Gardiner's Sacred Melodies (28)

The hymn is used as it appears in *Hymns Ancient and Modern,* where it is said to have been taken, probably, from *The Salisbury Hymnal,* 1857. This form differs much from the original which appeared in the Rev. Mr. Everest's *Visions of Death, and Other Poems,* 1833. Twelve hymns by ten American writers are included in *Hymns Ancient and Modern,* the epoch-making book which did so much to standardize English hymnody on a high plane.

Charles William Everest was born at East Windsor, Connecticut, May 27, 1814. After education at Trinity College, Hartford, he entered the ministry of the Protestant Episcopal Church, and was appointed rector at Hampden, Connecticut, where he served thirty-one years, much of that time conducting a successful school in addition to his parish duties. His *Visions of Death, and Other Poems,* was published in 1833 when the author was only nineteen years old. He died at Waterbury, Connecticut, January 11, 1877.

"Germany," also called "Fulda," "Walton," "Beethoven," and "Melchisadec" has long been an enigma to specialists in hymn tunes. It comes from William Gardiner's *Sacred Melodies from Haydn, Mozart, and Beethoven, adapted to the best English poets, and appropriated to the use of the British church,* Vol. II, 1815. (See No. 28.) The compiler credits it to Beethoven, but scholars most familiar with the works of the great composer have failed to find anything resembling this tune in his writings. In the "Advertisement" of volume two, Gardiner suggests he will tell of the original sources of his many excellent arrangements "in an essay to be annexed to the second volume of the words." Apparently, this essay never appeared—a circumstance much to be regretted, for while most of the melodies found in Gardiner's book have been traced, this fine Long-Meter tune has avoided detection. In 1838, Mr. Gardiner published a book, *Music and Friends,* in which he speaks of this tune, saying "It is somewhere in the works of Beethoven, but where I cannot point out." It remains an enigma, for no one else has been able to point it out, though James Love has called attention to the similarity of the first line of the melody to the introduction to Mozart's air, "Possenti Numi," in his opera, *The Magic Flute.*

**261—Jesus, I my cross have taken—Henry Francis Lyte (77)**
Ellesdie—Wolfgang Amadeus Mozart
Arranged by Hubert Platt Main

The hymn first appeared signed "G" in the author's *Sacred Poetry,* 1824, with the text from St. Mark 10. 28, "Lo, we have left all, and followed thee." Without the Rev. Mr. Lyte's acknowledgment of its authorship in his *Poems Chiefly Religious,* it might have remained anonymous. Two stanzas have been omitted from the original six. For Henry Ward Beecher's moving story about this hymn, in a sermon on "The Supreme Allegiance," no support has been found.

"Ellesdie," or "Disciple," "Vondeventer," "Violet," and "Ocean," presents another of the hymn-tune puzzles which have seemed to defy solution. Students of Mozart have failed to give its source, if any have, indeed, found it. It is quite possible it did not come from Mozart at all. What may be a clue to its composer may be found in *Hymns of Praise,* compiled by George A. Bell (?) and Hubert P. Main in 1884. In this book this legend is found:

Joseph Philip Knight, 1827. Arr. by H. P. M. 1872.

Two years later, in another book, "The New Alleluia," compiled by Dr. M. Woolsey Stryker (558) and Hubert P. Main, it is said to be "arr. by Hubert P. Main, 1873," and to have been taken from *Winnowed Hymns,* which had been issued in 1873 by C. C. McCabe and D. T. MacFarlan, who gave as its source:

Air, Mozart, Arr. by H. P. M.

The arrangement by Mr. Main must have been only a four-part harmonization, for this melody, and a bass, with the exception of one note exactly as in the Main "arrangement," appeared as early as 1831 in Joshua Leavitt's *The Christian Lyre,* Vol. II, called "Disciple." In *The Wesleyan Psalmist,* compiled by M. L. Scudder (1814-1891), in 1842, it again appears, called "Disciple," with the following at the top of the page on which it is printed:

> *Note.*—A young lady in England, was much persecuted by her unconverted father, because she had embraced Jesus. He sought to divert her mind, and gave her a song to play and sing, called "Go forget me, why should sorrow &c,"—To his surprise she played and sung the following:

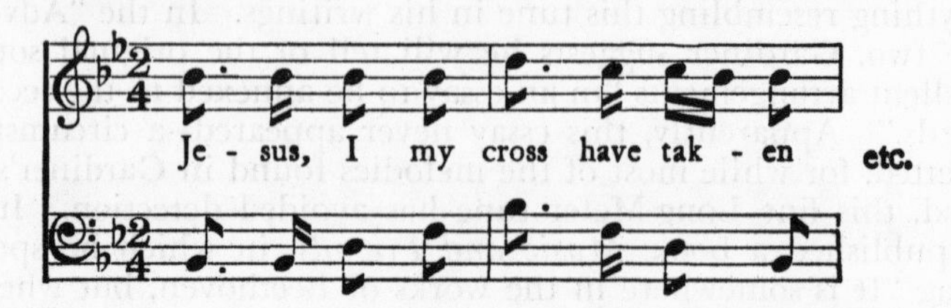


"Go, forget me,"[1] was a popular song written by Joseph Philip Knight, who was born July 26, 1812. A composer of many ballads (among them "Rocked in the cradle of the deep"), a clergyman of the Church of England, appointed to the Church of St. Agnes in the Scilly Isles, he made a concert tour in the United States in 1839, gaining such enormous popularity that he gave nine performances in New York City alone in the first half of the year. He died at Great Yarmouth, June 2, 1887. The following is taken from *The Amateur's Song Book,* 1843:

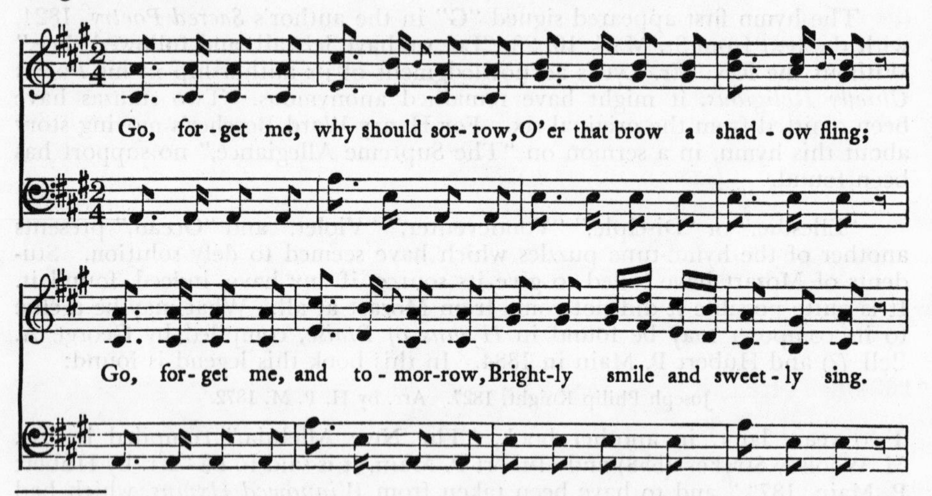


[1] Since writing the above the author has discovered a copy of the old song, "Go, Forget me." "Ellesdie" certainly is not this tune although musicians may see how the one might have suggested the other. The first part of Mr. Knight's song is:

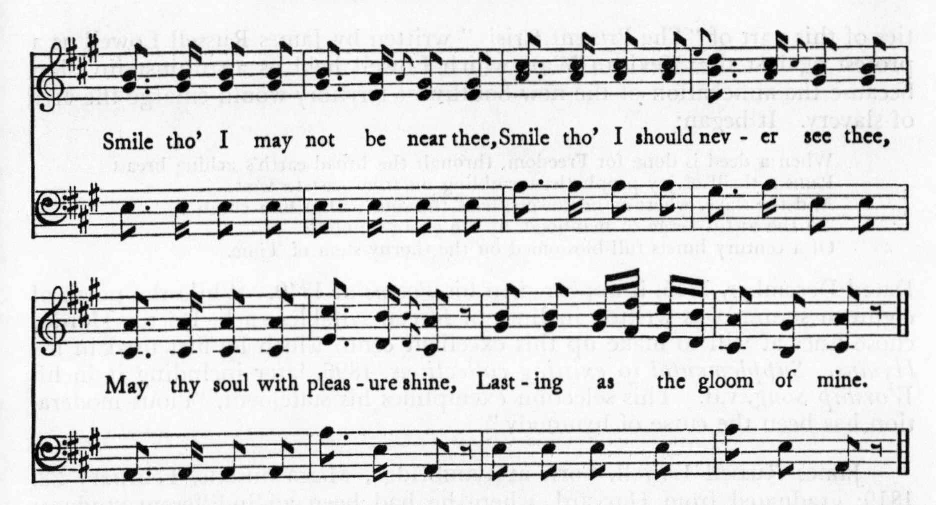
Smile tho' I may not be near thee, Smile tho' I should nev - er see thee,
May thy soul with pleas - ure shine, Last - ing as the gloom of mine.

No biographical sketch of Mozart seems necessary, however interesting it might be, as such accounts are given only of those whose offerings are sufficiently authenticated to be included in *The Methodist Hymnal.*

Hubert Platt Main, born August 17, 1839, at Ridgefield, Connecticut, was the son of Sylvester Main, junior partner in the firm of Bigelow and Main, successors to the W. B. Bradbury Company, and until recent years one of the most prominent music publishing firms in America. H. P. Main, from his boyhood interested in music, wrote his first tune when sixteen years of age. After a few years of general clerical work, he entered the employ of the Bradbury Company, with which he was connected eventually as general consultant and treasurer until his death. He has written and arranged hundreds of pieces of one kind or another—gospel songs, love songs, anthems, part songs, etc., and was a recognized authority in the field of hymnody. With Philip Phillips he edited the *Hymn and Tune Book,* 1866, for the Methodist Episcopal Church. His valuable library of early American songbooks was sold to the Newberry Library, Chicago, and is known as the Main Library. Mr. Main died October 7, 1925.

**262—God's trumpet wakes the slumb'ring world—Samuel Longfellow (42)**

**Corwin—J. W. Lerman**

This hymn by Samuel Longfellow first appeared in 1864 in *Hymns of the Spirit.* Copyright dates indicate the tune "Corwin" was written prior to 1908, but information as to when it was first used and concerning its composer, J. W. Lerman, has not been obtained. It is a stirring tune and makes a splendid processional.

**263—Once to every man and nation—James Russell Lowell**

**Ton-Y-Botel—Welsh hymn melody**

W. Garrett Horder, English hymnodist, first realized the hymnic possibilities of this part of "The Present Crisis," written by James Russell Lowell as a protest against the Mexican War, which Lowell held as an unjust invasion because the annexation of the new Southwest territory would enlarge the area of slavery. It began:

> When a deed is done for Freedom, through the broad earth's aching breast
> Runs a thrill of joy prophetic, trembling on from east to west,
> And the slave, where'er he cowers, feels the soul within him climb
> To the awful verge of manhood, as the energy sublime
> Of a century bursts full-blossomed on the thorny stem of Time.

Dated December, 1845, it appeared in his *Poems* of 1849. While the poem of eighteen stanzas was written in lines of fifteen syllables each, Doctor Horder chose lines at will to make up this excellent cento which he first used in his *Hymns. Supplemental to existing collections,* 1896, later including it in his *Worship Song,* v.d. This selection exemplifies his statement, "Pious moderation has been the curse of hymnody."

James Russell Lowell, born at Cambridge, Massachusetts, February 22, 1819; graduated from Harvard, where he had been an indifferent student; studied law, but failed as a practitioner; then became one of the outstanding men of letters of the nineteenth century. His love for his country was great, and he served her, not only as a fearless editorial writer, but as Minister to Spain and as Ambassador to Great Britain. He succeeded Henry W. Longfellow as Professor of Belles-Lettres at Harvard University; was the first editor of *The Atlantic Monthly;* and was associated in the conduct of *The North American Review* with Charles E. Norton, his literary executor. His prose writings cover a variety of subjects, but his best-known works are his volumes of poetry. He became the spokesman of the thoughtful and scholarly group in American life and made a deep impression on his generation, not only in his native country but abroad. His place as a leading poet and literary critic is secure. His death occurred at his estate, Elmwood, in Cambridge, Massachusetts, August 12, 1891.

"Ton-Y-Botel" ("tune in a bottle"), more properly "Ebenezer," was written as part of an anthem, "Light in the valley," by Thomas John Williams, who was born at Rhos, Pontardawe, Glamorganshire, Wales, in 1869, but apparently the tune was not printed until 1890, when it was included in *Llawlyfr Moliaint.* It is found in *The Baptist Book of Praise,* issued three years later, under the name "Assurance." The legend that it was found in a bottle washed ashore in a storm has no foundation. The name "Ton-Y-Botel" was given it as the result of a jest of a young man who had sung it at some social affair before it had become well known. When asked for its history he said it had been found by a boy on the coast of Lleyn in a sealed bottle where it had drifted to shore after a storm. This fantastic story has given it a curious name for a hymn tune, but has undoubtedly had much to do with calling attention to it, for the enthusiasm with which it swept over Wales was little less than phenomenal, and it is now being included in most hymnals. Its haunting melody has its beauty enhanced when sung by a large body of men.

**264—March on, O soul, with strength**—George Thomas Coster

**Arthur's Seat**—Arranged from John Goss

This hymn, based on Judges (R. V.) 5. 21, "O my soul, march on with strength," was written by the Rev. G. T. Coster, an English clergyman, in 1897, in an interval between pastorates at Stroud and Hessle. Its first appearance in an American hymnal was in 1904 in *The Pilgrim Hymnal,* edited by Dr. C. S. Noyes, who used five other hymns by the same author.

George Thomas Coster, born at Chatham, Kent, England, October 3, 1835, one of a family of thirteen children, all Christian workers, was a Wesleyan Methodist minister, who, though suffering from ill health, held several pastorates and was ever interested in the poor, the sick, and the afflicted. At Hull he instituted a series of Free Dinners for Poor Children, and established a Hospital for Poor Sick Children, now Victoria Hospital; in London he was instrumental in the establishment of shelters for cabmen; and later, at Hull, formed a branch of the Guild of Brave Poor Things, a self-help organization whose membership is composed of the blind and the crippled. He is best known as a poet and hymn writer, eight of his poems being included in W. Garrett Horder's *The Poets' Bible.* Retiring in 1902, the Rev. Mr. Coster spent his remaining years in editing his journals. He died at Rotherham, Yorkshire, August 29, 1912.

"Arthur's Seat" has not been found in any book published prior to 1874. In that year it appeared in *Hymns and Songs of Praise,* of which John K. Paine (1839-1906), then professor of music at Harvard University, and Uzziah C. Burnap (1834-1900), at the time organist of the Church on the Heights, Brooklyn, were the musical editors. More recent books state that this tune was arranged from Sir John Goss by U. C. Burnap.

John Goss, Mus. Doc., was born at Fareham, Hampshire, England, December 27, 1800, the son of the organist at Fareham; and became one of the children of the Chapel Royal. He served appointments as organist at several churches, among them St. Paul's Cathedral, London, and was honored by being made a composer to the Chapel Royal; by the knighthood in 1872; and by the degree Doctor of Music from Cambridge in 1876. Composer of much church music, he is best known by his anthem, "O Saviour of the World." He was a serious musician of attainment whose works are still in the repertoires of many choirs and which seem destined to have a long life. His death occurred at Brixton, a district of London, May 10, 1880.

**265—He who would valiant be**—John Bunyan

**Monk's Gate**—English traditional melody

The original from which this hymn evolved comes at the close of the conversation, in *Pilgrim's Progress,* between Mr. Valiant-for-Truth and Mr. Great-Heart, in which Valiant tells of his battle with the three men who tried to turn him from continuing his journey; of how Mr. Tell-True "had betaken himself to a pilgrim's life," and of the story of Christian and his travels, which had so affected him that his "heart fell into a burning haste to be gone after him," even though his parents did all in their power to dissuade him, for their arguments

> seemed but as so many nothings to me. . . . I still believed what Mr. Tell-True had said; and that carried me beyond them all. . . . I believed, and therefore came out, got into the way, fought all that set themselves against me, and by believing, am come to this place.

Then follows:

Who would true valor see,
Let him come hither;
One here will constant be,
Come wind, come weather;
There's no discouragement
Shall make him once relent
His first avow'd intent
To be a pilgrim.

Who so beset him round
With dismal stories,
Do but themselves confound
His strength the more is.
No lion can him fright,
He'll with a giant fight,
But he will have a right
To be a pilgrim.

Hobgoblin nor foul fiend
Can daunt his spirit;
He knows he at the end
Shall life inherit.
Then fancies fly away,
He'll not fear what men say;
He'll labor night and day
To be a pilgrim.

It was not said nor sung by Mr. Valiant, but seems to have been a summing up of what Bunyan felt was necessary "To be a pilgrim." While the above text has been followed literally in its use as a hymn in several English hymnals, American books have contented themselves with the use of the conventionalized version which was made in 1904 when Canon Percy Dearmer, general editor, and his associates, were preparing *The English Hymnal* for publication. It is Doctor Dearmer's opinion that it was a daring thing to do; but in their search for vigorous, masculine hymns this was chosen, and time seems to be vindicating their good judgment. But to have attempted to put words such as "Hobgoblin nor foul fiend" into the mouths of an American congregation engaged in public worship would have been disastrous: it was deemed advisable to use the modernized version which Mrs. Alice Meynell, who was suggested as Lord Tennyson's successor to the laureateship of England, included in her anthology, *The School of Poetry,* 1923. This "Pilgrim's Song" bids fair to become a popular hymn, for its challenge for one to be valiant " 'Gainst all disaster" should have an irresistible appeal to courageous youth.

John Bunyan, the son of a tinker (or "brasier"), was born at Elstow, not far from Bedford, England, in 1628, where he learned to read and write in the village school. Endowed with a powerful imagination and an extreme sensitiveness, as a boy he was haunted by religious terrors, his nights made hideous by dreams of fiends trying to fly away with him. His *Grace Abounding to the Chief of Sinners* gives details of his early life and its spiritual disturbances. For a time he was in the Parliamentary army, then joined a Non-conformist community at Bedford formed by John Gifford; became an itinerant preacher, and was thrown into prison, from which he might have been released had he been willing to abstain from preaching. His answer was, "If you let me out today, I will preach again tomorrow." Pardoned in 1672, he was again incarcerated for a short time in 1675, and it is now generally supposed he began *The Pilgrim's Progress,* which "won a place second only to the Bible," during this imprisonment. He died August 31, 1688, at London, as a result of exposure while on an errand of mercy.

"Monk's Gate" is an adaptation by Ralph Vaughn Williams (527[2]) of an old Sussex, England, folk song,

> Our captain calls all hands on board tomorrow,
> Leaving my dear to mourn in grief and sorrow.
> Dry up those briny tears and leave off weeping,
> So happy may we be . . . at our next meeting,

and was not sung by John Bunyan's Non-conformist congregation at Elstow, as has been suggested, for there was no singing indulged in there until some years after Bunyan's death. The tune is sturdy, quite able to stand by itself without any story being invented to attract attention to it. Apparently somewhat jerky because of its irregular rhythm, it will repay any congregation to take the time and have the patience necessary to learn it. The best and strongest tunes are not learned at one hearing.

**266—O young and fearless Prophet of ancient Galilee—Samuel Ralph Harlow**

Blairgowrie—John Bacchus Dykes (1)

Doctor Harlow has written:

> As to the story of the hymn. With my wife I was driving from Pittsfield to Northampton one spring morning. The words, "O young and fearless Prophet of ancient Galilee," kept ringing through my mind. Gradually the entire hymn came to me, and as we had to stop by the road, I repeated them to my wife, who wrote them down. Shortly after writing them down, we started again on our trip and passed a man poorly dressed and looking very tired. My wife suggested that if we lived up to the words of the hymn we ought to pick him up, which we did. He was most grateful and told us that he had walked from Boston to Albany and out to Rochester looking for work and finding none. He said: "Just as you passed I felt that I was at the end of my rope. Last night I sold my razor to buy food. I was sitting there washing my feet which are blistered from much walking when you called. Somehow when you think you are utterly forgotten, God shows you that you are not as forgotten as you think you are."
>
> Unfortunately, the verse that we related to this incident is not included in the Hymnal. It runs:
>
> Stir up in us a protest against unearned wealth,
> While men go starved and hungry who plead for work and health;
> Whose wives and little children cry out for lack of bread,
> And spend their years o'er weighted, beneath a gloomy dread.

This is the first appearance of this hymn in any book.

Samuel Ralph Harlow, Ph.D., who was born at Boston, July 20, 1885, was educated at Harvard and Columbia Universities; Union and Hartford Theological Seminaries. Ordained a minister of the Congregational Church in 1912, he has been since 1923 professor of religion and social ethics at Smith College. He saw service as a regional director for the Y. M. C. A., A. E. F., in France during the World War. Doctor Harlow engaged in various religious undertakings in the Near East, among them acting as chaplain and head of the Department of Sociology at International College, Smyrna, from 1912 to 1922. He is the author of many books and has contributed largely to various religious publications.

"Blairgowrie" was written by Doctor Dykes in February, 1872, to the words,

The voice that breathed o'er Eden,

for the wedding of a friend. It is one of the "stray tunes found in print," and listed by his biographer, the Rev. J. T. Fowler.

**267—Rise up, O men of God**—William Pierson Merrill

First tune: **Festal Song**—William Henry Walter

Second tune: **Oxnam**—Robert Guy McCutchan (9[2])

This hymn came through its author's deep interest in the Brotherhood movement, which gained such great headway during the early years of this century. Calvin W. Laufer, in *Hymn Lore,* quotes Doctor Merrill regarding its writing:

> There is not much to tell about the origin of the hymn. Nolan R. Best, then editor of *The Continent,* happened to say to me that there was urgent need of a brotherhood hymn. The Brotherhood Movement was then going strongly in the Presbyterian Church. He had written a hymn, "Made of one blood with all on earth," for which I had composed the music. It is still found in some hymnals. The suggestion lingered in my mind, and just about that time (1911) I came upon an article by Gerald Stanley Lee, entitled "The Church of the Strong Men." I was on one of the Lake Michigan steamers going back to Chicago for a Sunday at my own church, when suddenly this hymn came up, almost without conscious thought or effort. In the original draft the last two lines of the first stanza were in a much weaker form than now. It has given me very deep satisfaction to have the hymn obtain such general use. Several times each year I am asked for permission to include it in some new collection of hymns.

The Bishop of Ripon congratulated Doctor Merrill on his having written such a fine, practical hymn, saying, "I use it at every confirmation service in my diocese where young people are received into the church." It is one of a very few hymns, written by recent American authors, which seem to have found a place in English and Canadian hymnals.

William Pierson Merrill was born in Orange, New Jersey, January 10, 1867, educated at Rutgers College and Union Theological Seminary, and ordained a Presbyterian minister in 1890. He has held pastorates in Philadelphia, in Chicago, and in New York City. Since 1911 he has been pastor of the Brick Presbyterian Church, New York. Doctor Merrill, an author of repute, an outstanding preacher, an authority on hymns and tunes, has for nearly a half century battled for righteous causes in America's three largest cities.

"Festal Song" appeared first in 1894 in *The Hymnal Revised and Enlarged* (Protestant Episcopal), known as the "Last Tucker," edited by J. Ireland Tucker and William W. Rousseau. It was used with the hymn, "Awake and sing the song," by William Hammond, c. 1745. In 1903 Horatio W. Parker (314) set it to "Stand, soldier of the cross." Introduced into Canada by way of *The Book of Common Praise,* 1908, it was used twice, once with "Rejoice, ye pure in heart," and as the second tune for "Ye servants of the Lord." In 1912 it first became associated with Doctor Merrill's great hymn in *The Pilgrim Hymnal.* Here is as good a place as any to show the vicissitudes of a good hymn in search of a good tune. The following table, showing variation in settings, may be interesting to the hymnologist:

PUBLICATIONS IN THE UNITED STATES

| Date | Publication | Tune |
|---|---|---|
| 1912 | *Pilgrim Hymnal* | Festal Song |
| 1913 | *American Hymnal* | Alexandria |
| 1916 | *The Hymnal* (Protestant Episcopal) | Festal Song |
| 1920 | *Hymnal for American Youth* | Festal Song |
| 1922 | *Beacon Hymnal* | Heath |
| 1923 | *Hymns for the Living Age* | St. Thomas (227) |
| 1926 | *Hymns of the Christian Life* | Leighton |
| 1928 | *Abingdon Hymnal* | Festal Song |
| 1928 | *American Student Hymnal* | St. Thomas |
| 1930 | *Standard Hymnal* | Oxnam |
| 1930 | *New Hymnal for American Youth* | St. Thomas |
| 1931 | *Pilgrim Hymnal* | Festal Song |
| 1932 | *Praise and Service Hymns* | St. Thomas |
| 1933 | *The Hymnal* (Presbyterian) | Festal Song |

PUBLICATIONS IN ENGLAND

| Date | Publication | Tune |
|---|---|---|
| 1925 | *Songs of Praise* | St. Michael (Old 134th, which see at No. 39) |
| 1931 | *Songs of Praise* | Falcon Street (Silver Street, which see at No. 22) |
| 1933 | *Methodist Hymn Book* | Watchman (Not Lowell Mason's tune at No. 485. An English tune) |
| recent | *Hymns of the Kingdom* | St. Michael and Carno |
| recent | *Hymns for Today* | St. Michael |
| recent | *Congregational Hymnary* | Prague and Holy Rood |

PUBLICATIONS IN CANADA

| Date | Publication | Tune |
|---|---|---|
| 1930 | *The Hymnary of the United Church of Canada* | St. Michael |
| 1930 | *Songs of Worship* | St. Michael |

It is interesting to note how this fine hymn has had twelve different settings in twenty-four years. It is also interesting to find how editors, or committees, have changed their minds. The Congregationalist books (in the United States) have been consistent in their use of "Festal Song." This is also true of the Protestant Episcopal hymnals. But H. Augustine Smith, who edited five different books from 1920 to 1932, used this tune in his first and then turned to "St. Thomas" for the other four. The other editors have failed to select a common tune. In England, Vaughn Williams first used "St. Michael," then "Silver Street." The Canadian books have followed the first use of Vaughn Williams and adopted "St. Michael." In the United States "Festal Song" seems to be in the lead for supremacy, with "St. Thomas" in second place. It is a question whether either will eventually become the recognized setting for "Rise up, O men of God."

William Henry Walter, Mus. Doc., was born at Newark, New Jersey, in 1825, and died at New York City in 1893. After serving as organist in Episcopal churches in the cities of his birth and death, he was, in 1856, invited to become organist at Columbia University, which institution conferred on him the degree of Doctor of Music in 1865.

Robert G. McCutchan (9[2]) wrote the tune, "Oxnam," in 1929, soon after G. Bromley Oxnam had become president of DePauw University. The composer was so impressed with him as truly a man of God, giving "heart and mind and soul and strength to serve the King of kings," that it seemed fitting to name the tune "Oxnam." It first appeared in the *Standard Hymnal,* 1930.

**268—"Are ye able," said the Master**—Earl Marlatt (178)

**Beacon Hill**—Harry Silvernale Mason

Doctor Marlatt gives an account of the circumstances leading to the writing of this hymn to which he has given the name "Challenge":

> Although written for a Consecration Service at Boston University School of Religious Education in 1926, the Hymn, "Challenge," had its origin in the late Marcus D. Buell's classroom at Boston University School of Theology, where I was a student from 1919 to 1922. In his lectures on "The Gospel of John," Doctor Buell portrayed James and John, sons of Salome, so vividly as to make their holy gallantry a living symbol of ministry.
>
> "Jesus always threw out a challenge," he said. "When Salome asked for her sons a place in His Kingdom, He knew that just ahead of Him was Jerusalem and possibly crucifixion. He wondered if these young 'sons of thunder,' as He was accustomed to call them, had courage enough to follow Him that far. So He said to them, 'Are ye able to drink of the cup that I shall drink of and to be baptized with the baptism that I am baptized with?' They say unto Him, 'Lord, we are able.' "
>
> Two years later I went to Oberammergau. The most moving scene in the Passion Play was the Crucifixion and the most moving moment in that scene was one where a thief turned to Jesus and said, "Remember me when Thou comest into Thy kingdom." Jesus, seeing both the faith and penitence which flashed from those uplifted eyes, answered: "Today shalt thou be with me in paradise." As Anton Lang said those words, immortality suddenly became as real for me as the sunlight at that moment driving the clouds from the mountains, and I knew that nothing, nothing could ever shake my faith in that vision.
>
> Somehow those two moments got together when I was asked to write a hymn of self-dedication for the School of Religious Education. The words came so spontaneously to the music of a tune which Harry Mason had already written that the text seemed to write itself. I sang it to myself as I crossed the Boston Common one evening. By the time I reached my room on top of Beacon Hill the song was finished. I needed only to transcribe it for the quartet and congregation which sang it in Pilgrim Hall three days later. Subsequently it was sung at a similar consecration service in Robinson Chapel, after which it was adopted as one of the school songs of Boston University School of Theology, where I was then, and am still, a Professor of Religious Education. My students there have carried it out into their ministries

all over the world and eventually into the pages of *The Methodist Hymnal,* where its tune, for reasons which are obvious, was called "Beacon Hill."

"Beacon Hill" was written by Harry S. Mason in 1924 while a graduate student at Boston University School of Theology.

Harry Silvernale Mason, born in 1881, is now instructor in fine arts in religion at Auburn Theological Seminary, Auburn, New York.

## Trials and Conflicts

**269—Jesus, Saviour, pilot me**—Edward Hopper

**Pilot**—John Edgar Gould (196)

The hymn was first published anonymously in *The Sailors' Magazine,* 1871, and in *The Baptist Praise Book,* 1871, yet it was not until after its appearance in *Spiritual Songs,* 1878, that Dr. Edward Hopper acknowledged its authorship. It was written especially for sailors, who, in large numbers, attended Doctor Hopper's Church of the Sea and Land, in New York City.

Edward Hopper, D.D., born at New York City, February 17, 1816, graduated from New York University, completed his theological course at Union Theological Seminary, and was licensed to preach by the Third Presbytery of New York. With the exception of eleven years, while he preached at Sag Harbor, Long Island, all of his life was spent in his native city, where his last pastorate was at the Church of the Sea and Land. A sufferer from a weak heart, he died suddenly on April 23, 1888, while in the act of writing some lines on "Heaven." He wrote several poems, some of them hymns, which, because of an excessive modesty, he concealed under various odd pen names.

"Pilot," which was written as a setting for this hymn by John E. Gould just before sailing for Europe shortly before his death (196), was first published in *The Baptist Praise Book,* 1871.

**270—O for a faith that will not shrink**—William Hiley Bathurst

**Arlington**—Thomas Augustine Arne

The hymn is from the author's *Psalms and Hymns for Public and Private Use,* 1831, with the legend:

"The Power of Faith,"—Luke 17. 5

An excellent faith hymn, it has been changed at will by critics of its first form. The hymn has been improved by the omission of two stanzas, one of which, 4,

That bears unmov'd the world's dread frown,
Nor heeds its scornful smile;
That sin's wild ocean cannot drown,
Nor its soft arts beguile,

offers an example of why lines of hymns sometimes need to be changed.

William Hiley Bathurst, son of a member of the British parliament, the

Hon. Charles Bragge, who assumed the name "Bathurst" upon succeeding to his uncle's estates at Lydney Park, was born at Cleve Dale, Mangotsfield, near Bristol, August 28, 1796, and died at Lydney Park, Gloucestershire, November 25, 1877. Educated at Winchester and at Christ Church, Oxford, after holding one rectory for thirty-two years, he resigned and retired to private life because he could not reconcile his views with *The Book of Common Prayer.* Author of more than two hundred hymns and more than one hundred versions of the Psalms, the least that can be said of his originals is that they are simple and direct.

"Arlington," "Artaxerxes," or "Triumph," was taken from the minuet in the Overture to Doctor Arne's *Artaxerxes,* an opera produced in London in 1762. It was first arranged as a hymn tune by the Rev. Ralph Harrison (1748-1810), a member of a prominent Non-conformist family in England, who published it in his *Sacred Harmony* in 1784. In the older tune books the last half of the tune appears:

which is the way it was printed in *The Methodist Harmonist,* 1822, the hymn being,

On Jordan's stormy banks I stand.

The slow movement from which it evolved is:

although at first glance it may not be apparent.

Thomas Augustus Arne, Mus. Doc., who spent all of his life in London, being born March 12, 1710, and dying there March 5, 1778, was the foremost English composer of the eighteenth century. The son of an upholsterer, he had completed his law course and had acted as a clerk for three years before he could obtain his father's consent to follow music as his life's work. Being indifferent to his law studies and practice, he spent all of the time he could in playing on the flute and spinet. The spinet he had muffled in the home garret and had his father discovered it, Doctor Burney tells us, "he would probably have thrown the instrument out of the window, if not the player." After gaining his father's leave to practice openly, he charmed the family with his music. He taught his sister, Mrs. Cibber, to sing. This sister was the famous tragic actress and contralto for whom Handel composed the contralto solos in the *Messiah,* and who was chosen as one of the soloists for its first performance in Dublin. It is by his songs that Doctor Arne will continue to be known, although the greatest part of his writing in music was for the operatic stage, he being the composer at Covent Garden as well as at other theaters in London, notably Drury Lane. It was at Covent Garden, February 26, 1773, that Doctor Arne first introduced women's voices in an oratorio chorus for the singing of his own *Judith*. He will be remembered as long as there are patriotic Englishmen for having written "Rule Brittania."

**271—Lead us, O Father, in the paths of peace**—William Henry Burleigh

**Burleigh**—Joseph Barnby (31)

This hymn was written before 1859, for it appears in *The New Congregational Hymn Book* of that date. It appeared in C. D. Cleveland's *Lyra Sacra Americana,* 1868, which is usually given as its source. Its somberness seems somehow to enhance its attractiveness, for it is a general favorite.

William Henry Burleigh, born February 12, 1812, at Woodstock, Connecticut, was a Unitarian who learned the printer's trade when a young man, later becoming the editor and publisher of an abolition journal, *The Christian Freeman,* Hartford, Connecticut. After spending six years at Syracuse, New York, as agent for the New York State Temperance Society, he was appointed Harbor Master of New York City, making his home in Brooklyn, where he died March 18, 1871. His hymns, poetic, yet melancholy, are more in use in Great Britain than in America.

"Burleigh" was written for this hymn by Sir Joseph Barnby (31), first appearing in 1872.

**272—If thou but suffer God to guide thee**—Georg Neumark

**Bremen (Neumark)**—Georg Neumark

Georg Neumark was born in Thuringia, March 16, 1621, and received his undergraduate training at the gymnasia of Schleusingen and Gotha. Leaving the latter place in the fall of 1641 after completing his work, he started for the University at Königsberg, where he expected to study law. Shortly after leaving Marburg the party with which he was traveling was set upon by robbers, who took everything Neumark had except his prayer book and some little money he had sewed in his clothing. Finding it necessary to obtain employment, he returned to Marburg, but was unsuccessful in his quest for work, and the friends he had made there passed him on to others at Lüneburg. Here his Marburg experience was repeated, as was the case at Winsen and at Hamburg. It was not until he reached Kiel that he was successful, and then through the friendship of a former Thuringian, Nicolaus Becker, the chief pastor there, he secured employment in the home of Judge Stephen Heuning, where he remained until he was enabled to save enough money to allow his matriculation at Königsberg, in 1643, eighteen months after leaving Gotha. He remained there for five years, devoting much time to the study and writing of poetry. For the next three years he wandered about, seemingly aimlessly. In 1851 he returned to Thuringia, where he was fortunate enough to secure some sort of clerical position at the court of the Duke of Weimar, remaining there until his death, July 18, 1681. The last months of his life were spent in blindness.

"Bremen," or "Neumark," or "Augsberg," was written by Georg Neumark, probably late 1641 or early 1642, as a setting for his own hymn,

Wer nur den lieben Gott lässt walten,

the best-known translation being,

If thou but suffer God to guide thee,

by Catherine Winkworth (7), another, by the same translator, being,

Leave God to order all thy ways,

which was used in *The Methodist Hymnal* of 1905. Hymn as well as tune were composed at Kiel when, after many discouragements, he secured the position in the home of Judge Heuning. Neumark says of his good fortune,

> which good fortune, coming suddenly, and as if fallen from heaven, greatly rejoiced me, and on that very day I composed to the honor of my beloved Lord the here and there well-known hymn, "Wer nur den lieben Gott lässt walten:" and had certainly cause enough to thank the Divine compassion for such unlooked for grace shown me.

The tune, originally in 3 time, was written:

Bach evidently was very fond of this chorale-like tune, for he used it as the basis for his cantata by the same name; as the closing chorale of four other cantatas, and as the theme of one of his compositions for organ. Mendelssohn also used it as the chorale to the words "To Thee, O Lord, I yield my spirit," in his oratorio *St. Paul.* It is said to be so well loved, especially by the Lutherans, that it has been chosen as the setting for more than four hundred hymns. It is now known in the form used by Bach and Mendelssohn. It was first published in 1657 in Neumark's *Fortgepflanzter Musikalisch-Poetischer Lustwald.*

**273—O Love divine, that stooped to share**—Oliver Wendell Holmes (62)

**Hesperus (Quebec)**—Henry Baker

The hymn, written in 1849, was published ten years later in *The Atlantic Monthly* as one of the poems in *The Professor at the Breakfast Table,* which Oliver Wendell Holmes represented as having been heard by the Professor as he was passing a sick-room. Doctor Holmes entitled it,

Hymn of Trust,

and its little refrain,

Thou art near,

is found in Psalm 119. 151, "Thou art near, O Lord; and all Thy commandments are truth," than which it would be difficult to find a grander text for a sermon. The hymn is an exquisite expression of trust, and a work of art.

"Hesperus," or "Quebec," was written as a setting for "Sun of my soul," and appeared in the Rev. John Grey's *Hymnal for the Use of the English Church* in 1866, the first edition of which was published in 1857 and was the first book to contain hymn tunes by Doctor Dykes (1).

"Hesperus" had an interesting beginning. As told by J. T. Lightwood (453), there was some discussion concerning a suitable setting for Keble's "Sun of my soul" carried on in the columns of the London *Penny Post* in 1861. For more than a year contributors sent tunes to the paper; among them, without any means of identification and without a name, was this one, which received favorable comment as being a suitable setting for the evening hymn. After its appearance in Grey's book, Mr. Baker stated the tune in manuscript had been handed about among his friends for many years, he having written it while a student at Exeter College, Oxford, in 1854. He claimed it after its appearance without a composer's name in Bishop Bickersteth's book of 1871.

Henry Baker, an English civil engineer engaged for many years in railroad construction work in India, was born at Nuneham, Oxfordshire, in (?), 1835, and died at Wimbledon, April 15, 1910. Baker's possession of a marked talent for music caused Doctor Dykes to encourage him to take up its serious study, and he continued at it until he graduated a Music Bachelor from Exeter College, Oxford, in 1867. He never considered himself other than an amateur in the field. Several of his tunes were used by W. Garrett Horder in *Worship Song,* v. d.

**274—In the hour of trial**—James Montgomery (39)
Altered by Frances A. Hutton

**Penitence**—Spencer Lane

Written on October 13, 1834, this hymn appeared in James Montgomery's *Original Hymns,* 1853. The third and fourth stanzas were altered by Mrs. Frances A. Hutton (1811-1877) for *Supplement and Litanies,* n. d., compiled by Prebendary H. W. Hutton. Doctor Julian has given a detailed account of the different versions of this one of Montgomery's best-known hymns. Its scriptural basis is St. Luke 22. 32, "But I have prayed for thee, that thy faith fail not; and when thou art converted, strengthen thy brethren."

"Penitence" was composed by Spencer Lane because he did not like the tune set to a hymn his pastor had selected for use at an evening service at St. James' Church, Woonsocket, Rhode Island. Having been given the hymn numbers after the morning service, Mr. Lane wrote this tune while his wife was preparing their Sunday dinner. After hearing it sung, Bishop Clarke, of the Rhode Island diocese, told Mr. Lane the tune would make him famous. The Rev. Joseph L. Miller, rector, suggested it be sent to Dr. Charles L. Hutchins, editor of the Protestant Episcopal *Church Hymnal,* who included it in the edition of 1879.

Spencer Lane, the composer of "Penitence," was born April 7, 1843, at

Tilton, New Hampshire. Successively, a Union soldier in the Civil War, a student at the New England Conservatory of Music, a teacher of vocal and instrumental music in New York City, a proprietor of a music store, organist and choir director as well as composer of church music, he lived at Woonsocket, Rhode Island, at Monson, Massachusetts, at Richmond, Virginia, and at Baltimore, Maryland, where for seven years he was in charge of the music at All Saints' Protestant Episcopal Church. He died of apoplexy at Reedville, Virginia, August 10, 1903. Of his various hymn tunes, this is the only one in general use.

**275—Christian! dost thou see them**—Andrew of Crete
Translated by John Mason Neale (52)
First tune: **St. Andrew of Crete**—John Bacchus Dykes (1)
Second tune: **Greek Hymn**—Joseph Perry Holbrook (210[2])

This hymn, says Dr. C. S. Robinson,

> is one of the most vivid and dramatic presentations of our positions as Christians in the midst of an array of evil forces ever on the watch to overcome our resistance. A vigilance that never relaxes is our only safeguard; and as long as life lasts it is bound to be a struggle.

It is a battle cry whose words rouse and stir one. The words of Doctor Neale's translation, from *Hymns of the Eastern Church,* 1862, are even more vivid than those commonly used. Stanzas 1 and 2, which have undergone the greatest changes, are:

Christian! dost thou see them
On the holy ground,
How the troops of Midian
Prowl and prowl around?
Christian! up and smite them,
Counting gain but loss:
Smite them by the merit
Of the Holy Cross!

Christian! dost thou feel them,
How they work within,
Striving, tempting, luring,
Goading into sin?
Christian! never tremble!
Never be downcast!
Smite them by the virtue
Of the Lenten Fast!

Stanza 3 has been changed slightly in the fifth line, and stanza 4 differs from the original translation in only one word. Taken from the Greek of St. Andrew of Crete, it was composed of stichera[1] to be sung during the second week of Lent.

St. Andrew of Crete (or Jerusalem) was born about 660 and embraced the monastic life at Jerusalem, going from there to Constantinople where he became a Deacon of the Great Church and Warden of the Orphanage. Doctor Neale says:

---
[1] Responses appointed to be sung in the Greek Church after verses from the Psalms.

His first entrance in public life does no credit to his sanctity. During the reign of Philippicus Bardanes (711-714) he was raised by that usurper to the Archiepiscopate of Crete; and shortly afterwards was one of the Pseudo-Synod of Constantinople, held under the Emperor's auspices in A. D. 712, and which condemned the Sixth Œcumenical Council and restored the Monothelite heresy. At a later period, however, he returned to the faith of the Church, and refuted the error into which he had fallen.

It cannot be stated that he was the first writer of the Greek canon, but none of earlier date than his are extant. He died near Mitylene, Island of Hierissus, about 732.

"St. Andrew of Crete" was composed by Doctor Dykes for this hymn for the Appendix to *Hymns Ancient and Modern,* 1868. It is one of his best settings, for its changes from the relative minor key to its major strikingly bring out the question and answer form of the hymn. It is much the stronger and more virile of the two settings used.

"Greek Hymn," attributed to Joseph P. Holbrook, appeared anonymously in *The Hymnal* (Protestant Episcopal), 1870. It is too weak to carry adequately the combative spirit of the words, and is now found in only a few books. Its complete demise should not be regretted.

**276—Must Jesus bear the cross alone**—Thomas Shepherd and others

**Maitland**—George Nelson Allen

This hymn, without credit, is found in *The Oberlin Social and Sabbath School Hymn Book, compiled by Geo. N. Allen, Professor of Music in O. C. Institute,* Oberlin, James M. Fitch, 1844. This little book apparently has escaped the eyes of hymnodists, for the source of the hymn has been given as *The Social and Sabbath Hymn Book,* 1849, also compiled by George N. Allen. This book had but limited circulation, and it was not until Henry Ward Beecher issued his *Plymouth Collection* in 1855 that the hymn became widely known. The words are identical in the two books except that the first two lines of stanza 3 in the little book of 1844 were:

I'll bear the consecrated cross,
Till from the cross I'm free,—.

In the *Plymouth Collection* it was credited to G. N. Allen, which was simply an error. The text was rewritten from one of Thomas Shepherd's *Penetential Cries,* 1693, one of some half dozen independent singing books used before Doctor Watts issued his *Hymns and Spiritual Songs* in 1707. The first stanza of the Shepherd "Cry" has undergone the greatest change of any of the three. It was:

Shall Simon bear the Cross alone,
And other Saints be free?
Each Saint of thine shall find his own,
And there is one for me.

It is not known by whom the hymn was rewritten. Dr. L. F. Benson (38) gives the second stanza as Anon. c. 1810, and the third Anon. c. 1849.

Thomas Shepherd, son of a Non-conformist minister in England, was born in 1665, and died January 29, 1739. He took Holy Orders in the Church of England but seceded in 1694 and preceded Dr. Philip Doddridge (69) as pastor of the independent Castle Hill Meeting House at Nottingham, subsequently moving to Bocking, near Braintree, Essex, where he began his preaching in a barn. Seven years later, 1707, a chapel was built for his congregation. He wrote a few hymns, but most of his published works are sermons.

"Maitland," composed by George N. Allen some time in the 1840's, was said to be a "Western Melody" when it was used in the *Plymouth Collection,* 1855, and was called "Cross and Crown."

George Nelson Allen was born at Mansfield, Massachusetts, September 7, 1812. He entered the junior class at Oberlin College, graduated in 1838, and became an instructor in music there, organizing a chorus and orchestra, thereby laying the foundation for what since 1865 has been the Oberlin Conservatory of Music. He compiled at least two books of hymns, writing tunes and some hymns for them, and for a part of the time he was connected with Oberlin, taught geology. Retiring in 1864, he made his home at Cincinnati until his death, December 9, 1877. His burial was at Oberlin.

**277—My soul, be on thy guard**—George Heath
**Laban**—Lowell Mason (19)

The hymn was taken from *Hymns and Poetic Essays Sacred to the Public and Private Worship of the Deity,* 1781.

George Heath, born in 1750, was a student at Exeter and became an English Unitarian minister. He was for a time in charge of a Presbyterian church at Honiton, Devonshire, but was dismissed "for cause," and wrote this rallying cry as a warning to his fellow men. He died in 1822.

"Laban," also called "Conflict," was written by Lowell Mason in 1830.

## Activity and Zeal

**278—Lead on, O King Eternal**—Ernest Warburton Shurtleff
**Lancashire**—Henry Smart (77)

The hymn was written by Ernest W. Shurtleff for his graduating class, 1887, at Andover Theological Seminary, and was published the same year in the author's *Hymns of the Faith.* Being written for young men, it has a real appeal for them. It was sung with great gusto at the Methodist Centenary Celebration at Columbus, Ohio, in 1920, and has come into wide use both as a processional and a recessional, being especially appropriate as a recessional on baccalaureate occasions.

Ernest Warburton Shurtleff, born at Boston, April 4, 1862, was educated at Boston Latin School, Harvard University, and Andover Theological Seminary, and, entering the Congregational ministry, he held pastorates in Massachusetts and at Minneapolis, Minnesota. His greatest work, however, was the organizing and developing of the American Church at Frankfurt, Germany, and among American students in Paris. During the World War he was active, with his wife, in relief work. He was a good amateur musician and published several volumes of poetry. He died in France, August 29, 1917.

"Lancashire" was written by Henry Smart (77) in 1835 while living at Blackburn, England, the occasion being a "grand musical festival" celebrating the three hundredth anniversary of the Reformation. It was first printed on leaflets, and not until 1867 did it appear in a hymnal, *Psalms and Hymns for Divine Worship,* set to the missionary hymn, "From Greenland's icy mountains."

**279—God of grace and God of glory**—Harry Emerson Fosdick

**Cwm Rhondda** (165)—John Hughes (165)

This hymn was written by Doctor Fosdick for use as the processional hymn on the occasion of the dedication of Riverside Church, New York City, October 5, 1930. His theme for the occasion was "what matters in religion," in which he proposed as the guiding principle of the new church that "nothing matters in all this except the things that lead men into a more abundant life."

Harry Emerson Fosdick, LL.D., American Baptist clergyman, born at Buffalo, New York, May 28, 1878, was educated at Colgate, Union Theological Seminary, and Columbia University, and has received honorary scholastic recognition from Colgate, Brown, Yale, Princeton, Union, Boston University, Harvard, the University of Michigan, Rochester, Ohio University, and the University of Glasgow, Scotland. Eminent as a teacher and author, trustee of colleges, he stands pre-eminent among America's great preachers.

**280—Onward, Christian soldiers**—Sabine Baring-Gould (53)

**St. Gertrude**—Arthur Seymour Sullivan (15)

This processional hymn was written in 1864 for school children of Horbury Bridge, near Wakefield, Yorkshire, England, where the Rev. Mr. Baring-Gould was then curate in charge of mission work. The occasion was a school festival ("feast") and it was the author's desire to provide something appropriate for children to sing as they marched from one village to another. The tune used was one the author arranged from the slow movement of Haydn's Symphony in D, No. 15, but the arrangement has been forgotten. Some of the lines of the hymn have been objected to on various grounds, but attempts to change them have not been welcomed. Some of the changes made were not particularly poetic, one instance being that found in *Hymns Ancient and Modern,* where the editors, being literalists, changed the line,

We are not divided,

so that it read,

Though divisions harass.

It was published in the October 15 issue of *The Church Times* the year it was written, entitled,

Hymn for Procession with Cross and Banners.

Probably the name of Sabine Baring-Gould will be kept familiar through the singing of this hymn rather than through the reading of his numerous novels and other works.

"St. Gertrude" was written in 1871. Mrs. Gertrude Clay-Ker-Seymer in a letter to the *Musical Times*, London, of July, 1902, wrote:

> In answer to your letter regarding the composition of Sir Arthur Sullivan's tune to "Onward, Christian soldiers," which he dedicated to me, I can tell you that I believe it was written at Hanford, my home in Dorsetshire, while Sir Arthur was staying there, but it is so long ago I cannot be quite sure; what I do remember, however, is that we sang it in the private chapel attached to the house, Sir Arthur playing the harmonium, and having taught us the tune, as we had not the music. Therefore it was certainly not published then, but I think we may assume that it was written there. Sir Arthur often stayed with us for several weeks at a time, and composed several songs, &c, while at Hanford, after which place he named another of his hymn tunes, but not one of such striking merit as "Onward, Christian soldiers," which has now a world-wide reputation, and of which I am proud to be the sponsor.

It was published in *Musical Times* in 1871 and in *The Church Hymnary* the following year.

**281—Soldiers of the cross, arise!**—Jared Bell Waterbury

**Caledonia**—Scottish traditional melody

This militant hymn was one of seven by Jared B. Waterbury included in Volume I of Joshua Leavitt's *Christian Lyre,* 1830, each headed,

Written for the Lyre,

and signed "J. B. W." Bishop Warren thought so highly of it that he included it in his selection of *Fifty-two Memory Hymns.*

Jared Bell Waterbury, D.D., born at New York City, August 11, 1799, a graduate of Yale, 1822, was a Congregational minister holding pastorates at Hudson, New York, and Bowdoin Street Congregational Church, Boston, and an author of several religious works. He died at Brooklyn, December 31, 1876.

"Caledonia" is none other than the very old Scottish tune known as "Scots wha hae," which is so old no one has been able to discover its origin. It is one of those old melodies of which Robert Burns said, "Many of our Scots airs have outlived their original and perhaps many subsequent sets of verses." He seemed to be under the impression that this was the song Bruce's army sang at Bannockburn. It was mentioned by Gavin, Bishop of Dunkeld, in 1512, who called it "Now the Day Dawis," and who said it was a favorite with the people. Reference has been made to it from time to time in literature, but there is so little to work upon that a solution of the mystery of its source seems impossible. Writing in 1776, John Hawkins said:

> That the Scots melodies at the time when they were originally composed were committed to writing there can be no doubt; but it is to be feared that there are no genuine copies of any of them now remaining, they having for a series of years been propagated by tradition, and till lately existed only in the memory of the inhabitants of that kingdom.

Whatever its source, it is a grand old tune, which has been sung to this hymn in America for more than a century, being the setting used for it when it was first published in the *Christian Lyre,* 1830, there called "Wallace."

**282—Soldiers of Christ, arise**—Charles Wesley (25)

**Diademata** (170)—George Job Elvey (170)

Stanzas 1, 2, and 16 are taken from sixteen in *Hymns and Sacred Poems,* 1749. In the large *Collection* of 1780, and in each succeeding edition of the Methodist books, it was in three parts of four stanzas each, not being reduced to three stanzas until as late as 1905. The original title was,

The whole armor of God.

Founded upon Ephesians 6. 11-18, it was said by James King to be a spirited paraphrase of that passage which described the Christian soldier. Some striking portions have been omitted: the first part of stanza 7, one of the finest, being,

> But above all, lay hold
> On faith's victorious shield,
> Armed with that adamant and gold
> Be sure to win the field.

Canon Percy Dearmer speaks highly of this hymn and refers to its "mastered simplicity," "its faultless technique," and its "sagacity in the use of imperfect rhymes," as indications of high accomplishment. William T. Stead said it "is as inspiring as the blast of the bugle."

**283—Stand up, stand up for Jesus**—George Duffield, Jr.

**Geibel**—Adam Geibel

In a letter dated May 29, 1883, Doctor Duffield gives full details of the circumstances surrounding the writing of this hymn:

> "Stand Up for Jesus" was the dying message of the Rev. Dudley A. Tyng, to the Young Men's Christian Association, and the ministers associated with them in the Noon-Day Prayer Meeting during the great revival of 1858, usually known as "The Work of God in Philadelphia."
>
> A very dear personal friend, I knew young Tyng as one of the noblest, bravest, *manliest* men I ever met. . . . The Sabbath before his death he preached in the immense edifice known as Jaynes' Hall, one of the most successful sermons of modern times. Of the five thousand men there assembled, at least one thousand, it was believed, were "the slain of the Lord." His text was Exodus 10: 11, and hence the allusion in the third verse of the hymn.
>
> The following Wednesday, leaving his study for a moment, he went to the barn floor, where a mule was at work on a horse-power, shelling corn. Patting him on the neck, the sleeve of his silk study gown caught in the cogs of the wheel, and his arm was torn out by the roots! His death occurred in a few hours. . . .
>
> The following Sunday the author of the hymn preached from Eph. 6. 14, and the above verses were written simply as the concluding exhortation. The superintendent of the Sabbath school had a fly-leaf printed for the children—a stray copy

found its way into a Baptist newspaper—and from that paper it has gone in English, and in German and Latin translations all over the world. The first time the author heard it sung, outside of his own denomination, was in 1864, as the favorite song of the Christian soldiers in the Army of the James. . . .

Notwithstanding the many mutilations and alterations and perversions to which this hymn has been subjected, it is but proper to say, that since the night it was written, it has never been altered by the author in a single verse, a single line, or a single word, and it is his earnest wish that it shall continue unaltered until the Soldiers of the Cross shall replace it by something better.

Four stanzas of the original six are used without change, as desired by the author. Its first printing in any permanent publication in the form approved by the author, was in *Lyra Sacra Americana,* 1868. The first hymnal in which it appeared was *The Church Psalmist,* 1859, considerably altered. It has been honored by being translated into many languages, making its use extensive in all parts of the world.

George Duffield, Jr., D.D., born at Carlisle, Pennsylvania, September 12, 1818, membei of a family distinguished in Presbyterian church history, was educated at Yale and Union Theological Seminary and held pastorates in New York, New Jersey, Pennsylvania, Illinois, and Michigan. Upon his retirement in 1884 he made his home in Detroit, but was in the home of his son, the Rev. Samuel W. Duffield, author of *English Hymns, Their Authors and History,* at the time of his death, July 6, 1888.

"Geibel" was written for this hymn by Doctor Geibel. It first appeared in one of the publications of the Hall-Mack Company, with which the composer was connected for many years.

Adam Geibel, born in Baden, Germany, September 15, 1885, came to America in childhood; studied in Philadelphia, became active as organist and conductor, and formed the Adam Geibel Company, now the Hall-Mack Company, in Philadelphia. He was a striking example of the ability of the blind musician. Although he was born a normal child, he developed, at the age of eight or nine years, a slight eyelid infection, the treatment of which with too strong medicines caused the eyeballs to dissolve. In later years Doctor Geibel always contended that the loss of his sight enabled him to develop his God-given talent in music, and was never regretful that his sight had been taken from him.

Doctor Geibel had a great reputation as a writer in four parts for men's voices. Among his most successful quartets are the well-known "Kentucky Babe" and "Little Cotton Dolly." He made no claims for greatness as a musician, but devoted his time and talent to writing for the large body of people who, he believed, could enjoy and appreciate his music.

For many years he was organist at the Stetson Mission, Philadelphia. He died in the city, August 3, 1933.

**284—Am I a soldier of the cross**—Isaac Watts (3)

**Arlington** (270)—Thomas Augustine Arne (270)

This fine hymn which Doctor Watts used after one of his sermons on

Holy Fortitude, or Remedies against Fear,

the text from 1 Corinthians 16. 13, "Stand fast in the faith, quit you like men, be strong," was not included in his *Hymns,* nor is it found in many recent collections. Its tone may not please the fancy of modern Christians, but it teaches the best kind of discipline. The last paragraph of the sermon to which it was appended may well be quoted:

> Happy is that Faith that has no carnal Fear attending it, but is got above the Frowns and Smiles of this World. My Soul longs after it, and reaches at it, as something within the Power of her present Attainment through the Grace of Christ. I long to be armed with this sacred Courage, and to have my heart fortify'd round with these divine Munitions. I would fain be calm and serene in the midst of Buffetings and Reproaches, and pursue my Course steadily toward Heaven, under the Banner of Faith, through all the Arrows of Slander and Malice. Lord Jesus, I wait for thy divine Influences, to bestow this grace, and thy divine Teachings, to put me in the Way to obtain it.

The entire hymn is used, the only change being the last line of the fifth stanza, which Doctor Watts wrote:

> And seize it with thine eye.

**285—The Son of God goes forth to war**—Reginald Heber (1)

**All Saints, New**—Henry Stephen Cutler

The hymn, in eight four-line stanzas, appeared in Bishop Heber's posthumous *Hymns Written and Adapted to the Weekly Church Services of the Year,* 1827, the reference in the second stanza being to St. Stephen, for the celebration of whose day it was written. A few unimportant changes have been made.

"All Saints, New," written for this hymn, appeared in *The Church Hymnal* of the Protestant Episcopal Church, Dr. J. Ireland Tucker, 1872. In *The Methodist Hymnal,* 1905, it was called "Cutler."

Henry Stephen Cutler, Mus. Doc., was born at Boston in 1824, where he received a part of his education before going to Europe for further study. Upon his return he located in Boston, first as organist at Grace Church, then at the Church of the Advent, where he attracted attention with his surpliced choir, probably the first in the United States. Going to New York City in 1858, he served Trinity Church as organist and choirmaster for seven years, and here too he robed his choir and seated the members in the chancel, an innovation. After leaving Trinity he was active at Brooklyn, Providence, Philadelphia, and Troy, until his death in 1902.

**286—Fight the good fight**—John Samuel Bewley Monsell (114)

**Pentecost**—William Boyd

The hymn was written for the nineteenth Sunday after Trinity, the epistle for which is Ephesians 4. 17, *et seq.* It appeared in Doctor Monsell's *Hymns of Love and Praise,* 1863, and, though not an example of his best, it is by far the most popular of his nearly three hundred hymns.

"Pentecost" is a great favorite with British royalty, and it is always used at Royal confirmations—indeed at most English confirmations. Of this hymn, greatly enjoyed by soldiers and sailors, Lord Kitchener told its composer, "It is the most moving hymn I know." In the London *Times* of December 1, 1908, the Rev. William Boyd has given details of the writing of "Pentecost." It was written about 1864 at the request of Mr. Baring-Gould as a setting for the hymn, "Come, Holy Ghost, our souls inspire," to be included among the Whitsuntide hymns to be used at Horbury, where Baring-Gould was then curate. In 1868 there was published a book of *Thirty-two Hymn Tunes* by members of the University of Oxford, of which "Pentecost" was one. It was first sung, however, at a large meeting of Yorkshire colliers at Whitsuntide, and became very popular. Boyd was asked how it came to be associated with "Fight the good fight":

> Ah, that is a funny thing. One day as I was walking along Regent Street I felt a slap on my back and turning round saw my dear friend Arthur Sullivan. "My dear Billy," he said, "I've seen a tune of yours which I must have." (He was then editing *Church Hymns,* 1874.) "All right; send me a cheque and I agree." No copy of the book, much less a proof, was sent me, and when I saw the tune I was horrified to find that Sullivan had assigned it to "Fight the good fight." We had a regular fisticuffs about it, but judging from the favor with which the tune has been received, I feel that Sullivan was right in so mating words and music.

William Boyd, born at Montego Bay, Jamaica, in 1847, is said to come "from an old Scots stock of lowland Border thieves." Beginning to compose music at the age of ten, he was educated at Hurstpierpoint, where he was tutored by Sabine Baring-Gould (53), and at Worcester College, Oxford, where he was organ scholar. After serving the Church of All Saints, Norfolk Square, London, as vicar for twenty-five years, he lived in retirement from 1908 until his death at London, February 16, 1928.

**287—A charge to keep I have—Charles Wesley (25)**

**Boylston**—Lowell Mason (19)

The hymn, a great favorite and found in all editions of Methodist hymnals, is taken from *Short Hymns on Select Passages of the Holy Scripture,* 1762, where it is headed,

> Keep the charge of the LORD, that ye die not.—viii. 35 (Leviticus).

It was in two eight-line stanzas.

"Boylston," by Lowell Mason, first appeared in *The Choir,* 1832, set to

> Our days are as the grass.

It was sometimes written with a second ending:

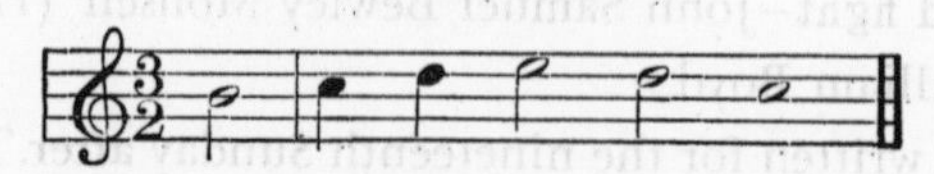

**288—Hark, the voice of Jesus calling—Daniel March**

**Ellesdie** (261)—Wolfgang Amadeus Mozart (?)
Arranged by Hubert Platt Main (261)

The hymn was first published in *The Hymnal of the Methodist Episcopal*

*Church,* 1878. On October 18, 1868, Dr. Daniel March, scheduled to preach for the Christian Association of Philadelphia, at a late hour found one of the hymns selected was not suited to his text,

Here am I; send me,

from Isaiah 6. 8. Hurriedly he wrote this hymn, which was sung from manuscript. Its first line was,

Hark! the voice of Jesus crying.

The "dangling modifier" (gladly) has been made the first word of line 5, stanza 3, instead of the last one. Originally in four stanzas, the three here used are 1, 2, and 4. Doctor March never became reconciled to the changes made in his lines.

Daniel March, D.D., a Congregational clergyman educated at Yale, was born July 21, 1816, at Millbury, Massachusetts. He served several Congregational and Presbyterian churches and published some prose works of a religious character, but so far as is known, this is his only hymn. He died March 2, 1909.

**289—O still in accents sweet and strong**—Samuel Longfellow (42)

**Mt. Calvary**—Robert Prescott Stewart

From *Hymns of the Spirit,* entitled,

Behold the Fields are White,

this hymn by Samuel Longfellow is unaltered and entire.

"Mt. Calvary" was written in 1874 by Sir Robert P. Stewart for Dr. J. M. Neale's hymn beginning,

O very God of very God,

a Christmas hymn for children.

Robert Prescott Stewart, Mus. Doc., was born December 16, 1825, at Dublin, Ireland, and died there, March 24, 1894. Because of his objection to acting longer without pay as organist at St. Patrick's Cathedral, Dublin, an arrangement was made whereby he was paid for acting as vicar choral with the understanding that he should continue as organist. He was knighted in 1872, and the same year composed a fantasia on Irish tunes for chorus, orchestra, and organ for the Peace Jubilee held in Boston. A man of broad culture and accomplishment, he was a noted organist, holding the positions of professor of music in Dublin University and musical editor of *The Irish Hymnal,* 1873. Indicative of the breadth of his interests, he was an authority upon bagpipes and was an extensive traveler and lecturer.

**290—Forth in Thy name, O Lord, I go**—Charles Wesley (25)

**Keble** (62)—John Bacchus Dykes (1)

The hymn, taken from *Hymns and Sacred Poems,* 1749, headed,

Before Work,

has been used with the original second and third stanzas omitted and with the second word of the second stanza of this hymn changed from "may" to "will."

**291—It may not be our lot to wield—John Greenleaf Whittier (120)**

**Abends (42)—Herbert Stanley Oakeley (42)**

The hymn is a part of an eight-stanza poem by John G. Whittier, entitled,

Seed-time and Harvest,

written about 1850, and published in the author's *Miscellaneous Poems.* The omitted stanzas, the first three, are:

1 As o'er his furrowed fields which lie
Beneath a coldly-dropping sky,
Yet chill with winter's melted snow,
The husbandman goes forth to sow,

2 Thus, Freedom, on the bitter blast
The ventures of thy seed we cast,
And trust to warmer sun and rain
To swell the germs and fill the grain.

3 Who calls thy glorious service hard?
Who deems it not its own reward?
Who, for its trials, counts it less
A cause for praise and thankfulness?

**292—Go, labor on! spend and be spent—Horatius Bonar (210)**

**Ernan—Lowell Mason (19)**

Of the hymn Doctor Bonar has said, "Written in 1843, and printed at Kelso in a small booklet of three or four hymns," it was intended as a means of encouraging some of his workers in a mission at Leith. The same year it was included in *Songs for the Wilderness,* with the title,

Labour for Christ,

and in 1867 in his *Hymns of Faith and Hope,* as,

The Useful Life.

Its eight stanzas have been used at will by hymnbook compilers, not always to the advantage of the hymn. It was Doctor Bonar's first hymn for adults.

"Ernan" was written by Lowell Mason for *Cantica Laudis,* 1850, one of the books which he published with the assistance of George J. Webb (487). In the Preface occurs a statement to the effect that the users of the book would be relieved from having *L. M.'s* and *G. J. W.'s* staring at them from every page, and would have the opportunity of making the acquaintance of Mozarts and Beethovens, "both old and new." In later books the compilers claimed as their own many of the tunes which appeared earlier unsigned.

**293—Work, for the night is coming—Annie Louise Coghill**

**Work Song—Lowell Mason (19)**

This "work song," written by an eighteen-year-old author, Miss Annie L.

Walker, while she was spending some time in Canada, was first published in 1854 in a Canadian newspaper. It might well have been based on St. John 9. 4: "The night cometh when no man can work." In 1861 this and others of her poems were collected and published at Montreal in a small book called *Leaves from the Backwoods.* After her marriage she continued writing, publishing six novels and, in 1890, her complete poetical collection *Oak and Maple,* in which the approved text of the hymn appears. The text is not sung, however, as she approved it, for the tune which Lowell Mason wrote for it required only five syllables in the last line of each stanza where six had been written. Mrs. Coghill indignantly wrote:

> I am utterly unable to see what advantage there can be in any alteration that has been proposed. I cannot sign, or in any way agree to what I extremely dislike.

This is, nevertheless, another clear instance in which a good tune has given life to a poem.

Annie Louise Coghill, née Walker, was born at Brewood, Staffordshire, England, in 1836; came to Canada, where her brothers were railway engineers, in her girlhood; returned to England about 1863; became a governess, reviewed books, and made her home for a time with her second cousin, Mrs. Margaret Oliphant, novelist and historical writer, whose *Autobiography and Letters* she edited. After her marriage to Harry Coghill, a wealthy merchant, she lived at Coghurst Hall, near Hastings. Her death occurred in 1907 at Bath.

"Work Song," by Lowell Mason, appeared in *The Song Garden,* 1864, Second Book, which the Preface says was one of "a series of music books for schools and families progressively arranged."

## Integrity

**294—Father in heaven, who lovest all**—Rudyard Kipling

**Germany** (260)—William Gardiner's Sacred Melodies (28)

These words are from Rudyard Kipling's *Puck of Pook's Hill,* 1906. Written as a patriotic song for English boys, it is quite as appropriate for adults, not only of England but of all other countries as well.

Rudyard Kipling, English poet, was born at Bombay, India, December 30, 1865. After his education at the United Services College, Westward Ho, North Devonshire, England, he was for a time assistant editor of the *Civil and Military Gazette,* and *The Pioneer,* in India, where he first began publishing the stories which made him famous. Recipient of honorary degrees from educational institutions in all parts of the world; winner of the Nobel Prize for Literature in 1907; sometime rector of the University of St. Andrew's; the author of novels, short stories, histories, war books, and many miscellaneous works in addition to his poetical works, he became one of the foremost and best-known writers of modern times. James Moffatt has said he was "a singer of the faith that has made Britain great." He died January 18, 1936, at London, while stopping, because of illness, on his way to southern France for the winter.

**295—Lord, as we Thy Name profess**—Edwin Pond Parker

**Savannah**—John Wesley's Foundery Collection

This hymn was written by the Rev. Edwin P. Parker in 1890.

Edwin Pond Parker, Congregational minister, probably best known for having arranged the tune "Mercy" (47), was born January 13, 1836, at Castine, Maine. After graduating from Bowdoin College and Bangor Theological Seminary he was ordained a minister of the Congregational Church and for half a century was located at Center Church, Hartford, Connecticut. Aside from his parish duties his greatest interest was in hymnology, and he was an able editor of hymnbooks. He died at Hartford, May 28, 1925.

"Savannah," or "Herrnhut," is from the *"Foundery" Collection,* 1742, compiled by John Wesley, but its source is not known. The names associated with it would lead to the conjecture that it was of German origin and that John Wesley may have heard it sung by the Moravians.

*A Collection of Tunes, set to Music, as they are commonly sung at the Foundery* should interest all Methodists, for it was the first collection of tunes provided for them. Modern congregational hymn singing may be said to date from the beginnings of the Wesleyan Revival, about 1740, when the Wesleys issued their book of *Hymns and Sacred Poems* of that year. Taking his cue from Martin Luther, John Wesley realized the necessity of singing to the success of religious work. Of the few old psalm tunes familiar to the people, most were looked upon with the disdain that goes with overfamiliarity. New tunes John Wesley must have and, always alert, he lost no time in providing them. Possibly because of haste, possibly because of economy, when his famous *"Foundery" Collection* came from the press in 1742, it proved to be one of the worst of all examples of the printers' art. Even worse than its printing was the number of errors found in the music and the impossible passages written for the voices to sing. One glaring instance, quoted by Lightwood (453), was that of "Jericho Tune," taken from one of Handel's operas, *Richard I,* where the first-violin part of the orchestral score had been copied for the soprano part. Set to "Commit thou all thy griefs," the part ran:

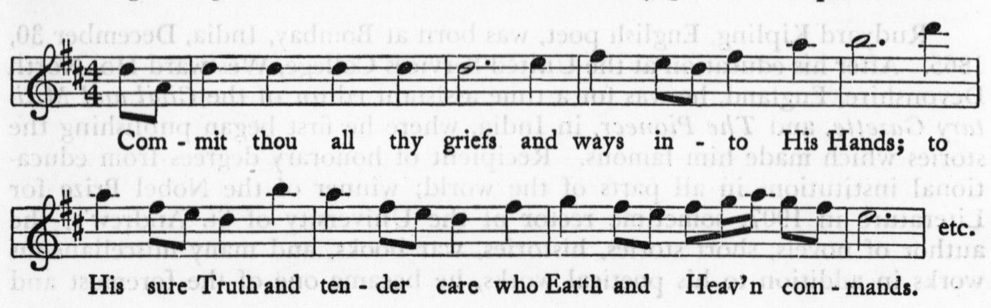
Com - mit thou all thy griefs and ways in - to His Hands; to
His sure Truth and ten - der care who Earth and Heav'n com - mands.
etc.

Only one edition of the book was printed, and it is now very scarce. With all of its faults, however, it has a very great historical interest for Methodists.

The book took its name from the "Foundery," an old building purchased by John Wesley in 1739, which he restored and made into the first Methodist meetinghouse in London. It was used by the British government as a plant for the casting of cannon until 1716, when, during the recasting of some of the guns captured by the Duke of Marlborough, there occurred an explosion which blew the top off the building and killed several of the workmen. The government then abandoned it, and it was little less than a ruin when it was secured by John Wesley.

**296—Go forth to life, O child of earth**—Samuel Longfellow (42)

**Rhys**—Rhys Thomas

The hymn is taken from Samuel Longfellow's *Hymns of the Spirit,* 1864, prepared in collaboration with Samuel Johnson. This was the book which endeavored to exclude all hymns "which attributed a peculiar quality and special authority to Christianity, and recognized a supernatural element in the personality of Jesus."

"Rhys" was selected for this hymn from manuscripts of tunes submitted for this edition of *The Methodist Hymnal.*

Rhys Thomas was born in Wales, February 21, 1867, and died in London, October 16, 1932. He was educated at Cardiff, Wales, and at London, and while still a comparatively young man, went to Winnipeg, Canada, where for twenty-eight years he was active in the musical life of that city and as an adjudicator at Canadian musical festivals. Prominent as a chorus conductor, choirmaster, and baritone soloist at Knox Church in Winnipeg, he composed many anthems, hymn tunes, and part songs. From 1925 he made his home in London.

**297—Draw Thou my soul, O Christ**—Lucy Larcom

**St. Edmund**—Arthur Seymour Sullivan (15)

The hymn is taken from Miss Larcom's *At the Beautiful Gate,* 1892, and began appearing in hymnals in the early 1900's.

Lucy Larcom was born at Beverly Farms, Massachusetts, March 5, either 1824 or 1826, and when a girl began working in a mill in Lowell, where her poetry, published in the *Lowell Offering,* attracted the attention of John Greenleaf Whittier, who became interested in her and was her lifelong friend. The *Lowell Offering,* the first magazine ever written exclusively by women, was the organ of the "Improvement Circle," the first factory-women's club. Working in a factory in Lowell in the early part of the nineteenth century was looked upon as a privilege, for the "Lowell factory system" was such that it attracted girls from such good families that a position in the mills there was somewhat of a social asset. Such were the privileges afforded the workers that the type of girl who now helps herself through college then went to Lowell for her education. Miss Larcom went to Illinois when about twenty years of age and began teaching in a rural school at Looking Glass. Always eager to improve herself intellectually, she was able to attend Monticello Seminary at Alton, Illinois, by doing some teaching of elementary subjects. Returning to New England after her graduation, she was successful as a teacher in advanced schools, and was able for a time to attend Wheaton Seminary at Norton, Massachusetts. When her health failed, she engaged in literary work, editing several books of poetry with John G. Whittier, and issuing others of her own. "Hannah Binding Shoes," frequently referred to as "Poor Lone Hannah," is perhaps her best-known single poem. She died on April 17, 1893.

"St. Edmund," or "Fatherland," by Sir Arthur Sullivan, was first published in *The Hymnary,* 1872, as the setting for T. R. Taylor's hymn beginning,

We are but strangers here,
Heaven is our home.

**298—Courage, brother, do not stumble**—Norman Macleod

**Courage, Brother**—Arthur Seymour Sullivan (15)

One of the most forcible hymns in the English language, this, by Norman Macleod, appeared in January, 1857, in *The Edinburgh Christian Magazine,* of which he was the editor for some years.

Norman Macleod, D.D., born at Campbelton, Argyleshire, Scotland, June 3, 1812, was a recognized leader of the Established Church in Scotland and was made Moderator of its General Assembly in 1869. Educated at the Universities of Edinburgh and Glasgow, and in Germany, he served parishes in Ayreshire and Glasgow; became one of the Queen's chaplains; wrote much that was popular, and from 1860 was editor of *Good Words.* He was also for some time editor of *The Edinburgh Christian Magazine,* and was a member of the General Assembly's hymnal committee. His death occurred at Glasgow, June 16, 1872.

"Courage, Brother," was written for this hymn by Sir Arthur Sullivan, in 1872. It was first published in the magazine, *Good Words.*

**299—I want a principle within**—Charles Wesley (25)

**Gerald**—Louis Spohr

John Wesley selected just one half of the original of this hymn for his large *Collection* of 1780, using five four-line stanzas, though when first printed in *Hymns and Sacred Poems,* 1749, with the title,

For a tender conscience,

each stanza consisted of eight lines. This hymn has been improved by several changes which have been made in its wording. Dean Tillett (117) thinks "it is well for the young Christian to commit this hymn to memory." Dr. Benjamin Gregory, English clergyman, in recalling certain youthful difficulties, says he had the notion that

> in case of any clouding of conscience, I must receive from heaven a direct and indubitable manifestation, or as it were, *notification* of my acceptance; not, perhaps, so vivid as at first, but yet assuring and enlivening. I had not yet learnt the practical theology of the lines—
>
> O may the least omission pain
> My well-instructed soul,
> And *drive me to the blood again*
> *That makes the wounded whole!*
>
> I had not learnt the art or acquired the habit of a prompt recurrence to, and a perfect rest in, the atonement and advocacy of our blessed Saviour. How truly Luther says, "He is a good (practical) theologian who has a firm hold on this truth"!

"Gerald" is the name given to this tune which is said to have been an adaptation of a number from Louis Spohr's oratorio, *Calvary*. Written in 1834, while its composer was mourning for his wife, who died that year, the oratorio was first performed at Cassel on Good Friday, 1835. Though called "Spohr" in *The Methodist Hymnal* of 1905, its name was changed for this edition because the tune called "Simpson" in the 1905 book is commonly known in America as "Spohr"; and in the last edition that name has been restored to it. There has been confusion as to the accepted names and sources of two of Spohr's tunes: this one and that used at Nos. 363 and 366.

Louis Spohr, born at Brunswick, Prussia, April 5, 1784, a man of herculean stature, was one of the greatest violinists of all time. A prodigy in music, he undertook his first concert tour when he was but fourteen years of age, became recognized as a great virtuoso, a composer of ability, and a conductor of note, and won an immense popularity in England, which country he visited six times. He was so extremely self-centered and such a confirmed stylist that he had difficulty in sensing good work in others. His severe criticism of Beethoven is explainable only on these grounds. Wagner seems to have been the only one of the great composers over whom he could become enthusiastic. Even though he wrote much in other fields his works for violin will probably be remembered longest. He died at Cassel, October 22, 1859.

**300—Be strong! We are not here to play**—Maltbie Davenport Babcock (72)

**Fortitude**—David Stanley Smith

Bishop Warren spoke of this as a "rugged hymn, knotted like the muscles of a torso of Hercules." It is taken from *Thoughts for Everyday Living,* edited by its author's widow shortly after his death in 1901.

"Fortitude" was written by David Stanley Smith in 1904 for this hymn, at the request of Dean Peter C. Lutkin (132) for use in *The Methodist Hymnal* of 1905, Dean Lutkin being one of its musical editors.

David Stanley Smith, Mus. Doc., one of America's best-known composers, was born at Toledo, Ohio, July 6, 1877; educated at Yale and in Germany; conductor of the New Haven Symphony Orchestra; and, since 1925, Battel Professor of Music in Yale. Perhaps his best-known work is his *Prince Hal* overture.

## Prayer and Guidance

**301—Guide me, O Thou great Jehovah**—From the Welsh
Peter Williams, stanza 1
William Williams, stanzas 2, 3

**Cwm Rhondda** (165)—Welsh hymn melody
John Hughes (165)

William Williams, known as "the sweet singer of Wales," was born at Cefn-y-coed, Wales, February 11, 1717, and died at Pantecelyn, near Llandovey, January 11, 1791. Educated in medicine, he became a deacon in the Established Church of England, but did not take Holy Orders for the reason that he was the subject of discipline many times for refusing to confine his preaching to the parish assigned to him. Becoming a Calvinistic Methodist, he went about Wales evangelistically preaching with great success for forty-five years, during each of which he averaged 2,230 miles. He was a friend of Daniel Rowland, of George Whitefield, and of Lady Huntingdon. It was when Williams was challenged to write better hymns than were then possessed by the Calvinistic Methodists that he wrote this one. It first appeared in a book of hymns which he issued at Bristol, in 1744, with the title *Alleluia*. Dr. Elvet Lewis said, "What Paul Gerhardt has been to Germany, what Isaac Watts has been to England, that and more has William Williams, of Pantecelyn, been to Wales."

While Peter Williams was a student at Carmarthen College, his tutor warned the young men not to go to hear "Whitefield, that fanatical preacher"; but they went, and Peter Williams was converted. He it was who added one stanza of his own composition to his English translation of three stanzas of William Williams's hymn, when he published it in his *Hymns on Various Subjects*, 1771. William Williams then adopted this English hymn; and, in its new form, doubtless early in 1772, issued it in a leaflet with this heading:

A Favorite Hymn
Sung by
Lady Huntingdon's young Collegians.
Printed by the desire of many Christian friends.
Lord, give it Thy blessing!

It then went into Lady Huntingdon's *Collection* of 1772.

Richard Knill, the missionary and missionary advocate who gave Charles H. Spurgeon sixpence to learn "God moves in a mysterious way," and who predicted that Spurgeon would grow into a great preacher, had this hymn constantly on his lips when he lay dying. He often asked his daughter to sing it, saying, "I cannot sing," and she did so, using the tune "Greenville" (187).

But even though her father could not sing, he always attempted the last stanza, beginning,

When I tread the verge of Jordan,
Bid my anxious fears subside.

Peter Williams (1722-1796) was one of the most prominent figures in the Methodist Revival in Wales. He occupies no place as a writer of hymns, his only contribution being the one stanza noted here, and not all hymnodists are in agreement as to his authorship of that.

**302—Sweet hour of prayer**—William W. Walford (?)

**Sweet Hour**—William Batchelder Bradbury (133)

For this hymn are used the first three stanzas of four by William W. Walford, a blind minister who lived in England the first part of the last century. Nothing more is known of him except that he dictated the words to Thomas Salmon, an English Congregational minister, who, in turn, sent them to the editor of the *New York Observer,* who printed them in that journal on September 13, 1845. It has erroneously been ascribed to Fanny Crosby by Doctor Julian and others.

"Sweet Hour," also called "Consolation," and "Walford," was said by W. B. Bradbury, its composer, in his *Anthem Book,* 1860, to have been taken from *Musical Tracts.*

**303—Prayer is the soul's sincere desire**—James Montgomery (39)

**Campmeeting**—Early American melody

The hymn was written upon the request of the Rev. E. Bickersteth in 1818, and was published the same year with three other prayer hymns in a pamphlet for use in Non-conformist Sunday schools near Sheffield, England. The next year it appeared in Bickersteth's *Treatise on Prayer.* It was headed,

What is Prayer

when included in *The Christian Psalmist,* 1825, and was included in Montgomery's *Original Hymns,* 1853. It has been omitted from several important books presumably because it is merely a series of statements concerning prayer. It is a great hymn, however, which Doctor Dearmer (79) says, "teaches the principles and practice of prayer with truth and power." James Montgomery testified that he received more inquiries concerning the worth of this hymn than of any other that he wrote—some four hundred. The night before he died he conducted family prayers with unusual devotion and spirit. In the morning he was found unconscious on the floor of his room, dying the same afternoon without regaining consciousness. He entered heaven with prayer—it was his last voice:

Prayer is the Christian's vital breath,
The Christian's native air,
His watchword at the gates of death;
He enters heaven with prayer.

The second line of the first stanza was changed slightly for this book in order to afford a better singing accent.

"Campmeeting" was an old camp-meeting chorus of the early days, usually sung to the words,

> I will believe, I do believe
> That Jesus died for me, etc.,

or, earlier,

> I do believe, I now believe,
> I can hold out no more;
> I sink by dying love compelled,
> And own Thee conqueror.

**304—Heavenly Father, bless me now**—Alexander Clark

**Seymour** (200)—Carl Maria von Weber (200)

This hymn was written in 1872 and published the same year in *The Voice of Praise.* Doctor Clark, its author, was a member of the Committee which prepared this book for the use of the Methodist Protestant Church.

Alexander Clark, D.D., was born in Jefferson County, Ohio, March 10, 1834. Educated for the most part under the eye and care of his father, a classical scholar, he commenced teaching at the age of seventeen, and also early embarked in journalism as the editor and publisher of the *School Visitor,* afterward the *Schoolday Magazine,* which after an existence of nearly twenty years was merged with *St. Nicholas.* Later he was the editor of the *Methodist Recorder* (Protestant), official organ of his Church, Pittsburgh, and of some Sunday-school papers. He preached and lectured extensively, wrote for other magazines, and found time to prepare several books, including a small volume of poems. As a preacher, lecturer, author, and editor, Doctor Clark gained fame outside the confines of his own Church.

While on a lecture tour in Georgia, he became ill at Atlanta and was taken by Governor Colquitt from his hotel to the Executive Mansion, where, after three weeks of suffering, he died, July 6, 1879.

**305—O gracious Father of mankind**—Henry Hallam Tweedy (182)

**St. Michel's** (118)—From W. Gawler's Hymns and Psalms (118)

The author furnishes the following interesting story of the writing of this excellent hymn:

> "O gracious Father of mankind" was written in 1925, and so far as I know first appeared in *Christian Song,* the hymnal edited by Dr. Louis F. Benson, which was published in 1926. The way in which I came to write it is this: I had set my class in Public Worship the task of studying the hymns in a certain hymnal, criticising the religious values as well as the character of the lyric poetry. I must confess that we dealt with some of the material rather vigorously, coming to the conclusion that one of the great needs of the modern church was some new hymns. In our study of Isaac Watts we had told the old story of the beginnings of his labors—his criticism of the hymns of his church and the challenge of its officers to give them something better. That seemed to be much fairer and more constructive than mere fault-finding, and it occurred to me that there would be no harm in trying it. I had never written a hymn, though I had dabbled more or less in what purported

to be poetry. At that time *The Homiletic Review* offered a prize for a new hymn. Writing a hymn for a prize did not especially appeal to me. It would, however, test my product and be an interesting experiment. It falls to my lot to speak almost every Sunday in some school or college; and on one of my journeys I occupied the time in writing this hymn. When I learned through a letter of Edwin Markham, who I believe was the chairman of the committee, that I had been awarded the prize, I confess to a generous amount of astonishment. I chose prayer as my theme because I found some of the older hymns on that theme unsatisfactory.

**306—My God, my Father, while I stray—Charlotte Elliott (198)**

**Hanford—Arthur Seymour Sullivan (15)**

This hymn, which Bishop Bickersteth thought "most beautiful," first appeared in Miss Elliott's *Invalid's Hymn Book,* 1834, entitled,

Thy Will be Done,

and, later, with some alterations, in *Hours of Sorrow Cheered and Comforted; or Thoughts in Verse,* 1836. Slight changes only have been made from Miss Elliott's revision, but the original fifth stanza has been omitted for obvious reasons:

Should pining sickness melt away
My life in premature decay,
My Father, still I strive to say,
"Thy will be done!"

"Hanford" was written by Sir Arthur Sullivan for another of Miss Elliott's hymns,

Jesus, my Saviour, look on me,

and appeared in *Church Hymns,* 1872, a book sponsored by the Society for the Promotion of Christian Knowledge. For additional comment on the tune "Hanford," see the letter quoted in the discussion of No. 280.

**307—Lord of our life, God whom we fear—Samuel Francis Smith (489)**

**Louvan—Virgil Corydon Taylor**

A search through many of the hymnals published since 1892, the date of the first printing of this hymn, has failed to discover its inclusion in any other than *The Methodist Hymnal.* It was written by Doctor Smith for *Historic Hymnists,* Dr. Charles S. Nutter's *Portrait Gallery of Great Hymn Writers,* in November, 1891, and was published in that book in 1893. The last stanza, as written by Doctor Smith, was:

We love Thy name, we heed Thy rod,
Thy word, our law; our guide, Thy nod;
We wait Thy will, on Thee we call,
Our light, our life, our God, our all.

As Dr. Samuel Francis Smith is so much better known for having written our National Hymn, his short biographical notice will be found at No. 489.

"Louvan" was first published in *The Sacred Minstrel,* 1846, and has held its own in the regard of compilers of hymnbooks, appearing in the latest ones, although generally used with

Lord of all being, throned afar,

by Oliver Wendell Holmes (62). It first appeared, however, set to the hymn of Thomas Moore:

There's nothing bright above, below.

"Louvan" is the only tune of its composer now in use.

Virgil Corydon Taylor, born at Barkhamsted, Connecticut, April 2, 1817, was an American musician, for a time organist at Hartford, Connecticut, then at Poughkeepsie, Brooklyn, and Niagara Falls, New York; and at Des Moines, Iowa, where he died, January 30, 1891. He issued a number of songbooks of the character common to the middle of the nineteenth century, one of which was the well-known *Sacred Minstrel.*

**308—Jesus, kneel beside me—Allen Eastman Cross**
**Eudoxia—Sabine Baring-Gould (53)**

This hymn, entitled

The Great Companion,

was written in 1907, the author writes:

> in a time of extreme personal worry and strain. I felt the ineffectualness of my prayer life, and the ineffectiveness of workaday service. The Son of man seemed to possess all that I lacked. I was drawn to him by sheer difference, as well as by far-off kinship. I turned to him as to a superlative companion, and spoke out of my need: "Jesus, kneel beside me, teach me how to pray." Later a hymn was asked for by a society of workers in the Old South Church in Boston. I gave them the verses, calling it by the above title. It was sung by them to the music of "Merrial," by Barnby, and has since been set to several lovely tunes.

Allen Eastman Cross was born at Manchester, New Hampshire, December 30, 1864; his preparatory school was Phillips-Andover; his college was Amherst; and at Andover Seminary he prepared for the Congregational ministry. He chose this "calling" "in the last year of college life, with the simplest and most audacious motive, to help God to help people." From his initial activity as minister with the building of a little church at Cliftondale, Massachusetts, he went on to Springfield Park Church, and to the Old South Church in Boston as associate pastor from 1901 to 1911, under the influence of that challenging and dynamic personality, Dr. George A. Gordon. In 1911 and 1912 he went round the world, and

> by visiting our mission stations, received the impulse and found the reality of our great missionaries. I was at Milford, Massachusetts, in the most loyal and grateful pastorate of my life for eleven years. Then I came back to my old home in Manchester, New Hampshire, to give me more freedom for composition and self-expression. When I gave up the ministry of the pulpit, to give myself to the ministry of writing, I tried to recreate my old compositions, that still had sparks of life, and to compose living poems, and hymns.

The Rev. Mr. Cross has published a book of verse called *Pass on the Torch,* issued in 1929. The cordial welcome accorded his first book encouraged him to publish another in 1936.

> I have a place of "retreat," just outside my home. It looks like a cabin on a high hill, but to me "Pinecrest" is both a place of meditation and a mystic shrine.

"Eudoxia" was written by Sabine Baring-Gould as a setting for his own evening hymn,

Now the day is over,

and they were together included in the Appendix to *Hymns Ancient and Modern,* 1868. It was a reminiscence of a German melody which the composer had heard in his youth, but which he was unable to identify. It still remains unknown.

**309—Talk with us, Lord, Thyself reveal—Charles Wesley (25)**
**Soho—Joseph Barnby (31)**

In the first line of the second stanza of this hymn Charles Wesley, doubtless unconsciously, quoted from John Milton's *Paradise Lost,* where Eve, speaking to Adam, says:

With thee conversing I forget all time.
All seasons and their change; all please alike.

As appearing in *Hymns and Sacred Poems,* 1740, the singular number occurs in the first two stanzas. The present version of the hymn, headed,

On a Journey

is exactly as John Wesley changed it for his *Collection* of 1780. The first stanza of the original, omitted here, was:

Saviour, who ready art to hear,
(Readier than I to pray,)
Answer my scarcely utter'd prayer,
And meet me on the way.

"Soho," or "Springtide Hour," was written by Sir Joseph Barnby for Dr. J. S. B. Monsell's children's hymn:

The springtide hour
Brings leaf and flower,
With songs of life and love;
And many a lay
Wears out the day
In many a leafy grove,

for which it was a much more appropriate setting than for this hymn. It first appeared in *The Methodist Sunday School Hymn and Tune Book,* London, while Sir Joseph was organist at St. Anne's, Soho.

**310—Blessed Jesus, at Thy word—Tobias Clausnitzer**
**Translated by Catherine Winkworth (7)**
**Liebster Jesu, wir sind hier—Johann Rudolph Ahle**

This is one of the many translations of Tobias Clausnitzer's hymn beginning,

Liebster Jesu, wir sind hier, Dich und Dein Wort anzuhören,

and was first published in *Altdorffisches Gesang-Büchlein,* 1663, to be used on

Sundays before the sermon. It was included, with the author's name, in the *Nürnberg Gesangbuch,* 1676. The translation, by Miss Winkworth, is from her *Lyra Germanica,* Second Series, 1858, unaltered and entire.

Tobias Clausnitzer, born at Thurn, near Annaberg, Saxony, February 5, 1619, was educated in various universities, including Leipzig, from which he graduated in 1643. After his appointment, the following year, to the chaplainship of a Swedish regiment, he preached the thanksgiving sermon celebrating the accession of Queen Christina to the Swedish throne in 1645, and that celebrating the Peace of Westphalia at the field service commanded by General Wrangle at Weiden, January 1, 1649. That same year he was appointed first pastor at the church at Weiden, where he remained until his death, May 7, 1684.

"Liebster Jesu, wir sind hier" is one of many forms of a tune which originally appeared in one of Johann R. Ahle's collections of songs for the various Sundays, published at Mühlhausen in 1664. It was set to the hymn (anonymous):

Ja, er ists, das Heil der Welt,

Later it was transferred to Clausnitzer's hymn, and appeared in many German collections. The form of the melody was considerably altered by Bach, who also harmonized it. Bach's version, a six-line hymn tune, is the "Later form" used at No. 390. It has been further altered for modern use, one form being this, while another, perhaps better known, called "Dessau," may be found at No. 390.

Johann Rudolph Ahle, a well-educated German organist and composer, was born at Mühlhausen, Thuringia, December 24, 1625, and died there, July 8, 1673. Educated at the universities of Göttingen and Erfurt, he was elected cantor at St. Andreas' Church and director of the music school at the latter place in 1646, where he stayed for three years. Being given the post of organist at St. Blasius' Church, Mühlhausen, he became an influential citizen and was made Burgomaster in 1661. While at Erfurt he became known as one of the most radical of the reformers of church music. He wrote more than four hundred "spiritual" songs of one kind or another for the different Sundays, Festivals, and other special days in the Calendar. Living at a time when florid writing was in vogue, he confined himself to the simple chorale style. Many of his songs are still popular in Protestant churches in Thuringia, but variants of "Liebster Jesu, wir sind hier," are all that have survived in England or America.

**311—Come, O Thou Traveler unknown—Charles Wesley (25)**
**Candler—Scottish traditional melody**
**From The Hesperian Harp**

This masterpiece of devotional poetry is from *Hymns and Sacred Poems,* 1742, where it had the title,

Wrestling Jacob.

It was founded on Genesis 32. 24-26: "And Jacob was left alone; and there wrestled a man with him until the breaking of the day. And when he saw that he prevailed not against him, he touched the hollow of his thigh; and the hollow of Jacob's thigh was out of joint, as he wrestled with him. And he said, Let me go, for the day breaketh. And he said, I will not let thee go, except thou bless me." This was one of Charles Wesley's favorite sermon subjects. In his *Journal* for Sunday, May 24, 1741, he wrote, after preaching in Kingswood:

> I preached on Jacob wrestling for the blessing. Many then, I believe, took hold on His strength, and will not let Him go, till He bless them, and tell them His name.

Charles Wesley has made mention of six other similar occasions when he used this theme.

One who was present at the service held by John Wesley at Bolton a fortnight after his brother Charles's death, has given this report of it:

> The venerable man, himself eighty-five years of age, commenced the service in the usual way, with singing and prayer; for the second hymn he selected "Wrestling Jacob," and gave out the first verse with peculiar emphasis. When he came to the words,
>
> "My company before is gone,
> And I am left alone with Thee,"
>
> his emotion became uncontrollable, and he burst right out into a flood of tears, and sat down in the pulpit, covering his face with both hands. The effect upon the congregation was such as might be expected—the people ceased to sing, and, in many parts of the chapel, sat down weeping and sobbing aloud. . . . After a while Mr. Wesley recovered himself, arose, and gave out the lines again; and then there was such singing as I never heard before; it seemed as if the sound would lift the roof off the building.

When John Wesley presented the obituary of his brother to the Conference of 1788, he said:

> His least praise was his talent for poetry, although Doctor Watts did not scruple to say that that single poem, "Wrestling Jacob," was worth all the verses he himself had written.

John Kirk praises it:

> The dramatic form, so singular in hymnic composition, shadowing forth the action of the conversation; the great force of its thoroughly English expression; the complete finish and rhythm of its verse; its straightforward ease without any straining at elegance; and the minuteness and general beauty of its application of the narrative, have won the commendation of all competent critics.

James Montgomery, in *The Christian Psalmist,* says:

> Among Charles Wesley's highest achievements may be recorded "Come, O thou Traveler unknown," in which, with consummate art he has carried on the action

of a lyric drama: every turn in the conflict with the mysterious Being against whom he wrestles all night being marked with precision by the varying language of the speaker, accompanied by intense, increasing interest, till the rapturous moment of discovery when he prevails. . . .

Dean Arthur P. Stanley referred to it in Ward's *English Poets* as being not only a hymn, but a philosophical poem filled with depth and pathos. Because of its worth, and, also, because of the inaccessibility of much of the poem, it here is given entire:

Come, O thou Traveler unknown,
Whom still I hold, but cannot see,
My company before is gone,
And I am left alone with Thee;
With Thee all night I mean to stay,
And wrestle till the break of day.

I need not tell Thee who I am,
My misery or sin declare,
Thyself has called me by my name,
Look on Thy hands and read it there;
But who, I ask Thee, who art Thou?
Tell me Thy name, and tell me now.

In vain Thou strugglest to get free,
I never will unloose my hold;
Art Thou the Man that died for me?
The secret of Thy love unfold;
Wrestling, I will not let Thee go
Till I Thy name, Thy nature know.

Wilt Thou not yet to me reveal
Thy new unutterable name?
Tell me, I still beseech Thee, tell;
To know it now resolved I am;
Wrestling, I will not let Thee go
Till I Thy name, Thy nature know.

'Tis all in vain to hold Thy tongue,
Or touch the hollow of my thigh;
Though every sinew be unstrung,
Out of my arms Thou shalt not fly;
Wrestling, I will not let Thee go
Till I Thy name, Thy nature know.

What though my shrinking flesh complain,
And murmur to contend so long,
I rise superior to my pain,
When I am weak then I am strong;
And when my all of strength shall fail,
I shall with the God-man prevail.

My strength is gone, my nature dies,
I sink beneath Thy weighty hand,
Faint to revive, and fall to rise;
I fall, and yet by faith I stand—
I stand, and will not let Thee go
Till I Thy name, Thy nature know.

Yield to me now, for I am weak,
But confident in self-despair;
Speak to my heart, in blessings speak,
Be conquer'd by my instant prayer:
Speak, or Thou never hence shalt move,
And tell me if Thy name is Love?

'Tis Love! 'tis Love! Thou diedst for me;
I hear Thy whisper in my heart;
The morning breaks, the shadows flee,
Pure Universal Love Thou art;
To me, to all Thy bowels move—
Thy nature and Thy name is Love.

My prayer hath power with God; the grace
Unspeakable I now receive;
Through faith I see Thee face to face—
I see Thee face to face and live;
In vain I have not wept and strove;
Thy nature and Thy name is Love.

I know Thee, Saviour, who Thou art—
Jesus, the feeble sinner's Friend;
Nor wilt Thou with the night depart,
But stay and love me to the end;
Thy mercies never shall remove—
Thy nature and Thy name is Love.

The Sun of Righteousness on me
Hath rose with healing in His wings;
Wither'd my nature's strength, from Thee
My soul its life and succour brings;
My help is all laid up above—
Thy nature and Thy name is Love.

Contented now upon my thigh
I halt, till life's short journey end;
All helplessness, all weakness, I
On Thee alone for strength depend;
Nor have I power from Thee to move—
Thy nature and Thy name is Love.

Lame as I am, I take the prey,
Hell, earth, and sin with ease o'ercome;
I leap for joy, pursue my way,
And as a bounding hart fly home,
Through all eternity to prove
Thy nature and Thy name is Love.

"Candler" is an adaptation of the old Scottish tune commonly known as "Bonnie Doon." Robert Burns, writing to a friend in 1794, said, among other things:

There is an air called "The Caledonian Hunt's delight," to which I wrote a song that you will find in Johnson. "Ye Banks and Braes o' bonnie Doon." . . . Do you know the history of the air? It is curious enough. A good many years ago Mr. James Miller . . . was in company with our friend Clarke; and talking of Scottish music, Miller expressed an ardent desire to be able to compose a Scots air. Mr. Clarke, probably by way of joke, told him to keep to the black keys of the harpsichord, and preserve some kind of rhythm, and he would infallibly compose a Scots' air. Certain it is that in a few days Mr. Miller produced the rudiments of an air, which Mr. Clarke, with some touches and corrections fashioned into the tune in question. . . . Now, to show you how difficult it is to trace the origin of airs, I have heard it repeatedly asserted that this was an Irish air; nay, I have met with an Irish gentleman who affirmed that he had heard it in Ireland among the old women, while, on the other hand, a countess informed me that the first person who introduced the air into this country was a baronet's lady of her acquaintance, who took down the notes from an itinerant piper in the Isle of Man. How difficult then to ascertain the truth respecting our poesy and music!

The setting used here was taken from *The Hesperian Harp*, of 1847, one of the best songbooks among rural singers of the South in the period preceding the Civil War. It was compiled by one George Hauser, of Georgia, a preacher, teacher, editor, doctor, singer, composer of hymn tunes, who, it is said, worked for eleven years on his book before its publication.

**312—Come, ye disconsolate**—Thomas Moore
Altered by Thomas Hastings (204)

**Consolation** (Webbe)—Arranged from Samuel Webbe (35)

A hymn of three stanzas entitled,

Relief in Prayer

appeared in Thomas Moore's *Sacred Songs*, 1816, which began,

Come, ye disconsolate, where'er you languish,
Come, at God's altar kneel,

which Thomas Hastings revised and used in his *Spiritual Songs for Social Worship*, issued with Lowell Mason (19) in 1832. He substituted his own stanza 3 for Moore's, which was:

Go, ask the infidel what boon he brings us,
What charm for aching hearts he can reveal,
Sweet as that heavenly promise Hope sings us—
Earth hath no sorrow that God cannot heal.

Thomas Moore, born in Dublin, Ireland, May 28, 1779, was educated at Trinity College, Dublin; studied law; held a government position in Bermuda for some time; and died at Sloperton, Wiltshire, February 26, 1852. Although the great literary merit of his writings gives distinction to the thirty-two hymns he wrote and published as *Sacred Songs* in 1816, Thomas Moore cannot be counted among the great in the family of writers of sacred verse.

"Consolation" (Webbe) is an alteration of a tune by Samuel Webbe, published in *A Collection of Motetts* in 1792. In the earlier days of its life it was sung as a solo with the last two lines of the hymn in two, three, or four parts, but now it is in the conventional four parts throughout. It is also known as "Alma" or "Alma Redemptoris."

**313—Dear Shepherd of Thy people, hear**—John Newton (27)

**Somerset**—William Henry Hewlett

Written by John Newton in 1769 and published in *Olney Hymns* just ten years later, stanzas 2, 4, 6, and 5 of the original seven are used for this hymn. The first line of the fourth stanza of this selection was originally written,

The feeling heart, the melting eye.

In *Olney Hymns* it was given the title,

On opening a Place for Social Prayer,

and its first stanza was:

O Lord, our languid souls inspire,
For here, we trust, Thou art!
Send down a coal of heavenly fire
To warm each waiting heart.

When John Newton and William Cowper realized their prayer meetings were attracting so many persons that it would be necessary to use the large room of the Great House at Olney each wrote a hymn for the first meeting. This was Newton's contribution.

"Somerset" was written for this hymn by William H. Hewlett for *The Methodist Hymn Book* of Canada.

William Henry Hewlett, Mus. Doc., born at Bath, Somerset, England, January 16, 1873, came to Canada with his parents in 1884. A student in music at Toronto, Berlin, and London, he became Bachelor of Music, Trinity University, Toronto, and in 1936 was made Doctor of Music *honoris causa* by the University of Toronto. Organist at various churches in Toronto and London, Ontario, he was for more than twenty-five years at Centenary Church, Hamilton, Ontario, where he was principal of the Hamilton Conservatory of Music and sometime conductor of the Elgar Choir. He died June 13, 1940.

**314—Lord, for tomorrow and its needs**—Sybil F. Partridge

**Vincent**—Horatio Richmond Palmer

For a great many years the authorship of this hymn was attributed to some member of the famous Wilberforce family of England. When, in 1910, a convict in the Kingston, Ontario, Canada, penitentiary claimed to have written it, much interest was aroused in its true source. In an extensive fact-finding investigation made by James Edmund Jones, secretary and convener of the Compilation Committee of the General Synod of Canada, responsible for the *Book of Common Praise* (authorized by the General Synod of Canada, in September, 1905), it was found that this hymn, in its original form, first appeared in *The Messenger of the Sacred Heart of Jesus,* a Roman Catholic monthly publication issued in London, in January, 1880. One page was devoted to

Dates and Topics of Prayer for members of the Apostleship of Prayer in the Holy League of the Sacred Heart of Jesus,

and the lines of this hymn were a part of an eight-stanza four-line poem printed there under the heading,

TODAY
Dignare, Domine. die esto, sine peccato nos custodire.

In 1910 *The Toronto Globe* gave the name of the nun who wrote the poem, but she has expressed the desire to be referred to merely as "a sister of Notre Dame, of the Community of Mount Pleasant, Liverpool." Apparently, its first appearance in America was in *Songs of Rejoicing,* Cincinnati, 1888. It was included, with this tune, "Vincent," in *The Plymouth Hymnal,* edited by Dr. Lyman Abbott, in 1893. It seems not to have come into use in England until 1894, when it appeared in the *Union Mission Hymnal.* Various selections of lines from the poem have been used in different hymnals, some few having been changed slightly in order to make them suitable for Protestant use.

"Vincent" was written for this hymn by Dr. H. R. Palmer for *The Plymouth Hymnal,* 1893.

Horatio Richmond Palmer, Mus. Doc., was born April 26, 1834, in New York state, came from a musical family; was educated at Rushford Academy of Music in New York, of which he became director when only twenty years of age. Later he studied music at Berlin and Florence. Residing in Chicago from 1861 to 1874, he established there the musical magazine, *Concordia,* and published *The Song Queen* and *The Song King,* the sales of which reached enormous proportions. After moving to New York City in 1874, he took charge of the Church Choral Union, which grew in its third year to a membership of more than forty-two hundred. For several years he was associated with Doctor (later Bishop) Vincent as dean of the School of Music at Lake Chautauqua. Both Chicago and Alfred Universities conferred on him the degree of Doctor of Music. Doctor Palmer died November 15, 1907, at his beautiful home at Park Hill-on-Hudson.

## Trust and Assurance

**315—How firm a foundation—"K" in Rippon's Selection, 1787**

First tune: **Adeste Fideles (Portuguese Hymn)**—From John Francis Wade's Cantus Diversi, 1751

Second tune: **Foundation**—Early American melody

This hymn, which has been the subject of much inquiry, was first found in Rippon's *Selection,* 1787, with the signature "K—," and the title,

Exceeding great and precious promises.

It has been ascribed to one "Kirkham" in modern editions of Rippon; to "George Keith," and to an unidentified "Keen." For the latter claim Doctor Julian says there is some basis in the fact that A. Fletcher's *Collection of Hymns* (Baptist), 1822, contains this hymn, credited to "Kn," and extended in his 1835 edition to "Keen." Doctor Fletcher was assisted in the work of compiling his book by Thomas Walker, who as editor of Doctor Rippon's *Tune-Book,* might have known the source of the hymn. Unless further evidence is found, however, the authorship must remain anonymous.

"Adeste Fideles," or "Portuguese Hymn," has also been the subject of a great deal of inquiry and controversy. The earliest printed book in which this tune is found is *An Essay on the Plain Chant,* London, 1782, although it has been found in manuscript form, dated 1751, in the library of Stonyhurst College, Lancashire, England. At that time Stonyhurst was in the possession of a wealthy Roman Catholic family by the name of Sherburn, some member of which had employed an itinerant music copyist to provide a songbook for use in the family chapel. The volume is entitled,

> Cantus Diversi pro Dominicis et Festus per annum.
> Gloria Patri. Post Introitum. Kyrie. Gloria in excelsis. Credo. Sanctus and Agnus Dei.
> Cum Hymnis et Antiphonis ad Elevationem and Benedictionem.
> Et ex praecordiis sonent praeconia.
> Nicolaus King, Ejus Cantus.
> Johannes Franciscus Wade, Scriptor.
> Anno Domini, MDCCLI.

The "Adeste Fideles," tune and hymn (96), is the second from the last selection in the book. Only recently has there been discovered another similar manuscript book in the Henry Watson Musical Library, at Manchester, England, which appears to date from a year earlier than the Stonyhurst volume.

John Francis Wade seems to have occupied at least a part of his time going about the country copying musical manuscripts for wealthy Catholic families. That is all that is known definitely about this famous tune and its copyist.

Two stories about the writing of the "Adeste Fideles" now seem to have been definitely disposed of. One is that the tune was assigned to one of three English musicians named John Reading. The opinion of the late Dr. W. H. Cummings that the John Reading (died 1692), one time organist of Winchester Cathedral, wrote the tune was based upon the conjecture that, as this Reading had written other tunes to Latin words, he might have written this one also. But it has not been possible from this conjecture to assign the composition definitely to any of the three John Readings.

The other story, which has had considerable circulation among American Methodists, is that which attributes the tune's composition to a one-time chapel master in the service of a king of Portugal. In *English Hymns,* 1886, by Dr. S. W. Duffield, there is this account:

> The "Portuguese Hymn" . . . was the composition of Marcas Portugal. He was the chapel master of the king of Portugal and died at Rio Janeiro over fifty years ago. The tune was originally employed as an offertory piece, and Dom João VI, in whose service the composer had a position, came to Brazil in 1808. Marcas Portugal accompanied him thither, and remained when his royal master returned to Europe. When Dom Pedro II, who is the grandson of Dom João, was a little boy, the old composer still led the chapel services, and Doctor Fletcher, in his *Brazil and the Brazilians,* fixes the date of his death in 1834. In the preface to the ninth edition of Doctor Fletcher's work this fact is authoritatively stated, and it is added that Marcas (or Marcos) Portugal wrote several operas as well as much sacred music. These were popular in the early part of the present century, both in Portugal and Italy. The claim, therefore, that Reading (otherwise Redding) was the composer of this celebrated tune, falls to the ground.

The proper name of "Marcas Portugal," commonly referred to as "Il Portogallo," was Marcos Antonio da Fonesca, a Portuguese operatic composer who was born at Lisbon, March 24, 1762, and who died at Rio de Janeiro, February 7, 1830. Like the John Reading story, this claim also "falls to the ground" when it is noted that the "Adeste Fideles" had been in use for at least a dozen years before "Il Portogallo" was born. (See No. 96.)

The manner in which this tune came to be called "Portuguese Hymn" is explained in a paragraph of a biography of Vincent Novello (1781-1861), who for twenty-five years, from 1797, was the organist at the Portuguese Chapel in London:

> The Adeste Fideles, although a composition by an Englishman named John Reading, . . . obtained the name of "The Portuguese Hymn" from its having been heard by the Duke of Leeds at the Portuguese Chapel, who imagined it to be peculiar to the service in Portugal. Being a Director of the Ancient Concerts, his Grace introduced the melody there, and it speedily became popular under the title he had given it.

"Foundation," too, has baffled those interested in tracing hymn tunes to their sources. By some strange circumstance this tune has been said to have been written by Anne Steele (389), the hymn writer. Frank J. Metcalf, in his *Stories of the Hymn Tunes,* 1928, has discovered the probable reason for this error. He says:

> How comes it that it should be ascribed to Anne Steele as its composer? The only person of that name known to hymnologists was a writer of religious verse, and many of her pieces have been introduced into the hymn books of the various denominations. We cannot believe that she ever composed a tune, at least for print. The hymnal of the Methodist Episcopal Church, South, c. 1889, furnishes the probable solution of the problem. Here the tune "Foundation" is set on the lower half of the page, following a hymn by Anne Steele, and her name, on account of the crowding of that page, comes so near the place over the tune where the name of the composer usually stands that someone, who borrowed the tune from this book, wrongfully took also the name of the writer of the upper hymn for the composer of the tune below, and the error has been copied from book to book without question as to the real fact.

The "real fact" is that "Foundation" is an old tune called "Bellevue," which appeared in a pamphlet compilation entitled *The Cluster of Spiritual Songs, Divine Hymns and Sacred Poems,* by the Rev. Jesse Mercer, D.D., and which, by 1817, reached a third edition. Doctor Mercer was a well-known Baptist preacher in Georgia in the early part of the last century, "the churches which he served being in the midst of a dense population, and embracing a considerable amount of intelligence and refinement." The famous *Sacred Harp,* first issued in 1844, has this tune set to

How firm a foundation,

with this credit line:

Mercer's Cluster, p. 411. Z. Chambless.

Who "Z. Chambless" was has not as yet been discovered. This great tune is now finding a deserved place in some of the most carefully edited books, among them *The Harvard Hymnal,* where, called "Convention," with Anne Steele named as its composer, it is used twice. It came into Methodist use through the *Hymn and Tune Book of the Methodist Episcopal Church, South,* 1889, where it is called "How Firm a Foundation." This was shortened to "Foundation" in *The Methodist Hymnal* of 1905. After one has heard a great congregation, thoroughly familiar with this tune, sing it to these words, he should be content to allow "Adeste Fideles" to be used only with the beautiful nativity hymn,

O come, all ye faithful,

and to use "Foundation" only to

How firm a foundation.

**316—I sought the Lord, and afterward I knew—Anonymous**

Peace—George Whitefield Chadwick

It has been suggested that this hymn was written by Jean Ingelow, but the suggestion has not been verified. First publication dates are given as c. 1878 and c. 1904.

"Peace" was written by G. W. Chadwick in 1890, but its first publication date has not been ascertained.

George Whitefield Chadwick, LL.D., who was born at Lowell, Massachusetts, November 13, 1854, began playing the organ when fifteen years of age; and after graduation from the Lawrence High School, took some piano lessons at the Boston Conservatory of Music. At twenty-one he decided to give up work in his father's insurance office at Lawrence and to teach music. By a position at Olivet College, Michigan, he was able to save enough money to spend three years in further study in Europe, and upon his return in 1880, he began teaching privately in Boston. In 1882 he joined the faculty of the New England Conservatory of Music, becoming its director in 1897. He was one of America's foremost teachers, organists, conductors, composers, and conservatory directors. He died at Boston, April 4, 1931.

**317—From every stormy wind that blows—Hugh Stowell**

Retreat—Thomas Hastings (204)

Entitled

Peace at the mercy seat,

this hymn by Canon Stowell first appeared in 1828 in a periodical, *The Winter's Wreath, A Collection of Original Compositions in Prose and Verse,* an illustrated annual published at London from 1828 to 1832. In its rewritten form the text has been included in the author's *Psalms and Hymns,* and in many other hymnals. Originally in six stanzas, 4 and 6 have been omitted, and there are a few minor changes in the wording of those used.

Hugh Stowell, born at Douglas, on the Isle of Man, December 3, 1799, was educated at St. Edmund Hall, Oxford; was ordained in 1823; and held several curacies until 1831, when he was made rector at Christ Church, Salford. Later he became Honorary Canon in Chester Cathedral and Chaplain to the Bishop of Manchester. He was an able and popular preacher, and a writer of note, especially for children. His *Psalms and Hymns, Suited to the Services of the Church of England,* 1831, contained forty-three hymns of his writing. He died at Salford, October 8, 1865.

"Retreat" was written by Thomas Hastings in 1840 and first published in his *Sacred Songs,* 1842. It was written for this hymn.

**318—O Love that wilt not let me go—George Matheson**

**St. Margaret—Albert Lister Peace**

Doctor Matheson wrote this tender hymn on the evening of June 6, 1882. He has written:

> My hymn was composed in the manse of Innellan, . . . I was at that time alone. It was the day of my sister's marriage, and the rest of the family were staying over night in Glasgow. Something had happened to me, which was known only to myself, and which caused me the most severe mental suffering. The hymn was the fruit of that suffering. It was the quickest bit of work I ever did in my life. I had the impression rather of having it dictated to me by some inward voice than of working it out myself. I am quite sure that the whole work was completed in five minutes, and equally sure that it never received at my hands any retouching or correction. The Hymnal Committee of the Church of Scotland desired the change of one word. I had written originally "I climbed the rainbow in the rain." They objected to the word "climb" and I put in "trace."

In another communication he said, "I was suffering from extreme mental distress, and the hymn was the fruit of pain." Just what had happened to cause his "extreme mental distress" he did not divulge, but John Telford, in *The New Methodist Hymn-Book Illustrated,* London, 1934, says it was written "when the lady to whom he had been engaged felt that his blindness prevented their marriage." Dr. Alexander MacMillan, however, has this to say in his *Hymns of the Church,* Toronto, 1935:

> A groundless story has unfortunately been frequently told to the effect that the cause of the suffering to which Doctor Matheson referred was a disappointment in love. There is nothing to support this idea, especially as Doctor Matheson had been blind more than twenty years before he wrote this hymn. Whatever the cause of the mental suffering may have been, it certainly was not because some one "refused to go through life with a blind man."

The hymn was first published in 1883 in *Life and Work,* the Church of Scotland magazine, and passed the next year into *The Scottish Hymnal.*

George Matheson, D.D., son of a wealthy Glasgow, Scotland, merchant, was born in that city, March 27, 1842. The condition of his eyesight had been a matter of concern with his parents from his early boyhood, and while he never became totally blind, he had moments of "shadowy eyesight," throughout his course at the University of Glasgow. After his graduation he was entirely dependent upon others. His devoted sisters learned Hebrew, Greek, and Latin the better to aid him in his studies. An ambitious and ardent student, his affliction seemed only to spur him to further endeavor. A minister of the Church of Scotland, he became a brilliant preacher, an author of distinction, and a scholar of note, delivering the Baird and St. Giles lectures on successive years. During the eighteen years he served the parish at Innellan, the popular seaside resort not far from the mouth of the River Clyde in western Scotland, many families came to the resort, year after year, in order to benefit from his preaching. During all of his busy life he was ever punctilious in his pastoral duties. In making calls he was always accompanied by a sister who lived with him. Going to St. Bernard's Church, Edinburgh, in 1886, he served a membership of nearly two thousand until the last few years of his life, which were spent in literary labors. He died at North Berwick, on the Firth of Forth, August 28, 1906.

"St. Margaret," by Dr. A. L. Peace, was written for Doctor Matheson's hymn in 1884 at Brodick Manse, Arran, a small island west of the Firth of Clyde, western Scotland, upon the request of the editors of *The Scottish Hymnal,* 1885. He said:

> It was composed . . . during the time the music of *The Scottish Hymnal,* of which I was the musical editor, was in preparation. I wrote it at Brodick Manse, where I was on a visit to my old friend, Mr. M'Lean. There was no tune of that particular metre available at that time, so I was requested by the Hymnal Committee to write one especially for Dr. Matheson's hymn. After reading it over carefully, I wrote the music straight off, and may say that the ink of the first note was hardly dry when I had finished the tune.

There has been much controversy over the suitability of this tune for this hymn. Whatever its merits, it will probably continue to be used, for it apparently has those qualities which make it appeal to the imagination of ordinary worshipers, who never give the slightest thought to the likes or dislikes of the critical musician. People love the combination of hymn and tune and few hymnals are found without it. The pragmatic test is usually a good one.

Albert Lister Peace, Mus. Doc., born at Huddersfield, Yorkshire, England, January 26, 1844, was a musical prodigy, giving evidence of the possession of the sense of absolute pitch before his fifth year, and at nine being engaged as organist in the parish church at Holmfirth. Serving other churches in that vicinity until the age of twenty-one, he moved to Glasgow to become organist at Trinity Congregational Church. He advanced to the position of organist at the University, and at Glasgow Cathedral. After graduating as Bachelor at Glasgow University, he took his Doctorate in music at Oxford. His last appointment was as successor to W. T. Best at St. George's Hall, Liverpool, in 1897. A remarkable technician, his reputation as an organist was more than church-wide.

> In church worship his playing was marked by strongly marked time and thunderous pedaling; he would often use the pedals to beat out in semi-staccato style the measure, like the double bass in the orchestra.

One eminent divine stated that when he preached in a church where Doctor Peace was organist, he feared to give out the hymn, "Peace, perfect peace," lest it be taken as a personal compliment by the organist. He died at Liverpool, March 14, 1912.

**319—When by fear my heart is daunted**—Percy Dearmer (79)

**Tantum Ergo**—Melody from Samuel Webbe's (35) Antiphons

This hymn was written by Canon Dearmer for *Songs of Praise,* 1925, because, as he states, the editors of the book wanted another hymn on confidence in God as text for a Welsh tune, "Ardudwy," which they wished to include in that book. When the hymn was carried over into *Songs of Praise, Enlarged Edition,* 1931, the author changed the first word of the last line from "Gaily" to "Bravely."

"Tantum Ergo" is taken from *A Collection of Motetts or Antiphons,* 1792, written by Samuel Webbe for the use of his choir while he was serving as organist at the Sardinian Chapel, London. Lightwood says the tunes were "tuneful, devotional, and easy to sing." In 1792 Webbe issued this *Collection* as well as *A Collection of Masses . . . for the use of Small Choirs.* This tune is taken from the second part of the setting for the "Tantum Ergo"[1] which appears in both works. This form of the tune is exactly as the original with the exception of a change in the seventh measure.

**320—Teach me, my God and King**—George Herbert (8)
Altered by John Wesley (36)

**Mornington** (25)—Arranged from a chant by Garret Wellesley (25)

John Wesley, a great admirer of George Herbert, took the first stanza of Herbert's poem, *The Elixir,* from *The Temple,* 1633, and used it as the basis of this hymn. The original is given so that the extensive alterations may be noted:

Teach me, my God and King,
In all things Thee to see,
And what I do in anything,
To do it as for Thee.

Not rudely, as a beast,
To run into an action;
But still to make Thee prepossest,
And give it his perfection.

A man that looks on glass,
On it may stay his eye;
Or if he pleaseth, through it pass,
And then the heav'n espy.

All may of Thee partake:
Nothing can be so mean,
Which with his tincture (for Thy sake),
Will not grow bright and clean.

A servant with this clause
Makes drudgery divine;
Who sweeps a room, as for Thy laws,
Makes that and th' action fine.

This is the famous stone,
That turneth all to gold;
For that which God doth touch and own
Cannot for less be told.

[1] The words beginning the last two stanzas of the hymn "Pange lingua," by St. Thomas Aquinas, sung (in the Roman Church) when the Eucharist is carried in procession. Through being sung also at the Benediction and certain other services in connection with the Eucharist, it has received some especial attention from church musicians.

At another place (8) attention has been called to George Herbert's naïve gift for using the most commonplace things in his teachings. He knew that

> A verse may find him who a sermon flies,
> And turn delight into a sacrifice.

**321—If, on a quiet sea**—Augustus Montague Toplady (204)

**Selvin**—Arranged by Lowell Mason (19)

This hymn is based on A. M. Toplady's

> Your harps, ye trembling saints,

but has been so greatly altered as to make it quite a different hymn. While it is not known who made the alterations, it is probable that it is the product of many hands.

"Selvin," is one of Lowell Mason's numerous "arrangements" which was first published in his *New Carmina Sacra,* 1850, set to

> If, through unruffled seas,

another cento from Toplady's hymn.

**322—My times are in Thy hands**—William Freeman Lloyd

**Ferguson**—George Kingsley (61)

Sometimes appearing

> Our times are in Thine hand,

this extensively used hymn has been said to have been published in 1835, but it has not been found in any book before its appearance, in 1838, in *Hymns for the Poor of the Flock.* The fifth of the original six stanzas has been omitted, and whatever slight changes have been made in the text are inconsequential.

William Freeman Lloyd, born at Uley, Gloucestershire, England, December 22, 1791, was from his boyhood greatly interested in the work being done in the Sunday schools, and as soon as he became equipped for it, he engaged in teaching in Oxford and London. In time, 1810, he was appointed one of the secretaries of the Sunday School Union, and six years later became identified with the Religious Tract Society. Josiah Miller, in his *Singers and Songs of the Church,* 1869, says of him:

> He commenced the *Sunday School Teachers' Magazine,* conducted for years the *Child's Companion* and the *Weekly Visitor,* and suggested the preparation of a large number of books for children and adults. His own literary productions were various, including several useful Sunday-School books for teachers and scholars, and numerous tracts. He was also much engaged in compilation and revision.

Mr. Lloyd died at the home of his brother at Stanley Hall, Gloucestershire, April 22, 1853.

"Ferguson" was first published in *The Harp of David,* 1843.

**323—Not so in haste, my heart—Bradford Torrey**
**Dolomite Chant**—Austrian melody
Harmonized by Joseph Thomas Cooper

This beautiful prayer hymn was for long ascribed to Bayard Taylor, as it appeared in *The Boston Transcript,* c. 1875, signed "B. T.," which initials W. Garrett Horder assumed "may or may not have stood for Bayard Taylor." It was so credited in *The Pilgrim Hymnal,* 1904, but by the time the 1912 edition was issued the error had been discovered and it was properly signed, Bradford Torrey.

Bradford Torrey, American ornithologist and naturalist, born at Weymouth, Massachusetts, October 9, 1843, was educated in the public schools of his native town. After teaching for a time he was engaged in business in Boston, and, for fifteen years, from 1886 to 1901, was a member of the staff of *The Youth's Companion.* Upon his retirement he moved to Santa Barbara, California, where he died October 7, 1912. He wrote much, among his books being *Birds in the Bush* and *Nature's Invitation,* while he edited Thoreau's *Journal.*

"Dolomite Chant" is an old Austrian melody arranged as a hymn tune by J. T. Cooper for *The Hymnal Companion to the Book of Common Prayer,* London, 1879.

Joseph Thomas Cooper, who was born May 25, 1819, and died November 17, 1879, was a well-known organist and writer on church music in London, where he spent all of his life. He collaborated with his close friend, Bishop E. H. Bickersteth (354), in the compiling and editing of the 1877 edition of *The Hymnal Companion to the Book of Common Prayer.*

**324—God is my strong salvation**—James Montgomery (39)
**Aurelia**—Samuel Sebastian Wesley

This rendering of Psalm 27. 1, "The Lord is my light and my salvation; whom shall I fear? The Lord is the strength of my life; of whom shall I be afraid?" appeared in James Montgomery's *Songs of Zion* in 1822. This is but one of many of his hymns based on the Psalms which he found a constant source of inspiration for his writings.

"Aurelia" was written in 1864 by S. S. Wesley as a setting for

The voice that breathed o'er Eden,

a wedding hymn by John Keble (35), but before it was published in that association he was asked, in that same year, to edit the music edition of a *Selection of Psalms and Hymns* by the Rev. Charles Kemble, which included a number of tunes from his pen. In this book he used this tune for three sections of St. Bernard's hymn,

(a) Brief life is here our portion,
(b) For thee, O dear, dear country,
(c) Jerusalem, the golden,

selecting its name from the last word, the Latin *aurum,* "gold." This association is almost unknown, it most often being found with

The Church's one foundation (381).

When this tune was selected as one of those to be used to celebrate the recovery of the Prince of Wales from a serious illness, in a service at St. Paul's Cathedral, London, February 27, 1872, Dr. H. W. Gauntlett (442) wrote an article for *The Choir,* a church-music periodical, denouncing it in no uncertain terms. Doctor Gauntlett said it was not only "inartistic, and not fulfilling the conditions of a hymn-tune," but went so far as to say it was "secular twaddle." The critic would seem to have been a poor prophet judging from the tune's continuing popularity.

Samuel Sebastian Wesley, Mus. Doc., born at London, August 14, 1810, was the grandson of Charles Wesley, Methodism's great hymn writer, and the son of Samuel Wesley, one of the greatest musicians England has produced, much of whose genius he inherited. When but a small boy he began playing the organ and held posts as organist from his tenth year. A great lover of outdoor life, and especially an enthusiastic fisherman, he is said to have been determined in his choice of positions by the character of the fishing in the near-by streams. There is a story told that he sent an assistant to open an organ on one occasion because a stream they had to cross, en route to the church with the new organ, looked too inviting for Wesley to resist. The assistant was to report that Wesley had been unavoidably detained. He was a queer character, quarreling constantly with his superiors. During his time church music was at such a low ebb in England that he was constantly irritated because of lack of interest and sympathy, and because of inadequate facilities. Yet he was true to his ideals, and those who knew him well could not fail to appreciate his idealism, his kindness and sympathy, in spite of a manner reserved and retiring, and at times even eccentric. He felt deeply, aimed high, and greatly enriched the repertory of music in the Church of England. Because of his ability to combine in his hymn tunes ease of singing with churchly dignity he is looked upon as one of a few whose contributions have resulted in uplifting the quality of the music sung by the masses. He died April 19, 1876.

**325—I look to Thee in every need—Samuel Longfellow (42)**

**O Jesu—Melody from Hirschberg Gesangbuch**

Few hymns have in them that which gives such encouragement and spiritual strength to the mentally weary and discouraged as this, by Samuel Longfellow, published in his *Hymns of the Spirit,* 1864. It is another of those fine poems by American writers which were discovered by W. Garrett Horder and introduced as hymnic material in England before becoming known in this country.

"O Jesu," the melody of which appeared first in the *Hirschberg Gesang-*

*buch,* 1741, is taken, with slight changes, from J. B. Riemann's *Sammlung alter und neuer Melodien Evangel. Lieder, etc.,* 1747.

**326—Children of the Heavenly King**—John Cennick (199)
**Pleyel's Hymn**—Ignace Josef Pleyel

Originally in twelve stanzas, 1, 2, 7, and 8, with only slight changes in the first two, have been chosen for this cento. The hymn appeared without heading in John Cennick's *Sacred Hymns for the Children of God, in the Days of Their Pilgrimage,* 1742. This book, which was issued while Cennick was still Whitefield's assistant, and upon which he looked with favor, also contained "Jesus, my All, to heav'n is gone" (199).

"Pleyel's Hymn" is taken from the slow movement of his fourth Quartet, op. 7. It appeared as a L. M. tune in *Arnold and Callcott's Psalms,* 1791, used with Joseph Addison's hymn, "The spacious firmament on high" (66).

Ignace Josef Pleyel, born at Ruppersthal in Lower Austria, June 1, 1757, the twenty-fourth child of an Austrian schoolmaster, was a favorite pupil of Haydn (30), who considered him very efficient. He gained fame as a composer, as a conductor, and then as a business man. In 1791 he found himself a rival conductor of Haydn in London, and although the rivalry was keen for a time, Pleyel and his friends had to retire in favor of the great master. Neither Haydn nor Pleyel seemed to have any feeling in the matter, for the quarrel between their friends was none of their doing. Haydn said, "I go to all of his concerts, for I love him," and late the same year wrote:

> Since his arrival, Pleyel has been so modest to me that my old affection has revived; we are often together, and it does him honor to find that he knows the worth of his old father. We shall each take our share of success and go home satisfied.

Mozart (261) also thought well of Pleyel, for he wrote his father:

> Some quartets have come out by a certain Pleyel, a scholar of Jos. Haydn's. If you don't already know them, try to get them, it is worth your while. They are very well written and very agreeable. . . It will be a happy time for music, if when the time arrives, Pleyel should replace Haydn for us.

The number of his compositions was enormous, primarily instrumental, for although he wrote for voice, his work in that field was not his best. In 1807 he founded the famous piano manufacturing house of Pleyel & Co., still in existence, which has always maintained a high standard of excellence and is well and favorably known in Europe. Before engaging in the manufacture of pianos he was a music seller and publisher. He died at Paris, November 14, 1831.

**327—O Holy Saviour, Friend unseen**—Charlotte Elliott (198)
**Flemming**—Frederick Ferdinand Flemming

Shortly after the death of Miss Elliott's father, in 1834, she wrote this hymn and the same year published it in an edition of her *Invalid's Hymn Book,* with the title,

**Clinging to Christ.**

Different selections of stanzas from the original nine have been used with few textual changes. In some instances the last line has been lengthened to make a long meter, but this has not proven an advantage.

"Flemming" was written in 1811 by Doctor Flemming for a chorus of men's voices to the famous ode of Horace, "Integer vitae." It is a great favorite with college men not only in this country but in England and Germany. There are few more satisfactory hymn tunes.

Frederick Ferdinand Flemming, M.D., was born at Neuhausen, Saxony, February 28, 1778, and died at Berlin, May 27, 1813. After completing his medical course at Wittenberg, Jena, Vienna, and Trieste, he settled in Berlin, where he not only became a successful practitioner of medicine, but a well-known and able composer of part songs for male choruses. *Grove's Dictionary of Music and Musicians* frankly states the notice given him is owing to his composition of the excellent tune usually sung to "Integer vitae."

**328—I worship Thee, most gracious God**—Frederick William Faber (76)

**Abergele**—John Ambrose Lloyd

This hymn appeared in Father Faber's *Jesus and Mary; or, Catholic Hymns for Singing and Reading,* 1849. In fourteen stanzas beginning,

> I worship Thee, sweet will of God,

it was entitled,

> The Will of God.

In the Preface to this book the author states he sought to emulate the simplicity and fervor of the *Olney Hymns* and those by John and Charles Wesley.

"Abergele" comes from J. A. Lloyd's *Aberth Moliant,* a collection of Welsh hymn tunes issued in 1873.

John Ambrose Lloyd, who was born June 14, 1815, at Mold, Flintshire, North Wales, and who died at Liverpool, September 14, 1874, was an influential Welsh musician, largely self-taught. He was much sought after as an adjudicator for the national Eisteddfodau. Compiler of two collections of excellent hymn tunes, his *The Prayer of Habakkuk* was the first cantata published in Wales, while his fine part song, *Blodeuyn Olef,* is looked upon as a Welsh classic.

**329—I know that my Redeemer lives**—Samuel Medley (168)

**Truro** (126)—From Psalmodia Evangelica, 1789 (126)

> I know that my Redeemer lives;
> What comfort this sweet passage gives!

is the manner in which Samuel Medley began his hymn of nine stanzas, interpreting, in the light of New-Testament events, the passage found in Job 19. 25, "For I know that my redeemer liveth." It first appeared without signature in George Whitefield's *Psalms and Hymns,* 1775.

**330—My Jesus, as Thou wilt—Benjamin Schmolck**
**Translated by Jane Borthwick (73)**

**Jewett—From Carl Maria von Weber (200)**

This translation, a rendering of Benjamin Schmolck's hymn beginning,

Mein Jesu, wie du willst,

was published in Jane Borthwick's *Hymns from the Land of Luther,* first series, 1854. The original hymn, published in 1709, in the fourth edition of the author's *Heilige Flammen,* was founded on St. Mark 14. 36: "And he said, Abba, Father, all things are possible unto thee; take away this cup from me: nevertheless not what I will, but what thou wilt." It is a simple hymn teaching us to bend our wills in submission to Jesus, as Jesus bent His to that of His Father.

Benjamin Schmolck was born at Brauchitzchdorf, near Liegnitz, Silesia, December 21, 1672. After his return from five years' study at the Gymnasium at Lauban, he preached for his father a sermon which so impressed the latter's patron that he provided funds for Benjamin's theological course at Leipzig. His father's assistant for five years after graduation, he was appointed diaconus at the Friedenskirche at Schweidnitz, where he remained until his death, February 12, 1737. By the terms of the Peace of Westphalia, the Lutherans of Schweidnitz had been hampered by many restrictions; they were allowed only one church, which was built of timber and clay without tower or bells and erected outside the walls of the city. Though serving the greater part of his life in such a situation, Schmolck was so unusually tactful in his preaching, and so remarkably devoted to his duties, that he was highly esteemed. His books, particularly the hymns which were included therein, gained for him an audience throughout all Germany. In addition to some nine hundred hymns he wrote the texts for many cantatas, funerals, and other special occasions.

> A deep and genuine personal religion, and a fervent love to the Saviour, inspire his best hymns; and as they are not simply thought out but felt, they come from the heart to the heart.

"Jewett" is an arrangement of the introduction to the Overture to the opera, *Der Freischütz,* by Weber, which opens with this theme scored for four horns. It has long stood as a model of four-part writing for brass instruments. The composer was three years working on this opera, and the Overture was the last number completed—May, 1820. Weber's favorite motto was "As God wills." It is said his last words when dying in London were,

Let me go back to my own home and then
"God's will be done."

One wonders if this were known to whoever first used this tune with this hymn. Earlier than this well-known arrangement made by Joseph P. Holbrook (210[2]) in 1862, the melody, with an equally good harmonization, will be found in *The Wesleyan Sacred Harp,* 1854, a book which seems to have contained much that appealed to some of the compilers of books of sacred song in the years immediately following its publication.

**331—Christ's life our code, His cross our creed**—Benjamin Copeland

**Copeland**—Karl Pomeroy Harrington (10)

Doctor Copeland wrote this hymn in his study in the parsonage of the Frank Street Methodist Episcopal Church, Rochester, New York, in the early spring of 1900. It was published in May of the same year, in *The Daily Christian Advocate,* the official organ of the General Conference which authorized the appointment of a Commission to revise the *Hymnal* of 1878. The poem claimed the immediate attention of the members of the Commission, and the hymn's first appearance in any hymnal was in *The Methodist Hymnal* of 1905.

Benjamin Copeland, one of four brothers of Pilgrim-Puritan lineage who are ordained ministers, was born at Clarendon, New York, June 14, 1855. Educated at Genesee Wesleyan Seminary, his first call was to serve the rapidly developing territory of the then largely unchurched circuit centering in Bradford, Pennsylvania. In 1877 he was admitted on trial to the Genesee Conference, was admitted to full membership two years later, and for forty-two years labored in western New York, serving about equally in city and village appointments. It has been his privilege to found five new churches, four of them in Buffalo, where he has continued making his home since his retirement from active service in 1921. He is the author of four volumes of verse. In 1917 Syracuse University conferred on him the S. T. D. degree.

"Copeland" was written by Professor Harrington for Doctor Copeland's hymn for *The Methodist Hymnal,* 1905, and it has proven so satisfactory that, so far as is known, none other has been made.

**332—Thou art the Way: to Thee alone**—George Washington Doane (47)

**St. Bernard**—John Richardson

This is the only hymn by Bishop Doane, and one of few by American writers to be included in *Hymns Ancient and Modern,* 1861. It was first published in his *Songs by the Way,* 1824. Its scriptural basis is St. John 14. 6: "Jesus saith unto him, I am the way, the truth, and the life: no man cometh unto the Father, but by me."

"St. Bernard" is usually attributed to John Richardson. In a book published in Cologne in 1741 the following melody appears with a hymn to the Virgin Mary:

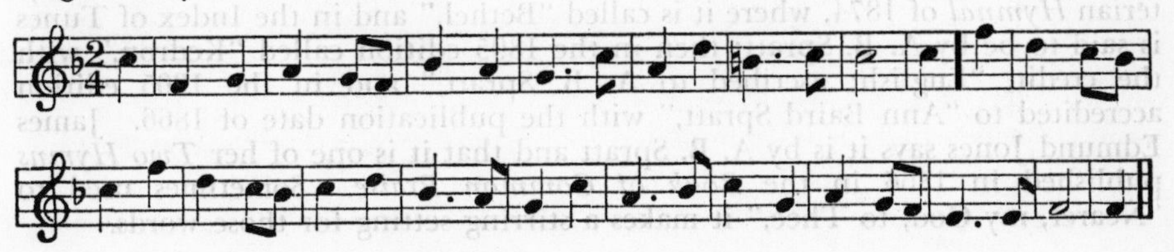

In another German book issued in 1767, it appears thus:

In this form it is found in the second volume of *Cantica Spiritualia,* Munich, 1847, and it is probably from this last-named book that John Richardson rearranged the melody and used it in *Easy Hymn Tunes . . . for Catholic Schools,* n.d., but which the British Museum catalogue gives as 1851. It was set to

Jesus, the very thought of Thee,

and was headed

Hymn of St. Bernard.

John Richardson, born at Preston, England, December 14, 1816, attracted attention in his boyhood by the beauty of his alto voice. Because of his unusual interest in music while yet young, he sang in Catholic choirs for several years and gave up a distasteful apprenticeship under a house painter and decorator, to begin a successful career as a church musician. Becoming an able organist and teacher, he spent most of his active life in Liverpool, where, in addition to his duties at St. Nicholas' Church, he composed several masses, including a Requiem Mass, and a Benediction Service, and won several prizes for glees. Upon the failure of his health, in 1860, he returned to his birthplace, where, after several years of invalidism, he died, April 13, 1879.

**333—No, not despairingly**—Horatius Bonar (210)

**Kedron**—Ann Baird Spratt

With the title,

Confession and Peace,

Doctor Bonar published this hymn in the third series of *Hymns of Faith and Hope,* 1867. Dean Tillett thinks this is one of the most successful of Doctor Bonar's hymns, for it brings out the "exceeding sinfulness of sin," frankly confesses it, has a note of "forgiveness and cleansing," and expresses "happy results."

"Kedron," one of our most beautiful hymn tunes, is another whose source is obscure. Apparently it first appeared in American hymnbooks in the Presbyterian *Hymnal* of 1874, where it is called "Bethel," and in the Index of Tunes is said to be by A. B. Spratt; then in the 1895 edition called "Kedron," with the credit, "English; ascribed to A. B. Spratt," and in the 1905 edition accredited to "Ann Baird Spratt," with the publication date of 1866. James Edmund Jones says it is by A. B. Spratt and that it is one of her *Two Hymns* published in 1866 in the *Book of Common Praise.* Sometimes used to "Nearer, my God, to Thee," it makes a stirring setting for those words.

Ann Baird Spratt is said to be an English woman born in 1829. It is a matter of great regret that no more is known of this composer and of the very worshipful tune she has written.

**334—My Lord, how full of sweet content**—Madame Guyon
Translated by William Cowper (24)
Altered by others

**Hamburg**—From a Gregorian chant
Arranged by Lowell Mason (19)

Madame Guyon included this hymn in *Poésies et Cantiques Spirituels,* published in 1722, its first line being,

Amour que mon âme est contente.

An abridged and altered form of William Cowper's nine-quatrain translation of 1801 was included in Edwin F. Hatfield's *Church Hymn Book,* 1872, from which this is taken entire and without change.

Madame Guyon, Jean Marie Bouvier de la Mothe before her marriage at sixteen years of age to a wealthy invalid many years her senior, was born at Montargis, France, April 13, 1648. One of the leaders of the seventeenth century Quietist movement, the doctrines of which are reflected in her hymns, she was imprisoned for a time in the Bastille because of her teachings and unconventional conduct. After her release in 1703, she lived quietly at the home of her brother near Blois, spending her time in writing and in "charitable and pious exercises" until her death there, June 9, 1717.

"Hamburg" was written by Lowell Mason in 1824 while he was living at Savannah, Georgia, and it was first sung at the First Presbyterian Church in that city. Henry L. Mason, grandson of Lowell Mason, writes that "Hamburg" is "in the spirit of, rather than arranged from, I think, Gregorian Chant I." Tone (Chant) I, ending 1 is:

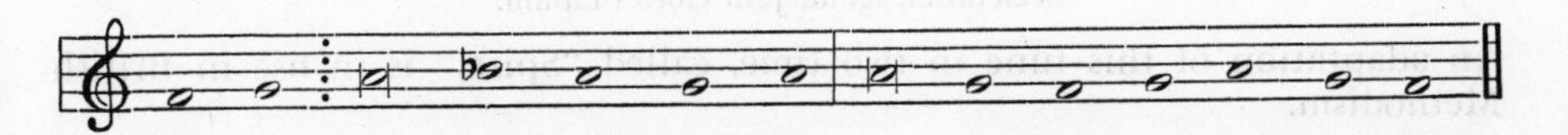

It was published in the third edition of *The Boston Handel and Haydn Society Collection of Church Music,* 1824.

**335—Jesus, I live to Thee**—Henry Harbaugh

**Lake Enon**—Isaac Baker Woodbury (137)

The "Mercersburg Hymn," as this is popularly known, was written in 1850 by Doctor Harbaugh, and was published in his *Hymns and Chants for Sunday Schools,* 1861.

Henry Harbaugh, D.D., born near Waynesborough, Pennsylvania, October 28, 1817, and unable on account of lack of means to complete his course at Marshall College, Mercersburg, Pennsylvania, was ordained a minister in the German Reformed Church, and served churches at Lewisburg, Lancaster, and Lebanon before answering a call to the professorship of theology at Mercersburg in 1863, where he remained until his death at that place, December 28, 1867.

"Lake Enon" was included by its composer, I. B. Woodbury, in *The Cythara,* 1854, set to a hymn by Anne Steele (389) beginning,

While my Redeemer's near.

The signature to the music was W**.

**336—Jesus, still lead on**—Nicolaus Ludwig Zinzendorf (205)
Translated by Jane Borthwick (73)

**Seelenbräutigam**—Adam Drese
Harmonized by Samuel Sebastian Wesley (324)

This hymn is a cento made, probably by Christian Gregor, from two hymns of Count Zinzendorf:

(a) Seelenbräutigam, O du Gottes-Lamm, and
(b) Glanz der Ewigkeit,

making that beginning,

Jesu, geh' voran,

which Miss Borthwick translated and published first in *The Free Church Magazine,* 1846, and in a slightly altered form in her *Hymns from the Land of Luther,* First Series, 1854. A splendid hymn for children, especially popular in Germany, it is here used in its altered form.

"Seelenbräutigam," "Darmstadt," "Haarlem," or "Zinzendorf," was composed by Adam Drese for use in his family devotions, and was first published in a *Gesangbuch* printed at Halle in 1697. It was associated with the composer's hymn,

Seelenbräutigam, Jesu Gottes-Lamm.

An adaptation of this tune in two time, called "Spire," is in use in British Methodism.

Adam Drese was born at Weinral, in Thuringia, in December, 1620, and died at Arnstadt, February 15, 1701. He studied music at Warsaw and held appointments as musical director at Weimar, to the Duke of Brunswick, at Arnstadt, and at Jena, where he became Mayor of the town. Services for the sect of Pietists, to which he belonged, were held at his house, and for them he wrote hymns and tunes. He contributed some tunes for Georg Neumark's (272) *Lustwald,* Jena, 1657.

**337—Saviour, like a shepherd lead us**—From Hymns for the Young
Ascribed to Dorothy Ann Thrupp

**Bradbury**—William Batchelder Bradbury (133)

Miss Thrupp included this hymn in her *Hymns for the Young,* Fourth

Edition, 1836, edited for the Religious Tract Society, London, and although the authorship is somewhat doubtful, it is usually ascribed to her.

Dorothy Ann Thrupp was born in London, June 20, 1779, and died there, December 14, 1847. A few of her extensively used hymns were contributed to *The Friendly Visitor* and *Children's Friend,* usually signed "Iota" or "D. A. T." Some of those attributed to her are done so with certain reservations (such as the one here considered), for all those contained in her *Hymns for the Young* are there given anonymously.

"Bradbury," written for this hymn and named for its composer, appeared in the 1859 edition of *Oriola,* a popular Sunday-school singing book issued by W. B. Bradbury.

## Peace and Joy

**338—Jesus, Lover of my soul**—Charles Wesley (25)

First tune: **Martyn**—Simeon Butler Marsh

Second tune: **Hollingside** (191)—John Bacchus Dykes (1)

Third tune: **Aberystwyth**—Joseph Parry

Charles Wesley gave "Jesu, Lover of my soul" the title "In time of prayer and temptation," later changing it to "In temptation." Printed first in *Hymns and Sacred Poems,* 1740, it is not known when it was written. There is general agreement that it is one of the greatest hymns, if not the greatest hymn, of all time. Alan Sutherland says this hymn shares with the Twenty-third Psalm first place in the hearts of countless thousands, "and the two together voice the creed, the hope, and the prayer of Christendom." Alexander MacMillan thus interprets the hymn:

> In melodious word and musical cadence it voices the need of the soul in time of dire distress and temptation; and with intense yet restrained passion exercises that divine aspiration after the highest, which finds its realization only in the life which is hid with Christ in God.

David R. Breed states:

> There can be no question with regard to the most acceptable of all of (C.) Wesley's hymns. There is one which the entire Church, with absolute unanimity, assigns to the first place, "Jesus, Lover of my soul."

Jeremiah B. Reeves concurs:

> This is one of the supreme hymns of the world. It has gone to the corners of the earth with the English language and has been translated into virtually every language there is. The song has become a treasury of spiritual wealth. A thousand legends cluster about it as about some ancient shrine or about the memory of some gentle and famous saint. Countless children through successive generations have learned and kept its lines by heart; countless men and women have found in it deep refreshment of spirit as from a cool spring and shade by the road when tired and thirsty; and uncounted ones have passed out of this life with its words on their lips.[1]

[1] *The Hymn as Literature.* D. Appleton-Century Company.

George Saintsbury, the eminent critic, says of it: "The mere word music of it is figured throughout in the most absolutely adequate manner."

John Telford pays this tribute: "This is the crown of Charles Wesley's work—one of the greatest hymns of the Universal Church. 'The finest hymn in the English language.'"

Samuel W. Duffield, a great hymnologist, comments: "There is scarcely any hymn which, for wide usefulness and acceptance, can dispute the supremacy with this."

Three stories connected with its composition have had quite general acceptance. One is that a bird, escaping from a hawk, flew through a window into a room in which Charles Wesley was sitting. Another is that Wesley, fleeing from a mob, secreted himself in a hedge, writing the hymn while in that place of refuge. The third, most generally credited, is to the effect that it was written during a storm while Wesley was on board a ship. A seabird, beaten by the storm, flew into Wesley's cabin through an open porthole. None of these stories has been substantiated. Doctor Breed suggests that the lyric "does not have need of them to enhance its beauty." And Dr. Percy Dearmer says, "It is more likely that the hymn was connected with the great spiritual change that he [Charles Wesley] underwent in 1738, since it was printed two years after that date." It would require a good-sized book to print all the incidents told in connection with "Jesus, Lover of my soul."

Lyman Beecher had great love for this hymn. His son, Henry Ward Beecher, speaking of this, said:

> I would rather have written that hymn of Charles Wesley's
>
> "Jesu, Lover of my soul,
> Let me to Thy bosom fly,"
>
> than to have the fame of all the kings that ever sat on the earth. It is more glorious. It has more power in it. I would rather be the author of that hymn than to hold the wealth of the richest man in New York. He will die. He *is* dead and does not know it. He will pass, after a little while, out of men's thoughts. What will there be to speak of him? What will he have done that will stop trouble, encourage hope? His money will go to his heirs and they will divide it. It is like a stream divided, growing narrower by division. And they will die, and it will go to their heirs. In three or four generations everything comes to the ground for redistribution. But that hymn will go on singing until the last trump brings forth the angel band; and then, I think, it will mount up on some lip to the very presence of God.

George Duffield, Jr., author of "Stand up, stand up for Jesus" (283), said:

> One of the most blessed days of my life was when I found after my harp had long hung upon the willows, that I could *sing* again; that a new song was put into my mouth; and when, ere ever I was aware, I was singing, "Jesu, Lover of my soul." If there is anything in Christian experience of joy and sorrow, of affliction and prosperity, of life and death—that hymn is *the* hymn of the ages!

Preachers cannot use too much care in the selection of their hymns, for they never know what their effect may be. Spurgeon tells of a man coming into a meeting where he was to preach, who, after hearing this hymn sung, said: "Does Christ love me? Then why should I live in enmity to Him?" And he became converted.

Dr. Louis F. Benson uses it to illustrate most of the subjects under which he lists good hymns, such as Poetry, Personal Experience, Prayer, etc. He says:

> We are dealing with the best-loved hymn in the language; the favorite of learned and illiterate, high and humble. And why is it so? No critic urged its acceptance. Average Christians could not analyze its appeal; its tenderness is a part of that, but hundreds of the Wesleyan hymns are equally tender. Its spiritual reality is a part of the explanation, but the hymns in general have as much. And after due tribute to these qualities the suspicion remains that the secret of its appeal lies in a poetic beauty that the average man feels without analyzing it, and in a perfection of craftsmanship that makes him want to *sing* it simply because it awakens the spirit of song in him rather than a mood of reflection. . . .
>
> John Wesley desired that the text of his brother's and his own hymns, furnished in his large *Collection* . . . (1780) should be final. As for hymn tinkerers, he said in the Preface: "I desire they would not attempt to mend them; for they really are not able. None of them is able to mend either the sense or the verse." The reference here very likely was to Whitefield or Toplady, both of whom had altered the hymns they had appropriated. After Wesley's death his wishes were disregarded even by the publishers of his own book. Charles Wesley's hymns suffered long at editorial hands that were all thumbs. His "Jesu, Lover of my soul," being the most lyrical, suffered the most, and only in our day has been restored to its original beauty. . . . How intolerable have been the changes in "Jesu, Lover of my soul"![1]

The hymn, particularly the first stanza, has been tinkered with by a long line of editors. As Doctor Benson says, it is only in our day that it has been restored to its original beauty and simplicity. The first four lines have been twisted around more than a similar number of lines in any other hymn. Doctor Julian says: "As an editorial curiosity these four lines are in their transformation unique." And why was it tinkered with? There were objections to the use of the word "Lover." And there was much argument as to why only the "nearer waters roll." Doctor Dearmer says that hymnbook compilers do not always realize that a "little poetic understanding is necessary for their work." Even Doctor Julian devotes much space to discussing the action of the waves in different kinds of storms!

Its simplicity is outstanding. In our book we use four stanzas. Of the 188 words used, 157 are of one syllable, leaving only 31 polysyllabic words. Note the overwhelming third stanza—only three words of more than one syllable! Of the many-syllabled words, which Charles Wesley loved to use, this, his greatest production, uses but few.

Time is required for the understanding of great works. Bach was forgotten for one hundred years. Although this hymn was first printed in 1740 in *Hymns and Sacred Poems,* John Wesley did not include it in his *Collection . . . for the people called Methodists,* 1780, and it did not appear in the *Methodist Hymn Book* until 1797.

It has worn out several generations of tunes. It would be interesting to know the tune to which it was first sung. In 1765, when John Wesley was preparing his tune book, *Sacred Melody,* the tune "Hotham," by the Rev. Martin Madan, was contributed for use with this hymn. It was generally sung to this tune in England until 1861, when, in *Hymns Ancient and Mod-*

[1] *The Hymnody of the Christian Church.* Harper and Brothers.

*ern,* it was set to "Hollingside," by Dr. John B. Dykes (1). This tune served admirably until the last few years, when Joseph Parry wrote "Aberystwyth" for it, one of three settings used in *The Methodist Hymnal* of 1935. In America its tune history has been even more varied and interesting. In *The Harmonist,* first official tune book of the Methodist Episcopal Church, 1821, the tune is "Alma," a variant of "Come, ye disconsolate." In later editions, 1837-1844, the English tune "Hotham" is used. In the *New Lute of Zion,* I. B. Woodbury, 1865, "Martyn" is used, and also the tune "Watchman" (Tell us of the night), dignified by a different number. This book, while not officially denominational, was compiled for "congregations generally, but more especially for the Methodist Episcopal Church." In the 1878 book of the Methodist Episcopal Church, two tunes, "Refuge" and "Martyn," are given, "Martyn" retiring to second place. These same tunes are used in the 1889 book of the Methodist Episcopal Church, South, but here "Martyn" still retains first place. By 1905, when the two churches united in issuing the book in use for the past thirty years, the Dykes tune had made its way to America and was chosen as the first setting for this hymn. Here we find three settings: "Refuge" was dropped but "Martyn" was retained; however, "Martyn" was given third place and a Joseph Barnby tune, "St. Fabian," second place. After thirty years "Martyn" and "Hollingside" are retained, and "Aberystwyth," immensely popular in England and beginning to become known in this country, is added. In the *Methodist Protestant Church Hymnal,* 1901, "Martyn" was the only tune used. The old, long-loved "Martyn" is given preference in the new *Methodist Hymnal,* "Hollingside" is second, and the new "Aberystwyth" will stand third. If "Aberystwyth" shows sufficient merit, it may displace the others by the time the next revision appears.

The popular type of songbooks has tried other tunes, but only strong ones have been able to hold their place for any length of time. The tune "Watchman" (called "Defense" in Asa Hull's *Pilgrim Harp,* 1869, and "Lover of my Soul" in Charles Dunbar's *Union Harp, or Revival Chorister,* 1859) seems to have attained some popularity for a time as a suitable setting, but owing to its association with "Watchman, tell us of the night," it now is never thought a suitable setting for any other hymn. A great hymn needs its own great tune.

"Aberystwyth" was written by Joseph Parry, born of poor parents in the iron district of southwest Wales, May 21, 1841. His mother was a superior woman and quite musical. At ten, Parry left school to work as a puddler in the iron furnaces. From the Welsh workmen, who do much singing and playing in bands, the boy picked up enough music to demonstrate his unusual talent. He came to America with his family in the 1850's and entered as many Eistedfodd contests as he could, later boasting that he never lost a contest. In a composition contest at Swansea in 1863 he entered a hymn tune which attracted so much attention that a collection was taken to enable him to enter the Royal Academy of Music in London. Making the most of every opportunity, he advanced to his Mus. Bac. degree, and seven years later to his Mus. Doc., both from Cambridge University. He served as Professor of Music at University College, Aberystwyth, and as lecturer at University College of South Wales, Cardiff. He died at Penarth, February 17, 1903. Although well known as a composer and educator, Doctor Parry will probably be remembered as the composer of the sterling tune, "Aberystwyth."

"Martyn" was written in the fall of 1834 while Mr. Marsh was on his way to one of his singing schools. He dismounted from his horse and wrote out the melody, which he associated with the words "Mary, at her Saviour's tomb." It has been used with the hymn "Saviour, when in dust to Thee," but it was Thomas Hastings (204) who discovered its affinity for "Jesus, Lover of my soul." These words of Charles Wesley and "Martyn" have become so strongly linked that a modern hymnal hardly seems complete without the combination. Greatly loved as it is by older people, the tune does have a certain dullness and lack of appeal for young people trained in music in the public schools. To relieve its monotony, some changes have been made in the voice leadings.

Simeon Butler Marsh, who wrote the tune "Martyn," born June 1, 1798, at Sherburne, New York, was a choir singer and leader nearly all of his life, for he joined a children's choir when he was seven years old. After securing what musical education he could, he began conducting singing schools. For some time he lived at Sherburne, New York, where he was superintendent of the Sunday school, organist, and choir leader. He wrote some other hymn tunes, some anthems, and two cantatas. The last years of his life were spent in Albany at the home of his son, where he died July 14, 1875.

In May, 1849, Dr. John B. Dykes (1) was appointed precentor of Durham. In a letter to a sister announcing the fact, he says:

> I am thinking seriously of starting a small establishment and trying a little bachelor housekeeping. The fact is there is at present a very pretty little cottage to be let about a mile from Durham, with a nice bit of garden and a very fine prospect. . . .

On the evening of May 1, 1850, about a year from the announcement of the appointment, he moved to Hollingside Cottage, and wrote to his fiancée, Susan Kingston:

> I cannot go to bed on this very first night at the Cottage, without entreating you to join in the very earnest prayer that the Divine Blessing may rest upon me in this house, to which by His Good Providence, I have at last arrived.

In his *Life of Dr. Dykes,* J. T. Fowler tells us that

> On St. James' Day, July 25, 1850, John Dykes was married to Susan Kingston at St. Michael's Church, Malton, and after their wedding tour in the English Lakes, he brought his bride to their charming home, Hollingside Cottage, near Durham. . . . This house gave its name to the hymn-tune "Hollingside," written a few years later for the first edition of *Hymns Ancient and Modern,* to the words "Jesu, Lover of my soul."

**339—Thou hidden Source of calm repose—Charles Wesley (25)**

**St. Petersburg—Dimitri Stepanovitch Bortniansky (45)**

The hymn is from *Hymns and Sacred Poems,* 1749, entitled,

For the Morning.

Charles Wesley wrote the last line,

My life in death, my heaven in hell,

concerning which Doctor Stevenson said:

> The poet's idea in this hymn is to exalt Christ, and he selects various circumstances in life which he gives in striking antithesis to set this forth. Christ is the Christian's rest in toil, his ease in pain, his peace in war, his gain in loss, his liberty in bondage, and last of all comes this marvelous climax—his heaven in hell! This, of course, cannot be taken as it is literally expressed; it is a poet's license with language which requires to be received in a careful and modified symbolical sense.

After quoting the above, Dean Tillett (117) adds, "While the change in the text removes an expression liable to be misunderstood, it destroys the climax of the hymn."

"St. Petersburg," also known as "Wells," "Wellspring," and "Shangana," was set to one of Gerhard Tersteegen's (185) hymns,

Ich bete an die Macht der Liebe,

in I. H. Tscherlitsky's *Choralbuch,* 1825, according to Lightwood (453), where it is said to be from a mass written by Bortniansky in 1822. Lightwood, who has investigated the source of this tune, questions Bortniansky's having written it because authorities on Russian music whom he has consulted know nothing of masses by this composer, although *Grove's Dictionary* states that he wrote one. One of Lightwood's correspondents, writing in 1904, told him that this tune was not used in Russian churches, but on certain feast days of a semireligious character such as that of the "blessing of the waters," which formerly took place on each January 6th at St. Petersburg. He says, further, that it is played on the chimes of certain churches. Vassily Ilich Safonov (1852-1918), famous Russian pianist and composer, said "St. Petersburg" was a Russian folk song, "Kol sla-ven," but this statement has not been verified. This very fine composition has been used with thrilling effect by some of the excellent Russian bands of singers which have toured extensively in America in recent years.

According to former editions of *Grove's Dictionary,* the "Zapfenstreich," or tattoo, was played before the emperor and other high officials, on the last night of the annual maneuvers of the old German army, by many hundreds of players in the massed bands of all of the participating regiments. At the close of a suitable program, the drummers started a long roll, very softly, crescendo, then fortissimo, breaking into a short introduction to the proper "Zapfenstreich." This was followed immediately by the combined cavalry bands playing a Retreat (*Retraite*); then, after a short "call" by fifes and drums, followed this "Prayer," played slowly by all the massed musicians. Whether that melody, now called "St. Petersburg," was used as a part of this ceremony prior to its appearance in 1825 in the *Choralbuch* referred to, has not been ascertained. The custom of playing such "tattoos" for very special occasions has extended to other countries.

The word "Zapfenstreich" seems to have come into use during the Thirty Years' War, when General Wallenstein found his soldiers were spending too many nights in drinking. In order to prevent these nightly revels he ordered a "tattoo," or curfew, to be sounded, after which the men were to go to their quarters, while police officers went to the booths serving drinks and drew a chalkline over the bungs of the barrels in order that the morning inspection might show whether or not any drink had been drawn after the last call. The drawing of the chalkline interested the men so much that it became a sort of ceremony and brought forth the word "Zapfenstreich," meaning, literally, "bung line."

**340—All as God wills, who wisely heed—John Greenleaf Whittier (120)**

**Stracathro—Charles Hutcheson**

This is another selection of stanzas from a poem by an American poet, John G. Whittier, in which W. Garrett Horder saw hymnic possibilities. He used a part of Whittier's poem "My Psalm," from *The Panorama and Other Poems,* 1856, in *Congregational Hymns,* 1884.

"Stracathro" first appeared in Charles Hutcheson's *Christian Vespers,* Glasgow, 1832. It was first sung at St. George's Church, Glasgow, of which the composer was a member.

Charles Hutcheson, a native of Glasgow, Scotland, was born in 1792, and died there in 1860. A musical amateur with an excellent voice, he took much interest in music, especially psalmody, and did some creditable composing, published *Christian Vespers,* a book of hymn tunes in three and four parts, in 1832, and was one of the founders of the Glasgow Dilettanti Society. A personal friend of his has said, "He was an interesting and attractive personality, and one of those who carry music in their hearts."

**341—'Mid all the traffic of the ways—John Oxenham**

**St. Agnes—John Bacchus Dykes (1)**

The words of this hymn were taken from *The Vision Splendid,* 1917. This book of verse is one of sixty-seven publications issued by John Oxenham in the period 1898-1934. Written during the turmoil of the World War, the hymn is a prayer to make

> My heart a quiet place, . . .
> A little shelter from life's stress.

John Oxenham, English poet and man of letters, gives neither the date nor the place of his birth in the biographical account of himself in the English *Who's Who.* He attended Old Trafford School and Victoria University, Manchester; for some years engaged in business; lived in France and the United States, and has traveled extensively in Europe and Canada. A visit to the Southern states for the purpose of investigating the possibilities in cotton growing or in sheep raising convinced him that he did not wish to engage in either, and he went home. He began writing as a relief from business, enjoyed it more, and, as he expresses it, "dropped business and stuck to writing." "John Oxenham" is the *nom de plume* of William Arthur Dunkerley.

"St. Agnes" was written for the first part of the lengthy hymn,

> Jesus, the very thought of Thee,

and first appeared in a hymnal for use in the English Church, compiled by the Reverend, the Honorable John Grey, 1866. In England it is known as "St. Agnes, Durham," to distinguish it from another "St. Agnes."

**342—Dear Lord and Father of mankind—John Greenleaf Whittier (120)**
**Rest (Elton)—Frederick Charles Maker (9')**

It is interesting to note that while John G. Whittier felt he had no gift for hymn writing, some of those which have been most helpful and successful in public worship have been culled from his poems on various themes. This is as striking an example as may be found. W. Garrett Horder selected stanzas suitable for use as a hymn from *The Brewing of Soma,* a poem of seventeen stanzas, telling of the brewing of an intoxicating drink by members of a certain sect in India:

The faggots blazed, the cauldron's smoke
Up through the green wood curled;
"Bring honey from the hollow oak,
Bring milky sap," the brewers spoke
In the childhood of the world.

And brewed they well or brewed they ill,
The priests thrust in their rods,
First tasted, and then drank their fill,
And shouted, with one voice and will,
"Behold the drink of gods!"

"Drink, mortals, what the gods have sent,
Forget your long annoy,"
So sang the priests. From tent to tent
The Soma's sacred madness went,
A storm of drunken joy.

As in that child-world's early year,
Age after age has striven
By music, incense, vigils drear,
And trance, to bring the skies more near,
Or lift men up to heaven.

And yet the past comes round again,
And new doth old fulfil;
In sensual transports wild as vain
We brew in many a Christian fane
The heathen Soma still.

Thus calling attention to equally pagan practices today, he then writes:

Dear Lord and Father of mankind
Forgive our foolish ways,

extolling the restfulness and quietude of the higher life.

"Rest" or "Elton," was written for this hymn by Frederick C. Maker for *The Congregational Hymnary,* London, 1887, edited by the Rev. Dr. G. S. Barrett.

**343—Jesus, my strength, my hope—Charles Wesley (25)**

**Richmond—Asa Brooks Everett**

Stanzas 1, 3, 4, and 6, from seven, are taken verbatim from Charles Wesley's hymn with the title,

A Poor Sinner,

which appeared in *Hymns and Sacred Poems,* 1742. The original seventh stanza, while peculiar, states a truth as an eager petition:

I want with all my heart
Thy pleasure to fulfill,
To know myself, and what Thou art,
And what Thy perfect will.
I want I know not what,
I want my wants to see,
I want, alas! what want I not,
When Thou art not in me.

"Richmond" has not been found in any book published prior to 1859: *The Wesleyan Hymn and Tune Book,* edited by L. C. Everett for "The Southern Methodist Publishing House," Nashville. The tune was there associated with

A charge to keep I have.

Asa Brooks Everett, Mus. Doc., who was born in Virginia in 1828, and who died near Nashville in September, 1875, gave up the study of medicine to join his brother, L. C. Everett, in following the profession of music. Closely associated, the two, with R. M. McIntosh, formed the L. C. Everett Company, a concern which compiled and published many song books. This company employed and kept in the Southern states for many years a corps of more than fifty teachers of music who were engaged in carrying on singing schools and musical conventions. It is said each teacher received a salary of one hundred dollars monthly and his expenses. Asa Brooks Everett, after studying music in Boston and teaching in the South, spent four years in Leipzig, Germany, in further study. In his later years he devoted himself almost wholly to the writing of sacred music, mostly gospel songs. His best-known book is *The Sceptre,* published by Bigelow and Main, New York. The Everetts were to the South what Lowell Mason and his associates were to the North in the period just prior to the Civil War.

**344—O Thou who camest from above—Charles Wesley (25)**

**Eisenach**—Johann Hermann Schein
Harmonized by Johann Sebastian Bach (52)

Based upon Leviticus 6. 13, "The fire shall ever be burning upon the altar; it shall never go out," this hymn, in two eight-line stanzas, was one of the *Short Hymns on Select Passages of the Holy Scriptures,* 1762. John Wesley changed "my sacrifice" in the last line, to "the sacrifice" in order to efface the antithesis between *"Thy* endless mercies" and *"my* sacrifice." In some recent books "mean altar" has been changed to "low altar" in recognition of the change in meaning of the words since the time of the Wesleys, and the second stanza has been dropped because of the difficulty congregations find in overcoming such successions of syllables as "in-ex-tin-guish-a-ble." So unsuccessful have been efforts to change the line containing this word, that some editors have frankly confessed their way out of the difficulty was omission of the stanza altogether. Methodists, however, have been content to attempt its use unaltered, remembering that Charles Wesley told his friend, Samuel Bradburn, in 1781, when they were together in Yorkshire, that his "experience might almost at any time be found" in the first two stanzas of this hymn.

"Eisenach" first appeared on a single sheet: *Trost-Liedlein über den seligen Hintritt der Frawen Margariten, des Herrn Caspar Werners . . . Hausfrawen . . . Componirt und Musicirt von Johan-Herman Schein,* 1628, passing into the second edition of *Cantional oder Gesangbuch Augsburgischer Confession* (the famous hymnbook for the Lutheran Church), 1645, containing seventy-nine tunes by Schein, its editor. J. S. Bach's arrangement is the one he uses in his *Johannespassion* and *Choralgesänge.*

Johann Hermann Schein, son of a Lutheran minister, was born at Grunhain, Saxony, January 20, 1586, and died at Leipzig, November 19, 1630. Educated in music, philosophy, and theology, he became kapellmeister[1] at Weimar and cantor[1] to the Thomasschule at Leipzig. While he was one of the pioneers in recognizing the significance of the Italian influence on German church music in the early seventeenth century, he is chiefly known now for his *Cantional.*

**345—Jesus, Thou Joy of loving hearts**—Authorship uncertain
Ascribed to Bernard of Clairvaux (188)
Translated and arranged by Ray Palmer (176)

**Rimington**—Francis Duckworth

This is a part of Bernard's lengthy hymn beginning,

Jesu dulcis memoria,

and is one of three hymns in *The Methodist Hymnal* from the same source, the others being No. 188,

Of Him who did salvation bring,

translated by Anthony W. Boehm, and No. 348,

Jesus, the very thought of Thee,

translated by Edward Caswall. This rendition by Doctor Palmer has been

[1] The title "cantor," which is so often noted in reference to the old German Protestant music, while equivalent in many respects to "kapellmeister," differed in that the "cantor" was connected with a municipality rather than with a Cathedral or court, and had as a part of his duties some of the responsibility for civic education. He might be connected with a single school or church, or have control of all of the music of the community—the "Town Musician," as, indeed, he was frequently called. The post of cantor to the Thomasschule of Leipzig has been an honored one; its list of incumbents is complete from 1531 to the present day.

included with one other of his hymns in *Hymns Ancient and Modern,* where it was taken from *The Sabbath Hymn Book,* Andover, 1859.

When Doctor and Mrs. Palmer celebrated their golden wedding anniversary in 1882, Dr. Richard R. Storrs paid this fine tribute to Doctor Palmer:

> The grandest privilege which God has ever given to His children upon earth and which He gives to comparatively few, is to write a noble Christian hymn, to be accepted by the churches, to be sung by reverent and loving hearts in different lands and different tongues, and which still shall be sung as the future opens its brightening centuries.

"Rimington," although not published until 1904, and then in leaflet form, had been written by Francis Duckworth many years earlier. While only a young boy he heard an uncle and some friends discussing the relative merits of certain hymn writers. Isaac Watts was mentioned, and his hymn, "Jesus shall reign where'er the sun," was cited as being a great hymn. Young Duckworth, a musical lad, then and there decided he would some time write a tune worthy of that hymn. It was many years before his resolution bore fruit, but in time "Rimington" was composed and in only a few instances have hymn tunes gained such extraordinary popularity. Included in many hymnals, it has been carried into all parts of the world by members of the Salvation Army. Its hold on people is remarkable. On the Sunday following the fall of Jerusalem during the World War, it was sung on Mount Calvary.

Francis Duckworth, born at Rimington, Ribblesdale, England, in 1862, went at the age of five with his family to their new home at Stopper Lane. His few subsequent music lessons, given him at a cost of about ten shillings, were the sole formal musical training with which he became organist at the local Wesleyan Chapel. When twenty years of age, he went into business at Colne, Lancaster, since his home, and where he was deputy organist, then organist at Albert Road Wesleyan Chapel. He retired from this post in 1929 after service as an organist for fifty years.

**346—O Thou, in whose presence my soul takes delight**—Joseph Swain

**Beloved**—Freeman Lewis
Arranged by Hubert Platt Main (261)

This hymn is from Joseph Swain's *Redemption, a Poem in Five Books,* 1791, a posthumous work.

Joseph Swain, born at Birmingham, England, in 1761, and left an orphan in early life, was apprenticed to an engraver. Influenced by the purchase of a Bible, he began a serious study of the Scriptures; and converted under the preaching of Doctor Rippon, he prepared for the work of the ministry in the Baptist Church. At thirty years of age he was given charge of a mission in Walworth, London. Having written hymns since the beginning of his interest in religion, he published, in the second year of his connection with the London mission, *Walworth Hymns.* His death occurred April 14, 1796, at the early age of thirty-five years, and the following year his *Redemption, in Five Books, with a Life of the Author* appeared.

"Beloved," called "Meditation" in *The Methodist Hymnal,* 1905, and having been given so many different names as to make it difficult to trace, was without doubt included in one songbook, *The Beauties of Harmony,* compiled by Freeman Lewis in 1813, as a number of books issued subsequently give that year as the date of its first appearance. A very popular tune a century ago, it was "arranged" by Hubert P. Main in 1869.

Freeman Lewis, concerning whom but little is known, was born in 1780 and died in 1859. He issued *The Beauties of Harmony* in 1813, which reached a third edition in 1818. Music was his avocation, his profession being that of surveyor, which he carried on at Uniontown, Pennsylvania.

**347—How sweet the name of Jesus sounds**—John Newton (27)
**Holy Cross**—Adapted by James Clifft Wade

Here are four stanzas from seven taken from *Olney Hymns. Book First. Hymns on Select Passages of Scripture,* 1779, where they have the heading,

The Name of Jesus. Cant. i. 3.

The passage from the Song of Solomon is,

Thy name is an ointment poured forth.

John Wesley inserted it in his *Arminian Magazine* in 1781, but did not use it in any of his hymnbooks, and it came into British Methodism only in 1875, when it was included in the *Wesleyan Hymn Book,* in six stanzas. Since the middle of the last century it has found a place in all official hymnals of the American churches which have joined in the making of the present book.

"Holy Cross" presents a puzzle as to its source. It appears in four time in many books, among them the series of Presbyterian hymnals edited by Dr. L. F. Benson (38). In the 1895 edition Doctor Benson has the credit,

Arr. by James C. Wade,

and in the forty-fourth printing (October, 1926) of that one copyrighted in 1911,

Arr. by Samuel Smith from Thomas Hastings, 1831.

Dr. Charles S. Robinson, in *A Selection of Spiritual Songs,* 1878, says it is "from Mendelssohn"; *Carmina for the Sunday Schools,* Mudge and Turner, 1898, ascribes it to John Stainer; Dr. E. J. Hopkins in his *Congregational Hymnal,* London, 1887, gives no composer. Among modern editors, however, there seems agreement with the statement of James Love, in *Scottish Church Music,* Edinburgh, 1891:

"Holy Cross" . . . was adapted . . . from an anonymous organ "Andante," which was said to be based on a theme by Mozart.

But no light has been thrown upon which work of Mozart containing the theme upon which the "Andante" was based, nor upon the book from which it is taken, nor upon the date.

James Clifft Wade, born January 26, 1847, at Coven, Staffordshire, England, was an organist who held several different appointments before becoming director of the music at St. Mary's Church, Maidenhead, Berkshire, where he also conducted the Orchestral Society.

**348—Jesus, the very thought of Thee**—Authorship uncertain
Ascribed to Bernard of Clairvaux (188)
Translated by Edward Caswall (31)

**St. Agnes** (341)—John Bacchus Dykes (1)

This translation of a part of St. Bernard's great hymn,

Jesu dulcis memoria,

was published in *Lyra Catholica,* 1849, by Edward Caswall. This translation vies with that of Dr. Ray Palmer (345) for popularity and wide use.

"St. Agnes" was written for this hymn. See No. 341.

**349—How tedious and tasteless the hours**—John Newton (27)

**Contrast**—Early American melody

Concerning this hymn of John Newton's, Dr. C. S. Nutter makes this statement:

> This joyous hymn has been in every edition of our hymnbook from the first. It truly represents the fact that communion with Christ makes a heaven on earth.

"How tedious and tasteless the hours" is taken from *Olney Hymns. Book First. Hymns on Select Passages of Scripture,* 1779, headed,

None upon earth I desire beside Thee.—Psalm lxxiii. 25.

The popularity of this hymn has not been confined to Methodists, for the Baptists are also partial to it. The omission of this hymn, and others, with a strong hold on Baptists, especially in the South, called forth such a vigorous protest against the otherwise excellent book, *The Psalmist,* 1843, by Baron Stow and S. F. Smith, that four years later a Supplement, compiled by Richard Fuller, of Baltimore, and J. B. Jeter, of Richmond, was published, remedying the difficulty. In the Preface to the edition containing the Supplement, Doctors Fuller and Jeter stated:

> Old songs, like old friends, are more valued than new ones. A number of the hymns best known, most valued, and most frequently sung in the South are not found in the *Psalmist.* Without them, no hymnbook, whatever may be its excellences, is likely to become generally or permanently popular in that region. To supply this deficiency in the *Psalmist,* as far as may be, is the design of the following Supplement.
>
> These hymns have been mostly selected, not on account of their poetic beauty, but their established popularity. They will, we think, be found not seriously defective as metrical compositions; but their chief excellence consists in their adaptation to interest and affect the heart. They are, with few exceptions, inserted as they are known and sung among us, without abridgment, or any attempt at improvement. If we are not deceived, they will form an acceptable appendix to the *Psalmist.* Adapted chiefly to social worship, they will, we trust, contribute greatly to the interest and profit of our prayer and protracted meetings.
>
> Though this selection has been made with special reference to the South, we know no reason why it should not be acceptable to other portions of the country. Many of the hymns in the Supplement are of high reputation in all parts of our

country, as appears from the fact that they are found in almost every collection enjoying a local popularity.

Supplying the place of the Chants in the *Psalmist,* which, in many portions of our country are seldom used, the Supplement will add very little to the bulk, and nothing to the price, of the book.

"How tedious and tasteless the hours" was included in this Supplement, as were, among others, "Amazing grace" (209), and "How happy every child of grace" (522), which, through the camp meetings, had become well known and were sung enthusiastically by all in attendance, regardless of denominational leanings. The "good old hymn" is losing favor in some quarters, but the Baptists and Methodists still cling to it.

"Contrast" is evidently a common melody from the early part of the last century, but editors have not been in agreement in naming or accrediting it. It appeared in *The New Lute of Zion,* 1856, I. B. Woodbury, where it was set to the hymn, "Ye angels! who stand 'round the throne," by Maria de Fleury, was called "De Fleury," and was said to be an "Old Ballad." Included in Charles Dunbar's *Union Harp and Revival Chorister,* 1859, to the words "How tedious and tasteless the hours," it is again called "De Fleury." The next year, as "De Fleury," it is found in W. B. Bradbury's *Eclectic Tune Book,* where it is said to be "arranged by W. B. B." Philip Phillips called it "Contrast," but ascribed it to De Fleury in *An Offering of Praise,* for the Methodist Episcopal Church, in 1866. This book was reprinted in 1902 for the African Methodist Episcopal Church, but was evidently re-edited, for here the tune is called "Contrast" by "Defurby." In *The Hymnal of the Methodist Episcopal Church* of 1878 Lewis Edson was given as its composer, but the editors of the 1905 edition said it was "German." Official books of the Methodist Episcopal Church, South, give both "De Fleury" and "Contrast" as names for it, and the Methodist Protestants have said it was written by De Fleury. It has also been called "Green Fields," "Greenfield," and "Newton."

**350—Come unto me, when shadows darkly gather**—Catherine Harbison Esling

First tune: **Adrian**—Thomas Franklin Rinehart

Second tune: **Henley**—Lowell Mason (19)

With the title,

Come unto Me,

the poem from which this hymn is taken was published in 1839 in *The Christian Keepsake,* an annual, by Miss Catherine H. Watterman, the next year Mrs. Esling, of Philadelphia. Originally in nine stanzas, the hymn is here made up of 3, 8, and 9, with minor changes.

Catherine Harbison Esling, née Watterman, born in Philadelphia, Pennsylvania, April 12, 1812, wrote and published her poems under her maiden name before her marriage to Captain George J. Esling, of the Merchant Marine. From 1840, the year of her marriage, until the death of her husband four years later, she lived at Rio de Janeiro, where she continued her writing. In 1850, after her return to Philadelphia, her poems were published as *The Broken Bracelet and Other Poems.* She died at Philadelphia in 1897.

"Adrian" was written by Professor T. F. Rinehart, who gives this account:

> During a severe fit of sickness in Adrian, the first quatrain of the well-known hymn, "Come unto me, when shadows darkly gather," kept running through my head, and, while still confined to my bed, I made up the tune, "Adrian," to fit those beautiful words. Shortly afterward (1901) a new edition of the Methodist Protestant hymnal was about to be published, and I sent my tune on to Dr. T. H. Lewis, head of the publishing Committee, who placed it in the collection.

Thomas Franklin Rinehart, born July 16, 1860, at Pittsburgh, Pennsylvania, graduated from the music department of Adrian College in 1877, and from the literary course in 1883. He continued his studies in music at the Cincinnati Conservatory of Music, the Peabody Institute, Baltimore, and for two years in Leipzig, Germany. Returning to America, he became director of the work in music at the Methodist Protestant College at Westminster, Maryland, and has lived ever since his removal, seven years later, in Adrian, Michigan, where he held a similar position at Adrian College for six years. For nearly forty consecutive years Professor Rinehart was organist at Plymouth Methodist Protestant Church, Adrian, and for twenty years served the Masonic fraternity in a similar capacity.

"Henley" was first published in *The Hallelujah,* 1854, compiled by its composer, Lowell Mason.

**351—Sometimes a light surprises—William Cowper (24)**

**Petition—Francis Joseph Haydn (30)**

With the omission of but one word ("E'en," line 7, stanza 2) this is taken from *Olney Hymns,* 1779, where it has the title,

Joy and Peace in Believing.

"Petition" is an arrangement suggested by melodies from Haydn and Mehul: the chorus, "God of light," from *The Seasons,* 1801, and an air, "Ere fancy's bud," from *Joseph,* 1807. The tune, as used here, comes from *Wesley's Hymns, and New Supplement with Tunes,* London, 1876.

The theme of the Haydn chorus is,

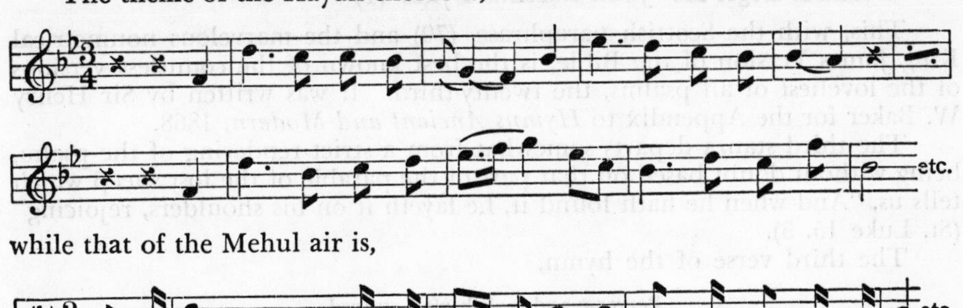


while that of the Mehul air is,

etc.

Note the comment on these themes at No. 378 in connection with the statement concerning "Manoah."

**352—In heavenly love abiding—Anna Laetitia Waring**

**Day of Rest—James William Elliott**

Miss Waring's hymn was first published in *Hymns and Meditations by A. L. W.*, 1850, entitled,

Safety in God,

and is reminiscent of the twenty-third psalm.

Anna Laetitia Waring, of whom little is known, was born April 19, 1823, at Neath, Glamorganshire, South Wales, and in her late years lived at Clifton, near Bristol, England. She published two books of hymns and is known to have contributed some verse to the *Sunday Magazine*. In order to read Old-Testament poetry in the original, she learned Hebrew and made a practice of reading her Hebrew Psalter daily. She died at Bristol, May 22, 1910.

"Day of Rest" was written as a setting for Wordsworth's hymn, "O day of rest and gladness" (396), and first appeared in *Church Hymns*, 1874, by J. W. Elliott, who assisted Sir Arthur Sullivan (15) in its preparation.

James William Elliott, born at Warwick, England, February 13, 1833, trained as a chorister at Leamington, after serving some minor appointments as organist, went to London, and in 1862 began playing at Saint Mark's Church, St. John's Wood, where he remained for thirty-six years. Sir Arthur Sullivan sought his aid in the work of preparing *Church Hymns*, 1874, for publication and acknowledged his obligation to him "for the very valuable assistance he has rendered by his good counsels, his sound judgment, and his untiring energy. . . ." His music for *Nursery Rhymes* is delightful, and his fine song, "Hybrias the Creton," is in the repertoire of many singers. Some months before his death, February 5, 1915, he resigned his position at Saint Mark's.

**353—The King of love my Shepherd is—Henry Williams Baker**

**Dominus Regit Me—John Bacchus Dykes (1)**

This, with the Scottish paraphrase (70) and the marvelous nonmetrical King James Version of the Bible, is the best known of the countless versions of the loveliest of all psalms, the twenty-third. It was written by Sir Henry W. Baker for the Appendix to *Hymns Ancient and Modern*, 1868.

The third stanza departs somewhat from a strict rendering of the psalm, being without doubt based on that part of the parable of the lost sheep which tells us, "And when he hath found it, he layeth it on his shoulders, rejoicing" (St. Luke 15. 5).

The third verse of the hymn,

Perverse and foolish oft I strayed,

were the last words spoken by the author, and Doctor Julian says, "This tender sadness, brightened by a soft, calm peace, was an epitome of his poetical life."

While other renditions of this universally loved psalm are more familiar, there is none more beautiful than that of George Herbert:

The God of love my Shepherd is,
And He that doth me feed;
While He is mine and I am His,
What can I want or need?

Or if I stray, He doth convert,
And bring my mind in frame
And all this not for my desert,
But for His holy name.

He leads me to the tender grass,
Where I both feed and rest;
Then to the streams that gently pass:
In both I have the best.

Yea, in death's shady black abode
Well may I walk, not fear;
For Thou art with me, and Thy rod
To guide, Thy staff to bear.

Surely Thy sweet and wondrous love
Shall measure all my days;
And, as it never shall remove,
So neither shall my praise.

It is a matter of regret that it is to be found in no modern American hymnal.

Sir Henry Williams Baker was born at London, May 27, 1821, and educated at Trinity College, Cambridge, where he took his B. A. Ordained in 1844, he became vicar of Monkland, near Leominster, and succeeded to the baronetcy in 1851. He lived at Monkland the remainder of his life, his death occurring there February 12, 1877. A writer of hymns and tunes, he was largely instrumental in the organization of the committee which issued *Hymns Ancient and Modern,* 1861, and became its first chairman. For many years he remained at the head of the Committee that carried on the development of this work, and exercised freely his prerogative of editing material submitted for publication—so much so that one contributor said "H. A. and M." meant "hymns asked for and mutilated." Time has vindicated his judgment.

"Dominus Regit Me" was composed by John Bacchus Dykes for this hymn for the Appendix to *Hymns Ancient and Modern,* 1868, and since its first appearance has been definitely associated with it. Another very popular musical setting for these words is the familiar anthem by Harry Rowe Shelley (1858- ) which has been sung by two generations of church quartets.

**354—Peace, perfect peace—Edward Henry Bickersteth**

**Pax Tecum—George Thomas Caldbeck**
**Arranged by Charles John Vincent (215)**

Doctor Bickersteth spent the summer of 1875 at Harrogate, the principal watering place in the north of England, where, one Sunday in August, he heard Canon Gibbon, vicar of Harrogate, preach a sermon on Isaiah 26. 3, "Thou wilt keep him in perfect peace, whose mind is stayed on thee: because he trusteth in thee," in which Canon Gibbon called attention to the fact that in the Hebrew the word "peace" was repeated, and that the 1611 translation had the rendering "perfect peace." He was so much impressed with the words "perfect peace" that the same afternoon while visiting Archdeacon Hill of Liverpool, a relative then on his deathbed, Doctor Bickersteth wrote this hymn in a few minutes at the bedside of the Archdeacon, and read it to the dying man. It was published on a card and hundreds of them were given to children whom the author confirmed. The year it was written it was published in *Songs in the House of Pilgrimage,* a tract of five hymns, and was included in *The Hymnal Companion,* second edition, 1877.

Bishop Bickersteth's biographer said:

> Its popularity spread rapidly. It is loved and sung by persons of all ranks and conditions. It is said to have been a favorite of Queen Victoria. It has been translated into many languages; and the Bishop heard it sung in Japanese and Chinese on his tour in the East.

Richard le Gallienne, poet and critic, says,

> It would be difficult to name any other hymn so filled with the sense of man's security as this, which tranquillizes me at certain moments to a remarkable degree.

The form of the hymn, the first line of each couplet being a question while the second is the answer, makes it suitable for antiphonal singing.

Edward Henry Bickersteth, D.D., was born at Islington, England, January 25, 1825; graduated from Cambridge University, and filled various appointments as curate, rector, and vicar; he was made Dean of Gloucester in 1885 and the same year was appointed Bishop of Exeter. He published twelve volumes of his poetry, but is best known for his *Hymnal Companion to the Book of Common Prayer,* issued first in 1870, and in a much revised form in 1877. Doctor Julian says this work in its Anglican representativeness "is at the head of all hymnals in the Church of England."

Bishop Bickersteth loved hymns as few men have done. His son says,

> It was his invariable custom to expect each one of us on Sundays at tea to repeat a hymn, and he did the same, unless, as frequently happened, he wrote us a special hymn himself, in which way many of his hymns were first given to the Church.

He retired from active work some five years before his death at London, May 16, 1906.

"Pax Tecum" is something of a mystery. There are two reports of its writing, neither of which has been fully authenticated. G. T. Caldbeck, its composer, is said by James Moffatt to have written it while a student and precentor at Islington Theological Seminary. James Love says that while Caldbeck was a missionary in China, he wrote as best he could a melody for "Peace, perfect peace," which he sent to Doctor Bickersteth. Whatever may be the truth of the matter, the tune was so revised and reharmonized by Charles J. Vincent (215) before publication in *The Hymnal Companion* of

1877 as to make it virtually his product, although editors still persist in assigning it to Caldbeck.

George Thomas Caldbeck, born in 1852 and educated at Islington Theological Seminary, is said to have abandoned his plans for work in the foreign-missionary field because of ill health. Going to Ireland, where he taught school for some time before becoming an evangelist, he returned to London and became prominent as a free-lance out-door preacher, his eccentricities and independence making it impossible for others to work with him. For many years he led a precarious existence, being reduced to selling tracts from house to house. On one occasion he was arrested for not having a peddler's license, but was released when the magistrate before whom he was taken learned he was the composer of "Pax Tecum." Though living in extreme poverty he even then presented a gentlemanly and scholarly appearance. Finally disappearing from view, it is not known what became of him. His death is supposed to have occurred in 1912.

**355—Sing praise to God who reigns above**—Johann Jakob Schütz
Translated by Frances Elizabeth Cox

**Mit Freuden Zart**—From the Bohemian Brethren's Gesangbuch, 1566

This translation by Miss Cox of

Sei Lob und Ehr dem höchsten Gut,

by Johann J. Schütz, appeared in *Lyra Eucharistica,* 1864. The hymn, which attracted attention from its first appearance and which has played a large part in German religious life, was founded on Deuteronomy 32. 3, "Because I will publish the name of the Lord: ascribe ye greatness unto our God," and was headed,

Hymn of Thanksgiving.

It first appeared in nine stanzas in *Christliches Gedenckbüchlein,* by Schütz, in 1675.

Johann Jakob Schütz, born September 6, 1640, at Frankfurt-am-Main, Germany, studied law and for a time practiced his profession in Frankfurt, in his later years having the title of "Rath." A man of great piety as well as learning, he was a close friend of P. J. Spener, and it was at his suggestion that Spener started his *Collegia Pietatis,* a prayer meeting, which was the beginning of the Pietist movement. Schütz became a Separatist and discontinued his attendance at Lutheran services. He died at Frankfurt, May 22, 1690.

Frances Elizabeth Cox, born at Oxford, England, in 1812, shares with Catherine Winkworth (7) the honor of being among the best translators of German hymns into English. She published two volumes of her translations: *Sacred Hymns from the German,* 1841, and *Hymns from the German,* 1864, the latter a revision of much of the material contained in the former, with the addition of some new material. She is said to have consulted with Baron

C. C. J. von Bunsen, minister from Germany to the Court of Saint James from 1841 to 1854, as to worthy hymns which should be translated. She died in 1897.

"Mit Freuden Zart" is from an old pre-Reformation melody. Many of these old tunes were used by Martin Luther (67) in his early singing books. This tune comes from the Bohemian Brethren's *Kirchengesänge* of 1566, which was the singing book of the old Brethren Church of Moravia and Bohemia, but it is said to have been much changed. A happy tune, as its name implies, it should not be sung too slowly.

**356—O how happy are they—Charles Wesley (25)**

**Rapture—R. D. Humphreys (?)**

This hymn, from *Hymns and Sacred Poems,* 1749, was written in sixteen stanzas in two parts, all of which appeared in the old *Pocket Hymn Book* and in others until 1849, when it was reduced to nine. This is the hymn containing the stanzas which have caused some of Charles Wesley's devotees to question whether he really wrote such ridiculous lines as are found in the omitted fifth and sixth stanzas:

On the wings of His love
I was carry'd above
All sin, and temptation, and pain;
I could not believe
That I ever should grieve,
That I ever should suffer again.

I rode on the sky,
Freely justify'd I!
Nor envy'd Elijah his seat;
My soul mounted higher
In a chariot of fire,
And the moon it was under my feet.

The wonder is that more writing equally poor was not done by Charles Wesley, who, in his more than six thousand hymns, should be permitted to indulge in some flights of fancy without being overly criticized.

The hymn was first written in triplet form although others in the same meter are in six-line stanzas. It has been slightly altered, in most cases to comply with metrical requirements, though not enough to warrant notice here. In the American *Pocket Hymn Book* it was one of five hymns classified under "Convinced of Backsliding."

"Rapture" is called "Rapture of Love" in many of the old books, and "Comfort" in others. In the *Hymnal of the Methodist Episcopal Church,* 1878, it is said to be by one R. D. Humphreys, but the author of this MANUAL has not found his name elsewhere and has been unable to find anything about him. In other books it is said to be a "Western Melody," but in the majority of cases no credit of any kind is given.

This tune was not used with this hymn in the *Methodist Hymnal* of 1905, because the august members of the commission which compiled it felt it was entirely too happy. When Dean Lutkin (132), commissioned to write another tune for it, produced "City Road," No. 311 in that book, he thought so little of his effort that he signed "John Jones" as its composer. It was so published in the first few printings, but later Dean Lutkin received credit for having written it. In the *Biographical Index of the Composers of Tunes* for the 1905 Methodist book, Doctor Nutter has this notation:

> Jones, John (1730-1796). An English organist, composer and author.
> *Tune*—City Road, 311

Dean Lutkin told this story with great glee to the author many years ago, but asked that it not be published until after his death.

When the committees for the retention of old tunes and for the selection of new ones for the present *Hymnal* discussed an appropriate setting for this hymn, it was the consensus that it would be just as well to go back to the old tune that had so long been associated with it.

**357—Joy is a fruit that will not grow**—John Newton (27)

**Elizabethtown**—George Kingsley (61)

This hymn, retained in the present *Methodist Hymnal* because it is a favorite with the Negroes in certain sections of the South, comes from *Olney Hymns. Book First. Hymns on Select Passages of Scripture,* 1779, headed,

> The Joy of the Law is our strength,

based on Nehemiah 8. 10: "Then he said unto them, Go your way, eat the fat, and drink the sweet, and send portions unto them for whom nothing is prepared: for this day is holy unto our Lord: neither be ye sorry; for the joy of the Lord is your strength." It was originally in nine stanzas, the last being omitted here.

"Elizabethtown," by George Kingsley, appeared first in his *Sacred Choir,* 1838, set to William Cowper's hymn, "O for a closer walk with God" (228).

**358—Rejoice, ye pure in heart**—Edward Hayes Plumptre

**Marion**—Arthur Henry Messiter

One of the most popular of our processional hymns, this was written by Doctor Plumptre for that purpose, the occasion being a choir festival held in May, 1865, at Peterborough Cathedral, one of the most important Norman churches now standing in England. With a special musical setting it was first published the same year and then again, in 1865, but without music, in Doctor Plumptre's *Lazarus and Other Poems,* second edition. Three years later it was launched on a successful career by being included in the Appendix to *Hymns Ancient and Modern.* Its great popularity is deserved.

Edward Hayes Plumptre, D.D., was born at London, August 6, 1821, and educated at King's College, London, and at University College, Oxford. One time Fellow of Brasenose, he took Holy Orders and rapidly forged to the front as a preacher and theologian, holding many appointments and finally becoming Dean of Wells. His literary contributions in the fields of history, divinity,

Biblical criticism, biography, poetry, and the classics have been numerous and important. Doctor Julian says,

> The rhythm of his verse has a special attraction for musicians, its poetry for the cultured, and its stately simplicity for the devout and earnest minded.

He died at the Deanery, Wells, February 1, 1891.

"Marion" was written in 1883 for this hymn and was included by Doctor Messiter in the *Hymnal with Music,* 1889. This was the

> preliminary report of the committee on the Hymnal appointed by the General Convention of 1886, modified with music as used in Trinity Church, New York,

and was edited by Doctor Messiter. This tune, so admirably suited to the thought of Dean Plumptre's hymn, gave it the impetus which placed it among the choicest of processionals.

Arthur Henry Messiter, Mus. Doc., was born at Frome Selwood, Somersetshire, England, April 1, 1834. After beginning the serious study of music when he was seventeen years old, he articled to a prominent musician in Northampton for four years, then took some additional work in piano and voice, in preparation for a teaching career. Upon his coming to America in 1863, he sang for a time as a volunteer in Trinity Church Choir in New York, where he was later to be identified with some unusual developments. After a time at Philadelphia and at Poultney, Vermont, he returned to New York City early in 1866 to take charge of the music at Trinity Church and to act as organist there. At the time of his appointment a New York musical paper said: "We hear that the authorities of Trinity Church have appointed an organist from Philadelphia. We suppose that at the next vacancy they will try Coney Island." Doctor Messiter remained at Trinity Church for thirty-one years, retiring in 1897. He wrote an interesting *History of the Choir and Music of Trinity Church,* 1906, and edited the *Hymnal with Music as used in Trinity Church.* His death occurred in New York City, July 2, 1916.

# Hope and Aspiration

**359—Awake, my soul, stretch every nerve**—Philip Doddridge (69)

**Christmas** (88)—Arranged from George Frederick Handel (88)

Doctor Doddridge wrote this hymn to follow a sermon he had preached, based on Philippians 3. 12-14: "Not as though I had already attained, either were already perfect: but I follow after, if that I may apprehend that for which also I am apprehended of Christ Jesus. Brethren, I count not myself to have apprehended: but this one thing I do, forgetting those things which are behind, and reaching forth unto those things which are before, I press toward the mark for the prize of the high calling of God in Christ Jesus." Dr. C. S. Robinson says it is a "matchless challenge—ringing like a trumpeter's note to start the athletes." It appeared in Doddridge's *Hymns,* 1775, with the title,

> Pressing on in the Christian Race.

**360—O Thou, to whose all-searching sight**—Nicolaus Ludwig Zinzendorf (205)
Translated by John Wesley (36)

**Bera** (196)—John Edgar Gould (196)

In John Wesley's *Psalms and Hymns,* 1738, appears his free translation of Count Zinzendorf's

Seelenbräutigam, O du Gottes-Lamm,

doubtless taken from the *Herrnhut Gesang-Buch,* 1735, although the original had appeared ten years earlier, in the *Sammlung geistlicher und lieblicher Lieder.* Wesley's hymn has as its third stanza a translation of one stanza from "Wer ist wohl wie du," by Johann A. Freylinghausen (1670-1739). In this stanza Wesley originally translated the first line,

Where rising floods my head o'erflow,

but changed "head" to "soul" in his *Collection* of 1780. Doctor Telford thinks the change "robs the fourth line of its point, but it is Wesley's own change." In the last half of line 3, stanza 1, "years" has been substituted for "parts." The title of the hymn was

The Believer's Support

**361—Dear God, our Father, at Thy knee confessing**—Katharine Lee Bates (101)

**Deeper Life**—Lindsay Bartholomew Longacre

Miss Bates wrote this hymn at the request of Dr. Earl Marlatt (178) for the *American Student Hymnal,* 1928, of which he was an associate editor. His request was that she provide a hymn on "the immanence of God." In his Memorial Address, "Hail and Farewell," delivered at Wellesley College Chapel in May, 1929, Doctor Marlatt, in recounting the incident, said Miss Bates seemed "appalled" at the prospect, but after some persuasion consented, and two days later handed him this hymn which she entitled,

For Deeper Life.

"Deeper Life" was written for this hymn for *The Abingdon Hymnal,* 1928; like the hymn, it was written upon request. Dr. Earl E. Harper (112), having the book in preparation, and wanting a new tune for the new hymn, which had been written to go with Mendelssohn's "Consolation" (40), asked Doctor Longacre to supply it. This he did, giving the tune as its name the full title Miss Bates had given the hymn, "For Deeper Life."

Lindsay Bartholomew Longacre, Ph.D., professor of Old Testament literature and religion at Iliff School of Theology, Denver, Colorado, was born January 26, 1870, at Pottsville, Pennsylvania. Graduating as a mining engineer from the School of Mines, Columbia University, he attended Drew Theological Seminary, the University of Jena, Germany, and New York University, Ph.D., 1908. Ordained a minister of the Methodist Episcopal Church in 1896, he held several pastorates in New York state until 1910, when he was called to his present Professorship. An author of distinction in his field, he compiled and edited, with Dr. Ira S. Dodd, *The Riverdale Hymn Book,* 1912.

**362—Nearer, my God, to Thee**—Sarah Flower Adams
**Bethany**—Lowell Mason (19)

This hymn, which comforted William McKinley in his last hours, beloved of Queen Victoria, Theodore Roosevelt, Edward VII, and a host of others, is based, of course, on Genesis 28. 10-22, the story of Jacob at Bethel. The hymn is invested throughout with the imagery of the story. Doctor Marlatt (178) speaks of it as being "a mighty expression of trust and triumph in the crises of life." Though some question has been raised concerning its basis in fact, the story persists that the band on the fated "Titanic" played this hymn as the great ship sank shortly after its collision with an iceberg in the north Atlantic, Sunday, April 14, 1912. Many are the incidents related of its comforting helpfulness in times of great stress. It is justly one of the most celebrated of all hymns, more than one critic lauding its fine artistic integrity.

It was written by Mrs. Adams in November, 1840, and is one of thirteen hymns she contributed to *Hymns and Anthems,* 1841, published by her minister, the Rev. W. J. Fox, for the members of his congregation.

Sarah Flower Adams was born February 22, 1805, at Harlow, Essex, England. She was the daughter of Benjamin Flower, who was imprisoned at Newgate and fined for publishing an alleged libelous attack on the Bishop of Llandaff. Shortly after his release he married Miss Eliza Gould, who had visited him in prison. Ambitious from her girlhood to become an actress, Sarah Flower had an unquestioned dramatic instinct, and as she became older the belief grew in her that the actress's plane of life should be as high and noble as the thoughts they expressed through their spoken lines. After her marriage in 1834 to John B. Adams, a civil engineer and inventor in the early days of the development of steam locomotion, she was encouraged by her husband to go on the stage, and she made her first appearance as "Lady Macbeth" in 1837 at the Richmond Theatre. Her success was such that she received an engagement at the Bath Theatre, but her strength proved unequal to the task of public performance, and she thereafter devoted herself to literary work, contributing to the *Monthly Repository,* and writing lyric verse and dramatic poems. Her most ambitious effort was *Vivia Perpetua—a Dramatic Poem,* 1841, without permanent place in literature. She is now remembered solely for having written this one hymn, "Nearer, My God, to Thee." Although Mrs. Adams was a member of the Unitarian Church, this hymn is sung in Trinitarian churches in every part of the Christian world.

Mrs. Adams has been described as being "tall and singularly beautiful, with noble and regular features; in manner gay and impulsive, her conversation witty and sparkling" by an intimate friend, Mrs. Bridell Fox, who wrote at another time:

> How she composed her hymns can hardly be stated. She certainly never had any idea of composing them. They were the spontaneous expression of some strong impulse or feeling at the moment; she was essenially a creature of impulse. Her

translations would be, of course, to a certain extent, an exception; also, perhaps, when she was writing words for music already in use at South Place Chapel. Otherwise she wrote when she felt that the spirit moved her.

She died August 11, 1848, at London, of tuberculosis, having, it is thought, contracted the disease from her sister, Eliza, who had fallen its victim two years previously.

"Bethany" made "Nearer, my God, to Thee" one of the best-loved hymns in America. It had been included in Henry Ward Beecher's *Plymouth Collection* of 1855, to the following tune, which was impossible even in those days:

The next year, 1856, Lowell Mason wrote for it the tune that has become generally identified with it. It was first published in the Andover *Sabbath Hymn and Tune Book,* 1859. Lowell Mason arranged as a hymn tune any melody that struck his fancy. This was doubtless suggested by the air sung to "Oft in the stilly night":

**363—O for a heart of calm repose—Anonymous**

**Spohr—Adapted from Louis Spohr (299)**

This hymn by an unknown author came from *Hymns of the Ages,* third series, 1864, the last of a succession of volumes numbering approximately 325 pages each, whose two compilers signed the Preface with their initials only. The books are dated, respectively, 1858, 1860, and 1864. This hymn is included in that section of volume three headed "Quiet."

"Spohr" came to be a hymn tune by way of an anthem by James Stimpson (1820-1886). He adapted "As pants the hart" to the music of "Though all my friends prove faithless," a solo and chorus from Spohr's oratorio, *Calvary,* 1834 [also known as the *Crucifixion*], whose text dealt with "the last hours of the Saviour." The anthem became very popular, and its first few measures were adapted, by some unknown person, as a hymn tune. The air upon which the anthem was based is:

Though all my friends prove faith - less, Though all for - sake and flee,

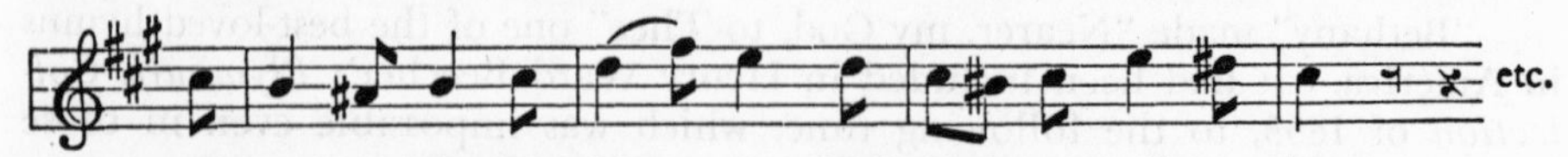
Thy love, all gra - cious Mas - ter, Shall bind me still to thee.
etc.

The naming of this tune has been discussed at No. 299.

**364—More love to Thee, O Christ**—Elizabeth Payson Prentiss

**More Love to Thee**—William Howard Doane (231)

Dr. George L. Prentiss, husband of the author of this hymn, tells in his biography of his wife something of the writing of it:

> The hymn, "More Love to Thee, O Christ," belongs probably as far back as the year 1856. Like most of her hymns, it is simply a prayer put into the form of verse. She wrote it so hastily that the last stanza was left incomplete, one line having to be added in pencil when it was printed. She did not show it, not even to her husband, until many years after it was written; and she wondered not a little that, when published, it met with so much favor.

Printed first as a leaflet in 1869, the next year it was included by Doctor Doane in his *Songs of Devotion,* in four stanzas, the third being omitted here.

Elizabeth Payson Prentiss was born at Portland, Maine, October 26, 1818, and when only sixteen years of age began contributing both poetry and prose to *The Youths' Companion.* After teaching school for some years in Portland, Maine, Ipswich, Massachusetts, and Richmond, Virginia, she married an eminent divine, Dr. George L. Prentiss, professor at Union Theological Seminary in New York City. Although her health was never robust, Mrs. Prentiss published several volumes of her works, the best known being *Stepping Heavenward.* Among her publications are *Religious Poems,* 1873, and *Golden Hours, or, Hymns and Songs of the Christian Life,* 1874. Her husband published her *Life and Letters* soon after her death in New York City, August 13, 1878.

"More Love to Thee" was written by Dr. W. H. Doane for this hymn for his *Songs of Devotion,* 1870.

**365—We hope in Thee, O God**—Marianne Hearn

**Resignation**—Moses Smith Cross

The exact source of this hymn has not been discovered. It has had limited use and is not known to Julian, nor is it mentioned in *Baptist Hymn Writers,* although each has a biographical account of Miss Hearn and mentions other hymns by her. It probably was first published in *The Sunday School Times* or in a newspaper, *The Christian World,* as she was a contributor to both publications.

Marianne Hearn, born at Farningham, Kent, England, was known during her active literary life only as Marianne Farningham, the *nom de plume* under which she wrote. She published three books of poems, mostly collected from her contributions to *The Christian World* and to *The Sunday School Times,* of which she was the editor.

"Resignation," written by Dr. Moses S. Cross for this hymn, first appeared in *The Methodist Hymnal* of 1905.

Moses Smith Cross, D.D., son of the Rev. Aaron Cross, a Methodist Episcopal minister of the Rock River Conference, was born in 1854. Admitted in 1890 to the California Conference, he joined the faculty of the University of the Pacific, Stockton, a year later, and was sometime its acting president and vice-president. He was an accomplished linguist and amateur musician. Doctor Cross died at Esparto, California, April 20, 1911.

**366—As pants the hart for cooling streams**—Psalm xlii
Tate and Brady, 1696 (14)
Altered by Henry Francis Lyte (77)

**Spohr** (363)—Adapted from Louis Spohr (299)

The first, second, and last stanzas of this rendering of the familiar forty-second psalm are, with the exception of the last line of the fourth stanza, exactly as they appeared in the *New Version of the Psalms of David fitted to the tunes used in churches by N. Brady, D.D., Chaplain in Ordinary, and N. Tate, Esq.; Poet-Laureat to His Majesty* (to give all of the title page except the imprint), first issued in 1696, the whole, including the third stanza, taken from H. F. Lyte's *Spirit of the Psalms,* 1834. The last line of this version was written,

Thy health's eternal spring,

and the lines which were the basis for the present third stanza were:

I sigh whene'er my musing thoughts
Those happy days present,
When I with troops of pious friends
Thy temple did frequent.

In a paper read before a convention held in the autumn of 1905 to promote the claims of the Psalms in worship, under the direction of the General Assembly of the United Presbyterian Church of North America, the Rev. David Reed Miller said:

In Psalm xlii we have the plaintive threnody of the Babylonian captive. And what can be more tenderly pathetic than this patriotic yearning for the old church where he used to worship, back on the Judean hills? Here is the touching metaphor in which he describes that longing:

"As the hart panteth after the water brooks,
So panteth my soul after Thee, O God."

**367—Make me a captive, Lord**—George Matheson (318)

**Leominster**—George William Martin

Arranged by Arthur Seymour Sullivan (15)

Written by Doctor Matheson in 1890 at Row, Dumbartonshire, Scotland, and published the same year in his *Sacred Songs,* this hymn was entitled

Christian Freedom

and was based on Ephesians 3. 1: "For this cause I Paul, the prisoner of Jesus Christ for you Gentiles."

"Leominster," arranged by Sir Arthur Sullivan from a part song called "The Pilgrim Song," by George W. Martin, first appeared in Vol. II of *The Journal of Part Music,* 1862. Sullivan's arrangement appeared in *Church Hymns with Tunes,* in 1874. In this work, it was stated that the tune was an old melody, but in *Hymn Tunes composed by Arthur Sullivan,* it was credited to G. W. Martin.

George William Martin, born at London, March 8, 1828, was a choir boy at St. Paul's Cathedral, where he received his early musical training. He was Professor of Music at the Normal College for Army Schoolmasters, music master at St. John's Training College, Battersea, and organist at Christ Church there. Martin had a peculiar aptitude for training choirs of school children and some of his public performances by them were very successful. He wrote many songs of the glee and madrigal type, was successful in winning prizes with some of them, and edited cheap editions of the more popular works of Haydn, Handel, and others. He fell into bad habits, drank heavily, and died from want and exposure at a London hospital April 16, 1881, where his identity would have been unknown save for the loyalty of one friend who stood by him to the end.

**368—Sunset and evening star**—Alfred Tennyson (206)

**Crossing the Bar**—Joseph Barnby (31)

Lord Tennyson's son wrote:

> "Crossing the Bar" was written in my Father's eighty-first year, on a day in October (1889) when we came from Aldworth to Farringford. Before reaching Farringford he had the moaning of the bar in his mind, and after dinner he showed me this poem written out. I said: "That is the crown of your life's work." He answered: "It came in a moment." He explained the "Pilot" as "that Divine and Unseen who is always guiding us." . . . A few days before my Father's end (1892), he said to me, "Mind you put 'Crossing the Bar' at the end of all my poems."

It is needless to say the poet's wish has been complied with, and this "delicate work of art" always appears last in collections of his poems.

"Crossing the Bar" was composed for Lord Tennyson's words by Sir Joseph Barnby for the *Home and School Hymnal,* 1892. Another tune by the same name was written for this poem by Sir John F. Bridge for Lord Tennyson's funeral service, held at Westminster Abbey, October 12, 1892.

**369—Blest are the pure in heart**—John Keble (35)

**Greenwood** (217)—Joseph Emerson Sweetser (217)

Stanzas 1 and 2 are the first and last from a seventeen-stanza poem in Keble's *Christian Year,* 1827, entitled,

THE PURIFICATION

Blessed are the pure in heart: for
they shall see God.—St. Matthew v. 8.

The third stanza is from the *New Mitre Hymn Book,* 1836, and was doubtless written by W. J. Hall (1793-1861), an English clergyman, one time Priest of the Royal Chapel, St. James's. This book received its name from the miter stamped on its cover. This text omits one stanza and has changes in line 3, stanza 3, from that authorized by John Keble. The change made the line read,

O give the pure and lowly heart,

where the Rev. Hall had written,

Give us a pure and lowly heart.

**370—O for a heart to praise my God**—Charles Wesley (25)

**Belmont** (28)—From William Gardiner's Sacred Melodies

The hymn is from *Hymns and Sacred Poems,* 1742, and is based on the prayer-book version of Psalm 51. 10:

Make me a clean heart, O God.

The original has "an heart" in place of "a heart" in each case; Wesley wrote "My dear Redeemer" instead of "My Great Redeemer" in the second stanza; began the third "An humble"; and had "dearest Lord" in the first line of the last stanza instead of "gracious Lord." John Wesley made these corrections before including the hymn in his large *Collection* of 1780.

John Wesley said:

I find scarcely any temptations from anything in the world: My danger is from persons.

O for a heart to praise my God,
A heart from sin set free.

To John Fletcher of Madeley, "such a hymn was meat and drink." He said, "Here is undoubtedly an evangelical prayer for the love which restores the soul to a state of sinless rest and scriptural perfection."

There is a story told of an old English Congregational minister and his wife who talked much of "Christian perfection," but decided they could not be far wrong if they sang this hymn with their whole hearts.

"Belmont" is one of the most famous tunes of the nineteenth century, even though doubt exists as to its source. (See Nos. 28 and 260.)

## Christian Perfection

**371—Jesus, Thine all-victorious love—Charles Wesley (25)**

**Azmon** (162)—Carl Gotthelf Gläser (162)
Arranged by Lowell Mason (19)

From *Hymns and Sacred Poems,* 1740, in twelve stanzas, entitled,

Against Hope, Believing in Hope,

stanzas 4, 9, 11, and 12 comprise this cento. Charles Wesley wrote lines 2 and 3, stanza 4,

Can now no longer move;
Jesus is all the world to me.

The first stanza, as Charles Wesley wrote it, is,

My God! I know, I feel Thee mine,
And will not quit my claim,
Till all I have be lost in Thine,
And all renew'd I am.

**372—Love divine, all loves excelling—Charles Wesley (25)**

**Love Divine**—John Zundel

This hymn first appeared in four stanzas in the rather curiously named

HYMNS
FOR THOSE THAT SEEK
AND THOSE THAT HAVE
REDEMPTION
IN THE BLOOD OF
JESUS CHRIST

in 1747, entitled,

Jesus, show us thy salvation.

John Wesley omitted stanza 2 from his *Collection* of 1780, but it is found in the *Pocket Hymn Book,* York, 1786. In the *Methodist Pocket Hymn Book,* the line,

Take away our power of sinning,

as written by Charles Wesley, was changed to,

Take away our bent of sinning.

The "bent of sinning" was changed to "bent to sinning," as it now reads, by 1829. This second stanza has seemed to be a matter of concern from its first writing. Charles Wesley in the 1747 pamphlet italicized "power," evidently anticipating the criticism of his use of that word which followed. John Fletcher, of whom John Wesley said, "We were of one heart and one soul. We had no secrets between us. For many years we did not purposely hide anything from each other," asks of the line,

Take away our power of sinning,

> Is not this expression too strong? Would it not be better to soften it by saying, "Take away the love of sinning"? (or the bent of the mind towards sin). Can God take away from us our *power of sinning* without taking away our power of free obedience?

Remaining unaltered in Methodist hymnals until 1935, the other doubtful line in the second stanza,

> Let us find that second rest,

was made to read,

> Let us find the promised rest.

The Primitive Methodists in England, however, had made the change fifty years before; and the author of this MANUAL finds the stanza written in long hand, in an old late eighteenth-century tune book, in this form:

> Breathe! O breathe Thy loving spirit
> Into ev'ry troubled Breast!
> Let us all in Thee inherit,
> Let us find Thy promised Rest:
> Take away the Love of sinning
> Alpha and Omega be
> End of Faith, as its Beginning,
> Set our Hearts at Liberty.

The name "Sarah Maria Knipe" appears, written apparently by the same hand, in ink, above the first hymn, indicating her ownership, but who she was is, of course, unknown. Remarkably, she anticipated the action of the Joint Commission of the Revision of *The Methodist Hymnal* by more than a century.

Doctor Dearmer calls attention to the fact that this is one of the few earlier hymns that dwell on the thought of God as love, and thinks that its continued popularity may be accounted for because it does address God in that way.

"Love Divine," more generally known as "Beecher," and also called "Zundel," was included in John Zundel's *Christian Heart Songs,* 1870. Zundel's harmonization has been criticized by purists because of the "octaves" between the soprano and tenor. The only explanation for it, if one is needed, is that it is three-part writing, and that Zundel must have known just what he was doing when he wrote it and wanted these voices "doubled," for he did it three times.

The Rev. F. Luke Wiseman in his *Charles Wesley, Evangelist and Poet,* tells us that in the hymns of Charles Wesley:

> Here and there are to be found phrases borrowed or suggested by other writers. . . The curious can find in his songs frequent echoes of the English poets, Milton,[1] Dryden, Pope, Prior, Young, and others. . . .
>
> Occasionally the poem will start him on a crusade of rescue just as did a good melody allied to indifferent words. To both causes may be ascribed the origin of

[1] See No. 309, "Talk with us, Lord, Thyself reveal."

one sublime hymn, "Love divine, all loves excelling." Without doubt his muse was set going by the "Song of Venus," from Dryden's play *King Arthur.* Probably, however, it was not the words but Purcell's entrancing aria to which they were set which haunted his ear. At any rate, the hymn was sung to this melody. At one and the same time, therefore, our Sir Galahad rescued this captive melody from Dryden's amorous words, and the great word "Love" from its bondage to the heathen goddess, united the two, and set them free for the glorious service of their heavenly Lord. So Dryden's words,

> "Fairest Isles, all Isles excelling,
> Seat of Pleasures and of Loves;
> Venus here will chuse her dwelling,
> And forsake her Cyprian groves.
>
> "Cupid from his Fav-rite nation
> Care and Envy will remove;
> Jealousy and poysons Passion
> And Despair that dies of love,"

are transfigured into

> "Love divine, all loves excelling,
> Joy of heaven, to earth come down;
> Fix in us thy humble dwelling,
> All thy faithful mercies crown:
>
> "Jesu, thou art all compassion,
> Pure, unbounded love thou art;
> Visit us with thy salvation,
> Enter every trembling heart."

In John Wesley's 1761 tune book, *Sacred Melody,* under the new name "Westminster," Purcell's lovely melody is wedded to Charles Wesley's delightful hymn:

John Zundel was born at Hochdorf, Germany, December 10, 1815, and after receiving his education, went to Russia. For seven years organist and bandmaster in Saint Petersburg, he came to America, where he remained for thirty years—from 1847. All the time he was in this country he lived in New York and Brooklyn, except for a few months spent in Detroit, as organist at Central Methodist Episcopal Church. This was just before his return to Germany, where he died at Cannstadt, in July, 1882. He is best known from his long association with Henry Ward Beecher at Plymouth Church, Brooklyn. At Doctor Beecher's request Darius E. Jones, with the assistance of Zundel, compiled and issued *Temple Melodies* in 1851. This did not satisfy Doctor Beecher, so he, with the assistance of his brother, Charles, and Mr. Zundel, produced the famous *Plymouth Collection* in 1855. Zundel issued other books of varied character and edited and published the *Monthly Choir and Organ Journal.* He had a very marked effect on church music in America. Doctor Beecher once said of him: "Mr. Zundel has co-operated with me for nearly twenty years in building up congregational singing in Plymouth Church."

**373—For ever here my rest shall be—Charles Wesley (25)**

**Martyrdom (Avon) (70)—Hugh Wilson (70)**

The first two stanzas of the original of this hymn based on I Corinthians 1. 30: "But of him are ye in Christ Jesus, who of God is made unto us wisdom, and righteousness, and sanctification, and redemption," and entitled,

Christ our Righteousness,

have been omitted. They are:

Jesus, Thou art my Righteousness,
For all my sins were Thine:
Thy death hath bought of God my peace,
Thy life hath made Him mine.

Spotless and just, in Thee I am;
I feel my sins forgiven;
I taste salvation in Thy name,
And antedate my heaven,

and the original of stanza 2, line 3, was,

Sprinkle me ever in thy blood,

and of stanza 4, line 3,

Till hope shall in fruition die.

The hymn was first published in *Hymns and Sacred Poems,* 1740.

**374—O how the thought of God attracts**—Frederick William Faber (76)
**Sawley**—James Walch

Here are the first five stanzas, unaltered, taken from Faber's *Jesus and Mary,* 1852, where this meditation was entitled,

Holiness Desired.

"Sawley" was composed for a children's anniversary celebration in 1857, and was first published, with other tunes for private circulation, in 1860.

James Walch, born at Egerton, near Bolton, Lancashire, England, June 21, 1837; studied organ with his father and with Henry Smart (77); was organist at Duke's Alley Congregational Church, Bridge Street Wesleyan Chapel, and St. George's Church, Bolton; and became director of the Bolton Philharmonic Society in 1870. From this he retired in 1874, going, in 1877, to engage in a music business at Barrow-in-Furness, where he acted as honorary organist of the parish church. He is better known for having written "Tidings" (475), although he composed other hymn tunes and many pieces for the piano. Four of his tunes were in *The Methodist Hymnal* of 1905. He died at Barrow-in-Furness in 1901.

**375—Thou hidden Love of God, whose height**—Gerhard Tersteegen (185)
Translated by John Wesley (36)

**New 113th**—William Hayes

John Wesley preached a sermon at St. Mary's Church, Oxford, on January 1, 1733, in which, among other things, he said, "Love is the fulfilling of the law, the end of the commandment." In his *Plain Account of Christian Perfection,* he says:

In the same sentiment did my brother and I remain (with all those young gentlemen in derision termed Methodists) till we embarked for America, in the latter end of 1735. It was the next year, while I was at Savannah, that I wrote the following lines:

> Is there a thing beneath the sun,
> That strives with thee my heart to share?
> Ah! tear it thence, and reign alone,
> The Lord of every motion there!

Stanzas 1, 4, 6, and 8 comprise this selection from Wesley's eight-stanza translation. He wrote the last line,

> To taste Thy love be all my choice.

Two other changes were made by the editorial committee of the 1935 *Methodist Hymnal.* Line 4, stanza 1, began, "Inly I sigh" and was made "And inly sigh," and lines 3 and 4, stanza 3, were changed from,

> Chase this self-will through all my heart,
> Through all its latent mazes there,

so as to be,

> Chase this self-will from all my heart,
> From all its hidden mazes there.

Ralph Waldo Emerson agreed with Oliver Wendell Holmes when he said there was only one supreme hymn, most of them being cabinet work, not poetry, and referred to "Thou hidden love of God," as being that one.

John Wesley translated Gerhard Tersteegen's hymn beginning,

> Verborgne Gottes Liebe du,

which had appeared in Tersteegen's *Geistliches Blumengärtlein,* 1729, and published it in his *Charlestown Collection* of 1737. St. Augustine perhaps suggested the thought of the hymn, as in the well-known opening paragraph of his *Confessions* he says,

> Thou movest us to delight in praising Thee; for Thou hast formed us for Thyself, and our hearts are restless till they find rest in Thee.

"New 113th" appeared in William Hayes's *Sixteen Psalms . . . set to music for the use of Magdalen Chapel in Oxford,* about 1774, and was set to James Merrick's version of Psalm 134. How the tune came to be called "New 113th" is a mystery. It is a good example of the type of hymn tune produced during the middle-eighteenth-century period, perhaps one of the better ones. The flatted seventh in the fifth line seems exactly suited to the sentiment expressed by the words:

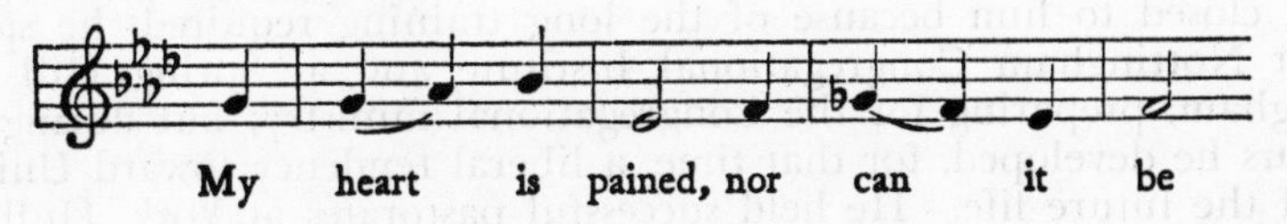
My heart is pained, nor can it be

William Hayes, Mus. Doc., was born at Hanbury, Worcestershire, England, in December, 1706, or 1707, *Grove's Dictionary* giving the latter date as opposed to other authorities agreeing on the former. He was articled to

William Hine (1687-1730), noted organist of Gloucester Cathedral, under whom Hayes became a chorister, and he is said to have become

> excellent in playing church music and extempore voluntaries. Few men knew the power of that instrument better; and by a very happy facility of expressing the genius of various stops was often attended to by the admirers of that species of playing with heartfelt satisfaction.

Five years after the expiration of his articles he was called to the position of organist and master of the choristers at Magdalen College, Oxford, where he remained forty-three years, becoming Professor of Music in 1742, and being granted the Doctorate in Music in 1749. On that occasion, when he was presented for the honor, Doctor Bradley, Professor of Astronomy, described him

> not only as a man eminent in his faculty, but as one whose sweetness of temper vied with that of his art.

A man of unusual culture and learning, he died July 27, 1777, at Oxford.

**376—Dear Master, in whose life I see**—John Hunter

**Hursley** (56)—Adapted from Katholisches Gesangbuch, 1774 (56)

Doctor Hunter's intensively devotional hymn first appeared in the *Monthly Calendar* of his church, Trinity, in Glasgow, and, later, in 1896, in *Hymns of Faith and Life.* It has not been improved by the generally accepted alterations made by the editors of the *Church Hymnary, Revised.* The two lines of the first stanza as Doctor Hunter wrote them were,

> Dear Master, in whose life I see
> All that I long, but fail to be,

and his original form of the second stanza was,

> Though what I dream and what I do
> In my poor days are always two.

The wisdom of changing "long" to "would," and "poor" to "weak" may at least be questioned as an example of unnecessary alteration; yet Doctor Hunter did not fail to make such changes as he desired in the works of others, subjecting himself to severe criticism by doing so. There are few finer examples of concise expression than this hymn.

John Hunter, D.D., born at Aberdeen, Scotland, July 12, 1848, apprenticed to a draper at the age of thirteen years, felt called to preach after his conversion during the Revival of 1859-61. Finding the ministry of the Scottish Church closed to him because of the long training required, he spent five years at Nottingham Congregational Institute and at Spring Hill College, Birmingham, preparing for the Congregational ministry; but during his college years he developed, for that time, a liberal tendency toward Universalist ideas of the future life. He held successful pastorates at York, Hull, and at Trinity Church, Glasgow. Doctor Hunter was persuaded, in 1901, to go to Weigh House Church, London, but after three depressing years of arduous work he returned to his former Glasgow congregation, where he remained until his health failed him in 1913. Upon his retirement to London, his friends prevailed upon him to preach once each Sunday at Aeolian Hall until, in 1917, he was compelled by illness to stop work altogether. He died at Hampstead, September 15, the same year. Aided by his personal example and inspiration, his *Devotional Services for Public Worship,* a pioneer book in its field, did much to bring about his great desire for developing a higher standard of worship in nonliturgical churches.

**377—O come and dwell in me—Charles Wesley (25)**

**Old 134th (St. Michael) (39)—Adapted from the Genevan Psalter (3)**

This hymn is made up of the first half of the first, the first half of the second and the entire third stanza of the selection from various stanzas in *Short Hymns on Select Passages of Scripture* made by John Wesley for his *Collection* of 1780. The first stanza of this cento was originally headed,

> Where the Spirit of the Lord is, there is liberty.—iii. 17. (II Corinthians)

The second,

> Old things are passed away; behold, all things are become new.—v. 17. (II Corinthians)

And the last two,

> Before his translation, he had this testimony, that he pleased God.—xi. 5. (Hebrews)

While the hymn in its present form is, except for one word, as John Wesley used it in his 1780 *Collection,* he had made certain minor changes from Charles's original. The first line was written,

> Come then, and dwell in me;

the third line of stanza 3,

> According to Thy mind and word;

and the last stanza,

> I seek no higher state,
> Indulge me but in this
> And soon or later then translate
> To Thine eternal bliss.

The one word which differs from John Wesley's editing is in line 3, stanza 2; "done" has replaced "past." This change occurred in the supplement to the *Methodist Pocket Hymn Book Compiled under the direction of Bishop Asbury,* as ordered by the General Conference of 1808.

**378—Walk in the light! so shalt thou know—Bernard Barton**

**Manoah—From Henry Wellington Greatorex's Collection, 1851**

The hymn was included in Bernard Barton's *Devotional Verses,* London, 1826, one of ten volumes issued by him. The distinctive notions of the Quakers, of whom he was one, influenced him to write this hymn about the "inner light." It was based on 1 John 1. 7: "But if we walk in the light, as he is in the light, we have fellowship one with another, and the blood of Jesus Christ his Son cleanseth us from all sin."

Bernard Barton, the English "Quaker Poet," was born of Quaker parents, January 31, 1784, at London, and was educated at the Quaker School at Ipswich. He was apprenticed to a shopkeeper at Halstead, Essex, in 1796, where he remained until 1806, when he went into the corn and coal business with a brother at Woodbridge, Suffolk. Heartbroken over the death of his wife only one year after their marriage, he went to Liverpool, where he obtained employment as a tutor, but shortly returned to Woodbridge to secure a clerical position in the local bank, where he remained for forty years. At Woodbridge he came to know Edward Fitzgerald, translator of *The Rubáiyát of Omar Khayyam,* who became the husband of Mr. Barton's daughter. He also had the friendship of Charles Lamb, Lord Byron, and other distinguished men, and carried on a correspondence with Sir Walter Scott, Robert Southey, and others. Doubtless he would have devoted himself wholly to literary pursuits had he not followed the good advice of Charles Lamb, who wrote him:

> Throw yourself on the world, without any rational plan of support beyond what the chance employ of booksellers would afford you! Throw yourself rather, my dear sir, from the steep Tarpeian rock, slap-dash headlong upon iron spikes. If you have but five consolatory minutes between the desk and the bed, make much of them, and live a century in them, rather than turn slave to the booksellers. They are Turks and Tartars when they have poor authors at their beck. Hitherto you have been at arm's length from them—come not within their grasp. I have known many authors want for bread—some repining, others enjoying the blessed security of a countinghouse—all agreeing they had rather have been tailors, weavers, what not? rather than the things they were. I have known some starved, some go mad, one dear friend literally dying in a workhouse. Oh, you know not—may you never know—the miseries of subsisting by authorship!

It was well that he listened to his good friend, his talents not being suited to the production of writing for the general market, for he wrote nothing striking nor had he much originality. An English periodical, in a cordial criticism, said:

> Mr. Barton's style is well suited to devotional poetry. It has great sweetness and pathos, accompanied with no small degree of power, which well qualify it for the expression of the higher and purer feelings of the heart;

and his daughter, who was his biographer, had this to say of his literary character:

> He was not learned—in language, science, or philosophy. Nor did he care for the loftiest kind of poetry, "the heroics," as he called it. His favorite authors were those who dealt most in humor, good sense, domestic feeling, and pastoral feeling.

A lovable person, kind, gentle, sweet-natured, he was a brilliant conversationalist, and his writings appeal to cultivated tastes.

> So punctual and methodical was he that as he returned from the office each midday, the housewives knew it was the correct time to put their potatoes into water as he passed their doors, and they liked to watch him, as, meeting a friend, he stopped to offer a pinch of snuff or tell a good story from Boswell.

From 1841 he received a state pension of £100 a year, which had been recommended by Sir Robert Peel. His daughter published a *Memoir* the year of his death, which occurred at Woodbridge, February 19, 1849.

"Manoah" appeared in *Greatorex's Collection of Church Music,* 1851. It has been assumed that Greatorex "arranged" this as a setting for a hymn in his book, yet there is nothing in the index of tunes, where composers' names are given, to indicate he had anything to do with it. It has been suggested that it might have come from some work of Haydn or Rossini, but if such is the case, no one has as yet identified it. James Edmund Jones, Canadian hymnodist, says it may have come partly from Mehul's *Joseph* and partly from Haydn's *Seasons,* but Lightwood has given those as the source of "Petition" (351). Some light upon the source may be shed by a comparison of "Manoah," "Petition," and the following setting, said to be "from Mehul," for "When, His salvation bringing," which appeared in *The Hymnal,* 1894 (known as "The last Tucker"):

This was followed by a codalike ending to the words, "Hosanna, Hosanna to Jesus they sang." Walter B. Gilbert (1829-1910), who had much to do with the musical part of the book, doubtless had the theme from *Joseph* in mind when he made this setting, but it is not "Manoah." See No. 351.

Henry Wellington Greatorex was born at Burton-on-Trent, England, in 1811, the son of Thomas Greatorex, eminent musician, who for a time conducted the famous Ancient Concerts in London and was organist at Westminster Abbey, and from whom Henry received most of his musical training. He was called to Hartford, Connecticut, in 1838, to become organist at Center Congregational Church, of whose organ, installed in 1835, Nathaniel Hawthorne wrote, "Organ building may in the future be carried further than this, but I am by no means sure that it is possible." One Sunday, May 17, 1835, when this organ was first played, Lowell Mason was present to lecture on Church Music and George James Webb to play. A report of the occasion says:

> When the organ was first played, it shook the windows so, the audience thought they would fall out. They rattled, to the dismay of the organist. He was warned to control his power, and Mr. Ezekiel Williams later found the "subbass" too much for his nerves and petitioned that it be dispensed with at the morning service.

Greatorex, it seems, was a remarkable player and was very popular in

Hartford, but he stayed there only two years, going to New York to St. Paul's and to Calvary Protestant Episcopal Church, remaining in the city twelve years before entering upon his new work at Charleston, South Carolina, where he contracted yellow fever and died, in 1858.

*Greatorex's Collection of Church Music* made the name of Henry W. Greatorex favorably known throughout the country, which was at the time being flooded with books by followers of Lowell Mason. In his Preface, Greatorex says:

> The Editor of this work trusts that the following pages will be found generally useful in the service of the church. His aim has been to furnish good music, rather than light, frivolous melody—to restore, as nearly as practicable, the old standard tunes and chants to their original harmonies, while, in the selection of the new, he has endeavored to avoid vulgarity, or straining after effect.

This book passed through many editions and generally had a wholesome effect on church music, especially in the larger cities.

# THE LIVING CHURCH

## The Church

**379—I love Thy Kingdom, Lord**—Timothy Dwight

**St. Thomas** (227)—From Williams' Psalmody, 1770 (227)

Doctor Dwight had this hymn, in eight stanzas, as Part III [that is, the last of three renderings, or versions] of Psalm 137 in what became known as "Dwight's Watts." Perhaps it should be said that it was neither a translation nor a paraphrase of this psalm, but was merely suggested by stanzas 5 and 6: "If I forget thee, O Jerusalem, let my right hand forget her cunning. If I do not remember thee, let my tongue cleave to the roof of my mouth; if I prefer not Jerusalem above my chief joy." It is found in *The Psalms of David, Imitated in the Language of the New Testament, and applied to the Christian Use and Worship, by I. Watts, D.D. A New Edition, in which the Psalms omitted by Dr. Watts are versified, local passages are altered, and a number of Psalms are versified anew, in proper Metres, by Timothy Dwight, D.D., President of Yale College. At the Request of the General Association of Connecticut. To the Psalms is added a Collection of Hymns,* published in 1801, and as the Presbyterian General Assembly had concurred in the request of the General Association, it at once found a place in the churches of both denominations, especially in Connecticut, where, Doctor Benson assures us, it was used in Congregational Churches, "perhaps without an exception." Of Doctor Dwight's contribution of thirty-three originals to the book, this is the only one now in common use.

Timothy Dwight, whose mother was the daughter of Jonathan Edwards, was born at Northampton, Massachusetts, May 14, 1752. From 1769, when he graduated from Yale, until 1795, when he became President of that institution, he was, successively: a grammar-school teacher in New Haven, a tutor in Yale, a chaplain in the American Army, a farmer and preacher, the representative of Northampton in the state legislature, and pastor of the Congregational Church at Greenfield, Connecticut. Doctor Moses Coit Tyler, in a sketch, says his life was

> not uncommonly long, almost never exempt from severe bodily pain, but pervaded throughout by singular activity, power, and productiveness, and challenging the public admiration, then and since then, by its breadth, versatility, and robust sense; its brilliance, its purity, its dignity of tone, its moral aggressiveness, its many-sided and benign achievement.

His precocity was amazing. As soon as he could talk, he began receiving instruction from books; at four he read the Bible; at six he entered grammar school; and, though his father insisted he was too young to study Latin, he found the texts of the other students when they were at play and "learned the whole of *Lily's Grammar.*" His desire for learning seemed insatiable and his associates thought "his knowledge was nearly boundless." One of his pupils said:

> I never knew the man who took so deep an interest in everything—the best mode of cultivating a cabbage, as well as the phenomena of the heavens, or the employments of angels. He was as pleased to talk with lowly people as with lofty ones—his kitchen servant, the college janitor, blacksmiths, hostlers, boatmen, ploughmen; he drew from them what they best knew, and he well paid them in kind for what they gave.

He became President of Yale College at the age of forty-three, and it is said that its greatness dates from the day he was inaugurated. His duties were manifold: the responsibility of a president; all of the instruction of the senior class in ethics, metaphysics, and logic; he was Professor of Literature and Oratory; Professor of Theology, and the College Chaplain. His greatest work, however, was his championship of Christianity. Dr. W. W. Sweet reminds us that when Doctor Dwight went to Yale, there were there no more than four or five professing Christians. Through his frank discussions with the students and the series of sermons on "Theology Explained and Defended" which he delivered in the college chapel, he changed for the better the whole moral and religious attitude on the campus. The revival which followed claimed one third of the student body, and was instrumental in inaugurating similar awakenings at Dartmouth, Amherst, and Williams.

Timothy Dwight was one of the most important of early American hymnodists, an author of repute, and one of the greatest educators America has produced. He died at Philadelphia, January 11, 1817.

**380—Jesus, with Thy church abide**—Thomas Benson Pollock

Litany—Melody by Frederick Alfred John Hervey

This is taken from the Rev. Mr. Pollock's *Metrical Litanies for Special Services and General Use,* 1870, and is composed of stanzas 2, 5, 9, 15, 12, and 18, from twenty, published in the Revised Edition of *Hymns Ancient and Modern,* 1875.

A litany was a prayer of general supplication used in processions in the early days of organized Christianity. It is the long series of responsive prayers beginning, "O God the Father, of heaven: have mercy upon us miserable sinners," and includes further invocations as well as deprecations, intercessions, and supplications, closing with the *Agnus Dei*[1] and the *Kyrie eleison.*[2] In the earliest days the litany consisted of the repetition of the *Kyrie,* over and over again, often as many as one hundred times. Charles Wheatly, in his

[1] O Lamb of God: that takest away the sins of the world.

[2] Lord, have mercy upon us.
Lord, have mercy upon us.
Lord, have mercy upon us.
Christ, have mercy upon us.
Christ, have mercy upon us.
Christ, have mercy upon us.
Lord, have mercy upon us.
Lord, have mercy upon us.
Lord, have mercy upon us.

*Rational Illustration of the Book of Common Prayer of the Church of England,* says:

> . . . and so it is used by the most ancient heathens, viz. "for an earnest supplication to the gods made in time of adverse fortune; and in the same sense it is used in the Christian Church, viz. for a supplication and common intercession to God, when his wrath lies heavy upon us." Such a kind of supplication was the fifty-first psalm, which may be called David's litany. Such was that litany of God's appointing in Joel, (ii. 17) where, in a general assembly, the priests were *to weep between the porch and the altar,* and to say, *Spare thy people, O Lord.* And such was that litany of our Saviour, (St. Luke xxii. 44) which he thrice repeated *with strong crying and tears* (Hebrews v. 7.).

The form in which litanies are now used in the English Church, indeed, appears to be very ancient. St. Basil refers to their use in the church before his time, and St. Ambrose left a form of litany which bears his name. By the year 400 people, walking barefoot in procession, very devoutly repeated them, and about the year 600 Gregory the Great arranged the famous sevenfold litany from all those then in use. A place fixed for the litany in King Edward's first *Book of Common Prayer* of 1549 since has had its special assignment in the Order for certain days.

Many of the Non-conformist churches followed—some more, some less—the form of litany used in the English Church,[1] and while some elements were omitted, the terms designating them, and sometimes modified forms of them, as in the case of litanies, were used, optionally, in services of worship. So it came to be in modern times that metrical prayers of supplication for certain occasions or things were written in hymn form. Thus we have litanies "of the Four Last Things," "of the Incarnate Word," "of Penitence," "of the Church," "for Children," etc.

Thomas Benson Pollock was born at Strathallan, Isle of Man, May 28, 1836, and was educated at Trinity College, Dublin, where he received the Vice-Chancellor's prize for English verse. Taking Holy Orders, he held curacies at St. Luke's, Leek, Staffordshire, and at St. Thomas's, Stamford Hill, London, before going to St. Alban's, Bordesley, Birmingham, as curate for thirty years to his brother, upon the failure of whose health he succeeded as vicar. The Rev. Mr. Pollock refused offers of preferment, choosing to stay in the miserably poor district of St. Alban's and to minister to its people. While the "living" at St. Alban's was worth only £150 a year, the brothers maintained a large staff to carry on their work and raised a half million dollars to defray the expenses of the church and school work there. As a result of the strenuous labor of many years, his failing health, like that of his brother, forced him to give over his work, in 1895, and he died at Birmingham, December 15, 1896.

The Rev. Mr. Pollock served for a time as a member of the committee of *Hymns Ancient and Modern,* and was a successful writer of metrical litanies,

[1] See the "Order of Worship III, An Order for morning and evening prayer, adapted from the Sunday service of John Wesley," on page 506 of the edition of *The Methodist Hymnal,* 1935, for the Methodist Episcopal Church, and the comment on "The Sunday Service of John Wesley" on page 503. This service, it will be noted, does not contain the Litany.

selections from his *Metrical Litanies for Special Services and General Use,* 1870, having greatly enriched modern hymnody.

"Litany," by the Rev. Mr. Hervey, appeared in *Hymns Ancient and Modern,* Revised Edition, 1875, set to the "Litany of the Incarnate Word," but was omitted from the New Edition of 1904 and from subsequent ones.

The Rev. Frederick Alfred John Hervey, C. V. O., born at London, May 18, 1846, educated at Marlborough, and Trinity College, Cambridge; rector of Sandringham; canon of Norwich; was, from 1901 until his death, August 8, 1910, Domestic Chaplain to the King. He was the son of the first Marquis of Bristol.

**381—The Church's one foundation**—Samuel John Stone

**Aurelia**—(324)—Samuel Sebastian Wesley (324)

This famous "Processional for Festivals" is taken from the revised form of the hymn as it appeared in the Appendix to *Hymns Ancient and Modern,* 1868. Written for the Rev. Samuel Stone's *Lyra Fidelium,* 1866, a small book of twelve pieces founded upon the Apostles' Creed, it is based on the article, "I believe in the Holy Catholic Church; the communion of saints." Originally in seven stanzas, it was expanded to ten in 1885 for use in Salisbury Cathedral. From this expanded form, revised as mentioned above, stanzas 1, 2, 5, in full, and the first and last halves, respectively, of 9 and 10, have been selected, unaltered, for this hymn. The Rev. Mr. Stone was so stirred by Bishop Gray, of Capetown, South Africa, in his defense of the Catholic faith against Bishop Colenso's teachings, that he wrote the hymn, and in the omitted third stanza expressed his strong feeling as to the controversy then waging:

Though with a scornful wonder
Men see her sore opprest,
By schisms rent asunder,
By heresies distrest;
Yet saints their watch are keeping,
Their cry goes up, "How long?"
And soon the night of weeping
Shall be the morn of song.

This hymn was chosen for use as the Processional at services held at Canterbury, Westminster, and St. Paul's Cathedrals for the Lambeth Conference of 1888, when representative high churchmen from all parts of the world met in England. The comment of one who attended the great meeting at St. Paul's is interesting:

> The effect of the hymn was almost appalling. Sung by a large congregation, some people say this hymn was really more than they could bear. "It made them feel weak at the knees, their legs trembled, and they felt as though they were going to collapse."

So profoundly affected was Bishop Nelson, of New Zealand, that he wrote:

Bard of the Church, in these divided days
For words of harmony to thee be praise:
Of love and oneness thou dost strike the chords,
And set our thoughts and prayers to tuneful words.

The Church's one Foundation thou didst sing,
Beauty and Bands to her thy numbers bring.
Through church and chancel, aisle and transept deep,
In fullest melody thy watch-notes sweep;
Now in the desert, now upon the main,
In mine and forest, and on citied plain:
From Lambeth towers to far New Zealand's coast,
Bard of the Church, thy blast inspires the host.

Samuel John Stone, English clergyman, born at Whitmore, Staffordshire, April 25, 1839, was educated at the Charterhouse and at Pembroke College, Oxford; took Holy Orders, and became curate of Windsor, and of St. Paul's, Haggerston, where he succeeded his father as vicar, in 1874. He published four volumes of poetical works as well as the *Order of the Consecutive Church Service for Children, with Original Hymns.* For the greater part, his hymns

are strongly outspoken utterances of a manly faith, where dogma, prayer, and praise are interwoven with much skill. Usually the keynote of his song is Hope.

Mr. Stone died at the Charterhouse, November 19, 1900.

**382—Glorious things of thee are spoken**—John Newton (27)

**Austrian Hymn**—Francis Joseph Haydn (30)

This hymn is taken from *Olney Hymns,* Book I, where it occurs in five eight-line stanzas headed,

Zion; or the City of God.—Isaiah xxxiii. 20, 21.

Look upon Zion, the city of our solemnities: thine eyes shall see Jerusalem a quiet habitation, a tabernacle that shall not be taken down; not one of the stakes thereof shall ever be removed, neither shall any of the cords thereof be broken.

But there the glorious Lord will be unto us a place of broad rivers and streams; wherein shall go no galley with oars, neither shall gallant ship pass thereby.

Though Newton gave only this scriptural reference, other reflections of the Bible occur in the hymn: the words in Psalm 87. 3,

Glorious things are spoken of thee, O city of God,

suggest the commanding opening, and the first part of the third stanza is a reflection of Exodus 13. 22: "He took not away the pillar of the cloud by day, nor the pillar of fire by night, from before the people." Of the original five stanzas, the first two entire, the first four lines of the third, and the first four of the first, unaltered, are used. Now improved by the omission of the other lines, this "glorious burst of praise" ranks as one of the greatest of John Newton's offerings.

"Austrian Hymn" was composed by Francis J. Haydn for the hymn "Gott erhalte Franz den Kaiser," by the poet Hauschka, and was first performed on the occasion of the birthday of the Emperor, February 12, 1797, during the excitement caused by the activities of the French revolutionary armies. It has also been used by the composer as the theme for the first movement of his string quartet Op. 76, No. 3, known as "The Emperor."

**383—How lovely is Thy dwelling place**—From Psalm 84
Scottish Psalter, 1650 (70)

**Salzburg**—Johann Michael Haydn (4)

This rendering of Psalm 84 supersedes that of Isaac Watts, "How pleasant, how divinely fair," which was used in the 1905 edition of *The Methodist Hymnal.* Of the twelve quatrains in the Psalter, the first five are here used, with slight changes in the rendering. "Vehemently" was changed to "ardently" as the last word, first line, second stanza, and the last line of the third stanza has been changed from,

Hath purchased a nest

to read,

Provided hath a nest.

"Salzburg" is one of at least three hymn tunes adapted from movements of a Mass composed "for the use of country choirs," by J. M. Haydn, brother of the better known Francis Joseph. The particular movement from which this is taken is in 6/8 time, beginning

The tune is named for the town where this Haydn lived for the last thirty-four years of his life, and for which he had an extraordinary affection. One reason for his love for the place was his great love and admiration for a clergyman named Rettensteiner.

**384—O where are kings and empires now**—Arthur Cleveland Coxe (116)

**St. Anne**—Probably by William Croft (169)

This hymn is a cento from Doctor Coxe's ballad, "Chelsea," which first appeared in *The Churchman,* 1839, and in his *Christian Ballads,* the following year. The ballad began,

When old Canute the Dane
Was merry England's king;
A thousand years agone, and more,
As ancient rymours sing;
His boat was rowing down the Ouse,
At eve, one summer day,
Where Ely's tall cathedral peered
Above the glassy way.

Written in ten eight-line stanzas this selection consists of the first half of stanza 6, last half of 8, first half of 7, and the last half of 7, with a goodly number of word changes which do not in any way affect the meaning its author intended to convey. Dr. Samuel W. Duffield quotes an interesting incident of its use at the 1873 General Conference of the Evangelical Alliance in New York City, related by one who was present, and it would seem not amiss to repeat it in these similar skeptical days:

It was at the time when so much had been said about the "prayer test," and when we scarcely knew whether the faith of the Church might not have been shaken for the moment by the universal storm of scepticism. President Woolsey was giving the opening address. After referring to the prevalent scepticism, he looked up with that peculiar twinkle of the eye which we all recollect—at once expressive of denial and satisfaction—and repeated the first stanza of Bishop Coxe's hymn:

"Oh, where are kings and empires now,
Of old that went and came?—
But, Lord! thy Church is praying yet,
A thousand years the same!"

For a moment there was silence. In another moment the full significance of the reference had flashed on every mind, and the response was instantaneous and universal. Shouts, waving of handkerchiefs from the ladies, clapping of hands, stamping of feet—I never knew anything like it. Round after round continued, until the storm of applause ended in a burst of grateful tears. No one doubted that the Church still believed in prayer and that the tempest had passed without the loss of a sail!

"St. Anne," a very famous tune, is generally credited to Doctor Croft, even though there has been some controversy over its composer. A part of the first phrase is found in a motet by Palestrina published in 1569, thus:

but after these four notes there is no further resemblance. There is no good reason for believing the whole was not original with Croft. The tune, with the name "St. Anne," appears in *A Supplement to the New Version of the Psalms by Dr. Brady and Mr. Tate,* sixth edition, 1708, set to Psalm 42, New Version. It is written for soprano and bass, as follows:

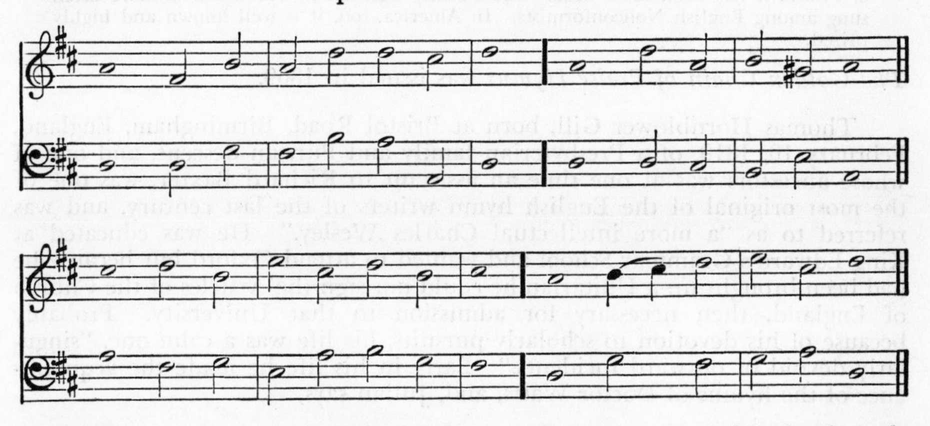

Though here indexed as a nameless new tune, it is connected in books published some twelve and fifteen years later, with the name of Doctor Croft, who is believed to have had something to do with issuing the Tate and Brady book in which it first appeared. John Church, who published one of these books crediting the tune to Doctor Croft, was Master of the Choristers at

Westminster Abbey while Croft was organist at St. Anne's, Westminster, and should have known who composed it. The claim that the tune was written by a "Mr. Denby" does not seem to have much foundation. J. S. Bach has a fugue that has as its subject the first strain only of Doctor Croft's tune, known in all English-speaking countries as "St. Anne's Fugue." A detailed account of the famous tune may be found in any edition of *Grove's Dictionary of Music and Musicians.*

**385—We come unto our fathers' God—Thomas Hornblower Gill**

**Luther—From Klug's Gesangbuch, 1535**

Mr. Gill has said:

> The birthday of this hymn, November 22, 1868 (St. Cecilia's Day), was almost the most delightful day of my life. Its production employed the whole day, and was a prolonged rapture. It was produced while *The Golden Chain* was being printed, just in time to be a link therein.

In response to an inquiry from the Rev. John Brownlie, author of *The Hymns and Hymn Writers of the Church Hymnary,* 1899, the author wrote:

> The hymn beginning "We come unto our fathers' God," built on verse 1 of Psalm 90, and intended to set forth the continuity and unity of God's people in all ages, had a somewhat remarkable birth. It was inspired by a lively delight in my Puritan and Presbyterian forefathers of East Worcestershire. Descended from a Moravian martyr and an ejected minister, I rejoice not a little in the godly Protestant stock from which I spring. A staff handed down from him, and inscribed with the date 1692, was in my hand when I began the hymn. Its composition occupied and gladdened a wet Sunday in the November of 1868, and seldom have I spent a day so delightful. In accordance with the delights of its production, has been the warmth and fulness of its acceptance. Of the 290 hymns which comprise *The Golden Chain of Praise,* it has been most widely and warmly welcomed. No hymn is more often sung among English Nonconformists. In America, too, it is well known and highly prized.

*The Golden Chain of Praise Hymns* was issued in 1869.

Thomas Hornblower Gill, born at Bristol Road, Birmingham, England, February 10, 1819, of a Presbyterian family and Puritan descent, and one of whose ancestors was at one time an assistant to Richard Baxter, was one of the most original of the English hymn writers of the last century, and was referred to as "a more intellectual Charles Wesley." He was educated at King Edward's Grammar School and wanted to attend Oxford but because he had been brought up a Unitarian he could not sign the Articles of the Church of England, then necessary for admission to that University. Probably because of his devotion to scholarly pursuits, his life was a calm one, "singularly devoid of outward incidents." Early in his life he made the acquaintance of the hymns of Doctor Watts, and, Julian says,

> In after years, the contrast between their native force and fullness and their dwindled presentation in Unitarian hymnbooks began that estrangement from his hereditary faith which afterwards became complete.

Mr. Gill spent his late years at Blackheath, and he died at Grove Park, Kent, in 1906.

"Luther" comes from the *Gesangbuch,* 1535, published by Joseph Klug as a setting for Martin Luther's first congregational hymn "Nun freut euch, lieben Christengemein," which had another tune. Hence, "Luther," or "Nun freut Euch," was transferred to the "German Dies Irae," "Es ist gewisslich an der Zeit," and came into English use through its association with its English rendering, "Great God, what do I see and hear?" There is no good reason for believing that Luther wrote the melody, for definite proof that he did so is lacking. There is only one known copy of the 1535 book by Klug, *Geistliche Lieder* (*Gesangbuch*), a second edition of a collection published in 1529. As there is no copy of the earlier book extant, it is not known whether Luther had any tunes in it. The legend that Luther heard a peasant singing a song with this melody and wrote it down is interesting but without foundation. Lightwood suggests Luther would have added to his laurels as the first collector of folk songs were the story true.

The melody, as has been the case in nearly all similar instances, has been modified, and it has been variously harmonized. The melody, as commonly used, is as it is found in *Psalmodia Germanica,* 1722, while the following is the earlier form:

# The Holy Scripture

**386—O word of God incarnate**—William Walsham How (197)

**Munich**—Neuvermehrtes Meiningisches Gesangbuch, 1693
Arranged by Felix Mendelssohn-Bartholdy (7)

Bishop How wrote this hymn for the 1867 Supplement to *Psalms and Hymns,* published by him in co-operation with the Rev. Thomas Baker Morrell, first in 1854. It was headed with the scriptural text from Proverbs 6. 23:

> The commandment is a lamp, and the law is light.

Dr. C. S. Robinson says this hymn finds illustration in a part of Bishop How's address when he assumed his high office:

> I am resolved not to be a Bishop of any party, but while openly avowing my own views and preferences, to help and encourage, so far as in me lies, all who are honestly laboring in the great cause and faithfully setting forth to their people the Gospel of our common Lord and Master.

"Munich" appeared in concrete form in the *Meiningisches Gesangbuch,* 1693, but Johannes Zahn (1817-1895), in his studies of the sources of German chorale melodies, thinks it was constructed from parts of melodies found in *Lobsingende Harffe,* by J. L. Prasch (?), 1682. Its early form was:

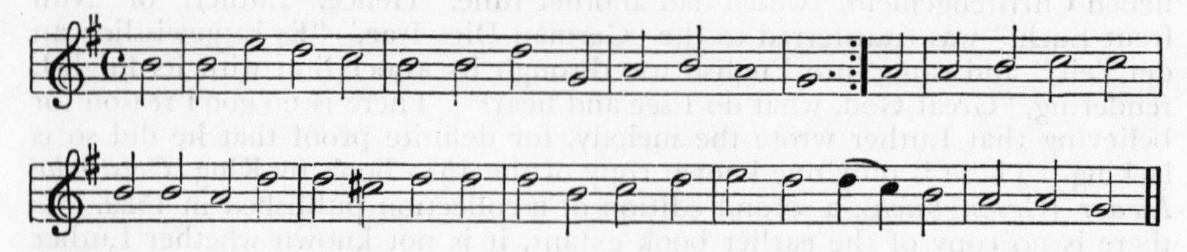

Known in Germany as the "Königsberg Choral," it was first used to "O Gott, du frommer Gott." Mendelssohn used the later form as the basis for his fine chorale, "Cast thy burden on the Lord," in the oratorio *Elijah.*

**387—Break thou the bread of life**—Mary Artemisia Lathbury (44)
**Bread of Life**—William Fiske Sherwin (44)

This is another hymn and tune by the "poet laureate of Chautauqua" and one of its favorite chorus directors and composers. Miss Lathbury wrote the hymn in the summer of 1877 upon Bishop Vincent's request that she provide one as a "study hymn" for the "Chautauqua Literary and Scientific Circle"; and Professor Sherwin supplied the music which has become so thoroughly wedded with the words that probably they will always be used together, neither having another association. This is as it should be. Would it not go a long way toward uniting more closely our Protestant Christians were they all to sing common hymns to common tunes?

"Bread of Life" was written at Lake Chautauqua and included in the "C. L. S. C." publications shortly after it was composed in 1877.

**388—A glory gilds the sacred page**—William Cowper (24)
**Burlington**—John Freckleton Burrowes

From *Olney Hymns, Book II,* 1779, this hymn begins with the second stanza of a five-stanza hymn. The first stanza is:

The spirit breathes upon the word,
And brings the truth to sight;
Precepts and promises afford
A sanctifying light.

The stanzas are used unaltered, and the whole is headed

The Light and Glory of the Word.

William Cowper dated his conversion from the day in July, 1764, he read Romans 3. 24, 25: "Being justified freely by His grace through the redemption that is in Christ Jesus: whom God hath set forth to be a propitiation through faith in His blood, to declare His righteousness for the remission of sins that are past, through the forbearance of God." Recounting the experience, he said:

Immediately I received strength to believe, and the full beams of the Sun of

> Righteousness shone upon me. I saw the sufficiency of the atonement Christ had made, my pardon in his blood, and the fullness and completeness of his justification. In a moment I believed and received the Gospel.

"Burlington" first appeared in 1830 according to tune-book editors, but no specific information has been found concerning it.

John Freckleton Burrowes, English composer and organist, was born at London, April 23, 1787, and died there, March 31, 1852. His works include an overture, songs, and piano pieces, and he was the author of the popular *Thorough-Bass Primer* and *Pianoforte Primer,* both of which passed through several editions. Burrowes gained a favorable reputation as a serious composer, but entered the more profitable field of writing ballads and piano pieces of the lighter sort. For nearly forty years he was organist at St. James's Church, Piccadilly.

**389—Father of mercies, in Thy word**—Anne Steele

**Gräfenberg**—From Johann Crüger's Praxis Pietatis Melica, 1653

This short hymn on the Holy Scriptures is taken from a selection of six stanzas, from the original of twelve, which was used in the Bristol, England, *Baptist Collection* of 1769. The original was first published in Miss Steele's *Poems on Subjects Chiefly Devotional, by Theodosia.* The last line of this cento was,

> And view my Saviour there,

"view" being changed to "find" by the editorial committee of *The Methodist Hymnal,* 1935. It is one of the most popular of this writer's hymns.

Anne Steele, daughter of William Steele, a timber merchant and unsalaried Baptist preacher, was born in 1716 at Broughton, Hampshire, England, where she spent her entire life, being a semi-invalid from childhood. Her literary gift showed early, and it was her custom to entertain her friends by reading and reciting her own compositions. The delicate condition of her health was intensified by the shock resulting from the drowning, on the day set for their wedding, of the young man she had expected to marry. Many of her hymns were written to lighten her own burden of grief. She lived quietly at her home in Broughton until her death there in November, 1778. On her gravestone in Broughton churchyard are these lines:

> Silent the lyre, and dumb the tuneful tongue
> That sung on earth her great Redeemer's praise;
> But now in heaven she joins the angel's song,
> In more harmonious, more exalted lays.

It was not until she was more than forty years of age that she could be prevailed upon to submit any of her writings for publication, and then she did so under the *nom de plume* "Theodosia." Her father wrote in his diary, under date of November 29, 1757:

> This day Nanny sent part of her composition to London to be printed. I entreat a gracious God, who enabled and stirred her up to such a work, to direct in it, and bless it for the good of many—I pray God to make it useful, and keep her humble.

Two years later he made this entry:

> Her brother brought with him her poetry, not yet bound. I earnestly desire the blessing of God upon that work, that it may be made very useful.

The reference is to *Poems on Subjects Chiefly Devotional,* which was published in two volumes in 1760.

Miss Steele was the first of the English women hymn writers, and Lord Selborne thought her, with the single exception of Doctor Doddridge, the "most popular, and perhaps the best" of the followers of Isaac Watts. She is frequently alluded to as the "Frances Havergal of the eighteenth century."

"Gräfenberg" is supposed to be the composition of Johann Crüger, who issued the fine *Praxis Pietatis Melica* and included this tune in the fifth edition in 1653. It was set to "Nun danket all und bringet Ehr," and has retained its early form more nearly than most of the tunes of that date:

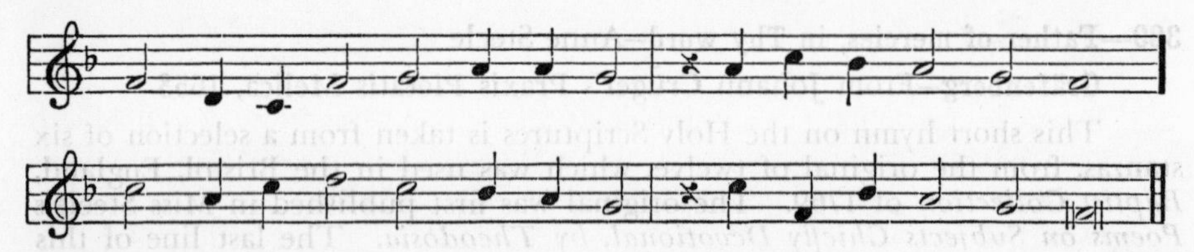

It formerly was called "Nun danket all," from the first words of the chorale to which it was set, but the use of the name "Gräfenberg" is coming into favor in order that the older name may not be confused with the better known "Nun Danket" (7).

**390—Book of books, our people's strength**—Percy Dearmer (79)

**Dessau (Liebster Jesu)**—Melody by Johann Rudolph Ahle (310)

Doctor Dearmer says he wrote this hymn to give a modern expression to the Bible. It first appeared in *Songs of Praise,* 1925.

"Dessau," or "Liebster Jesu," by J. R. Ahle, is an arrangement of a melody found in *Neue geistliche auf die Sonntage durchs gantze Jahr gerichtete Andachten*—Mühlhausen, 1664, where it is associated with the hymn, "Ja, er ists, das Heil der Welt." Later collections from Germany have this melody in varied form. The original form of the melody is shown at No. 310, "Liebster Jesu, wir sind hier," being a variant of the tune.

**391—Behold a Sower! from afar**—Washington Gladden (259)

**Bethlehem**—Gottfried Wilhelm Fink

Doctor Gladden's fine hymn of faith on the efficacy of God's Word was first published in *The Pilgrim Hymnal,* 1904.

"Bethlehem" in this form appeared in *Church Hymns with Tunes,* 1874, edited by Sir Arthur Sullivan (15) for the Society for Promoting Christian Knowledge, London. Set to "While shepherds watched their flocks by night"

(88), it was called an "Old Carol"; but it seems, rather, to have been an adaptation of a setting, by G. W. Fink, for a song by one M. Claudius beginning, "War einst ein Riese Goliath," as follows:

The melody is said to have been composed in 1842 and to have appeared in Fink's *Musikalischer Hausschatz der Deutschen* in 1843.

Gottfried Wilhelm Fink, born at Sulza on the Ulm, Thuringia, March 7, 1783, was educated as a chorister at Naumburg and in theology at Leipzig. Though a prolific scholarly writer about music, for a time professor of music at the University of Leipzig, he is best known for his popular arrangements of German popular songs and hymns, which he began publishing in 1810. Fink conducted a school at Leipzig; published his sermons and a book of *Devotions;* was editor of *The Musical Gazette,* Leipzig, for a number of years; and gained a considerable reputation as a music critic. He died at Halle, August 27, 1846.

**392—Lord of all power and might—Hugh Stowell (317)**

**Stowell—Isaac Hickman Meredith**

This hymn was written by Canon Stowell in the meter of "God save the King" for the Jubilee of the British and Foreign Bible Society, March 7, 1853, and appeared in *Hymns, By the late Rev. Canon Stowell,* 1868, edited by his son.

"Stowell" was written by I. H. Meredith as a setting for "My country, 'tis of thee," calling it "Myland." When the tune came into the hands of the Committee on the Selection of New Tunes for *The Methodist Hymnal,* 1935, the editor of the *Hymnal* asked, and received, Mr. Meredith's permission to use it with another hymn of the same meter, with the suggestion of the name "Stowell" as more fitting. It is published here for the first time.

Isaac Hickman Meredith, president of the Tuller-Meredith Company, now living in New York City, was born at Norristown, Pennsylvania, March 21, 1872; received his education in the public schools; and at nineteen years of age began a successful career as a gospel soloist, continuing in Christian work ever since. He began composing gospel songs and has about three thousand to his credit, many of them written for festival occasions. Since its organization he has been the musical editor of the company he now heads.

## The Lord's Day

**393—Safely through another week**—John Newton (27)

**Sabbath**—Lowell Mason (19)

This hymn appeared with the heading,

Saturday Evening,

in *Psalms and Hymns,* 1774, and then in Book II of *Olney Hymns,* 1779, in five stanzas, the second being omitted here. Inasmuch as the hymn was desired for use in Sunday-morning services the necessary changes were made so that it might be suitable.

"Sabbath," called "Sabbath Morn" in the *Methodist Hymnal,* 1905, and in other like books, was written for John Newton's hymn in 1824.

**394—Welcome, delightful morn**—"Hayward" in John Dobell's Selection, 1806

**Lischer**—Friedrich Schneider

John Dobell (1757-1840), published, in 1806, a book with this formidable title:

> *A New Selection of Seven Hundred Evangelical Hymns for Private, Family, and Public Worship (Many Original) from more than two hundred of the best Authors in England, Scotland, Ireland, and America, Arranged in Alphabetical order; Intended as a Supplement to Dr. Watt's Psalms and Hymns. By John Dobell.*

In this book, with the title,

Sunday Morning,

this hymn appeared signed "Hayward." Little other than the source is known of this hymn or of its mythical author.

"Lischer" came into Methodist tune books in *An Offering of Praise,* where it is said to be by Lowell Mason. This book was edited by Philip Phillips in 1866, and issued in 1868, as a new setting of tunes for the 1849 *Methodist Hymnal.* In other books it is said to have been arranged by Lowell Mason in 1841.

Johann Christian Friedrich Schneider, to give his full name, was born at Alt-Waltersdorf, near Zittau, Saxony, January 3, 1786, and died November 24, 1853, at Dessau. A Doctor of Philosophy and member of several academies, among them Berlin, he gained fame through his oratorio *The Deluge,* a short-lived work not now in the repertory of singing societies. He composed a symphony at ten years of age and during his life produced an enormous number of works. He had nine oratorios published and wrote seven others; has to his credit more than four hundred songs for men's voices, and two hundred for a single voice. The complete list of his works is staggering. Though jealous of Mendelssohn because of the latter's revival of Bach's works, the two were friends at the time of Mendelssohn's death. When the train bearing Mendelssohn's body passed through Dessau, Schneider's home, on its way to Berlin, Schneider met it with his choir, which sang a lament composed expressly for the occasion.

His name is included in the list of those whose compositions Lowell Mason found on his trip to Germany and which he published in *The Modern Psalmist,* 1839, mentioned at No. 69.

**395—Welcome, day of the Lord**—Percy Dearmer (79)

**Welcome**—Rowland Leach

This hymn was written at the request of Doctor Dwelly, Dean of Liverpool, who wanted a hymn in elegiac couplets "for use on a Sunday, with the Lord's Day for its theme." It appeared in *Songs of Praise, Enlarged Edition,* 1929, in five stanzas, the first being repeated as a refrain. Doctor Dearmer gave his consent for the hymn to be used in *The Methodist Hymnal* with the omission of the third original stanza, the omission of which, he felt, would not detract any from its value:

> Day of hilarity bright, of health and serene recreation;
> Kindreds and friends unite, fathers and children can play.

"Welcome" was written for this hymn for this edition of *The Methodist Hymnal* by Rowland Leach.

Rowland Leach, born at Haverhill, Massachusetts, April 26, 1885, was educated in the public schools of Haverhill, the Wellesley High School, Beloit College (A.B., 1908) and Yale (Mus. Bac., 1910). He earned his way through Beloit teaching violin. Professor Leach has had much experience as a successful teacher of violin and theory, successively at New Haven, Connecticut; Rockford College, Illinois; Calgary, Alberta, Canada; Bush Conservatory of Music, Chicago; DePauw University, Indiana; and the University of Redlands, California, where he is now Professor of Violin and Theory. He is a successful orchestral and operatic conductor, the composer of many works in various forms, a recognized concert violinist, and the author of a fine harmony text.

**396—O day of rest and gladness**—Christopher Wordsworth (153)

**Mendebras**—Arranged by Lowell Mason (19)

This is the opening hymn of Bishop Wordsworth's *Holy Year,* 1862, in six stanzas. The author wrote the sixth line of stanza 1,

> Before the Eternal throne,

but it has been made,

> Through ages joined in tune.

"Mendebras" was arranged from a German melody. Henry L. Mason, the composer's grandson, writes:

> I do not know that it was from a German folk song although I presume "Melody" is practically tantamount to folk song. Date 1839. First sung to, and written for, the hymn by Christopher Wordsworth.

It appeared in Lowell Mason's *The Modern Psalmist,* copyright, 1839, as a double short-meter tune to "I love Thy kingdom, Lord." In the index

"Mendebras" is accompanied with a star, which means, according to the Preface, that it had

> been arranged, adapted, or composed for this work, or taken from other recent works of the editor.

**397—This is the day of light—John Ellerton (28)**

**Dominica—Herbert Stanley Oakeley (42)**

The hymn was written in 1867 and published in *Hymns for Special Services* in Chester Cathedral, compiled by John Saul Howson (1816-1885), Dean of Chester, in 1867. It was published in five stanzas, but the one used in some collections beginning,

> This is the day of bread,

has been omitted. Canon Ellerton did not include it in his authorized text.

"Dominica" was written for this hymn by Sir Herbert S. Oakeley for the Revised Edition of *Hymns Ancient and Modern,* 1875.

**398—Softly fades the twilight ray—Samuel Francis Smith (489)**

**Holley—George Hews**

This lovely "Sabbath Evening" hymn, as it was entitled, was written by Dr. S. F. Smith in 1832 and published in *The Psalmist,* 1843, which he, with Baron Stowe, edited for the Baptist Church. The Supplement to this book has received somewhat extended mention at No. 349.

"Holley" was written by George Hews for the evening hymn, "Softly now the light of day" (47), with which it was published in *The Boston Academy's Collection* of 1835.

George Hews, born in Massachusetts in 1806, concerning whom little is known, was a professional musician and connected with the piano industry in Boston, where from 1830, or earlier, he was actively interested in the Handel and Haydn Society, and was a teacher and organist. W. S. B. Matthews mentions him in his *A Hundred Years of Music in America,* in the chapter on "The Progress of Oratorio to 1840," where he says Hews was the "countertenor" of the Handel and Haydn Society after 1830. He died at Boston, July 6, 1873.

## The Ministry

**399—Let Zion's watchmen all awake—Philip Doddridge (69)**

**Arlington (270)—Thomas Augustine Arne (270)**

The hymn, originally in five stanzas, was written by Doctor Doddridge for the ordination of a minister, probably at Floor, Northamptonshire, England, where it was dated October 21, 1736. It was headed,

> Watching for Souls in the View
> of the Great Account.

and was based on Hebrews 13. 17: "Obey them that have the rule over you, and submit yourselves: for they watch for your souls, as they that must give account, that they may do it with joy, and not with grief: for that is unprofitable for you." It was first published, posthumously, in 1755, in Doddridge's *Hymns Founded on Various Texts in the Holy Scriptures,* published from the author's manuscript by Job Orton.

**400—Jesus! the Name high over all**—Charles Wesley (25)

**Gräfenberg** (389)—From Johann Crüger's Praxis Pietatis Melica, 1653 (60)

This hymn, one of Charles Wesley's best, "has stamped itself deep in the religious life of Methodism," says the Rev. John Telford. It is composed of stanzas 9, 10, 13, 18, and 22, from a long hymn of twenty-two stanzas. In G. J. Stevenson's *The Methodist Hymn Book, illustrated with Biography, History, Incident, and Anecdote,* annotations on the hymnal of 1876 used by British Methodists, the following paragraph is found:

> This hymn has long been a great favorite with the Methodist people generally, and several well-authenticated instances are known of its having been used by godly persons to exorcise the devil. The facts which suggested the composition are recorded by Charles Wesley in his *Journal* under date of 6th August, 1744. Having been preaching in the small church at Laneast, in Cornwall, and condemning the drunken revels of the people, whilst urging them to repent and be converted, one in the congregation contradicted and blasphemed. Charles Wesley asked, "Who is he that pleads for the devil?" The reviler stood boldly forward, the preacher fearlessly exposed his iniquity, and showed the whole congregation their state by nature. Mr. Wesley's withering exposure drove the man in disgrace out of the church. These circumstances are believed to have suggested the writing of the hymn.

It appeared in *Hymns and Sacred Poems,* 1749, headed,

After preaching in a church.

In *Epworth Singers,* the Rev. S. W. Christophers says this hymn

> has been unhappily dealt with. John's selection from it is in the "Methodist Hymn Book," beginning with,
>
> Jesus, the Name high over all,
>
> but the abridgment of the original hymn impairs its strength, breaks its unity, and mars its grandeur. With what clarion-like music Charles's own song rings through the soul, especially when sung with the spirit which fired its author—
>
> Jesus, accept the grateful song,
> My Wisdom and my Might,
> 'Tis Thou hast loosed the stammering tongue,
> And taught my hands to fight.
>
> Thou, Jesus, Thou my mouth hast been;
> The weapons of Thy war,
> Mighty through Thee, I pull down sin,
> And all Thy truth declare.
>
> Not without Thee, my Lord, I am
> Come up into this place,
> Thy Spirit bade me preach Thy name,
> And trumpet forth Thy praise.
>
> Thy Spirit gave me utterance now,
> My soul with strength endued,
> Harden'd to adamant my brow,
> And arm'd my heart with God.

Thy powerful hand in all I see,
Thy wondrous workings own,
Glory, and strength, and praise to Thee
Ascribe, and Thee alone.

Gladly I own the promise true,
To all whom Thou dost send,
"Behold, I always am with you,
Your Saviour to the end."

Amen, amen, my God and Lord,
If Thou art with me still,
I still shall speak the Gospel Word,
My ministry fulfil.

Thee I shall constantly proclaim,
Though earth and hell oppose,
Bold to confess Thy glorious Name,
Before a world of foes.

The next stanza is the first one of this hymn. Coming under the *Hymnal* classification of "The Ministry," as this hymn does, it seems not beside the point to print the above stanzas.

The old tune to which it was sung in Wesley's time was "Liverpool":

which dates back to 1761, according to Stevenson. It is interesting, if for no other reason than that it is evidence that not all of the "old Methodist tunes" were of the "Hallelujah" type.

**401—Lord of the living harvest—John Samuel Bewley Monsell (114)**
**Missionary Hymn—Lowell Mason (19)**

This comes from Doctor Monsell's *Hymns of Love and Praise,* second edition, 1866, with the heading,

For Ember Days[1] and Ordinations.

[1] Ember Days, or Ember-days, are certain days in each season of the year set apart for fasting and prayer. The Sundays immediately following the Ember-days are appointed by the canons of the church of England for the ordination of priests and bishops. The Ember-days are the Wednesday, Friday, and Saturday after the first Sunday in Lent; after Whit-Sunday (seventh Sunday after Easter); after September 14, and after December 13.

"Missionary Hymn" was written by Lowell Mason in 1824 and appeared in 1829 in the ninth edition of *The Boston Handel and Haydn Society Collection.* It has also been called "Gospel Banner" and "Heber," after the author of the hymn for which it was written, "From Greenland's icy mountains." J. T. Lightwood says this tune will not soon be forgotten if "modern editors will leave the simple, original but effective harmonies alone."

**402—And are we yet alive**—Charles Wesley (25)

**Dennis** (69)—From Hans Georg Nägeli (69)
Arranged by Lowell Mason (19)

This hymn is taken from John Wesley's large *Collection* of 1780, with the change of but one word. It is composed of the first four lines of the first double stanza, the entire second stanza, and the first four lines of stanza 3. The word "hides" in the last line of this stanza 3 was "hide" in the 1780 *Collection.*

The hymn, originally in four eight-line stanzas, was published in *Hymns and Sacred Poems,* 1749, one of Wesley's "Hymns for Christian Friends." Some few minor changes were made by John Wesley for his large *Collection.* It has been used in untold instances as the opening hymn of the Methodist Conferences for more than a century and a half, in all parts of the world.

**403—And let our bodies part**—Charles Wesley (25)

**Boylston** (287)—Lowell Mason (19)

This is another of Charles Wesley's "Hymns for Christian Friends," in *Hymns and Sacred Poems,* 1749. Entitled,

At Parting,

it was in two parts, the whole comprising ten eight-line stanzas. John Wesley reduced it to twelve quatrains for his 1780 *Collection,* with changes in several lines. This selection is made of stanzas 1, 3, 4, and 5, from John Wesley's *Collection,* with "farther" changed to "further" in line 4, stanza 2, and "their Lord" to "the Lord," in line 1, stanza 3.

This is frequently sung by Methodist preachers at the close of their Annual Conferences, just after the appointments have been read, and, in the case of many, before going to their new homes.

**404—Blest be the dear uniting love**—Charles Wesley (25)

**Tiplady**—John Porter (8)

This is another "At Parting" hymn with associations similar to those of the preceding hymn, found in *Hymns and Sacred Poems,* 1742, in eight stanzas. There is only one change from the original in the stanzas used here; the last line of stanza 1 was written,

We still are joined in heart.

When this hymn is sung just before the time for reading the "appointments," the second line of stanza 2 has a peculiar significance:

> Where He appoints we go.

Bishop Warren A. Candler, in his *Life of Coke,* tells that this hymn was sung by his congregation when Coke set out as a missionary.

"Tiplady" was written late one afternoon in 1931 at the home of the composer, while he had as his guest the Rev. Thomas Tiplady, of London, then in America attending the Ecumenical Conference. He admired the tune, and it was named for him. Later, when the Commission desired a new common-meter tune for this hymn, it chose "Tiplady."

**405—Life of ages, richly poured—Samuel Johnson**
**Orientis Partibus—Pierre de Corbeil (?)**

This hymn comes from *Hymns of the Spirit,* 1864, of which Samuel Johnson was coeditor with Samuel Longfellow (173).

Samuel Johnson was born at Salem, Massachusetts, October 10, 1822; and was educated both in the Arts and in Theology at Harvard. For seventeen years, from 1853, pastor at Lynn, of a Free Church which he had formed, he did not affiliate with any religious denomination but was generally looked upon as a Unitarian. Although his hymnic contributions were less numerous than those of his associate, Samuel Longfellow, they were equally meritorious. He died at North Andover, Massachusetts, February 19, 1882.

"Orientis Partibus" is thought to have been written by Pierre de Corbeil, Archbishop of Sens in the thirteenth century. Known as the "Sequence [or Prose] of the Ass" and found in the *Office de la Circoncision à l'usage de la ville de Sens,* the tune was sung at church festivals in France as early as the first quarter of the thirteenth century. This Festival, celebrated on January 14, afforded occasion for the medieval play known as the *Feast of the Ass,* which commemorated the Flight into Egypt. In this little play a young girl representing the Virgin Mary, with a doll in her arms to represent the Infant Child Jesus, rode through the streets of the town and into the church on the back of a donkey. At the proper place in the service the priests and the people chanted a form of this tune, to a curious mixture of French and Latin. John F. Rowbotham in his *History of Music,* and others, have regarded this "Prose of the Ass" as a piece of burlesque, but M. Félix Clément (1822-1885), noted writer on musical history and archaeology, who has traced the melody to a manuscript (the *Office* referred to) in the Library of Sens, says in his *Notices sur les chants de la Sainte Chapelle,* 1852:

> Among the items composing this office, there is a piece which has been called Prose of the Ass (Prose de l'âne). Nothing in this piece justifies the opinion, which several writers hostile to Catholicism have endeavored to maintain in regard to a feast, in which the ass played a burlesque and ridiculous rôle.

M. Clément quotes the melody from the Sens manuscript as follows:

This melody, in somewhat different form, is also found in a manuscript from Beauvais, now in the British Museum, and in another at Madrid. Rowbotham gives the following translation, which, except for the first phrase, is similar to the Beauvais manuscript:

O - ri - en - tis par - ti - bus ad - ven - ta - vit As - i - nus,
Hez! Sire As - nes, car chan - tez, Bel - le bou - che re - chi - gnez.
Pul - cher et for - tis - si - mus, Sar - ci - nis ap - tis - si - mus.
Vous au - rez du foin as - sez, et de l'a - voin-e a plan - tez.

To this there was appended this phrase:

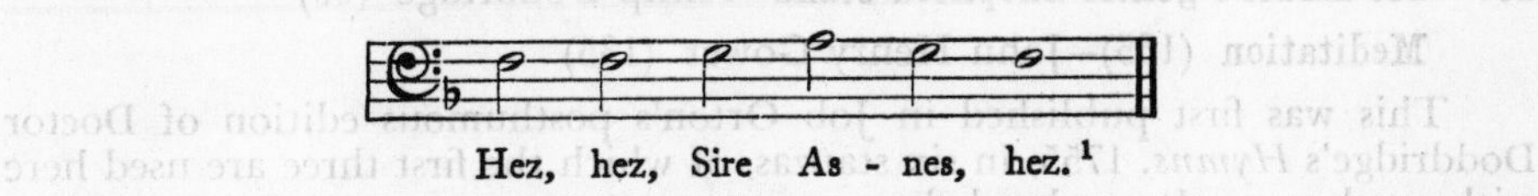
Hez, hez, Sire As - nes, hez.[1]

Richard Redhead (207) arranged a version of the tune, in common time, for his *Church Hymn Tunes,* 1853, which has been followed in some later collections; but this, in three time, seems more in keeping with the rhythm of the words and the notation of the Sens manuscript.

---

[1] A free translation of the "Orientis partibus" is:

> "From eastern parts hastened up an ass
> Fair and very strong; for burdens most suited.
>
> "Hail! Sir Ass, do sing, fair surly mouth
> You will have lots of hay, and of oats plenty.
> Hail, hail, Sir Ass, hail."

# The Sacraments

## Baptism

**406—Friend of the home: as when in Galilee**—Howell Elvet Lewis

**Ffigysbren**—Welsh hymn melody

This is from Doctor Lewis's *Sweet Singers of Wales,* 1889, a book which gives translations of Welsh hymns.

Howell Elvet Lewis, D.D., born April 14, 1860, a Congregational minister; won the Bardic Crown at the national Eisteddfod in 1888; was chairman of the Congregational Union of England and Wales in 1933-1934; contributed nine hymns and translations to the recent edition of *The Congregational Hymnary;* and served as a member of the Committee which compiled it. He is now the minister of the Welsh Tabernacle, Kings Cross, London.

"Ffigysbren" is from *Caniadau Seion* (Songs of Zion), by R. Mills (?), and is ascribed to him. It is known in Wales as "Clôd" (Praise), and is a variant of an earlier form:

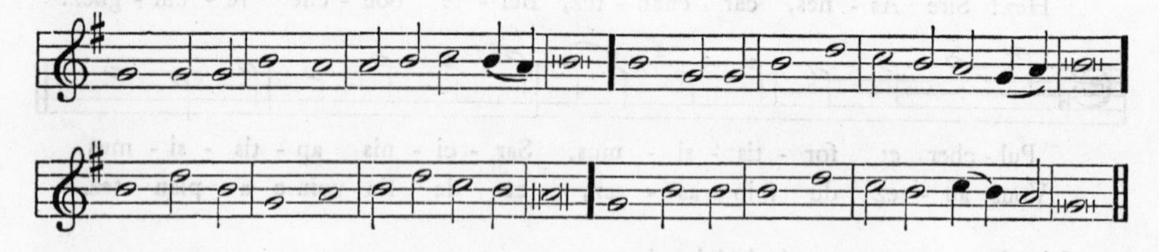

**407—See Israel's gentle Shepherd stand**—Philip Doddridge (69)

**Meditation** (135)—John Henry Gower (135)

This was first published in Job Orton's posthumous edition of Doctor Doddridge's *Hymns,* 1755, in six stanzas, of which the first three are used here without change. It was headed,

Christ's condescending Regard for little Children,

and was based on a part of St. Mark 10. 14: "Suffer the little children to come unto me, and forbid them not: for of such is the kingdom of God."

## The Lord's Supper

**408—Be known to us in breaking bread**—James Montgomery (39)

**Dundee (French)** (68)—Scottish Psalter, 1615 (68)

This hymn was included by James Montgomery in this form in his *Christian Psalmist,* 1825, where it was entitled,

The Family Table.

Although it is one of the finest of the Communion hymns, it need not be limited to that purpose in public worship, but may be put to many uses suggested by the words—for example, the asking of grace at the family table.

**409—The King of heaven His table spreads**—Philip Doddridge (69)

**Dundee (French)** (68)—Scottish Psalter, 1615 (68)

Stanzas 1, 2, 4, and 6 are taken, with changes of three words, from Doctor Doddridge's six-stanza hymn published posthumously by Job Orton in *Hymns founded on Various Texts in The Holy Scriptures,* 1755; in the second line Doddridge wrote "dainties," not "blessings"; in line 3, stanza 2, "And the rich blood" has been changed to "Through the rich blood"; and the Editorial Committee of *The Methodist Hymnal,* 1935, changed "Crowd to your places" to "Come to your places." This last change is a commentary upon the fact that no longer do congregations crowd to the communion altar.

**410—According to Thy gracious word**—James Montgomery (39)

**St. John's, Westminster**—James Turle

This hymn comes from James Montgomery's *Christian Psalmist,* 1825, where the text and the title are from St. Luke 22. 19: ". . . this do in remembrance of me."

"St. John's, Westminster" comes from *Psalms and Hymns for Public Worship, with Appropriate Tunes,* edited by James Turle, in 1863.

James Turle, born at Taunton, Somerset, England, March 5, 1802, was for sixty-three years connected with Westminster Abbey. Nature endowed him with such extraordinarily large hands that he was able to span an octave and a half with ease. Chorister at Wells Cathedral, organist at Westminster Abbey succeeding Thomas Greatorex [the father of Henry W. Greatorex (378)], whose assistant he had been for twelve years, from 1819, he remained active until relieved of much of the arduous work by the appointment of J. F. Bridge as his own assistant in 1875. His sole interest was in serving the Church and he wrote little but hymn tunes, chants, and anthems. His daughter collected his *Psalm and Hymn Tunes,* published in 1885, three years after his death. An excellent teacher, he had many pupils who became prominent in the profession of music. He died at London, June 28, 1882.

**411—Jesus spreads His banner o'er us**—Roswell Park

**Autumn** (166)—Arranged from François Hippolyte Barthélémon (166)

This hymn consists of the second and third stanzas of six taken from Doctor Park's *Poems* 1836, without alteration. In the beginning of the hymn,

> While the sons of earth retiring,
> From the sacred temple roam;
> Lord, thy light and love desiring,
> To thine altar fain we come.
> Children of our Heavenly Father,
> Friends and brethren would we be;
> While we round thy table gather,
> May our hearts be one in thee,

Doctor Park had in mind those churches where the members of the congregation not wishing to partake of the Lord's Supper are given an opportunity to retire before the invitation is extended.

Roswell Park, D.D., minister of the Protestant Episcopal Church, was born at Lebanon, Connecticut, October 1, 1807, and educated at Union College and at West Point Military Academy. Before his ordination he served in the Engineering Corps of the United States Army, and was Professor of Chemistry at the University of Pennsylvania. After serving as President and Chancellor of Racine College, Wisconsin, from 1852 until 1863, he established a school in Chicago, where he remained until his death, July 16, 1869.

**412—For the bread, which Thou hast broken**—Louis Fitzgerald Benson (38)

**Agapé**—Charles John Dickinson

This hymn was first published in Doctor Benson's private collection entitled *Hymns* in 1925. Mrs. Robert E. Jefferys, daughter of the author, writes that the first stanza of the hymn "was suggested by Bonar's 'For the bread and for the wine,' and was written to fill the place of the post-communion hymn." The first draft seems to have been made on November 21, 1924. Doctor Benson stated:

> I showed it to Dr. Henry Sloane Coffin at our house, and he spoke favorably of it but wanted an additional verse bringing in Service and Kingdom. (Sunday 23 Nov. '24). After he left next day I sat down and wrote the verse.

"Agapé" comes from *The Irish Hymnal,* 1873, where it is called "Sanctuary," and is set to Bishop Heber's hymn, "Bread of the world in mercy broken" (414). It appeared earlier, however, in the composer's *Hymn Tunes,* 1861. There are several other tunes bearing the name "Agapé" which should not be confused with this one.

Charles John Dickinson has the title "Reverend" given him in *The Irish Hymnal,* and James Edmund Jones gives 1822-1883 as the dates of his birth and death. To the writer nothing is known of him or his work other than that he issued a collection of his own tunes in 1861 and that he contributed five tunes to *The Irish Hymnal,* one of them being used three times.

**413—In memory of the Saviour's love**—Thomas Cotterill

**Salzburg** (383)—Adapted from Johann Michael Haydn (4)

This selection of stanzas 3, 5, and 6, of Thomas Cotterill's six-stanza hymn beginning, "Blest with the presence of their God," and headed,

For the Sacrament,

appeared in R. Whittingham's (?) *Collection,* 1835. The full hymn was included in a *Selection of Psalms and Hymns, for Public and Private Use,* 1805, edited by the Rev. Jonathan Stubbs, d. 1810, who was assisted in its compilation by Cotterill and others. This was the first of a series of books issued for local use in Staffordshire, England.

Thomas Cotterill, son of a dealer in wool (wool-stapler) in Cannock, Staffordshire, England, was born December 4, 1779. He graduated from St. John's College, Cambridge, became a Fellow, took Holy Orders, and came, in 1817, to the Perpetual Curacy of St. Paul's, Sheffield, where he died December 29, 1823. He is less favorably known as a writer of hymns than as a compiler, his *Selection of Psalms and Hymns* having had a marked effect on modern hymnals. (See No. 207.)

**414—Bread of the world in mercy broken—Reginald Heber (1)**

**Eucharistic Hymn—John Sebastian Bach Hodges**

This hymn comes from Bishop Heber's posthumous *Hymns Written and Adapted to the weekly Church Services of the year,* 1827, where it was headed,

Before the Sacrifice.

It has very extensive use.

"Eucharistic Hymn," a tune well named, has always been associated with this hymn of Bishop Heber. It is beautiful in its simplicity. Appearing in 1869 in *The Hymnal* of the Protestant Episcopal Church, it is sometimes called "Panis."

John Sebastian Bach Hodges, born at Bristol, England, 1830, was the son of the illustrious organist, Edward Hodges, Mus. Doc., 1796-1867, who came to America in 1838, and remained here until four years before his death. In 1845 the older Hodges sent for John, his son, and Faustina, his daughter, who came to this country. Educated at Columbia University and at the General Theological Seminary, John S. B. Hodges became a noted divine in the Protestant Episcopal Church. Influenced, however, by his father's musical interest (the elder Hodges was an excellent organist), he compiled *The Book of Common Praise,* 1868, and had much to do with the successive revisions of the Episcopal *Hymnal.* He founded in Baltimore the earliest choir school in the United States. His death occurred at Baltimore, May 1, 1915.

**415—Here, O my Lord, I see Thee face to face—Horatius Bonar (210)**

**Penitentia—Edward Dearle**

This hymn, by Dr. Horatius Bonar, though first published, in ten stanzas, in his *Hymns of Faith and Hope,* first series, 1857, had been written by the request of his brother, Dr. John J. Bonar, in October, 1855, for the leaflet which he customarily gave out after each communion service at St. Andrews' Free Church, Greenock, Scotland. Dr. Horatius Bonar went once each year to assist his brother, Dr. John James Bonar, at a communion service.

"Penitentia" is from *Church Hymns with Tunes,* London, 1874, edited by Sir Arthur Sullivan (15).

Edward Dearle, Mus. Doc., born at Cambridge, England, March 2, 1806, was an English organist and composer, especially of vocal music, both sacred and secular. He died at Camberwell, London, March 20, 1891.

## Fellowship

**416—Blest be the tie that binds**—John Fawcett (26)

**Dennis** (69)—From Hans Georg Nägeli (69)
Arranged by Lowell Mason (19)

Josiah Miller, 1832-1880, in his *Singers and Songs of the Church,* 1869, says:

> This favourite hymn is said to have been written in 1772, to commemorate the determination of its author to remain with his attached people at Wainsgate. The farewell sermon was preached, the waggons were loaded, when love and tears prevailed, and Dr. Fawcett sacrificed the attractions of a London pulpit to the affection of his poor but devoted flock.

The London pulpit was Carter's Lane, an attractive Baptist church whose minister had died; but Miller was content to remain in Yorkshire, England, even though he had been but a few years in the ministry and had found "his family increasing more rapidly than his income." "As a good soldier of Christ, he . . . endured hardness for far more than half a century." His reward has been great. It has been given to few men to write that which has brought comfort and gratitude to millions of souls as it was given to John Fawcett.

Positive evidence of the connection between the contemplated removal and the writing of the hymn is lacking, but internal evidence supports the truth of the story. The hymn was first published in Doctor Fawcett's *Hymns Adapted to the Circumstances of Public Worship and Private Devotion,* 1782. The first line of the last stanza formerly read,

> When we asunder part.

**417—All praise to our redeeming Lord**—Charles Wesley (25)

**Armenia**—Sylvanus Billings Pond

This comes from *Hymns for Those that Seek and Those that Have Redemption in the Blood of Jesus Christ,* 1747, the little book of sixty-eight pages that also contained "Love divine, all loves excelling" (372), and "Come, sinners, to the gospel feast" (186). The hymn was in three eight-line stanzas, of which the second is omitted. One word has been changed: In line 3, stanza 3, Charles Wesley wrote "sensual minds," not "worldly minds." It had the title,

> At meeting of Friends.

"Armenia" appeared in 1841 in S. B. Pond's *United States Psalmody.*

Sylvester Billings Pond, 1792-1871, was born near Worcester, Massachusetts, and moved before 1820, to Albany, New York, where he engaged in his trade of piano making. In 1832 he moved to New York and joined the firm of Firth and Hall, piano makers. In 1847 the firm added W. A. Pond to its personnel, and when John Firth retired from its membership in 1863, it became known as William A. Pond and Co. S. B. Pond compiled Sunday-school books and wrote tunes for them. In 1841 he issued the *United States Psalmody,* of which I. B. Woodbury (137) said, "Mr. Pond is author of many fine psalm tunes, and his collection of church music is deservedly valued for the sterling tunes it contains."

**418—Father of men, in whom are one—Henry Cary Shuttleworth**

**Llangoedmor**—Welsh hymn melody

This hymn first appeared in the *St. Nicholas Cole Abbey Hymnal Appendix,* 1879, and with music by the author, in *The Church Monthly,* 1898. It was written for "Friendly Societies."

Henry Cary Shuttleworth, professor of pastoral and liturgical theology, and lecturer in other subjects, in King's College, London, was born at Egloshayle, Cornwall, England, October 20, 1850, and died at London, October 24, 1900. An ardent ritualist, he became prominently identified with the Christian Socialist movement in the days of the Guild of St. Matthew. His published works include *The Place of Music in Worship; Hymns for Private Use.* Professor Shuttleworth was a much better than average musical amateur and wrote a number of carols and hymns.

"Llangoedmor," meaning "The church in the woods by the sea," is from *Y Gwyliedydd,* 1826.

**419—Jesus, united by Thy grace—Charles Wesley (25)**

**Beatitudo**—John Bacchus Dykes (1)

This is from a long hymn in four parts entitled,

A Prayer for Persons Joined in Fellowship,

which was included in *Hymns and Sacred Poems,* 1742. Stanzas 1 and 4 are the corresponding stanzas from Part IV, verbatim, and 2 and 3 are, respectively, 3 and 5 from Part I, with the first line of this stanza 3 changed from,

Up into Thee, our living Head,

to,

Up unto Thee, our living Head,

and the last line of the same from,

And sinless here below,

to,

And spotless here below.

"Beatitudo" was written by Doctor Dykes for the Revised Edition of *Hymns Ancient and Modern,* 1875, to the words "How bright these glorious spirits shine!"

## Christian Unity

**420—City of God, how broad and fair**—Samuel Johnson (405)

**Gräfenberg** (389)—From Johann Crüger's Praxis Pietatis Melica, 1653 (60)

This is from *Hymns of the Spirit,* 1864. Dr. Percy Dearmer (79) thinks it is one of the exceptionally fine hymns from American authors, and seems proud of the fact that he introduced it to English congregations through *The English Hymnal,* 1906.

**421—No form of human framing**—Henry van Dyke (12)

**Alford**—John Bacchus Dykes (1)

Dr. Tertius van Dyke, son of Dr. Henry van Dyke, the author of this hymn, has given the following information:

> It is one of seven hymns written after 1920 and chiefly during the winter of 1921-22. These seven hymns first appeared in a small volume which took its title from the first line of the first hymn:
>
> "Thy Sea is Great
> Our Boats are Small."
>
> To these seven new hymns were added three hymns of earlier composition. In the Foreword my father writes: "As they (i. e. the hymns) stand, they are at the service of all who ask and receive the permission of the publishers to use them." He also makes the statement:
>
> "These verses are simple expressions of common Christian feelings and desires in this present time,—hymns of today that may be sung together by people who know the thought of the age, and are not afraid that any truth of science will destroy religion, or any revolution on earth overthrow the kingdom of heaven. Therefore these are hymns of trust and joy and hope."

"Alford" was composed by Doctor Dykes for the hymn "Ten thousand times ten thousand," for the Revised Edition of *Hymns Ancient and Modern,* 1875. Sir Henry W. Baker wrote a letter to Doctor Dykes' widow at the time of his death, in which he said, "We are going to sing *only his* Tunes to every hymn all next Sunday, and the Dies Irae after evensong—*for him;* followed by 'Ten thousand times ten thousand.' "

## The Communion of Saints

**422—Come, let us join our friends above**—Charles Wesley (25)

**Dundee (French)** (68)—Scottish Psalter (68)

This is the first of the *Funeral Hymns,* Second Series, 1759, originally in five eight-line stanzas, of which all of stanzas 1 and 2 and the last half of stanza 4 are taken. The alterations, while inconsequential, are worth noting: In stanza 1, line 4, Wesley wrote "joy" instead of "joys"; the last two lines of stanza 5 were,

> **Part of His host hath cross'd the flood,**
> **And part is crossing now,**

and "blood-redeeméd bands" has been substituted for "blood-besprinkled bands" in the same stanza. In some of its many forms, for the entire hymn is seldom if ever used, it is in use in all English-speaking countries, especially for funeral occasions.

Without question this is one of Charles Wesley's greatest hymns, and among funeral hymns no other is so filled with grandeur and such an energetic statement of a conviction of belief in "the communion of saints." His imagery of an army of saints in heaven and on earth comprising "One Church" is strikingly vivid:

. . . . . . . . . .

One Church above, beneath,
Tho' now divided by the stream,
The narrow stream of death;

One army of the living God,
To His command we bow:
Part of His host have crossed the flood,
And part are crossing now.

The Bishop of Hereford, England (Doctor Percival), told W. T. Stead that he considered these lines among "the finest in the whole range of hymnology," and the fact that John Wesley and his congregation in Staffordshire were singing this hymn at the very hour his beloved brother was passing on

to sing
With those to glory gone,

gives it a peculiarly pathetic interest.

In the words of Richard Watson:

> The funeral hymns have but little of the softness of sorrow, perhaps too little, but they are written in that fulness of faith which exclaims over the open tomb, Thanks be to God which giveth us the victory, through our Lord Jesus Christ.

Dr. Abel Stevens, Methodist historian, in his *History of Methodism,* says:

> Many of his elegies [Charles Wesley's] have an unearthly power; a sadness of the grave pervaded by the rapture of heaven. His Funeral Hymns, occasioned, with hardly an exception, by actual deaths, constitute the most perfect part of the Methodist psalmody, and for a hundred years and more these testimonials of the dying triumphs of their early brethren have been sung at the death-beds and funerals of Methodists throughout the world.

When Joseph Hodges Choate, 1832-1917, eminent American diplomat and President McKinley's appointee to the ambassadorship at the Court of St. James, was about to return home after his resignation from this illustrious post for the excellent reason that he was homesick, he was tendered a banquet, May 6, 1905, at the Mansion House, London. In his address on that occasion he said:

> My friends on this side of the water are multiplying every day in numbers and increasing in the ardor of their affections. I am sorry to say that the great host of my friends on the other side are as rapidly diminishing and dwindling away.
>
> Part of the host have crossed the flood,
> And part are crossing now,
>
> and I have a great yearning to be with the waning number.

John Wesley, referring to Dr. Isaac Watts's (3) reference to Charles's *Wrestling Jacob* (311), was heard to say,

> O what would Dr. Watts have said if he had lived to see my brother's two exquisite Funeral Hymns, beginning, "How happy every child of grace" (522), and "Come, let us join our friends above"?

**423—We cannot think of them as dead—Frederick Lucian Hosmer (43)**
**St. Flavian—Adapted from Day's Psalter, 1562**

Written in 1882, this fine hymn by Doctor Hosmer comes from his *The Thought of God in Hymns and Poems,* first series, 1885, entitled,

My Dead.

It was a very personal expression beginning,

I cannot think of them as dead.

"St. Flavian" is taken from the tune set to Psalm 132 in *Day's Psalter,* 1562, so called because the book was printed by John Day, in London. It is better known as the "Old Version," or "Sternhold and Hopkins." This was the completed form of the *English Psalter* which was patterned after the earlier *Genevan Psalter,* 1542, of John Calvin. The interesting title page reads:

> *The whole Booke of Psalmes, collected into Englysh metre by T. Starnhold, I. Hopkins & others; conferred with the Ebrue, with apt Notes to sing them withal, Faithfully perused and alowed according to thordre appointed in the Quenes maiesties Iniunctions. Very mete to be used of all sortes of people priuately for their solace & comfort: laying apart all vngodly Songes and Ballades, which tende onely to the norishing of vyce, and corrupting of youth.* [This is followed by two scriptural texts and an imprint.] *An. 1562.*

It is from this book that many of the "old" tunes come. In *The Methodist Hymnal* are found "Old 100th" (3), "Old 113th" (513), and "Old 134th" (39).

This tune is the first half of the setting for Psalm 132, with some slight alterations. The following is the complete tune:

It is also known as "Day" or "Prescott."

John Day, or Daye, was a printer who is said to have been born in St. Peter's parish, Dunwick, Suffolk, England, in 1522, although there are no records to verify the date. Sometime before the middle of the sixteenth century he had settled in London and established himself as one of the earliest of the English printers. Dibdin says, "There are very few of our earlier printers to whom both literature and typography are more deeply indebted." He produced about two hundred and thirty works, among them being such important ones as the first editions of *Queen Elizabeth's Prayer Book* and Foxe's *Book of Martyrs.* Little more is known of him except that he must have had a certain wit. On many of his title pages are found the inscription:

| ARISE ╳ I SAY |
|---|
| FOR IT ╳ IS DAY |

**424—Give me the wings of faith to rise—Isaac Watts (3)**
**St. Peter—Alexander Robert Reinagle**

This hymn, with the heading,

Examples of Christ and the Saints,

which appeared in Book II of Doctor Watts's *Hymns and Spiritual Songs,* Second Edition, 1709, in five stanzas, has been but slightly altered: Line 1, stanza 2, has "that" substituted for "which," and "They gained" has replaced "Possess" at the beginning of the last line of the same stanza. The second stanza has been omitted.

Dr. Philip Doddridge (69) wrote Doctor Watts:

> I was preaching in a barn last Wednesday, to a company of plain country people. After a sermon from Heb. vi. 12, we sang one of your hymns, commencing, "Give me the wings of faith to rise," and had the satisfaction to see tears in the eyes of several of the auditory. After the service some of them told me they were not able to sing, so deeply were their minds affected with it; and the clerk in particular told me he could hardly utter the words of it. These were most of them poor people who work for their living.

How many are the "poor people who work for their living" who have been comforted and encouraged by the thought that they might have "wings of faith to rise"!

"St. Peter" comes from A. R. Reinagle's *Psalm Tunes for the Voice and Pianoforte,* c. 1830. It was called "St. Peter's, Oxford," in the 1905 *Methodist Hymnal.*

Alexander Robert Reinagle, who was born at Brighton, England, August 21, 1799, and who died at Kidlington, near Oxford, April 6, 1877, came from a musical family. His grandfather, Joseph, Sr., was a Hungarian, who late in life became "trumpeter to the King," presumably in Scotland, for at the time he lived at Edinburgh. This Joseph's eldest son, Alexander, was also a musician and lived in America, at Baltimore, for more than twenty years, until his death in 1809. The second son, Joseph, Jr., became prominent in musical circles in England. Alexander Robert, the second Joseph's son, early in life moved with his father's family to Oxford, where, later, he became organist at St. Peters-in-the-East. He was the composer and editor of many books used in the teaching of violin and violoncello, and his wife was prominent as a pianist and teacher.

**425—For those we love within the veil—William Charter Piggott**

**Meyer (Es ist kein Tag)**—From Johann David Meyer's Geistliche Seelenfreud, 1692

This hymn was written in 1915 for a war commemoration service, and its first appearance in a hymnal was in *Songs of Praise,* 1925.

William Charter Piggott, born at Leighton Buzzard, Buckshire, England, August 9, 1872, was educated for the Wesleyan ministry at Huddersfield College and Headingley College. After entering the Congregational ministry in 1902, he served charges at London, and Bedford before his return to London as the successor to C. Silvester Horne (492) at Whitefield's Chapel, Tottenham Court Road, London. He is now at Streatham.

"Meyer" or "Es ist kein Tag," is credited to Johann David Meyer, or Mejer, in *Geistliche Seelenfreud,* a book edited by him at Ulm in 1692. Nothing more is known of the composer than that he was at one time a town councilor in his native city, and it appears that his work as a musician was limited to the issuing of the book from which this tune was taken.

# THE CHRISTIAN HOME AND FAMILY

**426—Lord of life and King of glory—Christian Burke**

**Sicilian Mariners' Hymn** (26)—Arranged from a Sicilian melody

The hymn was written in December of 1903 by Miss Burke and was published in *The Treasury* in February, 1907, where it was headed,

Prize Hymn for a Mothers' Union Service

Miss Christian Burke was born at London, in 1859. Her earlier poetic writings were collected and published in 1896 in a volume with the title *The Flowering of the Almond Tree.*

**427—O happy home where Thou art loved the dearest—Carl Johann Philipp Spitta**

Arranged from a translation by Sarah Borthwick Findlater

**Alverstoke**—Joseph Barnby (31)

This hymn, originally from Spitta's *Psalter und Harfe*, Leipzig, 1833, and written in the fall of 1826, began,

O selig Haus, wo man dich aufgenommen.

Founded on St. Luke 19. 9, "And Jesus said unto him, This day is salvation come to this house, forsomuch as he also is a son of Abraham," and headed,

Salvation is come to this house,

it was a picture of the happy Christian home life of the author. It came into popularity in Germany through its inclusion in the *Württemberger Gesangbuch*, of 1842. This version of a translation by Mrs. Findlater was included in *Hymns from the Land of Luther*, Third Series, 1858, which appeared in the Scottish *Church Hymnary*, 1898, in "a more singable metre," an alteration which did not receive the approval of the translator. The hymn was in six stanzas, two and three being omitted. As they more completely fill the picture of the Christian home, they are given here.

O happy home, where two in heart united
In holy faith and blessed hope are one,
Whom death a little while alone divideth,
And cannot end the union here begun!

O happy home, whose little ones are given
Early to Thee, in humble faith and prayer,
To Thee, their Friend, who from the heights of heaven
Guides them, and guards with more than mother's care!

Carl Johann Philipp Spitta, D.D., born at Hanover, Germany, August 1, 1801, was, according to Dr. Philip Schaff, "upon the whole, the most popular

(German) hymnist of the nineteenth century. . . . His hymns are characterized by deep evangelical piety and simplicity." He began writing verse when only eight years old, but abandoned all thought of a literary career in his eleventh year, when taken with an illness that lasted four years. He was then apprenticed to a watchmaker but, although he was faithful and efficient, the occupation was not to his liking. He never gave expression to this dislike, and his true feelings remained unknown even to the members of his immediate family until, in grieving over the death of a younger brother who had been preparing for the Lutheran ministry, he inadvertantly disclosed it to a close personal friend. It was with delight that he embraced the opportunity to adopt a similar career and by hard study prepared himself in less than a year's time for his examinations for entrance into the highest class in the gymnasium. Completing his theological course at the University of Göttingen, he acted as a tutor in a private family for four years, when he was ordained in 1828 as assistant pastor at Sudwalde, near Hoya, and two years later was appointed assistant chaplain at the garrison at Hameln. Charged with being a Pietist and mystic, he failed to succeed to the full chaplaincy. For ten years he was Lutheran superintendent at Wittingen, Peine, and Bergdorf. Soon after entering upon his duties at Bergdorf, he died suddenly of a heart attack while sitting at his study table, on September 28, 1859. He had written and published a number of songs and secular poems while at the University, but began writing hymns in 1824 after a marked spiritual change. In 1826 he wrote to a friend, saying:

> In the manner in which I formerly sang I sing no more. To the Lord I consecrate my life and my love, and likewise my song. His love is the one great theme of all my songs; to praise and exalt it worthily is the desire of the Christian singer. He gave to me song and melody; I give it back to Him.

It is said that his *Psalter und Harfe* was looked upon in Germany much as Keble's *Christian Year* was in England. Doctor Spitta's son, Julius August Philipp, 1841-94, was the author of the monumental *Life of Bach.*

Sarah Findlater, née Borthwick, born at Edinburgh, Scotland, November 26, 1823, was the sister of Jane Laurie Borthwick (73), and with her translated German hymns issued in four series, from 1854 to 1862, under the title, *Hymns from the Land of Luther.* Fifty-three of the translations were by Mrs. Findlater. Her daughter, in writing of her, has said:

> She was a woman of great individuality, almost eccentric in many ways, and with a curious simplicity of nature. She never had and never wanted any of the things that most people prize most. The only use she had for money was to give it away, and she used to say to us when we complained of the restrictions of poverty, "It is the lightest of all trials." Her home life with my father was almost idyllically happy, in the small manse at Lochearnhead, where there never was enough of money, yet where my parents exercised unceasing hospitality—almost foolish hospitality. They were both great readers, and used to read aloud to each other for hours. My mother was an excellent linguist, and her German translations were a great pleasure to her. That simple little hymn of hers which begins "O happy home," is really an epitome of her home life with my father—they were so single-eyed in their longing to serve God: it came first with them always. I often wonder if there are such simply "good" men and women now. No doubt they were not altogether enlightened in their methods, but the sincerity of their purpose was amazing.

Mrs. Findlater died at Torquay, in 1907.

"Alverstoke" was written by Sir Joseph Barnby for the hymn "Still, still with Thee" (40), giving it no name. This name was supplied by some later editor. Many of his hymn tunes were originally issued on leaflets and were known only by the first line of the hymn to which they were set. The tune was first published in 1883 in a collection of original tunes by the composer. The first hymnal which included it was the *Methodist Free Church Tune-Book*, in 1892.

**428—Happy the home when God is there**—Henry Ware, the younger

**St. Agnes** (341)—John Bacchus Dykes (1)

This first appeared in *Selection of Hymns and Poetry for the Use of Infant and Juvenile Schools and Families,* third edition, 1846, Mrs. Herbert Mayo, entitled:

The Happy Home

Henry Ware, D.D., son of the eminent Professor of Divinity at Cambridge Theological School, Henry Ware, D.D., was born at Hingham, Massachusetts, April 21, 1794, graduated with high honors from Harvard in 1812, and became an assistant at Exeter Academy in New Hampshire. After being licensed to preach by the Boston Unitarian Association in 1815, he was, two years later, ordained pastor of the Second Unitarian Church of that city, where for a time, in 1829, Ralph Waldo Emerson was his assistant. The same year he was appointed Professor of Pulpit Eloquence and Pastoral Care in the Cambridge Theological School, where, from 1830, he remained for twelve years. He died, September 25, 1843, at Framingham, where he had retired. He was editor of *The Christian Disciple,* later *The Christian Examiner.* His works were collected by the Rev. Chandler Robbins and published in four volumes in 1847.

The following paragraph is taken from *The Life of Henry Ware, Jr.,* by his brother:

> If he had properly a worldly ambition for anything, it was for the fame of a poet. He had constantly in view great objects to accomplish and he therefore derived the greatest satisfaction from those accomplishments which promoted them. But, apart from this source of interest, he took more pleasure in poetical composition than in any other occupation; and although he indulged himself in it but little, when his mind was entirely unbent, when he had no immediate purpose to accomplish, as in traveling or in sickness, he almost instinctively turned to poetry for rest or refreshment.

**429—Shepherd of tender youth**—Clement of Alexandria
Translated by Henry Martyn Dexter

**Kirby Bedon**—Edward Bunnett

This hymn should not be referred to as a translation, for it is not. Doctor Dexter has said that after he first translated a Greek hymn attributed to Clement of Alexandria literally into prose, he "transfused as much of its language and spirit" as he could into verse. In 1846, while preparing a sermon from the text "Remember the days of old," Deuteronomy 32. 7, on "Some prominent characteristics of the early Christians," Doctor Dexter for use at the service wrote this hymn, based on the old Greek poem with which he was familiar. First printed in *The Congregationalist,* December 21, 1849, it soon was included in various hymnals.

Clement of Alexandria wrote a book—one of ten—which is known as *The Instructor,* or *The Tutor,* the date of which is unknown. This book is in three parts, the first describing "The Instructor" (the Word Himself), the children (Christian men and women) trained by Him, and the method of instruction. The second gives instruction as to daily living, and the third inveighs against extravagances, particularly in the dress of both men and women. Appended to this book are two hymns, the first, entitled a *Hymn of the Saviour,* the basis for Doctor Dexter's lines. This hymn is included in *The Methodist Hymnal* because of its historical interest as the oldest Christian hymn extant. Efforts to make a modern service hymn out of it have been unsuccessful. If it is to be used at all, it is better to take it for just what it is and leave it as Doctor Dexter wrote it.

Clement of Alexandria is thought to have been born at Athens about 170, but nothing is known certainly either as to the time or place of his birth. He was the head of the Catechetical School at Alexandria, the center of Christian scholarship, from about 190 until 202. A pagan philosopher in his younger days, he embraced Christianity and became a teacher of note. Driven from Alexandria by the persecutions of Severus in 202-03, he became a wanderer and nothing is known of his later years. He is thought to have died shortly before 220.

Henry Martyn Dexter, D.D., Congregational minister and for many years editor of *The Congregationalist and Recorder,* was born at Plympton, Massachusetts, August 13, 1821, and graduated from Yale in 1840; ordained after graduation from Andover Theological Seminary in 1844, he served pastorates at Manchester, New Hampshire, and at Boston. In addition to his pastoral duties at Boston he acted as editor of *The Congregationalist* and *The Congregational Quarterly,* until, after 1867, he devoted all of his time to *The Congregationalist and Recorder.* He was a scholar and a man of letters, writing verse only as an occasional matter, and none other than the hymn, "Shepherd of tender youth," has been published. He died in his sleep, November 13, 1890.

"Kirby Bedon" was composed by Edward Bunnett and appeared in *The Congregational Hymnary* of the Congregational Union of England and Wales.

Edward Bunnett, Mus. Doc., was born at Norwich, England, June 26, 1834 or 1835, and died there January 5, 1923. He was a prominent English organist and composer of church music, including *Twenty-four Original Tunes to Favorite Hymns.*

**430—O Love divine and golden—John Samuel Bewley Monsell (114)**

**Blairgowrie (266)—John Bacchus Dykes (1)**

This "common vernacular" hymn is taken from Doctor Monsell's *Spirit-*

*ual Songs for the Sundays and Holy Days Throughout the Year,* published in 1857.

**431—O perfect Love, all human love transcending**—Dorothy Blomfield Gurney

**O Perfect Love**—Arranged from Joseph Barnby (31)

Mrs. Gurney gave the following account of the writing of this very popular hymn for holy matrimony:

> It was written one Sunday evening in a quarter of an hour, sixteen years ago (1883), for my sister's marriage with Mr. Hugh Redmayne, of Brathay Hall. We had all been singing hymns, and had just sung No. 12 in *Hymns Ancient and Modern* ("O strength and stay upholding all creation"), when my sister remarked that it was her favourite tune ("Strength and Stay"—Dykes), and that she wished the words were suitable to a wedding. "What is the use of having a sister who writes poetry," she added, "if she cannot write me words for that tune?" I said I would, and there and then took the hymn-book into the library, and wrote the hymn with hardly a pause. I wrote it at Pull Wyke, Ambleside. After that, it was sung privately at most of the London weddings for two or three years; and then was put into the revised edition of *Hymns Ancient and Modern.* Sir Joseph Barnby set it for the wedding of Princess Louise of Fife, and it has been sung at all the subsequent royal weddings.

At another time Mrs. Gurney wrote:

> The writing of it was no effort whatever after the initial idea had come to me of the two-fold aspect of perfect union, love and life, and I have always felt that God helped me to write it.

Dorothy Frances Gurney, née Blomfield, born at London in 1858, was the eldest daughter of Prebendary F. G. Blomfield, and the granddaughter of Doctor Blomfield, Bishop of London. She married Gerald Gurney, who, upon graduation from Oxford, became an actor, later being ordained in the Church of England. In 1919 both Mr. and Mrs. Gurney joined the Roman Catholic Church. Mrs. Gurney published two books entitled *Poems,* and a third, *A Little Book of Quiet.* Perhaps her best-known lines are from her poem, "God's Garden":

> The kiss of the sun for pardon,
> The song of the birds for mirth:
> One is nearer God's heart in a garden
> Than anywhere else on earth.

A correspondent to the London *Times* at the time of her sudden death at London, June 15, 1932, wrote:

> Thousands of people at thousands of weddings must have sung, or heard sung, "O Perfect Love!" without knowing that Mrs. Gurney wrote the hymn. It was always to her a matter of amused regret that she did not get a royalty for each performance. . . . But it is not as an author that she will be best remembered by her many friends. . . . A wide circle of friends of every creed and class knew that they could take to her all their troubles, great or small, and come away with the burden of them lightened or removed.

"O Perfect Love" is taken from the anthem composed by Sir Joseph Barnby for the marriage of the Duke of Fife to Princess Louise of Wales, July 27, 1889.

**432—Thou gracious God whose mercy lends**—Oliver Wendell Holmes (62)
**Rimington** (345)—Francis Duckworth (345)

Doctor Holmes wrote this hymn in 1869 to be read or sung at the fortieth annual reunion of the class of 1829 at Harvard University. In that class were other distinguished men, among them Judge George Tyler Bigelow, of Massachusetts; J. Freeman Clarke, founder of the Disciples; and Samuel F. Smith, who wrote "America." Beginning in 1855, Doctor Holmes, for almost all of the remainder of his life, wrote a poem either to be read or sung by him at his annual class reunions. When first written, the first line read,

Thou gracious Power, whose mercy lends,

but "God" was substituted for "Power" with the consent of Doctor Holmes for *The Home and School Hymnal,* London.

**433—Bless the four corners of this house**—Arthur Guiterman
**Home**—Van Denman Thompson (153)

This is the first appearance, with musical setting, in any hymnal, of Arthur Guiterman's lovely verses admirably adapted for use in the dedication of a Christian home. No hymn could be found more admirable for the beautiful custom of young married couples of dedicating their new homes to Almighty God. Mr. Guiterman gladly gave his consent to have his poem put to such use.

The author has written interestingly of his little poem:

> I wrote "House Blessing" about September, 1916. While I don't think the matter important, the poem has had an unusually varied career, which has been interesting and amusing to me.
>
> To begin with, I sent it to (a well-known journal), only to have it returned with the following note from one of the editors:
>
> "I liked your 'House Blessing' very much, and gave Mr. ——— a chance at it. But he felt that it got down too much to the details of a house, which to his mind is inartistic—especially in poetry. So he turned it down. I am sorry."
>
> Then I sent it to (another well-known journal), fully aware that it was not at all the sort of verse favored by that periodical, but feeling that it might have some effect on the editors of that excellent but rather snooty outfit. Here is the note that came back with it:
>
> "These are such pretty lines that we are sorry to think that they are less suited to (our publication) than to some magazine which presides with greater placidity over the domestic scene."
>
> While I have an antiquated idea that "placidity" is desirable in "the domestic scene," I didn't venture to convert this heathen editor, but sent the poem to *House and Garden,* which published it with an illustration, and then the poem started out on its travels.
>
> Apparently, it was plagiarized in England by someone who put it into "olde Englysshe" with the usual exaggerations of spelling; and about four years ago I learned, from a newspaper clipping, that it had been "discovered" as an old English hymn for the dedication of a house, set to music, and sung at the dedication of the new Girl Guides headquarters in London in the presence of Lord Baden-Powell and the Princess Mary, who expressed her delight over this "newly discovered old English hymn." This made it imperative for me to claim my property, and I am glad to say that I had no difficulty in getting apologies and acknowledgments. Since then it has been published widely on greeting cards and wall cards, with and without permission in this country, England, and Ireland.

Arthur Guiterman was born of American parents in Vienna, Austria, November 20, 1871. Because of the anxiety of his mother, a native of Ohio, that there should be future doubt of his citizenship, his name was registered at the American Consulate within twenty-four hours after his birth. He was educated mainly in New York; at Grammar School No. 69, with an interval of two early years at Bridgeport, Connecticut, and at the College of the City of New York, from which he was graduated in 1891 with the degree of Bachelor of Arts. During his college years he was active in lacrosse, tennis, and rowing, was captain of the bicycle club, class secretary and poet, and leading "lady" of the dramatic club. As the best sprinter of his year he was a member of the college track team in the Inter-Collegiate Games in 1891. At his graduation he was awarded the Ward Medal for highest standing in English composition. He has been elected to the Phi Beta Kappa Society in recognition of his literary work.

Since 1909 Mr. Guiterman has been a principal contributor of verse to *Life,* in which magazine he originated the widely imitated "Rhymed Reviews" and other features. He is also a frequent contributor to *Harper's Magazine, The Saturday Evening Post, The Youth's Companion, Ladies' Home Journal,* and many other leading periodicals. Joyce Kilmer, in an article in *The Independent,* characterized him as "the most American of poets."

Mr. Guiterman began to write verse during his eighth year and has written verse, serious and humorous, on any and all themes that have interested him and aroused his enthusiasm; thus his work has an extraordinarily diversified appeal, including historic and legendary ballads, folk tales, lyrics, society verse, outdoor and nature poems, political and social satires, occasional verses, couplets and quatrains embodying Oriental and other proverbs, and many other poems, grave and gay.

Mr. Guiterman is still considered a good skater, tennis and hockey player, is fond of canoeing, fishing and tramping, and he and Mrs. Guiterman usually manage to spend a month or two each summer deep in the Maine woods or on country roads and mountain trails with their packs on their backs. The question is frequently asked, "How is the family name pronounced?" Several years ago one of his editorial friends tried to enlighten an anxious inquirer on this point by printing the explanatory couplet,

"There ain't no better, fitter man,<br>
Than Mister Arthur Guiterman."

He is a splendid speaker, always individual, always entertaining and with a background rich in experience as a human being, a poet, and a speaker.

"Home" was written by Doctor Thompson for *The Methodist Hymnal,* 1935, as a setting for this poem. It was deliberately written in a somewhat modern style because it will be sung by the members of the oncoming generations who are quite familiar with such an idiom. It is not intended to be used by a congregation, but by much smaller groups, and on a personal and intimate occasion.

# HYMNS FOR CHILDREN

**434—Away in a manger, no crib for a bed**—Stanzas 1, 2, Anonymous
Stanza 3, John Thomas McFarland

**Müller**—Carl Müller (?)

This hymn has long been ascribed to Martin Luther (67). The first two stanzas have not been traced to any of Luther's works and are so unlike any of his other hymns that they can only be labeled anonymous. Bishop William F. Anderson has given the story of the writing of the third stanza:

> When I was Secretary of the Board of Education, 1904-08, I wanted to use "Away in a manger," which I found with the designation "Martin Luther's Cradle Song," in the Children's Day program one year. It had but two stanzas, 1 and 2. Dr. John T. McFarland, then Secretary of our Board of Sunday Schools, was my near neighbor in his office at 150 Fifth Avenue (New York). I asked him to write a third stanza. He went to his office and within an hour brought me the third stanza beginning, "Be near me, Lord Jesus, I ask Thee to stay." I used it, which was the first time it was ever published. I am pleased to see that it is now being used very widely. The honor of it belongs to that great and good man, Dr. John T. McFarland.

It is interesting to the author to note that this story reached him on the eighty-sixth anniversary of Doctor McFarland's birth, January 2, 1937.

John Thomas McFarland, LL.D., was born at Mount Vernon, Indiana, January 2, 1851, and died suddenly at his home at Maplewood, New Jersey, December 22, 1913. While he graduated from Simpson College, most of his undergraduate work was done at Iowa Wesleyan University. After completing his graduate work at Boston University School of Theology, he held various ministerial appointments in Iowa, Illinois, Rhode Island, New York, and Kansas, became Secretary of the Sunday School Union, and, in 1904, Editor of Sunday School Literature for the Methodist Episcopal Church. His most signal editorial contribution was the placing of the Graded Lessons before the Sunday-school world. For this innovation he was criticized, but the General Conference of 1912 gave him a vote of confidence "such as the prime minister of any great nation might covet." An article which appeared in *The Christian Advocate* (New York), three days after his death, continues:

> The Church has . . . steadily advanced in its appreciation of his work and in its approval of his policy of appropriating the best results of pedagogical science for use in Sunday-school instruction.

"Müller," the tune, is also of unknown source, though it is much in the style of the German folk song.

Carl Müller is as much of a mystery as both the first two stanzas of the hymn and the tune. The whole presents an interesting problem for research.

**435—I am so glad that our Father in heaven**—Ascribed to Emily Sullivan Oakey
Doubtless by Philip Paul Bliss
(254)

**Gladness**—Philip Paul Bliss (254)

In *Memoirs of Philip P. Bliss,* 1877, by Major D. W. Whittle, long an associate of Mr. Bliss, the following account of the writing of this gospel song is given:

> I think it was in June, 1870, that "Jesus Loves Me" was written. Mr. and Mrs. Bliss were at the time members of my family, at 43 South May Street, Chicago. One morning Mrs. Bliss came down to breakfast and said, as she entered the room: "Last evening, Mr. Bliss had a tune given him that I think is going to live and be one of the most used that he has written. I have been singing it all the morning to myself and cannot get it out of my mind." She then sang over to us the notes of "Jesus Loves Me." The idea of Mr. Bliss in writing it was that the peace and comfort of a Christian were not founded upon his loving Christ, but upon Christ's love to him, and that to occupy the mind with Christ's love, would produce love and consecration in keeping with Romans v. 5:
>
> "The love of God (to us) is shed abroad in our hearts by the Holy Ghost, which is given to us."
>
> . . . How much God has used this little song to lead sinners and fearful timid Christians to "look away to Jesus" eternity alone can tell.

Doctor Julian, in his article on Philip P. Bliss, says that this, as well as "Sowing the seed by the daylight fair," is usually attributed to Mr. Bliss, who, in his own *Gospel Songs,* Cincinnati, 1874, claims the music only. It will be noted, however, that Major Whittle does not say definitely that Mr. Bliss wrote the words, yet he gives that impression. In the carefully edited *Church Hymnary* of the United Church of Canada, Dr. Alexander MacMillan ascribes the text to Annie S. Oakey without any question other than that implied by the word "ascribed." The author of this MANUAL is willing to accept the statement of Dr. George C. Stebbins (50), who knew both Mr. Bliss and Major Whittle well, that both words and music are by Mr. Bliss.

Emily Sullivan Oakey was born at Albany, New York, October 8, 1829, and died there May 11, 1883. A writer of gospel songs, she is perhaps best known for her "Sowing the seed by the daylight fair."

**436—The shepherds had an angel**—Christina Georgina Rossetti (94)

**May Song**—Traditional English carol

This was written by Miss Rossetti in 1856, and was entitled,

A Christian Carol. For my God-children.

It is found first in *Sing Song,* a book of nursery rhymes, in her *Poetical Works,* 1904, and in *The Sunday School Hymnary* (English), 1905, where it was first used as a hymn.

"May Song" is an arrangement of an arrangement of "Heave away, my Johnny," an old Somerset folk tune.

**437—Father, lead me day by day**—John Page Hopps

**Orientis Partibus** (405)—Pierre de Corbeil (?) (405)

This "child's prayer for divine guidance" is taken from Mr. Hopps's *Hymns, Chants, and Anthems for Public Worship,* 1877. When the Editorial Committee of *The Methodist Hymnal* was discussing this hymn at its meeting held at Chautauqua, New York, in the summer of 1933, it was thought desirable to find a more forceful word than "sweet" in the second line of the first stanza. Dean Shailer Mathews, of the University of Chicago Divinity School, who was visiting the Committee, suggested the word "good" be used in its stead. The suggestion was adopted at once and the change made.

John Page Hopps, born at London, November 6, 1834, was educated at a Baptist college at Leicester, England, but left that denomination after preaching two years and became identified with the Unitarians. He retained much of the evangelical fervor of the Baptists, as is shown in many of his hymns. He compiled several books of hymns, three of which were for the home, children, and youth. In 1863 he founded the monthly periodical, *The Truthseeker,* which he edited until his death, in 1911.

**438—Holy Spirit, hear us**—William Henry Parker

**Ernstein**—James Frederick Swift

This hymn was one of three introduced by Mr. Parker's pastor, the Rev. W. R. Stevenson, through *The School Hymnal* (English), issued in 1880, and was included in *The Children's Book of Praise* the following year.

William Henry Parker was born at New Bosford, Nottingham, England, March 4, 1845, and was apprenticed in the machine construction department of a large lacemaking plant in Nottingham, remaining in the employ of the same company for the greater part of his life. When only a small boy he began writing verse, and after uniting with the General Baptist Church and becoming interested in Sunday-school work, he began composing hymns for anniversary festivals. This he continued doing for many years, producing one or more each year. These verses were published in newspapers and other periodicals and in his volume *The Princess Alice and Other Poems,* 1882. He died in 1929.

"Ernstein" was composed by J. F. Swift for "Summer suns are glowing," and it first appeared in the British *Methodist Sunday School Tune Book* of 1881.

James Frederick Swift was born in Manchester, England, December 28, 1847, and at an early age moved with his family to Liverpool, where his aptitude for music developed rapidly enough for him to secure a position as organist in the Cranmer Street Wesleyan Chapel at the age of fourteen. He was a popular choral conductor as well as a competent organist, and for a time directed three choruses at Liverpool. In addition to his church music, under the pseudonym "Godfrey Marks," he wrote and published more than two hundred songs and ballads, among them the ever-popular "Sailing," which is sung the world over. He died at Liscard, Cheshire, in 1931.

**439—The wise may bring their learning**—Anonymous

From the Book of Praise for Children, 1881

**Ellon**—George Frederick Root

This anonymous hymn has received considerable recognition in recent years, which is not to be wondered at when it has so much to commend it. Its lesson, that the youngest and most poorly equipped may be of real service in Christ's kingdom, is a useful one for children to learn:

We'll bring the little duties
We have to do each day;
We'll try our best to please Him,
At home, at school, at play.
And better are these treasures
To offer to our King,
Than richest gifts without them;
Yet these a child may bring.

"Ellon" was probably first published in *The Crown of Sunday School Songs,* 1871, a book edited by L. H. Dowling, consisting principally of the works of George F. Root and P. P. Bliss (254), where it was called "Because He Loves Me So." It was set to

I love to hear the story
Which angel voices tell,

written by Mrs. Emily H. Miller (445) as a sort of companion piece, or sequel, to "Tell me the old, old story" and "I love to tell the story" (249). In 1879 George F. Root used both text and tune, which he called "Angel's Story," in *The New Choir and Congregation, A Collection of Hymns, Tunes, Anthems, Chants, and Responsive Services for the Choir and "All the People."* Owing to the designation of tunes as "Angel's Story" and "Angels' Story," that name has no particular significance when used with this anonymous hymn; thus, the name was changed to "Ellon," but when, or why, or by whom has not been discovered. Besides being an apparently perfect setting for these words, it is an ideal melody for children to sing. When it is sung by adults, as it is being sung more and more, let them sing it as the little children do—quickly and with light tone.

George Frederick Root, Mus. Doc., born at Sheffield, Massachusetts, August 30, 1820, studied music with B. F. Baker in Boston, and when he was nineteen years of age he became associated with A. N. Johnson as a teacher and as his assistant organist at Winter Street and Park Street churches.

In 1841 he assisted Lowell Mason (19) as a teacher of music in the Boston City Schools, removing in 1844 to New York, where he taught in Jacob Abbott's Young Ladies' School, Rutgers Female Institute, Union Theological Seminary, and the New York Institute for the Blind, where he had Fanny Crosby (231) as his pupil. In response to the popular vogue for "musical institutes," he organized and conducted many during his active life, and was naturally led to compose and to publish music. Going to Chicago in 1859 to join the firm of Root and Cady (his brother, E. T. Root, and C. M. Cady), he was caught in the fervor of the excitement brought on by the approaching civil conflict, and wrote many "war songs" that had an immense popularity. He also wrote popular ballads, such as "Hazel Dell" and "Rosalie, the Prairie Flower," under the name of "G. Friedrich Wurzel," which were sung by members of Christy's famous minstrel troupe. Among some seventy collections of various kinds which he compiled, edited, and published, were several cantatas which were performed by singing organizations all over America. He was one of the less able followers of Lowell Mason. His death occurred at his summer home on Bailey's Island, off the coast of Maine, August 6, 1895.

**440—I think when I read that sweet story of old**—Jemima Thompson Luke

**Sweet Story**—A Greek melody
Arranged by William Batchelder Bradbury (133)

This hymn was written by Mrs. Luke to fit a Greek melody she had heard and which had caught her fancy. She had gone one day in 1841 from her home to the Normal Infant School in Gray's Inn Road not far away to learn something of the teaching methods used there. She heard the children singing a marching song which, upon inquiry, she found to be a Greek tune known as "Salamis." This melody intriguing her, she set about to find words which would fit it, but was unsuccessful. She has written:

> Having been recalled home, I went one day on some missionary business to the little town of Wellington, five miles from Taunton, in a stage coach. It was a beautiful spring morning, it was an hour's ride, and there was no other inside passenger. On the back of an old envelope I wrote in pencil the first two of the verses now so well known, in order to teach the tune to the village school supported by my stepmother, and which it was my province to visit. The third verse was added afterwards to make it a missionary hymn.

Her father, Thomas Thompson, "a friend of every good cause," had charge of a Sunday school at Blagdon, where it was his custom to allow the pupils to choose the opening hymn for their services. On one occasion when the children had sung this song, he asked where it came from and was astonished at the reply: "Oh, Jemima wrote it." The next day he sent it to *The Sunday School Teachers' Magazine,* where it appeared the next month. It appeared anonymously in *The Leeds Hymn Book* in 1853, and since has gone into numberless other books and has been learned by countless children all over the world.

The tune "Salamis," or "Athens," as it was called in the recent *Methodist Hymnal,* which Mrs. Luke heard was as follows:

In making the four-line tune "Sweet Story" from "Salamis," William B. Bradbury lost much of the interest of the eight-line Greek tune. The Bradbury version is much more familiar in America than the original, and attempts to have the latter used have not been successful. An eight-line version was used in *The Methodist Hymnal* of 1905, with the unhappy result that this very fine children's hymn was not sung so much as it should be. It was thought wise to use the Bradbury arrangement in the present book.

Jemima Luke, *née* Thompson, was born at Colebrooke Row, Islington, London, August 19, 1813, and married the Rev. Samuel Luke, a Congregational minister, in 1843. At the age of thirteen she was an anonymous contributor to *The Juvenile Magazine,* and subsequently published several books. She is now known solely for having written this one hymn. Her death occurred February 2, 1906.

**441—Tell me the stories of Jesus—Wiliam Henry Parker (438)**

**Stories of Jesus—Frederic Arthur Challinor**

This child's hymn on the "Life of Christ" appeared in *The Sunday School Hymnary* (English) in 1885.

"Stories of Jesus" was written for these words and it first appeared in one of the publications of the National Sunday School Union, London.

Frederic Arthur Challinor, a composer who also has the poetic ability to write suitable lyrics for his vocal settings, was a poor boy, born at Longton, Staffordshire, England, November 12, 1866. His father was a miner, and the boy found it necessary to enter some gainful occupation early in life. When only ten years old he began working in a brick-making plant, keeping at such back-breaking labor for two years, when he found employment in a coal mine. At fifteen he was able to secure work in a china manufacturing plant; but being ambitious for a musical career, he employed all of his time when not working in the study of harmony, doing his exercises while at his meals and at other moments when he could use his hands for making notes. The coming of a small piano into the home as a part of a legacy greatly stimulated the boy's interest. By hard work he was able, in 1897, to complete the required work for his Mus. Bac. degree. After a few years he gained recognition and success as a composer, producing such worthwhile cantatas as *Bethany* and *The Gardens of the Lord.* Not satisfied with his accomplishments, he passed to the degree of Doctor of Music in 1903. He has specialized in the field of writing for voices and has more than four hundred published compositions to his credit.

**442—Once in royal David's city—Cecil Frances Alexander (135)**

**Irby—Henry John Gauntlett**

This, one of Mrs. Alexander's most attractive and successful hymns for children, was published in her *Hymns for Little Children,* 1848, and was based on the words of the Apostles' Creed:

> Was conceived of the Holy Ghost.
> born of the Virgin Mary.

It was another of her hymns written to help little children understand the teachings of the Creed. Dr. John Telford says the gospel story has never been more attractively told to children than in "There is a green hill far away" (135) and "Once in royal David's city." This book, *Hymns for Little Children,* went through more than one hundred editions in England, so popular was it with its illustrations and its musical settings by Doctor Gauntlett.

"Irby" was written for Mrs. Alexander's child's hymn by Dr. H. J. Gauntlett, and it first appeared in *Christmas Carols, four numbers,* 1849, with no name. In this little book and in *Hymns for Little Children, set to music,* etc., 1858, it was written for but one voice with piano accompaniment. In 1861 it was harmonized for four voices, named "Irby" and published in the Original Edition of *Hymns Ancient and Modern.*

Henry John Gauntlett, Mus. Doc., born at Wellington, Salop, England, July 9, 1805, originally a lawyer, was one of the most remarkable of the long list of writers of hymn tunes. Mendelssohn wrote of him:

> His literary attainments, his knowledge of the history of music, his acquaintance with acoustical laws, his marvelous memory, his philosophical turn of mind, as well as his practical experience, rendered him one of the most remarkable professors of the age.

The ease with which he wrote was remarkable, it being said that "St. Alphage," one of his tunes, was composed during the progress of a dinner while a messenger waited for it. Moffatt says he composed thousands of tunes. He was made Doctor of Music by the Archbishop of Canterbury, the first for more than two hundred years to be so honored. Doctor Gauntlett was an organist of ability, holding his first position as such at nine years of age, and had much to do with the improvement of organs mechanically, securing patents for applying electric or magnetic action to them. He died suddenly of a heart attack in London, February 21, 1876.

**443—It fell upon a summer day**—Stopford Augustus Brooke

**Childhood**—From A Students' Hymnal
University of Wales, 1923

This hymn comes from Doctor Brooke's *Christian Hymns,* 1881, in ten stanzas, entitled,

Christ blessing little children.

Miss Honor Brooke, daughter of the author, writes:

> This hymn was written by my father for his congregation to sing whilst a collection was made to send London "sparrows" away for a three weeks' holiday in the country. In those days very little was being done. Never shall I forget the gathering of poor children labelled for their country destinations at all London's great stations. It was then a big work; now it is a mighty stream!

Stopford Augustus Brooke, LL.D., born at Glendoen, Letterkenny, Donegal, Ireland, November 14, 1832, was educated at Trinity College, Dublin, took Holy Orders in London, and held curacies at St. Matthew's, Marylebone and St. Mary Abbott's, Kensington, before becoming chaplain to the British Embassy in Berlin in 1862. Returning to London in 1865, he became one of the foremost preachers in London, being appointed chaplain to Queen Victoria in 1867, who wished to give him an appointment as a canon at Westminster. The same liberality of views which made this impossible, however, finally induced him to resign his Orders in the English Church, in 1880. For a time he preached as an Independent. For many years he had devoted much time to critical and scholarly literary work, and after his retirement from the Church, not only continued in this field but gained a reputation as a great authority on Old and Middle English literature. He was also successful as a lecturer. He died at Four Winds, Surrey, March 18, 1916.

"Childhood" is referred to in the Preface to *Hymns of the Kingdom,* one of the forms of which is *A Students' Hymnal,* for use in Welsh schools and colleges, in this wise:

> Some of the tunes in this book whose authorship is collectively marked "University of Wales" have been composed by a small community of minds. In two cases no less than five melodists took an essential part in a four-line tune. The actual selection of tunes for the whole book has been made by many minds, but finally referred to one, so that the Editor became personally responsible for all flaws of choice.

**444—Gentle Jesus, meek and mild**—Charles Wesley (25)

**Gentle Jesus**—Martin Shaw

F. A. Jones, in his *Famous Hymns and Their Authors,* says:

> Though Charles Wesley was fond of children and wrote many hymns for their benefit, it cannot be said that he was ever very successful as a writer for the young. The reason, as a contemporary has pointed out, is not very far to seek. "He started with the wrong idea, attempting to lift children up to the level of adults, merely adapting his compositions to them by simplicity of diction." With the exception of "Gentle Jesus, meek and mild," not one of the many hymns he wrote for children has lived to be sung to-day.

The hymn beginning, "Gentle Jesus, meek and mild," is one of six hymns for children which appeared in *Hymns and Sacred Poems,* 1742, and which were reprinted in *Hymns for Children,* 1763. The four stanzas used here are taken from the hymns numbered 72 and 73 in that collection, stanza 1 from the former and the others from the latter. The Rev. John Telford quotes Dr. A. E. Gregory as having said this hymn is

> associated with the happy infancy of tens of thousands.
>
> Watts wrote some simple lyrics which seem to have suited our prim little ancestors; and Charles Wesley wrote, "Gentle Jesus, meek and mild," but even the manners and beliefs of the devout souls of that time cannot altogether excuse some of his hymns, which must have frightened many a poor little Methodist out of his wits.

"Gentle Jesus" was written for Charles Wesley's beautiful hymn for children by Martin Shaw, who used it in *Additional Tunes and Settings in use at St. Mary's, Primrose-Hill,* 1915. It is charming in its simplicity, and, as was intended, will be very easily learned by children.

Martin Shaw, born at London, March 9, 1876, was a pupil of Sir Charles Stanford at the Royal College of Music, and has been for the greater part of his life an organist and church musician with wide interests, being especially interested in freeing "English Church Music from a load of sentimentality," and in promoting the use of folk music and community singing. It took him some little time to make himself felt, and after his student days he "embarked upon a large period of starving along." One time musical director for Ellen Terry, he toured Europe as conductor for Isadora Duncan. His own compositions are numerous and vary in character from light opera to orchestral music, church music, and songs of a high grade. Canon Scott Holland's comment on his *Te Deum* characterizes all of his music for the church for it possesses "dignity, massiveness, and reserve. Everything about it is wholesome and manly, and there are no fanciful or artificial episodes." He was associated with Canon Dearmer (79) and Ralph Vaughn Williams (527) in issuing *Songs of Praise,* 1925, the Enlarged Edition of 1931, *The Oxford Book of Carols,* 1928, and he also edited *The English Carol Book.* He is Master of Music at the Guildhall, London. His recent autobiography, *Up to Now,* was cordially received, and justly so, for it is most entertaining and clearly written.

**445—Tell the blessed tidings**—Emily Huntington Miller

**Deva**—Edward John Hopkins (29)

The date of the writing of this hymn is uncertain. Mrs. Miller has written:

> It was written for the Young People's Jubilee in connection with one of our branch missionary meetings, and has been often used since as a processional for similar occasions. I cannot give the exact date—perhaps 1903.

Emily Miller, née Huntington, was born at Brooklyn, Connecticut, October 22, 1833, the daughter of the Rev. Thomas Huntington, D.D., a Methodist minister. A graduate of Oberlin College, becoming the wife of Professor John E. Miller in 1860, she was a writer of both prose and poetry, specializing in children's literature. For some years she was the editor of *The Little Corporal,* published at Chicago, which was later merged with *St. Nicholas.* She was also, for some years, the Dean of Women at Northwestern University, which conferred on her in 1909 the honorary degree of L. H. D. She died at the home of her brother in Northfield, Minnesota, November 2, 1913.

"Deva" was written by Dr. E. J. Hopkins for the New-Year hymn, "Standing at the portal," for his *Congregational Church Hymnal,* London, 1887, which also used it as the setting for two other hymns.

**446—Brightly gleams our banner**—Thomas Joseph Potter

Altered and abridged

**St. Theresa**—Arthur Seymour Sullivan (15)

This alteration and abridgment of Mr. Potter's favorite children's processional hymn is taken in part from the Appendix to *Psalms and Hymns,* 1869, a publication of the Society for the Promotion of Christian Knowledge, London. In the original form, appearing first, with music, in *Holy Family*

*Hymns,* Roman Catholic hymnal, it was unsuitable for Protestant use. The third stanza comes from *Church Hymns,* London, 1871, where there was also a slight revision in stanza 1, from the version in the 1869 *Psalms and Hymns.*

Thomas Joseph Potter, born at Scarborough, England, in 1827, joined the Roman Catholic Church in 1847, later taking Holy Orders. He became Professor of Pulpit Eloquence and English Literature at the Foreign Missionary College, All Hallows, Dublin, Ireland. Although the author of various books dealing with the subject of preaching and of a number of hymns for Catholic books, he is known to Protestants by this one hymn. Mr. Potter died at Dublin, in 1873.

"St. Theresa" was written in 1874 for this hymn for *Church Hymns with Tunes,* of which its composer, Sir Arthur Sullivan, was the editor.

**447—All things bright and beautiful—Cecil Frances Alexander (135)**

**Royal Oak—Old English melody**

This comes from Mrs. Alexander's *Hymns for Little Children,* 1848, and is based on "Maker of heaven and earth" in the Apostles' Creed, and that part of Genesis 1. 31, which reads, "And God saw everything that he had made, and, behold, it was very good." Three stanzas have been omitted; one,

The rich man in his castle,
The poor man at his gate:
God made them high and lowly,
And ordered their estate,

because it is not entirely in keeping with Christian teachings; and the others because the hymn is complete without them.

"Royal Oak" is an arrangement of an attractive English traditional melody made by William H. Hewlett (313). It was first used as a hymn tune by Martin Shaw (444), who had it printed on a sheet for community singing in 1915. It should be sung briskly and always in unison.

**448—In our work and in our play—Whitefield Glanville Wills**

**Rosslyn—English melody**

This charming child's prayer hymn was written for *School Hymns* (English), 1891, and was entitled,

Children of God.

Whitefield Glanville Wills was born at Bristol, England, October 28, 1841, and died at Esling, October 2, 1891. He published a small collection of original *Hymns for Occasional Use,* in 1881.

"Rosslyn" is taken from the Supplement to the *Primitive Methodist Hymnal,* 1912, where it is said to have been "Adapted and harmonized by C. B., 1896."

**449—Saviour, teach me, day by day**—Jane Elizabeth Leeson

**Innocents** (81)—From The Parish Choir, 1850 (81)

Originally in four eight-line stanzas, Miss Leeson's hymn appeared first in her *Hymns and Scenes from Childhood,* 1842. The second half of stanzas 1 and 2, and the first half of 3 and 4 have been omitted. It may well have been suggested by 1 John 4. 19: "We love him, because he first loved us," for she uses almost those words in the refrainlike last line of each stanza. Dean Tillett thinks " 'Love's sweet lesson' has perhaps never been more beautifully presented to the young than in this little love-lyric of one who was pre-eminently gifted in writing hymns for the young."

Jane Elizabeth Leeson, an Englishwoman, details of whose life are strangely lacking, was born in 1807, and died in 1882. She issued at least two volumes of hymns, contributed hymns to the collections of others, and was the author of additional miscellaneous religious books. Some of her hymns are reported to have been improvised as "prophetical utterances," one observer stating that the hymn "was delivered slowly, with short pauses between the verses, a pause three times as long as any one would ordinarily make in reading." She was an active member of the Catholic Apostolic Church, to the hymnal of which she contributed nine hymns and translations. Late in her life she joined the Roman Catholic communion.

**450—God make my life a little light**—Matilda Barbara Betham-Edwards

**Capel**—English traditional melody

This hymn, by Miss Betham-Edwards, appeared in 1873 in the magazine *Good Words,* with an evening hymn beginning,

The little birds now seek their nest.

Matilda Barbara Betham-Edwards was born at Westerfield, near Ipswich, Suffolk, England, March 4, 1836. She wrote verse other than hymns, and popular stories. She died at Suffolk, January 4, 1919.

"Capel" is a tune which Miss Lucy Broadwood, authority on English traditional melodies, wrote down from the singing of some Gypsies, in 1893, near Capel, a village near Horsham, Surrey, England. The Gypsies were singing it to a curious old ballad, "King Pharim" ("Pharaoh"), beginning,

King Pharim sat a-musing,<br>A-musing all alone;<br>There came a blessed Saviour,<br>And all to him unknown.

The tune is an old one known as "King Pharaoh and the cock." Both tune and ballad are mentioned in *The Oxford Book of Carols,* and additional information may be found in Miss Broadwood's *English Traditional Songs and Carols.*

**451—Hushed was the evening hymn**—James Drummond Burns (37)

**Samuel**—Arthur Seymour Sullivan (15)

This hymn is taken from *The Evening Hymn,* 1857, a small volume issued by James D. Burns, containing a hymn and a prayer for each evening of the month. This is the only hymn of the Rev. Mr. Burns that has had common use. It is one of a few hymns that admit of being successfully dramatized. In case it should be put to such use, care should be taken that the second stanza should always be sung—not recited. There seems to be a desire on the part of small boys to insert a comma after "watch" in the third line of that stanza, and to omit the one after "Levite" in the fourth line, which alters the intended meaning quite too much:

His watch, the temple child,
The little Levite kept!

"Samuel," composed for this hymn by Sir Arthur Sullivan, was included in his *Church Hymns with Tunes,* 1874. Originally composed for treble voices in unison, this arrangement was made for *The Presbyterian Hymnal* (English) of 1877 by the composer.

**452—Jesus, tender shepherd, hear me**—Mary Lundie Duncan

**Dijon**—Old German melody

This is one of twenty-three hymns which Mrs. Duncan wrote for her own children and which were not published until after her death. They were written between July and December, 1839. Early in January, the following year, she died of a severe fever following a cold. In the next year, 1841, her mother published a *Memoir* containing these hymns. They also appeared separately as *Rhymes for My Children* in 1842.

Mary Duncan, née Lundie, whose father was the Rev. Robert Lundie, parish minister at Kelso, Scotland, and whose younger sister married Dr. Horatius Bonar (210), was born at Kelso, April 26, 1814, and married the Rev. William Wallace Duncan, parish minister of Cleish. She was a beautiful woman with a beautiful character—a devoted wife and mother, amiable and accomplished. She died, January 5, 1840, after three and a half years of happy married life. Her husband left the Church of Scotland at the time of the Disruption, joining the Free Church and ministering at Peebles until his death in 1864.

"Dijon," set to the words, "Müde bin ich, geh zur Ruh," appeared in 1842 in *Lieder-Buch für Kleinkinder-Schulen . . . von Theodor Fliedner.* The original form of the melody was:

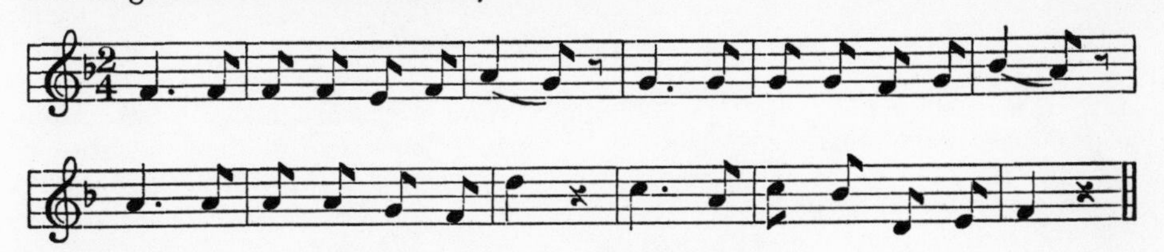

**453—Lord, when we have not any light**—Annie Matheson

**Lytham**—James Thomas Lightwood

This child's evening prayer was written by Miss Matheson for a *School*

*Hymnal,* 1880, compiled by the Rev. W. R. Stevenson, English Baptist minister, a book Julian says was of "high merit."

Annie Matheson, eldest daughter of a Congregational minister, was born at Blackheath, London, March 29, 1853. From the publication of her first hymn in *Good Words,* when she was only thirteen years of age, she was a contributor to the better magazines for children. Julian says her hymns were characterized by a pleasing combination of simplicity and refinement. She died March 16, 1924, at London.

"Lytham" was written for this hymn by James T. Lightwood for *The Methodist School Hymnal,* London, 1910. Mr. Lightwood has another tune, in 6/8 time, by the same name which should not be confused with this one.

James Thomas Lightwood, son of the Rev. Edward Lightwood, Wesleyan minister, was born at Leeds, England, December 29, 1856. After education at Kingswood School, Bath, he was for three years in a drapery establishment at Lincoln, before his thirty-two years (1878-1910) as schoolmaster at Lytham, Lancaster. There, with his brother, Edward R. Lightwood, he established the justly famed Pembroke House School. In 1910 he established *The Choir,* under the auspices of the Methodist Publishing House, London, and took the position of editor, which he held until his retirement in December, 1936. An enthusiastic cyclist since 1878, he is now Vice-President of the Cyclists' Touring Club.

Mr. Lightwood is the acknowledged English authority on hymn tunes, his *Hymn Tunes and Their Story* and *The Music of the Methodist Hymn Book* being source works. He is also the author of *Charles Dickens and Music,* and *Samuel Wesley, Musician.* Mr. Lightwood continues to make his home at Lytham.

# THE KINGDOM OF GOD

## Service

**454—The voice of God is calling**—John Haynes Holmes

**Meirionydd** (194)—Welsh hymn melody

This hymn, written on the Atlantic Ocean in the early fall of 1913 during the author's homeward voyage from England, first appeared in *The Christian Register*.

John Haynes Holmes, D.D., was born at Philadelphia, November 29, 1879; graduated A. B., *summa cum laude,* and Phi Beta Kappa from Harvard University in 1902; S. T. B. from the same institution in 1904. He has been honored by having the degree Doctor of Divinity conferred on him by the Jewish Institute of Religion and by St. Lawrence University. After his ordination as a Unitarian minister in 1904 at Dorchester, Massachusetts, he went, in 1907, to the Community Church, New York City, formerly the Church of the Messiah, which became independent in 1919. A noted preacher and lecturer, an extensive traveler, the author of many books on a wide variety of subjects, contributor to many periodicals, and for some years editor of *Unity,* Chicago, Doctor Holmes is noted as an authority in the field of racial relationships. He lives in New York City.

**455—Awake, awake to love and work**—Geoffrey Anketell Studdert-Kennedy

**Sheltered Dale**—German traditional melody

This is a selection from G. A. Studdert-Kennedy's poem, "At a Harvest Festival," first published in *The Sorrows of God, and Other Poems,* 1921.

Geoffrey Anketell Studdert-Kennedy was born in St. Mary's Vicarage, Quarry Hill, Leeds, Yorkshire, England, June 27, 1883, the seventh son of the Vicar of St. Mary's, Leeds. He was educated privately, at Leeds Grammar School, and at Trinity College, Dublin. Taking Holy Orders, he was curate at Rugby, succeeded to his father's former appointment at St. Mary's, Leeds, and became vicar of St. Paul's, Worcester. During the World War as the popular chaplain known to the soldiers as "Woodbine Willie," he became "a Good Samaritan to hosts of men who found him a staunch friend and a strong helper." After the War he was appointed chaplain to the King and was made rector of St. Edmund King and Martyr, London. During a visit to the United States in the spring of 1924 he won many friends to add to the long list he had already made. From 1916 until his death at Liverpool, March 7 or 8, 1929, he wrote much, among his works being *Rough Rhymes of a Padre, Lies, I Believe,* and *Food for the Fed-Up.*

"Sheltered Dale," known in England as "The Millwheel" and in Germany as "Das zerbrochene Ringlein" ("The Broken Ring"), is a German folk song sung to words by Joseph von Eichendorff, the air from a melody by J. L. F. Glück, 1814.

**456—We give Thee but Thine own**—William Walsham How (197)

**Schumann**—From Cantica Laudis, 1850

This hymn, a composition dating from about 1858, appeared in Morrell and How's *Psalms and Hymns* in 1864. It is one of the most popular of all hymns dealing with Christian liberality. John Wesley once said:

> You will have no reward in heaven for what you lay up: you will for what you lay out; every pound you put into the earthly bank is sunk: it brings no interest above. But every pound you give to the poor you put into the bank of heaven. And it will bring glorious interest.

In his notes on this hymn in *The New Methodist Hymn-Book Illustrated,* the Rev. John Telford tells the story, from the *Talmud,* of Rabbi Jochanan,

> who was riding with some of his pupils outside the walls of Jerusalem, when they saw a poor woman picking up the grain that had fallen round the troughs where the cattle of some Arabs were feeding. She begged help from the rabbi, who asked, "What has become of the money thou didst receive on thy wedding-day?" She answered, "Ah, is there not a saying in Jerusalem, 'The salt was wanting to the money'?" The Jews believed that charity preserved money as salt preserved meat. When the rabbi asked about her husband's money, she replied, "That followed the other." The rabbi told his pupils, "I remember when I signed her marriage contract. Her father gave her a million of gold dinars. Her husband also was wealthy." Then he bestowed upon her what he could, and wept with her over her hard lot.

Dr. George Matheson (318) said:

> "We give Thee but Thine own" sounds the real humanitarian note to the fatherless and widows. Hymnology is feeble and ineffective when it ignores the humanitarian side of religion.

"Schumann" is from *Cantica Laudis, The American Book of Church Music,* issued by Lowell Mason (19) and George J. Webb (487) in 1850. Called "White" in this book, the tune is said to be "Arranged from Robert Schumann." When James Love submitted the tune to Madame Schumann with an inquiry as to the particular work of her husband from which it was taken, she replied that she was doubtful if it had been adapted from any of Robert Schumann's compositions. Other experts have found nothing among his musical writings from which it could have been derived.

**457—God of the strong, God of the weak**—Richard Watson Gilder (10)

**Godwin**—William Godwin Blanchard

This hymn was written by Doctor Gilder for a memorial service for Dr. J. L. M. Curry held by the Southern Education Conference at Richmond, Virginia, April 26, 1903. Here are used the first four of six stanzas in the poem.

"Godwin" was written by William G. Blanchard in 1934 for use with this hymn to appear in this *Hymnal.* Its style conforms to the musical thinking of the modern young composer.

William Godwin Blanchard, son of Dean William M. Blanchard, of DePauw University, a prominent Methodist layman and delegate to the General Conferences of 1920, 1924, and 1932, was born at Greencastle, Indiana, September 5, 1905. He was educated in the public schools of Greencastle, at the School of Music of DePauw University, and at the School of Music of the University of Michigan. A very versatile musician, he is now a member of the music faculty of Pomona College, California.

**458—We thank Thee, Lord, thy paths of service lead**—Calvin Weiss Laufer (130)
**Field**—Calvin Weiss Laufer (130)

The hymn was written by Doctor Laufer after he had dined one evening with his friend, the Rev. Herbert H. Field, pastor of the Flatbush Presbyterian Church, Brooklyn, and the tune was written so the new composition might be used at Doctor Field's church for a service in September, 1919. In *The Handbook to the Hymnal,* 1935, of which the author and composer was the associate editor, the following quotation from Bishop Simpson's fine statement of the task of the Church, is used as part of the comment on the hymn:

> The Church must go into the field with the farmer, into the tent with the soldier, into the forecastle with the sailor, into the pit with the miner, into the counting room with the merchant; it must go into the alleys and purlieus of the city, and grope its way up the rickety stairs and kneel on the bare floor beside the loathsome sufferer. Like the atmosphere, it must press equally on all surfaces of society, like the sea, it must crowd into every nook on the shore line of humanity, like the sun, it must shine on things foul and low as well as things fair and high. For the Church was redeemed and organized and equipped and commissioned for the moral and spiritual renovation of the whole world.

A friendship that has grown through the years lies back of this hymn. For more than ten years Doctor Laufer and his friend, the Rev. Mr. Field, lunched together on the average of once a week. At that time Doctor Laufer was a traveling secretary of the Board of Publication and Sabbath School Work of the Presbyterian Church, and the joint experiences of a busy pastor in a city parish and an equally busy Board secretary quite naturally formed the basis of conversation and mutual profit.

It was at one such luncheon in the fall of 1919 that the inspiration came to reproduce in the words of this remarkable hymn the theme of that day's conversation, based on the dual aspect of Christian service. The theme of the hymn is fitly found in the opening lines:

> We thank Thee, Lord, Thy paths of service lead
> To blazoned heights and down the slopes of need.

Throughout the hymn this thought is continued, and each stanza sings of the life of service to mankind closely knit with the life of communion with God, such as the true Christian must daily lead.

On a similar occasion when the author and his friend had spent the luncheon hour in delightful fellowship, the music was composed. The tune forthwith dedicated to Doctor Field was very shortly thereafter used in a service in his church.

**459—Behold us, Lord, a little space—John Ellerton (28)**

**St. Agnes (341)—John Bacchus Dykes (1)**

This hymn is characteristic of Canon Ellerton's work at its best, and is, as Canon Dearmer suggests, one of the first of the hymns to recognize art and science as a part of God's work. It is as modern now as when it was written nearly seventy years ago. Written in 1870 for "Mid-day service in a London city church," it was first published in *Church Hymns,* 1871.

**460—Lord, speak to me that I may speak—Frances Ridley Havergal (221)**

**Gratitude—Paul Ami Isaac David Bost**

Miss Havergal gave the title,

A Worker's Prayer,

at the head of the original manuscript of this hymn, written at Winterdyne, April 28, 1872, which was printed on a leaflet with music the same year. It was based upon Romans 14. 7: "For none of us liveth to himself, and no man dieth to himself." It is of such a personal and intimate nature as to militate against its wide use in public worship, yet Bishop Bickersteth (354) thought highly of it as "the choicest of the many choice contributions" of Miss Havergal to the "Church's treasure of song."

"Gratitude" was adapted by Thomas Hastings (204) from a tune by Ami Bost in 1837 for his *Manhattan Collection.*

Paul Ami Isaac David Bost, 1790-1874, is said by Dr. C. S. Nutter, in his "Biographical Index of the Composers of Tunes" to *The Hymns and Hymn Writers of the Church,* 1911,[1] to be "A native of Geneva, Switzerland, composer of psalmody and church music." The author has been unable to secure any other information concerning him.

**461—Heaven is here, where hymns of gladness—John Greenleaf Adams**

**Austrian Hymn (382)—Francis Joseph Haydn (30)**

This is an altered form of John G. Adams's "Heaven is here, its hymns of gladness," which appeared in *The Pilgrim Hymnal* of 1904, where it was erroneously credited to John Quincy Adams. It was contributed, originally, to *Hymns for Christian Devotion,* 1846. The hymn, in its original form, was:

HEAVEN HERE

1. Heaven is here; its hymns of gladness
Cheer the true believer's way,
In this world where sin and sadness
Often change to night our day.

[1] When Dean Tillett (117) and Doctor Nutter divided the work entailed in the preparation of their book, *The Hymns and Hymn Writers of the Church,* it fell to the lot of Doctor Nutter to prepare the short biographical notes on the composers of the music for *The Methodist Hymnal* of 1905.

2. Heaven is here; where misery lightened
Of its heavy load is seen,
Where the face of sorrow brightened
By the deed of love hath been:

3. Where the bound, the poor, despairing
Are set free, supplied and blest;
Where, in others' anguish sharing,
We can find our surest rest.

4. When we heed the voice of duty
Rather than man's praise, or rod;
This is heaven,—its peace, its beauty,
Radiant with the smile of God.

John Greenleaf Adams, D.D., was a Universalist minister, born at Portsmouth, New Hampshire, July 30, 1810. Most of his education was obtained in the Portsmouth schools. With Dr. E. H. Chapin he edited the Universalist *Hymns for Christian Devotion,* 1846, and he alone compiled and edited *The Gospel Psalmist,* 1861. In addition to his interest in philanthropic and moral reforms, Doctor Adams was the editor of the *Star in the East, Gospel Teacher, Myrtle,* and *Sunday School Helper,* and the author of about twenty books and pamphlets, mostly decidedly Universalist in character. *The Universalist Register* of 1888 says, "He was a Universalist in all his convictions and sympathies and was untiring in his efforts for the spread of the knowledge of the truth." He died at Melrose Highlands, Massachusetts, May 4, 1887.

**462—From Thee all skill and science flow—Charles Kingsley**

**Gräfenberg** (389)—From Johann Crüger's Praxis Pietatis Melica, 1653 (60)

This hymn is a selection of stanzas 3-6 from a six-stanza, four-line hymn by Charles Kingsley. The author's widow gave the following account of its writing:

> On the 4th of December, 1871, Lord Leigh laid the foundation stone of the working men's block of the Queen's Hospital at Birmingham with masonic honours, and the following simple hymn, which Mr. Kingsley had been requested to compose for the occasion, was sung by a choir of 1,000 voices:—
>
> Accept this building, gracious Lord,
> No temple though it be;
> We raise it for our suffering kin,
> And so, good Lord, to Thee.

Charles Kingsley, the author of stories and poems which have become English classics, was born June 12, 1819, at Holne Vicarage, Devon, England, educated at Magdalene College, Cambridge, and served as rector of Eversley, canon of Chester, canon of Westminster, and other important appointments. As author of *Hypatia, Westward Ho!* and *Water-Babies,* he is known to all who enjoy reading English at its best. It has been said that "this little hymn is an epitome of his life, and a mirror of his mind and heart." He died at Eversley, January 23, 1875.

**463—"Thy Kingdom come," on bended knee—Frederick Lucian Hosmer (43)**

**Irish** (14)—Melody from A Collection of Sacred Hymns and Poems (14)

This hymn, says Canon Dearmer (79), is "one of the noblest hymns in the language; and this does express the eternal hope of the Prayer." He calls attention to the fact that this is one of two hymns written throughout the whole of the nineteenth century to express the petition, "Thy kingdom come," in the Lord's Prayer. The other was "Thy Kingdom come, O God," by Lewis Hensley, 1824-1905. Doctor Hosmer's hymn was written on June 12, 1891, for the commencement exercises of Meadville Theological Seminary, Meadville, Pennsylvania, and was included in the second series of his *Thoughts of God,* 1894.

**464—Master, no offering—Edwin Pond Parker (295)**

**Love's Offering**—Edwin Pond Parker (295)

Hymn and tune were composed by Doctor Parker in 1888, while he was pastor and director of music at Center Church, Hartford, Connecticut. Both appeared in *The Christian Hymnal,* 1889. The hymn was first written to be read after one of Doctor Parker's sermons.

# Brotherhood

**465—Where cross the crowded ways of life—Frank Mason North**

**Germany** (260)—From William Gardiner's Sacred Melodies (28)

A chance meeting of Doctor North and Professor Caleb T. Winchester (561), in 1903, at the New York headquarters of Methodism, resulted in the writing of this hymn classic. Professor Winchester, as a member of the Commission which prepared *The Methodist Hymnal* of 1905, had made a trip to New York City from his home at Middletown, Connecticut, on business having to do with the proposed book and, meeting Doctor North, took advantage of the occasion to ask him to write a missionary hymn for it. Doctor North protested that he was no hymn writer,[1] but gave his promise to try to write one. Being at the time the Corresponding Secretary of the New York City Missionary and Church Extension Society, which is now the New York City Society of the Methodist Episcopal Church, and deeply interested in the many perplexing problems encountered in his work, he naturally thought of the field of missionary work in the city. About this time Doctor North was preparing a sermon upon the text from St. Matthew 22. 9, "Go ye therefore into the highways, and as many as ye shall find, bid to the marriage," and had noted the American Revised Version rendering, "Go ye therefore unto the partings of the highways, and as many as ye shall find, bid to the marriage feast," which suggests quite a different picture. Intrigued by the phrase, "the partings of the highways," he pictured in his sermon some of the world's

[1] In a letter to the writer dated September 28, 1935, Doctor North wrote: "I am not a hymn writer, as that term is ordinarily used."

great centers where streets converge into a square, or platz, or place: Herald Square, Leipziger-Platz, Place de la Concorde. This suggested the first line of the hymn,

Where cross the crowded ways of life,

and the remainder of the hymn is full of references to conditions found in all large cities.

Quite generally looked upon as one of the really great hymns of modern times, it was first published in 1903 in the organ of the city missionary society, of which Doctor North was then the editor, *The Christian City*. The fact that the first hymnal in which it appeared was *The Methodist Hymnal* of 1905 has given rise, doubtless, to the oft-repeated statement that the hymn was first published in 1905. Probably no other hymn in recent years has been included in so many different types of books of sacred song.

Frank Mason North, D.D., born at New York City, December 3, 1850, graduated from Wesleyan University, Connecticut, and was ordained a minister of the Methodist Episcopal Church, entering the New York Conference in 1873. After serving various charges he transferred to the New York East Conference in 1887, going to Middletown, Connecticut, where he remained for five years. In 1892 he was chosen Corresponding Secretary for the New York City Missionary and Church Extension Society, continuing that work until 1912, when he was made Corresponding Secretary for the Board of Foreign Missions of his Church. He represented his Conference at several General Conferences, was a trustee of his Alma Mater and other educational institutions; served on many commissions, and for years was actively engaged in various forms of Christian activity. He died December 17, 1935, at his home in Madison, New Jersey.

**466—O brother man, fold to thy heart thy brother**—John Greenleaf Whittier (120)

**Ilona**—J. W. Lerman

The hymn is from John G. Whittier's poem "Worship" written in 1848 and published in his *Poems* in 1850. It was made by using stanzas 13, 11, and 14 from the fifteen-stanza poem beginning,

The Pagan's myths through marble lips are spoken,
And ghosts of old Beliefs still flit and moan
Round fane and altar overthrown and broken,
O'er tree-grown barrow and gray ring of stone.

At the head of the poem is the passage from James 1. 27: "Pure religion and undefiled before God and the Father is this, To visit the fatherless and the widows in their affliction, and to keep himself unspotted from the world." The first line of the second stanza of the hymn reads,

For he whom Jesus loved hath truly spoken,

and continues:

The holier worship which He deigns to bless . . .
feeds the widow and the fatherless.

The poem was not written under the "stress of the antislavery movement," as Dr. Edward S. Ninde has implied, but at the close of the Mexican war, and it was written to show his opposition to, and contempt for, elaborate rites and ceremonies in worship.

As if the pomp of rituals, and the savor
Of gums and spices, could the Unseen One please;
As if His ear could bend, with childish favor,
To the poor flattery of organ keys!

. . . . . . . . . . . . .

He asks no taper lights, on high surrounding
The priestly altar and the saintly grave,
No dolorous chant nor organ music sounding,
Nor incense clouding up the twilight nave.

His Quaker simplicity prompted him to emphasize "the holier worship" which "feeds the widow and the fatherless," and which is the essence of "Brotherhood" in the "Kingdom of God."

"Ilona" was written in 1908 by J. W. Lerman, concerning whom no information has been obtained. The inner voices have been changed slightly from the original harmonization to avoid a certain monotony. Though the only use of "Ilona" seems to have been associated with this hymn, the hymn appears to have had no specific tune commonly associated with it; in twenty-one books examined, eleven different tunes for it were found. Frequently it takes years, sometimes generations, for hymns to find adequate settings. (See Nos. 267 and 338 for further comment on musical settings for hymns.)

**467—Not in dumb resignation**—John Hay
**Llangloffan**—Welsh hymn melody
From D. Evans' Hymnau a Thonau, 1865

This hymn was first published in three stanzas in *Harpers New Monthly Magazine* of October, 1891, and was first used as a hymn in Dr. Lyman Abbott's *Plymouth Hymnal* of 1894.

The original, entitled,

Thy Will be Done,

contained three stanzas, the second being omitted here. The first word of the sixth line of the first stanza was "Who," not "That," and the first line of the second stanza was written:

Thy Will! It bids the weak be strong.

The omitted stanza was a vigorous statement which carried over into the last one:

When tyrant feet are trampling
Upon the common weal,
Thou dost not bid us bend and writhe
Beneath the iron heel.

In Thy name we assert our right
By sword or tongue or pen,
And even the headsman's axe may flash
Thy message unto men.

John Hay, statesman, diplomat, and author, was born at Salem, Indiana, October 8, 1838, was educated at Brown University, Rhode Island, and studied law in the office of Abraham Lincoln at Springfield, Illinois, being admitted to the bar in that city in 1861. Shortly afterward he became assistant private secretary to President Lincoln, serving with John G. Nicolay until the President's death. He was a diplomat and statesman of note, being Ambassador to the Court of St. James and Secretary of State under President McKinley. He represents the best in American literature, his *Pike County Ballads,* containing "Little Breeches," being worthy of ranking with Bret Hart, and his monumental *Abraham Lincoln* being indispensable to students of the Civil War period. His place among America's great men has become definitely fixed. He was Secretary of State at the time of his death, which occurred at his estate near Newport, New Hampshire, July 1, 1905.

"Llangloffan" is an old Welsh melody whose source is not now known. It is taken from the Rev. D. Evans' *Hymnau a Thonau* (Hymns and Tunes), 1865.

**468—The light of God is falling—Louis Fitzgerald Benson (38)**
**Laufer—Emily Swan Perkins**

The hymn was written in 1910 and appeared with the tune "Greenland" in the 1911 revision of the Presbyterian *Hymnal,* of which Doctor Benson, its author, was the editor. This "song of brotherhood" is one of the best of his hymns, its strength lying in the emphasis placed on the common virtues of the true Christian.

At a special memorial service held for Doctor Benson at Philadelphia, November 2, 1930, Dr. Henry van Dyke (12) counseled the churches to cultivate Doctor Benson's ideals for hymns: reverence, spiritual reality, beauty, and cheerfulness. He said that "When singing in all our churches has these marks, the joy of worship will revive and the churches will fill up."

"Laufer" was written for this hymn in 1925 by Miss Perkins at the request of Doctor Benson, then preparing for publication a volume of his hymns. The hymn had made a particular appeal to Miss Perkins, who felt the tune "Greenland," formerly used with it, was so unsatisfactory that she made this setting. In spite of the fact that Doctor Benson approved of it and used it in his book, Miss Perkins is modest in stating that the tune does not "measure up to the hymn." Others apparently think differently, for it is appearing in books that have selected "The light of God is falling" as a desirable hymn.

Emily Swan Perkins, born at Chicago, October 19, 1866, for many years has been a resident of Riverdale-on-Hudson, New York City. Coming from a hymn-singing family, Miss Perkins has had a lifelong interest in hymns. In 1921 she published privately a collection of fifty-four of her hymn tunes, for four of which she had also written the words. The following year she organized the Hymn Society, of which she has since been corresponding secretary. Now numbering among its members the foremost hymnologists of the United States, this Society has become a real force for a better hymnody. Its success has been due in large measure to the untiring interest of Miss Perkins.

**469—At length there dawns the glorious day**—Ozora Stearns Davis

**St. Michel's** (118)—From W. Gawler's Hymns and Psalms (118)

The hymn was first printed, with others (see No. 471), in a pamphlet used at the convention of the National Congregational Brotherhood held at Minneapolis, in the fall of 1909. One day, while Doctor Davis was walking through the woods near his summer cottage at Lake Sunapee, New Hampshire, musing over his desire to "express the inner meaning of Christian brotherhood as the unifying force in humanity," the words of this hymn shaped themselves into this form. The author admirably succeeded with them in expressing to the members of the convention two moods, "the outer and the inner phases of Christian experience."

Ozora Stearns Davis, D.D., born July 30, 1866, at Wheelock, Vermont, spent his boyhood years in the same state, at White River Junction, where he became an expert telegrapher when only fifteen years old. Ambitious to secure an education, he attended St. John's Academy, Dartmouth College, Hartford Theological Seminary, and the University of Leipzig. Upon his return to America he held pastorates in Springfield, Vermont; Newtonville, Massachusetts; and New Britain, Connecticut, and from 1909 to 1920 served as President of the Chicago Theological Seminary. An outstanding theologian of the Congregational Church, he was, in 1927, elected Moderator of its National Council. He died March 15, 1931.

**470—O Jesus, Master, when today**—Charles Stedman Newhall

**Beloit**—Carl Gottlieb Reissiger

This hymn was written by Mr. Newhall in 1913 and was published in *The Survey* for January 3, 1914. Its first appearance in a hymnal was in *Social Hymns of Brotherhood and Aspiration*, 1914.

Charles Stedman Newhall, soldier in the Civil War, Congregational minister, naturalist, and author, was born at Boston, Massachusetts, October 4, 1842. Educated at Amherst and at Union Theological Seminary, he served pastorates from 1872 until his identification, in 1898, with the United States Forestry Service in California. An authority on the trees, shrubs, and vines of the Northeastern states, he has written of the relation of the United States Reserves to sheep, fire, and lumbering. After his retirement in 1905 he made his home at Berkeley, California, where he died April 11, 1935.

"Beloit" is doubtless an arrangement of one of Carl G. Reissiger's many songs, but definite information concerning it is lacking.

Carl Gottlieb Reissiger, born at Belzig, near Wittenberg, Germany, January 31, 1798, was a prolific writer, producing more than two hundred works, but, it is said, he was "utterly devoid of originality." He was well educated and a figure of considerable force in Germany during the first half of the last century. He succeeded Weber (200) as Court Kapellmeister at Dresden, where he died, November 7, 1859.

**471—We bear the strain of earthly care**—Ozora Stearns Davis (469)

**Azmon** (162)—Carl Gotthelf Gläzer (162)
Arranged by Lowell Mason (19)

This was one of two hymns (see No. 469) which Doctor Davis was commissioned to write for the convention of the National Congregational Brotherhood held at Minneapolis, Minnesota, in the fall of 1909, and like "At length there dawns the glorious day," was written at his summer home on Lake Sunapee, New Hampshire. It is a simple statement of Doctor Davis's faith, which should be that of all professing Christians.

**472—Lift up our hearts, O King of kings**—John Howard Bertram Masterman

**Samson**—George Frederick Handel (88)

These three stanzas are taken from four written by Doctor Masterman for *A Missionary Hymn Book,* "first published in 1922 under the auspices of the Missionary Council of the National Assembly of the Church of England, the successor of the Central Board of Missions," one of the publications of the Society for Promoting Christian Knowledge. This selection consists of stanzas 2, 3, and 1, of what was written as a missionary hymn, the omitted last stanza being the prayer:

> Hear Thou the prayer Thy servants pray,
> Uprising from all lands today,
> And o'er the vanquished powers of sin,
> O bring Thy great salvation in.

The discovery of the scarcity of worth-while hymns on Christian brotherhood led to the selection of these appropriate stanzas.

John Howard Bertram Masterman, D.D., who was born at Tunbridge Wells, England, December 6, 1867, became Lecturer at St. John's College, Cambridge, after his graduation therefrom, and filled many positions of responsibility and honor in the field of religion and education in England. He published many scholarly works. From 1923 until his death, November 25, 1933, he was Suffragan Bishop of Plymouth.[1]

"Samson" is taken from the chorus, "Then round about the starry throne," in Handel's oratorio of that name, written in 1742. There are two

[1] A Suffragan Bishop is one consecrated to assist a regular bishop disabled by age, illness, or other cause, but he has no power to exercise jurisdiction.

somewhat similar arrangements of this chorus in common use, neither of which resembles closely what Handel wrote:

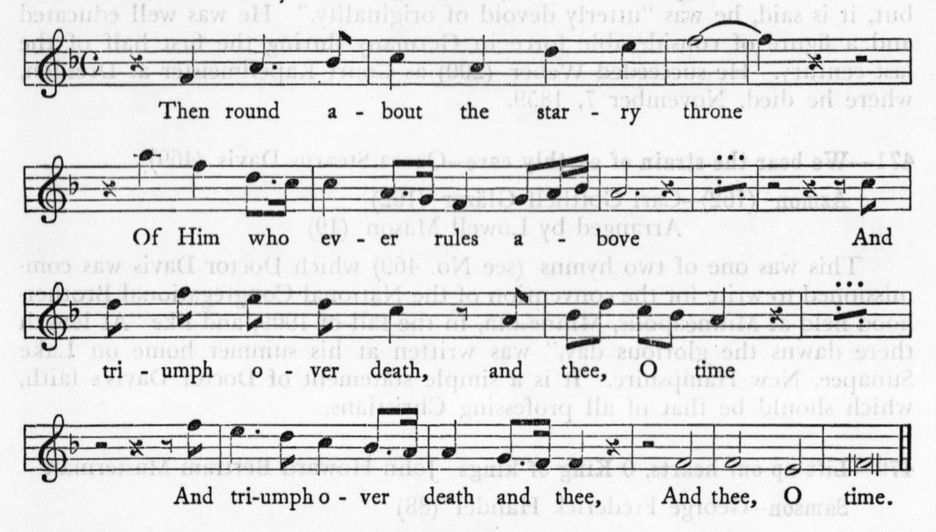
Then round a - bout the star - ry throne
Of Him who ev - er rules a - bove And
tri - umph o - ver death, and thee, O time
And tri-umph o - ver death and thee, And thee, O time.

**473—King of the City Splendid**—George Thomas Coster (264)
**City of Light**—Arthur Vennell Coster

This hymn was based on a part of Ezekiel 48. 35: ". . . and the name of the city from that day shall be, The Lord is there." Written by the Rev. G. T. Coster in 1897 in the interval between two pastorates, it was first published in *The Fellowship Hymn-Book,* London, 1909, and shortly thereafter included in the Supplement to *The Primitive Methodist Hymnal.* This is its first appearance in any American book.

"City of Light" was composed for this hymn by A. V. Coster, son of its author. Its first appearance in a hymnal was, like the hymn for which it was written, in *The Fellowship Hymn-Book,* 1909. Hymn and tune are so firmly wedded that they seem destined to remain one.

Arthur Vennell Coster, who was born December 25, 1864, and who died May 14, 1931, was a professional draughtsman, engineer, and inventor. He lived the greater part of his active life in Manchester, England. A Christian worker, especially interested in temperance reform, he did much speaking in that cause before Bands of Hope. His son, Vernon B. Coster, holder of the copyright of this tune, made as his only stipulation for its use the publishing of his address, in order that others desiring to use the hymn and tune might be able to have their communications reach him easily.

**474—O holy city, seen of John**—Walter Russell Bowie
**Ford Cottage**—Frederick Charles Maker (9[1])

The first appearance of this hymn was in *The Fellowship Hymn Book,*

London, 1909. Reference, of course, is made to the last chapter of the Revelation of St. John the Divine.

Walter Russell Bowie, D.D., is a native Virginian, born at Richmond, October 8, 1882. He was educated at Harvard, receiving his B. A. degree, with Phi Beta Kappa honors, in 1904, and his M. A. the following year. Becoming a priest of the Protestant Episcopal Church in 1909, he served pastorates at Greenwood and Richmond, Virginia, before going to Grace Church, New York, in 1923. He declined elevation to the Episcopacy for the reason that he felt his work in New York was not finished. A man of varied activities and interests, Doctor Bowie has been a scholar, the Chaplain of a Base Hospital during the World War, and in addition to being a great preacher and leader in the fight for social righteousness, he has been sometime editor, and a writer of sacred poetry representative of the best in American hymnody. At the celebration of the 125th anniversary of the organization of Grace Church, in December, 1933, Doctor Bowie said:

> It is not enough that we live in the best spirit and knowledge of today. We must be alert and sensitive to see the meanings of tomorrow. We live in a critical age when only those institutions will deserve to endure which are seeking to fulfill those better possibilities for human life, individual, social, national, and international, which the thought of the Kingdom of God requires.

Give us, O God, the strength to build
The City that hath stood
Too long a dream, whose laws are love,
Whose ways are brotherhood,
And where the sun that shineth is
God's grace for human good.

"Ford Cottage" seems to have first appeared in 1909 as the setting for Doctor Bowie's hymn in *The Fellowship Hymn Book*.

# Missions

**475—O Zion, haste, thy mission high fulfilling—Mary Ann Thomson**

Tidings—James Walch (374)

Mrs. Thomson has told of the writing of this hymn:

> I wrote the greater part of the hymn, "O Sion, Haste," in the year 1868. I had written many hymns before, and one night, while I was sitting up with one of my children who was ill with typhoid fever, I thought I should like to write a Missionary hymn to the tune of the hymn, "Hark, Hark, My Soul, Angelic Songs are Swelling," as I was fond of that tune, but as I could not then get a refrain I liked, I left the hymn unfinished and about three years later I finished it by writing the refrain which now forms part of it.
>
> I do not think my hymn, "O Sion, Haste," is ever sung to the tune for which I wrote it. Mr. Anketell [the Rev. John Anketell] told me, and I am sure he was right, that it is better for a hymn to have a tune of its own, and I feel much indebted to the author of the tune "Tidings," for writing so inspiriting a tune to my words.

As will be noted in the paragraph on the tune, "Tidings," Mrs. Thomson was mistaken.

The hymn was one of four by Mrs. Thomson to appear in *The Church Hymnal,* 1894, of the Protestant Episcopal Church.

Mary Ann Thomson has also written of herself:

I am an English woman and was born, baptized, and confirmed in London, and I am, and for many years have been a member of the Church of the Annunciation, Philadelphia.

I am the wife of John Thomson, the Librarian of the Free Library of Philadelphia, and he is the Accounting Warden of the Church of the Annunciation.

She was born December 5, 1834, and died at Philadelphia, March 11, 1923. She contributed more than forty hymns and poems to *The Churchman,* New York, and *The Living Church,* Chicago. Her husband was the first Librarian of the Free Library of Philadelphia.

"Tidings" was written by James Walch for "Hark, hark, my soul!" (532) because neither the Henry Smart (77) nor the J. B. Dykes (1) setting pleased him. While his tune failed to become a well-known third setting for the Faber hymn, it did perhaps become better known in its present association than either of the others in theirs. It is interesting to note that the hymn, "O Zion, haste," which had been written to be sung to the tune for "Hark, hark, my soul!" and the tune "Tidings," written for the latter hymn, should now be so definitely fixed in their relation, one to the other.

**476—Eternal God, whose power upholds**—Henry Hallam Tweedy (182)

**Everyland, No. 1**—Lily Rendle (57)

This hymn was the first choice of the Hymn Society from among the more than one thousand missionary hymns submitted in its prize contest, announced in November, 1928, the award being made in July, 1929. Since its enthusiastic acceptance at the Riverdale, New York, Presbyterian Church, on May 30, 1930, where it was first sung, it has been welcomed as a valuable addition to the all-too-meager supply of missionary hymns.

Doctor Tweedy has written:

In 1928 the Hymn Society offered a prize for a missionary hymn. I dislike to mention this fact, for it looks as if my motive in writing hymns were purely mercenary! It did start me off, however, on another attempt[1] and the result was "Eternal God, whose power upholds." It has appeared in a number of hymnals both here and abroad.

"Everyland, No. 1," was written especially for Doctor Tweedy's missionary hymn and was published for the first time in the 1935 edition of *The Methodist Hymnal.*

**477—Thou, whose almighty word**—John Marriott

**Righini**—Vincenzo Righini

This hymn was first printed in the *Evangelical Magazine* in June, 1825, the year of its author's death, and again, the next month, in *The Friendly Visitor,* without signature, entitled,

Missionary Hymn.

[1] See comment at No. 305.

Julian says this was one of a few hymns printed before the death of the author, but without his permission. The fourth line of the third stanza was,

Move on the water's face,

instead of its present reading,

Move o'er the water's face,

and line 3, stanza 4, was written,

Wisdom, Love, Might.

Charles Marriott, the author's son, "The Man of Saintly Life," described in Dean Burgon's *Twelve Good Men,* stated the hymn was written "about 1813."

John Marriott, English clergyman, born in 1780, at Cottesbach, near Lutterworth, England, where John Wycliffe died, was educated at Rugby and Christ Church, Oxford. While for a time tutor in the family of the Duke of Buccleuch at Dalkeith Palace, he became the friend of Sir Walter Scott, who dedicated to him the second canto of *Marmion:*

For we had fair resource in store
In classic and in Gothic lore:
We mark'd each memorable scene,
And held poetic talk between:
Nor hill, nor brook, we pass'd along
But had its legend or its song.

Though retaining throughout his life the appointment to the "living"[1] of Church Lawford, Warwickshire, he was compelled because of his wife's ill health to make his home in Devonshire, where he served several curacies. His modesty prevented the publication of any of his hymns during his lifetime. He died at Broadclyst, near Exeter, March 31, 1825.

"Righini" appeared in the following form in the books of the last quarter of the nineteenth century, when this tune seems to have come to light in our hymn books:

[1] The ecclesiastical living in England is a preferment to which rank or public office is attached, and is technically a benefice.

Vincenzo Righini, born at Bologna, Italy, January 22, 1756, a conductor of opera in Berlin, was a prolific composer, and had he not had Mozart as a contemporary would doubtless be better known, even though he does not come within the first rank. He was an excellent teacher of singing and has contributed some vocal studies that are among the best. Righini was much beloved, modest and courteous. He died at Bologna, August 19, 1812.

**478—Father, whose will is life and good**—Hardwicke Drummond Rawnsley

**Tallis' Ordinal**—Thomas Tallis (51)

This hymn is taken entire and unchanged from *A Missionary Hymn Book with Tunes,* 1922, and is the only one in *The Methodist Hymnal* so specifically to exalt medical missionary work.

Hardwicke Drummond Rawnsley was born at Shiplake-on-Thames, England, September 28, 1851, and during his education came under two powerful influences—that of his godfather, Edward Thring (see No. 41), at school in Uppingham, and that of John Ruskin, at Balliol College, Oxford. His literary interests are indicated in numerous works, including *Memories of the Tennysons.* After taking Holy Orders and serving as curate and vicar at various appointments, he was appointed, in 1909, as one of the canons of Carlisle Cathedral and made a chaplain to the King of England. Greatly loved by the people for his insistence on their right to have access to the beautiful Lake District in England, he was the founder of the National Trust for Places of Historic Interest and National Beauty. As a mark of respect to him, after his death, several beauty spots on Derwentwater, perhaps the loveliest of the English lakes, were acquired by public subscription and given to the National Trust in memory of one "who, greatly loving fair things in Nature and art, set all his love to the service of God and man." He died at Grasmere, Westmorland, May 28, 1920.

"Tallis' Ordinal" is from *The whole Psalter translated into English Metre, which contayneth an hundreth and fifty Psalmes,* a book with no date and no author's name. It is known, however, to be the work of Matthew Parker, Archbishop of Canterbury during the latter part of the reign of Queen Mary, and is thought to have been printed in 1651. At the close of this book there are nine tunes by Thomas Tallis, this being the last of the nine, and it is used as the setting for the Ordination Hymn, "Veni Creator" (636). The first eight tunes in Archbishop Parker's *Psalter* are written each in a different one of the eight modes, of which the eighth is the "Evening Hymn" noted at No. 51. In "Notes on Certain Tunes," W. H. Havergal, in his *Psalmody,* 1871, says "Tallis' Ordinal" "is simplicity itself. A child may sing the tune, while manly genius will admire it."

**479—Jesus shall reign where'er the sun**—Isaac Watts (3)

**Duke Street** (17)—John Hatton (17)

This "greatest of all missionary hymns," a rendering of Psalm 72 into "Christian song," first appeared in Doctor Watts's *Psalms,* of 1719. The version used in *The Methodist Hymnal* consists of stanzas 1, 4, 5, and 8, of the eight stanzas comprising Part II of the psalm. It has come down through the years with surprisingly few changes from the original text of Watts. A reading of the Preface to his Psalms will explain his apparently anachronistic introduction of the name of Jesus in his renderings of the Psalms and, in this particular instance, also the reason for his bold expression of confidence in the eventual full and complete victory of Jesus Christ:

> Where the original runs in the form of prophecy concerning Christ and his salvation, I have given an historical turn to the sense; there is no necessity that we should always sing in the obscure and doubtful style of prediction, when the things foretold are brought into open light by a full accomplishment.

Warranted by the fact that this is the first confident missionary pronouncement in modern hymnody, the following inclusion of the eight stanzas of the original rendering will indicate alterations.

1 Jesus shall reign where e'er the sun
Does his successive journeys run;
His kingdom stretch from shore to shore,
Till moons shall wax and wane no more.

2 Behold! the islands, with their kings,
And Europe her best tribute brings:
From North to South the princes meet
To pay their homage at his feet.

3 There Persia, glor'ous to behold,
There India shines in Eastern gold;
And barb'rous nations, at his word,
Submit and bow, and own their Lord.

4 For this shall endless pray'r be made,
And praises throng to crown his head;
His name, like sweet perfume, shall rise
With ev'ry morning sacrifice.

5 People and realms of ev'ry tongue
Dwell on his love with sweetest song;
And infant-voices shall proclaim
Their early blessings on his name.

6 Blessings abound where e'er he reigns,
The pris'ner leaps to loose his chains;
The weary find eternal rest,
And all the sons of want are blest.

7 Where he displays his healing pow'r,
Death and the curse are known no more;
In him the tribes of Adam boast
More blessings than their father lost.

8 Let ev'ry creature rise and bring
Peculiar honors to our King;
Angels descend with songs again,
And earth repeat the long Amen.

**480—O Master of the waking world—Frank Mason North (465)**

**Melita—John Bacchus Dykes (1)**

Doctor North described the origin of this fine "World Service Hymn" as follows:

> In 1927 Dr. Henry H. Meyer was moved to give emphasis to "world service" in the first issue of *The Church School Journal* for 1928. He asked me to write a hymn.

My unrelenting interest in the Missionary Movement refused to let me excuse myself. I was in constant touch with men and women who were giving their lives to the "work of missions,"—who was I, that I should not at least try to put into verse what was in their hearts, and mine, and, if the verse could be sung, so much the better. The task was not simple; this hymn was the result. It was first published in *The Church School Journal,* January, 1928.

"Melita" was written by Doctor Dykes for William Whitings's hymn "on behalf of those at sea," beginning,

Eternal Father, strong to save,

for the Original Edition of *Hymns Ancient and Modern,* 1861. It is one of the seven tunes by Doctor Dykes which were accepted for the first edition of this epoch-making hymnal.

**481—Christ for the world we sing**—Samuel Wolcott

**Kirby Bedon** (429)—Edward Bunnett (429)

At the Ohio State Convention of the Y. M. C. A., held at Cleveland in 1869, there was placed over the stage a motto,

Christ for the world, and the world for Christ,

made from branches of evergreen. The Rev. Samuel Wolcott, then a pastor in Cleveland and a delegate to the Convention, was so greatly impressed by these words, that while walking home through the streets of the city, he put the implications of the motto into the form of a hymn. For many years it has been sung as the opening hymn of each semester at Yankton College, South Dakota.

Samuel Wolcott was born at South Windsor, Connecticut, July 2, 1813, graduated from Yale and Andover Theological Seminary, and went to Syria as a missionary. Compelled by ill health to return to America, he was ordained a Congregational minister, and served churches at Providence, Rhode Island; Chicago, Illinois; and Cleveland, Ohio. Later he acted as Secretary of the Ohio Home Missionary Society. Not until he was fifty-six years of age did he write any hymns, but from that time until his death at Longmeadow, Massachusetts, February 24, 1886, he wrote more than two hundred, most of which have already been forgotten.

**482—Heralds of Christ, who bear the King's commands**—Laura Scherer Copenhaver

**National Hymn**—George William Warren

Mrs. Copenhaver has written the author:

The great hymns of the church, I sometimes think, should come out of a mood which compels the writing, whether or not there is a specific need for such hymns. The hymn "Heralds of Christ" and others of mine have always been written to meet a need, and I wonder whether they might not have been better if they had not been done "by request."

Yet they would not have existed at all if someone had not said, "We have no hymn for this convention or for this meeting or for this pageant. You must write one."

In writing "Heralds of Christ" for one of the Summer Conferences at which I used to lecture, I was moved with a deep sense of unity with the builders of the

> King's Highway in far lands, next door to me in America, and even with those great ones I had known as a child now gone on with the immortals by way of Africa and India.

In an article, "The Builders," which appeared in *Onward,* of April, 1934, apropos of this hymn, she says:

> Today in every land Christians are uniting to build a Kingdom which shall have no geographical bounds, no limitations of race, no barriers of caste or class.
>
> Many feet are on the Highway today. Many hands are building. Not all are using the same tools or the same tempo, but all are building with their eyes fixed on the same Leader, Jesus Christ. There are many roads, but no matter whether they stretch over mountain or river, through open plains or dark jungle, the Highway will be firm and straight because it reaches to one goal, the Kingdom of God.

Laura Scherer Copenhaver was born at Marion, Virginia, August 29, 1868, where she lived most of her life at Marion College, founded by her father. There for about thirty years she taught English literature. She was interested in and influenced by the missionaries and ministers who were frequent visitors at the college, and has spent many summers lecturing at summer Mission schools. Mrs. Copenhaver has written a number of pageants and has been a contributor to magazines. In her best-known article, the story of Madame Russell, sister of Patrick Henry, published in *Scribner's Magazine* for June, 1928, Mrs. Copenhaver says of Madame Russell that she "was one of Bishop Asbury's most interesting converts, and the things she said and did deserve wider quotation than they have had." Mrs. Copenhaver, for some years past, has devoted much of her time to developing handicrafts among a group of Virginia mountain women.

"National Hymn," written at the request of Dr. J. Ireland Tucker for a tune for Daniel C. Roberts's hymn, "God of our fathers" (496), first appeared in the 1894 Episcopal *Hymnal.*

George William Warren, born August 17, 1828, at Albany, New York, spent his life in studying and playing organs. Though largely self-taught in music, he had his general education at Racine University. As organist, he served churches in Albany, Brooklyn, and New York City, and in 1888 published *Hymns and Tunes as sung at Saint Thomas' Church,* New York. His death occurred at New York, March 17, 1902.

**483—From all the dark places**—Mary Bridges Canedy Slade

**The Kingdom Coming**—Emilius Laroche (?)

This missionary gospel song, so amazingly popular for Methodist missionary meetings, first appeared in 1873 in *The School Festival.*

Mrs. Mary Bridges Canedy Slade was the wife of a clergyman in Fall River, Massachusetts, where she lived from her birth, in 1826, to her death, in 1882. She was a teacher, a one-time assistant editor of *The New England Journal of Education,* and the founder of *Wide Awake.* She wrote a number of gospel song texts for R. M. McIntosh, 1836-99, well-known Southern church musician.

Emilius Laroche is said by Frank J. Metcalf to be a *nom de plume* of R. M. McIntosh.

**484—From Greenland's icy mountains**—Reginald Heber (1)
**Missionary Hymn** (401)—Lowell Mason (19)

A facsimile of the original manuscript of this hymn has the following account of it, penned on the fly-leaf, by Thomas Edgworth, an attorney of Wrexham, England, who was living there when the copy was made:

> On Whitsunday, 1819, the late Dr. Shipley, Dean of St. Asaph and Vicar of Wrexham, preached a sermon in Wrexham Church in aid of the Society for the Propagation of the Gospel in Foreign Parts. That day was also fixed upon for the commencement of the Sunday evening lectures intended to be established in the Church, and the late Bishop of Calcutta (Heber), then rector of Hodnet, the Dean's son-in-law, undertook to deliver the first lecture. In the course of the Saturday previous, the Dean and his son-in-law being together in the vicarage, the former requested Heber to write "something for them to sing in the morning;" and he retired for that purpose from the table, where the Dean and a few friends were sitting, to a distant part of the room. In a short time the Dean inquired: "What have you written?" Heber, having then composed the first three verses, read them over. "There, there, that will do very well," said the Dean. "No, no, the sense is not complete," replied Heber. Accordingly he added the fourth verse, and, the Dean being inexorable to his repeated request of "Let me add another, oh, let me add another," thus completed the hymn, of which the annexed is a fac-simile, and which has since become so celebrated. It was sung the next morning, in Wrexham Church, the first time.

The tune to which it was first sung, was traditionally that of an old ballad, "'Twas when the seas were roaring."

The hymn was brought to general notice shortly after Heber's appointment as Bishop of India, when it was published in *The Christian Observer* in February, 1823, in both the English and American editions. It was through this journal that the attention of Miss Mary W. Howard of Savannah, Georgia, was called to it. By her request Lowell Mason wrote a tune with which it might be associated.

Bishop Heber lived during the period of growing interest in the missionary movement in England; this general interest fired his imagination to write what is without doubt our greatest missionary hymn. Would that others had been similarly inspired. There is a distressing absence of missionary hymns having merit, as all hymnbook makers will agree.

In the author's text the first and third lines of stanza 2, as here printed, began with "Can we." This was changed to "Shall we" in the 1905 *Methodist Hymnal,* and has again been altered for the 1935 edition, where the first four lines of the stanza now read:

> Can men whose souls are lighted
> With wisdom from on high,
> Can they to men benighted
> The lamp of life deny?

The original second stanza has been omitted.

**485—Watchman, tell us of the night**—John Bowring (75)
**Watchman**—Lowell Mason (19)

The hymn, based on the repeated inquiry,

> Watchman, what of the night?
> Watchman, what of the night?

from Isaiah 21. 11, was included in Sir John Bowring's *Hymns,* 1825. He is said to have told a friend in China, years after he had written it, that he first heard it sung in Asiatic Turkey sometime in 1835 by a group of American missionaries in a prayer meeting.

"Watchman" was written by Lowell Mason in 1830 in the following form:

Few hymns are written in the form of conversation as is this, and few lend themselves so excellently to antiphonal singing. The composer had in mind its use as a duet between soprano and tenor with the congregation participating only in repeating the reply of the watchman in the last line of each stanza. Lowell Mason called it a

Missionary or Christmas Hymn.

It may easily be dramatized for use in a Christmas service.

It may not be amiss to repeat what has been so frequently said, that the author of the hymn and the composer of the tune were literally contemporaries, being born in the same year, 1792, and dying in the same year, 1872.

**486—From ocean unto ocean**—Robert Murray

**Lancashire** (278)—Henry Smart (77)

This is from *The Hymnal of the Presbyterian Church in Canada,* 1880, and is a favorite home-missions hymn. Doctor Murray was one of the leaders in the movement to unify the Presbyterians of Canada, and it is a matter of regret that he did not live to see the consummation of the larger union of churches in his country. To the Canadian Presbyterian *Hymnal* mentioned he contributed another hymn, envisioning the United Church for which he yearned:

Our blessed bond of union
Thou art, O Christ, our Lord!
The rule of our communion
Is Thine own faithful word.

. . . . . . . .

We grasp the promise given,
We set before our eyes
One faith, one hope, one heaven,
One battle, and one prize.

Robert Murray, D.D., eminent Canadian Presbyterian divine, and for fifty years editor of *The Presbyterian Witness,* was born in the country near Truro, Nova Scotia, Canada, December 25, 1832. At the age of ten years, it is said, he began writing poetry. A graduate of the Free Church College of Halifax, he was for a time its governor. Although licensed to preach, he was chosen editor of *The Presbyterian Witness* because of his recognized aptitude for editorial work. Several of his poems, first appearing (usually anonymously) in his paper, found their way into *The Hymnal,* 1880, and into *The Church Hymnary* of 1898. Doctor Murray died at Halifax, December 10, 1910.

**487—The morning light is breaking**—Samuel Francis Smith (489)

**Webb**—George James Webb

Dr. Samuel F. Smith, the author of this stirring missionary hymn, wrote it in 1832 and placed it in the hands of Lowell Mason (19) and Thomas Hastings (204), who used it in *Spiritual Songs for Social Worship,* 1833. It has been translated into many languages and is sung in all parts of the world.

"Webb," named after its composer, is widely known and very popular. Mr. Webb wrote this tune while on board ship bound for America, to the secular words, "'Tis dawn, the lark is singing." He has said he did not know who adapted this tune to the sacred words, "The morning light is breaking," nor when. "Webb" is interesting in that it is wedded to two hymns, "The morning light is breaking" and "Stand up for Jesus." The Rev. Samuel W. Duffield, author of *English Hymns,* says, "So nearly as can be ascertained, it was W. B. Bradbury who (in 1861) adapted the tune 'Webb' to it." It appeared in this connection in *The Wesleyan Psalmist,* 1842. See No. 261.

George James Webb was born near Salisbury, England, June 24, 1803. He had adequate musical training, his father, a prosperous farmer, being in sympathy with his desire to follow the musical profession. He wished to come to America and had engaged passage on a boat sailing to New York, but the captain of a boat sailing for Boston prevailed upon him to change his plans, which was fortunate for him, for shortly after his arrival in Boston he was engaged as organist at Old South Church, where he played for many years. Forming a close personal friendship with Lowell Mason, the two collaborated in various musical projects. With Mason he founded the Boston Academy of Music, assisted him in the conducting of children's classes, and together they issued a number of singing books. He lived forty years in Boston, moving to Orange, New Jersey, in 1871, where Doctor Mason had preceded him. A cultivated gentleman and a competent musician, he died at Orange, October 7, 1887.

**488—Hail to the brightness of Zion's glad morning**—Thomas Hastings (204)

**Wesley**—Lowell Mason (19)

Thomas Hastings wrote this hymn in 1830 and published it in *Spiritual Songs for Social Worship,* 1833, which he compiled jointly with Lowell Mason. This hymn has come down through all the years with little or no editing since its composition in 1830 and its first appearance in *Spiritual Songs.* The word "gliding," line 2, stanza 3, has been changed to "flowing"; the word "Jehovah," line 2, stanza 4, to "the Saviour"; and "fall'n are the weapons," line 3, stanza 4, to "fallen the weapons." The first two of these alterations were made by the Editorial Committee of *The Methodist Hymnal* of 1935.

"Wesley," called "Hail to the Brightness," was written for this hymn by Lowell Mason, and appeared with it in the same book at the same time, 1833.

## National and International Life

**489—My country, 'tis of thee**—Samuel Francis Smith

**America**—Henry Carey

Dr. Henry S. Burrage gives, in his *Baptist Hymn Writers and Their Hymns,* an interesting account of the writing of our National Hymn:

> Dr. Smith's well-known hymn,
>
> My country, 'tis of thee,

> also grew out of his intimacy with Lowell Mason. While Dr. Smith was a student at Andover, Mr. William C. Woodbridge returned from Germany, bringing with him a large number of German hymn books, with music, which he put into the hands of Mr. Mason. Mr. Mason brought them to Mr. Smith, saying, "You can read these books, but I cannot tell what is in them." The music of one of the hymns pleased Dr. Smith, and he dashed off the words of this hymn, without any expectation that it would ever become a favorite with anybody, much less a national hymn. He gave the hymn to Mr. Mason, and it was first sung at a Fourth of July Sunday-school celebration in Park Street Church, Boston, in 1832. It soon became popular in children's celebrations, patriotic meetings, thanksgivings, and having come into general use in this country, it has traveled round the globe, and is everywhere known as the American national hymn.

It was written on an afternoon in February, 1832. As a young student, he noted the patriotic character of a German poem, and tells us:

> I instantly felt the impulse to write a patriotic hymn of my own, adapted to the tune. Picking up a scrap of waste paper which lay near me, I wrote at once, probably within half an hour, the hymn "America" as it is now known everywhere. The whole hymn stands today as it stood on the bit of waste paper.

The German hymn which was Doctor Smith's inspiration was "Gott segne Sachsenland," which was the basis for "God bless our native land" (490). Doctor Smith's hymn is simple, direct, and moving in its homely patriotic and religious appeal and is by far the most popular of our "national" hymns.

Samuel Francis Smith, D.D., eminent nineteenth-century Baptist clergyman, was born at Boston, Massachusetts, October 21, 1808. He was educated at Harvard University and at Andover Theological Seminary, and for a short time after graduating from Andover acted as editor of *The Baptist Missionary Magazine.* For twenty years he ministered at Waterville, Maine, where he also taught modern languages at Waterville, now Colby College, and at Newton Center, Massachusetts. From 1854 until his death at Newton Center, November 16, 1895, he devoted himself to the work, both secretarial and editorial, of the American Baptist Missionary Union. With Dr. Baron Stowe he compiled *The Psalmist,* an excellent collection published in 1843. He was the author of about one hundred hymns, four of which are in *The Methodist Hymnal.* While Doctor Smith was well and favorably known as an author and editor during his life, he will be better known to generations of Americans for having written "My country, 'tis of thee."

"America" is the tune of the British National Anthem, "God save the King," and there is as much controversy over the composer of the tune as there is over the source of the words of the anthem. It is traced variously, to John Bull, who performed it on an organ in 1607; to an old Christmas carol found in *Songs and Fancies,* Aberdeen, 1682, which had been taken from Ravencroft's *Melismata,* 1611; to a passage in one of Henry Purcell's sonatas; to a hymn said to have been sung in the private chapel of James II on the occasion of the apprehended invasion of England by the Prince of Orange. Elsewhere it is said to be a Jacobite composition; to be French in origin and composed by Lully; to have been composed by, or its modern revival attributed to, James Oswald, a hack-writer for the editor of the early issues of the tune. The claims for most of these theories have been abandoned, and the majority of the writers on the subject seem to be of the opinion that it was composed by Henry Carey; yet there seems to be reliable evidence that it may have been the work of James Oswald. Certainly, this tune now common as a setting for many different patriotic verses, is not the sole property of any one country. It was a great favorite of Weber's, who used it in his cantata, *Kampf und Sieg,* his *Jubal Overture,* and twice set it for four voices. Beethoven wrote seven variations on it for piano, introduced it into his Battle Symphony, and arranged it for solo and chorus with accompaniment by violin, cello, and piano. Many lengthy articles and some books have been written dealing with its source.[1]

Doctor Smith, author of the hymn, said the use of the same tune for the National songs of both England and America was a "beautiful bond of union between the mother country and her daughter."

Henry Carey, who was born about 1690, and who died at Clerkenwell, October 4, 1743, an English musician possessing considerable natural ability, has always been considered second rate. Nevertheless, he wrote the music for a good many farces and light, ballad, and burlesque operas, as well as other pieces, which were performed at the best theaters of his day. He also had some reputation as a poet. It is for having written "Salley in Our Alley" that he is most favorably known. Although Carey may have been only a popular entertainer, Sir John Hawkins (1719-1789), seems to be not quite fair to him when he says

> the extent of his abilities seems to have been the composition of a ballad air, or at most a little cantata, to which he was just able to set a bass. Being thus slenderly accomplished in his art, his chief employment was teaching at boarding schools and among people of middling rank in private families. . . . As the qualities that Carey was endowed with were such as rendered him an entertaining companion, it is no wonder that he should be, as he frequently was, in straits. . . . About the year 1744, in a fit of depression, he laid violent hands upon himself, and at his house in Warner-street, Coldbath fields, put a period to a life which had been led without reproach. As a musician Carey seems to have been one of the first of the lowest rank; and as a poet, the last of that class of which D'Urfey was the first, with this difference, that in all the songs and poems written by him, on wine, love, and such kind subjects, he seems to have manifested an inviolable regard for decency and good manners.

At any rate, that is more than can be said for the most of Carey's contemporaries.

**490—God bless our native land**—Siegfried Augustus Mahlmann

Translated by Charles Timothy Brooks and John Sullivan Dwight

Stanza 3, William Edward Hickson

**America** (489)—Henry Carey (489)

This is a rather free rendering of the German hymn which was S. F.

[1] The most complete discussions of "God save the King" are to be found in: *Grove's Dictionary* (all editions), the article "God save the King"; *Dictionary of Hymnology,* Julian, same heading; *Stories of Famous Songs,* S. J. Adair Fitz-Gerald, Chapter xx; *Encyclopedia Britannica,* article "National Anthems"; Richard Clarke's *Account of the National Anthem,* 1822; W. H. Cummings, *God save the King,* 1902; Frank Kidson, *The Minstrelsy of England,* 1901; William Chappell, *History of Music;* Richard Grant White, *National Hymns,* 1862.

Smith's inspiration for *My country, 'tis of thee* (489). The original German version as revealed in G. W. Fink's *Musikalischer Hausschatz der Deutschen,* 1842, was:

Gott segne Sachsenland,
Wo fest die Treue stand
In Sturm und Nacht!
Ew'ge Gerechtigkeit,
Hoch über'm Meer der Zeit,
Die jedem Sturm gebeut,
Schütz' uns mit Macht!

Blühe, du Rautenkranz,
In schöner Tage Glanz
Freudig empor!
Heil, Friedrich August, dir!
Heil, guter König, dir!
Dich, Vater, preisen wir
Liebend im Chor!

Was treue Herzen flehn,
Steigt zu des Himmels Höh'n
Aus Nacht zum Licht!
Der unsre Liebe sah,
Der unsre Thränen sah,
Er ist uns huldreich nah,
Verlässt uns nicht!

Gott segne Sachsenland,
Wo fest die Treue stand
In Sturm und Nacht!
Ew'ge Gerechtigkeit,
Hoch über'm Meer der Zeit,
Die jedem Sturm gebeut,
Schütz' uns mit Macht!

The Rev. Charles T. Brooks translated (in two stanzas) a part of the German hymn while he was a member of the Divinity School at Cambridge, some time during the years 1832-35. Some years afterward Dr. John S. Dwight, a Boston music critic, altered some of its lines. Both gentlemen furnished texts for use by Lowell Mason (19) in his various singing books, and perhaps worked together on this. As it stands the first five lines of the first stanza may be attributed to Doctor Brooks (c. 1832-35) and the remainder of the first two stanzas to Doctor Dwight (c. 1844). They may be found in *The Psaltery,* Mason and Webb, 1845, although a slightly different text was used by Mason in his *Carmina Sacra* of 1841.

The third stanza is the fourth of a four-stanza hymn having the same first line as this, which was written by William E. Hickson, an Englishman, as a "new national anthem" in 1835. The original form of this stanza which appeared in the "Second Class Tune Book," No. 3, of *The Singing Master,* 1836, is as follows:

And not this land alone,
But be thy mercies shown
From shore to shore.
Lord, make the nations see
That men should brothers be,
And form one family,
The wide world o'er.

Neither Doctor Julian nor Doctor Benson (38) seems to have been familiar with the original. In a communication to *The Outlook* of July 9, 1909, the Rev. James Mearns, then assistant editor of the *Dictionary of Hymnology,* gives the German original with the notation:

> Gott segne Sachsenland! 1815. Author August Mahlmann. First printed in the "Zeitung für die elegante Welt," 1815 . . . and first sung on 13 November, 1815, in the presence of the King of Saxony.

Siegfried Augustus Mahlmann was born at Leipzig, Saxony, May 13, 1771, and died there December 16, 1826. Best known as a song writer, he was the editor of *Zeitung für die elegante Welt* from 1805 to 1816.

Charles Timothy Brooks, D.D., was born at Salem, Massachusetts, June 20, 1813. Educated at Harvard and the Divinity School at Cambridge, he held a pastorate at Newport, Rhode Island, for thirty-four years, from 1837. Compelled to resign because of failing eyesight and health in 1871, he died there June 14, 1883.

John Sullivan Dwight was born at Boston, May 13, 1813, and died there September 5, 1893. Graduating from Harvard and the Cambridge Divinity School, his early charge was that of a small Unitarian Church at Northampton, Massachusetts, from which he resigned after serving only one year. Suffering from a natural timidity and shrinking from any outward expression of religious feeling, he in time lost all interest in the organization and methods of the church and ceased attending its religious services. In 1852 he founded *Dwight's Journal of Music,* in which he made himself felt as an able critic and did a great service through stressing music as a branch of liberal culture. Though accused of being a *Germanophile,* and having, as John Tasker Howard says, little sympathy for what was being done in America by American musicians, nevertheless he was just in his criticisms. He was one of the founders of the Harvard Musical Association (1837), still an active organization.

William Edward Hickson, an English boot manufacturer, was born at London, January 7, 1803; retired from business in 1840; and removed to Kent, where he died at Fairseat, Seven Oaks, March 22, 1870. He compiled *The Singing Master* in 1836.

**491—O beautiful for spacious skies—Katharine Lee Bates (101)**

**Materna**—Samuel Augustus Ward

This hymn classic, which every American school child should know, was written on an evening in 1893 after Miss Bates had returned to Colorado Springs from a visit with a party of friends to the summit of Pike's Peak. According to her own account, they

> gazed in wordless rapture over the expanse of mountain ranges and sealike sweep of plains. . . . It was then and there that the opening lines of "America the Beautiful" sprang into being.

In the *Journal* of the National Education Association she is reported to have said:

> My friend took me to the great World's Fair, whose White City made such strong appeal to patriotic feeling that it was in no small degree responsible for at least the last stanza of "America the Beautiful." It was with this quickened and deepened sense of America that we went on, my New England eyes delighting in the wind-waved gold of the vast wheatfields.

It was Miss Bates's first trip into the great West. She was spending a part of the summer of 1893 teaching in a summer school in Colorado Springs, when there came to her these experiences revealing the beauty and wonder of her country, and inspiring her to a patriotic outburst that has seldom been equaled. Her prayers: "God mend thine every flaw," "May God thy gold refine," and the repetition emphasizing "God shed His grace on thee," more than justify its inclusion in any book of sacred song.

In 1928 Miss Bates was in attendance at the Sixty-sixth Annual Meeting of the National Education Association of the United States, held July 1-6 in Minneapolis. At one of the sessions at which "America the Beautiful" was sung by a chorus of girls representing twenty different nationalities, Miss Bates was introduced to the members of the convention and said, in part:

> It is not work to write a song; it is a great joy, and this is, in reality a very simple song, a simple framing of words. . . . I remember writing the opening stanzas in a notebook that was traveling with me, a notebook that I did not open again for two years. It was not until the summer of 1899 that I came upon that notebook and copied out this song and sent it to a Boston concern which very kindly published it. To my great surprise, people began immediately that very year to write music for it. It has been sung to many tunes.
>
> All through these years requests have come to use the song in one way or another in our colleges, in hymn books, in one form or another. I am only too glad to give it free as my own slight gift to my country, but my only condition is that they hold to the authorized text, so that we may not have as many texts as we already have tunes.
>
> One of the suggestions that was most insistently made in these later years was that I add a stanza to express international brotherhood. It has not seemed easy to do that, for although I long for world brotherhood and am among those who look forward eagerly to the day when the United States shall enter the League of Nations, yet the song is long enough already, and is written for one special thing. So the best suggestion I can make is that when you sing the first stanza, you think of "From sea to shining sea," as applying from the Pacific to the Atlantic, around the other way, and all the states in between, and that will include all the nations and all the people from sea to shining sea.

"Materna" was written by Samuel A. Ward in 1882 as a setting for the hymn "O mother dear, Jerusalem," and the combination of hymn and tune appeared in the Protestant Episcopal *Hymnal* of 1894. Not long after Miss Bates's "America the Beautiful" became known, the tune became somehow inseparably associated with her words.

Samuel Augustus Ward was born at Newark, New Jersey, December 28, 1847, and died there, September 28, 1903. He was a dealer in musical merchandise and was prominent in musical circles in his native city, being for fourteen years conductor of its Orpheus Club.

**492—For the might of Thine arm we bless Thee**—Charles Silvester Horne

**Cormac**—Irish traditional melody

This hymn was suggested to Doctor Horne by Mrs. Hemans's "Hymn of the Vaudois Mountain Christian," which begins:

For the strength of the hills we bless thee,
Our God, our Fathers' God;
Thou hast made thy people mighty
By the touch of the mountain sod,
Thou hast fixed our ark of refuge
Where the spoiler's feet ne'er trod,
For the strength of the hills we bless thee,
Our God, our Fathers' God.

Doctor Horne's hymn first appeared in *The Fellowship Hymn Book,* 1909, in four stanzas, of which the last, omitted in *The Methodist Hymnal* of 1935, is:

May the shadow of Thy presence around our camp be spread;
Baptize us with the courage with which Thou bless'd our dead;
O keep us in the pathway their saintly feet have trod;
For the might of Thine arm we bless Thee, our God, our fathers' God.

Doctor Horne wrote the hymn for use at Whitefield's Tabernacle, Tottenham Court Road, London, where he ministered from 1903 to 1914.

Charles Silvester Horne, brilliant and powerful English preacher, was born at Cuckfield, Sussex, England, April 15, 1865, the son of a Congregational minister who gave up preaching to publish a local newspaper and engage in the printing and book-selling business at Newport, Shropshire. He was educated at the Newport Grammar School, at the University of Glasgow, and at Mansfield College, Oxford, where he was a member of the first class entering. Because of his unusual ability to preach he was called to the conspicuous pulpit of Allen Street Church, Kensington, two years before he had completed his theological course. Being ordained there in 1889, he continued his successful ministry until 1903, when he responded to the call to the newly organized institutional church known as Whitefield's Tabernacle, Tottenham Court Road, London. Prominent in Brotherhood work and in the Congregational Union, he was elected to Parliament in 1910. He came to America in 1914 to deliver the Yale Lectures on Preaching, arriving in this country on April 13. While taking the boat from Niagara to Toronto, soon after the Yale Lectures, he fell dead on its deck, at his wife's feet, just as the boat entered the harbor at Toronto, May 4, 1914.

"Cormac," from *Feis Ceoil Collection of Irish Music,* is a fine traditional Irish melody, known for its use with the Irish song, beginning,

Down by the salley gardens.

It is especially effective when sung in unison by a large body of men.

**493—O God, beneath Thy guiding hand—Leonard Bacon**

**Duke Street** (17)—John Hatton (17)

This anniversary hymn was written by Dr. Leonard Bacon for the Bicentenary of New Haven, Connecticut, celebrated in his Center Church, April 25, 1833. It has been abbreviated and somewhat altered from the original, which began,

The Sabbath morn is as bright and calm.

In its revised form it was included in *Psalms and Hymns for Christian Use and Worship,* 1845, of which Doctor Bacon was one of the compilers.

Leonard Bacon, D.D., was born on February 19, 1802, at Detroit, where his father was a missionary to the Indians. Educated at Yale and Andover Theological Seminary, he was, in 1825, ordained pastor of Center Church, New Haven, Connecticut, where he remained forty-one years, until 1866. Appointed Professor of Theology in Yale Divinity School the same year, he resigned this appointment in 1871, but until his death at New Haven, December 23, 1881, he was Lecturer on Church Polity at that institution. It is significant of one so long interested in hymnody that while yet a student at Andover, he edited, in September, 1823, a small collection of *Hymns and Sacred Songs for the Monthly Concert* of prayer for missions. His later services to hymnology as a writer and compiler were important. He was the author of the formerly popular mission hymn, "Wake the song of jubilee," which he included in his *Monthly Concert,* now a rare piece of Americana.

**494—Our fathers' God, to Thee we raise**—Benjamin Copeland (331)

**Theodore**—Peter Christian Lutkin (132)

This hymn, written by Doctor Copeland during his pastorate at the Richmond Avenue Methodist Episcopal Church in Buffalo, New York, at the close of the Spanish-American War, was first published in *Zion's Herald,* November 18, 1903, under the title,

Thanksgiving Day.

Its introduction as a hymn came through its inclusion in *The Methodist Hymnal,* 1905.

The timely reference in the second line of the fourth stanza to "our widening bounds" is significant, for only a short while before Doctor Copeland wrote the hymn, both Porto Rico to the east and the Philippine Islands, far to the west, had come under the American flag.

"Theodore" was written for this hymn by Dean Lutkin for *The Methodist Hymnal* of 1905. Some years ago the author of this Manual received from Dean Lutkin, his friend of many years, a letter referring, among other matters, to his tunes in *The Methodist Hymnal,* 1905, of which he was one of the musical editors. He said:

> My hymn tunes have been very casual productions indeed, and I have never taken the trouble to ever keep them or make any memorandum of when they were composed. As you will see, most of them were written for the M. E. Hymnal. The Hymn Committee had collected about thirty-five new hymns to insert into the collection, and we had these hymns printed and sent to a number of prominent composers, most of whom paid no attention to them. Arthur Foote wrote back that he would rather write an overture than a hymn tune. David Stanley Smith sent us a few tunes, two of which are used. Arne Oldberg and Alfred Wathall contributed one and seven tunes respectively. At the last moment we had quite a number of nymns left for which we had hoped to get original tunes, and in desperation I wrote seventeen tunes, most of which I am not proud of. I think I wrote one tune on the train going to Committee meeting in New York, but I have forgotten which one it was.

. . . . I think you recall the hymn Theodore. The Rev. Benjamin Copeland asked me why I named it Theodore, as he had lost a child by that name shortly before, and when I wrote him it was called Theodore because the tune was supposed to be rather a strenuous character, he was greatly pleased, because he had also named his son, Theodore for the same reason, when Mr. Roosevelt had an official position in New York in the earlier part of his career. Later, a friend of mine was visiting Mr. Roosevelt at Oyster Bay, and told him of the incident, and Mr. Roosevelt sent me a note thanking me for the supposed honor.

**495—O valiant hearts, who to your glory came**—John Stanhope Arkwright

**Langran**—James Langran

Published in *The Supreme Sacrifice and other Poems in Time of War,* 1919, this finest hymn for Armistice Day came through *Songs of Praise,* 1925. Should it be desired to print it on programs to be used in services where hymn books are not available, the greater familiarity of the suggested alternative tune, "Ellers," may give the hymn more extended use than the excellent setting, "Langran."

John Stanhope Arkwright, English barrister, member of Parliament for twelve years from 1900, and Chief Steward of the City of Hereford, was born in London in 1872, and educated at Eton and Christ Church, Oxford. Among his publications are *The Last Muster* and *The Supreme Sacrifice and other Poems in Time of War.*

"Langran," known in England as "St. Agnes," was written by James Langran for the hymn, "Abide with me," and was published first on leaflets in 1861 or 1862. In 1863, called "Evensong," it was included in John Foster's *Psalms and Hymns adapted to the Services of the Church of England.* The successor of this book was *The New Mitre Hymnal,* 1875, so-called from the embossed miter on its cover.

James Langran was born in London, November 10, 1835; studied with J. B. Calkin (502) and Dr. J. F. Bridge; was an able organist in London; and graduated Mus. Bac. from Oxford University at the age of forty-nine years. He wrote music for church use and was the musical editor of *The New Mitre Hymnal,* 1875. He died at London at his residence, June 8, 1909.

**496—God of our fathers, whose almighty hand**—Daniel Crane Roberts

**National Hymn** (482)—George William Warren (482)

This was written for a Fourth of July celebration held in the little town of Brandon, Vermont, in 1876. Its unusual merit caused it to be published in several newspapers about that time, and in 1894 it was included in *The Hymnal* of the Protestant Episcopal Church. It has been selected for use for a number of extraordinary celebrations, among them that in New York City of the Centennial of the adoption of the Constitution of the United States and at the Bicentenary of Trinity Church, New York, where it was used as the processional hymn.

The author told Dr. L. F. Benson (38) that he had written the hymn to be sung to the "Russian Hymn" (505), but when it was included in *The*

*Hymnal* of 1894, the tune "National Hymn" appeared with it, for George W. Warren had composed the new setting especially for the use of this hymn at the Centennial of the Constitution. (See No. 482.)

Daniel Crane Roberts, minister of the Protestant Episcopal Church, was born at Bridgehampton, Long Island, November 5, 1841. Graduating from Kenyon College in 1857, he was ordained in 1866, and for many years was rector of St. Paul's Church, Concord, New Hampshire. He died there October 31, 1907.

**497—God of our fathers, known of old**—Rudyard Kipling (294)
**Melita** (480)—John Bacchus Dykes (1)

This "warning against the pride of imperialism" was written by Rudyard Kipling, England's "uncrowned poet laureate," for Queen Victoria's Diamond Jubilee in 1897. The London *Times* asked Kipling to write a poem suitable for the occasion, and he has said:

> That poem gave me more trouble than anything I ever wrote. When it came due I had nothing that satisfied me. The *Times* began to want the poem badly, and sent letter after letter asking for it. I made many more attempts, but no further progress. Sitting down with all my previous attempts before me, I searched through those dozens of sketches till at last I found just one line I liked. That was "Lest we forget." Round these words "The Recessional" was written.

It was first published in *The Times* of July 17, 1897, and later as "Recessional" in *Five Nations,* 1903. Although a storm of protests arose concerning the allusions in stanzas 2 and 3 to the Jubilee Procession and the previous Naval Review held on June 26, the English people now accept it as one of their great literary productions.

**498—O Lord, our fathers oft have told**—Psalm 44
Tate and Brady (14)
**St. Anne** (384)—Probably by William Croft (169)

The paraphrase of the first eight stanzas of Psalm 44 constitutes Part I of the psalm as published in *A New Version of the Psalms of David Fitted to the Tunes used in the Churches,* 1696. Strictly speaking, this is a much altered version of verses 1, 3, 4, and 8, of the Tate and Brady rendering. The King James version of the first eight verses and the Tate and Brady rendering are given in parallel columns:

| King James Version | Tate and Brady |
|---|---|
| 1 We have heard with our ears, O God, our fathers have told us, what work thou didst in their days, in the times of old. | 1 O Lord our fathers oft have told, in our attentive ears,<br>Thy wonders in their days perform'd, and elder times than theirs: |
| 2 How thou didst drive out the heathen with thy hand, and plantedst them; how thou didst afflict the people, and cast them out. | 2 How thou, to plant them here, didst drive the heathen from this land,<br>Dispeopled by repeated strokes of thy avenging hand. |

| | |
|---|---|
| 3 For they got not the land in possession by their own sword, neither did their own arm save them: but thy right hand, and thine arm, and the light of thy countenance, because thou hadst a favor unto them. | 3 For not their courage, nor their sword,<br>to them possession gave;<br>Nor strength, that, from unequal force,<br>their fainting troops could save;<br>But thy right hand, and pow'rful arm,<br>whose succour they implor'd;<br>Thy presence with the chosen race,<br>who thy great name ador'd. |
| 4 Thou art my King, O God: command deliverances for Jacob. | 4 As thee their God our father's own'd,<br>thou art our sov'reign King;<br>O! therefore, as thou didst to them, to us<br>deliv'rance bring. |
| 5 Through thee will we push down our enemies: through thy name will we tread them under that rise up against us. | 5 Thro' thy victorious name, our arms the<br>proudest foe shall quell;<br>And crush them with repeated strokes, as<br>oft as they rebel. |
| 6 For I will not trust in my bow, neither shall my sword save me. | 6 I'll neither trust my bow nor sword, when<br>I in fight engage: |
| 7 But thou hast saved us from our enemies, and hast put them to shame that hated us. | 7 But thee, who hast our foes subdu'd, and<br>sham'd their spiteful rage. |
| 8 In God we boast all the day long and praise thy name for ever. Selah. | 8 To thee the triumph we ascribe,<br>from whom the conquest came:<br>In God we will rejoice all day,<br>and ever bless his name. |

The five stanzas of the selection as they appear in the *Hymnal* are also given so that all may be compared:

1 O Lord, our fathers oft have told,
In our attentive ears,
Thy wonders in their days performed,
And in more ancient years.

2 'Twas not their courage nor their sword
To them salvation gave;
'Twas not their number nor their strength
That did their country save;

3 But Thy right hand, Thy powerful arm,
Whose succor they implored,
Thy providence protected them
Who Thy great Name adored.

4 As Thee their God our fathers owned,
So Thou art still our King:
O, therefore, as Thou didst to them,
To us deliverance bring!

5 To Thee the glory we ascribe,
From whom salvation came;
In God, our shield, we will rejoice,
And ever bless Thy Name.

When and by whom the alterations were made is not known.

**499—Lord, while for all mankind we pray—John Reynell Wreford**

**Manoah (378)—From Henry Wellington Greatorex's Collection (378)**

This was written by Doctor Wreford about the time of Queen Victoria's accession to the throne of the British Empire in 1837. It was published "with other loyal and patriotic pieces" in *Lays of Loyalty,* and contributed to the Rev. J. R. Beard's *Collection of Hymns for Public and Private Worship* in 1837.

John Reynell Wreford, D.D., was born at Barnstaple, Devonshire, England, December 11, 1800, and was educated for the Unitarian ministry at Manchester College, York. For five years, from 1826, he acted as copastor at the New Meeting, Birmingham, but compelled by the failure of his voice to relinquish this work, he opened a school at Edgbaston. Thereafter he published a number of works, most of which were devotional poetry. He died, July 2, 1881, at Bristol, where he had spent the last years of his life.

**500—See how great a flame aspires**—Charles Wesley (25)

**Culford**—Edward John Hopkins (29)

From *Hymns and Sacred Poems,* 1749, this is the last of four hymns following the heading,

After Preaching to the Newcastle Colliers.

Thomas Jackson, in his *Life of Wesley,* says, "Perhaps the imagery was suggested by the large fires connected with the collieries, which illuminate the whole of that part of the country in the darkest nights." The third stanza of the original four has been omitted. There have been no changes in the text. The last stanza is based on the experience of Elijah on Carmel, as related in 1 Kings 18. 43-45:

> And said to his servant, Go up now, look toward the sea. And he went up, and looked, and said, There is nothing. And he said, Go again seven times. And it came to pass at the seventh time, that he said, Behold, there ariseth a little cloud out of the sea, like a man's hand. And he said, Go up, say unto Ahab, Prepare thy chariot, and get thee down, that the rain stop thee not. And it came to pass in the mean while, that the heaven was black with clouds and wind, and there was a great rain.

"Culford" was set to the hymn, "Songs of praise the angels sang," in *The Temple Church Choral Service,* 1867, of which Dr. E. J. Hopkins, the composer, was the editor. He was organist at Temple Church, London, for fifty-five years.

**501—We've a story to tell to the nations**—"Colin Sterne"

**Message**—Henry Ernest Nichol

This rousing missionary song was written, both words and music, by H. Ernest Nichol in 1896, the year of their publication in *The Sunday School Hymnary* (English). "Colin Sterne" is the *nom de plume* used by the writer in signing those hymns for which he wrote the music.

Henry Ernest Nichol, English poet and musician, was born at Hull, England, December 10, 1862. He was apprenticed to civil engineering in 1877 but abandoned it in 1885 for serious study in music and received his degree of Bachelor of Music from Oxford University in 1888. He has written for Sunday-school festival occasions a number of services which contain one hundred and thirty of his own tunes. His death occurred in 1928.

**502—Fling out the banner! let it float**—George Worthington Doane (47)

**Doane**—John Baptiste Calkin

Bishop Doane wrote this hymn at Riverside, Massachusetts, in December, 1848, and it was first published in *Verses for 1851 in Commemoration of the Third Jubilee of the S. P. G.* It was written upon request for a flag-raising ceremony to be held at St. Mary's School, Burlington, New Jersey, which the Bishop had founded, and which keeps his memory alive by singing his "Softly now the light of day" at its weekly vespers. (See No. 47.) Dr. David R. Breed speaks glowingly of this hymn and tune in his *The History and Use of Hymns and Hymn Tunes,* saying that the missionary spirit surely cannot be subsiding so long as its message is sung in such stirring, triumphant tones.

"Doane," known by a variety of names, was written by J. B. Calkin for a variant of this hymn beginning,

Uplift the banner! Let it float,

for *The Hymnary,* London, 1872, of which Sir Joseph Barnby (31) was the musical editor. The tune lends itself admirably for processional use.

John Baptiste Calkin, F. R. C. O., was born in London, March 16, 1827; studied music under his father, James Calkin; was for a time connected with St. Columba College, Ireland; and served as organist at several London churches. He was a professor at the Guildhall School of Music and a Member of Council, Trinity College. His pupil, James Langran (495), says of this composer of many published works:

> Besides being an accomplished performer he was a composer quite at home in all styles—the part-song, the church service, anthems, organ music, and music for his own particular instrument, all are excellent, and bear the mark of a highly cultured musician.

He died at London, May 15, 1905.

**503—There's a voice in the wilderness crying**—James Lewis Milligan

**Hereford**—Francis Donaldson Heins

This missionary hymn was contributed to *The Hymnary of the United Church of Canada,* 1930, by the Rev. J. Lewis Milligan, who writes that it was written upon the consummation of the union of the Canadian churches. He says:

> There is a second verse which was omitted by the hymnal committee. It runs:
>
> Like the sun in his glory advancing
> On the dark domain of night,
> The face of the Lord appearing
> Shall flood the land with light:
> The East with a song shall greet Him,
> The West take up the strain,
> While the tribes in wonder listen
> In the lands beyond the main.
>
> This is written from memory, but I fancy it is correct.

James Lewis Milligan was born at Liverpool, England, February 1, 1876, and as his Scotch-Irish father and his Welsh mother were Anglicans, he naturally attended Anglican schools, until, at twelve years of age, he went to work. While working in the building trades he was always a student and a contributor to the London papers. He won the Hemans Prize for Lyrical Poetry at the University of Liverpool in the year 1910, when a collection of his verse was published by a London house. He emigrated, in 1911, to Canada, a married man with four children, and became lay pastor on a Methodist circuit in Hastings County, Ontario. About two years later he became editor of the Peterborough *Daily Review,* and shortly joined the editorial staff of the Toronto *Globe.* As editor and publicity director for the Presbyterian Bureau of Literature and Information during the Church Union movement, he had more to do with its success than is generally known. For some years he was publicity director for the Ontario Department of Mines and is now the editorial writer for the Stafford *Beacon-Herald.* His second book of verse, *The Beckoning Skyline,* was published in 1920, and a play, *Judas Iscariot,* in 1930. Mr. Milligan says he now has no time for writing poetry, but, "like Samson, is tied to the grist mill."

"Hereford" was written for this hymn for the Canadian *Hymnary* for the United Church in 1930.

Francis Donaldson Heins, assistant conductor of the Toronto Symphony Orchestra, under Sir Ernest MacMillan (107), was born at Hereford, Herefordshire, England, February 19, 1878. Coming from a musical family, he began the study of violin at the age of four years; entered the Royal Conservatorium at Leipzig at fourteen; and five years later at the time of his graduation, he played a sonata for violin and piano of his own composition. Returning to England, he continued his studies until 1902, when he came to teach at Ottawa, Canada. In that city he numbered among his pupils the Princess Patricia. Organizer of the Ottawa Symphony Orchestra and of instrumental music classes in the public schools of that city, Mr. Heins, in 1927, went to Toronto to join the faculty of the Toronto Conservatory of Music. He is well known in Canada and the States as a composer, teacher, and violinist of note.

**504—Break, day of God, O break—Henry Burton (123)**

**Darwall (171)—John Darwall (171)**

On Christmas Eve, 1900, as Doctor Burton was returning from an engagement to his home at Blundellsands, near Liverpool, England, he wrote the first stanza of this hymn while on the railway bridge,

> Where I lingered on my way home,

and completed it upon his arrival there. It was included in *The Methodist Hymn Book,* London, 1904. The second stanza of the original, omitted here, is:

Break, day of God, O break!
The night has lingered long;
Our hearts with sighing wake,
We weep for sin and wrong:
O Bright and Morning Star, draw near;
O Sun of Righteousness, appear.

**505—God the Omnipotent! King, who ordainest—Henry Fothergill Chorley
John Ellerton (28)**

**Russian Hymn—Alexis Feodorovitch Lvov**

There are so many versions and combinations of versions of this hymn that, without considerable research, it would be impossible to give its exact history. Briefly, its story is this: In 1842, H. F. Chorley wrote a hymn to be sung to "Russian Hymn," which he entitled,

In Time of War,

although at the time England was at peace with all nations. This hymn, in four quatrains, was published in John Hullah's *Part Music* the same year. The first stanza began:

God the all-terrible! King, who ordainest
Great winds Thy clarions, the lightnings Thy sword,

and continued as in *The Methodist Hymnal,* 1905.

On August 28, 1870, just four days before the Battle of Sedan, during the Franco-German War, Canon John Ellerton (28) wrote a hymn of the same length, and following the style of Chorley's, which began:

God the Almighty One, wisely ordaining.

From these two hymns, with various alterations, the selection in the present *Methodist Hymnal* is made. Just when, or by whom, the slight changes have been made has not been definitely ascertained. The cento is comprised of stanzas 1 and 3, Chorley; 2 and 4, Ellerton. This statement is based on information secured from such reliable sources as Julian, Jones, Telford, and others.

Henry Fothergill Chorley, born at Blackleyhurst, Lancashire, England, December 15, 1808, was educated for commercial pursuits at the Royal Institution, Liverpool. Early showing literary tendencies, in which he was encouraged by Mrs. Hemans, he became music critic and reviewer for *The Athenaeum,* London, continuing in that connection for thirty-five years, and publishing some novels and a number of songs. He died at London, February 15, 1872.

"Russian Hymn" was written, in 1833, by Alexis F. Lvov by command of the Emperor Nicholas of Russia. In his memoirs, Lvov has given full particulars concerning the circumstances of its writing:

In 1833 I accompanied the Emperor Nicholas on his journeys to Prussia and Austria. On returning to Russia, I was informed by Count Benkendorff that the sovereign had expressed a regret that we Russians possessed no national hymn; being, moreover, tired of the English tune which had been used as a stop-gap for a very long time, he commissioned me to make an attempt to write a Russian anthem.

This momentous duty seemed likely to prove difficult of accomplishment. In recalling the British anthem, "God Save the King," which is so imposing, the French song, so full of originality, and the Austrian hymn, of which the music is so touching, I felt and fully appreciated the necessity of accomplishing something which would be robust, stately, stirring, national in character, something worthy to reverberate either in a church, through the soldiers' ranks, or amongst a crowd of people, something which would appeal alike to the lettered and the ignorant. This consideration absorbed me, and I was perplexed by the problem of fulfilling all these needs.

One night, on returning to my quarters at a very late hour, I composed and wrote out the tune of the hymn on the spur of the moment. Next day I went to Joukovsky and asked him to suggest some words; but he was by no means musical and had a lot of trouble in adapting them to the minor close of the first cadence. Subsequently I was able to inform Count Benkendorff that the hymn was ready. The Emperor expressed a desire to hear it, and came on November 23, 1833, to the Court Chapel, accompanied by the Empress and the Grand-Duke Michael. I had assembled the whole choir and it was supported by two orchestras.

The sovereign ordered the hymn to be played over several times, and asked to hear it sung without accompaniment, then he had it played by each orchestra in turn and finally with the united body of performers. His Majesty then said to me in French: "It is really superb," and there and then he commanded Count Benkendorff to inform the Minister of War that the hymn was adopted for the army. This measure was officially ratified on December 4, 1833. The first public performance took place on December 11, at the Grand Theatre, Moscow. The Emperor was apparently desirous of submitting my work for the approval of the Moscow public. On December 25, the hymn resounded through the halls of the Winter Palace on the occasion of the blessing of the colours.

The sovereign graciously presented to me a gold snuff-box adorned with diamonds, as a mark of the imperial pleasure, and also ordered that the words "God protect the Czar" should be added to the armorial bearings of the Lvov family.

The "Russian Hymn" was used by Gounod (575) as the theme for a fantasia for piano and orchestra, and by Tschaikowsky in his popular *Overture 1812,* where it is heard in contrast to the "Marseillaise."

Alexis Feodorovitch Lvov (or Lwoff) was born at Reval, Esthonia, June 6, 1799. Under the guidance of his father Feodore Lvov, he prepared himself for a musical career, excelling in his violin playing, and became proficient in his general musicianship. According to the Russian custom of regarding music not so much as a career for a means of livelihood as a serious avocation, young Lvov joined the army, eventually attaining the rank of general. He was recognized as an excellent violinist, a fine quartet player, and a composer, writing a good deal of church music. Berlioz spoke of him as "a composer of rare talent," but this has been discounted as Berlioz was a candidate for the post of director of the Russian Imperial Opera, of which Lvov was then director, and had been invited to Russia to give a series of concerts. Nor is Wagner's estimate of him as "a very insignificant person . . . in spite of the orders hanging from his neck," to be taken any more seriously, for he had had unfortunate business dealings with Lvov. A just estimate is a compromise between these two extremes. There is nothing about this tune that is national in character, nor that has any particular affinity with Russian popular song. All that may honestly be said about it is that it is somewhat better than the average hymn tune. Nevertheless, it has made Lvov known widely and had he not written it, his works would have been shortly forgotten, as, indeed, most of them have been. He died near Kovno, Lithuania, December 16, 1870 or 1871.

**506—Our thought of Thee is glad with hope**—John Greenleaf Whittier (120)

**Beloit** (470)—Carl Gottlieb Reissiger (470)

Unable to attend a reception, honoring Mrs. John A. Logan, at Concord, Massachusetts, in 1890, J. G. Whittier sent this poem, written especially for the occasion, and this accompanying note:

> I cannot be with you on the 14th, owing to the state of my health; but I send you some lines which I hope may not seem inappropriate. I am very truly thy friend.
>
> (signed) John G. Whittier.

The poem was in ten stanzas, of which 1, 2, 8, and 9 have been chosen for this hymn.

Dean Tillett's fine comment on this hymn should be preached from all of the pulpits in Christendom:

> This song by our Quaker poet shows how truly Christianity is conducive to patriotism. But the most perfect patriotism is international as well as national. Songs of patriotism that inculcate virtue and righteousness as the foundation of national greatness should hold an honored and influential place in the literature and life of every Christian nation. The flag of a truly Christian nation stands for peace and not for war, for the reign of Christian ethics and altruism and not for selfishness and greed.

**507—In Christ there is no East or West**—John Oxenham (341)

**St. Peter** (424)—Alexander Robert Reinagle (424)

This hymn, written in 1908, and used in the *Pageant of Darkness and Light,* given extensively in England and the United States for several succeeding years, is from John Oxenham's *Bees in Amber.* It not only expresses the hope for good will among nations but also carries a challenging missionary message.

**508—All people of the earth**—Leonard Beecher McWhood

**Hymn of Nations**—Leonard Beecher McWhood

Of this hymn and tune, Doctor McWhood says he wrote it in 1933 "in an endeavor to provide a hymn that might embody, for all mankind, the spirit of good will and understanding." It was first printed on leaflets and first sung at a Rotary Club meeting at Hanover, New Hampshire, in May, 1933, and one year later was printed in *The Rotarian,* at Detroit, in June, 1934, when it was sung at the great international meeting of representatives of this organization from all over the world, this sentiment being expressed in its introduction:

> It has become clear that we cannot legislate peace into the hearts of men; it is difficult to reason it in; why not sing it in?

Both hymn and tune have their first appearance in any book in *The Methodist Hymnal,* 1935.

Leonard Beecher McWhood, Mus. Doc., Professor of Music at Dartmouth College, New Hampshire, was born at Brooklyn, New York, December 5, 1870. He obtained his early education at Newark, New Jersey, and graduated from Columbia University in 1893, continuing there for five years as a graduate student and Fellow in Psychology under Edward A. MacDowell. He was adjunct professor at Columbia for some years, and also taught at Vassar, at Drew Theological Seminary, and at the National Park Seminary in Washington, and for a time had charge of the music in the Newark High School. In addition to his composition of cantatas, a light opera, and many songs and pieces for instruments, he has been a successful conductor of choruses and orchestras. Since 1918 he has been connected with Dartmouth.

**509—Great God of nations, now to Thee**—Alfred Alexander Woodhull

**Mendon**—German traditional melody
Arranged by Samuel Dyer

This hymn, written in 1828, when the author was only eighteen years of age, was first published in *Psalms and Hymns,* a Presbyterian book, published at Princeton, New Jersey, the following year. It was entitled,

Thanksgiving Hymn,

and began,

God of the passing year, to Thee.

Stanzas 1, 2, 3, and 6, of the original six, make up this selection. Alterations have been made in each stanza.

Alfred Alexander Woodhull, M.D., son of a Presbyterian clergyman, was born at Cranbury, New Jersey, March 25, 1810, graduated first from Princeton, and then, in medicine, from the University of Pennsylvania. He followed his profession in Marietta, Pennsylvania, and in Princeton, where he died at the age of twenty-six, October 5, 1836.

"Mendon" was introduced to American tune books by Samuel Dyer in the *Supplement of Samuel Dyer's Third Edition of Sacred Music,* 1828, where the tune, called "German Air," had one more note in each line and a different last line, from the form now familiar. The omission of the additional note in the fourth edition of the book was accompanied with this notation: "It is believed that the present arrangement is the original form." It is thought Lowell Mason (19) altered the last line when he began using it in his publications and that he gave it its present name.

Samuel Dyer, a native of Wellshire, England, born November 7, 1785, came to America in his twenty-sixth year, and established himself in New York as a choir leader and teacher of sacred music. He remained there only for about a year, moving to Philadelphia for a three years' stay. After a visit to England in 1815 he was induced to settle in Baltimore, where he published his *New Selection of Sacred Music,* first in 1817. His *Philadelphia Collection of Sacred Music,* 1828, second and third editions, contain valuable sketches of composers and much information about Dyer himself. He taught singing schools in the Southeastern states, was a member of the Musical Fund Society of Philadelphia and for a time conductor of the New York Sacred Music Society. He died at Hoboken, New Jersey, July 20, 1835.

**510—Come! Peace of God, and dwell again on earth**—May Rowland (57)

**Pax**—Lily Rendle (57)

Miss Rowland writes that this hymn was "written about 1928, when there was much talk about the peace of the world and a great desire for it amid the unrest of the nations." It was submitted in manuscript to the Commission preparing *The Methodist Hymnal* of 1935 and its inclusion in this book marks its first publication.

"Pax," written by Miss Rendle for Miss Rowland's hymn, "Come! Peace of God," in 1928, is also published for the first time in this last edition of *The Methodist Hymnal.*

**511—O God of love, O King of peace**—Henry Williams Baker (353)

**Theodore** (494)—Peter Christian Lutkin (132)

This is one of the hymns for use in "Times of Trouble" included in the Original Edition of *Hymns Ancient and Modern,* 1861, written by Sir Henry W. Baker, who, with the Rev. Francis H. Murray, was one of the originators of the project to issue that fine collection.

**512—These things shall be: a loftier race**—John Addington Symonds

**Truro** (126)—From T. Williams' Psalmodia Evangelica (126)

These four stanzas come from "A Vista," a long poem included in J. Addington Symonds's *New and Old: A Volume of Verse,* 1880. The author's daughter has said:

> It was probably thrown off hurriedly during some moments of deep longing, a longing for the betterment of the people . . . which his study of Whitman and his own later life among a prosperous and democratic people helped so much to foster.

The hymn was widely used in the World War camps, becoming familiar to thousands of soldiers. At first being used at other than specifically religious services, it came into denominational hymnody through *The Methodist Hymn Book* of 1904, published in London. There has been an unwarranted change of the word "inarmed" to "unarmed" in the second line of the third stanza in some books. "Inarmed," meaning "arm in arm," gives the broader meaning Symonds wished to convey—he wanted men more closely bound together than they might be were they merely "unarmed."

The last stanza, while not so well adapted for singing as those selected for the hymn, is well worth quoting:

> These things—they are no dream—shall be
> For happier men when we are gone:
> Those golden days for them shall dawn
> Transcending aught we gaze upon.

John Addington Symonds, brilliant student at Harrow and Balliol College, Oxford, was born at Bristol, England, October 5, 1840. The threat of tuberculosis to his naturally weak constitution obliged Mr. Symonds to give up his heavy and confining work and to live the greater part of his active life in the healthful Swiss Highlands, at Davos Platz. A scholar of attainment, an author of repute, a gentleman with a wide circle of cultured friends, he lived an abundant life. His greatest contribution in the field of scholarship was his monumental *Renaissance in Italy,* in six volumes. He died at Rome, April 19, 1893.

# THE ETERNAL LIFE

**513—I'll praise my Maker while I've breath**—Isaac Watts (3)
Altered by John Wesley (36)

**Old 113th (Lucerne)**—From a melody in The Strassburg Psalter, 1539
Arranged by Ernest MacMillan (107)

George John Stevenson, 1818-1888, was for some years owner and editor of *The Wesleyan Times,* an English Methodist newspaper. Before and after his newspaper experience he was in the printing and book-selling business in London, and in 1883 published a book, *The Methodist Hymn Book Illustrated with Biography, Incident, and Anecdote,* dealing with *The Methodist Hymn Book* of 1875, which Doctor Julian said was "the most complete account of Methodist hymnody extant." Though, as Doctor Julian says, his knowledge in other fields of the subject was superficial, in that of his own denomination he was a student and an authority, and "In that department he had no equal."

Few hymns have as great interest for Methodists as this one by Isaac Watts, altered by John Wesley. Its first line Wesley himself struggled to repeat with his last breath. All recent accounts of the hymn are dependent upon Mr. Stevenson's authoritative account:

> This memorable composition forms Dr. Watts' version of Psalm cxlvi., published 1719. The original has six verses, the second and third being omitted. The first line John Wesley has altered from "I'll praise my Maker with my breath;" and verse three in the original reads thus—
>
> "The Lord hath eyes to give the blind,
> The Lord supports the sinking mind."
>
> These and other judicious alterations, made by John Wesley, add much to the value of the hymn. The thought of the poet in the third verse seems to be borrowed from Pope's "Messiah"—
>
> —"All ye blind, behold!
> He from thick films shall purge the visual ray,
> And on the sightless eyeballs pour the day."
>
> The venerable founder of Methodism died in great peace. On Monday, 28th February, 1791, he was exceedingly weak, slept much, and spoke but little. On Tuesday morning he sang two verses of a hymn, then, lying still, as if to recover strength, he called for pen and ink, but could not write. Miss Ritchie proposed to write for him, and asked what to say. He replied, "Nothing, but that God is with us." In the forenoon he said, "I will get up." While they were preparing his clothes, he broke out in a manner that astonished all who were about him in singing—
>
> "I'll praise my Maker while I've breath;
> And when my voice is lost in death,
> Praise shall employ my nobler powers;
> My days of praise shall ne'er be past,
> While life, and thought, and being last,
> Or immortality endures."

Having finished the verse, and got him into his chair, they observed him change for death. But he, regardless of his dying body, said with a weak voice, "Lord, Thou givest strength; speak to all our hearts, and let them know that Thou loosest tongues." He then sung one of his brother's doxologies—

"To Father, Son, and Holy Ghost,
Who sweetly all agree."

Here his voice failed. After gasping for breath, he said, "Now we have done all." He was then laid on the bed, from which he rose no more. Later in the day he tried again to speak, and with all his remaining strength said, "The best of all is, God is with us." During the night following, and early on Wednesday morning, 2nd March, he often attempted to repeat Dr. Watts' Psalm cxlvi., but could only get out—

"I'll praise; I'll praise."

His end drew near. His old and faithful friend, Joseph Bradford, now prayed with him; and the last word he was heard to articulate was "Farewell." A few minutes before ten o'clock on Wednesday morning, 2nd March, 1791, while a number of friends were kneeling round his bed, died John Wesley, in his eighty-eighth year.

"Old 113th," or "Lucerne," was a favorite tune with John Wesley. Probably as a boy in Epworth Church, he had learned this tune which was the last he sang in this life, and which he used in all of his tune books. Though it may be traced as far back as *The Strassburg Psalter* of 1539, it was popularized by *The Genevan Psalter* (3). Known in its early days in England as "Patriarch's Tune," it was one of the first of the German chorales to become popular with the English people.

John Calvin, being forced to leave Geneva in 1538, went to Strassburg, another center where the Reformers had gathered, and there began the publication of his songbooks. The first, with the title *Aulcuns Pseaulmes et Cantiques mys en chant, A Strassburg,* was issued in 1539, and became the precursor of the French Huguenot Psalter, the *Genevan,* on which all metrical psalters in every other country, including England and Scotland, were founded. This rare book was believed by nineteenth-century scholars never to have achieved the dignity of print. The announcement of its discovery in the Library of Munich, c. 1875-76, created a sensation among bibliologists. Sir Richard R. Terry, Mus. Doc., F. R. C. O., noted English scholar and authority on the music of Bach, discusses it fully in his *Calvin's First Psalter,* London, 1932.

"Old 113th" was used as the setting for Psalm 36, and differs from the now accepted version at only two points, "not to the disadvantage of the original" (see illustration). It is the only one of the tunes in the Strassburg book to be included in modern hymnals, which is not easily understood when one considers their dignity and virility, as well as their individuality, and the distinction of their melodies.

Originally it was one of the longest of psalm tunes, being in twelve lines, but was shortened to a six-line tune early in the eighteenth century. It was probably in this shortened form that John Wesley sang it; yet so late as 1904

22
Tour le plaisir dung captif deliure.

O toy chascun ie te veulx faire entendre,
Et te monstrer la voye ou tu doibs tendre,
En ayant loueil droict dessus toy plante
Pour tadresser cōme experimente.

Ne ressemblez le cheual & la mulle,
Qui nont en eulx intelligence nulle,
De mors & frain leurs bouches vas domptāt
Que contre toy ne viennēt resistant.

L home endurcy sera dompte de mesmes,
Par maulx sans nōbre & par doleurs extremes.
Mays qui en dieu son espoir asserra,
Enuironne de mercy se verra.
Or prenez doncq en dieu resiouyssance,
Justes esleuz qui aues cognoyssance
De verite, menez ioye or endroict,
Chascun de vous qui auez le cueur droict.

Psalme XXXVI.

EN moy le se cret pen se ment,
Car il se complaist en ses faictz,

23
Du maling par le clairement, Cest q'ua
Tant que haine sur ses mesf faictz Et ius
Dieu il ne pen se, Son parler tend a
ge ment ad uan ce.
decep uoir Il ne cherch' en tendre et
scauoir, N'aussi vng seul bien fai re,
Il pen se mal e stant couche. Sudroict
B iiij

24
che min est de bauche, Sans au mal
se desp plai re.

Sire ez cieulx attaint ta bonte
Et ez nūes ta verite
Tant hault quon les regarde
Ta iustice sembl' ez haultz montz
Tes iugemens es lieux profondz
L hōm' & beste tu garde
Notoir' est ta benignite
Les humains auront seurete
Soubs lumbre de tes aelles
De tes biens se ressaisiront
Et du fleuu' abreuuez seront
De tes delices belles.

Car source de vie en toy as
Et ta clarte lere fuiras
Qui noz yeulx illumine
Poursuys ta bonte vers les tiens

Psalm 36 as it appeared in *The Strassburg Psalter* of 1539.

it was used in its full length in *The Methodist Hymn Book*, London. The tune, as it appeared in early Methodist books, is:

**514—Lead, kindly Light, amid th' encircling gloom**—John Henry Newman

First tune: **Lux Benigna**—John Bacchus Dykes (1)

Second tune: **Sandon**—Charles Henry Purday

No more beautiful hymn, nor one more dignified, has been written in English. For similar imagination and spirit of such exquisite phrases as "with the morn those angel faces smile," "o'er moor and fen, o'er crag and torrent," one must go back to the Elizabethan writers; and in such phrases as "encircling gloom," and "the garish day," there is a certain similarity of mood to Milton's "Il Penseroso." It was the outpouring of John H. Newman's heart in hours of agony. Distressed at the evidences of disruption in his beloved Church of England and chagrined at its supine policy, convinced that he had "a mission" to fulfill, sick in mind as well as body, "he breathed forth the impassioned and pathetic prayer,"

Lead, kindly Light, amid the encircling gloom,
Lead Thou me on.

In Cardinal Newman's *Apologia Pro Vita Sua,* 1864, he not only states, in a restrained but elaborate manner and style, his attitude toward both the English Church and that of Rome, but gives a full account of his circumstances leading up to, and at the time of writing the hymn.

> At this time I was disengaged from College duties, and my health had suffered from the labours involved in the composition of my volume. . . . I was easily persuaded to join Hurrell Froude and his father, who were going to the south of Europe for the health of the former. We set out in December, 1832. . . . The strangeness of foreign life threw me back into myself; I found pleasure in historical sites and beautiful scenes, not in men and manners. . . . Especially when I was left to myself, the thought came upon me that deliverance is wrought, not by the many but by the few, not by bodies but by persons. . . . I began to think I had a mission. . . . When we took leave of Monsignore Wiseman, he had courteously expressed a wish that we might make a second visit to Rome: I said with great gravity, "We have a work to do in England." I went down at once to Sicily, and the presentiment grew stronger. I struck into the middle of the island, and fell ill of a fever at Leonforte. My servant thought that I was dying, and begged for my last directions. I gave them, as he wished; but I said "I shall not die." I repeated, "I shall not die, for I have not sinned against light, I have not sinned against light." I never have been able to make out at all what I meant. I got to Castro-Giovanni, and was laid up there for nearly three weeks. Towards the end of May I set off for Palermo, taking three days for the journey. Before starting from my inn in the morning of May 26th or 27th, I sat down on my bed and began to sob bitterly. My servant, who acted as my nurse; asked what ailed me. I could only answer, "I have a work to do in England." I was aching to get home; yet for want of a vessel I was kept at Palermo for three weeks. I began to visit the Churches, and they calmed my impatience, though I did not attend any services. I knew nothing of the Presence of the Blessed Sacrament then. At last I got off in an orange boat bound for Marseilles. We were becalmed a whole week in the Straits of Bonifacio. Then it was that I wrote the lines "Lead, kindly light" [June 16, 1833], which have since become well known.

The poem was first printed in the *British Magazine,* March, 1834, with a motto: "Faith-Heavenly Leadings." In subsequent early printings other mottoes were used, probably a reflection of the various meanings the author attached to it at different periods of his life. Thus, when he contributed it to *Lyra Apostolica,* 1836, a book containing his poems as well as some from Keble (35) and others, the motto read: "Unto the godly there ariseth up light in the darkness." Later, in his *Occasional Verses,* 1868, it was: "The Pillar of the Cloud."

There has been much discussion and speculation over the meaning of the last two lines, as well as a few feeble attempts to alter some of the other lines of the hymn; for example, Bishop Bickersteth (354) thought he might improve it by adding a stanza. Nevertheless the hymn has been accepted just as Newman wrote it, and is now found in almost every church hymnal. There are those who have objected to it as being too personal for use in public worship, but if all such intimate and personal hymns were omitted from our hymnody, it would lead to a "needless impoverishment of our spiritual life."

Realizing its purely personal nature, this outburst of tense emotion, Cardinal Newman himself said the words of this poem are

> Not a hymn, nor are they suitable for singing; and it is that which at once surprises and gratifies me, and makes me thankful that, in spite of their having no claim to be a hymn, they have made their way into so many collections.

Captain John Lauder tells, in *A Minstrel in France,* how he was able to comply with the request of a badly wounded soldier who had said, an hour before his death, that he would like to hear "Lead, kindly Light," adding that he was very glad he had learned that hymn in Sunday school as a boy. Could it but be realized that in hours of real need, wholesome hymns and not light songs are those which help, would not more care be used in the selections chosen to be sung in our Sunday schools?

This hymn was a great favorite of the martyred President, William McKinley, and was the first hymn sung at his funeral. On the first anniversary of his death it was sung at memorial services in countless churches throughout the land.

John Henry Newman, D.D., was born in London, February 21, 1801, the son of a banker with strong religious convictions, who carefully trained his boy in the truths of the Word of God. A brilliant student at Trinity College, Oxford, he earned a Fellowship at Oriel and was vice-president at St. Alban's Hall. For fifteen years, from 1828, he was vicar of the University Church, St. Mary the Virgin, and his preaching there had a profound effect upon Oxford. A leader in the Oxford Movement, it has been said that as John Keble sang it, John Henry Newman preached it. The Church of England was in sore need of a revival of religion, yet, while Newman and others set their minds to bringing it about, they turned "resolutely to the past," and Newman, especially, dreamed of a revival of the "mystical glories of the Middle Ages." Disappointed in the apathy of the church leaders, he turned to Roman Catholicism as the best means of accomplishing the reforms he deemed necessary. For years after his reception into the Roman Church, in 1845, he lived a lonely, disappointed life, and it was not until 1879, when he was made a Cardinal, that he became "quietly happy." He died August 11, 1890, at Edgbaston, Birmingham, where, at the Oratory of St. Neri, he had lived so long, "a great Englishman, and a great saint."

"Lux Benigna" first appeared in a book of *Psalms and Hymns for the Church, School and Home,* London, 1867, edited by the Rev. D. T. Barry, and was called "St. Oswald." In the next year, however, with some slight changes (among them the change of key from G to A flat), it was published in the Appendix to *Hymns Ancient and Modern.*

Doctor Dykes's biographer, J. T. Fowler, has this to say concerning "Lux Benigna":

> August 29th: (1865) Leeds.—Began writing out a tune for 'Lead, kindly light.'
>
> On the subject of this tune, "Lux Benigna," which was wedded to Cardinal Newman's beautiful words, Dr. Dykes' cousin (the Rev. George Huntington, Rector of Tenby) gives the following details:—I had been paying Cardinal Newman a visit. . . . I happened to mention his well known Hymn 'Lead, kindly light,'—which he said he wrote when a very young man, as he was becalmed on the Mediterranean, for a week, in 1832. I ventured to say, "It must be a great pleasure to you to know that you have written a Hymn treasured wherever English-speaking Christians are to be found; and where are they not to be found?" He was silent for some moments and then said with emotion, "Yes, deeply thankful, and more than thankful," then, after another pause, "But you see it is not the Hymn, but the Tune that has gained the popularity! The tune is Dykes', and Dr. Dykes was a great Master." Dr. Dykes' friends remember his telling them that the *tune* to "Lead, kindly light" came into his head while walking through the Strand in London. This is not unlikely, as he had been in London, and, while there, to St. Paul's, before his visit to Leeds—when he notes in his Diary that he was writing the tune. Thus the hymn, inspired while the poet was becalmed on the still water of the Mediterranean Sea, became wedded to the melody rising from the heart of the musician, as he walked through the noisy, crowded thoroughfare of the great city.

"Sandon" first appeared in *The Church and Home Metrical Psalter,* 1860, edited by the composer of this tune, C. H. Purday. It was written especially for these words and, being somewhat simpler in form than "Lux Benigna," is looked upon with favor as a desirable alternative tune.

Charles Henry Purday, born at Folkestone, England, January 11, 1799, was a publisher of music; a lecturer on musical subjects. Favorably known as a composer and writer, he was one time a vocalist of repute, being precentor at the Church of Scotland in Crown Court, Drury Lane, London. In the "Introduction" to one of his books he gives some excellent advice about congregational singing.

> The Editor is of opinion that if every church were to be supplied with its tune-book in sufficient numbers for each individual of the congregation to have one, many more persons would join in singing the praises of the Great Redeemer of the World; and there would be a greater amount of solemn and dignified praise uttered than is now generally found in our places of worship. And it is further suggested that, if every family would take the pains to have their children taught to sing at sight, and use their tune-books at home, we should have no lack of good congregational singing in the church; and less complaint when the precentor, choir, or organist introduces new tunes. Singing should be made a necessary part of the education of all classes, that everybody might be enabled to join in choral music, sacred and secular; and until such is really the case, we shall never have good congregational singing in our churches.

He died at London, April 23, 1885.

**515—One sweetly solemn thought—Phoebe Cary**

**Dolce Domum**—Robert Steele Ambrose

This poem, called "Nearer Home," was written directly upon Miss Cary's return from church on a Sunday in 1852, without the author's slightest anticipation that it would ever become a hymn. It was the first selection in the author's *Religious Poems and Hymns.* It has been badly mutilated in order to make it fit the arrangement of the tune with which it has been associated in this edition of *The Methodist Hymnal.*

Phoebe Cary, younger sister of Alice, and equally gifted as a poet, was born near Cincinnati, Ohio, September 4, 1824. The sisters, utterly devoted to each other throughout their lives, began writing poetry at a very early age, and two years after the publication of their first volume of *Poems* in 1850, moved to New York, where their courage and mutual affection drew to them many friends and attracted widespread attention. Her death, hastened by the loss of her sister six months before, occurred on July 31, 1871, while she was on a visit to Newport, Rhode Island.

"Dulce Domum" is no more than a corruption of a popular anthem by R. S. Ambrose.

Robert Steele Ambrose was born at Chelmsford, Essex, England, March 7, 1824. He came to Canada with his parents in his first year and later prepared himself for the profession of music, being successively organist at St. George's Church, Guelph, St. George's Cathedral, Kingston, and of the Church of the Ascension, Hamilton, Ontario, as well as musical director at Hamilton Ladies' College. Although he composed in various forms, he was best known for his sacred songs, particularly "One sweetly solemn thought," which he later republished as an anthem. Mr. Ambrose died at Hamilton, March 31, 1908.

**516—Lord, it belongs not to my care—Richard Baxter**

**St. Agnes** (341)—John Bacchus Dykes (1)

This hymn comes from Richard Baxter's *Poetical Fragments,* 1681, and was therein entitled,

> Heart Employment with God and itself:
> The Concordant Discord of a Broken-
> hearted Heart,

and was dated,

> London, at the Door of Eternity: Richard Baxter,
> Aug. 7, 1681.

In a later edition of the book, 1689, it has the title,

> The Covenant and Confidence of Faith,

and the author has added this note:

> This covenant, my dear wife, in her former
> sickness, subscribed with a cheerful will.

It had been sung to her during her last illness.

The hymn was originally in eight double quatrains, and was based on Philippians 1. 21, "For me to live is Christ, and to die is gain."

The changes have been but few, the most important being line 4, stanza 2, which originally was written,

> That shall have the same pay.

This hymn was a great favorite of James Clerk Maxwell, Professor of Experimental Physics at Cambridge, discoverer of the electro-magnetic character of light. He frequently repeated it during his last illness in 1879. It was Maxwell who said:

> I think men of science as well as other men need to learn from Christ, and I think Christians whose minds are scientific are bound to study science that their view of the glory of God may be as extensive as their being is capable of.

Richard Baxter, best known for having written *The Saints' Everlasting Rest,* was born at Rowton, Shropshire, England, November 12, 1615, and took Orders in the Church of England, although his formal education, obtained at Wroxeter School, was but meager. Remarkable, in the light of his large literary output of more than two hundred and fifty publications, is the fact that he never attended a university. While nominally a Presbyterian, he was never more than a moderate Non-conformist. He is usually remembered in connection with his long and remarkable service as curate of Kidderminster, but he was for a time a chaplain in Cromwell's army, and refused the bishopric of Hereford offered to him by Charles II. He was a man without fear, suffering for what he believed to be right, and not hesitating to rebuke Cromwell for his assumption of supreme power in the state, the while defending the old monarchy. When he was being tried before Chief Justice George Jeffreys in 1685 on the ridiculous charge of libeling the Church in his *Paraphrase on the New Testament,* he replied to Jeffreys's taunt, "Richard, I see the rogue in thy face," with, "I had not known before that my face was a mirror." As a result of this trial, one of the most infamous in the whole history of English court procedure, he was sentenced to lie in prison until a fine of five hundred marks was paid. After eighteen months the government, hoping to win him to its side, released him from prison and remitted the fine. Although he had been warned not to preach, he would not be restrained.

Always in a weakened physical condition, he was so feeble at the time he was writing his *Everlasting Saints' Rest,* 1650, that it was necessary for two men to support him when he was in his pulpit. He said:

> Weakness and pain helped me to study how to die; that set me on studying how to live, and that on studying the doctrine from which I must fetch my motives and comforts; beginning with necessities, I proceeded by degrees, and am now going to see that for which I have lived and studied.

Although one of the most devoted of the Puritan clergy, who, as is well known, disapproved of music, he was nevertheless always its champion:

> I have made a psalm of praise in the holy assembly the chief delightful exercise of my religion and my life, and have helped to bear down all the objections which I have heard against Church music.

He died at London, December 8, 1691, his last years being filled with peace and honor. His funeral was largely attended by churchmen and dissenters alike, and two centuries later a monument was erected in his honor at Kidderminster, where his influence for good was still felt.

**517—I know not what the future hath—John Greenleaf Whittier (120)**
**Cooling (174)—Alonzo Judson Abbey (174)**

This cento is from John G. Whittier's poem of twenty-two four-line stanzas entitled:

The Eternal Goodness,

written in 1865 and included in *The Tent on the Beach, and Other Poems,* 1867. The stanzas have been rearranged as to order, being 16, 17, 22, 19, and 20. Various other selections of stanzas from this poem have been made for use as hymns, most of them beginning with the line, "I bow my forehead in the dust," or "Who fathoms the eternal thought?" The poem begins:

> O friends, with whom my feet have trod
> The quiet aisles of prayer,
> Glad witness to your zeal for God
> And love of man I bear.

John Bright has spoken of this fine meditation on trust on God as a

> poem which is worth a crowd of sermons which are spoken from the pulpits of our sects and churches, which I do not wish to undervalue. It is a great gift to mankind when a poet is raised up among us who devotes his great powers to the sublime purpose of spreading among men principles of mercy, and justice, and freedom.

Were John Bright writing in the turbulent times of the first half of the twentieth century, he might well have expressed a yearning for all men to believe that

> . . . in the maddening maze of things
> And tossed by storm and flood,
> To one fixed trust my spirit clings;
> I know that God is good.

**518—Servant of God, well done!—Charles Wesley (25)**
**Mornington (25)—Arranged from a chant by Garret Wellesley (25)**

John Wesley preached the funeral sermon of George Whitefield, November 18, 1770, at the Tabernacle, Tottenham Court Road, London, and repeated it at Moorfields the same day. This hymn, which has never been included in British Wesleyan publications, was printed at the close of this sermon. It was not included in *The Primitive Methodist Hymnal* until 1889, but forty years previously had appeared in *Hymns for the use of the Methodist Episcopal Church* in the United States. Just one half of the original hymn, unchanged, was selected for the present *Methodist Hymnal.*

**519—When on my day of life the night is falling—John Greenleaf Whittier (120)**
**Journey's End—William Ketcham Anderson**

Written in 1882, ten years before Whittier's death, this rarely beautiful poem bore the title,

At Last.

It was included in his volume of poems, *The Bay of Seven Islands,* 1883. In the complete edition of Whittier's *Poetical Works* is this note:

> Recited by one of the little group of relations who stood by the poet's bedside as the last moment of his life approached.

The second stanza of the poem, which has been omitted, is:

> Be near me when all else is from me drifting;
> Earth, sky, homes, pictures, days of shade and shine,
> And kindly faces to my own uplifting
> The love which answers mine.

One of Phoebe Cary's (515) last poems was "John G. Whittier." The first and last stanzas are:

> Great master of the poet's art!
> Surely the sources of thy powers
> Lie in that true and tender heart
> Whose every utterance touches ours.
> . . . . . . . .
> But not thy strains, with courage rife,
> Nor holiest hymns, shall rank above
> The rhythmic beauty of thy life,
> Itself a canticle of love.

"Journey's End" was composed in 1930, and in a very real sense grew out of the serious illness of Mrs. Fanny Spencer Anderson, wife of the composer, William K. Anderson. The shock following a major operation had caused the attending physicians to give up hope of saving her life. During the days of her illness the words of Whittier's beautiful poem were constantly running through the consciousness of her husband, and perhaps, he has said,

> the tune might have been gradually taking form at the same time. After the danger had passed, with these words still running through my mind, I sat down at the piano and the tune was born, substantially as it is, with the exception of the last three measures.

It is first printed in *The Methodist Hymnal,* 1935.

William Ketcham Anderson, D.D., son of Bishop William F. Anderson, was born April 27, 1888, in a Methodist parsonage in what is now the Bronx Borough, New York City. He was educated at Holbrook's Military Academy, Wesleyan University, Union Theological Seminary, and Columbia University. Admitted on trial to the North-East Ohio Conference in 1912, he transferred to the Ohio Conference in 1915, and to the Pittsburgh Conference in 1920. He is now pastor of the Franklin Street Methodist Episcopal Church, Johnstown, Pennsylvania.

Doctor Anderson says he began his "composing activities" in 1924, when he entered one of his tunes in the Hymn Society's contest for a setting for Doctor Farrington's "I know not how that Bethlehem's Babe" (112). He wishes now he had paid more attention to the music lessons he began taking while a boy in New York City.

**520—Abide with me: fast falls the eventide**—Henry Francis Lyte (77)
**Eventide**—William Henry Monk

When in early September, 1847, Henry F. Lyte was ordered to leave his home in Brixham, England, for southern France, because of his failing health, his family became alarmed over his announcement that before his departure he would hold a communion service. He preached on the morning of September 4, assisting at the sacrament afterward. In giving the history of this hymn, the author's daughter, Mrs. Anna Marie Maxwell Hogg, continues:

> Though necessarily much exhausted by the exertion and excitement of this effort, yet his friends had no reason to believe it had been hurtful to him. In the evening of the same day he placed in the hands of a near and dear relative the little hymn "Abide with me," with an air of his own composing, adapted to the words.

Tradition has it that he had walked down the path through his garden to the seashore, and had then returned to his study, where he seems to have composed the hymn.

In *The Spectator,* London, October 3, 1925, the Rev. H. T. Bindley has an article which gives another account of the writing of these famous lines, which does not conflict, essentially, with Mrs. Hogg's record. He says they were written in 1820, when Lyte, then a young clergyman, was visiting with friends at Wrexham.

> He went to see an old friend, William Augustus Le Hunte, who lay dying, and who kept repeating the phrase "abide with me." After leaving the bedside Lyte wrote the hymn and gave a copy of it to Sir Francis Le Hunte, William's brother, amongst whose papers it remained when they passed to his nephew, the Rev. Francis Le Hunte. No doubt, when Lyte felt his own end approaching, his mind reverted to the lines he had written so many years before, and then it was that they became first popularly known. These details were given to me some years ago by Sir George Ruthven Le Hunte, grandson of William Augustus, and I have recently had them confirmed by members of his family.

Whatever the facts of its writing, it is not an evening hymn as it has been classed so often, probably because of its first two lines. Canon Ellerton (28), in the folio edition, 1881, of his *Church Hymns,* says, in a note:

> This is a curious instance of the misapprehension of the true meaning of a hymn by those among whom it is popular; for a very little consideration will suffice to shew that there is not throughout the hymn the slightest allusion to the close of the natural day: the words of St. Luke xxiv. 29 are obviously used in a sense wholly metaphorical. It is far better adapted to be sung at funerals; . . . but it is almost too intense and personal for ordinary congregational use.

The hymn was first printed on a leaflet with the author's music in September, 1847, and appeared in 1850 in his *Remains,* by his daughter, and in *Miscellaneous Poems,* 1868, with slight variations in text. Originally in eight stanzas, the first two and the last three are usually selected for inclusion in hymnals.

No words could be more appropriate and comforting than these for use on funeral occasions. Shortly before his death, Adoniram J. Gordon (234), gifted Baptist leader, called his wife to his side and said: "If anything should happen, do not have a quartet choir. I have selected four hymns I want sung by the people." The first hymn on his list was "Abide with me."

It was this hymn that John Callahan, long Superintendent of the Hadley Mission on New York's Bowery and known as "the Bishop of the Bowery," heard sung in a mission, years after having heard it at his mother's funeral, that brought him to his senses and made him realize he "was not traveling the right road."

No hymns were sung at the funeral service of the late President William Howard Taft, but the bells of All Soul's Church in Washington pealed forth the melody of the familiar tune, recalling to all present the words,

> Abide with me: fast falls the eventide.

"Eventide" was written for this hymn by Dr. William H. Monk for the Original Edition of *Hymns Ancient and Modern,* 1861. J. T. Lightwood in *The Music of the Methodist Hymn-Book,* 1935, says Doctor Monk's widow gave this statement in answer to an inquiry concerning it:

> The tune was written at a time of great sorrow—when together we watched, as we did daily, the glories of the setting sun. As the last golden ray faded he took up some paper and pencilled that tune, which has gone all over the world.

James Love in *Scottish Church Music,* 1891, comments:

> "Eventide," says Dr. Monk, was written for the hymn to which it is set, immediately before "Hymns Ancient and Modern" was published, no other having been found suitable. As he sat writing it, one of his assistants was within two yards of him playing a Thalberg *Fantasia.*

The Historical Edition of *Hymns Ancient and Modern,* 1909, gives an account of both stories but makes no comment.

William Henry Monk, Mus. Doc., who wrote but one musical setting for secular words, was born in London, March 16, 1823, and is remembered not only for his very great influence on English Hymnody, but for his great work as musical editor of the first edition of *Hymns Ancient and Modern* to have musical settings for its hymns. He suggested its title and "he had the sole musical initiative and veto on the original edition, and no other musical counsel was called in until the position of the book had been made." He continued as musical editor for the various editions which followed in 1868, 1875, and 1889. On the day before his death on March 1, 1889, he sent the final proofs of the complete edition of *Hymns Ancient and Modern* to the publishers with word that although he had completed the work, he did not expect to live to see the printed book. His influence on the book was so marked that for a time after its first publication it was known as "Monk's Book."

Doctor Monk's early love for church music attracted him to the concerts of the Sacred Harmonic Society, where the foundation was laid for his work that was to develop with increasing forcefulness through the years. He held various appointments as organist in London churches, but is best known in that connection for his work at St. Matthias, Stoke Newington, where he was able to maintain a daily choral service with only a volunteer choir.

His interest in the changes in music required by the Oxford Movement was such that with others he founded *The Parish Choir* (see No. 81), a musical journal which became the organ of the movement. He personally edited it after its fortieth number, until its discontinuance in 1853. Congregational worship music was Doctor Monk's greatest interest, and he directed all of his talents to its development and betterment.

**521—It singeth low in every heart—**John White Chadwick

**Auld Lang Syne—**Scottish melody

Doctor Chadwick wrote this hymn, which he gave the title,

In Memoriam,

in 1876, for the twenty-fifth anniversary of the dedication of the Second Unitarian Church, of Brooklyn, New York, where he had been ministering since 1864. It is finding a place in an increasing number of hymnals in America, and its merit so appealed to W. Garrett Horder that he included it in his *Worship Song,* London, 1905.

John White Chadwick was born at Marblehead, Massachusetts, October 19, 1840; graduated from Cambridge Divinity School in July, 1864; and was ordained minister of the Second Unitarian Church, Brooklyn, in December of that same year. He was a frequent contributor to *Harper's Magazine, The Christian Examiner,* and other periodicals, all of which published poems by him. His hymn, "Eternal Ruler of the ceaseless round," written for the commencement exercises of the Cambridge Divinity School at the time of his graduation, is of superior merit. He died December 11, 1904.

"Auld Lang Syne" is said by S. A. FitzGerald in his *Stories of Famous Songs,* 1898, to have been composed by William Shield as a melody in the overture to his opera *Rosina.* Alfred Moffatt, the editor of *The Minstrelsey of Scotland,* disputes Shield's claim to having written this classic, but his case does not seem founded on sufficient evidence to be taken seriously. In the overture mentioned, the melody now known as "Auld Lang Syne" from its association with the ballad of an unknown writer, was given to the oboe with a drone bass by the bassoon in imitation of the Scottish bagpipe. Shield's opera, *Rosina,* was first produced on New Year's Eve, 1782, but it was twenty years before this tune became associated with "Auld Lang Syne."

The Editor of *The Methodist Hymnal* was commissioned in the summer of 1933 to find a fitting tune for Doctor Chadwick's memorial hymn. For many weeks he sought for a tune which might be satisfactory. Although the melody of "Auld Lang Syne" kept recurring to him, at the time he did not know Doctor Chadwick had written his hymn with the Scottish melody in mind, nor that the two had been used together at the anniversary service for which the hymn had been written. Knowing the prejudice against the use of secular melodies as hymn settings held by some of the members of the Commission, he hesitated to recommend it. Finally, in despair of finding any other setting that would be more fitting, he suggested this tune, which was enthusiastically received by the majority of the Commission members. The tune is so generally known and loved that it would seem more fitting to call it "Universal melody" than "Scottish melody."

William Shield, composer of English operas, was born at London, March 5, 1748, the son of a singing master. Being not greatly infatuated with his music lessons, which started when he was but six years old, his father apprenticed him to a shipbuilder. During the time of his apprenticeship he was able to take some lessons in elementary composition and to learn something about playing the violin, so that when he was free to do so, he had not much difficulty in making his way by means of music. For a time he played second violin in the opera orchestra of Giardini (2). After having written a successful opera, he was engaged as composer for Covent Garden, where he remained, with the exception of about one year, until 1797. He gave up all connection with the theater in 1807 and was appointed Master of the King's Musick in 1817. He died at his home in Bemers Street, London, January 25, 1829, and was buried in Westminster Abbey.

**522—How happy every child of grace—Charles Wesley (25)**

**Alida**—Early American melody
D. B. Thompson (?)

The second series of *Funeral Hymns,* London, 1759, contains this hymn without title. The first two of the original eight stanzas are all that are found in *The Methodist Hymnal.* Two changes have been made: line 6, stanza 1, was written, "Yet O, by faith," not, "Which yet by faith"; and the last line of the second stanza has been completely changed.

Our earthen vessels filled,

has been replaced by,

His life in us revealed.

Comment has been made on John Wesley's reference to this hymn at No. 422.

"Alida," said to have been written by one unknown D. B. Thompson, was a popular melody at the religious gatherings along the Middle Western frontier even before the Civil War. The manner in which it came to be included in the *Hymnal* as a setting for this happy funeral hymn may be of interest.

The tune "Materna," to which this hymn was set in the 1905 edition of *The Methodist Hymnal,* was so unsatisfactory in every way that there was a general demand for another setting. In this case, as in many others, the Editor was asked to find a suitable one. An old tune which he remembered from hearing his mother sing while he was a child kept coming to him and crowded out all others that he had tried. He wrote it out from memory and submitted it, not being able at first to give any other source for it. After it had been adopted, the Editor discovered this tune set to this hymn in the *Methodist Collection of Hymns and Tunes,* published by Carlton and Porter in 1857. Here it was said to have been taken from *The New Lute of Zion,* compiled by Isaac B. Woodbury (137) in 1856. This book, "A Collection of Sacred Music designed for the use of congregations generally, but more especially the Methodist Episcopal Church," credited the tune to *The Devotional Harmonist,* Charles Dingley, 1853. It was also discovered to have been used in the last

*Methodist Protestant Church Hymnal.* The hymn had been set to "Devizes" in the 1878 *Hymnal of the Methodist Episcopal Church,* a sorry enough tune, but in the 1889 *Hymn and Tune Book of the Methodist Episcopal Church, South,* it was given to a very lugubrious one, in A minor, called "Solemnity"! Neither was a very happy choice, and it is no wonder that there was little interest shown in singing the hymn. "Materna," which was used in the 1905 *Hymnal,* was little better, although it did have somewhat more life. It is hoped that with the restoration of this fine old camp-meeting tune the hymn will again come into general use.

**523—On Jordan's stormy banks I stand**—Samuel Stennett (220)

**Varina** (528)—George Frederick Root (439)

This hymn, long famous among Methodists, has appeared in each *Hymnal* since Bishop Asbury used it in his *Supplement to The Pocket Hymn Book,* ordered by the General Conference of 1808. Eight lines of the original thirty-two have been omitted, thereby greatly improving the hymn:

> There gen'rous fruit that never fails,
> On trees immortal grow:
> There rocks, and hills, and brooks, and vales,
> With milk and honey flow.
>
> There, on those high and flow'ry plains,
> Our spirits ne'er shall tire;
> But in perpetual, joyful strains,
> Redeeming love admire.

The last four lines of stanza 3 were written:

> Fill'd with delight, my raptur'd soul
> Would here no longer stay!
> Though Jordan's waves around me roll,
> Fearless I'd launch away.

This hymn, contributed to *Rippon's Selection,* 1787, may have been patterned after Doctor Watts's "There is a land of pure delight" (528). Compare the last half of stanza 1 of this hymn with the first part of stanza 2 of the older one.

**524—Rise, my soul, and stretch thy wings**—Robert Seagrave

**Amsterdam**—From The Foundery Collection

This hymn, entitled,

> The Pilgrim's Song.

first appeared in *Hymns for Christian Worship, Partly Composed and Partly Collected from Various Authors,* issued by its author, Robert Seagrave, in 1742.

Robert Seagrave, born November 22, 1693, at Twyford, Leicestershire, England, was educated at Clare College, Cambridge, graduating in 1714. Soon after he took Holy Orders he almost immediately became greatly interested in the work of the Wesleys and Whitefield, and for fifteen years wrote a series of pamphlets designed to stimulate the clergy and to arouse in them a deeper interest in their work. At some time during his eleven years of preaching at Lormer's Hall, London, he issued his *Hymns for Christian Worship,* to which he contributed fifty hymns of his own writing. He also preached occasionally at Whitefield's Tabernacle. He is thought to have died about 1759, but the exact year is unknown.

"Amsterdam," from *The Foundery Tune Book,* 1742, was one of the German chorales with which John Wesley grew familiar through his association with the Moravian Brethren. Its source, however, is not known.

**525—I will sing you a song—Ellen Huntington Gates**

**Home of the Soul—Philip Phillips**

Philip Phillips has written that he sent the following from Bunyan's *Pilgrim's Progress* to Mrs. Gates, with the request that she use it as the basis for "a suitable hymn":

> Now I saw in my dream that these two men [Christian and Hopeful] went in at the gate; and lo, as they entered, they were transfigured; and they had raiment put on them that shone like gold. There were also those that met them with harps and crowns and gave them to them; the harps to praise withal, and the crowns in token of honor. Then I heard in my dream that all the bells in the city rang again for joy, and that it was said unto them: "Enter ye into the joy of your Lord!" . . . Now, just as the gates were opened to let in the men, I looked in after them, and behold, the city shone like the sun; the streets also were paved with gold; and in them walked many men, with crowns on their heads and palms in their hands, and golden harps to sing praises withal. . . . After that, they shut up the gates which, when I had seen, I wished myself among them.

He continues:

> When the verses were forwarded to me, in 1865, I seated myself in my home with my little boy on my knee, and with Bunyan's immortal dream-book in my hand, and began to read the closing scenes where Christian and Hopeful entered into the city,—wondering at Bunyan's rare genius, and like the dreamer of old wishing myself among them. At this moment of inspiration I turned to my organ, with pencil in hand, and wrote the tune. This hymn seems to have had God's special blessing upon it from the very beginning. One man writes me that he has led in the singing of it at a hundred and twenty funerals. It was sung at the funeral of my own dear boy, who had sat on my knee when I wrote the tune.

Ellen Gates, née Huntington, youngest sister of Collis P. Huntington, was born at Torrington, Connecticut, 1835, and made her home for many years in New York City. She was quite well known as a writer of gospel song texts, especially "If you cannot on the ocean," sometimes said to have been President Lincoln's favorite hymn. She also contributed many poems to *Harper's Magazine*. Her death occurred at New York City, October 23, 1920.

Philip Phillips, known as the "Singing Pilgrim," was born on a farm in Chautauqua County, New York, August 13, 1834; sang first in public when only five years old; attended his first singing school and joined the village choir at sixteen; and began teaching music at singing schools of his own at nineteen. Only a little studying and teaching was possible, however, in the few leisure hours left him from an apprenticeship to a farmer and cheese-maker. Upon the arrival of his twenty-first birthday he began peddling songs of his own writing through the countryside, stopping at the farmhouses, playing on his melodeon, and singing his wares. Following this occupation in the summer months and holding singing schools during the winter, he was enabled to save enough money to make a start in the music business in Fredonia, New York. Successful in other and larger business enterprises, a publisher of gospel song books, this evangelistic singer literally sang his way around the world, and gave some thirty-two hundred "song services."

Bishop J. H. Vincent paid this fine tribute to Mr. Phillips:

> No one claims perfection for Mr. Phillips; but from a personal knowledge of him for nearly twenty years, from intimate association with him in Sunday-school and church work, from long weeks of travel in his company on both sides of the continent, I am glad to be able to pay this willing tribute to his genuineness as a man, his earnestness, fidelity, and conscientiousness as a Christian, his simplicity and effectiveness as a singer for the cause of humanity and Christ.

Philip Phillips died at Delaware, Ohio, June 25, 1895.

**526—Now the laborer's task is o'er**—John Ellerton (28)

**Requiescat**—John Bacchus Dykes (1)

John Ellerton's biographer says of this hymn:

> It has been sung, and will continue to be sung, at the grave-side of princes, divines, statesmen, poets, artists, authors, as well as of many a Christian laborer in human life.

It was written for the Society for the Promotion of Christian Knowledge and was published in their *Church Hymns,* London, 1871. Canon Ellerton says of it:

> The whole hymn . . . owes many thoughts, and some expressions, to a beautiful poem of the Rev. Gerald Moultrie's, beginning, 'Brother, now thy toils are o'er.'

"Requiescat" was written for this hymn by Doctor Dykes for the Revised Version of *Hymns Ancient and Modern,* 1875.

**527—For all the saints who from their labors rest**—William Walsham How (197)

First tune: **Sarum**—Joseph Barnby (31)

Second tune: **Sine Nomine**—Ralph Vaughan Williams

This was first published in *Hymns for Saints' Days, and other Hymns by a Layman,* issued in 1864 by Earl Nelson, nephew of the celebrated Admiral Nelson. Found generally in the best collections of English hymns, this popular hymn of Bishop How originally began,

> For all Thy saints,

but was changed to "the saints," by the author himself.

"Sarum," called originally "St. Philip," and in some contemporary hymnals "For all the Saints," was written for Bishop How's hymn by Sir Joseph Barnby and was first published in *The Sarum Hymnal,* compiled by Earl Nelson (see above), who had as his musical editor Theodore E. Aylward, 1844-1933, long an eminent musician in Cardiff, Wales.

"Sine Nomine" was especially written for this hymn for *The English Hymnal,* 1906, by Dr. Vaughan Williams. There it was hailed with delight by those musicians who have scoffed at Barnby's "Sarum" because they felt the latter tune was not worthy of Bishop How's words. "Sine Nomine," however, is not easy for congregations to sing, and until it has been heard frequently enough to be somewhat familiar, it may be most successfully used by choirs, after rehearsing it adequately, as a special number or, somewhat questionably, as a processional. It has a strong melody and is no doubt one of the finest hymn settings from modern composers.

Ralph Vaughan Williams, born at Down Ampney, Gloucestershire, England, October 12, 1872, is one of the distinguished present-day English musicians. Between his school days at Charterhouse and his University course at Trinity College, Cambridge, he took up the study of music at the Royal College of Music, London, returning there for further study after his graduation from Cambridge, although that institution had given him the degree of Bachelor of Music while he was yet an undergraduate. He studied piano, organ, and composition at London, Berlin, and Paris, under some of the world's greatest teachers in their respective fields, and is now recognized himself as one of the masters. His major interest has been in choirs and their singing, and he has produced some of the most remarkable of modern works for choral bodies. His music reflects his great interest in folk song and his love for the old modal forms of medieval polyphonic writing. He is intensely British, and his is a new voice in English music. In an article in the *Magazine* of the Royal College of Music, he has said:

> Have not we all about us forms of musical expression which we can take and purify and raise to the level of great art? For instance, the lilt of the chorus at a music-hall joining in a popular song, the children dancing to a barrel organ, the rousing fervour of a Salvation Army hymn, St. Paul's and a great choir singing in one of its festivals, the Welshmen striking up one of their own hymns whenever they win a goal at an international football match, the cries of the street pedlars, the factory girls singing their sentimental songs. Have all these nothing to say to us?

Perhaps those queries may help us to understand why his music has taken such a strong hold on the English mind.

Vaughan Williams was the musical editor of *The English Hymnal,* 1906, and was coeditor, with Martin Shaw (444) and Percy Dearmer (79), of *Songs of Praise,* 1925, its enlarged edition of 1931, and of *The Oxford Book of Carols,* 1928. After serving in France as a Lieutenant R. G. A. in the World War he returned to the Royal College of Music as a teacher of composition, a position he now holds.

**528—There is a land of pure delight—Isaac Watts (3)**

**Varina**—George Frederick Root (439)

This was first published in Doctor Watts's *Hymns and Sacred Songs, Book II,* 1707, in six stanzas of four lines with the heading,

> A prospect of Heaven makes death easy.

Here are found the first three and the last stanzas. The imagery of this hymn was suggested, it is said, by the view of lovely Southampton Water and the Isle of Wight from the window where young Watts sat in poetic meditation.

"Varina," one of the best-known tunes of George F. Root, first appeared in *The Sabbath Bell,* 1856, where it is said to be

From Rink, by G. F. R.

The tune seems entirely wedded to the Doctor Watts hymn, to which it was set.

The old fuguing tune, "Exhortation," was a great favorite with Methodist preachers in the South a generation or more ago, and Dean Tillett says that "to hear them go through the six stanzas, at some of the Conferences, *like a whirlwind,* was an experience never to be forgotten." Many present-day Methodists, preachers and laymen alike, have never heard a "fugue tune" nor seen one in print. For their benefit "Exhortation," as it was sung to these words, is printed on page 511.

**529—Jerusalem the golden**—Bernard of Cluny
Translated by John Mason Neale (52)
**Ewing**—Alexander Ewing

Bernard of Cluny, or Morlaix, as he is perhaps better known, was born of English parents, at Morlaix, Bretagne, France, early in the twelfth century. Nothing is known of his life other than that he entered the Abbey of Cluny some time after 1122, while Peter the Venerable was at the head of that institution. Of this monastery Dr. J. M. Neale has written:

> In the twelfth century, the Abbey of Cluny, under its celebrated head, Peter the Venerable, was at the very height of monastic reputation. Its glorious church, the most magnificent in France, the fullness and exactness of its ritual, and the multitude of its brethren, raised it to a pitch of fame which, perhaps, no other house ever attained.

Scattered over Europe were many similar establishments, renowned and opulent, considered by Bernard of Clairvaux (188) to be places of gross self-indulgence:

> Who could say, to speak of nothing else, in how many ways eggs are cooked and worked up? with what care they are turned in and out, made hard or soft, or chopped fine; now fried, now roasted, now stuffed; now they are served mixed with other things, now by themselves. Even the external appearance of the dishes is such that the eye, as well as the taste, is charmed, and when the stomach complains that it is full, curiosity is still alive.

It was in such surroundings that Bernard of Cluny spent his life, and during his leisure hours wrote that "wondrous satire" on the evil conditions of the time in which he lived, known by Bernard's title, *De Contemptu Mundi.* It is a long poem of about three thousand lines supposed to have been written about 1145. Quoting Doctor Neale again:

> The greater part is a bitter satire on the fearful corruptions of the age. But as a contrast to the misery and pollution of earth, the poem opens with a description of the peace and glory of heaven, of such rare beauty as not easily to be matched by any medieval composition on the same subject.

The Eternal Life
511
There is a land of pure de-light, Where saints im -
mor - tal reign;
In -
In - fi - nite day ex -
In - fi - nite day ex-cludes the night, And
fi - nite day ex - cludes the night, And pleas - ures ban - ish
cludes the night,
And pleas - ures ban - ish pain, In -
pleas - ures ban - ish pain,
pain,
And pleas - ures ban - ish pain.
fi - nite day ex - cludes the night,
EXHORTATION

It is composed in

> dactylic hexameters, with the leonine (sometimes a trisyllable or dactylic), and tailed rhyme, each line being broken up into three parts thus:—
>
> Hóra noviss*ima* | | tempora péss*ima* | | sunt: vigil*emus*!
> Ecce mina*citer* | | imminet ar*biter* | | ille supr*emus*!
> Imminet, im*minet* | | ut mala ter*minet* | | aequa cor*onet*
> Recta remu*neret* | | anxia li*beret* | | aethera *donet*.

This "rhythm of intense difficulty" is such as to make anything approaching an acceptable literal translation impossible.

Bernard, in dedicating his work to the Abbot Peter, wrote:

> I say it in nowise arrogantly, but with all humility, and therefore boldly: that unless that Spirit of Wisdom and Understanding had been with me, and flowed in upon so difficult a metre, I could not have composed so long a work.

Doctor Neale, who was too wise in matters of translation to attempt the impossible, chose the simple ballad rhythm (7s 6s double) for his rendering. He was the first to translate any part of the long poem, and it is notable that though many other translations have been made, his only is now in use. In his *Rhythm of Bernard de Morlaix, Monk of Cluny, on the Celestial Country,* 1858, Neale published two hundred and eighteen lines, beginning with the first:

> Hora novissima, tempora pessima sunt, vigilemus.

From these lines some eight centos have been made into hymns, four of which have had very extensive use:

> (a) The world is very evil,
> (b) Brief life is here our portion,
> (c) For thee, O dear, dear country,
> (d) Jerusalem the golden.

All four were included in *The Hymnal of the Methodist Episcopal Church,* 1878, and two each in *The Hymn and Tune Book of the Methodist Episcopal Church, South,* 1889, and *The Tribute of Praise,* Methodist Protestant hymnal, 1882. "Jerusalem the golden" is the only one of the four to survive in the recent revision of the *Hymnal,* and the centos based on this section of the *Rhythm* are much more widely used than those based on any other.

John Brownlie insists Bernard's hymns reveal to us only monkish conceptions of heaven, beautiful though they be.

> Heaven is apt to assume various complexions, according to the circumstances and conditions of our present life. To the poor and hungry it is a place of plenty, where poverty never pinches; to the solitary and friendless a place of communion and friendship; to the toiling and careworn and sad, a place of rest and gladness. What was it to Bernard? A city, a place in whose busy streets one can have constant intercourse with one's fellow men. . . .
>
> The whole conception of the world as expressed in those hymns is monastic. That good man had been sickened with the sin of the world, had so brooded over it that he had come to transfer evil from souls to things, from men's hearts to the world. It was the world that was bad, and it was the world that had to be got rid of, and Bernard and others like him tried in their own way to get rid of it. Hence the pictures of the new Jerusalem. There is little spiritual about it. It is a material heaven. Having denied themselves those earthly blessings for which a wise Creator had

> designed them, having removed themselves from the scene of discipline for which God had intended them, they have to pay the penalty. They seek those blessings and expect that discipline where they have no right to expect them, and where they are not to be had. It is a truth that while the man who shuts himself out from the world is the man to whom heaven becomes most material, the man who faces the world, lives in it, using it lawfully, and fighting with its evils, is the man whose conception of heaven becomes most spiritual.

"Ewing" was composed in 1853 by Alexander Ewing and was published in leaflet form the same year. The tune was frequently attributed to his uncle, Bishop Ewing, but William Carnie told the true story of its authorship. At the close of a meeting of the Aberdeen Harmonic Choir, Mr. Ewing approached Mr. Carnie, its distinguished leader, and told him he had been trying his hand at hymn-tune writing, asking that the tune be sung by the choir. This was done, and it was found acceptable. He had set the tune to the part of Bernard's hymn beginning "For thee, O dear, dear country," not "Jerusalem the golden," the part of the same hymn to which it is now universally sung. It was written in 3 time and was first published in 1857 in *A Manual of Psalm and Hymn Tunes,* J. Grey. The following part of the melody will show how it appeared in this form:

When it appeared in *Hymns Ancient and Modern,* 1861, the time was changed to 4, as it now appears, but without the composer's knowledge or consent, he being absent in a distant country at the time. Mr. Ewing said: "In my opinion the alteration of the rhythm has very much vulgarized my little tune. It now seems to me a good deal like a polka. I hate to hear it." Dr. J. M. Neale, whose translation of Bernard's lines was used by Mr. Ewing, wrote in 1861:

> I have so often been asked to what tune the words of Bernard may be sung, that I may mention that of Mr. Ewing, the earliest written, the best known, and with children the most popular; no small proof in my estimation of the goodness of church music.

Alexander Ewing, born at Aberdeen, Scotland, January 3, 1830, studied law in his home city at Marischal College, but because of his interest in music went to Heidelberg, Germany, where he studied that art. He learned to play the violin, cello, and cornet well, and was much interested in choral music, being an enthusiastic member of the Haydn Society and the Harmonic Choir of Aberdeen, the latter being an organization whose purpose was to study madrigals and anthems. Both organizations were under the leadership of William Carnie. At the outbreak of the Crimean War Ewing joined the army and attained the rank of lieutenant-colonel. He married Juliana Horatio Gatty, the celebrated writer of children's stories. Colonel Ewing was held in high regard as an amateur musician. He died at Taunton, England, July 11, 1895.

**530—The Homeland, O the Homeland**—Hugh Reginald Haweis

**Homeland**—Arthur Seymour Sullivan (15)

American hymnals give H. R. Haweis as the author of this hymn; some English hymnals, however, give the credit to William Lindsay Alexander (?). Its authorship has not been definitely established nor is it known where it first appeared, although the date 1855 has been assigned to it in the Presbyterian *New Psalms and Hymns,* 1901. This was said to have been the favorite hymn of the great Spurgeon. He requested that it be sung to him just before his death, and the children of the Stockwell orphanage sang it at his funeral.

Hugh Reginald Haweis, 1838-1901, was for thirty-five years, from 1866, Incumbent of St. James's, Marylebone, England, where he "introduced Sunday evenings for the people." His *Music and Morals* was widely read.

"Homeland" is reported to be Sir Arthur Sullivan's first published tune. It appeared in *Good Words* in 1867, having been written at the request of its editor.

**531—Ten thousand times ten thousand**—Henry Alford

**Alford** (421)—John Bacchus Dykes (1)

"A Processional for Saints' Days" was first published by Dean Alford in his *Year of Praise,* 1867, a book intended primarily for use in Canterbury Cathedral. Very appropriately, it was chosen as the hymn to be sung in the churchyard at the close of the Dean's funeral exercises. A memorandum was found among his papers with these words, an injunction, it is needless to say, which was faithfully obeyed:

> When I am gone, and a tomb is to be put up, let there be, besides any indication of who is lying below, these words, and these only, *Deversorium viatoris proficiscentis Hierosolymam,* i. e., the inn of a traveler on his way to Jerusalem.

Henry Alford was born in London, October 7, 1810, and won distinction as a student at Trinity College, Cambridge, where he graduated in 1832. On his sixteenth birthday he wrote in his Bible:

> I do this day, in the presence of God and my own soul, renew my covenant with God, and solemnly determine henceforth to become his and to do his work as far as in me lies.

After his ordination in 1833 he became known as an able and eloquent preacher and was respected for his eminent scholarship, his chief work, upon which he labored for twenty years, being his four-volume edition of the Greek Testament. For some years he was the editor of *The Contemporary Review.*

In 1857 Lord Palmerston, then Prime Minister, made him Dean of Canterbury, where he remained until his death, January 12, 1871.

"Alford" was written for this hymn by Doctor Dykes. (See No. 421.)

**532—Hark, hark, my soul! angelic songs are swelling**—Frederick William Faber (76)

**Pilgrims**—Henry Smart (77)

This hymn comes from F. W. Faber's *Oratory Hymns,* 1854, in seven stanzas of four lines, with the refrain. In his *Hymns,* 1862, it was headed,

The Pilgrims of the Night.

In stanza 4, line 3, Faber wrote:

All journeys end in welcome to the weary.

The last two lines of the hymn were changed to their present form by the editors of *Hymns Ancient and Modern.* They were, originally:

While we toil on and soothe ourselves with weeping,
Till life's long night shall break in endless love.

Canon Ellerton (28) said of this hymn: "We enquire in vain into the meaning of the 'Pilgrims of the Night': congregations are carried away by the rhythm and musical ring of the lines." In its popular anthem form by Harry Rowe Shelley, 1858- , it has been sung in thousands of churches.

"Pilgrims" was written by Henry Smart for this hymn for the Appendix to the Original Edition of *Hymns Ancient and Modern.*

# SPECIAL SEASONS AND SERVICES

## The Changing Year

**533—O God, our help in ages past**—Isaac Watts (3)

**St. Anne** (384)—Probably by William Croft (169)

Canon Dearmer (79) suggested that we call this "Watts' Ninetieth," that it might be classed with Old Hundredth. One of the greatest hymns in our language, this is a rendering of the first part of Psalm 90, and appeared in *The Psalms of David,* 1719, with the heading,

Man frail and God Eternal.

Watts wrote line 2 of stanza 2,

Thy saints have dwelt secure,

line 3, stanza 5,

Be thou our guard while troubles last,

and John Wesley altered the original first line of the first and last stanzas which began, "Our God, our help," to "O God, our help." Stanzas 1, 2, 3, 5, and 9 of the original nine are used. It was written about 1714, shortly before the death of Queen Anne, during the time of anxiety in England as to who might be her successor. Thackeray has referred to it in the closing chapters of *Henry Esmond,* and other literary references to it are plentiful. F. J. Gilman, after calling it "the great ceremonial hymn of the English nations," says Watts's Memorial in Westminster Abbey would have been justified for his having written it if for nothing else.

**534—Another year is dawning**—Frances Ridley Havergal (221)

**Bremen**—Melchior Vulpius

This was written in 1874 by Miss Havergal as the text for an ornamental New Year's card, and was included in her *Under the Surface* the same year.

"Bremen," "Vulpius," "Mein Leben," or "Christus der ist," comes from *Ein schön geistlich Gesangbuch . . . Durch Melchiorem Vulpium Cantorem zu Weymar. Jehna,* 1609. It was set to a hymn of unknown origin beginning,

Christus, der ist mein Leben,

the original form of the melody being:

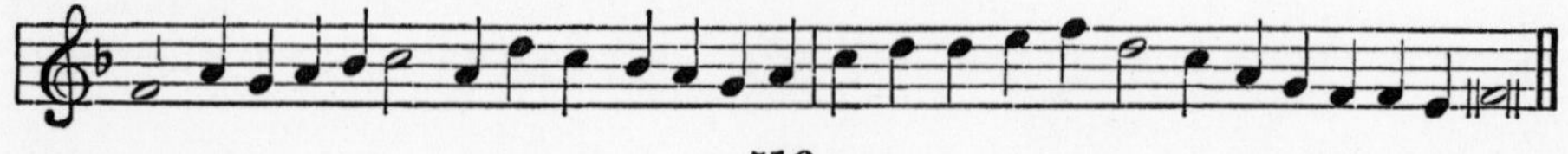

Lines three and four in the now familiar form are found in the *Praxis Pietatis Melica,* 1662 (60). Bach (52) used the later form of the melody in his *Choralgesänge.*

Melchior Vulpius was born at Wasungen, Henneberg, Thuringia, in 1560, and about 1600 became cantor at Weimar. In 1604 and 1609 he published editions of the *Gesangbuch* mentioned above, a valuable work. He died at Weimar, August 7, 1616. Goethe's wife was "née Vulpius of Weimar."

**535—Father, let me dedicate—Lawrence Tuttiett**

**Dedication**—George Alexander MacFarren

This fine hymn of dedication for the New Year is from Canon Lawrence Tuttiett's *Germs of Thought on The Sunday Special Services,* 1864. It may be found in different collections with variations in text. The original version is used with stanzas 3 and 4 interchanged. In reply to an inquiry the author said there was no particular incident connected with its writing. Noting the scarcity of hymns for the New Year, he wrote this in his desire to help supply a recognized need.

Lawrence Tuttiett, son of a surgeon in the British Navy, was born at Colyton, Devonshire, in 1825. He was educated for the profession of medicine at Christ's Hospital and King's College, London, but abandoned his intention and turned to the Church, being ordained in 1848. While acting as curate on the Isle of Wight in 1854, he made with his preaching a great impression on Lord Norton, who advanced him to the living at Lea Marsten, Warwickshire. After remaining there for sixteen years, he removed to St. Andrews, Scotland, to become the Incumbent of the Episcopal Church. Ten years later he was made a canon of St. Ninian's Cathedral, Perth. After his retirement in 1893 he lived at Pitlochry. He died, May 21, 1897, at St. Andrews, where he had returned for a visit.

"Dedication," with the name, "Father, let me dedicate," was contributed as the setting for Canon Tuttiett's hymn in the Supplement to *Hymns Ancient and Modern,* 1889, but was not included in the New Edition of 1904.

George Alexander MacFarren, Mus. Doc., was born at London, March 2, 1813. Early in life he showed a marked predilection for music and began its formal study at the Royal Academy of Music at the age of fourteen, his major interests being composition and trombone playing. His record as a student was such that in his twenty-second year he was admitted to the faculty of the institution, which he had entered only seven years previously. He maintained his connection with the Royal Academy of Music until his death, October 31, 1887. He was chosen to succeed Sterndale Bennett, not only as Principal of the Academy, but as Professor of Music at Cambridge University. In company with Arthur Sullivan (15) and George Grove, of *Grove's Dictionary* fame, he was knighted in 1883.

Sir George was noted for his phenomenal memory. It has been said that he remembered for years the errors his students had made in their harmony exercises. Dates in musical history were easily remembered, and apparently retained in his memory were details he had learned in his student days. On one occasion, a story goes, he had heard an unusual melodic and harmonic progression in Raff's *Leonora* symphony, and upon being asked if he did not think it "strikingly original," replied: "Oh, no! I wrote a passage just like that in one of my symphonies forty-five years ago. I don't like it."

After constantly increasing difficulties with his eyesight for many years, he became totally blind, but for the last twenty years he kept on with his work, dictating his music to an amanuensis. Little of the great quantity of music he wrote is now heard, and he is better known for his successful teaching, his lecturing, and his writings about music.

**536—Come, let us anew—Charles Wesley (25)**

**Lucas—Early American Melody**
James Lucas

This is numbered the fifth of the seven hymns contained in the collection called *Hymns for New-Year's-Day*. One word has been changed: Charles Wesley wrote "might" instead of "may" in the first line of the third stanza. The meter in which it is written is one of those that must have given rise to what our fathers called "Peculiar Meter." Peculiar it is, but from the number of hymns Charles Wesley wrote in meters quite similar to this, the inference is that he was particularly fond of it. In the little book containing this hymn, in the author's possession, it is printed thus:

Come, let us anew
Our journey pursue
And never stand still, till the Master appear;
His adorable will
Let us gladly fulfill,
And our talents improve
By the patience of hope, and the labor of love.

The early Methodists apparently were fond of these "peculiar meters" and sang them lustily. Surely they were better vocalists than those of the twentieth century, for it would be difficult to imagine a 1937 Watch Night crowd singing the old tune, "New Year's Day," from 1761, which is shown in the illustration on page 519.

The Watch Night service had a singular origin. Crowther's *Portraiture of Methodism* says:

> 1742. The first Watch-night was held in London. The custom originated with the colliers of Kingswood, near Bristol, who had been in the habit, when slaves of sin, of spending every Saturday at the ale house. They now devoted that night to prayer and singing of hymns. Mr. Wesley, hearing of this, and of the good that was done, resolved to make it general. At first he ordered *Watch-nights* to be kept once a month, when the moon was at the full, and afterwards fixed them for once a quarter.

Robert Southey, one time Poet Laureate of England, commented:

> The reclaimed colliers having been accustomed to sit late on Saturday nights at the ale house, transferred their weekly meetings, after their conversion, to the school house, and continued there praying and *singing hymns far into the morning*.

G. J. Stevenson (513) quotes an interesting incident from Tyerman's *Life of Fletcher:*

> The Rev. John Fletcher, of Madeley, was a man of great simplicity of living. He one morning visited a school of young ladies, and sat with them during the breakfast hour; at its close he invited them all to visit him next morning at the vicarage at seven o'clock. On their arrival, Mr. Fletcher took his basin of bread and milk, and asked the girls to look at his watch and tell him how much time he took for breakfast. When he had finished they said, "Just a minute and a-half." The vicar then said, "My dear girls, we have fifty-eight minutes of the hour left, let us sing—
>
> 'Our life is a dream—our time as a stream
> Glides swiftly away,
> And the fugitive moment refuses to stay.'"
>
> He gave them a lecture on the value of time, and the worth of the soul, and after praying with them at eight o'clock, they returned to school more deeply impressed than ever before.

"Lucas" is found in *The Choir,* 1832, Lowell Mason (19), with no mention of a composer. Just when James Lucas's name was associated with the tune the author is unable to say. One not too reliable reference says James Lucas was an Englishman, but gives no facts to support the assertion. It sounds as if it might have originated in the camp meetings.

**537—Ring out, wild bells, to the wild sky**—Alfred Tennyson (206)

**Wild Bells**—Henry Lahee

This hymn, as "Strong Son of God, immortal Love" (206, which see), is from Lord Tennyson's *In Memoriam.* Six of the eight stanzas of section cvi are used without change. The omitted third and fifth stanzas of the original are:

Ring out the grief that saps the mind,
For those that here we see no more;
Ring out the feud of rich and poor,
Ring in redress to all mankind.

Ring out the want, the care, the sin,
The faithless coldness of the times;
Ring out, ring out my mournful rhymes,
But ring the fuller minstrel in.

"Wild Bells" was written by Henry Lahee for these lines by Lord Tennyson. The composer's son, Henry C. Lahee, of Boston, in a personal letter, tells how, on a visit to his old home, he "heard the bells of St. Luke's, Chelsea, which inspired my father to write 'Wild Bells,' which won a prize in some competition."

Henry Lahee was born at Chelsea, England, April 11, 1826, and died at Croydon, April 29, 1912. For about thirty years he was organis at Holy Trinity Church, Brompton, and was especially apt at writing glees, madrigals, and part songs, winning many prizes. His music of the cantata *The Sleeping Beauty* contains some lovely writing for women's voices.

**538—Sing to the great Jehovah's praise**—Charles Wesley (25)

**Evangelist**—Felix Mendelssohn-Bartholdy (7)

This is the last of the seven *Hymns for New-Year's-Day,* published in Bristol in 1750, to sell for only a penny. Charles Wesley wrote "Demands" instead of "Inspires" as the first word of the last line of the first stanza; "Whose providence" in place of "His providence," line 1, stanza 2; "Thy still continued care," not "And Thy continued care," as line 2, stanza 3. The hymn was originally in three stanzas of eight lines each, the last being:

Our residue of days or hours
Thine, wholly Thine shall be,
And all our consecrated powers
A sacrifice to Thee:
Till Jesus in the clouds appear
To saints on earth forgiven,
And bring the grand sabbatic year
The jubilee of heaven.

"Evangelist" is the melody of the first measures of the chorus, "How lovely are the messengers," from Mendelssohn's *St. Paul,* Part II, which was completed at Leipzig, April 18, 1836.

**539—Great God, we sing that mighty hand**—Philip Doddridge (69)

**Federal Street** (185)—Henry Kemble Oliver (185)

The first four stanzas, unaltered, of five from the posthumous *Hymns*

*Founded on Various Texts in the Holy Scriptures,* 1755, comprise this hymn. Originally its heading was:

Help obtained of God. Acts xxvi. 22
For New Year's-Day.

The scriptural basis was: "Having therefore obtained help of God, I continue unto this day, witnessing both to small and great, saying none other things than those which the prophets and Moses did say should come."

**540—Come, let us use the grace divine—Charles Wesley (25)**

**St. Martin's (172)—William Tans'ur (172)**

From *Short Hymns on Select Passages of Scripture,* 1762, the first two of three double quatrains, based on that part of Jeremiah 50. 5, which is, ". . . . Come, and let us join ourselves to the Lord in a perpetual covenant that shall not be forgotten." Wesley wrote the first line of the second quatrain:

Give ourselves up through Jesu's power.

This hymn is used by Methodists both in England and America at the renewing of the Covenant, although it was not originally designed for such a purpose.

In 1934 The Abingdon Press issued a booklet entitled *A Service for such as would make or renew their Covenant with God.* The introductory note, called "The Covenant Service," was:

In his *Journal* for December 25, 1747, Wesley writes: "Both this and the following days I strongly urged the wholly giving up ourselves to God, and renewing in every point our Covenant that the Lord should be our God."

There is no further reference to the subject till August 6, 1755, when he writes: "I mentioned to the congregation another means of increasing serious religion, which had been frequently practiced by our forefathers and attended with eminent blessing, namely, the joining in a Covenant to serve God with all our heart and with all our soul. I explained this for several mornings following, and on Friday many of us kept a fast unto the Lord, beseeching him to give us wisdom and strength to promise unto the Lord our God and keep it." On the Monday he explained once more the nature of such an engagement, and the manner of doing it acceptably to God. "At six in the evening," he says, "we met for that purpose at the French Church in Spitalfields. After I had recited the tenor of the Covenant proposed, in the words of that blessed man, Richard Alleine, all the people stood up, in testimony of assent, to the number of about eighteen hundred persons. Such a sight I scarce ever saw before. Surely the fruit of it shall remain for ever."

Wesley introduced the Service at Bristol in October and at Dublin the following April. After the renewal of the Covenant in 1775 "many desired to return thanks, either for a sense of pardon, for full salvation, or for a fresh manifestation of his grace, healing all their backslidings." Wesley did not issue a separate Form of Service till 1780, though in 1753 he had printed in Vol. 30 of the *Christian Library* that recommended by Richard Alleine.

For nearly two hundred years the use of the Covenant Service has drawn believers into the secret place of the divine presence and sent them forth with new courage and deeper devotion. It is hoped that this service, which has been revised to give the people a larger part in the devotions, will help those who share in it to realize how rich in mercy is their Covenant-keeping God and to be strengthened in their personal love and service to him.

This would be an excellent hymn for use in such a service.

## Thanksgiving

**541—O Lord of heaven and earth and sea**—Christopher Wordsworth (153)

**Oldbridge** (41)—Robert Newton Quaile (41)

This, considered by many to be the finest of all offertory hymns, was first published in the third edition of Christopher Wordsworth's *The Holy Year,* 1863, with the title,

Charitable Collections.

While the hymn is unquestionably a fine offertory hymn, and in *The Methodist Hymnal* is suggested for services of thanksgiving, its use should not be restricted, for it is a hymn of praise as well as thanksgiving and teaches God's grace in redemption as well as in His providence.

Canon Ellerton (28) has commented:

> It is not in the least poetical; it is full of halting verses and prosaic lines. And yet, it is such true praise, so genuine, so comprehensive, so heartfelt, that we forget its homeliness.

**542—When all Thy mercies, O my God**—Joseph Addison (66)

**Manoah** (378)—From Henry Wellington Greatorex's Collection (378)

This hymn, sung to "Manoah," is one of the greatest songs of praise and thanksgiving in all our hymnody. The grand sweep of the melody in the third line, with its broad, full close, is thrilling when sung heartily by a great crowd of worshipers. Its use should be general, not confined to use as a Thanksgiving Day hymn; man should express his gratitude to God for "all Thy mercies" much more often, for, as George Herbert said,

Ev'n eternitie is too short to extoll Thee.

Appearing as the second of Joseph Addison's hymns in *The Spectator* of August 9, 1712, it was thus introduced:

> I have already obliged the public with some pieces of divine poetry which have fallen into my hands; and as they have met with the reception which they deserve, I shall, from time to time, communicate any work of the same nature which has not appeared in print, and may be acceptable to my readers.

Addison had written, as a part of an essay, "Gratitude," of which this hymn forms the conclusion:

> There is not a more pleasing exercise of the mind than gratitude. It is accompanied with such an inward satisfaction, that the duty is sufficiently rewarded by the performance. If gratitude is due from man to man, how much more from man to his Maker! Every blessing we enjoy, by what means soever it may be derived upon us, is the gift of Him who is the great Author of good, and Father of mercies.

**543—Not alone for mighty empire**—William Pierson Merrill (267)

**Hyfrydol** (11)—Melody by Rowland Hugh Prichard (11)

This hymn first appeared in *The Continent,* a Presbyterian paper formerly published in Chicago, in 1911.

**544—We plow the fields and scatter**—Matthias Claudius
Translated by Jane Montgomery Campbell

**St. Anselm**—Joseph Barnby (31)

This is the "Peasants' Song" from Claudius's *Paul Erdman's Feast,* a picture of the charming harvest festivals held in north Germany. In his story of the occasion Claudius says:

> They sang the Peasants' Song as here follows. I don't know what sort of effect the song has when it is read; but I know well what that was when the peasants sang it. The music, they said, was Italian. I have here set it down as well as I could catch it. Let any one improve it, or make another one.

The song was in seventeen four-line stanzas, each followed by a refrain which Miss Campbell translated thus:

> All good gifts around us
> Are sent from heaven above;
> Then thank the Lord, O thank the Lord,
> For all His love.

In 1800 there appeared in Hanover a book for use in schools, which included stanzas 3-10 of this piece set to the well-known somewhat boisterous "Wir Pflügen," by J. A. P. Schulz, 1747-1800. It immediately attained a popularity with German children and adults which it still maintains. It was from this song that Miss Campbell made her translation which appeared in England in 1861 in *Garland of Songs,* C. S. Bere.

Matthias Claudius, son of a Lutheran minister, was born at Reinfeld, Holstein, near Lübeck, August 15, 1740. He studied theology at Jena, but influences there caused him to take up law and languages. Turning to journalism, he edited the *Wandsbeck Messenger* for some years, in 1776 receiving an appointment as a Commissioner of Agriculture and Manufactures at Hesse Darmstadt. The influence of Goethe, with whom he became acquainted, and other free thinkers at Darmstadt caused him to renounce the religion of his younger days; but a serious illness "wrought powerfully on his spirit" and he returned to his father's faith. He gave up his position with its assured adequate income and returned to his editorial work at Wandsbeck, where he remained until he was given a bank auditorship at Altona, Schleswig-Holstein. His death occurred January 21, 1815, shortly after he had retired to live with his daughter at Hamburg.

Jane Montgomery Campbell, born at London in 1817, contributed some translations from the German to C. S. Bere's *Garland of Songs, or an English Liederkranz,* 1861, and to his *Children's Choral Book,* 1869. Miss Campbell taught in the parish school of her father, the Rev. A. M. Campbell. She died at Bovey Tracey, November 15, 1878.

"St. Anselm," written by Sir Joseph Barnby in 1868, was published in his *Original Tunes,* 1869, to "O day of rest and gladness," and in *The Hymnary,* London, 1872.

**545—Come, ye thankful people, come**—Henry Alford (531)

**St. George's, Windsor**—George Job Elvey (170)

This, the most popular of Dean Alford's hymns, first appeared in his *Psalms and Hymns,* 1844, but was considerably altered by him for inclusion in his *Year of Praise,* 1867, and his *Poetical Works,* 1868. The version in *The Methodist Hymnal* is the author's approved text from the *Year of Praise.* The text in *Hymns Ancient and Modern,* which was altered from the Dean's first edition, never received his approval.

"St. George's, Windsor," or "St. George," was written by Sir George J. Elvey as a setting for "Hark, the sound of jubilee," James Montgomery (39), and first appeared in *A Selection of Psalm and Hymn-Tunes,* London, 1858, edited by E. H. Thorne, the tune book to accompany the word book having the same title, compiled by the Rev. Thomas H. Morrell and Bishop William W. How (197). The tune was first associated with this hymn in the Original Edition in *Hymns Ancient and Modern,* 1861.

**546—For all the blessings of the year**—Albert H. Hutchinson

**Oldbridge** (41)—Robert Newton Quaile (41)

Nothing is known to the author of this book of the source of this simple, yet beautiful, hymn of gratitude for the common things of life; nor has any information been obtained concerning its author, Albert H. Hutchinson.

## Dedications

**547—O living Christ, chief Corner Stone**—Maud Merrimon Cuninggim

**Arlington** (270)—Thomas Augustine Arne (270)

Mrs. Cuninggim wrote this hymn in 1926 for the ceremonies accompanying the laying of the corner stone of the beautiful Belle H. Bennett Memorial, including Wightman Chapel, on the campus of the Scarritt College for Christian Workers at Nashville, Tennessee.

Maud Merrimon Cuninggim, born at Raleigh, North Carolina, March 7, 1874, came of distinguished and scholarly lineage; her father, Augustus Merrimon, was a Chief Justice of the State Supreme Court after having served as United States Senator from 1873 to 1879. It was during her father's last illness that his youngest daughter, then a girl of eighteen, occupied the night watches with her first attempts at poetry. Quite characteristically, some of these were given expression in hymns which later found their way into various periodicals. Later this talent was to serve her well, since it developed that she had a remarkable facility in writing what are known as "verses for occasions."

Mrs. Cuninggim developed a rare aptitude for teaching through eleven years' experience in that calling. Her self-dedication to the training of Christian workers came to full flower through her wholehearted absorption in the work of Scarritt Bible and Training School (now Scarritt College), of which her husband, Dr. J. L. Cuninggim, is president.

**548—On this stone now laid with prayer—John Pierpont**

**Pleyel's Hymn** (326)—Ignace Josef Pleyel (326)

This dedication hymn has probably been used at more corner-stone-laying services than any other since it was written in 1839. All such hymns seem to have been written for some special occasion. This one was the laying of the corner stone of the Suffolk Street Chapel, for the ministry of the poor, in Boston, May 23, 1839.

John Pierpont, born at Litchfield, Connecticut, April 6, 1785, "turned a pulpit into a field piece." He was the most prolific "poet of occasions" of his time, providing laureates for any and all occasions. Pierpont graduated from Yale in 1804 and the following year went to South Carolina as tutor in a private family. Not finding this to his liking, he returned north to Massachusetts; studied law and opened an office in Newburyport in 1811; left that to enter the dry-goods business in Boston; and tried opening other similar establishments in Baltimore and in Charleston, South Carolina. But only disaster followed this early chain-store enterprise; his family was reduced to the need of selling its silver, piece by piece. While Pierpont was in this condition of poverty, his second daughter, Juliet, destined to become the mother of J. Pierpont Morgan I, was born.

After his failure in business, Pierpont chose the ministry as his profession. On the proceeds derived from the sale of his *Airs of Palestine* and other books he was able to enter and graduate from Harvard Divinity School. He became the minister of the Hollis Street Church, Boston, and remained there for twenty-six years. Becoming involved in a controversy with certain of his parishioners over the temperance and other issues, he was charged, in part, with failing to give his "undivided attention" to the work of his ministry. This statement appears in a formal resolution against him, dated September 30, 1839:

> When his attention was drawn from these duties by the making of *Books,* and the manufacture of *Stoves,* and *Screws,* and *Razor-Strops*—and by entering into every exciting topic that the ingenuity of the fanatic at home, or the imported mountebank could conjure up to disturb and distract the public mind, such as *Imprisonment for Debt, The Militia Law, Antimasonry, Phrenology, Temperance,* and last and above all, the *Abolition of slavery,* a question which threatens more than all else, the distruction of our *Glorious Union,* it would be wonderful indeed if his people were made of such materials as to sit quietly and tolerate such freedom.

His detailed reply greatly affronted the dignity of the Hollis Street Church officials, and he was ousted. After leaving Hollis Street Church, he went to the First Unitarian Society, Troy, New York, four years, then to First Congregational (Unitarian) Church, West Medford, Massachusetts, for nine years. Although he was seventy-six years of age at the opening of the Civil War, he volunteered as chaplain of the Twenty-second Massachusetts Volunteers and went with them to the front, but Senator Charles Sumner influenced him to resign and secured for him a clerkship in the Treasury Department at Washington, D. C. He edited many school books "for the use of my own children, and those of my parishioners and countrymen generally." On his eightieth birthday, Bryant, Whittier, and Holmes sent greetings in the form of verse. He returned to Medford a few months before he died, August 26, 1866.

**549—Thou, whose unmeasured temple stands**—William Cullen Bryant

**Dundee (French)** (68)—From the Scottish Psalter (68)

Written for the dedication of a chapel in Prince Street, New York, in 1835, this hymn has had wide use in both England and America. In addition to this version of the hymn, there is another revised and included in *Hymns, by William Cullen Bryant,* thought to have been published in 1869. The revised form, which was that chosen by W. Garrett Horder for his *Congregational Hymns,* London, 1884, follows:

How Amiable Are Thy Tabernacles

Thou, whose unmeasured temple stands,
Built over earth and sea,
Accept the walls that human hands
Have raised, Oh God! to thee.

And let the Comforter and Friend,
Thy Holy Spirit, meet
With those who here in worship bend
Before thy mercy seat.

May they who err be guided here
To find the better way,
And they who mourn, and they who fear
Be strengthened as they pray.

May faith grow firm, and love grow warm,
And hallowed wishes rise,
While round these peaceful walls the storm
Of earth-born passion dies.

William Cullen Bryant, born at Cummington, Massachusetts, November 3, 1794, noted journalist and the first of America's greater poets in point of time, was not a successful hymn writer. The Rev. F. M. Bird says Bryant's "genius was cool, meditative, and not distinguished by lyric fire. His hymns are correct and solid, but none reach the highest rank."

After spending two years as a student at Williams College, Bryant studied law and practiced the profession for about ten years at Plainfield and Great Barrington. He had always been interested in writing, having published his first book of poems at the age of fourteen and written *Thanatopsis* when only eighteen; so, disliking the law, he went to New York in 1825 to engage in literary work. After a year of precarious fortune he became one of the editors of *The Evening Post,* only a little later securing complete control of its editorial policy and becoming its chief owner. A religious eclectic, he was brought up in a Congregational home, was for a time a Unitarian, in New York worshiped with the Episcopalians, and at his country home on Long Island attended a Presbyterian church. Finally, on a day in 1858, his biographer says, while walking in Naples, Italy, with a ministerial friend who was a Baptist, he spoke with softened heart of the new beauty that he felt in the old truth, and proposed to his friend to baptize him. With prayer, and hymn, and spiritual meditation, a little company of seven in a large upper room, as in the Christian story, partook of the Communion, and with his good grey head bowed William Cullen Bryant was baptized.

His interest in hymns came from reading those of Isaac Watts (3). About 1869 he published a small volume of nineteen of his own composition, for private circulation. He died, June 12, 1878, in accordance with his wish, as expressed in his poem, "June":

I gazed upon the glorious sky,<br>
And the green mountains round,<br>
And thought that when I came to lie<br>
At rest within the ground,<br>
'Twere pleasant, that in flowery June,<br>
When brooks send up a cheerful tune,<br>
And groves a joyous sound,<br>
The sexton's hand, my grave to make,<br>
The rich, green mountain-turf should break.

**550—Come, O Thou God of grace**—William Edwin Evans

**Italian Hymn (Trinity)** (2)—Felice Giardini (2)

This hymn was written by Doctor Evans for the dedication of Park Place Methodist Episcopal Church, South, Richmond, Virginia, while he was its minister. It was included in *The Methodist Hymnal,* 1905.

William Edwin Evans was born at Baltimore, Maryland, July 11, 1851. Educated for the ministry at Randolph-Macon College, he joined the Baltimore Conference of the Methodist Episcopal Church, South, in 1872, but transferred at once to the Virginia Conference, where he filled various appointments. In 1892 he transferred to the communion of the Protestant Episcopal Church and was for some years located at Birmingham, Alabama, as rector of the Church of the Advent. He died at Richmond, Virginia, May 22, 1915.

**551—O Thou, whose hand hath brought us**—Frederick William Goadby

**Webb** (487)—George James Webb (487)

This hymn "for the opening of a place of worship" was included in *The Baptist Hymnal,* London, 1879. Most of the hymns by its author, F. W. Goadby, were written for special occasions.

Frederick William Goadby, member of an English family prominent in the Baptist Church, was born at Leicester, England, August 10, 1845. He entered Regent's Park College in 1862 and six years later graduated Master of Arts from the London University. After serving churches at Bluntesham and Watford, he died at the latter place October 15, 1879, at the early age of thirty-four years. He was looked upon at the time as one of the most promising young men in the English Baptist ministry.

**552—All nature's works His praise declare**—Henry Ware, Jr. (428)

**Bethlehem** (391)—Gottfried Wilhelm Fink (391)

This was written for the dedication of an organ and was dated November 9, 1822. It was included in W. Garrett Horder's English *Congregational Hymns,* 1884.

## Travel

**553—Eternal Father, strong to save**—William Whiting

**Melita** (480)—John Bacchus Dykes (1)

There are three different versions of this hymn of supplication for those exposed to perils of the sea, the texts varying widely. Written in 1860 by William Whiting, it was revised by the compilers of *Hymns Ancient and Modern,* 1861; the revised form, used in *The Methodist Hymnal,* is the most common.

William Whiting, born at Kensington, London, November 1, 1825, and educated at Clapham and Winchester schools, was for many years Master of the College Choristers' School, Winchester. He is known to hymnody solely for having written this one hymn. He died at Winchester, May 3, 1878.

**554—Father, who art alone**—Edith Jones (?)

**Samuel** (451)—Arthur Seymour Sullivan (15)

This hymn appeared in 1885 in *The Home Hymn Book, A Manual of Sacred Song for the Family Circle,* London. Julian says he knows no book of equal comprehensiveness and merit for use in the home, and praises especially its music. This book was compiled by Mrs. Hester P. Hawkins, née Lewis, whose home was in Bedford, England. It contained seven of her own hymns.

Edith Jones, or "E. J.," has expressed the desire that she remain unknown.

**555—O God Creator, in whose hand**—Harry Webb Farrington (112)

**Byrd**—Rob Roy Peery

Rob Roy Peery, who wrote the tune "Byrd," has given interesting information concerning "The Airmen's Hymn." He says it was one of a number of hymns resulting from a weekly collaboration between Doctor Farrington and himself when he was a student in New York City in the winter of 1928-1929. Mr. Peery writes further:

> We met regularly each Thursday night for many months, sometimes in my cramped quarters, usually at his own home. He would bring his new hymns to these meetings and read them to me; I would bring my settings of hymns he had given me at an earlier meeting. Thus we would work together, he encouraging my lagging inspiration, I suggesting certain changes which lent themselves to better musical treatment.
>
> "The Airmen's Hymn" came to light in that period of aviation history made colorful by the epochal flight of Charles A. Lindbergh. Aware of the existing hymns

for the safety of those on land and sea, our contribution was what I believe to be the first and only hymn for "those in air." Dr. Farrington's petition for "those who now command the ships that brave the sky" was to me a moving prayer for world fellowship, which deserved a strong, rugged musical treatment. My tune "Byrd" was written in just a few moments. I remember well the author's delight when I first played the melody for him. He called his wife into the room with enthusiasm and had me repeat it for her. Of course we did not then know that this newly born work would take its place in the hymnals of the day.

It was first published in *A Cycle of Hymns,* consisting of six hymns of our joint authorship, as a special edition for the Sixtieth Anniversary of the Woman's Foreign Missionary Society of the Methodist Episcopal Church in 1929.

Rob Roy Peery was born at Saga, Japan, January 6, 1900, the son of parents who were doing missionary service in that country at the time. The family returned to America in 1903, first living at Denver, where Rob Roy attended the public schools, and at the age of eight began the study of piano under his mother's guidance, and at eleven started lessons on the violin. His father becoming president of Midland College, then at Atchinson, Kansas (now located at Fremont, Nebraska), the young student graduated A. B. therefrom in 1920. Subsequently he studied and taught at Omaha and Denver, later going to Lenoir-Rhyne College, Hickory, North Carolina, as teacher of violin and organ. After further study at Chicago, Oberlin Conservatory of Music (Mus. Bac., 1925), and New York City, where he also did postgraduate work at the School of Sacred Music, Union Theological Seminary, he taught at Catawba College, Salisbury, North Carolina. In 1931 he joined the editorial staff of the Theodore Presser Company, Philadelphia, later becoming its chief music critic. For the last decade, among other steps to renown, he has become known as the composer of some excellent examples of pure and melodic hymn-tune writing.

**556—When the great ships, passing**—May Rowland (57)

**Mariners**—Lily Rendle (57)

Miss Rowland writes that the hymn was written in 1928, and that it "was a hymn for mariners. Having written a 'Prayer Hymn for Airmen,' I intended this hymn to be a prayer for all who voyage."

"Mariners" was written by Miss Rendle as a setting for this hymn. Both hymn and tune appear for the first time in *The Methodist Hymnal,* 1935.

**557—God be with you till we meet again**—Jeremiah Eames Rankin

**God be with you**—William Gould Tomer

This inordinately popular farewell hymn appeared in 1880 in *Gospel Bells,* a book compiled by Dr. J. E. Rankin, Congregational minister of Washington, D. C., his organist, John W. Bischoff, and his Sunday-school superintendent, Otis F. Presbrey. Doctor Rankin says:

It was written as a Christian good-bye, and first sung in the First Congregational Church of which I was minister for fifteen years. We had gospel meetings on Sunday nights, and our music was intentionally of the popular kind. I wrote the first stanza, and sent it to two gentlemen for music. The music which seemed to me best suited to the words was written by W. G. Tomer, teacher of public schools in New Jersey, at one time on the staff of General O. O. Howard. After receiving the music (which was revised by Dr. J. W. Bischoff), . . . I wrote the other stanzas.

Hackneyed though it may be, it nevertheless has a firm hold on the affections of millions of Christians of all denominations all over the world. It was a great favorite among the British soldiers in the South African War. Its familiar number in the famous Ira D. Sankey collection—494—was used by the men as a password. The author of *Chaplains in Khaki* says that on sentry the soldiers would meet and whisper, "Four-nine-four"; that they wrote these numbers in their letters, and that they shouted them as they, or their comrades, were going into battle. The founder of the Christian Endeavor Society, Dr. F. E. Clark, has said that this song followed him as a benediction hymn all around the world.

Jeremiah Eames Rankin, LL.D., was born at Thornton, New Hampshire, January 2, 1828. After completing his college course at Middlebury College and his theological course at Andover, he was ordained a minister of the Congregational Church, held various pastorates, and became President of Howard University, at Washington, D. C. He wrote a number of poems and a few hymns. Doctor Rankin died at Cleveland, Ohio, November 28, 1904.

William Gould Tomer, born October 5, 1833, died September 26, 1896, was a soldier in the Union Army, detailed at the headquarters of General O. O. Howard, was in the employ of the national government at Washington, and for some years taught music in the public schools of New Jersey. When he wrote his tune, "God be with you," he was in charge of the music at Grace Methodist Episcopal Church, Washington.

## Schools and Colleges

**558—Almighty Lord, with one accord**—Melancthon Woolsey Stryker

**Patten**—Peter Christian Lutkin (132)

This was first printed in *The New York Evangelist,* February 27, 1896, when it was entitled,

A College Hymn.

In the same year it was included in *The College Hymnal,* New York. One stanza of the original has been omitted from *The Methodist Hymnal* of 1935. Quite appropriately, it is sung as a Commencement hymn in many Christian colleges. For such use, when tune books are not available, "Azmon" (162) will serve admirably as a familiar tune for it.

Melancthon Woolsey Stryker, D.D., was born at Vernon, New York, January 7, 1851, and was educated at Hamilton College, New York, and at Auburn Theological Seminary. He was an eminent Presbyterian minister, serving churches in Auburn and Ithaca, New York, Holyoke, Massachusetts, and Chicago, Illinois. In 1892 he was called to the presidency of Hamilton

College, his Alma Mater. He was a student in the field of hymnology and compiled several hymnals and books of sacred song. He died at Clinton, New York, December 6, 1929.

"Patten" was written by Dean Peter C. Lutkin for this hymn for use in *The Methodist Hymnal* of 1905.

**559—O Thou whose feet have climbed life's hill—Louis Fitzgerald Benson (38)**

**St. Magnus** (78)—Jeremiah Clark (78)

According to his own statement in *Hymns Original and Translated,* Doctor Benson wrote this hymn at Philadelphia, February 2, 1894. It was first printed in *The Hymnal* (Presbyterian), 1895, and revised for the 1911 edition of the same book.

**560—Lord and Saviour, true and kind—Handley Carr Glyn Moule**

**Boyce (Sharon)**—William Boyce

This hymn first appeared in *The Council School Hymnal,* London, in 1905. It was entitled,

Jesus, the Guide of Youth.

Handley Carr Glyn Moule, born at Fordington, Dorset, England, December 23, 1841; educated at Trinity College, Cambridge, where he became a fellow; was Assistant Master at Marlborough; Dean of Trinity College; and became Bishop of Durham in 1901. Author of many books of prose and poetry, many of the latter containing hymns, this saintly man was a forceful figure in the Anglican Church, and won many honors. He died on May 8, 1920.

"Boyce," "Sharon," or "Halton Holgate," was written by Doctor Boyce as a setting in two parts for Psalm 4 in his *Melodies for the Psalms of David, according to the version of Christopher Smart, A. M.,* 1765.

William Boyce, Mus. Doc., a chorister of St. Paul's, was born in London, February 7, 1710, the son of a cabinetmaker. Variously, this distinguished musician was organist at a number of London churches; conductor of the famous "Three Choirs" of Gloucester, Worcester, and Hereford; Master of the King's Band; one of the organists of the Chapel Royal; and composer to the Chapel Royal. The impairment of his hearing in young manhood caused him but to work the harder, and not until he was about sixty years of age did it seriously conflict with his duties. After that date he gave up playing and teaching, removed to Kensington, and employed himself in collecting, compiling, and editing materials for the work which brought him his greatest fame:

> *Cathedral Music, being a collection in score of the most valuable and useful compositions for that service by the several English Masters of the last two hundred years.*

This monumental work, in three volumes, although projected by Dr. Maurice Greene, Boyce's predecessor at St. Paul's Cathedral, was carried through by

Doctor Boyce, eighteen years elapsing between the issuing of the first volume (1760) and the last (1778). As a composer he is best known for his anthems, a few of which are still sung. He may be looked upon as the last of the old school of English church musicians. An excellent musician, a good man, he died at Kensington, February 7, 1779.

Doctor Boyce was a friend of Charles Wesley and showed an interest in Wesley's two musical sons. (See No. 633b.) Upon hearing of his death in 1779, Charles Wesley addressed a poem to him beginning:

> Father of harmony, farewell!
> Farewell for a few fleeting years!
> Translated from the mournful vale,
> Jehovah's flaming ministers
> Have borne thee to thy place above,
> Where all is harmony and love.

**561—The Lord our God alone is strong—Caleb Thomas Winchester**

**Truro** (126)—From T. Williams' Psalmodia Evangelica (126)

Professor Winchester wrote this hymn in 1871 to be used at the dedication of the Orange Judd Hall of Natural Science, Wesleyan University, Middletown, Connecticut, from which he had graduated two years previously. It was first published in *The Hymn and Tune Book of the Methodist Episcopal Church,* 1878.

Caleb Thomas Winchester, LL.D., was born at Montville, Connecticut, January 18, 1847. Four years after his graduation from Wesleyan University in 1869, he became its Professor of English Literature. A scholar of note, Doctor Winchester was the author of several books, among them *The Life of John Wesley*. Of all his nonreligious books, his *Literary Criticism* is best known, still being a standard text in the field. To his painstaking labors as a member of the Joint Commission which compiled *The Methodist Hymnal* of 1905, may be attributed much of the excellence of that book. Dickinson College conferred upon him the honorary degree of Doctor of Literature in 1892. He died at his home in Middletown, Connecticut, March 24, 1920.

**562—The world's astir! The clouds of storm—Frank Mason North (465)**

**All Saints, New** (285)—Henry Stephen Cutler (285)

Doctor North gave the following information concerning this hymn:

> This was written in 1917, in response to an earnest appeal by Dr. Abram W. Harris, then, as Corresponding Secretary of The Board of Education, planning his program for "Children's Day," for a hymn with which the multitude of our young people, pressing outward from our schools toward the alluring, but untested world, might meet its fresh and fascinating appeal. I believed in Dr. Harris and in his ideals. We were indeed friends. Thirty years before when he was an instructor in Wesleyan University and I the pastor of the Methodist Church in Middletown, he was the delightful Superintendent of my Sunday School. Then came also the compulsion of the memory of my father, Charles Carter North, Esq. who, with Dr. George R. Crooks, when they were members of the Centenary Committee in 1866, had thought out "Children's Day" and started the Children's Fund. Through the years I had written much, even occasional verses, but no hymn for fourteen years. It was used with Dr. Harris's publications that year, 1917, as "The Student's Hymn," a title which still describes it.

## The Wesley Graces

**563—Be present at our table, Lord—John Cennick (199)**

**Uxbridge (186)—Lowell Mason (19)**

**564—We thank Thee, Lord, for this our food—John Cennick (199)**

**Hursley (56)—Adapted from Katholisches Gesangbuch, c. 1774 (56)**

These two *Metrical Graces* are more generally known and widely used by English-speaking people than any of the many others which have been written. John Cennick wrote them and included them in his *Sacred Hymns for the Children of God, In the Days of Their Pilgrimage*, 1741, as follows:

HYMN cxxx.
*Before* Meat.

Be present at our Table, Lord;
Be Here, and Ev'ry Where ador'd;
Thy Creatures bless, and grant that we
May feast in PARADISE with Thee.

HYMN cxxxi.
*After* Meat.

We bless Thee, Lord, for this our Food;
But more for Jesu's Flesh and Blood;
The *Manna* to our Spirits giv'n,
The Living Bread sent down from Heav'n;
Praise shall our Grateful Lips employ,
While Life and Plenty we enjoy;
Till worthy, we adore thy Name,
While banqueting with CHRIST, the LAMB.

The first has remained unchanged, but the second has been improved by the alterations which have been made. They are commonly called "The Wesley Graces." There are other modifications that are widely used. One of the treasures of City Road, London, is the teapot used by John Wesley, upon which he had engraved both the "Grace before Meat" and the "Grace after Meat."

Our Lord gave his sanction to the old Jewish custom of "giving thanks" and saying "a blessing" in the home at table. That the custom was followed by the early Christians, and that it had the approval of the Church is attested by the writings of the Church Fathers. Prose expressions were in general use until about the middle of the sixteenth century, but with the prominence given the metrical forms in the *Primer* of Henry VIII in 1545 the latter were generally accepted and have found a place in every English *Primer* since. In the Elizabethan *Primer*, this "Grace after Dinner" was given, with some prefatory remarks to which the twentieth century might well give heed:

Now You have well refreshed your bodyes, remember the lamentable afflictions and miseries of ye thousandes of your neighboures and brethren in Christ visited by the hand of God, some with mortall Plagues and diseases, some with imprisonmentes, some with extreme pouertye, and necessitie, so that eyther they cannot or they have not to feede on as you have done, remember therefore how muche and how deepely ye presente are bound to the goodness of God for your healthe wealth libertye, and many other his benefittes geuen vnto you.

Take hede ye neuer abuse the same,
Giue thankes to god for euerything;
And alwaie praise his holy name
Who doth not so is sore to blame
No euill ensample see that ye geue
Thus do the God's worde teache vs to lyve.

William T. Brooke asserts that the nonjuring and other influences upon John and Charles Wesley had much to do with the development of the English *Metrical Graces*. While John Wesley taught his followers the duty of "saying grace," it was his brother who provided adequately for its observance by writing a special booklet of *Twenty-six Graces,* which was published in 1746. In addition he included others in various works from 1739 to 1767. In recent years, probably owing to certain conditions which obtain in modern life, less attention is being given this beautiful custom than formerly. Would that all believers, everywhere, might say:

Thee let us taste in all our food,
And relish Thy free grace,
Always confess that Thou art good,
And always sing Thy praise.
Jesus, Thou art the living Bread,
That Bread which came from heaven:
For as Thy precious blood was shed,
For us Thy life was given.

# MUSIC FOR THE HOLY COMMUNION

Responses Doxologies

Ancient Hymns and Canticles

# RITUAL MUSIC FOR THE HOLY COMMUNION

## The Holy Communion

**565—Gloria Deo—** (a) John Merbecke
**566** (b) Marie Briel
**567** (c) Composer unknown

This is a modification of the "Gloria Tibi," the brief doxology, made to accord with the Order for the Administration of the Sacrament of the Lord's Supper in the Ritual of the Methodist Episcopal Church, but it need not be restricted to such usage. It may be said or sung as a prelude to, or may be considered as an announcement of, the reading of the Holy Scriptures, or at any other place in a service where the text might prove acceptable.

The "Gloria Tibi, Domini" (English form "Glory be to Thee, O Lord") was known in the Eastern Church as early as the fifth century, but not until later is it mentioned in the West. In the *Book of Common Prayer,* 1549, it was ordered to be said or sung before the reading of the Gospel.

John Merbecke was a sixteenth-century English church musician of more than ordinary importance, for it was he who in 1550 produced *The Booke of Common Praier noted,* which was the first setting to music of

*The Booke of the Common Prayer and Administracion of the Sacramentes, and other Rites and Ceremonies of the Churche, after the use of the Churche of England,*

authorized by the Act of Uniformity of 1549, and known as the First Prayer Book of Edward VI. When it is remembered that Merbecke's task was to supply music in keeping with the traditions of plainsong and at the same time adapt it to the accentual qualities of the English language, the difficulties which confronted him become apparent. That he acquitted himself creditably shows his unusual ability to recognize the necessities of the case.

Merbecke was not only a composer of ability, an organist at Windsor, and a Biblical student, but was an author of several theological controversial works which show him to have been an uncompromising Protestant.

In the dedication to Edward VI of his *Concordance,* 1550, he refers to himself as "altogether brought up in your highness Colledge at Wyndsore, in the study of Musike and plaiyng on Organs, wherin I consumed vainly the greatest part of my life." The date and place of his birth are not known. He died at Windsor, c. 1585.

Marie Briel, A. A. G. O., born at Peru, Illinois, February 14, 1896, Mus. Bac., 1919, Mus. M., 1925, Northwestern University School of Music, has taught at Marionville College, Missouri, Iowa Wesleyan College, and the

Columbia School of Music, Chicago, and is now a member of the faculty of the American Conservatory of Music, Chicago, and that of the National College of Education, Evanston. She is organist-director at Wilmette Methodist Episcopal Church.

**568—Gratia Tibi**—Thomas Tallis (51)

The "Gratia Tibi," "Thanks be to Thee, O Christ," is one of the minor elements of the "full service" ordered to be sung after the reading of the Gospel in *The Book of Common Prayer* of 1549.

The word "service" in church usage refers to a ritual or liturgical form prescribed for public worship consisting of a series of words and ceremonies. It is sometimes prefixed by a defining word, such as "Communion," "Burial," "Marriage," etc. In a musical sense it refers to a full set of musical settings of the chants, canticles, and other elements participated in by the choir or the congregation, or both, especially in the Anglican Church. None of the metrical hymns or anthems are included. The parts of the Morning and Evening Service include the Venite, Te Deum, Benedicite, Benedictus (Dominus), Jubilate, Kyrie, Nicene Creed, Sanctus, Agnus Dei, Benedictus (qui venit), Gloria in excelsis, Magnificat, Cantate Domino, Nunc Dimittis, and Deus Misereatur—not all, however, being included in any one service. In addition there are, or may be, certain minor elements such as the Amen, the Gloria Tibi, etc. In the "full service" it is usual to write all of the several parts in a common key; hence, they are designated not only by the name of the composer but also by the name of the key in which they are written. Thus "Wesley in F" is understood to mean his setting of the parts that comprise the Morning Service in the key of F.

**569—Gloria Patri**— (a) Charles Meineke

**570** (b) Henry Wellington Greatorex (378)

**571** (c) Parisian Tone

The Gloria Patri, called the "Lesser Doxology," although not an exact rendering of the Latin, "is ancient and adequate." Originally it consisted of:

> Glory be to the Father, and to the Son, and to the Holy Ghost, world without end. Amen.

The extended form resulted from the insistence of the orthodox parties to the Arian controversy that all possible points relating to the "consubstantiality" of the Father and the Son be emphasized. The phrase,

> As it was in the beginning, is now, and ever shall be,

was inserted and in time gained general acceptance. It was one of the brief responses in which the congregations of the early church participated. In the English Church it is appointed to be sung after the Psalm, and in most of the Nonliturgical churches using it, its place is after the Responsive Reading or after the Apostles' Creed or other Affirmation of Faith.

(a)—569—This setting is from the "Evening Prayer" in Charles Meineke's

*Music for the Church, containing Sixty-two Psalm and Hymn Tunes in Four Parts Together with Chants, Doxologies, and Responses . . . Composed for St. Paul's Church, Baltimore, by C. Meineke, Organist,* Baltimore: 1844. Its original form was:

Charles Meineke, 1782-1850, was a German pianist and organist, who was occupying the position of organist at St. Paul's Church, Baltimore, Maryland, in 1836. Between his departure from Germany in 1810 and his known residence in Baltimore from 1822, he lived sometime in England. He is not to be confused with a man by the same name who was one-time organist at Oldenburg.

(b)–570–This is Gloria Patri No. 1 from *Greatorex's Church Music,* 1851.

(c)–571–The same as the "Rouen Meditation," Tone V, ending 8:

This version was one of the late forms of the old Psalm Tones which came into use in France, especially in Paris and Rouen. It was known to the English as the "Parisian Tone."

**572—The Lord's Prayer—** (a) Gregorian
**573** (b) C. A. Wickes (?)
**574** (c) Vincent Novello

This is the prayer of our Lord which He uttered after saying to His disciples, "After this manner pray ye." It is in the form taken over from The Great Bible of 1539[1] into *The Book of Common Prayer.* James Moffatt says the admission that "because the Prayer which Christ taught His disciples is not only a pattern of prayer but itself a most comprehensive prayer, we recommend it to be used in the prayers of the Church," was one of the few sound features in *The Directory of Public Worship* which was taken over by the Church of Scotland, in the seventeenth century, from the English Puritans.

(a)–572–"Gregorian" is a general name given to the type of ritual music associated with the liturgy of the Roman Church, that is, plainsong or chant. It is one of the oldest of musical institutions, its use having extended over twelve or more centuries. It is a form of musical declamation primarily suited to prose texts and has no definite rhythmic or time structure. Being the only kind of music the use of which has ever been authoritatively commanded by the Roman Church, its acceptance was naturally universal up to the time of the Reformation, and since that time has been very general. It was

[1] See Note under No. 626.

based upon those ancient melodies which had been inherited by the early Christians, and which because of the persecutions, they were able to hand down from generation to generation by oral tradition only. Such a method of transmission continued over the years could lead only to their being grossly corrupted, if not hopelessly lost. To remedy these evils, Bishop Ambrose of Milan (38) gathered together all that were then in use, reduced them to their purest possible form, and set forth rules which greatly reduced the chances of future deterioration. Gregory the Great, about two centuries later, amplified the work of Ambrose by making a second collection, more extensive than that of Ambrose and based on a more comprehensive musical system. Whereas Ambrose had laid down four modes (scales) as the basis of his system, Gregory added eight or nine more; where Ambrose's tones (tunes) were those of the Psalms and the ancient Canticles of the Church, those of Gregory included ritual music, music for the Antiphons used during the whole ecclesiastical year, and many new hymns. This large collection became known as the *Cantus planus* ("plain chant"), later distinguished by the names "Ambrosian Chant" and "Gregorian Chant," respectively. The first is now used only in those churches which comprise the diocese of Milan, but the second, for centuries inseparably wedded to the Roman Catholic ritual, is now, and has been for some time past, finding a place alongside the Anglican chant for modern church use. It is impossible, with any degree of certainty, to assign a date of composition to any of the old Gregorian Chants.

(b)–573–The author of this MANUAL has been unable to secure information of any kind concerning the source of this chant or concerning its composer, C. A. Wickes.

(c)–574–From a *Service in A* by Vincent Novello.

Vincent Novello, founder of the great firm of music publishers, Novello & Co., Ltd., was born at London, September 6, 1781. Greatly interested in choral music, he was a chorister under Samuel Webbe (35) at the Sardinian Chapel, London; organist for twenty-five years (from 1797) at the Portuguese Chapel, and for a time at the Rouen Catholic Chapel, Moorfields; and pianist to the Italian Opera Company in London. His greatest contribution, by far, was his publishing of all kinds of the better class of music, making available a splendid catalogue. Upon his retirement from active work he made his home in Nice, where he died August 9, 1861. A memorial window honoring him was placed in the north transept of Westminster Abbey.

**575—The Ten Commandments**
**Our Lord's Summary of the Law**
**Response to the Commandments**—(a) Composer unknown
(b) Charles François Gounod
(c) Thomas Tallis (51)

The Ten Commandments are as in the King James Version of Exodus 20. 3-17.

Our Lord's Summary of the Law is based upon St. Mark 12. 29-31, and St. John 13. 34.

These responses, which have become known as the "English Kyrie," may be traced directly to the *Strassburg Litany* of Pullian, 1551.

The second *Book of Common Prayer,* having been revised under Calvinistic influences, was issued in 1552. It established the custom of reciting the Commandments during the Communion Service.

(a)—Composer and source unknown.

(b)—Charles François Gounod, whose father was a painter of distinction and whose mother was a fine pianist, was born at Paris, June 17, 1818. Unusually gifted in music, Gounod was so disappointed by the ill success of his early compositions that he determined to study for the priesthood. Though returning, upon wise counsel, to his work of composing, he gained from his two years in theological study a love for reading and literary attainment possessed by few musicians. Driven from France in 1870 by the horrors of the Franco-Prussian War, he spent some years in England. Always religious, in his late life he became especially so, devoting all of his time and thought to the composition of sacred music. It was at this period of his life that he wrote that which so appeals to the taste of English-speaking people. He is generally favorably known, although criticized for emphasizing the melodic element in his writing at the expense of variety and dramatic expression. Among his best known works are *Faust, The Redemption, Messe Solennelle* (St. Cecilia), and *Gallia.* He died at Saint-Cloud, October 17, 1893.

(c)—This form of the chant was included in William Boyce's *Cathedral Music,* Volume I, 1760 (560), and was set to the "Venite" in Thomas Tallis's *Service, Preces, and Litany in F.*

**576—Kyrie—** (a) John Merbecke (565)
**577** (b) From a Lutheran Service of 1528

The "Kyrie eleison" is that portion of the Ordinary[1] of the Mass which follows immediately after the Introit, preceding the Gloria in excelsis. This general cry for mercy is of very ancient origin. Historically speaking, it is the end of the Litany which preceded the Mass, and in the earliest days of the church was repeated *ad libitum.* The ninefold Kyrie which dates from the early medieval period consists of a threefold "Kyrie eleison," a threefold "Christe eleison," and a threefold "Kyrie eleison" repeated. The text of the Kyrie originated in the Greek Church and has never been changed to Latin.

(a)—576—The source is Merbecke's *The Book of Common Praier Noted,* 1550. (See No. 565.)

(b)—577—This comes from a Lutheran service of 1528. The Lutheran service followed closely that of the Roman Church except in the use of the German language, the prominence of the sermon, and the introduction of the chorales which admitted the congregation to much larger participation in public worship. Each Sunday had its prescribed Bible lesson, its versicles and prayers, most of the chorales used, and other music. The Lutheran liturgy

[1] The Ordinary is that part of the Mass which is unchanging from day to day. It has remained unchanged for centuries.

was especially favorable to music, as was that of both the Roman and the Anglican Church. It followed closely the order of the Roman High Mass, some parts of it being in Latin. Its elaborate musical features were: an organ prelude, often of considerable length; a motet, frequently in Latin; the Kyrie; the Litany; the Creed; a short cantata or a motet, known as the "principal music"; several chorales, often with elaborate interludes between the stanzas and with other embellishments by the organ or other accompanying agency; and, nearly always, another motet during the communion service. Such great care was taken with the preparation of the music for these services that much of it—such as the Bach cantatas, passion music, choral-preludes and elaborations, etc.—has survived in great favor even to the present time.

The services were lengthy, that of the ordinary Sunday beginning at seven o'clock in the morning and lasting at least four hours, including the long sermon and the communion service. The elaborateness of these services varied with the size of the towns. There was also an elaborate afternoon service similar to that of the morning, without the Eucharist. When special festivals were held, the time was frequently extended to more than one day. So extremely popular were these services that much of the enthusiasm of the German people today for the more intellectual type of music can be traced to their influence.

**578—Responses to the Beatitudes of our Lord**—Ancient Tone, as in The Church Hymnary, 1927

The Beatitudes, as in St. Matthew 5. 3-10, authorized version.

This "Ancient Tone," or tune, with slight rhythmic change, was that which was sung to the phrase of the Litany:

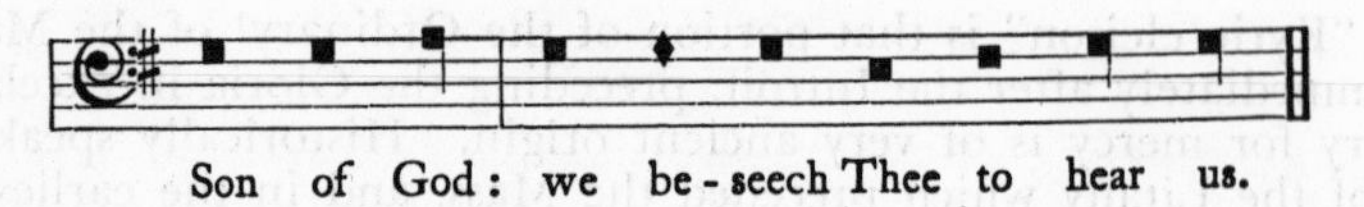
Son of God: we be-seech Thee to hear us.

**579—Responses to the Beatitudes of our Lord**—(a) Robert Guy McCutchan (9[2])

**580** —(b) Van Denman Thompson (153)

This form of the Responses to the Beatitudes was that recommended by the General Conference Commission on Ritual of the Methodist Episcopal Church and adopted by the General Conference of that Church held at Atlantic City, New Jersey, May, 1932. It was the desire of the Editorial Committee of the Joint Commission preparing *The Methodist Hymnal* of 1935 to have two forms of setting for these Responses, one melodic and the other in chant form. The Editor fulfilled the commission to provide them, by writing No. 579 himself and by prevailing upon his friend, Doctor Thompson, to write No. 580.

**581—Presentation of the Offering for the Needy**—(a) Ludwig van Beethoven (12)

**582** —(b) Jonathan Battishill

The first one of the Responses after the Presentation of the Offering for the Needy is from 1 Chronicles 29. 14. It is a part of King David's prayer as recorded in verses 10-19, of the same chapter. A reading of the historic setting will aid in making the meaning of this Response more vivid.

The second is from Hebrews 13. 16. It is the rendering used in *The Book of Common Prayer,* 1549, with "well" inserted before "pleased."

(a)—581—Beethoven's music for this Response is one of the best liked and most widely known of all responses and is in favor with congregations of all denominations.

(b)—582—This is from J. Battishill's *Fifty Double and Single Chants being the most favorite as perform'd at St. Paul's, Westminster, and most of the Cathedrals in England,* c. 1768.

Jonathan Battishill, born at London, in May, 1738, was a chorister at St. Paul's Cathedral; an organist in London churches; and a composer of much sacred and secular music of good quality. He died at Islington, December 10, 1801, and in accordance with his last wish, was buried in St. Paul's, near Doctor Boyce (560), for whom he had for a time officiated on the organ of the Chapel Royal.

**583—Sursum Corda**—John Camidge

Lamentations 3. 41 has been given as the source of the *Sursum Corda:* "Let us lift up our heart with our hands unto God in the heavens." This versicle, which is found in all of the ancient liturgies, is used in that of the Roman Church at the beginning of the Preface, and in the Anglican Communion office, inviting the people to join in thanksgiving to Almighty God. This setting is from a *Service in E,* but the date of its composition has not yet been ascertained.

John Camidge was the first of the line of a family of musicians prominent in Yorkshire, England, for more than a century. He was born at York in 1735, and died there April 25, 1803. Succeeding to the post of organist of York Minster upon the resignation of his Master, James Nares, in 1756, he remained there until his retirement in 1799.

**584—Sanctus, with Preface**—Composer unknown

It is a matter of regret that the composer of this beautiful setting of the Sanctus is unknown. The most effective way to use it is to have a solo voice, preferably a baritone, sing the Preface, the choir and the congregation joining at the beginning of the Sanctus, according to the early Latin rite.

This Cherubical Hymn, *Ter Sanctus,* the Ascription "Holy, holy, holy, Lord God of hosts, . . ." is the culmination of the Preface and leads up to the Prayer of Consecration. From its probable primitive origin, it was used in the ancient Jewish service as recorded in Isaiah 6. 3, and occupies a prominent place in all liturgies. A similar ascription is also a part of the Te Deum Laudamus (625). The early forms of musical setting were in the simplest chant form, but as the plainsong developed they became more elaborate and frequently had appended the "Hosanna in the highest."

**585—Sanctus**—Alexander Samuel Cooper

This setting is from *The Parochial Chant Book,* London, n.d. It was used by Dr. Charles L. Hutchins in his *Chant and Service Book,* 1894.

Alexander Samuel Cooper, F. R. C. O., organist and composer, was born at London, April 30, 1835. He served as organist at St. John's, Putney, St. Paul's, and Covent Garden; was awarded a prize by the Ely Diocesan Church Music Society for a setting of the Nicene Creed in 1869; was the composer of anthems, music for Holy Communion, chants, hymn tunes, songs, and part songs; and was the editor of *The Parochial Psalter* and *The Parochial Chant Book,* both of which have passed through many editions. The date of his death has not been ascertained.

**586—Agnus Dei**— (a) John Merbecke (565)
**587** (b) Giovanni Pierluigi da Palestrina (156)

The "Agnus Dei" is based on a part of St. John 1. 29: "The next day John seeth Jesus coming unto him, and saith, Behold the Lamb of God, which taketh away the sin of the world." Its place in the service of the Communion is after the Consecration and before the partaking of the elements. In the Roman Church it is a part of the Ordinary of the Mass—that is, its use is obligatory. In the Nonliturgical churches its use is, of course, optional.

The Agnus Dei was introduced into the Roman ritual by Pope Sergius I, d. 701, who wished to include in the liturgy of the Western Church some of the desirable features already in use in the Eastern Church. This is the one part of the Ordinary in which a change in the text is ever permitted. The *Miserere nobis,* later the *dona nobis pacem,* was changed to *dona eis requiem sempiternam* in the Requiem Mass—that for the dead.

(a)—586—This is from Merbecke's *Service in E minor* in *The Book of Common Praier Noted,* 1550.

While the Agnus Dei was included in the first English Prayer Book of 1549, it was omitted from that of 1552. That accounts for this beautiful adaptation by Merbecke from the plainsong. The chant has long since been restored to its place in the English service.

To make it most effective, there should be a short organ interlude after the first clause as well as after its repetition.

(b)—587—This is an example of the simplicity of style adopted by Palestrina in his settings for the more solemn and serious parts of the Communion Service.

**588—Gloria in excelsis**—Old Scottish chant

The Gloria in excelsis, known as "The Greater Doxology," is also called the "Angelic Hymn" because its opening words are from the song the Angels sang at Bethlehem, recorded in St. Luke 2. 13, 14: "And suddenly there was with the angel a multitude of the heavenly host praising God, and saying, Glory to God in the highest, and on earth peace, good will toward men." It is said to date from the time of St. Athanasius, 296-393.

This is known as the "enlarged form," an expansion of one of the earliest of Christian hymns. It still occupies its original opening place in the Mass, but in the Anglican use, since the revision of *The Book of Common Prayer* in 1552, it has stood at the close of the service after the Communion and the prayer of thanksgiving. To Cranmer, supposedly responsible in large measure for the revision of 1552, should go the credit for making this most admirable change in position.

The "Old Scottish Chant" is so well known that it is often designated simply as "Old Chant." The inability of extensive search to clear up the mystery of its source is extraordinary in the light of its long-continued use and familiarity.

# RESPONSES AND SENTENCES

## Opening

**589—The Lord is in His holy temple—**(a) Karl Pomeroy Harrington (10)
**590** (b) Calvin Weiss Laufer (130)
**591** (c) Karl Pomeroy Harrington (10)

This "Opening Response," perhaps more generally used than any other, is taken from Habakkuk 2. 20.

(a)—589—Professor Harrington wrote this at a time when he was teaching at the University of Maine. He has written:

> The "Invocation Sentence" was written at the request of President (Abram) Harris, then of the University of Maine, to introduce the chapel service at the University. He wanted something to quiet the audience at once at the beginning of the short period allotted for chapel. This invocation sentence was used regularly there from that time onward, I think, for some years. It began to be used at Wesleyan for the same purpose soon after the introduction of *The (Methodist) Hymnal* in 1905 and was used for a good many years until radical changes in the service took place. It was my custom to save time and accomplish Doctor Harris's purpose by using two notes only to introduce it, the first two notes of the little tune. I cannot tell exactly when this was composed, but I think it must have been as early as 1903.

(b)—590—This was written by Doctor Laufer in 1926, and was included in *The Hymnal* of the Presbyterian Church, 1933.

(c)—591—Written by Professor Harrington in 1932, his second setting of this opening sentence was first published in *The Methodist Hymnal* in 1935.

**592—Father of lights, in whom there is no shadow—**Elizabeth Wilson and Helen Thoburn

**Welwyn**—Alfred Scott-Gatty

Of the composition of this Response Miss Wilson has written:

> In the spring of 1913 Helen Thoburn was writing a pageant, *The Ministering of the Gift,* for the Fourth National Convention of the Young Women's Christian Associations of the U. S. A., which was to be held in Richmond, Virginia. One afternoon she came into my office in the headquarters building, New York City, asking whether I thought that an unpublished hymn of eight lines, based on Loyalty to Christ, which she had previously written for a Week of Prayer program, could be enlarged into a processional for the Richmond pageant, to be sung to Jeffrey's stirring tune, "Ancient of Days." Instantly the idea of God, the Father of Lights, sending His greatest gift, The Light of the World, flashed into my mind, and we began working those themes into the original verses, at intervals pacing up and down the long corridor singing to test the marching values of the rhythm and making changes where emphasis required. When our colleagues passed us as the offices closed, we were still putting our Recessional to this proof.
>
> The pageant was extremely successful and the Recessional began to be sung in all parts of all kinds of Association meetings, so that the original third line of stanza one, "Ere we depart, we seek Thy holy presence," we agreed to alter to read, "With

one accord, we seek Thy holy presence." Certainly this sounded better when we two attended a fashionable church wedding and saw the bridal party coming up the aisle to this music.

The first four lines of the two eight-line stanza "Hymn of the Lights" have been used for this Opening Response.

Elizabeth Wilson, born at Neenah, Wisconsin, August 19, 1867, is the daughter of the Rev. Thomas Coles Wilson, a member of the Wisconsin Conference. Educated at Lawrence University (now College); Oxford, England; the University of Jena, Germany; and the Bengal Government Weaving Institute, Serampore, India, and teaching at Lawrence for five years, she began her connection with the Young Women's Christian Association in 1889 and continued it until 1928, spending a part of this time in India as an Association secretary. Retiring from active work in the Association, she returned to her former home, Appleton, Wisconsin, where she now lives, an ordained minister of the Methodist Episcopal Church. One time an officer in the American Association of Women Preachers, she is also a member of the British Society for the Ministry of Women.

Helen Thoburn, born at Union City, Pennsylvania, June 17, 1885, and educated at Leland Stanford University, spent eight years in China as an editorial secretary of the Young Women's Christian Association. She made many trips from America to the Orient, interpreting each to the other. Upon her return to New York City she undertook special responsibility for the international educational program of the Association. She died suddenly at New York City, February 3, 1932.

"Welwyn," by Sir Alfred Scott-Gatty, is from the "Arundel Hymns," London, 1902.

Alfred Scott-Gatty (Sir Alfred Scott), born at Ecclesfield, Yorkshire, England, April 26, 1847, was an amateur musician who wrote a great number of popular songs of simple, unaffected melody and style. He is perhaps best known for his *Plantation Songs* in four volumes. His first compositions were published in *Aunt Judy's Magazine,* of which his mother was the editor in 1868. Among his contributions were several musical plays for children. Much interested in heraldry, he became Garter Principal King of Arms in 1904, and was knighted soon after he received this appointment. He died at London, December 18, 1918.

**593—Jesus, stand among us—**William Pennefather

**Vesper** (Mann)—Frederick A. Mann (?)

This simple, yet beautiful prayer, suited admirably for the opening of public worship, is from William Pennefather's *Hymns Original and Selected,* published posthumously in 1873. It was written and printed as a leaflet for use at the Barnet and Mildmay Conferences, which the author founded at Barnet in the 1850's.

William Pennefather, son of a Baron of the Irish Exchequer, was born at Dublin, Ireland, February 5, 1816. Educated at Westbury College and at

Trinity College, Dublin, and taking Holy Orders, he served an appointment as curate and one as vicar in Ireland before removing to England in 1848. The "Conferences" he inaugurated at Barnet, in England, and later carried on at Mildmay Park resulted in the establishment of the famous large charitable and religious institutions at Mildmay, his greatest work. It was at Mildmay that he introduced into England the Order of Deaconesses. He died at Muswell Hill, London, April 30, 1873.

The author of this MANUAL has been unable to secure any information concerning the tune "Vesper" or its composer, Frederick A. Mann.

**594—Let all mortal flesh keep silence**—Liturgy of St. James
Translated by Gerard Moultrie
Picardy—French traditional carol

This is known as the "Prayer of the Cherubic Hymn," is from The Liturgy of St. James, and is found in *Translations of the Primitive Liturgies,* 1868-69, Neale and Littledale. It had been put into metrical form by Gerard Moultrie for the second edition of *Lyra Eucharistica,* 1864, and three years later came into *The People's Hymnal,* when it was designated for use "Before Consecration."

The Liturgy of St. James, also known as The Liturgy of Jerusalem, is one of the five great original forms of service used for the celebration of the Eucharist upon which those of modern times are based. It is one of the earliest forms of Christian liturgical worship.

Gerard Moultrie, English clergyman, translator of Greek, Latin, and German hymns, and author of other original ones, was born at Rugby, September 16, 1829. He was educated at Rugby, and at Exeter College, Oxford. After taking Holy Orders, he became chaplain in Shrewsbury School, served in a number of other appointments, and in 1873 became warden of St. James's College, Southleigh. Many of his hymns, first appearing in *The Church Times* and other papers, dealt, for the most part, with subjects not usually treated by hymn writers. He died at Southleigh, April 25, 1885.

"Picardy" is a French carol, probably from the seventeenth century, but is in a mood quite different from most carols originating in France. It was entitled "Romancero" in Tiersot's *Melodies,* Paris, 1887. It should never be taken at a quick tempo. On the contrary, it should be sung very slowly in order to make clear its ceremonial character.

**595—O worship the Lord in the beauty of holiness**—From the Scriptures
Setting by John Porter
(8)

This opening sentence is based on 1 Chronicles 16. 29: "Give unto the Lord the glory due unto His name: bring an offering, and come before Him: worship the Lord in the beauty of holiness," and Psalm 100. 2: "Serve the Lord with gladness: come before His presence with singing." James Gibbon Huneker, in his *Steeplejack,* said that God cannot be worshiped beautifully enough.

# After Prayer

**596—Hear our prayer, O Lord**—George Whelpton

This response after Prayer has had very extensive use. It was written about 1900 and was first printed in a four-page leaflet containing other responses and a dismissal hymn which Mr. Whelpton had prepared.

George Whelpton, born at Redbourne, England, May 17, 1847, came to this country with his father's family in 1851. Entering the Union Army at the age of sixteen, he had some experience as an assistant pharmacist which enabled him to secure work in a drugstore and thus to defray the expense of going to high school. His only preparation for his later work in music was had in classes under H. R. Palmer (314) and with a private teacher in Boston. For many years a well-known choir director in Buffalo, from 1903 to 1925, when he retired from active work, he was engaged in the business of editing various publications. He died suddenly at Oxford, Ohio, November 25, 1930.

**597—Let the words of my mouth**—From Psalm 19
Setting from Adolph Baumbach

These are the words of the last verse of Psalm 19, than which no more beautiful and appropriate Response after Prayer has ever been penned.

This setting is taken from *Baumbach's Sacred Quartets, A Collection of Pieces for the Opening and Close of Service,* Boston, 1862. It is from a "Response" to these words which opens with a duet for alto and tenor:

Adolph Baumbach was born in Germany about 1830, and died in Chicago in 1880. He came to America and in 1855 was in Boston. He was a teacher of piano and organ, a composer of pieces for instruction on the piano, and compiled a collection for quartet choirs.

**598—Almighty Father, hear our prayer**—Setting arranged from Felix Mendelssohn-Bartholdy (7)

The source of the text of this prayer is unknown.

See No. 601 for the source of this setting.

**599—Through love to light! O wonderful the way**—Richard Watson Gilder (10)

**Finlandia** (73)—Jean Sibelius (73)
Arranged for The Hymnal, 1932

This is the "After Song" to *The New Day, A Poem in Songs and Sonnets,* found in Richard Watson Gilder's complete works.

**600—Saviour, hear us, we pray**—W. W. Ellsworth (?)

**Lucy**—Arranged from Johannes Brahms

This lovely little prayer appeared in *The Methodist Sunday School Hymnal,* 1911, edited by Dr. John R. Van Pelt and Dean Peter C. Lutkin (132).

W. W. Ellsworth is unknown to the author of this Manual and no information concerning him has been secured.

"Lucy," also called "Brahms," was arranged from Brahms's "Lullaby" for this prayer by Dean Lutkin for *The Methodist Sunday School Hymnal,* 1911.

Johannes Brahms, Mus. Doc., one of the greatest of the great among musicians, was born at Hamburg, Germany, May 7, 1833, and died at Vienna, April 3, 1897. His songs, symphonies, and the great *Requiem* have made him known as a composer of the first rank. It would be futile to attempt to do justice to a discussion of his five hundred works in such limited space as can be allotted here. He was a man of noble ideals, was a prodigious reader, had a widely cultivated mind, and was in every respect deserving of the praise that has been lavished upon him.

**601—Hear Thou in love, O Lord, our cry**—From Elijah

Arranged from Felix Mendelssohn-Bartholdy (7)

The text is taken from the oratorio *Elijah* and is a part of the prayer of the prophet and the people for rain, after the destruction of the prophets of Baal. As his own librettist, Mendelssohn drew largely upon his thorough knowledge of the Bible, which, for oratorio texts, he said "is always the best source of all."

William H. Callcott, 1807-82, wrote a tune, "Intercession," for use in *Psalms and Hymns for Divine Worship,* 1867, and Dr. Horatius Bonar (210) was asked

> to furnish a fitting refrain to the two lovely lines of Mendelssohn's, with which Callcott's tune "Intercession," ends. In searching for a Scripture theme containing some reiterated phrase almost of the nature of a refrain, he was struck with Solomon's prayer at the dedication of the temple (2 Chron. vi.), in which every separate petition concludes with substantially the same words. This idea was taken for the starting point, and Solomon's words, "Hear Thou from heaven, Thy dwelling place, and forgive," became the familiar couplet—
>
> Hear then, in love, O Lord, the cry,
> In heaven, Thy dwelling-place on high.

The hymn was "When the weary, seeking rest." It was the hymn numbered 509 in *The Methodist Hymnal* of 1905. Slight changes in its wording have been made.

The tune appears in the oratorio, *Elijah,* at the close of the dramatic "Baal scene," one of the most thrilling in all musical literature. This oratorio was completed at Leipzig, August 11, 1846.

## After Scripture

**602—Hosanna in the highest**—The setting from Charles François Gounod (575)

The acclamation, "Hosanna in the highest," is found in St. Mark 11. 10: "Blessed be the kingdom of our father David, that cometh in the name of the Lord: Hosanna in the highest," from which comes also the suggestion for the Benedictus qui venit following the Sanctus in the Roman and Anglican liturgies. It must not, however, be confused with the Benedictus at No. 628, from St. Luke 1. This ascription of praise to God has been in liturgical use from very early times. It is frequently used with the Benedictus qui venit.

This Hosanna in excelsis is the last phrase of the Benedictus in Gounod's *Messe Solonnelle,* the "St. Cecelia's Mass," which is thought to have been written during the five years (1845-50) he was living in seclusion.

**603—God be merciful unto us and bless us**

The Response is Psalm 67. 1-2, verbatim. The composer of the setting is unknown.

**604—Thy testimonies are very sure**—Setting by Robert Guy McCutchan (9*)

Responses after Scripture being few in number and an additional one being desired by the Editorial Committee of the Joint Commission revising *The Methodist Hymnal,* the editor, Robert G. McCutchan, was asked to provide another, and this is the result, the words being those from Psalm 93. 5.

**605—O Lord, open Thou our eyes**—Setting by John Camidge (583)

This is based on Psalm 119. 18.

The source of this setting by John Camidge has not been ascertained.

## Offertory

**606—Offertory Response** (581)—(a) Arranged from Ludwig van Beethoven (12)
**607** (b) Pelham Humfrey
**608** (c) George Alexander MacFarran (535)

(a)—606—This arrangement from a work of Beethoven is undoubtedly the most familiar of all the responses sung during or after the taking of the Offering. It is simple, tuneful, and reverent in its spirit.

(b)—607—This setting is from Pelham Humfrey's *Service in C,* where it was associated with the Venite (626).

Pelham Humfrey, English musician, born in 1647,[1] was one of the first set of children of the Chapel Royal when it was re-established in 1660, and showed such marked musical talent that Charles II sent him abroad to continue his studies. Upon his return from Italy and France he again was taken into the Chapel Royal, having been chosen for a vacancy which occurred during his absence, and upon the death of Captain Henry Cooke he was appointed Master of Children. Pepys, in his *Diary,* makes many references to him and his music. Humfrey was the composer of many fine anthems, and much other music, some of his best being that for the play, *The Tempest.* He died at Windsor, July 14, 1674, at the early age of twenty-seven years.

(c)—608—Taken from *MacFarran in C* as in *The Anglican Chant Book,* etc., edited by Edwin George Monk, 1850. It has been transposed to the lower key of B-flat for congregational use.

**609—Bless Thou the gifts our hands have brought**—Samuel Longfellow (42)
**Canonbury** (116)—Robert Schumann (116)

A stanza from Samuel Longfellow's hymn beginning, "Thou Lord of Life, our saving health."

**610—We give Thee but Thine own** (456)—William Walsham How (197)
**St. Andrew**—Joseph Barnby (31)

"St. Andrew" was written in 1866 by Sir Joseph Barnby for the hymn beginning,

Sweet is Thy mercy, Lord,

by Dr. J. S. B. Monsell (114), while Barnby was organist at St. Andrew's Church, London, 1863 to 1871. It was published without name in his *Hymn Tunes,* 1869. In the Preface of that book it is said to have been written for use at St. Andrew's. In his *Hymn Tunes,* published posthumously in 1897, it was called "St. Andrew."

[1] This is the spelling used by himself, but it will also be often found as "Humphrey" or "Humphreys," with every possible variety of spelling.

**611—All things are Thine: no gift have we**—John Greenleaf Whittier (120)
**Herr Jesu Christ**—From Pensum Sacrum, 1648
Arranged by Johann Sebastian Bach (52)

This was written in 1873 by John G. Whittier, in four quatrains, for the opening of Plymouth Church, St. Paul, Minnesota, and was published in *Hazel Blossoms* two years later, and in his *Complete Poetical Works* in 1876. It came into American hymnody by way of W. Garrett Horder's *Congregational Hymns*, London, 1884.

"Herr Jesu Christ" is found as No. 45 in an octavo volume published at Görlitz, Germany: *Pensum Sacrum, Metro-Rhythmicum, CCLXVII Odis . . . denuo expansum expensumque Opera et Studio Tobiae Hauschkonii* (1648). It has an Appendix which contains eighty melodies, without texts, suitable for the Latin odes in the volume. This melody occurs among several old hymn tunes, and, doubtless, dates from an older period than the volume published at Görlitz. The melody was sung to the hymn "Herr Jesu Christ, dich zu uns wend," in the following form:

The hymn has been attributed to William II, Duke of Saxony, but on insufficient and inconclusive evidence.

## Closing

**612—Now may He who from the dead**—John Newton (27)
**Solitude**—Lewis Thomas Downes

This is the first stanza of three from one of the Short Hymns from Book III, *Olney Hymns*, 1779, written by John Newton to be sung "After Sermon." It is based on Hebrews 13. 20-22: "Now the God of peace, that brought again from the dead our Lord Jesus, that great shepherd of the sheep, through the blood of the everlasting covenant, make you perfect in every good work to do His will, working in you that which is well-pleasing in His sight, through Jesus Christ; to whom be glory for ever and ever. Amen. And I beseech you, brethren, suffer the word of exhortation: for I have written a letter unto you in a few words."

"Solitude" was written for these words by Lewis Thomas Downes (July 9, 1824–June 16, 1910), an organist at Providence, Rhode Island. It was written in 1850 and has been widely used as a setting for a number of different hymns. Of late years its popularity has waned.

**613—The Lord bless thee and keep thee**—Setting by Lucy Rider Meyer

The text, the "Old Testament benediction," is taken literally from Numbers 6. 24-26.

This setting was made by Miss Lucy Rider, either late in 1884 or early in 1885, to be sung at the close of the evening chapel services held at Marquand Hall, Northfield Seminary, Massachusetts. It has become known as "The Northfield Benediction."

Lucy Rider Meyer was born September 9, 1849, at New Haven, near Middlebury, Vermont. Her early education was obtained in the schools in and near her home, where she was able to prepare herself for teaching. While still in her teens she taught in the high school at Brandon, Vermont, and in a school for freedmen at Greensboro, North Carolina. She entered Oberlin College in her twenty-first year, having prepared herself to enter the Junior class. Becoming engaged to a young man whose intention it was to become a medical missionary, Miss Rider entered the Women's Medical School in Philadelphia in order to prepare herself for the same career. The early death of her betrothed caused her to revise her plans completely. She said in later years, "There came a winter when all my plans were frustrated and my future was a blank."

Recovering her poise, Miss Rider's interest was engaged in the work Doctor Vincent was doing at Lake Chautauqua, and she was profoundly impressed by the personality of that great leader. She was for a time "Lady Principal" of the Troy Conference Academy, Poultney, Vermont, and Professor of Chemistry, at McKendree College, Illinois. Upon her return from being a delegate to the World's Sunday School Convention held at London in 1880, she became Field Secretary of the Illinois State Sunday School Association. In this position she became keenly conscious of the great need for adequately trained Christian leaders.

She spent the winter of 1884-85 as a teacher at Northfield Seminary, was married in the spring of 1885 to Josiah Shelley Meyer, a Methodist Episcopal minister of the Rock River Conference, and with him, the same year, opened the Chicago Training School for City, Home, and Foreign Missions, where she rendered conspicuous service as Principal for thirty-two years.

She had a variety of interests. An amateur musician, she wrote a number of gospel songs and Negro spirituals, some of the latter being published in *The Outlook.* Every good cause appealed to her. She has been called the "Mother of the Deaconess Movement." Her name has been linked with that of Frances E. Willard in the Woman's Christian Temperance Union and with that of Jane Addams in the work of the Social Settlement. That phase of her work nearest her heart, the training of Christian workers, is still being carried on at the Training School of Garrett Biblical Institute, Evanston. An ardent Methodist, her life was filled with good works. Mrs. Meyer died at Chicago, March 16, 1922.[1]

[1] Because of the extended use of the Northfield Benediction among youth groups, and because of the surprising lack of information concerning its composer, this somewhat extended, though inadequate, account of Mrs. Meyer has been given.

**614—The Lord bless you and keep you**—Arranged from Numbers 6. 24-26.

**The Lord bless you and keep you**—Peter Christian Lutkin (132)

This has proven one of the most effective and beautiful settings that has been made for the "Old Testament benediction." It was made by Dean Lutkin in 1900, and was dedicated "To my friend William Smedley." Published in octavo form, it has been so extensively used that it has been the most potent means of making the composer's name generally known. Its first appearance in a hymnal was in *The Methodist Hymnal* of 1905. The sevenfold Amen with which it closes was omitted as Dean Lutkin did not feel it was suitable for congregational use.

**615—Father, give Thy benediction**—Samuel Longfellow (42)

**Alla Trinita Beata**—From Laudi Spirituali, 1336 (?)

This one stanza of eight lines was published anonymously in Samuel Longfellow's *Hymns of the Spirit,* Boston, 1864.

"Alla Trinita Beata" is an arrangement of one of the *Laudi Spirituali* made by Charles Burney, 1726-1814, the author of the first *History of Music* to be published in English. He had heard a group of *Laudisti,* "psalm-singers," in Florence, Italy, while on a tour for the purpose of collecting material for his history. He says in *The Present State of Music in France and Italy,* London, 1771, a journal of his tour:

> The morning after my arrival in Florence, between six and seven o'clock, they passed by the inn where I lodged, in grand procession, dressed in a whitish uniform, with burning tapers in their hands. They stopped at the *duomo,* or great church, just by, to sing a cheerful hymn, in three parts, which they executed very well. In this manner, on Sundays and holidays, the trades-people and artisans form themselves into distinct companies, and sing through the streets, on their way to church.

The *Laudi Spirituali* is a name given to collections of music of a devotional character which were compiled for the use of the *Laudisti,* a religious group instituted at Florence in 1310. The poems were written wholly in Italian and show no evidence of classical derivation or influence. The music to which they were sung was at first very simple and in unison, but later some were set in parts. It is from a manuscript collection of these songs, dated 1336, in the Magliabecchi Library, Florence, that Burney took the "Alla Trinita Beata." The character of the songs so appealed to St. Fillipo Neri, d. 1595, that he had them performed in his chapel after the sermon or other devotional exercise. Some of these "spiritual songs" were interspersed with dialogues, and others, acquiring a dramatic character, were the germ from which the oratorio afterward developed.

**616—Praise God from whom all blessings flow**—Thomas Ken (34)

**Old 100th** (3)—From the Genevan Psalter (3)

The Long Meter Doxology, as this is called, is the closing stanza of Bishop Ken's Morning and Evening Hymn. See Nos. 34 and 51.

Thomas Johnson's engraving of "Mear," 1755

**617—To Father, Son, and Holy Ghost**—Tate and Brady (14)
**Mear**—Composer unknown

This doxology is the first of the "Gloria Patri, &c." at the close of the Psalms in the *New Version* of Tate and Brady.

"Mear" has been said to have been the first tune composed by an American composer, but the statement has not been verified. The author of this MANUAL has in his possession a copy of the *New Version* of Tate and Brady, published in Boston, in 1757, in the back of which are bound, without title, fifteen pages of music and one of "Rules of Singing," engraved by Thomas Johnson, Brattle Street, Boston, 1755. "Mear" is one of fifty-one hymn tunes included therein. (See illustration.) Though omitted from most recent tune books, this long-popular hymn tune has been continued in *The Methodist Hymnal* for historic reasons.

**618—To God the only wise**—Isaac Watts (3)
**Old 134th (St. Michael)** (39)—Adapted from the Genevan Psalter, 1551 (3)

These two stanzas are from a hymn of five which appeared in Isaac Watts's *Hymns and Spiritual Songs,* 1707.

## Amens

**619—(a) Sevenfold Amen**—John Stainer

**620—(b) Wykagyl Amen**—Philip James

**621—(c) Dresden Amen**

**622—(d) Threefold Amen**—Danish

**623—(e) Twofold Amen**—Orlando Gibbons

**624—(f) Twofold Amen**—Van Denman Thompson (153)

The Amen, with settings such as these, should be used in the sense of a solemn statement of concurrence in a prayer, a confession of faith, or other formal statement. When sung at the conclusion of a hymn, it is more in the nature of a concluding formula. There seems to be no good reason for the singing of an Amen at the close of each hymn, as is so frequently the case; the usual manner gives the impression that the Amen merely means "This is the last." There are quite valid reasons for omitting it except in the case of a few hymns, but there would be no gain by discussing them here.

The word "Amen" was taken over as a liturgical expression from the Jewish Church; and its use as a response meaning "So be it," is common to Christianity, Judaism, and Islam.

In the Preface to *A Students' Hymnal,* London, 1923, Sir Walfred Davies says:

> An Amen cannot be too good. It is music's chance to embody the great Christian affirmative. In singing an Amen it is well to pretend you may never sing

another, and put everything into it, recalling St. Paul's great saying: "In Him was Yea."

(a)—619—The Sevenfold Amen by John Stainer appeared in *A Choir-Book for the Office of Holy Communion,* 1873, of which he was the editor.

John Stainer, Mus. Doc., was born in London, June 6, 1840; became a chorister at St. Paul's Cathedral when seven years of age; wrote several anthems and chants during the eight or nine years he was there; graduated Mus. Bac., 1859, B. A., 1863, Mus. Doc., 1865, and M. A., 1866, from Oxford University; and after serving several different appointments as organist in London churches and in colleges, became Professor of Music at Oxford in 1889. A composer of much church music, one of England's foremost musicians in the last century, he was knighted in 1888. He died at Verona, Italy, March 31, 1901.

(b)—620—The Wykagyl Amen was written by Philip James in 1926 for use in the church at which he was organist at Wykagyl, New York.

Philip James was born in New York City, May 17, 1890, was educated in that city, and has served several churches there and in the metropolitan district as organist. He has given recitals in London and Paris; is a Fellow of the American Guild of Organists; a conductor of orchestral and choral bodies; and a composer whose works have been received highly favorably. During the World War he attained the rank of lieutenant and became known to thousands of soldiers as the director of "Pershing's Own Band." Formerly Instructor in Music at Columbia University, he is now Professor of Music at New York University.

(c)—621—The Dresden Amen is an old ecclesiastical cadence much used in the Court Church, Dresden. It has been made use of by several modern composers, notably Mendelssohn (7) in his *Reformation Symphony,* and Richard Wagner in his *Parsifal.*

(d)—622—This threefold Amen, widely used in Lutheran churches in Denmark, is from an unknown Danish source.

(e)—623—The twofold Amen of Orlando Gibbons is doubtless from his *Service in G,* or from one of his many anthems, but this surmise has not been authenticated.

Orlando Gibbons, Mus. Doc., born at Cambridge in 1583, one of the most noted of the early seventeenth-century English composers, became organist at the Chapel Royal in 1604. Receiving his degree of Doctor of Music from Oxford in 1622, he was appointed organist the following year at Westminster Abbey. Two years later summoned to Canterbury to attend the wedding of Charles I, for which he had composed music, he became ill and, after a short illness, died, June 5, 1625. He was buried in Canterbury Cathedral.

(f)—624—Dr. Van Denman Thompson wrote this twofold Amen for a service in which he used as the anthem his well-known "Show me Thy way, O

Lord," the first notes of which are the same as those in the first measure of the Amen. The date was 1930, and the church in which it was used was the Gobin Memorial Methodist Episcopal Church, Greencastle, Indiana.

# ANCIENT HYMNS AND CANTICLES

## Chants and Hymns

**625—Te Deum Laudamus**—Henry Lawes and Robert Cooke

The authorship of this famous hymn is obscure. There seems to be increasing agreement in assigning it to Nicetas, missionary bishop of Remesiana in Dacia, about 400; yet there is a tradition ascribing it to St. Ambrose and St. Augustine, according to a statement by Hincmar of Rheims, in 859, that it was made by the two saints at the time of the baptism of St. Augustine in the Church of St. John, Milan. Ambrose is said to have exulted, "We praise Thee, O God; we acknowledge Thee to be the Lord," and Augustine immediately replied, "All the earth doth worship Thee, the Father everlasting." The legend is that they continued in this manner, antiphonally, to the end of the second part which closes: "Make them to be numbered with Thy Saints in glory everlasting." The Te Deum probably assumed its present form early in the fifth century. It is not entirely an original composition, for in it are familiar parts from the Apostles' Creed, the Gloria in excelsis, and the Sanctus. Originally in two parts—verses 1-13 and 14-21—the third part was added at another time. Whatever may be its history, it is one of the grandest of paeans.

Mrs. Elizabeth R. Charles (146) told William T. Stead: "The Te Deum with its glorious subjectiveness, its tender humility, and its note of hope, has, perhaps, helped and inspired me through life more than any other hymn."

It is a pity it has not had more general use in American churches.

The setting used for the first and third parts is taken from *Lawes in C*, found in *Chants, Ancient and Modern, in score, Edited by John Goss*, 1841. There it is headed "Arranged from Lawes" but the original has not been successfully traced. That for the second part is from *Cooke in C minor*, found in the same work. They have been transposed a step lower in each instance in order to make them more suitable for congregational use.

Henry Lawes was born at Dinton, Wiltshire, England, and was baptized January 1, 1595 or 6. He was a member of the Chapel Royal and composed the music for Milton's *Comus*. It was he whom Milton addressed in the sonnet beginning:

> Harry, whose tuneful and well-measured song
> First taught our English music how to span
> Words with just note and accent.

He died at London, October 21, 1662.

Robert Cooke, born at Westminster, London, in 1768, became organist and Master of the Choristers of Westminster Abbey in 1802. While of unsound mind as consequence of a love affair, he drowned himself in the River Thames, August 22, 1814.

**626—Venite**—Psalm 95

(a) William Boyce (560)

**627** (b) John Robinson

The Venite, Exultimus Domino, is the rendering of all but the last phrase of the first seven verses of Psalm 95 as found in the "Great Bible" of 1539.[1] The last two verses of the canticle proper are from other sources. The Gloria Patri (569) is used with all of the canticles.

(a)—626—The setting is from *Boyce in D* and has been transposed one step lower. This chant is from *Divine Harmony, Being a Collection of Two Hundred and Seven Double and Single Chants in Score, Ancient and Modern. Sung at His Majesty's Chapels Royal.* London, 1770. In this book the chant is accredited to "Mr. Davis." Fourteen years later it is found in the Rev. Ralph Harrison's *Sacred Harmony* as a chant and as a short-meter tune with William Boyce's name attached in both instances. One Thomas Vandernan, the engraver and publisher of the 1770 book, was a Gentleman of the Chapel Royal while Doctor Boyce was organist there, and it is quite likely he knew the name of the composer of the chant. No light has been thrown on the identity of "Mr. Davis."

(b)—627—The chant is from *Robinson in E flat,* found in *Cathedral Music, being a collection in score of the most valuable and useful compositions for that Service by the several English Masters of the last two hundred years. The whole selected and carefully revised by Dr. William Boyce,* Vol. I, 1760.

John Robinson, born 1682, was a chorister of the Chapel Royal under Doctor Blow. He succeeded Doctor Croft (169) as organist at Westminster Abbey. John Hawkins, in his *History of Music,* 1776, speaks of him, in one place, as "a very florid and elegant performer on the organ, inasmuch that crowds resorted to hear him," and again:

> Mr. Robinson introduced a different practice . . . degrading the instrument, and instead of the full and noble harmony with which it was designed to gratify the ear, tickling it with mere airs in two parts, in fact solos for a flute and a bass.

Whatever his organ playing may have been, he will be long remembered for this fine double chant. He died at London, April 30, 1762.

**628—Benedictus**—St. Luke 1. 68-79

(a) Joseph Barnby (31)

**629** (b) Arranged from Ludwig van Beethoven (12)

This "Song of Zacharias," St. Luke 1. 68-79, "Great Bible" version, was used in public worship as early as the ninth century.

[1] The versions of all of the canticles are from the "Great Bible," so called because it was "the whole Bible of the largest volume in English," measuring 17¼ by 7½ inches. Its rendering of the Psalms was that which was used in the Prayer Book of Edward VI, and the Psalms retained that form when the revision of 1662 ordered that the lessons should be taken from the Authorized Version. At least 20,000 volumes of the "Great Bible" were issued.

(a)—628—From *Barnby in E.*

(b)—629—This is an arrangement of the first part of Beethoven's song *"In Questa Tomba,"* the words of which are those on the tomb of Shakespeare:

Good friend, for Jesus' sake, forbear
To dig the dust enclosed here;
Blest be the man that spares these stones
And curst be he that moves my bones.

**630—Jubilate Deo—Psalm 100**

(a) Henry Aldrich

**631** (b) Thomas Norris

Psalm 100, from the "Great Bible," 1539, was introduced into the *Book of Common Prayer* in 1552. It has been used, except at certain festivals, in the Synagogue service from ancient times. Engraved on the marble slab covering the grave of Edward Fitzgerald is:

It is He that hath made us, and not we ourselves.

He had expressed the wish that, should any text be used on his gravestone it should be this, for he had never seen it used in that way.

(a)—630—This is taken from *Aldrich in F.* While quite generally assigned to him, there is some question whether or not it is by Henry Aldrich. This arrangement is found in *A Collection of Tunes and Chants for Public Worship,* 1848, compiled by the Rev. William Harrison, but it is not found in earlier collections containing Aldrich's chants.

Henry Aldrich, born at Westminster in 1647, was a man of extraordinarily varied gifts. He was a theologian, a logician, a musician, an authority on heraldry, and such a successful architect that his plans were used for the building of Peckwater Triangle and the Church of All Saints, Oxford. He was a tutor of Christ Church, Oxford, became canon, and later became its dean. For three years, from 1692, he was Vice-Chancellor of the University. While his musical compositions are not extraordinary, they are a real achievement in a man whose interests were so many and of such uniformly high quality. He died at Oxford, December 14, 1710.

(b)—631—*Norris in A* was taken from *A Selection of Single and Double Chants,* c. 1810, compiled by John Clarke (Clarke-Whitfeld, Mus. Doc., Professor of Music at Cambridge University), 1770-1836. It also appeared about the same time in another collection used at Christ Church Cathedral, and St. John's College, Oxford, but it is not known which book was the first to be issued.

Thomas Norris, born at Mere, Wiltshire, England, was baptized August 15, 1741. A chorister at Salisbury Cathedral, he became organist at Christ Church and St. John's College, and lay clerk of Magdalen College, Oxford. He died at Himley Hall, Staffordshire, September 3, 1790.

**632—Magnificat**—St. Luke 1. 46-55

(a) Henry Smart (77)

**633** (b) Samuel Wesley

The Magnificat has been used at Vespers since the Middle Ages. It seems to be looked upon in the West as an evening song, but in the Eastern Church it is sung with the Morning Canticles. The song of Mary, it is called the "Song of Songs."

(a)—632—The source of this chant has not been ascertained.

(b)—633—The exact title and date of the book from which this chant is taken is not known, but it is thought to have been included in one of Vincent Novello's (574) collections for use in Roman Catholic churches. *Grove's Dictionary* lists only one complete Morning and Evening Service by him, that in F.

Samuel Wesley, son of Charles Wesley, was born at Bristol, England, February 24, 1766. Both Samuel and his elder brother, Charles, were possessed of extraordinary musical talents. While Samuel did not display his precocity so early as Charles, he played a tune when three years old; he learned to read words before he was five through looking over Handel's oratorio *Samson;* he taught himself to write; and between six and seven he learned to play by note. Before he had reached the age of eight he had written out, complete, an oratorio, *Ruth,* which received the commendation of Doctor Boyce (560). He acquired a knowledge of several languages, became a good classical scholar, had a fine taste for general literature, and even before he became of age was highly regarded as an organist, especially for extemporaneous performance. By many he is considered the greatest organist England has produced. In consequence of an accident which befell him when he had barely attained his majority, he was afflicted with a despondency and an irritability which greatly interfered with the success which might otherwise have been his. He became a Roman Catholic in 1784 and thereafter wrote much music for use in the churches of that communion. He died at London, October 11, 1837.

**634—Bonum Est**—Psalm 92

(a) Richard Farrant

**635** (b) John Alcock

This is the first four verses from Psalm 92, the "Great Bible," 1539.

(a)—634—The first setting is from *Farrant in F,* which he based on his well-known anthem, "Lord, for Thy tender mercies' sake."

Richard Farrant was born about 1530. He was a Gentleman of the Chapel Royal, Master of the Choristers at St. George's Chapel, Windsor, and organist and lay vicar there. For a number of years, from 1567, he had the responsibility each year for the presentation of a play before the Queen. He died at Windsor, November 30, 1580.

(b)—635—The source of this chant has not been ascertained. The only Service by John Alcock listed by Grove is that in E minor.

John Alcock, Mus. Doc., born at London, April 11, 1715, was a composer and an organist of more than ordinary distinction. He entered St. Paul's Cathedral as a chorister at seven years of age; was organist at several London churches; composed in a variety of styles for both voice and instruments, winning prizes for his glees; and was a scholar in musical history, turning over to Dr. Maurice Green, 1695-1755, much of the material later used by Doctor Boyce (560) in his monumental *Cathedral Music*. Doctor Alcock died at Lichfield in February, 1806.

**636—Come, Holy Ghost, our souls inspire**—Anonymous (9th or 10th century)
Translated by John Cosin
**Veni Creator**—Ancient plainsong
(Veni, Creator Spiritus)

This great hymn has been ascribed to Charlemagne, Ambrose, Gregory the Great, and Hrabanus Maurus, but positive evidence to support the claims of those who would assign it to any of these men is lacking. Its hold on the church at large is perhaps greater than that of any other medieval hymn, the Te Deum alone excepted. Its use at Pentecostal services may be traced as far back as the tenth century. An early translator said, "Whoever repeats this hymn by day or night, no enemy, visible or invisible, shall assail him." It has been sung at the most solemn functions in English history for a thousand years, and in the olden times its singing was an occasion for the ringing of bells and the use of lights and incense.

This translation by John Cosin was included in his *Collection of Private Devotions,* 1627, published while he was rector of Brancepeth. Canon John Ellerton (28) has said:

> For this book John Cosin translated the *Veni Creator,* not intending it to be sung in church, but said privately every morning at nine o'clock, in commemoration of the hour when God the Holy Ghost came down upon the Church. . . . He was one of the revisers of the Prayer Book in 1661-2, and thus it came to pass that his version of the *Veni Creator* was inserted in the Ordination Service.

John Cosin was born at Norwich, England, November 30, 1594, and was educated at Caius College, Cambridge. After taking Holy Orders he held several minor and major appointments before becoming Vice-Chancellor of Cambridge University in 1640. Suffering much persecution at the hands of the Puritans, after the Restoration he was made Dean, later Bishop, of Durham. He died at Westminster, January 15, 1672.

"Veni Creator" has been associated with this hymn from its earliest use in church services.

**637—Hail, gladdening Light**—Greek hymn from the 3rd century
Translated by John Keble (35)
**Sebaste**—John Stainer (619)

This ancient Greek hymn, known as the "Candlelight Hymn" because of its use at the Lighting of the Lamps, is quoted by St. Basil in the fourth century without date or author. A. E. Gregory says it is from the ancient Syrian Liturgy of St. James. In the Greek liturgical books it is ascribed to Sophronius, Patriarch of Jerusalem, and is in great favor among Russian composers, almost all of whom have made settings of this "Hymn to Sophronius," used extensively in the services of the Greek Church. It lends itself admirably to musical treatment. Longfellow's translation of this hymn, "O gladsome light," which he uses in his *Golden Legend,* is one of the most beautiful of its many translations. That used in this instance was made by John Keble and first appeared in 1834 in *The British Magazine,* going from there to *Lyra Apostolica,* 1836.

"Sebaste" was written by Sir John Stainer for this hymn and appeared first in the Revised Edition of *Hymns Ancient and Modern,* 1875. While in more general use than any other setting of Keble's rendering of the hymn, it is rather dull and uninteresting.

**638—O splendor of God's glory bright**—Ambrose of Milan (38)

**St. Venantius**—Rouen Church melody (16)

This, the *Splendor paternae gloriae,* is one of twelve hymns which have been definitely assigned to St. Ambrose by the Benedictine editors. It is a beautiful morning hymn which the Benedictine Monks sang at Lauds on Monday. Other monastic orders used it daily.

This translation is that signed "Tr. by R. B." (Robert Bridges?) in the *Yattendon Hymnal,* 1899.

**639—The Angelic Song**—From Luther's Service, 1524

Nothing is to be said about this other than it was used in Luther's early service book. The source of the tune has not been ascertained, but it is doubtless of plainsong origin.

**640—De Profundis**—Psalm 130

(a) From Henry Purcell
Arranged by James Turle (410)

**641** (b) William Croft (169)

In the Roman and Anglican churches this is one of the seven penitential psalms. This was the psalm, to the singing of which by the choir of St. Paul's Cathedral, London, John Wesley listened on the afternoon of May 24, 1738. On that evening, at Aldersgate, his "heart was strangely warmed," and Methodism was born.

(a)—640—The source of this chant in A flat has not been ascertained.

Henry Purcell was born between November 21, 1658, and August 11, 1659, but neither the exact date nor the place of his birth is known. He has been generously acclaimed as "the greatest and most original of English composers." He was a chorister of the Chapel Royal, and after his voice broke seems to have been kept on as a sort of supernumerary in order that he might continue his studies under Doctor Blow. In time he became organist at Westminster and wrote many fine anthems and three services. But it is as a writer of dramatic music that he became famous. His ability to set English to song has never been surpassed. He had a vivid imagination, a real creative sense, and was keenly sensitive. What he would have meant to English music had his life been prolonged can be only surmised. He was only twenty-seven years old when he died, November 21, 1695, at Westminster, yet his genius had been recognized by such writers as Tate, D'Urfey, Dryden, and other important poets who furnished texts for his music.

(b)—641—From *Croft in A minor,* found in Volume I, 1760, of Boyce's *Cathedral Music* (560).

**642—Nunc Dimittis**—St. Luke 2. 29-32

(a) Joseph Barnby (31)

**643** (b) Tonus Regius

**644** (c) Composer unknown

This "Song of Simeon," as the Nunc Dimittis is called, is from the "Great Bible" and was used at Compline[1] in the early days of the Church. It has been called the "greeting of the Old Dispensation to the New."

The Rev. John Telford, in *The New Methodist Hymn-Book Illustrated,* has the following quotation:

> Simeon represents himself under the image of a sentinel whom his master has placed in an exalted position, and charged to look for the appearance of a Star, and then announce it to the world. He sees this long-desired Star; he proclaims its rising, and asks to be relieved of the post he has occupied so long. In the same way, at the opening of Aeschylus's *Agamemnon,* when the sentinel, set to watch for the appearing of the fire that is to announce the taking of Troy, beholds at last the signal so impatiently expected, he sings at once both the victory of Greece and his own release.

(a)—642—The source of the Barnby chant in E has not been ascertained.

(b)—643—The Tonus Regius is the modern form of Tone VI. It is also referred to as a "French Chant."

(c)—644—This is a modern chant by an unknown composer.

[1] The last of the canonical hours. In the early Church these hours were specified times set during the day when certain offices were said, or intended to be said. Seven in number, they were:

a. Matins, which began properly at midnight and consisted of two services, Nocturns and Lauds. Nocturns consisted chiefly of psalms and prayers, and Lauds of songs or reiterated ascriptions of praise to God, preferably just as day was breaking.

b. Prime—to be said at the first hour after sunrise.

c. Terce—halfway between sunrise and noon.

d. Sext—midday.

e. Nones—originally said about 3 P. M.

f. Vespers—in England known as "Evensong."

g. Compline—originally said after the evening meal and just before retiring for sleep. Later it was said immediately after vespers.

# BOOK III

# A HYMN CALENDAR
# BIBLIOGRAPHY
# INDEXES

# A Hymn Calendar

| | *Born* | *Died* |
|---|---|---|
| | **January** | |
| 1: | Tiplady, Thomas<br>Lawes, Henry (Baptized)<br>See No. 310 | |
| 2: | Charles, Elizabeth R.<br>Coles, George<br>Gordon, George A.<br>McFarland, John T.<br>Rankin, Jeremiah E.<br>See No. 434 | Caswall, Edward<br>Perronet, Edward<br>Baring-Gould, Sabine |
| 3: | Ewing, Alexander<br>Fletcher, Douglas<br>Schneider, Johann C. F.<br>See No. 470 | Hawks, Annie S. |
| 4: | | Betham-Edwards, Matilda |
| 5: | Coffin, Henry S.<br>Ett, C. | Bunnett, Edward<br>Duncan, Mary L.<br>Matthews, Timothy R. |
| 6: | Fawcett, John<br>Peery, Rob Roy<br>See No. 339 | |
| 7: | Hickson, William E.<br>Stryker, Melancthon W. | Bradbury, William B.<br>Edmeston, James |
| 8: | Mason, Lowell | Collyer, William B. |
| 9: | See No. 60 | |
| 10: | Merrill, William P. | |
| 11: | Purday, Charles H. | Dwight, Timothy<br>Everest, Charles W.<br>Williams, William |
| 12: | | Alford, Henry<br>Schwedler, Johann C. |
| 13: | Parker, Edwin P.<br>Darwall, John (Baptized)<br>Shrubsole, William (Baptized) | Hérold, Louis J. F. |
| 14: | See No. 405 | Sears, Edmund H. |
| 15: | | Cosin, John |
| 16: | Hewlett, William H. | |
| 17: | | |
| 18: | Winchester, Caleb T. | Kipling, Rudyard<br>Shrubsole, William |
| 19: | See No. 1 | Twells, Henry |
| 20: | Schein, Johann H. | Auber, Harriet<br>Bambridge, William S. |
| 21: | Mote, Edward | Claudius, Matthias |

# A Hymn Calendar

| | *Born* | *Died* |
|---|---|---|
| | **January—Continued** | |
| 22: | Edson, Lewis<br>Righini, Vincenzo | Dykes, John B. |
| 23: | | Brooks, Phillips<br>Kingsley, Charles<br>Wyeth, John |
| 24: | Neale, John Mason | |
| 25: | Bickersteth, Edward H. | Shield, William<br>Prichard, Rowland H. |
| 26: | Longacre, Lindsay B.<br>Peace, Albert L.<br>Wade, James C. | |
| 27: | | Stocking, Jay T. |
| 28: | Baring-Gould, Sabine<br>Hérold, Louis J. F.<br>Longstaff, William D. | Barnby, Joseph<br>Wainwright, John (Buried) |
| 29: | | Oakeley, Frederick<br>Shepherd, Thomas |
| 30: | | Taylor, Virgil C. |
| 31: | Barton, Bernard<br>Reissiger, Carl G. | |
| | **February** | |
| 1: | Milligan, James L. | Plumptre, Edward H.<br>West, Robert A. |
| 2: | See No. 559 | Gordon, Adoniram J.<br>Luke, Jemima<br>Palestrina<br>Procter, Adelaide Anne |
| 3: | Doane, William H.<br>Lanier, Sidney<br>Mendelssohn-Bartholdy, Felix | Thoburn, Helen |
| 4: | See No. 225 | Davies, Samuel<br>Hopkins, Edward J. |
| 5: | Clausnitzer, Tobias<br>Pennefather, William | Elliott, James W. |
| 6: | | |
| 7: | Boyce, William | Boyce, William<br>"Portogallo, Il" |
| 8: | Gilder. Richard W. | |
| 9: | | |
| 10: | Gill, Thomas H.<br>Milman, Henry H.<br>Willis, Richard S. | |
| 11: | Gladden, Washington<br>Williams, William | Small, James G. |
| 12: | Burleigh, William H.<br>See No. 382 | Baker, Henry W.<br>Crosby, Fanny J.<br>Schmolck, Benjamin |

**FEBRUARY—Continued**

| | *Born* | *Died* |
|---|---|---|
| 13: | Elliott, James W. | |
| 14: | Briel, Marie | |
| 15: | Douglas, Charles W.<br>Praetorius, Michael | Chorley, Henry F.<br>Dresse, Adam<br>Praetorius, Michael<br>Sheppard, Franklin L. |
| 16: | See No. 53 | Boyd, William |
| 17: | Hopper, Edwara | Parry, Joseph |
| 18: | Burns, James Drummond | Luther, Martin<br>Sandys, William |
| 19: | Bacon, Leonard<br>Heins, Francis D. | Barton, Bernard<br>Clephane, Elizabeth C.<br>Johnson, Samuel |
| 20: | | |
| 21: | Newman, John H.<br>Thomas, Rhys<br>See No. 233 | Gauntlett, Henry J. |
| 22: | Adams, Sarah F.<br>Lowell, James R. | |
| 23: | Bode, John E.<br>Handel, George F. | Crüger, Johann<br>Vincent, Charles J. |
| 24: | Wesley, Samuel | Wolcott, Samuel |
| 25: | | |
| 26: | Stebbins, George C.<br>See No. 270 | Monod, Theodore<br>Moore, Thomas |
| 27: | Dearmer, Percy<br>See Nos. 324, 558 | Sill, Edward R. |
| 28: | Flemming, Frederick F.<br>See No. 513 | |
| 29: | Byrom, John | |

**MARCH**

| | *Born* | *Died* |
|---|---|---|
| 1: | Ingalls, Jeremiah<br>Redhead, Richard<br>See No. 66 | Monk, William H. |
| 2: | Berggreen, Anton P.<br>Dearle, Edward<br>Doane, William C.<br>Monsell, John S. B.<br>MacFarren, George A. | March, Daniel<br>Wesley, John |
| 3: | | Herbert, George (Buried) |
| 4: | Betham-Edwards, Matilda B.<br>Parker, William H. | Gould, John E. |
| 5: | Larcom, Lucy<br>Shield, William<br>Turle, James | Arne, Thomas A. |
| 6: | | |

MARCH—Continued

| | *Born* | *Died* |
|---|---|---|
| 7: | Ambrose, Robert S.<br>Cuninggim, Maud M.<br>Fink, Gottfried W.<br>Park, John Edgar<br>See No. 392 | Studdert-Kennedy, Geoffrey A. (or 8) |
| 8: | Martin, George W. | Studdert-Kennedy, Geoffrey A. (or 7) |
| 9: | Shaw, Martin | Barbauld, Anna L.<br>Barber, Mary A. S. |
| 10: | Clark, Alexander<br>Dykes, John B. | |
| 11: | Wallace, William V. | Thomson, Mary A.<br>Tours, Berthold |
| 12: | Arne, Thomas A.<br>Gerhardt, Paul<br>Lowry, Robert | Kocher, Conrad |
| 13: | Alexander, James W.<br>Warren, William F. | Kingsley, George |
| 14: | Sherwin, William F. | Peace, Albert L. |
| 15: | Gardiner, William<br>See No. 39 | Davis, Ozora S.<br>Gawler, William |
| 16: | Calkin, John B.<br>Monk, William H.<br>Neumark, Georg | Matheson, Annie<br>Meyer, Lucy R. |
| 17: | | Warren, George W. |
| 18: | Elliott, Charlotte | Bakewell, John<br>Burleigh, William H.<br>Brooke, Stopford A. |
| 19: | | Ken, Thomas |
| 20: | | Dearle, Edward<br>Wordsworth, Christopher |
| 21: | Bach, Johann S.<br>Meredith, Isaac H.<br>White, Henry K. | |
| 22: | | Hickson, William E. |
| 23: | Twells, Henry | |
| 24: | Crosby, Fanny J.<br>Threlfall, Jeanette<br>"Portogallo, Il" | Abbey, Alonzo J.<br>Stewart, Robert P.<br>Winchester, Caleb T. |
| 25: | Thring, Godfrey<br>Woodhull, Alfred A. | |
| 26: | | Beethoven, Ludwig van |
| 27: | Elvey, George J.<br>Lutkin, Peter C.<br>Matheson, George | |
| 28: | Harper, Earl E. | Charles, Elizabeth R. |

# A Hymn Calendar

| | *Born* | *Died* |
|---|---|---|
| | **March—Continued** | |
| 29: | Matheson, Annie | Bates, Katharine Lee<br>Keble, John<br>Palmer, Ray<br>Wesley, Charles |
| 30: | | |
| 31: | Haydn, Francis Joseph<br>Reed, E. M. G.<br>Wyeth, John | Ambrose, Robert S.<br>Burrowes, John F.<br>Marriott, John<br>Stainer, John |
| | **April** | |
| 1: | Messiter, Arthur H. | |
| 2: | Taylor, Virgil C. | Longstaff, William D. |
| 3: | Herbert, George | Brahms, Johannes<br>Heber, Reginald<br>Tersteegen, Gerhard |
| 4: | Shurtleff, Ernest W. | Ambrose of Milan<br>Chadwick, George W. |
| 5: | Conder, Eustace R.<br>Spohr, Louis | |
| 6: | Laufer, Calvin W.<br>Pierpont, John<br>Sears, Edmund H. | Ingalls, Jeremiah<br>Kennedy, Benjamin H.<br>Reinagle, Alexander R. |
| 7: | Lane, Spencer<br>Stocking, Jay T. | Shirley, Walter |
| 8: | | |
| 9: | Borthwick, Jane L.<br>Crüger, Johann | Monsell, John S. B. |
| 10: | Kremser, Edward | Van Dyke, Henry |
| 11: | Alcock, John<br>Lahee, Henry | Newhall, Charles S. |
| 12: | Esling, Catherine H.<br>Giardini, Felice de | |
| 13: | Guyon, Madame | Richardson, John |
| 14: | Collyer, William B.<br>Lewis, Howell E.<br>Wainwright, John (Baptized)<br>See Nos. 85, 362 | Handel, George F.<br>Sherwin, William F.<br>Swain, Joseph |
| 15: | Horne, Charles S.<br>See No. 148 | Baker, Henry |
| 16: | See No. 67 | Gläzer, Carl G.<br>Martin, George W. |
| 17: | | Larcom, Lucy |
| 18: | See No. 538 | |
| 19: | Gordon, Adoniram J.<br>Waring, Anna L. | Symonds, John A.<br>Wesley, Samuel S. |
| 20: | | Cross, Moses S. |
| 21: | Heber, Reginald<br>Ware, Henry, Jr. | |

# A Hymn Calendar

| | *Born* | *Died* |
|---|---|---|
| | **April—Continued** | |
| 22: | | Lloyd, William F. |
| 23: | Burrowes, John F.<br>Rinkart, Martin | Hopper, Edward<br>Purday, Charles H. |
| 24: | | |
| 25: | Keble, John<br>Stone, Samuel J.<br>See No. 493 | Camidge, John<br>Cowper, William<br>Moultrie, Gerard<br>Wesley, Samuel |
| 26: | Duncan, Mary L.<br>Leach, Rowland<br>Palmer, Horatio R.<br>Scott-Gatty, Alfred<br>See No. 457 | |
| 27: | Anderson, William K. | Burton, Henry<br>Doane, George W.<br>Redhead, Richard |
| 28: | See No. 460 | |
| 29: | Gilmore, Joseph H.<br>Sill, Edward R. | Lahee, Henry |
| 30: | Cooper, Alexander S. | Cennick, John<br>Conkey, Ithamar<br>Montgomery, James<br>Pennefather, William<br>Robinson, John |
| | **May** | |
| 1: | Addison, Joseph<br>Brown, Phoebe H.<br>See No. 338 | Hodges, John S. B.<br>Turner, William B. |
| 2: | Watson, Lawrence W. | |
| 3: | | Whiting, William |
| 4: | Gläzer, Carl G. | Adams, John G.<br>Horne, Charles S. |
| 5: | | |
| 6: | See No. 422 | |
| 7: | Brahms, Johannes | Clausnitzer, Tobias<br>Willis, Richard S. |
| 8: | Gottschalk, Louis M. | Moule, Handley C. G. |
| 9: | | Zinzendorf, Nicolaus L. |
| 10: | Coxe, A. Cleveland | Goss, John |
| 11: | Wooler, Alfred | Oakey, Emily S. |
| 12: | | |
| 13: | Dwight, John S.<br>Mahlmann, Siegfried A.<br>Sullivan, Arthur S. | |
| 14: | Dwight, Timothy<br>Rendle, Lily | Coster, Arthur V.<br>Greg, Samuel<br>Hughes, John<br>Kelly, Thomas |

# A Hymn Calendar

## May—Continued

| | *Born* | *Died* |
|---|---|---|
| 15: | Conkey, Ithamar<br>Phelps, Sylvanus D. | Calkin, John B.<br>Hastings, Thomas |
| 16: | Mann, Arthur H.<br>Price, Carl F. | Bickersteth, Edward H.<br>Ett, C. |
| 17: | James, Philip<br>Whelpton, George<br>See No. 378 | Doane, William C. |
| 18: | Hervey, Frederick A. J. | Babcock, Maltbie D. |
| 19: | | |
| 20: | See No. 25 | Vail, Silas J. |
| 21: | Parry, Joseph<br>Wesley, Charles (Converted) | Tuttiett, Lawrence |
| 22: | | Evans, William E.<br>Schütz, Johann J.<br>Waring, Anna L.<br>Wellesley (or Wesley) Garret |
| 23: | See No. 548 | |
| 24: | Marlatt, Earl B.<br>See Nos. 36, 311, 640 | Hart, Joseph<br>Selnecker, Nicolaus |
| 25: | Cooper, Joseph T.<br>Gower, John H. | Holst, Gustav T.<br>Webbe, Samuel |
| 26: | Nägeli, Hans G.<br>Zinzendorf, Nicolaus L. von | |
| 27: | Baker, Henry W.<br>Doane, George W.<br>Everest, Charles W. | Cook, Joseph S.<br>Flemming, Frederick F. |
| 28: | Fosdick, Harry E.<br>Hawks, Annie S.<br>Moore, Thomas<br>Pollock, Thomas B. | Parker, Edwin P.<br>Rawnsley, Hardwicke D. |
| 29: | | Dearmer, Percy |
| 30: | See No. 476 | |
| 31: | | Haydn, Francis Joseph<br>Neander, Joachim |

## June

| | *Born* | *Died* |
|---|---|---|
| 1: | Lyte, Henry F.<br>Marsh, Simeon D.<br>Masefield, John<br>Pleyel, Ignace | |
| 2: | | Knight, Joseph P. |
| 3: | Gladstone, William H.<br>Macleod, Norman<br>See No. 10 | Havergal, Frances R. |
| 4: | | Reed, E. M. G.<br>Tillett, Wilbur F. |
| 5: | | Gibbons, Orlando<br>Weber, Carl M. F. E. von |

# A Hymn Calendar

**JUNE—Continued**

| | *Born* | *Died* |
|---|---|---|
| 6: | Hamilton, Clarence G.<br>Lvov (or Lwoff), Alexis F.<br>Stainer, John<br>See No. 318 | Buckall, Henry J.<br>Bullinger, Ethelbert W.<br>Cummings, William H. |
| 7: | | Gerhardt, Paul<br>Grüber, Franz<br>Hosmer, Frederick Lucian |
| 8: | Schumann, Robert A.<br>Southgate, Thomas B. | Hassler, Hans L.<br>Langran, James |
| 9: | | Guyon, Madame<br>Robinson, Robert |
| 10: | Wigner, John M. | |
| 11: | | |
| 12: | Kingsley, Charles<br>See No. 463 | Bryant, William C.<br>Littlefield, Milton S. |
| 13: | Harrington, Karl Pomeroy<br>Rimbault, Edward F. | Denny, Edward<br>Hewlett, William Henry |
| 14: | Dix, William C.<br>Copeland, Benjamin<br>Lloyd, John A.<br>Stowe, Harriet Beecher | Brooks, Charles T.<br>Jeffrey, J. Albert |
| 15: | | Ellerton, John<br>Gurney, Dorothy F. |
| 16: | Chandler, John<br>See No. 514 | Downes, Lewis Thomas<br>Macleod, Norman |
| 17: | Gounod, Charles F.<br>Thoburn, Helen | Addison, Joseph<br>Huntingdon, Countess of |
| 18: | Clephane, Elizabeth C.<br>Longfellow, Samuel | Irons, William J.<br>Tappan, William B. |
| 19: | | |
| 20: | Barbauld, Anna L.<br>Brooks, Charles T.<br>Thrupp, Dorothy A. | |
| 21: | Walch, James | |
| 22: | Scholefield, Clement C.<br>See No. 246 | Baxter, Lydia |
| 23: | Medley, Samuel | |
| 24: | Allen, James<br>Webb, George J.<br>See No. 149 | |
| 25: | See No. 7 | Phillips, Philip |
| 26: | Bunnett, Edward<br>Doddridge, Philip<br>See No. 497 | |
| 27: | Studdert-Kennedy, Geoffrey A. | |
| 28: | Faber, Frederick W.<br>Rousseau, Jean J.<br>Wesley, John | Turle, James |
| 29: | | |
| 30: | Hopkins, Edward John | |

# A Hymn Calendar

**July**

| | *Born* | *Died* |
|---|---|---|
| 1: | | Chandler, John<br>Hay, John<br>Stowe, Harriet Beecher |
| 2: | Wolcott, Samuel | Gladden, Washington<br>Messiter, Arthur H.<br>Wreyford, John R. |
| 3: | | Rousseau, Jean J. |
| 4: | Dickinson, Charles A.<br>See No. 496 | Cennick, John<br>Gladstone, William H. |
| 5: | | |
| 6: | Smith, David S. | Clark, Alexander<br>Conder, Eustace R.<br>Duffield, George, Jr.<br>Hewes, George<br>Smart, Henry T. |
| 7: | | |
| 8: | See No. 30 | Ahle, Johann R. |
| 9: | Bliss, Philip P.<br>Downes, Lewis Thomas<br>Gauntlett, Henry J. | Grant, Robert |
| 10: | | Knapp, Mrs. Joseph F. |
| 11: | Evans, William E. | Ewing, Alexander |
| 12: | Hunter, John | |
| 13: | Kelly, Thomas<br>See No. 245 | |
| 14: | Bridges, Matthew<br>Farrington, Harry Webb<br>See No. 155 | Humfrey, Pelham<br>Marsh, Simeon B. |
| 15: | Caswall, Edward | |
| 16: | Rinehart, Thomas F. | Park, Roswell |
| 17: | Turner, William B.<br>Watts, Isaac<br>See No. 497 | Medley, Samuel<br>Watson, Lawrence W.<br>Wells, Marcus M. |
| 18: | Bambridge, William S. | Neumark, Georg |
| 19: | Wellesley (or Wesley) Garret | Werner, Johann G. |
| 20: | Harlow, S. Ralph | Barthélémon, François H.<br>Coxe, A. Cleveland<br>Dyer, Samuel |
| 21: | March, Daniel | |
| 22: | Benson, Louis Fitzgerald<br>Elliott, Emily E. S.<br>Oakeley, Herbert S. | |
| 23: | | Gilmore, Joseph H. |
| 24: | Holland, Josiah G.<br>Newton, John | |
| 25: | See No. 338 | Fawcett, John |
| 26: | | |

JULY—Continued

| | *Born* | *Died* |
|---|---|---|
| 27: | Barthélémon, François H.<br>See No. 431 | Hayes, William |
| 28: | | Bach, Johann S. |
| 29: | | Schumann, Robert A. |
| 30: | Adams, John G.<br>Davis, Ozora S. | Gower, John H. |
| 31: | | Alexander, James W.<br>Bonar, Horatius<br>Cary, Phoebe |

AUGUST

| | *Born* | *Died* |
|---|---|---|
| 1: | Spitta, Carl J. P. | Weissel, George |
| 2: | | |
| 3: | Babcock, Maltbie D.<br>Emerson, Luther O. | Elliott, Emily E. S.<br>Geibel, Adam |
| 4: | | |
| 5: | Tweedy, Henry H. | |
| 6: | Plumptre, Edward H.<br>Tennyson, Alfred<br>See Nos. 400, 540 | Neale, John Mason<br>Root, George F. |
| 7: | Sheppard, Franklin L.<br>See No. 516 | Jude, William H.<br>Vulpius, Melchior |
| 8: | | Hervey, Frederick A. J. |
| 9: | Piggott, William C.<br>See No. 542 | Draper, William H.<br>Novello, Vincent |
| 10: | Goadby, Frederick W.<br>Lathbury, Mary A.<br>Riley, J. Athelstan | Haydn, Johann Michael<br>How, William W.<br>Lane, Spencer |
| 11: | Waterbury, Jared B.<br>See No. 601 | Adams, Sarah F.<br>Canitz, Baron F. R. L. von<br>Mason, Lowell<br>Newman, John H.<br>Toplady, Augustus M. |
| 12: | Barnby, Joseph<br>Bates, Katharine Lee | Lowell, James R.<br>Oliver, Henry K.<br>Tate, Nahum |
| 13: | Dexter, Henry M.<br>Phillips, Philip | Fischer, William G.<br>Hopkins, John H., Jr.<br>Prentiss, Elizabeth P.<br>Sankey, Ira D. |
| 14: | Wesley, Samuel S. | Croft, William<br>Wilson, Hugh |
| 15: | Claudius, Mathias<br>Norris, Thomas (Baptized) | |
| 16: | | |
| 17: | Croly, George<br>Main, Hubert P.<br>Warren, George W. | |
| 18: | MacMillan, Ernest C. | |

| | *Born* | *Died* |
|---|---|---|
| | **August—Continued** | |
| 19: | Luke, Jemima<br>Wilson, Elizabeth | Righini, Vincenzo |
| 20: | | Bernard of Clairvaux |
| 21: | Atkinson, Frederick C.<br>Littlefield, Milton S.<br>Reinagle, Alexander R. | Hedge, Frederick H. |
| 22: | Cummings, William H.<br>See No. 625 | Cooke, Robert |
| 23: | See No. 66 | |
| 24: | Huntingdon, Selena, Countess of<br>See No. 210 | Stennett, Samuel |
| 25: | Tillett, Wilbur F. | Bourgeois, Loys (Louis) |
| 26: | | Pierpont, John |
| 27: | | Fink, Gottfried W. |
| 28: | Bathurst, William H.<br>Sankey, Ira D.<br>See No. 505 | Matheson, George |
| 29: | Copenhaver, Laura S.<br>Holmes, Oliver W.<br>See No. 514 | Coster, George T.<br>Shurtleff, Ernest W. |
| 30: | Root, George F. | |
| 31: | | Bunyan, John |
| | **September** | |
| 1: | | |
| 2: | | |
| 3: | | Norris, Thomas |
| 4: | Cary, Phoebe<br>Hatch, Edwin<br>See No. 520 | Holden, Oliver |
| 5: | Blanchard, William G.<br>Oakeley, Frederick | Dwight, John S. |
| 6: | Greg, Samuel<br>Novello, Vincent<br>Schütz, Johann J. | |
| 7: | Allen, George N. | Lanier, Sidney<br>Whittier, John G. |
| 8: | | |
| 9: | Baxter, Lydia<br>Buckoll, Henry J<br>Meyer, Lucy R. | Dix, William C. |
| 10: | Edmeston, James | Scholefield, Clement C. |
| 11: | | |
| 12: | Duffield, George, Jr.<br>Irons, William J. | King, John |
| 13: | McCutchan, Robert G.<br>Winkworth, Catherine<br>See No. 302 | Thring, Godfrey |

| | *Born* | *Died* |
|---|---|---|
| | **September—Continued** | |
| 14: | Haydn, Johann Michael | Lloyd, John A. |
| 15: | Geibel, Adam<br>Parker, Horatio W. | Hunter, John |
| 16: | Moultrie, Gerard | |
| 17: | See No. 67 | |
| 18: | Holden, Oliver | |
| 19: | Vincent, Charles J. | |
| 20: | See No. 71 | Smith, Walter C.<br>Thompson, Will L. |
| 21: | Holst, Gustav T.<br>Rowland, May | |
| 22: | | Elliott, Charlotte |
| 23: | | |
| 24: | | Milman, Henry H. |
| 25: | | Ware, Henry |
| 26: | | Faber, Frederick W.<br>Rimbault, Edward F.<br>Tomer, William G. |
| 27: | Robinson, Robert | |
| 28: | Rawnsley, Hardwicke D.<br>See No. 465 | Bortniansky, Dimitri S.<br>Byrom, John<br>Spitta, Carl J. P.<br>Ward, Samuel A. |
| 29: | | |
| 30: | Knecht, Justin H.<br>See No. 548 | Whitefield, George |
| | **October** | |
| 1: | Park, Roswell | Emerson, Luther O. |
| 2: | Denny, Edward<br>Wells, Marcus M. | Wills, William G. |
| 3: | Coster, George T.<br>See No. 520 | Longfellow, Samuel |
| 4: | Auber, Harriet<br>Newhall, Charles S. | Carey, Henry<br>Francis of Assisi |
| 5: | Symonds, John A.<br>Tomer, William G. | Woodhull, Alfred A. |
| 6: | Bradbury, William B.<br>Vail, Silas J. | Bode, John E.<br>Bridges, Matthew<br>Tennyson, Alfred |
| 7: | Alford, Henry<br>Converse, Charles C.<br>McGregor, Ernest F.<br>Pierpoint, Folliott S.<br>See No. 161 | Holmes, Oliver W.<br>Main, Hubert P.<br>Tans'ur, William<br>Torrey, Bradford<br>Webb, George J. |
| 8: | Bowie, Walter R.<br>Hay, John<br>Oakey, Emily S. | Stowell, Hugh |

| | *Born* | *Died* |
|---|---|---|
| | **October—Continued** | |
| 9: | Torrey, Bradford | |
| 10: | Johnson, Samuel | Benson, Louis Fitzgerald<br>Brown, Phoebe Hinsdale<br>Scriven, Joseph |
| 11: | | Wesley, Samuel |
| 12: | Vaughan Williams, Ralph<br>See No. 368 | Alexander, Cecil F.<br>Holland, Josiah G.<br>Wallace, William V. |
| 13: | See No. 274 | |
| 14: | Fischer, William G. | |
| 15: | Hastings, Thomas<br>See No. 280 | Goadby, Frederick W. |
| 16: | Hosmer, Frederick L. | Thomas, Rhys |
| 17: | Bowring, John | Gounod, Charles F. |
| 18: | See No. 288 | Converse, Charles C. |
| 19: | Chadwick, John W.<br>Perkins, Emily S. | White, Henry Kirke |
| 20: | Shuttleworth, Henry C.<br>See No. 36 | Hiles, Henry<br>Lathbury, Mary A. |
| 21: | Smith, Samuel F.<br>See No. 399 | Lawes, Henry |
| 22: | Miller, Emily<br>Schlegel, Katharine von | Spohr, Louis |
| 23: | Woodbury, Isaac B. | Gates, Ellen |
| 24: | Tappan, William B. | Shuttleworth, Henry C. |
| 25: | Hassler, Hans L. (or 26) | Farrington, Harry Webb |
| 26: | Jeffery, J. Albert<br>Prentiss, Elizabeth P.<br>Smart, Henry T.<br>Hassler, Hans L. (or 25) | Doddridge, Philip<br>Oakeley, Herbert S.<br>Woodbury, Isaac B. |
| 27: | | |
| 28: | Bortniansky, Dimitri S.<br>Harbaugh, Henry<br>Hopkins, John Henry, Jr.<br>Wills, William G.<br>See No. 117 | |
| 29: | | Gordon, George A.<br>Grigg, Joseph |
| 30: | Procter, Adelaide Anne<br>Wordsworth, Christopher | |
| 31: | | Allen, James<br>MacFarren, George A.<br>Roberts, Daniel C. |
| | **November** | |
| 1: | Whiting, William | |
| 2: | See No. 468 | Miller, Emily |

# A Hymn Calendar

| | *Born* | *Died* |
|---|---|---|
| | **November—Continued** | |
| 3: | Bryant, William C.<br>Davies, Samuel | Southgate, Thomas B. |
| 4: | Cennick, John<br>Matthews, Timothy R.<br>Montgomery, James<br>Toplady, Augustus M. | Mendelssohn-Bartholdy, Felix |
| 5: | Roberts, Daniel C. | |
| 6: | Hopps, John P.<br>Kennedy, Benjamin H.<br>Monod, Theodore<br>Tans'ur, William (Baptized) | |
| 7: | Dyer, Samuel<br>Thompson, Will L. | Reissiger, Carl G. |
| 8: | | Milton, John |
| 9: | See No. 552 | Berggreen, Anton P. |
| 10: | Langran, James<br>Luther, Martin<br>Van Dyke, Henry | Hatch, Edwin |
| 11: | | |
| 12: | Baxter, Richard<br>Challinor, Frederick A.<br>Hemy, Henri F.<br>Palmer, Ray | |
| 13: | Chadwick, George W. | Dexter, Henry M.<br>Mote, Edward |
| 14: | Brooke, Stopford A. | Pleyel, Ignace J. |
| 15: | | Campbell, Jane M.<br>Palmer, Horatio R. |
| 16: | | Gardiner, William<br>Smith, Samuel F. |
| 17: | | Cooper, Joseph T. |
| 18: | See Nos. 494, 518 | |
| 19: | | Mann, Arthur H.<br>Schein, Johann H.<br>Stone, Samuel J. |
| 20: | Guiterman, Arthur | Lyte, Henry F. |
| 21: | See No. 412 | Purcell, Henry |
| 22: | Seagrave, Robert<br>See No. 385 | Sullivan, Arthur S. |
| 23: | See Nos. 412, 505 | Bowring, John<br>Phelps, Sylvanus D.<br>Tallis, Thomas |
| 24: | Oliver, Henry K. | Croly, George<br>Schneider, Johann C. F. |
| 25: | Grüber, Franz<br>Tersteegen, Gerhard<br>See No. 56 | Bathurst, William H.<br>Lowry, Robert<br>Masterman, John H. B.<br>Watts, Isaac<br>Whelpton, George |

# A Hymn Calendar

**NOVEMBER—Continued**

| | *Born* | *Died* |
|---|---|---|
| 26: | Burton, Henry<br>Cowper, William<br>Findlater, Sarah | |
| 27: | Canitz, Baron F. R. L. von | Burns, James Drummond<br>Kremser, Edward |
| 28: | | Rankin, Jeremiah E. |
| 29: | Holmes, John H. | |
| 30: | Cosin, John | Farrant, Richard<br>Threlfall, Jeanette |

**DECEMBER**

| | *Born* | *Died* |
|---|---|---|
| 1: | See No. 286 | Knecht, Justin H. |
| 2: | Wilson, Hugh (Baptized) | |
| 3: | North, Frank Mason<br>Stowell, Hugh | |
| 4: | Cook, Joseph S.<br>Cotterill, Thomas<br>See Nos. 462, 505 | John of Damascus<br>Mohr, Joseph |
| 5: | McWhood, Leonard B.<br>Rossetti, Christina G.<br>Selnecker, Nicolaus<br>Smith, Walter C.<br>Thomson, Mary A. | |
| 6: | Masterman, John H. B.<br>See No. 66 | Warren, William F.<br>Stryker, Melancthon W. |
| 7: | | |
| 8: | Sibelius, Jean | Baxter, Richard<br>Rinkart, Martin |
| 9: | Milton, John<br>See No. 228 | Allen, George N.<br>Elvey, George J. |
| 10: | Nichol, Henry E.<br>Thompson, Van Denman<br>Zundel, John | Battishill, Jonathan<br>Murray, Robert |
| 11: | Mohr, Joseph<br>Wreford, John R.<br>See No. 505 | Chadwick, John W. |
| 12: | Cennick, John<br>Hedge, Frederick H. | |
| 13: | Brooks, Phillips<br>How, William W. | |
| 14: | Havergal, Frances R.<br>Richardson, John | Aldrich, Henry<br>Jacobi, John C.<br>Thrupp, Dorothy A. |
| 15: | Bullinger, Ethelbert W.<br>Chorley, Henry F. | Pollock, Thomas B. |
| 16: | Beethoven, Ludwig van<br>Ellerton, John<br>Kocher, Conrad<br>Stewart, Robert P.<br>Whitefield, George | Dutton, Deodatus, Jr.<br>Lvov (or Lwoff), Alexis F.<br>Mahlmann, Siegfried A. |

# A Hymn Calendar

| | *Born* | *Died* |
|---|---|---|
| | **December—Continued** | |
| 17: | Tours, Berthold<br>Whittier, John G.<br>See No. 83 | Giardini, Felice de<br>North, Frank Mason |
| 18: | Weber, Carl M. F. E. von<br>Wesley, Charles | Darwall, John<br>Gottschalk, Louis M.<br>Parker, Horatio W.<br>Scott-Gatty, Alfred |
| 19: | Bonar, Horatius<br>Draper, William H. | |
| 20: | | |
| 21: | Schmolck, Benjamin<br>Schwedler, Johann C.<br>See No. 429 | Newton, John |
| 22: | Dutton, Deodatus, Jr.<br>Lloyd, William F. | McFarland, John T. |
| 23: | Moule, Handley C. G. | Bacon, Leonard |
| 24: | Ahle, Johann R.<br>See Nos. 87, 106, 504 | Doane, William H. |
| 25: | Coster, Arthur V.<br>Murray, Robert<br>See Nos. 85, 93, 103, 505, 540 | |
| 26: | | Nägeli, Hans G. |
| 27: | Goss, John | Lutkin, Peter C. |
| 28: | Swift, James F.<br>Ward, Samuel A. | Harbaugh, Henry |
| 29: | Lightwood, James T.<br>Pott, Francis<br>See No. 254 | Bliss, Philip P.<br>Cotterill, Thomas<br>Rossetti, Christina G. |
| 30: | Cross, Allen E.<br>Kipling, Rudyard<br>Croft, William (Baptized) | |
| 31: | Hiles, Henry<br>See No. 521 | Waterbury, Jared B. |

# Bibliography

The following bibliography, while by no means complete, is included to aid those who are interested in study in the field of hymnology. No attempt has been made to include general reference sources, such as the many valuable encyclopaedias, general and biographical dictionaries, histories of music, and such, nor would it be practical to list the hundreds of hymnals and tune books of various kinds that have been examined, nor the mass of correspondence in the author's possession. No extended reference need be made here to publications such as *The Musical Times, The Choir, The Diapason,* and others published in England and in the United States.


*American Psalter, The,* The H. W. Gray Company, New York, 1930 (Preface).
ASBURY, SAMUEL E., and MEYER, HENRY E., *Old-Time White Camp-Meeting Spirituals,* Reprinted from Publications of the Texas Folk-Lore Society, Number X, 1932.
BARLOW, REV. J. HERBERT, *The Bach Chorale Book,* H. W. Gray Company, New York, 1922.
BARNBY, JOSEPH, *Hymns with Tunes,* Novello, Ewer and Co., London, 1869 (Preface).
BARNBY, JOSEPH, *Hymns with Tunes,* Vol. II, Novello, Ewer and Co., London, 1883 (Preface).
BARNBY, JOSEPH, *Hymn Tunes,* Novello, Ewer and Co., London, 1897.
BATES, REV. WILLIAM, *College Lectures on Christian Antiquities and the Ritual of the English Church,* John W. Parker, London, 1845.
BAUDOT, DOM JULES, *The Roman Breviary,* B. Herder, St. Louis, 1909.
BEERY, WILLIAM, *Stories about Hymns,* Brethren Publishing House, Elgin, Illinois, 1921.
BELCHER, JOSEPH, *Historical Sketches of Hymns,* Lindsay & Blakiston, Philadelphia, 1859.
BENSON, LOUIS F., *Hymns Original and Translated,* privately printed, Philadelphia, 1925.
BENSON, LOUIS F., *The English Hymn,* The Presbyterian Board of Publication, 1915.
BENSON, LOUIS F., *The Hymnody of the Christian Church,* George H. Doran Company, New York, 1927.
BENSON, LOUIS F., *The Hymns of John Bunyan,* The Hymn Society, New York City, 1930.
BENSON, LOUIS F., *Studies of Familiar Hymns,* first series, The Westminster Press, Philadelphia, 1903.
BENSON, LOUIS F., *Studies of Familiar Hymns,* second series, The Westminster Press, Philadelphia, 1923.
BIRD, JOSEPH, *Gleanings from the History of Music,* Benjamin B. Mussey & Co., Boston, 1850.
BIRGE, EDWARD BAILEY, *History of Public School Music in the United States,* Oliver Ditson Company, Boston, 1928. (Valuable material covering Lowell Mason and his contemporaries.)
BODINE, WILLIAM BUDD, *Some Hymns and Hymn Writers,* The John C. Winston Co., Philadelphia, 1907.
*Book of the Common Prayer, The,* 1549. Privately Reproduced in Facsimile from a Copy of the Original Edition for MR. G. MORETON, Seal Chart near Sevenoaks, Kent, 1896.
*Book of Praise, The,* from the best English Hymn Writers, Sel. & arr. by ROUNDELL PALMER, LORD OF SELBORNE, George Routledge and Sons, Ltd., London, E. P. Dutton and Co., The Muses Lib. Ed.
BOYD, CHARLES N., *The Organist and the Choirmaster,* The Abingdon Press, New York, 1936.
BRAWLEY, BENJAMIN, *History of the English Hymn,* The Abingdon Press, New York, 1932.
BREED, REV. DAVID R., *The History and Use of Hymns and Hymn-Tunes,* Fleming H. Revell Company, New York, 1903.
BROWN, JAMES D., and STRATTON, STEPHEN S. *British Musical Biography,* Stratton, Birmingham, 1897.
BROWN, THERON, and BUTTERWORTH, HEZEKIAH, *The Story of the Hymns and Tunes,* American Tract Society, New York, 1906.
BROWNLIE, JOHN, *The Hymns and Hymn Writers of the Church Hymnary,* Henry Frowde, London, 1911.
BUCHANON, E. S., *The Early Latin Song-Book,* Chas. A. Swift, Inc., New York, 1930.
BURGESS, FRANCIS, *The Rudiments of Gregorian Music,* William Reeves, London, n. d.
BURNEY, CHARLES, *Burney's Tour,* 3 Vols., London, 1771-1773 (a journal).
BURNEY, CHARLES, *History of Music,* Vols. I-IV, Published by the author, London, 1776-1789.
BURRAGE, HENRY S., *Baptist Hymn Writers,* Brown, Thurston & Company, Portland, Maine, 1888.
BUTTERWORTH, HEZEKIAH, *The Story of the Hymns,* American Tract Society, New York, 1875.
BUTTERWORTH, HEZEKIAH, *The Story of the Tunes,* American Tract Society, New York, 1890.
*Calvin's First Psalter,* edited with critical notes and modal harmonies to the melodies by SIR RICHARD TERRY, Ernest Benn Limited, London, 1932.
CARTWRIGHT, REV. PETER, *Fifty Years as a Presiding Elder,* Walden and Stowe, Cincinnati, 1871. (Preaching on the frontier.)
*Chants Chrétiens,* 3d ed., L.-R. Delay, Paris, 1841. (Preface.)
CHARLES, ELIZABETH R., *The Voice of Christian Life in Song,* Robert Carter & Brothers, New York, 1859.
CHRISTOPHERS, REV. S. W., *The Epworth Singers and Other Poets of Methodism,* Anson D. F. Randolph & Company, New York, 1874.
CHRISTOPHERS, REV. S. W., *Hymn-Writers and Their Hymns,* S. W. Partridge & Co., London, 1866.
*Church and the Hymn Writers, The,* from "The Living Church Series," Doubleday, Doran & Co., Inc., N. Y. C., n. d.
*Church Hymnal,* by permission of the General Synod of the Church of Ireland, edited by SIR ROBERT PRESCOTT STEWART, 3d ed., A. P. C. K., Dublin, 1878.
COLSON, ELIZABETH, *Hymn Stories,* The Pilgrim Press, Boston, 1925.
COWAN, WILLIAM, and LOVE, JAMES, *The Music of the Church Hymnary and The Psalter in Metre,* Henry Frowde, Edinburgh, 1901.
CREAMER, DAVID, *Methodist Hymnology: comprehending notices of the Poetical Works of John and Charles Wesley,* published by the author, New York, 1848.
CURTISS, GEORGE L., *Manual of Methodist Episcopal Church History,* Hunt & Eaton, New York, 1892.
CURWEN, J. SPENCER, *Studies in Worship Music,* First Series, J. Curwen & Sons, London, 1880.
CURWEN, J. SPENCER, *Studies in Worship Music,* Second Series, J. Curwen & Sons, London, 1885.
DANIELS, REV. W. H., *History of Methodism,* The Methodist Book Concern, New York, 1880.
DAVIES, REV. E., *Frances Ridley Havergal,* Holiness Book Concern, Reading, Mass., 1884.
DAVISON, ARCHIBALD T., *Protestant Church Music in America,* E. C. Schirmer, Boston, 1933.

# Bibliography


DEARMER, PERCY, WILLIAMS, R. VAUGHAN, and SHAW, MARTIN, *The Oxford Book of Carols*, Humphrey Milford, London, 1928.
DICKINSON, EDWARD, *Music in the History of the Western Church*, Charles Scribner's Sons, 1908.
DICKINSON, HELEN A., and DICKINSON, CLARENCE, *Excursions in Musical History*, The H. W. Gray Co., New York, 1917.
DIXON, JAMES, *Personal Narrative of a Tour through a Part of the United States and Canada*, Lane & Scott, New York, 1850.
DONNELLY, MOST REV. DR., *Magister Choralis*, Second (English) Edition, Frederick Pustet, Ratisbon, New York & Cincinnati, 1892.
DOUGLAS, ERNEST, *A Plain Song Service Book*, The Boston Music Company, 1906 (Preface).
DOUGLAS, WINFRED, *A Brief Commentary on Selected Hymns and Carols*, published by Northwestern University, 1936.
DOUGLAS, WINFRED, *Church Music in History and Practice*, Charles Scribner's Sons, New York, 1937.
DUTTON, W. E., *The Eucharistic Manuals of John and Charles Wesley*, Bull, Simmons and Co., London, 1794 (Reprint).
DUFFIELD, SAMUEL WILLOUGHBY, *English Hymns: Their Authors and History*, Funk & Wagnalls, New York, 1886.
DUFFIELD, SAMUEL WILLOUGHBY, *Latin Hymns*, Funk & Wagnalls, New York, 1889.
DUNLAVY, KATHARINE, *The Bases of the Early American Anthem*, Master's Thesis, DePauw University, Greencastle, 1935.
ELSON, LOUIS C., *American Music*, The Macmillan Company, New York, 1915.
EMMONS, NATHANAEL, *A Discourse Delivered at a Public Meeting of a Number of Singers Who Were Improving Themselves in Church Musick*, David Hawkins, jun., 1806.
ENGEL, CARL, *Reflections on Church Music*, Gustav Scheurmann and Co., London, 1856.
EWENS, J. BAIRD, *Let Us Sing*, The Epworth Press, London, 1935.
FETIS, F., *Biographie universelle, des musiciens et bibliographie generale de la musique*, 2d ed., Firmin-Didot, Paris, 1884.
FISHER, WILLIAM ARMS, *Notes on Music in Old Boston*, Oliver Ditson Company, 1918.
FISHER, WILLIAM ARMS, *Ye Olde New-England Psalm Tunes*, 1620-1820, Oliver Ditson Company, New York, 1930.
FITZ-GERALD, S. J. ADAIR, *Stories of Famous Songs*, John C. Nimmo, London, 1897.
FLOOD, W. H. GRATAN, *Early Tudor Composers*, Humphrey Milford, London, 1925.
FOSTER, MYLES BIRKET, *Anthems and Anthem Composers*, Novello and Company, London, 1901.
FOWLER, REV. J. T., *Life of Dr. Dykes*, John Murray, London, 1897.
FRASER, DUNCAN, *The Passing of the Precentor*, John Knox's House, Edinburgh, 1905.
GABRIEL, CHAS. H., *Church Music of Yesterday, To-day and for To-morrow*, The Rodeheaver Company, Chicago and Philadelphia, 1921.
GABRIEL, CHAS. H., *Gospel Songs and Their Writers*, The Rodeheaver Company, Chicago and Philadelphia, 1915.
GABRIEL, CHAS. H., *The Singers and Their Songs*, The Rodeheaver Company, Chicago and Philadelphia, 1916.
GABRIEL, CHAS. H., *Sixty Years of Gospel Song*, Hope Publishing Company, Chicago, n. d.
GARDINER, WILLIAM, *The Music of Nature*, Oliver Ditson & Co., Boston, n. d.
GILLMAN, FREDERICK JOHN, *The Evolution of the English Hymn*, The Macmillan Company, New York, 1927.
GORHAM, REV. B. W., *Camp Meeting Manual*, H. V. Degen, Boston, 1854.
GOULD, NATHANIEL D., *History of Sacred Music in America*, Boston, 1853.
GREGORY, A. S., *Hymns and the Faith*, The Epworth Press, London, n. d.
GREGORY, A. S., *Praise with Understanding*, The Epworth Press, London, 1936.
GROVE, SIR GEORGE, *Dictionary of Music and Musicians*, 6 Vols. (including American supplement), various eds., The Macmillan Company, New York, v. d.
*Guide for Methodist Choirs, A.*, A MINISTER, The Epworth Press, London, 1935.
GUNDY, PALMER VAN, *Some Ministers of Music*, published by First M. E. Church, Los Angeles, 1935.
HALL, REV. CHARLES CUTHBERT, and LASAR, SIGISMOND, *The Evangelical Hymnal with Tunes*, A. S. Barnes & Company, New York and Chicago, 1880.
HALL, J. H., *Biography of Gospel Song and Hymn Writers*, Fleming H. Revell Company, New York, 1914.
*Handbook of American Music and Musicians*, containing biographies of American Musicians, Edited by F. O. JONES, C. W. Moulton & Co., Buffalo, 1887.
*Handbook to The Hymnal*, Presbyterian Board of Christian Education, Philadelphia, 1935.
HART, WILLIAM J., *Hymns in Human Experience*, Harper & Brothers, New York, 1931.
*Harvard University Hymn Book, The*, Harvard University Press, Cambridge, 1926 (Biographical section).
HATFIELD, EDWIN F., *The Church Hymn Book with Tunes*, New York, 1872.
HAVERGAL, C. A., *Havergal's Psalmody*, Robert Cocks & Co., London, 1871 (Preface and Notes on Tunes).
HAWKINS, SIR JOHN, *History of Music*, 4 Vols., Novello, Ewer & Co., London, 1875.
HEWINS, JAMES M., *Hints Concerning Church Music*, Ide & Dutton, 1856.
HOPKINS, JOHN H., JR., *The Canticles Noted, with Accompanying Harmonies*, Hurd & Houghton, New York, 1866 (Preface).
HORDER, W. GARRETT, *The Hymn Lover*, J. Curwen & Sons, London, n. d.
HORTON, ISABELLE, *High Adventure*, The Methodist Book Concern, New York and Cincinnati, 1928.
HOWARD, JOHN TASKER, *Our American Music*, Thomas Crowell Company, New York, 1931.
HOWES, CHARLES, *Free Church Musicians*, Novello and Co., London, 1909.
*Hundred Years of Music in America, A*, W. S. B. MATHEWS, Associate Editor, G. L. Howe, Chicago, 1889.
HUNTER, STANLEY ARMSTRONG, Editor, *Music and Religion*, The Abingdon Press, New York, 1930.
HUNTER, STANLEY ARMSTRONG, Editor, *The Music of the Gospel*, The Abingdon Press, New York, 1932 (Sermons on Hymns).
HUTCHINS, REV. CHARLES L., *Annotations of the Hymnal*, M. H. Mallory and Co., Hartford, Conn., 1872.
*Hymns Ancient and Modern*, Historical Edition, William Clowe and Sons, Limited, London, 1909.
IDELSOHN, A. Z., *Jewish Music in its Historical Development*, H. Holt & Co., New York, 1929.
JACKSON, GEORGE PULLEN, *White Spirituals in the Southern Uplands*, University of North Carolina Press, 1933.
*Jewish Encyclopedia*, Funk & Wagnalls, 1906.
JOHNER, REV. DOM DOMINIC, *A New School of Gregorian Chant*, Fr. Pustet, New York and Cincinnati, 1906.
JOHNSON, FRANCES HALL, *Musical Memories of Hartford*, Witkower's, Hartford, Connecticut, 1931.
JONES, FRANCIS ARTHUR, *Famous Hymns*, 2d ed., Hodder and Stoughton, London, 1903.
JONES, F. O., *A Handbook of American Music and Musicians*, C. W. Moulton and Co., Buffalo, 1887.
JONES, JAMES EDMUND, *The Book of Common Praise*, Oxford University Press, Toronto, 1909.

# Bibliography

JONES, JAMES EDMUND, *In Fane and Forest*, Humphrey Milford, Oxford University Press, 1915.
JULIAN, JOHN, *A Dictionary of Hymnology*, Revised edition with new supplement, John Murray, London, 1925.
KENNEDY, REV. JAMES, *Christ in the Song*, Bradley & Woodruff, Boston, 1890.
KING, REV. JAMES, *Anglican Hymnology*, Hatchards, London, 1885.
KINLOCH, T. F., *An Historical Account of the Church Hymnary;* Revised Edition, W. Heffer & Sons, Ltd., Cambridge, 1926.
KNAUFF, CHRISTOPHER W., *Doctor Tucker, Priest-Musician*, A. D. F. Randolph Company, New York, 1897.
LANDON-HUMPHREYS, F., *The Evolution of Church Music*, Charles Scribner's Sons, New York, 1896.
LAUFER, CALVIN W., *Hymn Lore*, The Westminster Press, Philadelphia, 1932.
LEE, JESSE, *A Short History of the Methodists in the United States of America*, Magill and Clime, Baltimore, 1810.
LEONARD, WILLIAM A., *Music in the Western Church*, W. and F. Morgan, Bristol, 1872.
*Library of Southern Literature*, compiled under the direct supervision of Southern men of letters, The Martin and Hoyt Co., Atlanta, 1909, 16 Vols.
LIGHTWOOD, JAMES T., *Hymn Tunes and Their Story*, The Epworth Press, London, 1923.
LIGHTWOOD, JAMES T., *The Music of the Methodist Hymn-Book*, The Epworth Press, London, 1935.
*Liturgy and the Offices of Worship and Hymns of the American Province of the Unitas Fratrum or the Moravian Church, The*, Moravian Publication Office, Bethlehem, 1912 (valuable historical Preface).
LORENZ, EDMUND S., *Music in Work and Worship*, Fleming H. Revell Company, New York; 1925.
LORENZ, EDMUND S., *Practical Church Music*, Fleming H. Revell Company, New York, 1909.
LOVE, JAMES, *Scottish Church Music*, William Blackwood and Sons, Edinburgh and London, 1891.
LUCKOCK, HERBERT MORTIMER, *Studies in the History of the Prayer-Book*, Longmans, Green and Co., London, 1910.
LUNDQUIST, MATTHEW N., *Hymnological Studies*, Wartburg Publishing House, Chicago, 1926.
LUTKIN, PETER CHRISTIAN, *Hymn-Singing and Hymn-Playing*, Published by Northwestern University, 1930.
LUTKIN, PETER CHRISTIAN, *Music in the Church*, The Young Churchman Company, Milwaukee, 1910.
MACMILLAN, ALEXANDER, *Hymns of the Church*, The United Church Publishing House, Toronto, 1935.
MACMEEKEN, REV. J. W., *History of the Scottish Metrical Psalms*, McCulloch & Co., Glasgow, 1872.
MANTRIPP, J. C., *The Devotional Use of the Methodist Hymn Book*, The Epworth Press, London, 1934.
MASON, LOWELL, *Musical Letters from Abroad*, Oliver Ditson & Co., Boston, 1853.
MCCUTCHAN, ROBERT G., *The Deluge of New Hymnals*, A Reprint from the M. T. N. A. Proceedings, 1933.
MCCUTCHAN, ROBERT G., *The Congregation's Part in the Office of Music Worship*, Northwestern University, 1934.
MCCUTCHAN, ROBERT G., *American Church Music Composers of the Early Nineteenth Century*, Reprint from Church History, September, 1933, issue.
MCNAUGHER, JOHN, and others, *The Psalms in Worship*, The United Presbyterian Board of Publication, Pittsburgh, 1907.
*Memoirs of a New England Village Choir*, by a Member, 2d ed., Benjamin H. Greene, Boston, 1834.
MERRILL, WILLIAM P., *The Religious Value of Hymns*, The Hymn Society, New York City, 1931.
MESSENGER, RUTH ELLIS, *The Praise of the Virgin in Early Latin Hymns*, The Hymn Society, New York City, 1932.
METCALF, FRANK J., *American Psalmody*, Charles F. Heartman, New York, 1917.
METCALF, FRANK J., *American Writers and Compilers of Sacred Music*, The Abingdon Press, New York and Cincinnati, 1925.
METCALF, FRANK J., *Stories of Hymn Tunes*, The Abingdon Press, New York, Cincinnati and Chicago, 1928.
MOFFATT, PROF. JAMES, and PATRICK, REV. MILLAR, *Handbook to the Church Hymnary*, Revised Edition with Supplement, Humphrey Milford, London, 1935.
MONTAGU-NATHAN, M., *A History of Russian Music*, Wm. Reeves, London, 1914.
MOORE, JOHN W., *Encyclopedia of Music*, Oliver Ditson Company, Boston, 1880.
NASON, REV. ELIAS, and BEALE, J. FRANK, *Lives and Labors of Eminent Divines*, John E. Potter and Company, Philadelphia, 1895.
NEATBY, WILLIAM BLAIR, *A History of the Plymouth Brothers*, Hodder and Stoughton, London, 1901.
*New Hymn and Tune Book*, Edited by PHILIP PHILLIPS, Nelson & Phillips, New York, 1866.
NINDE, EDWARD S., *The Story of the American Hymn*, The Abingdon Press, New York and Cincinnati, 1921
*Notes and Queries*, English Periodical, Pub. London, v. d.
NUTTER, REV. CHARLES S., *Hymn Studies*, 3d ed., Eaton & Mains, New York, 1897.
NUTTER, REV. CHARLES S., *Historic Hymnists*, Published by the author, Boston, 1893.
NUTTER, REV. CHARLES S., and TILLETT, WILBUR F., *The Hymns and Hymn Writers of the Church*, The Methodist Book Concern, New York and Cincinnati, 1911.
NUTTER, REV. CHARLES S., *Hymn Studies*, Phillips & Hunt, New York, 1884.
OTIS, PHILO ADAMS, *The Hymns You Ought to Know*, Clayton F. Summy, Chicago, 1928.
PAINE, SILAS H., *Stories of the Great Hymns of the Church*, Flexo Printing Company, 1926.
PARKE, W. T., *Musical Memoirs*, Vol. I, Henry Colburn and Richard Bentley, London, 1830.
PATTEN, SIMON N., *Advent Songs*, B. W. Huebsch, New York, 1916.
PHELPS, AUSTIN, and PARK, EDWARDS A., *Hymns and Choirs*, Warren F. Draper, Andover, 1860.
PHILLIPS, PHILIP, *Song Pilgrimage Around the World*, Fairbanks, Palmer & Co., Chicago, 1880.
PLAYFORD, JOHN, *The Whole Book of Psalms*, J. Heptinstall, London, 1701 (Preface).
POTEAT, HUBERT MCNEILL, *Practical Hymnology*, The Gorham Press, Boston, 1921.
PLACE, CHARLES A., *The Early Forms of Worship in North America*, American Antiquarian Society, Worcester, Massachusetts, 1930.
PRATT, WALDO SELDEN, *The History of Music*, G. Schirmer, New York, 1907.
PRATT, WALDO SELDEN, *The Music of the Pilgrims*, Oliver Ditson Company, Boston, 1921.
PRATT, WALDO SELDEN, *The New Encyclopedia of Music and Musicians*, Carl Fischer, Inc., New York, 1924.
PRICE, CARL F., *The Music and Hymnody of the Methodist Hymnal*, The Methodist Book Concern, New York and Cincinnati, 1911.
PROCTOR, REV. FRANCIS, *A History of the Book of Common Prayer*, Macmillan and Co., Cambridge, 1856.
RAVENSHAW, THOMAS F., and ROCKSTRO, W. S., ESQ., *The Ferial Psalter*, J. Masters and Co., London, 1890 (Preface).
REDFORD, REV. A. H., *The History of Methodism in Kentucky*, 3 Vols., Southern Methodist Publishing House, Nashville, 1870.
REED, ANDREW, and MATHESON, JAMES, *A Narrative of the Visit to the American Churches by the Deputation from the Congregational Union of England and Wales*, 2 Vols., Jackson and Walford, London, 1835.
REEVES, JEREMIAH BASCOM, *The Hymn as Literature*, The Century Co., New York and London, 1924.

# Bibliography


RILEY, ATHELSTAN, *Concerning Hymn Tunes and Sequences*, A. R. Mowbray & Co., Ltd., London, 1915.
RITTER, DR. FREDERIC LOUIS, *Music in America*, Charles Scribner's Sons, New York, 1883.
RITTER, DR. FREDERIC LOUIS, *Music in England*, Charles Scribner's Sons, New York, 1883.
ROBINSON, CHARLES SEYMOUR, *Annotations upon Popular Hymns*, F. M. Barton, Cleveland, Ohio, 1893.
ROCKSTRO, W. S., *A General History of Music*, Scribner and Welford, New York, 1886 (Plainsong).
RODEHEAVER, HOMER, *Hymnal Handbook for Standard Hymns and Gospel Songs*, The Rodeheaver Company, Chicago and Philadelphia, 1931.
ROUNDELL, EARL OF SELBORNE, *Hymns*, Adam and Charles Black, London, 1892.
ROWBOTHAM, JOHN FREDERICK, *A History of Music*, Richard Bentley and Son, London, 1893.
RUDIN, CECILIA M., *Stories of Hymns We Love*, John Rudin & Co., Chicago, 1937.
SANKEY, IRA D., *My Life and the Story of the Gospel Hymns*, Harper & Brothers, New York, 1907.
SCHWEITZER, ALBERT, *J. S. Bach*, translation by Ernest Newman, Breitkopf, Leipzig, 1911.
SCUDDER, REV. M. L., *American Methodism*, S. S. Scranton & Co., Hartford, Conn., 1867.
*Service for Such As Would Make Their Covenant with God, A*, The Abingdon Press, New York, 1934.
SHIELDS, CHARLES W., *Presbyterian Book of Common Prayer*, Charles Scribner's Sons, 1902.
SMITH, H. AUGUSTINE, *Lyric Religion*, The Century Co., New York, 1931.
SMITH, NICHOLAS, *Hymns Historically Famous*, Advance Publishing Co., Chicago, 1901.
*Songs of Praise Discussed*, by DEARMER and JACOB, Humphrey Milford, London, 1933.
SPITTA, PHILIPP, *Johann Sebastian Bach*, 3 Vols., Novello and Company, London, 1899.
STAINER, SIR J., *The Present State of Music in England*, Horace Hart, Oxford, 1889.
STACY, REV. A. G., *The Service of Song*, Southwestern Book and Publishing Company, Saint Louis, 1871.
STEBBINS, GEORGE C., *Reminiscences and Gospel Hymn Stories*, George H. Doran Company, New York, 1924.
STEVENS, ABEL, *A Compendious History of American Methodism*, Carlton and Porter, New York, 1867.
STEVENS, ABEL, *History of the Methodist Episcopal Church*, Carlton & Porter, New York, 1866, 4 Vols.
STEVENSON, ARTHUR L., *The Story of Southern Hymnology*, published by the author, Salem, Va., 1931.
STEVENSON, GEORGE JOHN, *The Methodist Hymn Book*, Charles H. Kelly, London, 1898.
STONE, ALFRED, and others, *The Bristol Tune Book*, Novello, Ewer and Co., London, 1881 (Preface).
SUMMERS, THOMAS O., *Biographical Sketches of Eminent Itinerant Ministers*, E. Stevenson & F. A. Owen, Nashville, Tenn., 1858.
SUTHERLAND, ALLAN, *Famous Hymns of the World*, Frederick A. Stokes Company, New York, 1923.
SWEET, WILLIAM WARREN, *Circuit-Rider Days Along the Ohio*, The Methodist Book Concern, New York and Cincinnati, 1923 (Doctor Sweet makes frequent mention in his books of the significance of hymn-singing).
SWEET, WILLIAM WARREN, *Methodism in American History*, The Methodist Book Concern, New York, Cincinnati, Chicago, 1933.
SWEET, WILLIAM WARREN, *The Rise of Methodism in the West*, The Methodist Book Concern, New York and Cincinnati, 1920.
SWEET, WILLIAM WARREN, *The Story of Religions in America*, Harper & Brothers, New York, 1930.
TELFORD, JOHN, *The New Methodist Hymn-Book*, 2d ed., The Epworth Press, London, 1935.
TELFORD, JOHN, *The Treasure House of Charles Wesley*, The Epworth Press, London, 1933.
TERRY, SIR CHARLES SANFORD, *Bach's Chorales*, in 3 Vols., University Press, Cambridge, 1915-1921.
THOMPSON, F. FAGAN, *Music and Worship*, Whitmore & Smith, Nashville, Tenn., 1935.
TILLETT, REV. WILBUR F., *Our Hymns and Their Authors*, Barbee & Smith, Nashville, Tenn., 1900.
TOWLSON, CLIFFORD W., *A Mightier Music*, The Epworth Press, London, 1934.
WALKER, ALBERT H., *How to Receive and Use the New Methodist Hymn Book*, The Epworth Press, London, 1933.
WALKER, JOHN MANN, and others, *Better Music in Our Churches*, The Methodist Book Concern, New York and Cincinnati, 1923.
WARD, REV. J., *Round and Through the Wesleyan Hymn Book*, B. W. Sharp, Leeds, 1868.
WARRINGTON, JAMES, *Short Titles of Books Relating to or Illustrating the History and Practice of Psalmody*, privately printed, Philadelphia, 1898.
WASHBURN, CHARLES C., *Hymn Stories*, Whitmore & Smith, Nashville, 1935.
WATKINS, COLE, *A Study of Some American Developments in Congregational Church Song*, Master's Thesis, DePauw University, Greencastle, 1936.
WATTS, ISAAC, *Twelve Sermons on Various Subjects*, Wright & Sibley, Montpelier, 1811 (Hymns appended).
WATTS, ISAAC, *Sermons On Various Subjects*, Rogers and Fowle, Boston, 1746 (Hymns appended).
WELLS, AMOS R., *A Treasure of Hymns*, United Society of Christian Endeavor, Boston and Chicago, 1914.
WELSH, REV. R. E., and EDWARDS, F. G., *Romance of Psalter and Hymnal*, James Pott & Co., New York, 1889.
WHEATLEY, CHARLES, *A Rational Illustration of the Book of Common Prayer of the Church of England*, Henry G. Bohn, London, n. d.
WHITTLE, D. W., *Memoirs of Philip P. Bliss*, A. S. Barnes & Company, Chicago, 1877.
WILLIAMS, JAMES R., *History of the Methodist Protestant Church*, Book Committee of the M. P. Church, Baltimore, 1843.
*Who's Who in American Methodism*, edited by CARL F. PRICE, E. V. Treat & Co., New York, 1916.
WISEMAN, F. LUKE, *Charles Wesley*, The Abingdon Press, New York, 1932.
WOODS, LEONARD, *A Discourse on Sacred Music*, Joshua Cushing, Salem, 1804.

# Index of Scripture Texts

The letter *a* attached to a Scripture reference indicates the first part; *b*, the second.

# Index of Scripture Texts

# Index of Scripture Texts

# Index of Scripture Texts

# Index of Scripture Texts

# Index of Scripture Texts

# Index of First Lines of Stanzas of Hymns

(With the exception of the first lines of hymns)

# First Lines of Stanzas of Hymns

# First Lines of Stanzas of Hymns

# First Lines of Stanzas of Hymns

# First Lines of Stanzas of Hymns

# First Lines of Stanzas of Hymns

# First Lines of Stanzas of Hymns

# Index of Authors, Translators, and Sources of Hymns

# Authors, Translators, and Sources of Hymns

# Authors, Translators, and Sources of Hymns

# Index of Composers, Arrangers, and Sources of Tunes

# Composers, Arrangers, and Sources of Tunes

# Composers, Arrangers, and Sources of Tunes

# Alphabetical Index of Tunes

# Alphabetical Index of Tunes

# Alphabetical Index of Tunes

# Index of Responses and Sentences



# Index of Ancient Hymns and Canticles

# Index of First Lines of Hymns

# First Lines of Hymns

# First Lines of Hymns

# First Lines of Hymns

# First Lines of Hymns

# First Lines of Hymns

# Supplementary Index

# Supplementary Index

Date D